BANKS AND POLITICS
IN AMERICA

from the Revolution
to the Civil War

By Bray Hammond

T0272077

PRINCETON, NEW JERSEY

PRINCETON UNIVERSITY PRESS

PUBLISHED BY PRINCETON UNIVERSITY PRESS,
41 WILLIAM STREET,
PRINCETON, NEW JERSEY 08540
IN THE UNITED KINGDOM
BY PRINCETON UNIVERSITY PRESS, OXFORD

COPYRIGHT © 1957 BY PRINCETON UNIVERSITY PRESS;
RENEWED © 1985 BY PRINCETON UNIVERSITY PRESS
ALL RIGHTS RESERVED

LIBRARY OF CONGRESS CARD NO. 57-8667
ISBN 0-691-04507-0
ISBN 0-691-00553-2 (pbk.)
FIRST PRINCETON PAPERBACK PRINTING, 1967;
SECOND PRINTING FOR THE REISSUE OF THE PAPERBACK, 1991

PRINCETON UNIVERSITY PRESS BOOKS ARE PRINTED ON ACID-FREE
PAPER, AND MEET THE GUIDELINES FOR PERMANENCE AND
DURABILITY OF THE COMMITTEE ON PRODUCTION GUIDELINES FOR
BOOK LONGEVITY OF THE COUNCIL ON LIBRARY RESOURCES

10   9   8   7   (hbk.)
10   9   8   7   6   5   4   3   (pbk.)

PRINTED IN THE UNITED STATES OF AMERICA

TO

MELITTA DE KERN

HAMMOND

PREFACE

THIS is a book about politics and banks and history. Yet politicians who read it will see that the author is not a politician, bankers who read it will see that he is not a banker, and historians that he is not an historian. Economists will see that he is not an economist and lawyers that he is not a lawyer.

Had I been any of these, the book would not have been written, probably, and the world, in the opinion of my more critical readers, would have been no worse off. I agree. Yet it is written; and I prayerfully abide the outcome.

I was led into writing it from some familiarity with banking, because of which I had found myself puzzled frequently by two things. One was hearing history often invoked to support notions about money and banking which I doubted if it could in fact support. The other was that in respect to the Bank of the United States and Andrew Jackson, interpretations were offered and accepted without attention to the obvious resemblance of that institution to modern central banks. My quest disclosed much besides what I had set out to find. It disclosed, to my sense of evidence, that the Jacksonians were not peculiarly agrarian; that the Bank of the United States was not "the money power"; that Nicholas Biddle was not a schemer who deserved what he got; that debt in its significant sense is not something distressing which the poor get into; and, without going further, that Americans have not been mostly idealistic. I was also impelled to suspect that recent contemporaries who had dealt with the things I was investigating had relied rather more on inner enlightenment than on facts and that in consequence they compared so unfavorably with their predecessors as to disparage the doctrine that the world grows progressively better and better.

It seems to me that this book, whatever it should have been, is not simply a history of banking. Instead, banking is used in it as an approach to certain phenomena of early American history—or, better perhaps, as a point of observation whence one looks over the landscape and spies out things not to be so clearly seen from any other angle. The book is a history told with primary attention to what the Americans did politically about certain economic and cultural matters. In particular, it reflects the political and cultural force of business enterprise, which seems to me to have been the most powerful continuing influence in American life ever since Independence. The rival force in the early 19th century was agrarianism, formerly dominant but no longer so. These two fought about banks, because banks provide credit, and credit is indispensable to enterprise.

Enterprise won, it got banks by the thousand, and it devoted Americans to dollars. "What we want is more money," cried Colonel Mulberry Sellers, when engaged ardently in making America great. Basing the currency on gold was too restrictive; it might better be based on pork. Better still, let it be based on everything. Let money be cheap and abundant. That was what the factory-owner wanted, the railway-builder, the inventor, the merchant, and last of all the farmer himself, who tardily began to see, with the zeal typical of converts, the virtues in easy money that had been apparent from the first to the business man.

This conflict of farmer and entrepreneur for dominance over American culture provoked much of the basic political controversy of the period from the Revolution to the Civil War. So in judging the struggle between federal powers and states' rights, or the issues dividing Hamilton and Jefferson, or Nicholas Biddle and Andrew Jackson, one has to discuss the function of banks. Bank credit has been of immense importance to the Americans, whether for good or ill, as they have never failed to see. To some, as to Alexander Hamilton, it was a desirable means of making America the wealthy power that her resources gave promise of her becoming. To others, as to Thomas Jefferson, to the poets and Transcendentalists—to Emerson, Hawthorne, and Thoreau—it was an objectionable instrument of industrialization, materialism, and immorality. As the 19th century progressed, the Hamiltonian view pretty well spread from top to bottom and in ways that would have surprised Mr Hamilton himself. A devotion to dollars came to prevail, and a conviction that the more there were of them the better off every one would be.

Banks are the mediums of this abundance. Practically speaking, they do what Colonel Sellers wanted, for they do base their liabilities on everything and their liabilities constitute the major part of the money supply. The funds they lend originate in the process of lending and disappear in the process of repayment. This creative faculty was far easier to observe a century and a half ago than it is now; for then the monetary funds that banks provided were commonly in the form of their own circulating notes, handed over the counter to the borrower, and the expansion of the circulating medium was the palpable and visible aspect of the expansion of credit. Every one recognized that the more banks lent, the more money there was. That is why they were a political issue. That is why they were denounced by Thomas Jefferson and others who did not wish America to degenerate into a money market or an industrial economy. And it is why most Americans esteemed them, liking what Mr Jefferson had said about freedom but ignoring what he said about business. Nowadays banks give the borrower deposit credit, not circulating notes, and the result is that their function is less obviously monetary than it used to be but in magnitude more so.

The largest of all borrowers to-day is the federal government, its indebtedness to commercial banks, in late years, being more than half that of all other borrowers combined. But the government aside— for it was never a dominating borrower in the period of this study—the borrowers who are of most economic and political importance are and always have been business men and business corporations. In the early 19th century the borrowers were the merchants, speculators, enterprisers, and promoters who were building up the modern American empire. America, as Robert Morris already said in 1785, has grown rich by borrowing. The fact is obvious. Yet typical accounts read as if it were to be taken for granted that Americans have borrowed only when they have been in trouble, that debtors have all been poor agrarians, and that a chronic and significant condition of American life has been the distress of agrarian debtors, their oppression by creditors, and their struggles for relief. On the contrary, I should say, the chronic and significant condition has been the prosperous use of borrowed funds by business men. Until fairly well along in the 19th century farmers did not wish to borrow and lenders did not consider agriculture a very good credit risk. The debtors who owed the most and whose influence was greatest were business men; and their complaints were not that their debts were too heavy but that borrowing was not easy enough. The "poor debtor" does not explain Thomas Jefferson and Andrew Jackson. As an important factor in politics or in the economy before the Civil War, he was a myth.

To make my study comparative, I have given some attention to parallel history, political and economic, in Canada. The contrast between the experiences of the two countries is interesting, and I hope that no Canadian will find cause to resent the little invasion of the Provinces into which it has drawn me.

Bray Hammond

Meran, South Tyrol
1954

Thetford, Vermont
1956

CONTENTS

BANKS AND POLITICS
IN AMERICA
from the Revolution
to the Civil War

CHAPTER 1

The Setting

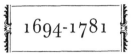

1694-1781

I. The Bank of England; the South Sea Bubble — II. Agrarianism and enterprise — III. Colonial paper money — IV. The business need of paper money — V. Rhode Island's success — VI. Official policy toward colonial paper money — VII. Continental bills — VIII. The agrarian paper money fallacy — IX. Steam and credit

I

IN 1694, in the reign of William and Mary, the English Parliament passed the Tunnage Act; in 1720, in the reign of George I, it passed the Bubble Act. The Tunnage Act provided funds for the current warfare with Louis XIV and authorized incorporation of the Bank of England to that end. It also provided the model for banking in the New World; for Alexander Hamilton, ninety-six years later, drew upon the Bank's example and charter in preparing legislation to the pattern of which American and Canadian banks still in varying degrees conform. The Bubble Act, whatever its original purpose, got its real and lasting force from the revulsion following collapse of speculation in South Sea Company stock. It also came in time to inspire opposition to banking in the New World; a President of the United States, Andrew Jackson, said more than a century later that ever since he read about the South Sea Bubble he had been afraid of banks.

The Parliamentary acts of 1694 and 1720 are associated, therefore, with two traditions, which being transplanted to America were for more than a century in growing conflict. The act of 1694 is a monument to faith in the power and beneficence of credit; the act of 1720 is a monument to distrust of it.* About 1832, credit triumphed, and since then the distrust of it has shown, only now and then, some feeble signs of life.

When banking began in America, about 1780, the bulk of it in

* 5 William and Mary, c. 20; 6 George I, c. 18.

Great Britain and Europe was in the hands of individuals, families, and partnerships, where it had been for centuries. And it continued so. Incorporated banks, such as the Riksbank of Sweden, the Bank of Spain, and the Bank of England, were outstanding, special, and few. Banking developed very differently in America. In the early 18th century there were occasional things called "banks," of which I shall speak shortly, but they were distorted imitations of what Europe had, and they meant little to the formation and practice of the real banks that came later. Instead, banking began in the New World of a sudden, under specific governmental sanction, with a pretentious assembly of capital, and in a forensic blaze of controversy. It began with incorporation, and with important exceptions incorporation remained the rule, both in the States and in Canada.

Many things worked together to make the difference. America was not, like Europe, an ancient and matured economy with accumulations of monetary capital accessible in numerous money markets. It had no money or other free capital; for capital, as fast as it was accumulated, became fixed in land, buildings, and tools. Nor had Americans the patience to drop back centuries and recapitulate the evolution of Europe. Instead, they would start where Europe had arrived. But for want of Europe's long accumulations, especially of cash and other liquid capital, they had to invent, improvise, covenant, and pretend. If they were to form banks at all, they had to do it by "clubbing together" their scanty funds, as Robert Morris said, and gain all the adventitious credit they could from public association and corporate charter.

In Britain, by now, such procedure had been rendered unlawful by the privileges of the Bank of England and by the terms of the Bubble Act. Laws protecting the former forbade banking by other corporations or by partnerships of more than six members "in that part of Great Britain called England," and the Bubble Act restrained if it did not prevent large scale banking elsewhere. According to this act, its restraints were occasioned by "dangerous and mischievous undertakings or projects" of recent occurrence and by "other unwarrantable practices (too many to enumerate)." Because of these evils it was declared that "the acting or presuming to act as a Body Corporate," by any organization not already formed at the passage of the act, should "forever be deemed to be illegal and void." The penalties were the harsh ones of the ancient statutes of praemunire: forfeiture of property and imprisonment at the King's pleasure.[1]

Despite the severity of this language, its purpose is obscure. The law seems to breathe antipathy for the corporate form of business organization and was eventually interpreted that way; yet it incorporated two new insurance companies and left existing corporations untouched. It undoubtedly purposed not so much to protect His Majesty's subjects from monopoly as to protect monopoly itself as possessed by the companies already chartered and by the South Sea Company particularly. This Company had been incorporated to trade abroad in much the same extensive fashion as the East India Company and the Hudson's Bay Company, but its interests were more heterogeneous. It had a monopoly of the traffic in slaves to parts of Spanish America, and it was a corporate holder of the public debt, the entire amount of which it undertook to acquire by offering its stock to investors in exchange. In the latter respect it was a Tory rival of the Bank of England, which was Whig. At the same time that it flourished, John Law presided in Paris over the operations of his Mississippi Company. Speculation in the shares of both the South Sea and Mississippi Companies collapsed in London and Paris respectively a few weeks apart in the summer of 1720.

In the course of six months, shares in the South Sea Company had risen from 200 to 1,000 and then fallen back below 200. The emotional reaction of both victims and spectators now gave the recent restraining act its popular name, "the Bubble Act," and also a fresh and adventitious purpose—as if the measure had followed the explosion instead of preceding it. Its prohibitions were found to be in the public interest, whatever their original intent. Once the bubble burst, then, in the words of Professor Julius Goebel, "Public hysteria no longer saw the company as a goose which laid eggs of gold but as a monster from the book of Revelation. . . . Nothing could have appealed more to the shopkeeping mind than the avowed purpose of the Act to restrain practices 'Dangerous to the Trade' of the Kingdom. . . ." It became, writes Professor DuBois, "for one hundred and five years the statutory framework by which (in legal theory at least) the business organizations of the time were restricted." It acquired the support of a prejudice against business ventures that were beyond the scope of individuals and partnerships. It found itself voicing a determination to maintain what in 20th

[1] 6 George I, c. 18, ¶ xviii (1720).

century America is called "small business." Obeyed in this spirit by three generations of the men who governed Britain, it made the procurement of corporate charters for business enterprise almost impossible. When the Bank of England was a century old, in 1794, there were but four other chartered banks in the British Isles. There were then already eighteen chartered banks in America, only thirteen years after incorporation of the first American bank.[2]

II

Yet in 18th century America economic conservatism was possibly stronger even than in 18th century England, for the people were more largely agrarian. Benjamin Franklin conjectured after the Revolution that for one artisan or merchant in America there were at least a hundred farmers. The popular economic precepts were those of frugality and avoidance of debt. Dr Franklin, himself a successful business man, recommended these virtues in his *Way to Wealth*. "He that goes a-borrowing goes a-sorrowing." And Poor Richard, seeing how artificial wants may well become more numerous and costly than natural ones, resolves to wear his old coat a little longer instead of buying stuff for a new one. The modern American economy thrives by no such precepts. The producer borrows and so does the consumer. But the virtues of debt, nowadays so obvious, were already being discerned in the 18th century by some of Poor Richard's contemporaries. Dr Franklin himself on occasion realized the advantages of borrowing. So 18th century America retained an agrarian conservativism in the main, though the business part of it, speculative and eager, became steadily more numerous and potent.

In the rivalry of yeoman and merchant which had followed the first settlers to the New World, the yeomen had more than the obvious advantage of numbers. They had also on their side the ancient prestige of pastoral and georgic poetry, the ideas of unworldly philosophers, the fervor of evangelical Christianity, and the brilliant contemporary influence of the French physiocrats. From all this and eventually from the eloquent spokesmanship of Thomas Jefferson, agrarianism derived an arsenal of distinguished and moving sentiments, ethical rather than economic, deeply cherished, and loyally obeyed—so long as considerations of gain were not too strong.

The natural situation of 17th and 18th century life in America had favored such views and selected, in a Darwinian sense, the per-

2 DuBois x (Introduction by Goebel) 2.

sons who held them. It had not favored the gentlemen adventurers seeking El Dorados in the wilds but the folk from Old World crofts and farms and trades. The New World confirmed for these people the influence of their Old World setting. They were typically in modest circumstances, always had been, and for a long time had few chances of being otherwise. Security from molestation and interference in their personal lives meant more to them than prospects of opulence. They were sturdy, self-reliant, contented with subsistence, and independent of landlords and masters. The freedom of their life and its constant challenge to endurance and ingenuity begot a mystical sense of superiority. "Those who labour in the earth," wrote Jefferson in his *Notes on Virginia*, "are the chosen people of God, if ever he had a chosen people, whose breasts he has made his peculiar deposit for substantial and genuine virtue." Benjamin Franklin also could describe the agrarian position as well as if he were a farmer. Nations, he said, could acquire wealth in three ways: by war, which was robbery; by commerce, which was generally cheating; and by agriculture. The last was "the only honest way." For by it "man receives a real increase of the seed thrown into the ground, in a kind of continual miracle wrought by the hand of God in his favour as a reward for his innocent life and his virtuous industry."[3]

Looking back at the agrarian faith from a remote distance, one can regard it with respect and nostalgia. For it accorded well with the New World before the Industrial Revolution took hold there, when America's eventual wealth was still unknown, when its iron and water power were only beginning to be important, when its coal was still an oddity, when its other minerals—copper, gold, silver, and oil—remained intact in the earth, when its forms of energy were mainly animal, and when land alone was its great resource. But later, when these other riches were disclosed, idealistic agrarianism became an ecological anomaly. In a land brimming with resources and possessed by an energetic and ingenious people, it had no place. It was yet to retain, however, a tremendous residual power in American thought and politics. In moments of doubt and fear or moral excitement, the familiar vocabulary was good to fall back on. So the agrarian shibboleths held, no matter how scarce or inconstant agrarians in person became. They held by virtue of their sentimental

[3] Jefferson (Ford) III, 268; Franklin V, 202.

attractiveness and political convenience. For most Americans—including business men—were of rural birth, and whatever their behavior might become, their native ideas remained rural.

In contrast to the venerable traditions of 18th century agrarianism, the emergent business tradition was not very uplifting. It had on its side the support of mercantilism, of realistic statecraft, and of lucrative self-interest, but the poetry inspired by it was poor. It utilized no higher faculties than energy, imagination, and ingenuity. Yet its attractions were insidious and irresistible. The best of agrarians would now and then speculate in lands or feel himself drawn by the advantages to his neighborhood of a mill or a foundry. And as the 18th century wore on into the 19th, and the 19th moved with increasing noise and stir into the 20th, the business tradition gained more and more the hearts and brains of Americans in general, though agrarian ideals retained control of their lips and of their idler fancies. But it was an essential characteristic of the metamorphosis from an agrarian to a business economy that business should expand at the bottom as well as at the top, and rather less through the investments of capitalists than through the diversification, expansion, and refinement of trades and skills.

It was at the end of the 18th century, after the Revolution, that enterprise suddenly shot forward into a place of commanding influence. Under the spokesmanship of Alexander Hamilton, it achieved political dominance as the party of nationalism, wealth, and power. In the constitutional discussions of 1787 and in the *Federalist*, one is struck by the consciousness of the unprecedented act of political creation in which the advocates of the federal union were engaged. And likewise, in Alexander Hamilton's reports upon the measures necessary to get the government of the Union under way, one is struck by the consciousness of the economic powers being evoked. At the same time that British authorities were still governed by the conservative spirit of the Bubble Act, Hamilton and the Federalists pushed the program of enterprise vigorously and creatively forward. The effect upon the economy was spectacular. "A people," observed Henry Adams, "which had in 1787 been indifferent or hostile to roads, banks, funded debt, and nationality, had become in 1815 habituated to ideas and machinery of the sort on a great scale." The new order of things had its critics—notably John Taylor of Caroline, who ponderously urged America to turn back to 1787—but in influence if not in number they were shrinking into a sentimental and objurgatory remnant.[4]

By 1815, indeed, enterprise had outgrown its Federalist nursery, destroying the party in the process. The American Revolution had fused with the Industrial Revolution, and the Republican party of Thomas Jefferson had gained the greater part of the Federalist inheritance. For enterprise in time had found the old fashioned conservatism of the Federalists unbrookable, and like the cow-bird it went to lay its eggs in the Jeffersonian nest. The sayings of Thomas Jefferson lent themselves readily to *laisser faire* and to a democratic dream that in America everybody might get rich. So the Jeffersonian party was become by 1800 one fold both for John Taylor of Caroline, the agrarian apostle, and for Daniel Ludlow, the Wall Street bank president. The trend was to go further, making Alexander Hamilton's son, a wealthy speculator in New York real estate, one of Andrew Jackson's personal aides and making the Jacksonian Revolution itself an entrepreneurial revolution—so much was business enterprise extended through all strata of society and money-making democratized.

The bipartisan triumph of enterprise in the American economy was still fresh when Albert Gallatin, himself become a New York banker but at heart Jeffersonian and a scion of the 18th century, mourned it in 1836 in these words: ". . . the bank-paper mania has extended itself so widely that I despair of its being corrected otherwise than by a catastrophe. The energy of this nation is not to be controlled; it is at present exclusively applied to the acquisition of wealth and to improvements of stupendous magnitude. Whatever has that tendency, and of course an immoderate expansion of credit, receives favor. The apparent prosperity and the progress of cultivation, population, commerce, and improvement are beyond expectation. But it seems to me as if general demoralization was the consequence; I doubt whether general happiness is increased; and I would have preferred a gradual, slower, and more secure progress. I am, however, an old man, and the young generation has a right to govern itself. . . ."[5]

III

In the 18th century America "banks" were known in three different senses. First, the word was used of corporate institutions—

[4] Henry Adams, *History* IX, 195-96.   [5] Henry Adams, *Gallatin*, 653.

the Bank of England, for example—of which, however, there was none in America till 1782. Second, it was used of an issue of bills of credit by a colonial government: Rhode Island, for example, might emit "a bank of £40,000." This use became obsolete before the century ended. Third, it was used of an association of private persons who issued their own bills of credit.

The bills of credit of the colonial governments had at first been issued to meet official expenses, especially for military expeditions against Indians and the French. Later they were issued principally by lending at colonial loan offices, which in exchange for the bills took mortgages on the borrower's real property. The former bills were spent, the latter lent. But the difference was of no necessary importance to the bills as money. Either might be over-issued; either might be kept equal to specie in value, or not. The private associations or "banks" put their bills in circulation by lending them on mortgage security as the loan offices did; and the two were therefore parallel or alternative methods of providing a circulating medium, the one public, the other private. Both moreover, in a sporadic fashion, were engaged in the banking function, viz., in the creation of liabilities generally serving as money and made available to the borrower in exchange for his promissory note or other obligation. In both procedures, the liabilities created by lending and used as money were in the form of circulating bills, whereas the liabilities nowadays created by lending and used as money are bank deposits. In the 18th century the borrower took his bills and by paying them to others as needed passed them into circulation. In the 20th century the borrower receives deposit credit and pays it by check to others. Either way the amount of silver and gold, as it was then, or of lawful money, as it is now, was or is far less than the amount of the medium of payment created by lending. The purpose, then as now, was to supply, by lending, a flexible, convenient, and inexpensive substitute for lawful money.

Notwithstanding these abstract resemblances, the public loan offices or other like associations in colonial America had little if any influence, in my opinion, upon the banks that have succeeded them. The modern bank is corporate, with a specialized, distinct, and continuing organization, with permanent staff and offices, and only relative limits on the volume of its business. The colonial loan office was a governmental activity. Its private counterpart was a loose association of subscribers, without capital other than the mortgages or other obligations which the subscribers individually provided; it was organized without corporate charter, to transact a limited volume of business in a limited period of time. Both arose from the need of a medium of exchange and a legal tender in the absence of specie, which the need of imports kept driving away. For as fast as specie was received, it was exported to pay for goods that could not be produced at home.

In its absence, a domestic medium of exchange was required, and even more a legal tender, for the law unrealistically assumed the existence of silver and gold, which accordingly had to be produced for the settlement of taxes and contracts. But the medium of exchange was so exhausted, wrote John Colman, a Boston merchant, in 1720, "that in a little time we shall not have wherewith to buy our daily bread, much less to pay our debts or taxes"; people in the country were lucky, he said, for they were not dependent on the "ready penny." Trade was languishing because "there is not money to buy with." Moreover there were lawsuits and writs against "good honest housekeepers" who had property enough and the will to pay their debts but could not raise the money—the reason being that there was none. In several colonies land and commodities were made legal tender in the absence of specie, but that involved disputes about values and was generally unsatisfactory. The development of the economy tended to make the problem worse, for development required imports, and the imports put specie more in demand than ever. It was this dearth of specie, the only legal tender, that in 1786 drove the Shays rebels in Massachusetts to demand a medium with which they could protect their farms from tax sales—though the dearth at that time coincided with no unusual surplus of imports. The difficulty was general and persisted into the 19th century. "The small farmers," according to Professor Abernethy, writing of Tennessee at a later period, "were often forced to accept depreciated paper currency for their produce at the same time that they were required to discharge obligations in specie, for only gold and silver were legal tender."[6]

In their efforts to meet the need of a domestic medium of exchange, several colonies were very successful. One was Pennsylvania. Benjamin Franklin had advocated her paper money and Thomas Pownall, who had been governor of Massachusetts and South Carolina, praised it in his study of colonial administration. "There never was a wiser

[6] A. M. Davis, *Colonial Currency Reprints* i, 398-409; Abernethy, 325.

or a better measure," he said, "never one better calculated to serve the uses of an increasing country, . . . more steadily pursued or more faithfully executed." Governor Pownall distinguished Pennsylvania's success from the "outrageous abuses" in other colonies and "the great injury which the merchant and fair dealer" had suffered from them. A group of London merchants who were engaged in trade with America, and with Pennsylvania in particular, petitioned Parliament in March 1749 in favor of that colony's money, which, they said, had been issued "in an advantageous manner" and interference with which "would lessen the trade and exports of this kingdom." Maryland, from the early part of the 18th century, issued an acceptable paper money, levied a tax for its redemption, and kept the unused funds invested in stock of the Bank of England.* Success attended the issue of bills of credit in other colonies also, notably New York, New Jersey, Delaware, Nova Scotia, and French Canada.[7]

IV

Despite these considerations, emphasized by many authorities—among them Alexander Hamilton and Albert Gallatin, both of whom acknowledged the usefulness as well as the imperfection of colonial currency—the notion has long been current that colonial Americans, and particularly agrarians, had a "craze" for paper money as a means of escaping payment of their debts and taxes. This notion arose in reaction to late 19th century Populism, to combat which it was said that earlier American experience with

---

* Independence raised delicate legal questions respecting ownership of the Maryland funds. Could the British trustees, whose American properties had been confiscated by Maryland, use the trusteed funds to indemnify themselves personally? The British courts held that they could not. Was the state of Maryland to be recognized as the successor to the colony of Maryland and owner of the trusteed funds? The British courts decided that the Crown and not the state of Maryland was the successor. But the Crown thereupon surrendered the funds to Maryland voluntarily. The case was prolonged many years by the claims of minor litigants and in diplomatic negotiation. The funds surrendered exceeded half a million dollars, a sum whose transfer was more than an ordinary transaction in international exchange.

[7] Pownall, 185-88; Stock v, 310-11; Hamilton (Lodge) III, 365; Gallatin III, 316-17; Madison, *Writings* (Hunt) II, 259-62; Franklin I, 307; v, 1-14; Ramsay II, 125ff; Adam Smith I, 310; Lester, 108-14, 140-41, 151; Kemmerer, *JPE*, XLVII (1939), 867ff; Rodney, 18ff; Knox, *History of Banking*, 563; Behrens, Crowl, Radoff, Gould, passim.

paper money had been wholly bad, wholly unnecessary, and wholly inspired by the frontier, which the Populist West of the 19th century roughly paralleled. The idea was expressed by Professor Frederick J. Turner in 1894 in his editorial introduction to a monograph by Professor O. G. Libby on the votes for and against ratifying the federal Constitution in 1787 and 1788. In this study the areas of paper money advocacy in the 1780's were identified with areas of hostility to the proposed Constitution. The author of the study, according to Professor Turner, had shown "the influence of frontier conditions and sparse settlement in permitting lax business honor, inflated paper currency, and wild-cat banking"; he had shown "that the colonial and revolutionary interior was the region whence emanated many of the worst forms of an evil currency." Further he said:

"The West in the War of 1812 repeated the phenomenon on the frontier of that day, while the speculation and wild-cat banking of the period of the crisis of 1837 occurred on the new frontier belt; and the present Populistic agitation finds its stronghold in those western and southern regions whose social and economic conditions are in many respects strikingly like those existing in 1787 in the areas that opposed the ratification of the Constitution. A phase of social transformation has passed westward and carried with it, in successive areas, similar agitations over questions of debt and taxation. Between paper money agitations in the colonial days and the present Western unrest and remedial proposals, there is a historical continuity. Like social conditions have wrought like effects. Thus each one of the periods of lax financial integrity coincides with periods when a new set of frontier communities has arisen and for the most part coincides in area with these successive frontiers. A primitive society can hardly be expected to show intelligent appreciation of the complexity of business interests in a developed society. The continual recurrence of these areas of paper-money agitation is another evidence that the similar social and economic areas can be isolated and studied as factors of the highest importance in American history."[8]*

* I am sorry to say that Professor Turner's statement seems to me wholly fallacious. The crises of 1812 and 1837, for example, were commercial; the speculation and wild-cat banking were not peculiar to the frontier or engaged

[8] Libby, vi-vii; from Turner, *Significance of the Frontier in American History,* Annual Report, AHA (1893), 223; also in Turner, *Frontier in American History,* 32.

The matter was restated no less symmetrically six years later by Professor Calvin J. Bullock, when William Jennings Bryan was making his second formal attempt to loosen America's bondage to gold and give it Populist salvation with greenbacks and free silver. Professor Bullock's statement was that "a strong movement in favor of cheap money has existed continuously in this country from the earliest period"; that "the persistence of such an agitation has been due, more than to any other single cause, to the constant spread of settlements westward"; that "with the growth of numbers, the rise of manufacturing and commercial industries, and the increase of wealth, the desire for a cheap currency has gradually diminished"; but that "this has no sooner taken place in the more populous states than the old phenomena have reappeared in newly settled districts, while any localities that have remained sparsely peopled and devoted chiefly to agricultural pursuits have always furnished a favorable field for the old propaganda."[9]

This is the view, commonly elaborated by writers around 1900, which seems still to govern what many if not most people think on the subject. But it involves serious difficulties in fact and reasoning. It avoids the basic fact that the 18th century Americans, being without specie to serve as a medium of exchange and legal tender, had to provide something. It conflicts with the fact that colonial and revolutionary paper currencies were the products of war, administrative need, and business interest. It conflicts with the fact that many of the colonies had a satisfactory experience with paper money. It ignores the fact that when the federal Constitution was being composed, paper money was condemned because of the experience with the continental bills issued to finance the Revolution and not because of colonial experience. It ignores the fact that Andrew Jackson and the agrarians of his day were fanatically opposed to paper money, whether issued by banks or by government. It conflicts with the fact that so far from demanding easy money and abundant credit as they spread westward, these agrarians restricted banks and

---

in by "a primitive society." Between "paper money agitation in colonial days" and 19th century Populism there was neither parallel nor continuity— no parallel, because one was commercial and the other agrarian—no continuity, even if a parallel be assumed, because the Jeffersonian and Jacksonian agrarians were a rigidly hard-money lot. The basic error is the assumption that easy money is peculiarly agrarian if agrarian at all.

[9] Bullock, 1-2.

bank currency to the point of prohibiting them, without supplying a substitute. It conflicts with the fact that the dominant and influential debtors have long been speculators and business men rather than farmers, and with the fact that the eventual multiplicity of banks and abundance of credit characteristic of the 19th and 20th century American economy are the result of an aggressive and persistent demand by these business men and speculators. The conventional theory of an agrarian "craze" for easy money is tenable in the United States, and also in Canada, for a relatively recent period only; and its attribution to the 18th century is a projection of ideas backward where they have no place.

The colonial shortage of money was first felt by the colonial governments, next by the merchants, and least of all by farmers. The governments felt it because cash was needed for wars and administrative expenses. Payments in kind would not do. The first American issues of paper money were occasioned by the expedition from Massachusetts against the French in 1690, and from then on issues and advocacy of issues never ceased. In 1720 John Colman, the Boston merchant whom I quoted earlier, urged the country folk to join the city in an effort to get paper money issued; "and tho' I confess you can do without Money better than we, yet our want of Money to Buy will very much lower the Prices of all your Produce." His division of the interest between country and city was confirmed by an opponent, the Reverend Edward Wigglesworth: "As to the Publick Loans, or Bank, as you call it, all the World knows that the General Assembly, especially the Country Part, had never thought of or consented to it, had it not been upon the great Sollicitation and pressing Importunity of the Trading Part." The same conviction was implied by Thomas Jefferson nearly a century later, in 1813, when he attributed complaints about the scarcity of money not to farmers but to "speculators, projectors, and commercial gamblers."[10]

The most famous 18th century advocate of paper money is Benjamin Franklin. In his *Modest Enquiry into the Nature and Necessity of a Paper Currency*, 1729, he mentions the stimulating effect abundant money will have on the prices of farm products, but mainly it is the advantage to trade that he emphasizes, to manufacturing, particularly shipbuilding, and to the wages of labor. The opponents

---

[10] A. M. Davis, *Colonial Currency Reprints* I, 407, 410; Jefferson (Ford) IX, 417n.

of paper money, he says, will be those "wanting Courage to venture in trade," the wealthy, and lawyers. Its proponents will be those who are "lovers of trade and delight to see manufactures encouraged." Later, in a memorandum written about 1764, he suggested that the colonial legislatures be empowered to issue any amount of paper money required for purposes of revenue, trade, business, and agriculture—the bills to be lent on collateral security, deficiencies in the security to be guarded against by funds obtained from taxes, and the interest on the loans to be used in meeting current expenses. Incidentally, "in emergencies, war, etc.," the money might be used directly in payment of expenses, but money so used was to be retired at a uniform rate in ten years.* In 1767, in his *Remarks and Facts Concerning American Paper Money*, he avers that in the middle colonies the money has increased their "Settlements, Numbers, Buildings, Improvements, Agriculture, Shipping, and Commerce."[11]

The best-known contemporary of Dr Franklin who opposed paper money was "the honest and downright Doctor William Douglass" of Boston, whom Adam Smith esteemed, though he was himself far more temperate about paper money than his downright doctor was. Dr Douglass, an intelligent physician who appears to have had much more authority with historians and economists than Benjamin Franklin, can not mention paper money without heat. Yet he never attributes the issues to farmers. Those who call most loudly for it, he says in his *Discourse*, about 1740, are "such as would take up money at any bad lay, viz., the Idle, those in desperate Circumstances, and the Extravagant." Paper money, he concedes, has given "some Men Opportunities of building vessels and running into trade," but they are men without substance, not "large traders," and he expects them to fail. He is scornful of the argument that a plenty of money enables the community to spruce itself up. "Boston, like a private man of small fortune, does not become richer but poorer

---

* It was on this proposal of Benjamin Franklin's that Thomas Pownall based his own proposal for an issue of bills by His Majesty's government to be lent in America on real estate security, remarking that in case of an American war the bills could also be used for expenditures in the colonies, so that it would be unnecessary "to send real cash thither." Governor Pownall seems to have been the one British statesman to offer a constructive proposal for the colonies' monetary needs.

[11] Franklin II, 139, 141; v, 14; Riddel, *PMHB*, LIV (1930), 52; A. M. Davis, *Boston "Banks,"* passim.

by a rich, goodly appearance." Debt is something that sensible persons avoid, a concomitant of distress and no possible source of good. "All private banks for large sums upon subscription have the same bad consequence which attends publick Loans, viz., a snare to the People by giving the unwary and the Prodigal Opportunities of borrowing, that is, of involving and ruining themselves." Debt serves a constructive purpose only "amongst Shopkeepers," who have a maxim, he says, that the readiest way to grow rich is through bankruptcy.[12]

His animadversions never suggest that he has agrarians in mind, nor what Professor Turner calls the more "primitive" elements of society. He declares "that all our paper-money-making assemblies have been legislatures of debtors, the representatives of people who from incogitancy, idleness, and profuseness have been under a necessity of mortgaging their lands." Incogitancy, idleness, and profuseness are not the frailties of farmers. That instead he is talking about business men becomes evident when he turns to Rhode Island, in contrast with which Connecticut is a "colony of industrious Husbandmen," who have "with much Prudence emitted only Small Quantities of Bills" to meet administrative needs, and retired them. The Rhode Islanders issue paper money "for private iniquitous ends," he says. "This handful of People have lately made a very profitable Branch of Trade and Commerce by negociating their own Paper Money in various Shapes." With it, they purchase in Massachusetts "British and foreign goods" which they then sell as competitors of the Massachusetts merchants, particularly in the rich West Indies markets. And one of the arguments used in Massachusetts for paper money, he reports, is that Massachusetts should imitate the Rhode Islanders and "partake with them in the plunder," instead of doing which she is "by some unaccountable Infatuation," and to her own hurt, giving Rhode Island's money a wide currency and her traders unconscionable profits.[13]

V

Rhode Island was generally considered the most reprobate of the colonies. From 1715 to 1750, she issued eight "banks" of paper money, mostly lent to borrowers. The preamble to the act authorizing the first of these "banks," one of £40,000, recalled the expense of

---

[12] Douglass, *Discourse*, 27-41.
[13] Douglass, *Discourse*, 11-13, 38; Douglass, *Summary* I, 310; II, 86-88n.

fighting the French and the Indians and other military charges that had "reduced the Money of the Colony and other Mediums of Exchange unto a very low Ebb that thereby Trade is sensibly Decayed, the Farmers thereby Discouraged, Husbandmen and others Reduced to great Want and all sorts of Business Languishing, few having wherewith to pay their Arrears and many not wherewithal to sustain their daily wants by Reason the Silver and Gold in the first place necessary to defray the Incident and Occasional Charges hath been exhausted. . . ." In 1721 a second "bank," of £40,000, was authorized and in 1728 a third, of the same amount—"at this juncture," according to the preamble, "there being so great a scarcity and want of a proper Medium of exchange, that . . . Trade and Commerce, which are the Nerves and Power of the Government," were beginning to "Decline, Stagnate, and Decay." Proposals for a fourth "bank," 1731, aroused spirited opposition, but the paper-money party won. A "bank" of £60,000 was brought in with an eye to "Encouragement of the Hempen Manufactury and of the Whale and Cod Fishery." In 1733 came the fifth "bank," of £104,000, again for "Promoting the Whale and Cod Fishery" and the construction of a harbor at Block Island; and in 1738 a sixth, of £100,000. In authorizing the latter the legislature found that the previous "banks" had "entirely answered those Ends for which they were emitted and have tended greatly to the interest and Advantage of the publick by encreasing and promoting Trade and encouraging all Kinds of Business." But now they were due to be retired, and so new issues must take their place. Moreover a new Colony House should be built in Newport and a new light house at Beaver Tail, "the Fishery and Hemp Manufactures" were growing but needed increased encouragement, and some £3,000 was to go into an enterprise for making duck. A seventh "bank," of £20,000, was authorized in 1740, and an eighth, of £40,000, in 1743. The principal of all these "banks" was lent to borrowers on the security of land and the interest was allocated to the improvements and enterprises named.[14]

Among the advocates of these paper money measures, members of the Wanton family were prominent. They were merchants and shipbuilders. One of them, John Wanton, was Deputy Governor of the colony. He was accounted the wealthiest merchant in Newport. In 1731, when the Governor, Joseph Jenckes, a professional land surveyor, had sought to prevent the "bank" then being authorized,

[14] Potter and Rider, 12, 23, 26ff, 40-41, 45-50, 52, 57, 182-86.

John Wanton had convened the Assembly and over-ridden the Governor. The latter appealed to the King and to the Board of Trade against the Assembly's behavior and its dismissal of his memorial "in this torn and tattered manner." But the appeal was futile. The legal opinion in Whitehall—indulgent to the American colonies in a fashion soon to be abandoned—was that the Assembly's act was valid under Rhode Island's liberal charter and that neither King nor Governor could set it aside. So Rhode Island got some more paper money, the Governor who tried to stop it was defeated for re-election, and William Wanton, the colony's leading ship-builder and a brother to John, was made Governor. John Wanton, who had convened the Assembly and got the paper money through, continued as Deputy Governor, and later became Governor himself.[15]

Some years later, in response to a request from the Lords Commissioners of Trade for the Foreign Plantations, Governor Richard Ward made a report on the colony's currency, 9 January 1740. He too was a Newport merchant, Deputy Governor when John Wanton was made Governor, and his successor when he died. Rhode Island at the time had about 18,000 inhabitants—Dr Douglass's troublesome "handful of people." In his report to Whitehall, the Governor observed first "that it is now but an hundred years since the English came into this Colony, then a hideous wilderness and inhabited by Indians only." He reviews one by one the paper money issues I have mentioned and describes the fruits of a monetary policy which later historians and economists have called ruinous. He says that after the colony was called upon in 1710 "to appear in the field for the honor and interest of Great Britain" and had been reduced by the expense of its expeditions "to a low ebb, . . . we . . . boldly ventured upon enlarging our trade, which God Almighty hath crowned with so great a success, that we follow the same path to this day."*

The colony, he says, now has above 120 sail of vessels "all constantly employed in trade" with Africa, Europe, the West Indies, and her neighboring colonies. She has equipped and manned five privateers, "now cruising against the Spaniards."

---

* The expeditions referred to were presumably incident to the War of the Spanish Succession, known in America as Queen Anne's War, which was concluded in 1713 by the Treaty of Utrecht.

[15] Bartlett, *Wanton Family*; Bartlett, *Records of the Colony of Rhode Island* IV, 457-58, 461; Potter and Rider, 26ff, 58n.

"These, may it please your Lordships, are matters of the utmost importance to us; for navigation is one main pillar on which this government is supported at present; and we never should have enjoyed this advantage had not the government emitted bills of credit to supply the merchants with a medium of exchange, always proportioned to the increase of their commerce. Without this, we should have been in a miserable condition, unable to defend ourselves against an enemy or to assist our neighbors in times of danger.

"In short, if this Colony be in any respect happy and flourishing, it is paper money and a right application of it that hath rendered us so. And that we are in a flourishing condition is evident from our trade, which is greater in proportion to the dimensions of our government than that of any Colony in His Majesty's American dominions.

"Nor have we served ourselves only by engaging so deeply in navigation. The neighboring governments have been in a great measure supplied with rum, sugar, molasses, and other West India goods by us brought home and sold to them here. Nay, Boston, itself, the metropolis of the Massachusetts, is not a little obliged to us for rum and sugar and molasses, which they distil into rum for the use of their fishermen, &c.

"The West Indies have likewise reaped great advantage from our trade, by being supplied with lumber of all sorts suitable for building houses, sugar works, and making casks. Beef, pork, flour, and other provisions, we are daily carrying to them, with horses to turn their mills, and vessels for their own use. And our African trade often furnishes them with slaves for their plantations. To all this we beg leave to add that the merchants of Great Britain have, within these twelve months or thereabouts, received seven or eight sail of ships from this Colony for goods imported here of late and sold to the inhabitants.

". . . Hereto, we beg leave to add, that within the space of about six or seven years, several of the merchants of Newport have contracted a correspondence in London, procured goods to be sent to them, and thereby so well supplied our shop-keepers that our dependence on Boston hath been in some measure taken off. In return for those goods, our merchants have remitted to their correspondents ships of our own building, logwood fetched from the Bay of Honduras in our own vessels, bills of exchange purchased of the planters in the West Indies, and other commodities, in such quantities that for these six years last past bills have continued to be equal to silver, at twenty-seven shillings per ounce."[16]

Now, I think one will see in this account more of the influence of Lord Keynes than of distressed agrarian debtors. And the following, though not peculiarly Keynesian, is certainly not agrarian either. A committee of the General Assembly of Rhode Island, February 1749, explains that Rhode Island currency is depreciated "because the inhabitants of New England constantly consume a much greater quantity of British manufactures than their exports are able to pay for." This "makes such a continual demand for gold, silver, and bills of exchange to make remittances with that the merchants to procure them are always bidding one upon another and thereby daily sink the value of paper bills with which they purchase them."

"And it is plain where the balance of trade is against any country, that such part of their medium of exchange as hath a universal currency will leave them, and such part of their medium as is confined to that country will sink in its value in proportion as the balance against them is to their trade. For what hath been the case with Rhode Island bills hath also been the common fate of all the paper bills issued by the other Colonies in New England; they have been all emitted at near equal value and have always passed at par one with another and consequently have equally sunk in their value. And this will always be the case with infant countries that do not raise so much as they consume: either to have no money or if they have it, it must be worse than that of their richer neighbors, to compel it to stay with them."[17]

Rhode Island was the least suitable of the provinces for an agrarian economy, because her land area was little, and little of that little was as good as what her neighbors had much of; at the same time, a large part of her gross area comprised excellent harbors and roadsteads for the light-draft vessels of the 18th century. Her people were free-thinking and independent. She was a haven for refugees from the theocracies of Massachusetts and Connecticut and a pioneer of religious and political tolerance. She had an exceptionally liberal and democratic charter. She was a progressive, unshackled community, thoroughly disliked by her larger, more conservative neighbors—and not least of all for her commercial prosperity. "The

---

[16] Potter and Rider, 143-63; Bartlett, *Records of the Colony of Rhode Island* v, 8-14.
[17] Potter and Rider, 188-89.

paper-money promoters" in Rhode Island, wrote a contemporary gentleman in Boston, 1743, "are the desperate and fraudulent, these being vastly the majority in the colony." He links her ascendancy with the practice in Rhode Island of electing "both legislative and executive parts of their government" annually, which was an abominable democratic heresy. "This poor small colony," containing no more than "20,000 men, women, and children, whites, Indians, and Negroes," had £400,000 in paper money outstanding; "and of this about three quarters is in the possession of people of neighboring colonies."*

These unfriendly words do not fit the paper money craze of poor farmers but the sophisticated monetary practice of an intelligent and energetic business community which not only fomented commerce and developed markets but obtained the capital for its enterprise, without interest, from its envious and conservative neighbors. Rhode Island's monetary practice was as characteristic of its success as were its ships. No other colony appears to have achieved so much or exemplified so much in monetary policy. But that is perhaps because no other was so largely commercial. The enterprising majority in Rhode Island was an enterprising minority elsewhere— inclined the same way but not so powerful. Yet throughout the colonies the same interest, in an economic setting more or less common to all, found in some degree the same solution to the problem

---

* There happens to be abundant evidence that the people of Rhode Island used to be very wicked. Many of them were Quakers, or worse. The men in power were dependent on the people, who were "cunning, deceitful, and selfish" and lived "almost entirely by unfair and illicit trading." Moreover, as Dr Douglass had observed, their judicial oath or affirmation did "not invoke the judgments of the omniscient God," and so entailed only this world's penalties for perjury. (*Summary* II, pp. 94-95.) The colony being in so wretched a state, "it has happened more than once that a person has had sufficient influence to procure a fresh emission of paper money, solely to defraud his creditors. . . ." This is the testimony of an energetic and excellent young man, the English traveler Andrew Burnaby, who subsequently became a clergyman. His dispassionate opinions confirm those of the honest and downright Dr Douglass, from whom he got them. (Burnaby, 127-29.)

On the other hand, Professor Hillman M. Bishop, answering the question as to "Why Rhode Island Opposed the Federal Constitution," in *Rhode Island History*, VIII (February 1949), 7, contends that the number of persons in Rhode Island who abused their creditors by payments in depreciated paper money "has been greatly exaggerated."

of money; and Adam Smith, commenting on the redundancy of paper money in America, and in Scotland, said that "in both countries it is not the poverty but the enterprising and projecting spirit of the people" that occasioned it.[18]

The jejune assumption of poverty among farmers or any other part of the colonial peoples is itself palpably out of accord with the facts. For all but a few, the conditions of living were primitive and severe but not miserable. They were far better than in Europe. "Some few towns excepted," wrote Hector St. John Crèvecoeur somewhat later, "we are all tillers of the earth, from Nova Scotia to West Florida," and everywhere was "a pleasing uniformity of decent competence." Andrew Burnaby, in the course of 1,200 miles, "did not see a single object that solicited charity." A scarcity of silver and gold was inconvenient to such people only when a tax or other obligation had to be paid in specie; it did not signify poverty or any scarcity of food, shelter, and apparel.[19]

VI

British policy with respect to the monetary schemes of the colonial Americans was at first indulgent but became at last arbitrarily negative, in the spirit of the Bubble Act. This retrogression owed much to the difficulties of the problem—difficulties arising partly from the colonies' inchoate state of economic development and partly from their number: there were nineteen of them from Newfoundland to West Florida, with their various monetary systems, constitutional rights, traditions, and other idiosyncrasies.* The sheer multiplicity of currencies was bad enough, but it was a multiplicity variously depreciated. Prices of the same commodities varied inordinately from colony to colony, and debtors were legally shielded from their outside creditors by the right to offer them payment in money whose value was less than the amount of the debt. In the reign of Queen Anne, Parliament had sought to establish order in the heterogeny by as-

---

* This was the maximum number from 1763 to 1776. They were Newfoundland, Prince Edward Island, Nova Scotia, Canada, New Hampshire, Massachusetts, Rhode Island, Connecticut, New York, New Jersey, Pennsylvania, Delaware (not wholly separate from Pennsylvania), Maryland, Virginia, North Carolina, South Carolina, Georgia, and the two Floridas, East and West. I do not include the West Indian colonies, which to the home government, however, were just so many more.

[18] Horace White, 81-82; Adam Smith II, 426.
[19] Crèvecoeur, 49, 50 (Letter III); Burnaby, 149.

certaining and publishing the comparative value of foreign coins current in each of the "plantations," but the good intent of this measure had been frustrated, Parliament complained, 25 April 1740, by subsequent issues in the various colonies with arbitrary values. A generation later, Adam Smith wrote that "£100 sterling was occasionally considered as equivalent in some of the colonies to £130 and in others to so great a sum as £1,100. . . ." These things Parliament knew, for she was being constantly reminded of them by exasperated creditors and colonial administrators. But what could she do? It seemed impossible to solve the problem without abandoning basic commitments on commercial and colonial policy; nor on the other hand could any prohibition of paper money be effectual without interfering with the common law right to borrow. For paper money was essentially an evidence of debt. Such interference, by a commercial people, was unlikely.[20]

In 1740 John Colman, the Boston merchant whom I have quoted, organized one of those associations called "banks," whose bills of credit, lent to members of the association on the security of real estate, were not redeemable in specie. Other merchants who mistrusted this "land bank" organized a rival association whose bills were to be redeemed after a period in silver. John Colman's land bank seems to have assumed the impossibility of getting specie together in any great amount, and the silver bank seems to have assumed the possibility of getting it together some years later. A third group petitioned Parliament to curb both projects. Meanwhile Governor Jonathan Belcher had interposed despotically against the land bank. He warned Parliament that "If some speedy stop be not put to these things, they will be more fatal consequences to the Plantations than the South Sea Bubble was, in the year 1720, to Great Britain." This was ridiculous, but Parliament listened. When she was told that John Colman's scheme "would here in Great Britain be an high offense and attended with heavy punishments and might easily be suppressed" as being within the Bubble Act but that "his Majesty's Attorney and Sollicitor-General . . . have reported their opinion that that act does not extend to America," she took pains to extend it there "by express words." The new act was passed early in 1741. It recited that persons had presumed to publish in America "a Scheme for Supplying a pretended Want of Medium in Trade" by setting up a bank on land security; that they

[20] Stock v, 49; Adam Smith i, 310.

promised "to receive the Bills which they should issue for and as so much lawful Money"; and that "sundry other Schemes, Societies, Partnerships, or Companies have been and may be set on Foot in America for the Purpose of raising publick Stocks or Banks and unlawfully issuing large Quantities of Notes or Bills there. . . ." On these grounds the Bubble Act of 1720, suppressing "mischievous and Dangerous undertakings," was extended to America.[21]

There was already vocal in the colonies a resentment at Parliament's growing disposition to rule British subjects without allowing them representation, and the act of 1741 caused an uproar. It was universally offensive on constitutional grounds, it produced suffering and injustice in Massachusetts, being an *ex post facto* measure, and it reversed the position taken by Whitehall ten years before in upholding Rhode Island's paper money. But it does not follow that Americans at large greatly resented its substance. They might have found the purpose of the act as congenial as their British contemporaries did, could it have been considered by itself. Most of the farmers and shopkeepers of the new world, and scarcely less the large land owners and conservative merchants, were not disposed to have large scale, corporate, monied organizations at their thresholds.*

Besides arousing bitter feelings, the act of 1741 failed to stop the Americans, especially in New England and particularly in Rhode Island. The Rhode Islanders, Parliament was told, authorized issues of paper money, borrowed it, purchased goods and other property, depreciated it with successive issues, used it when depreciated to repay their indebtedness, and realized egregious profits. So Parliament passed in 1751 "An Act to regulate and restrain Paper Bills of Credit in his Majesty's Colonies or Plantations of Rhode Island and Providence Plantations, Connecticut, the Massachusets Bay, and New Hampshire in America; and to prevent the same being legal Tenders in Payments of Money." It forbade that "any Paper

---

* So late as 1884 it was contended in the Massachusetts Supreme Court that the Bubble Act was still in force in that state, having been amongst the statutes taken over when Massachusetts became independent. The reasoning was logical, but the Court, whose opinion was given by Judge Oliver Wendell Holmes, rejected it on pragmatic grounds. The case was *Phillips* v. *Blatchford,* 137 Massachusetts 513.

[21] A. M. Davis, *Currency and Banking in Massachusetts* I, chap. VII; Osgood III, 353ff; DuBois, 25, 65-66, n138; Stock V, 97-100; 14 George II, c. 37 (1741).

Bills or Bills of Credit . . . be created or issued under any Pretence whatsoever" but permitted issues for current administrative needs or emergencies—a distinction pretty hard to define and observe in practice.[22]

Thirteen years later, 1764, Parliament passed the more general "act to prevent Paper Bills of Credit, hereafter to be issued in any of his Majesty's Colonies or Plantations in America, from being declared to be a legal Tender in Payments of Money." It bore on all the colonies and not on New England alone but seems to have left them free to issue paper money, so long as it was not legal tender. Certainly they did issue it: Nova Scotia continued to do so till Confederation in 1867. But the legal tender quality was of a practical importance hard to imagine nowadays, and the prohibition was another interference in domestic matters; and in consequence the new measure caused an uproar like that two decades earlier when the Bubble Act was extended to America. It was coupled in spirit with the Stamp Act, the Quartering Act, and Parliament's other assumptions of power to legislate for British subjects in America without allowing them representation. These violations of constitutional rights formerly defended by the British authorities affronted the Americans more than refusal to let them have paper money and make it legal tender, which was something that many of them did not wish to do anyway.* Three years later Benjamin Franklin told Parliament that the lessened respect Americans felt for it was in part due to "the prohibition of making paper money among themselves." His last two words are pregnant; being denied paper money is not the same as being denied the right to do something about one's own monetary system oneself.[23]

In 1773 in "an Act to explain and amend" the 1764 measure, Parliament confirmed and enlarged the freedom of the American colonies to issue paper money. It did so in consideration of "the Want of Gold and Silver Currency" in the colonies, in consideration

* In 1833 William Gouge, Jacksonian anti-bank authority, spoke approvingly of Parliament's interdict of 1764 respecting legal tender; though he said it had "caused much murmuring, for the speculating classes of society, who are always the most noisy, liked not to be deprived of so many opportunities of profit as a vacillating currency afforded them. . . ." Gouge II, 24.

22 Stock v, 448-50, 464-67; 24 George II, c. 53 (1751).
23 4 George III, c. 34 (1764); Franklin IV, 420.

of "the publick Advantage," and "in Justice to those Persons who may have Demands upon the publick Treasuries in the said Colonies for Services performed." The money might be issued in the form of "Certificates, Notes, Bills, or Debentures" and made "a legal Tender to the publick Treasuries" in payment of taxes and other dues. But this concession came too late.[24]

The Declaration of Independence, three years later, cited Britain's interference with domestic law-making among the causes which impelled the colonies to separation, but it did not include interference with paper money among the more specific of them. The new sovereign state of Virginia observed a like distinction in October 1777 when she enacted a law derived from Parliament's statute of 1764 but more drastic. It was "an act to prevent private persons from issuing bills of credit in the nature of paper currency." After reciting that "divers persons have presumed, upon their own private security, to issue bills of credit or notes payable to the bearer, in the nature of paper currency, which may tend . . . to the great injury of the publick by increasing the quantity of money in circulation . . . ," the law subjected persons who issued such bills to a forfeiture of ten times their amount. It did not merely forbid their being made a legal tender—which was all that Parliament had done in 1764—it forbade their being used at all. Virginia was brushing boldly against the common law right to borrow, which Parliament had not done, and evincing a grimmer intent against paper money *per se*. There is the difference that Virginia was dealing with private action alone, but this was a difference of jurisdiction only, not of principle. Her stated purpose was to curb inflation. And in October 1785, after the war, she passed a new act "to prevent the circulation of private bank notes," making it unlawful "for any person to offer in payment a private bank bill or note for money," the penalty again being forfeiture of ten times the amount involved. This was at a time, as James Madison testified, when money was so scarce it was doubtful if taxes could be paid; and for that reason the year following, the Shays rebellion broke forth in Massachusetts. The new Virginia statute was prepared by George Wythe, who with Thomas Jefferson was one of the revisors appointed to survey the Parliamentary statutes ante-dating Independence and select those which it was expedient for the state to re-enact. There is, to be sure, no direct phraseological evidence that the Virginia prohibitions were

24 13 George III, c. 57 (1773).

derived from the Parliamentary act of 1764. But there should be none; Mr Jefferson has explained why. The revisors decided, he said, "to reform the style of the later British statutes and of our own acts of Assembly, which, from their verbosity, their endless tautologies, their involutions of case within case and parenthesis within parenthesis, and their multiplied efforts at certainty by *saids* and *aforesaids*, by *ors* and by *ands*, to make them more plain, do really render them more perplexed and incomprehensible, not only to common readers but to the lawyers themselves." What the revisors "thought proper to be retained were digested into one hundred and twenty-six new acts in which simplicity of style was aimed at as far as was safe." No listing was made to indicate correspondence between the old and the new laws, but important changes were explained, among which no change of monetary measures was included.* George Wythe and Thomas Jefferson had been vigorous critics of Parliament's usurpations, but they were evidently in accord with Parliament's monetary principles.[25]

The same seems to have been true in Massachusetts, where in 1799 a law was enacted to the effect that "no person unauthorized by law" should "subscribe or become a member of any association, institution, or company, or proprietor of any bank" (unless an incorporated bank, of course) and that existing unincorporated associations were to cease issuing notes and lending. New York in March 1804 enacted the same law. By then such bans could have no other effect than that of protecting the monopoly of note issue by banks already incorporated. But Richard Hildreth, who was a contemporary, said that the Massachusetts law of 1799 was based on the 1741 act of Parliament, which at that time, he observed, "had almost produced a rebellion." Thus the series of statutes which the Bubble Act of 1720 initiated came round in the end, in America, to the purpose with which it evidently had started in Britain, viz., the shielding of monopoly; but for the greater part of the 18th century its purpose, in America as in Britain, was to protect the public interest. Verbally, the law remained the same; subjectively and juris-

* Why the law enacted in 1777 was altered in 1785, I do not know. But the revisors' measures were not adopted systematically, and my conjecture is that the 1777 law was enacted amongst the first, because it was thought important, and later was re-enacted in modified form with numerous other measures that had had the revisors' more deliberate attention.

[25] Hening ix, 175, 431; xii, 166; Jefferson (Boyd) ii, 316-17; Jefferson (Ford) i, 61; iii, 242-43.

prudentially, its purpose moved to the opposite and back again. And for the Americans as for the British its purpose was restrictive and expressed no craze for easy money.[26]

VII

The bills of credit issued during the Revolution were wartime expedients that stood on a very different footing from the colonial bills that preceded them. One may condemn the colonial bills and yet excuse those of the Revolution on the ground that there was no practicable alternative to issuing them, except giving up the struggle. Alexander Hamilton, called them "indispensable," though never again to be employed. Benjamin Franklin said they had worked as a gradual tax upon each person in whose hands they had lost value, and that with them the Americans had "supported the war during five years against one of the most powerful nations of Europe." David Ramsay, in his *History of the American Revolution*, published in 1789, wrote that "the United States derived for a considerable time as much benefit from this paper creation of their own, though without any established funds for its support or redemption, as would have resulted from a free gift of as many Mexican dollars." He observes that their issue was not intended for more than a temporary expedient but that the war outlasted expectations, and the issues had therefore to be continued.[27]

The individual states issued bills and so did the Continental Congress—the bills of the latter being called "continentals." They could not possibly be replaced by specie, and the amount of them could not be held down to normal needs for circulation. Instead the amount was determined by the needs of war. But the more there were issued, the less they were worth. In the end their value sank to nothing, as the phrase, "not worth a continental," survives to testify. They were not agrarian in any sense whatever; farmers indeed were their worst victims, for they were mostly used to supply the army with food, horses, fodder, carriage, and such. There had to be force to make farmers accept them.

VIII

In contending that colonial demand for paper money, aside from military and administrative needs, reflected nascent enterprise in-

26 Hildreth, *History of United States* v, 549.
27 Hamilton (Lodge) i, 307; Franklin ix, 231, 234; Ramsay ii, 127.

stead of distress and impoverishment, I have had some misgivings lest I be beating a dead horse. For a respectable number of recent works have pitched their discussion of colonial paper money in a new key. A younger generation than my own, born since the Populists frightened the country in the late 19th century, has felt no inspiration to see in the facts more than is there. In 1939 Professor Richard A. Lester in his *Monetary Experiments* showed that colonial paper money issues of Pennsylvania, New York, New Jersey, Delaware, and Maryland had done very well; the people of the colonies were realists and "managed the money supply with a considerable degree of skill and success." Studies of Maryland's colonial paper money by Kathryn L. Behrens and Philip Crowl had already indicated that that colony had not been so imbecile in money matters as the colonists were reputed in general to be. In 1946 Professor Joseph Dorfman, in his *Economic Mind in American Civilization*, observed of the colonies generally that "contrary to the tradition that historians have perpetuated, a critical analysis of the contemporary literature indicates that the proponents as well as the critics were not poor debtors or agrarians, but for the most part officials, ministers, merchants, and men of substance and learning in general." Professor H. F. Williamson, in 1951, in a volume edited by him, *Growth of the American Economy*, stated that some colonial issues were "highly successful in remedying an inadequate monetary supply."[28]

Yet the confused notion of paper money crazes and orgies for which poor debtors, usually agrarian, were responsible, survives openly still in many works and lurks mischievously between the lines in more. In Horace White's long-lived, entertaining, and influential *Money and Banking*, first published in 1894, "the pamphlets and records of the colonial period are filled with accounts of the distress and demoralization caused by depreciated paper money made legal tender." They are also filled with accounts of the benefits to business of paper money, for which, however, Mr White had only a frosty and unseeing eye. "The emission," he says, "of bills of credit on loan was, in effect, a conspiracy of needy landowners against the rest of the community." It is especially unfortunate that such ideas should have penetrated works of general history. They got into Professor Turner's at the very outset. Thirty years later they confused Professor H. L. Osgood in his volumes on the American colonies and produced there an odd incongruity between what he saw the facts

[28] Lester, 287, 307; Dorfman, 93, 142; Williamson, 227.

to be and what he accepted on faith. He is cognizant again and again of the pressing want of a proper circulating medium, of the froward-ness of the British government in forbidding what the colonists tried to do whilst proposing nothing better, and of the paper money issues advocated by merchants for the promotion of trade and in-dustry. Yet he also lets himself be persuaded to see in it all "a paper money craze," the work of "agrarian radicals." The enterprising and lucrative practice of Rhode Island's traders he calls "an expres-sion of her agrarian radicalism." In the *Dictionary of American Biography*'s article on Governor Richard Ward, whose account of Rhode Island's paper money I have quoted, it is remarked that "Ward as a merchant belonged to the conservative group, but he was unable to prevent the establishment of another bank of issue." Passing over the implication that Governor Ward ever wished to prevent paper money issues and that a bank in the corporate sense was involved somehow, I think the really notable error in this state-ment is couched in its bland assumption that merchants constituted a "conservative class" and presumably included no debtors at all but only creditors. In the volumes of Professor Charles M. Andrews, *The Colonial Period in American History*, published 1934 to 1938, these incongruities are absent. But so is the whole subject, prac-tically. Professor Andrews omits the customary clichés, and what he does say is respectful of the facts even though brief with them. "The one problem," he says, "that neither the government nor the mercantilists were ever able to solve was how to meet the need of hard money in the colonies or to provide an adequate medium of exchange for the doing of business. Though the Board of Trade well knew that the money situation in America was serious—and it knew this at least as early as 1707—it seemed quite incapable of finding an adequate solution."[29]

Among recent works I have encountered none in which the ideas to which I object are deliberately expounded; but there are plenty in which they are confusedly taken for granted and employed to enliven a few ancient paragraphs with orgies and disasters. In most that mention the matter anti-Populist cant reappears whenever colonial paper money comes up. In one or another, the classic narra-tives of Horace White or Calvin J. Bullock are cited for details, honest and downright Dr William Douglass is quoted respectfully,

[29] Horace White, 86-87; Osgood ii, 374-75; iii, 221, 258, 260-61, 280, 347, 349; Andrews iv, 350-51.

and poor befuddled Dr Benjamin Franklin is corrected and patron-
ized. One comes on "the craze for paper money" again and again, on
"the rapid depreciation," and "the utter demoralization of industry
and trade." Rhode Island "started upon her notorious career"; hers
was the "most extreme case"; her issues are "of infamous memory."
The colonial scene as a whole was one of monetary "confusion,"
"excesses," "abuses," "crazes," "manias," "orgies," and "rages."
There was little variety in all this. The experience was "monotonously
bad"; it was "almost everywhere the same: over-issue, delay, and
postponement of redemption, depreciation, and finally in some cases
repudiation. And yet with all its evils, the practice was persisted
in. . . ." The experience "only too well illustrates the temptations
and dangers involved in the resort to paper money. Once started on
the downward path. . . ." And so on.

Such words sustain a myth of colonial distress, ineptitude, and
dishonesty. They deny the austere and simple well-being of the
colonists. They ignore the difficulties that had to be faced and the
energy, enterprise, and success with which the Americans met them.
They appraise colonial resourcefulness by one criterion only, the
depreciation of paper in terms of silver and gold. They also disregard the conservative temper of agrarianism the world over. It can
be stubbornly rebellious, not because agrarians are experimental,
innovatory, and radical but because they are typically the opposite.
In America they have changed considerably since colonial days, but
as late as the era of Andrew Jackson they still clung to the typical
preference for metallic money, serving as a store of value, a medium
of exchange, and a legal tender. Money in this sense is not meant to
stimulate economic activity; its amount is to be limited to the needs
of trade and of legal payments; and to make its volume expansible
at will is mischievous. Thomas Jefferson, taking note that it was
considered a merit in banks that they could expand the circulating
medium, said that just that in his judgment was their demerit.[30]

But it is no less important that the agrarians be absolved from
the demand for colonial paper money than that business men be
credited with it. The demand did not connote the stagnant, oppressive burden that unproductive debt may be but the welcome obligation that the entrepreneur assumes when he has a chance to make
money. The merchant borrowed eagerly because the credit enlarged
his working capital and his profit. The farmer borrowed, if at all,

[30] Clarke and Hall, 93.

because accident forced him to. The effective demand for credit, accordingly, came from the prospering and enterprising part of the population; the politically powerful "poor debtors" of the clichés were really thriving business men, and their debts were mercantile and self-liquidating. They relied for credit in part on their British suppliers, who allowed them customarily eighteen months' time; but for domestic transactions they wanted paper money, which they could borrow on mortgage security—for like everyone they owned land—and which would provide a medium of payment. They would alternately buy with it and sell with it. After Independence they found themselves able to set up banks, which under British rule the Bubble Act had forbidden. The vast creative use to which credit was put in the 19th century arose from these beginnings in the 18th at the hands of sanguine pioneers of enterprise and not from the hypothetical straits of farmers and paupers floundering in debt and trying to evade its repayment.

The agrarian demand for paper money and easy credit which did at last appear in the States in the latter part of the 19th century arose from tardy recognition by the agrarians that they lived in a modern economy, not in dreamland, and in order to hold their own must use credit as business men did. It arose from a slow realization that farming must be a means of making money, not of withholding oneself from the world. Till then, observers who knew with what attention to profit farming was conducted in Europe were struck by the American farmer's inattention to it; and similarly Americans— from the North—were impressed by the expectation of Europeans that agriculture should pay. But in the face of business enterprise and industrialization, it became impossible for farming to remain unchanged. Stock had to be improved. Machinery had to be acquired. The elements of farm capital became diversified, the land itself ceasing to be the one ingredient of weight. Money and credit forced their way into the farmer's reckoning.[31]

This development diminished no whit the agrarian antipathy for city, commerce, and finance. It did not make the farmer love banks. Instead it led him, with the current of nationalism stimulated by the Civil War, to think more trustingly of the federal government than he had done when it was established. The central power that with Thomas Jefferson he had feared, he now saw he might control to his own advantage against the forces of enterprise that had set

[31] Danhoff, *JPE*, lxix (1941), 317ff.

it up. He concluded that the banks, especially under the National Bank Act, had usurped the sovereign power to create money.* He wanted it restored, so that he might get the funds he needed from the state, and not from private corporations. So wholly was the farmer won by this un-Jeffersonian concept of a benevolent central government, that he also dropped his Jacksonian aversion to paper money and became enthusiastic for greenbacks; though free silver at the ratio of 16 to 1 came closer to his hard money traditions and to his heart. This was Populism. It was now the business world, for which bank liabilities had become the accepted monetary medium, that became the so-called hard money party. And it was in defense of the existing "sound money" system, comprising mainly bank liabilities convertible into gold, that economists and historians identified contemporary Populism with 18th century agrarianism. Whether this historical analogy ever converted any Populists I doubt, but it confirmed the "sound money" party in the righteousness of their views and steeled them to resist the alarming nonsense of Mr William Jennings Bryan.

This effort made a half century ago to save the country from Mr Bryan and his Populists is one with which I have a congenital sympathy and in which I had an infant but enthusiastic part. For my liveliest political recollections are of the exciting presidential campaign of 1896—there has been none like it since—when I was nine years old and my breast was covered with badges attesting allegiance to the gold standard. My father, a country banker in Iowa, on occasion wore a waistcoat of golden yellow to the same purpose; he was a young man of great ardency, and as a member of the McKinley and Hobart glee club he sang derisive songs about greenbacks and the free and unlimited coinage of silver at the ratio of 16 to 1. I understand the anxious bias which omitted to say any good of paper money and which saw in history more warnings against contemporaneous agrarian monetary projects than were really there. But it is time that the 18th century be freed from the

* This point was made by Mr Jefferson himself in 1813. "Bank paper must be suppressed, and the circulating medium must be restored to the nation, to whom it belongs." But the Populist idea of doing this was not his. He wanted first to curb the banks; he wanted second to solve a fiscal problem for the Treasury. His proposal was the same that Alexander Hamilton had made fifteen years before and solely for the Treasury's benefit. Jefferson (Ford) ix, 399n.

19th century's polemics, which like the golden yellow waistcoat are now *démodé*.

IX

The agrarian dislike of banking under the Republic continued the agrarian dislike of paper money in colonial days, for the distinctive mark of banks was their circulating notes, and these notes were a variety of paper money. The dislike was aggravated by the recent experience with continental bills during the Revolution and by the fact that banks were corporations. It was a blend of acute understanding and of pardonable ignorance. When Thomas Jefferson explained in 1791 that the vaunted power of banks to expand the supply of money was not a virtue but an evil, he showed that he discerned the function of banks as well as Alexander Hamilton did. The difference between Hamilton and him was not as to the fact but as to the significance of the fact. The agrarians saw well that banks belonged to an order of things incompatible with their own and differentiated from it by predilections and moral choices that were basic.

In these circumstances such ignorance of banking as they exhibited was excused by an idealism which directed attention to the moral significance of things, not to their formal peculiarities, and which in consequence effaced differences and likenesses obvious to others. When the agrarians hated banks, they had, by a business man's standards, no clear idea what a bank was. Yet by their own standards they had a very clear idea. They were endeavoring tenaciously to preserve some primitive and virtuous simplicities in the labors of man and in his institutions. This purpose appears in the way the Bubble Act was applied and in the act of 1741 supplementary to it, in the currency act of 1764, in the Virginia statutes of 1777 and 1785, in repeal of the Bank of North America's charter in 1785, and later in the prohibition of banking in a number of western states. It is as if the greater part of the 18th century Anglo-Saxon world, in point of numbers, were drawing back premonitorily from the vast accomplishments of the entrepreneurial and industrial revolution in the centuries ahead—a revolution generated by steam and credit—to which the world is now so firmly committed that resistance to it seems quaint. To Thomas Jefferson it did not seem quaint.

There was, it is true, an important element of ignorance in the novelty of what was being brought to pass in the world by steam and credit, but it was not an ignorance peculiar to agrarians. No matter whether one welcomed these miracle-working factors in economic life or deplored them—either way one was confronted by something of which men had had no previous experience and of whose powers no one had more than inklings. The more conservative and thoughtful were deeply disturbed, for their observations were made in the early, confused phase of an evolution upon which we can look back calmly and teleologically. In the 20th century the strange and demoralizing forces that confront man are physical rather than economic. We take bank credit and machine production for granted, and think little of the circumstance that most of man's economic work is now done through the medium of artificial persons called corporations. Instead, what bothers us are novelties like nuclear fission and the second law of thermo-dynamics. In 1800 it was steam and credit. Most people, however, soon acquired a more cheerful view of the matter and left the gloom to the dwindling minority of agrarians, poets, and Transcendentalists. They took the view that Alexander Hamilton had expressed in 1781: "Most commercial nations have found it necessary to institute banks; and they have proved to be the happiest engines that ever were invented for advancing trade."[32]

The resistance of the minority to this complacent view died hard and slowly. In 1799 President John Adams wrote that "the fluctuations of our circulating medium have committed greater depredations upon the property of honest men than all the French piracies," which were then afflicting American commerce. In 1811 he wrote: "Our whole banking system I ever abhorred, I continue to abhor, and shall die abhorring." And in 1819 he wrote again that "banks have done more injury to the religion, morality, tranquillity, prosperity, and even wealth of the nation than they can have done or ever will do good." John Taylor of Caroline had said in 1794, "banking in its best view is only a fraud whereby labour suffers the imposition of paying an interest on the circulating medium"; and in 1814: "In the history of our forefathers we recognize three political beasts, feeding at different periods upon their lives, liberties, and properties. Those called hierarchical and feudal aristocracy, to say the worst of them, are now the instruments of the third," viz., of banks. In John Taylor's footsteps, William Gouge said in 1833 that banking was

[32] Hamilton (Lodge) III, 362.

"the *principal* cause of social evil in the United States," the italics being his. About the same time Senator Thomas Hart Benton demanded to know: "Are men with pens sticking behind their ears to be allowed to put an end to this republic?"[33]

Senator John C. Calhoun was more penetrating and descriptive of the sort of thing his contemporaries disliked, and less disturbed by it. He spoke objectively of "that peculiar description of property existing in the shape of credit or stock, public or private, which so strikingly distinguishes modern society from all that has preceded it."[34]

Some centuries earlier the only familiar form of property, aside from personal chattels, was real estate—as it still was in 18th century America, and as it still is in economically underdeveloped countries. There might be difficulty in selling property unless it had been held long enough for it to be commonly known who the owner was. Evidence of ownership lay largely in continuous, notorious, exclusive, adverse possession, and its transfer required witnesses and a primitive formality. The small portion of society comprising merchants and money lenders had other forms of property—mortgages, notes, bills, etc.—which were at first subjected to somewhat the same cumbrous, physical procedures as transactions in lands and houses. Written documents had not the eminent standing they have since acquired, and bankers would not recognize a written order to pay to a third party from a depositor's account; instead the depositor must go to the banker personally, accompanied by his creditor, and give oral instructions for the payment or transfer to be made on the banker's books. But the growth of commerce necessitated simpler procedures, with the result that in time, under the law merchant, the ownership of bills of exchange, orders, and claims became readily negotiable and transferable, by simple endorsement, successively, without witnesses, formalities, or the presence of the parties concerned. Joseph Chitty, the 18th and early 19th century authority for both Britain and America, explained the evolution in the following words, which Senator Calhoun must have known well:

". . . in the infancy of trade, when the bulk of national wealth consisted of real property, our courts did not often condescend to

---

[33] John Adams VIII, 660; IX, 638; X, 375; Taylor of Caroline, *Principles and Tendency*, Sec. III, 18; and *Principles and Policy*, 289; Gouge, Part I, 42, 133; Benton II, 60.

[34] Calhoun II, 349.

regulate personalty; but as the advantages arising from commerce were gradually felt, they were anxious to encourage it by removing the restrictions by which the transfer of interests in it was bound. On this ground the custom of merchants whereby a foreign bill of exchange is assignable by the payee to a third person—was recognized and supported by our courts of justice in the 14th century; and the custom of merchants rendering an inland bill transferable was established in the 17th century. In short, our courts, anxiously attending to the interests of the community, have in favour of commerce adopted a less technical mode of considering personalty than realty; and in support of commercial transactions have established the law merchant, which is a system founded on the rules of equity and governed in all its parts by plain justice and good faith."[35]

Mr Chitty, from a comfortable familiarity with the commercial world, wrote sympathetically of an evolution peculiar to that world. But these were things alien and distasteful to an agrarian society. People accustomed to property in its real form only, became aware of its taking unfamiliar, abstract, and intangible forms as well.* And they became aware also that in these forms it seemed to have a fearful vigor and infectiousness. New values arose which they had no competence to judge. Speculation, with its vicissitudes of fortune and ruin, seemed a wicked sleight-of-hand with pieces of paper. Of two documents bearing legal legends, one might be good as gold and the other worthless; yet the difference was one that simple people could not recognize themselves. They had to rely on what they were told. Where, in such circumstances, was their self-dependence and the freedom for which they prized America? Altogether, the ready and dynamic expansion of wealth was profoundly disturbing. Commerce at its best was a necessary evil, but bubbles, banks, funds, stocks, and all such were not only unproductive—they were useless, burdensome, malign. The source of wealth was the earth, and the

---

* In a passage of his memoirs, *Persons and Places* (p. 134), Mr George Santayana shows how strange the system of trust and credit is when approached from an economy where it does not prevail. He at first found it hard to feel at home in the system, but, he says, "I soon learned to swim happily with my eyes closed on this stream of business convention, which indeed at this moment is supplying me with a comfortable income coming, as far as my direct action or perception goes, from nowhere." Mr Santayana adjusted himself to the conventions of a credit economy without losing his sense of wonder; most people take them for granted.

[35] Usher I, 5ff, 28ff; Chitty, 8-9, 12.

producers thereof were those who tilled it and mined it and fished in its waters. The wealth possessed by bankers and stock-jobbers must have been taken somehow from these toilers. Whence otherwise could it come? The change in the form and instruments of wealth put all conservatives at a disadvantage and not agrarians alone. "The paper system," Alexander Baring told a committee of Parliament in 1819, "is undoubtedly particularly favourable to one class of people, viz., to enterprising speculators; and may be said to be unfavourable to persons of large capitals," who, of course, were typically creditors. The debtors were the enterprisers and speculators. Yet, Mr Baring continued, "it is impossible to deny that much of the aggregate wealth of the country has been derived from that spirit of enterprise"—an understatement that itself shows how novel was the thing of which he spoke.[36]

Though banks owed their growth mainly to business enterprise and its need of credit for monetary use, they also owed much of it to government and the need it too had for credit. For governments always have been borrowers, and repeatedly their dependence upon banks has been critical, especially in wartime. Since it is the function of banks to create money, and since it is characteristic of wars to cost money, the evolution of banking in the United States has received from wars some of its most powerful impulses. Thence indeed it had its start: the narrative taken up in the next chapter begins toward the end of the Revolutionary War, when the first American bank came into existence largely because of the desperate need of the Continental Congress for funds with which to maintain the Army.

[36] British Parliament, *Expediency of Resuming Cash Payments*, 128 (Query 158).

CHAPTER 2

The First American Bank, Philadelphia

1781-1787

I. Alexander Hamilton's first proposals for a bank — II. The Pennsylvania Bank — III. Alexander Hamilton's further proposals — IV. The Bank of North America established — V. The mutiny — VI. The attack upon the bank — VII. The agrarian charges — VIII. The charter revoked — IX. The appeal — X. The bank's victory

I

In the winter of 1779-1780, not quite two years before the surrender of Lord Cornwallis at Yorktown, the American revolutionary cause was in one of its darkest passages. The British held New York fast and were gaining ground in the South. The war was dragging on into its fifth year. Halfhearted as the enemy was, the Continental Army still had not the means to strike a decisive blow. Its soldiers were neglected and mutinous. It was "a mob rather than an army; without clothing, without pay, without provision, without morals, without discipline." Congress had failed to obtain the funds required for vigorous collective action, and its credit was gone in promises it could not keep. It had no power to tax but only to requisition the individual states with the hope that its requisitions would be respected, which much of the time they were not. Often its only resort for funds was Benjamin Franklin, its Minister in Paris, who, having once drawn lightning from the clouds, was expected to draw money from the coffers of the King of France with the same ease and whenever required.[1]

Lieutenant-Colonel Alexander Hamilton was then aide to General Washington in winter quarters with the army near Morristown, New Jersey. The words quoted in the foregoing paragraph are his. Four years in the Army had impressed him with the fact that military operations could not be made more effective without more money, and more money could not be procured without new means. To pay for its imports, the young country was dependent on loans and gifts from other enemies of Great Britain. To pay its domestic expenses

[1] Hamilton (Lodge) I, 221.

it issued bills of credit. It issued more and more—continental and state bills—and in the end they became valueless. The Army had to have food and equipment, as every patriot knew, but the soldier or farmer or dealer who accepted payment in revolutionary bills was making an inordinate contribution to the cause of independence, for the money he received would not buy the equivalent of what he had sold or of the service he had rendered. Patriotism grew thin in such circumstances, soldiers lost ardor, and farmers and dealers withheld supplies.

Amidst his military duties Alexander Hamilton found time to formulate a plan for radical reform of the revolutionary finances and to set it forth in a long letter whose date and address are both uncertain but which probably was sent in November 1779 to General John Sullivan, representative of New Hampshire in Congress. In this letter, from which his name was withheld, Colonel Hamilton urged that a bank be "instituted by authority of Congress for ten years, under the denomination of the Bank of the United States." Its nominal capital was to be $200,000,000—a fantastic sum, save that it represented the current depreciated continental paper money, whose retirement would be effected by exchange for bank stock and bank notes. This would provide a currency whose value would no longer rest on the promises of a weak government but on those of an institution with assets and credit derived from the union of private wealth and governmental authority. Farmers and merchants alike would accept this new currency in payment for the supplies needed by the Army.[2]

"I am aware," Hamilton wrote, "how apt the imagination is to be heated in projects of this nature." He was then about twenty-four. But nevertheless he thought that the scheme stood on a firm footing of public and private faith, that it linked the interest of the state intimately with the interests of rich individuals; and that it afforded, "by a sort of creative power," a circulating medium that would be "a real and efficacious instrument of trade." The plan also comprehended a foreign loan of two millions sterling and that the bank be recompensed by the government, which was to be its principal borrower and own half its stock. "Very beneficial contracts," the Colonel said, might be made between the bank and the government for supplying the Army. Its life was set tentatively at ten years, but

[2] Schachner, 98, n46; Hamilton (Lodge) III, 333-34. The retained copy of this letter in the Hamilton papers is without address or date. Lodge took it to have been addressed to Robert Morris in 1780. Schachner shows it to have been addressed more probably to John Sullivan in 1779.

Hamilton did not suppose that it would be discontinued, or that experience would fail to suggest how it should be improved. The plan had a kinship, which he recognized, "to the famous Mississippi scheme projected by Mr Law," who, however, he said, "had much more penetration than integrity." The foundation of that scheme was good, he thought, "but the superstructure too vast. The proprietors aimed at unlimited wealth, and the government itself expected too much."[3]

These early proposals by Alexander Hamilton, known then as a very able young military officer, probably reflected more ideas than they originated. They seem to have been without influence, but they indicate what the current ideas were and the early stages of his own prolific thought. In the developments that follow immediately, he seems to have had no part.

II

During the spring of 1780 things had continued to go badly for the Americans. General Tarleton's raids spread fright in the Carolina Piedmont, and in May Sir Henry Clinton captured Charleston. The next month, Congress received what it called the "liberal offer" of some ninety merchants and other men of substance who "on their own credit" were preparing "to supply and transport three millions of rations and 300 hogsheads of rum for the use of the army" and had "established a bank for the sole purpose of obtaining and transporting the said supplies." These men had pledged their property and credit for respective sums which aggregated £300,000. Congress accepted their offer, and James Madison wrote Thomas Jefferson that the greatest hopes of feeding the soldiers were founded on this "patriotic scheme of the opulent merchants" of Philadelphia.[4] The front page of the *Pennsylvania Packet*, 15 July 1780, was taken up by a dialogue in verse which included the following:

> "Has not the loss of Charlestown prov'd once more
> That where the soul's engaged
> Danger becomes a stimulus to action?
> Look at those large and honorable aids
> By voluntary contributions rais'd
> Which this fair city gives—her splendid Bank
> And liberal subscriptions; whence are they

[3] Hamilton (Lodge) III, 332-34, 338-39.
[4] Lewis, 18-23; Clarke and Hall, 9-10; Madison, *Writings* (Hunt) I, 66.

But from the arduous feeling of the soul
Rous'd by some new and unforeseen misfortune?"

A prospectus of the bank and a list of subscribers had already been published in the Philadelphia *Gazette*, 5 July 1780, and on the 15th the following business-like notice appeared in the *Packet*: "The Pennsylvania Bank will be open on Monday next two doors above Walnut Street in Front Street from nine to twelve in the morning and from three to five in the afternoon. All persons who have already lent money are desired to apply for bank-notes, and the Directors request the favor of those who may hereafter lodge their cash in the bank that they would tie it up in bundles of bills of one denomination, with labels, their names endorsed, as the business will thereby be done with less trouble and greater dispatch."

Besides accepting the offer of the subscribers, Congress resolved that since the associators in the bank meant "not to derive from it the least pecuniary advantage," it was just and reasonable that they be fully reimbursed and indemnified. It therefore pledged the faith of the United States to protect them against loss. The directors were authorized to "borrow money on the credit of the bank for six months or for less time and to emit notes bearing interest at the rate of six per cent." Operations began in Philadelphia 17 July 1780 and continued until the latter part of 1781. The subscribers were reimbursed by Congress for the purchases they had made, and the bank was fully liquidated in 1784. By means of this bank, wrote Thomas Paine, "the army was supplied through the campaign and being at the same time recruited was enabled to maintain its ground. . . ." According to Paine, it was with himself and not with the opulent merchants of Philadelphia that the idea of the Pennsylvania Bank originated. In 1780, he said, the American states were "in want of two of the most essential matters which governments could be destitute of—money and credit." The spring of that year "was marked with an accumulation of misfortunes. The reliance placed on the defense of Charleston failed and exceedingly lowered or depressed the spirits of the country. The measures of government, from the want of money, means, and credit, dragged on like a heavy loaded carriage without wheels and were nearly got to what a countryman would understand by a dead pull."[5]

When the Pennsylvania Assembly met in May in Philadelphia,

[5] Clarke and Hall, 10; Paine (Conway) II, 149-50, 153.

Paine went on, "what particularly added to the affliction was that so many of the members, instead of spiriting up their constituents to the most nervous exertions, came to the assembly furnished with petitions to be exempt from paying taxes. How the public measures were to be carried on, the country defended, and the army recruited, clothed, fed, and paid, when the only resource, and that not half sufficient, that of taxes, should be relaxed to almost nothing, was a matter too gloomy to look at. A language very different from that of petitions ought at this time to have been the language of every one." Meanwhile, a letter received by the Executive Council from General Washington was transmitted to the House. The doors were shut, and Mr Paine, as clerk, read the letter aloud. "In this letter," he said, "the naked truth of things was unfolded. . . . The General said that notwithstanding his confidence in the attachment of the army to the cause of the country, the distress of it, from the want of every necessary which men could be destitute of, had arisen to such a pitch that the appearances of mutiny and discontent were so strongly marked on the countenance of the army that he dreaded the event of every hour."

Thomas Paine himself felt that there was "something absolutely necessary to be done which was not within the immediate power of the House to do; for what with the depreciation of the currency and slow operation of taxes and the petitions to be exempted therefrom, the Treasury was moneyless and the government creditless. If the assembly could not give the assistance which the necessity of the case immediately required, it was very proper the matter should be known by those who either could or would endeavor to do it. . . . The only thing that now remained and was capable of reaching the case was private credit and the voluntary aid of individuals; and under this impression, on my return from the House, I drew out the salary due to me as clerk, enclosed five hundred dollars to a gentleman in this city, in part of the whole, and wrote fully to him on the subject of our affairs." Paine divulged to his correspondent the desperate news that the Assembly had heard and urged him to propose a voluntary subscription, in which his own five hundred dollars was to be included.

"While this subscription was going forward, information of the loss of Charleston arrived, and on a communication from several members of Congress to certain gentlemen of this city of the increasing distresses and dangers then taking place, a meeting was held of the subscribers and such other gentlemen who chose to attend, at the city tavern. This meeting was on the 17th of June, nine days after the subscription had begun. At this meeting it was resolved to open a security-subscription, to the amount of three hundred thousand pounds, Pennsylvania currency, in real money;* the subscribers to execute bonds to the amount of their subscriptions and to form a bank thereon for supplying the army."[6]

This was the Pennsylvania Bank. In September 1780, when it was barely two months old, Alexander Hamilton wrote that he had had hopes it would be "the embryo of a more permanent and extensive establishment." But he now had reason to believe he would be disappointed. "It does not seem to be at all conducted on the true principles of a bank." For, he said, "the directors of it are purchasing with their stock instead of bank-notes, as I expected, in consequence of which it must turn out to be a mere subscription of a particular sum of money for a particular purpose." Some years later, after the Pennsylvania Bank had ended its brief life, Robert Morris, who was one of its organizers, confirmed Colonel Hamilton's words. He said it was "in fact nothing more than a patriotic subscription of continental money . . . for the purpose of purchasing provisions for a starving army."[7]

Thomas Paine's name does not appear on surviving lists of subscribers to the Pennsylvania Bank, but his subscription may have been included in the larger one of his friend, the practice being common; for five hundred dollars in continental money was precious little. Nevertheless, though the lists include a hundred or more persons representing a substantial part of the commercial wealth of Philadelphia, the first to lay cash on the barrel head was evidently Thomas Paine. Noah Webster made the statement in 1806, or a little before, that banks were advocated in America "as early as 1776, first by Mr Paine" in *Common Sense*; and he quoted the following words in which Paine anticipated a famous remark of Alexander Hamilton's. "No nation ought to be without a debt," Paine had said. "A national debt is a national bond. . . ." In the 20th century the

---

* "Three hundred thousand pounds, Pennsylvania currency, in real money" would be, presumably, an amount of specie obtainable with three hundred thousand pounds of Pennsylvania currency, the latter being at a discount in relation to specie.

[6] Paine (Conway) II, 150-53.
[7] Hamilton (Lodge) I, 233; Sumner, *Financier and Finances* II, 22.

advocacy of a national debt does not obviously imply an advocacy of banks, because both in men's thinking and in fact the association of banking and a public debt is less close than the prominent example of the Bank of England made it in 1776 and than the nearer example of the Bank of the United States made it thirty years later. According to Noah Webster both public debt and banks were instruments of mercantile triumph over the survival of feudalism, and it was for such reasons that Thomas Paine advocated them.[8]

III

In September 1780, about nine months after his first proposal for a bank and about two months after inauguration of the Pennsylvania Bank, Alexander Hamilton restated his proposal in a letter to James Duane, representative in Congress from New York. This letter gives a foretaste of the Constitution, which it preceded by seven years. To Duane, Hamilton said less about the form of his proposed bank than he had to John Sullivan and more about the scheme of government in which the bank was to have place.

"Congress," he said, meaning the Confederation as distinct from the individual states, "should have complete sovereignty in all that relates to war, peace, trade, finance, and to the management of foreign affairs." It should have the right "of coining money; establishing banks on such terms and with such privileges as they think proper; appropriating funds and doing whatever else relates to the operations of finance." The providing of supplies, he said, was now "the pivot of everything else," and there were four ways of achieving it, "all of which must be united: a foreign loan, heavy pecuniary taxes, a tax in kind, a bank founded on public and private credit." The contemporary paper money rested on public credit alone; the joint credit of the public and of individuals was needed. The proposed bank should be authorized to issue notes to the amount of its capital. It should be authorized to coin money. The faith of the government must be pledged for its support, and the government must have the right to inspect it. It "should be one great company in three divisions: in Virginia, Philadelphia, and at Boston." It was to be hoped that it could be built on the Pennsylvania Bank, which at the time he wrote was still in existence.[9]

In February 1781 Congress made Robert Morris its Superin-

8 Blodget, 168; Paine (Conway) 1, 102.
9 Hamilton (Lodge) 1, 224-25, 229, 232-36.

tendent of Finance, or Financier. Colonel Hamilton, still with General Washington, had been considered for the appointment, evidently without his own knowledge. Two months later he resigned as Washington's aide, hoping to get a combat command, and the day he left headquarters, 30 April 1781, he sent Robert Morris the third argument he had elaborated for a "National Bank."[10]

The national bank was to be, of course, far more than a private enterprise. At the moment American independence was the object of all effort, and in Colonel Hamilton's words, "'Tis by introducing order into our finances—by restoring public credit—not by gaining battles, that we are finally to gain our object." He reviewed at length the capacity of the country for revenue and "the proportion between what it is able to afford and what it stands in need of," and found a difference between revenues and expenses of from four to four and a half million dollars, "which deficiency must of course be supplied by credit, foreign or domestic, or both." He considered the potentialities of France, Spain, and the Netherlands as lenders and found them inadequate. But America had her own resources, and these he would utilize more fully by a public bank which would "supply the defect of monied capital and answer all the purposes of cash," secure the independence of the country, "have the most beneficial influence upon its future commerce, and be a source of national strength and wealth." The tendency of such a bank, he said, would be "to increase public and private credit. The former gives power to the state for the protection of its rights and interests, and the latter facilitates and extends the operations of commerce among individuals. Industry is increased, commodities are multiplied, agriculture and manufactures flourish; and herein consists the true wealth and prosperity of a state."

The national bank was to be a corporation chartered for thirty years—"no other bank, public or private, to be permitted during that period." It was to have a capital stock of £3,000,000. Besides specie, this sum was to include "European funds" and "landed security"—i.e., real estate mortgages. About half the capital might be owned by the government, which would appoint four of the twelve directors. The bank was to issue pound notes—partly in large denominations bearing interest—but the whole issue should not exceed the amount of the bank's capital. It might coin metal to half of the amount of its capital. It was to receive deposits. It was to lend to

[10] Schachner, 126; Hamilton (Lodge) iii, 342ff.

the government and to the public. It was to be the agent for redemption of the government's outstanding paper money obligations at the ratio of forty units of the old for one of the new. It was to contract with both the French and American governments for the supply of the naval and military forces. It was to have three offices, as in his earlier plan, one in Pennsylvania, one in Massachusetts, and one in Virginia.[11]

These terms were closer to those of banking as subsequently known than were the terms that Hamilton had previously proposed. They specified a corporation whose principal powers were to lend, to issue notes and accept deposits, and to act as fiscal agency of the government. Moreover, the amount of capital was now more practicable and the transactions in merchandise were of reduced importance. As before, in his letters to Sullivan and Duane, Hamilton did not stake all on a bank alone: a foreign loan was indispensable, and there must also be fiscal and political reforms. And again as before, he sought to shift from the Spanish dollar, which was the unit of the depreciated revolutionary currency, to the pound, which was still current and in terms of which the proposed bank was to be capitalized and to issue its notes. He still hoped that the amorphous Pennsylvania Bank would contribute to establishment of the national bank he was proposing.

When the Financier, Robert Morris, received this letter, he was engaged on his own more modest plan for the Bank of North America, and it is unlikely that he thought Colonel Hamilton's ideas made any important changes necessary in what he had already done. But he wrote Hamilton that he felt strengthened in his own confidence by finding their ideas had much in common and that he would show the letter to the proposed bank's directors.[12]

IV

The Bank of North America, now proposed by Robert Morris, was to have a capital of $400,000, to be paid in gold and silver. Its notes were to be accepted by the government in payment of duties and taxes, and a statement of its note obligations and cash on hand was to be made daily to the Superintendent of Finances, who would have the right also at all times to examine into its affairs, with "access to all the books and papers." Congress, 26 May 1781, ap-

[11] Hamilton (Lodge) III, 343-56, 360-61, 367ff.
[12] Clarke and Hall, 14.

proved the plan for what it called "a national bank," which it resolved to promote and support.[13]

Mr Morris published the congressional resolution with a statement in which he offered the enticement to prospective subscribers that the bank's advances to the government would be profitable and secure, that its circulating notes would replace the depreciated government issues then current, and that its credit would be available to merchants. "To ask the end which it is proposed to answer by this institution of a bank, is merely to call the public attention to the situation of our affairs. A depreciating paper currency has unhappily been the source of infinite private mischief, numberless frauds, and the greatest distress. The national calamities have moved with an equal pace, and the public credit has received the deepest injury. . . . The exigencies of the United States require an anticipation of our revenue; while, at the same time, there is not such confidence established as will call out, for that purpose, the funds of individual citizens. The use, then, of a bank is to aid the government by their monies and credit, for which they will have every proper reward and security, to gain from individuals that credit which property, abilities, and integrity never failed to command, to supply the loss of that paper money which, becoming more and more useless, calls every day more loudly for its final redemption, and to give a new spring to commerce, in the moment when, on the removal of all its restrictions, the citizens of America shall enjoy and possess that freedom for which they contend."[14]

The response to these brave words was not too encouraging. Though many participants in the Pennsylvania Bank transferred their interests to the new institution, new subscribers came in sluggishly. The Financier also had trouble in getting together the funds the government was subscribing, but providentially "one of his most Christian majesty's frigates arrived at Boston and brought a remittance in specie of about four hundred and seventy thousand dollars," which was taken to Philadelphia by wagon. All that Morris could spare, "about 254,000 dollars," he subscribed for stock in the bank and immediately borrowed back. The money was part of a sum obtained by Benjamin Franklin from the French Treasury, some as a gift and some as a loan. It was fetched across the ocean by Colonel John Laurens, Alexander Hamilton's friend, and Thomas Paine, according to whom it took sixteen ox teams to transport the

---

13 Clarke and Hall, 10-12.   14 Lewis, 80-31.

money from Boston to Philadelphia; and it took the teams two months or more to make the journey. The money arrived in Philadelphia in October after the British surrender at Yorktown, and the task of organizing the bank was not completed till two months later.* On the last day of the year 1781, Congress passed an ordinance incorporating it as the President and Company of the Bank of North America.[15] This was the first real bank, in the modern sense, on the North American continent.**

A week after the action of Congress, Robert Morris addressed a circular letter to the Governors of the thirteen states, with which he transmitted copies of the congressional ordinance and of the resolutions "recommending to the several states to pass such laws as they may judge necessary for giving the said ordinance its full operation." "It affords me great satisfaction to inform your Excellency that this bank commenced its operations yesterday, and I am confident that with proper management it will answer the most sanguine expectations of those who befriend the institution. It will facilitate the management of the finances of the United States. The several states may, when their respective necessities require and the abilities of the bank will permit, derive occasional advantage and accommodation from it. It will afford to the individuals of all the states a medium for their intercourse with each other and for the payment of taxes, more convenient than the precious metals and equally safe. It will have a tendency to increase both the internal and external commerce of North America and undoubtedly will be infinitely useful to all the traders of every state in the union, provided, as I have already said, it is conducted on the principles of equity, justice, prudence, and economy."[16]

The Connecticut legislature a few days later made the bank's

* The bill of lading for this specie, put on board *La Résolue* at Brest, the receipt given for it by Governor John Hancock of Massachusetts in Boston, and the receipt given for it by Tench Francis in Philadelphia for Robert Morris, Superintendent General of Finances, are displayed in Carpenters' Hall, Philadelphia.

** In Canada banking did not start till establishment of the Bank of Montreal in 1817. In Mexico there seems to have been no banking, in the sense in which I am using the term, until about the year 1864, when the Banco de Londres y México was founded and the country's modern banking system had its beginning. Lobato Lopez, 135, 140, 158ff; McCaleb, chap. 1.

[15] Carey, 48; Paine (Foner) II, 720-21; Paine (Conway) I, 171-73, 213-15; II, 466.
[16] Lewis, 39-40.

notes receivable in payment of state taxes, and the Rhode Island legislature made punishable the counterfeiting of the bank's notes and theft of its funds. Massachusetts and New York went further and granted charters of incorporation which gave the bank a monopoly in the two states for the duration of the war. These state charters were occasioned by disbelief in the validity of the congressional charter; New York in its grant made the reservation, "That nothing in this act contained shall be construed to imply any right or power in the United States in Congress assembled to create bodies politic or grant letters of incorporation in any case whatever." That Congress had not the power was maintained by several of its own members and particularly by James Madison, its foremost legal authority. The bank's directors being themselves in doubt, barely a month passed before they sought a charter from the Pennsylvania Assembly. After considerable opposition and debate, one identical with that granted by Congress was enacted 1 April 1782 and accepted by the bank as the authority under which its operations were to be conducted. These measures with reference to the Bank of North America which were adopted in 1781 and 1782 by Congress and by Connecticut, Rhode Island, New York, Massachusetts, and Pennsylvania constituted the first bank legislation proper in North America, with the dubious exception of that respecting the Pennsylvania Bank.[17]

With the surrender of Yorktown several weeks before the bank was opened, the fighting had stopped, but the government was no stronger, the states were no more united, British troops still occupied New York, and Great Britain was in no hurry to conclude the formal recognition of American independence. The negotiations with her were to be prolonged for nearly two years. These were not the circumstances in which the bank had been expected to work, but its services were nevertheless useful; it facilitated the resumption of peacetime commerce and the administration of the public finances. The United States for a short time owned most of the bank's stock, having more than 600 of its 1,000 shares. For these shares, "the bank by special bargain lent them the whole money immediately, but it not being convenient for the Financier to repay the money when wanted by the bank," the shares were sold to other subscribers.[18] The president of the bank was Thomas Willing, one of Philadelphia's principal merchants. Its directors and proprietors, its gov-

[17] Cleaveland, xiin.   [18] Lewis, 135.

ernmental connection, and the fact that it was unique, made it an outstanding institution. But the private stockholders represented only a part of the mercantile community in Philadelphia, and the neglected merchants, who were mostly Quaker, decided that they should have a bank of their own. Their efforts to obtain a corporate charter from the Pennsylvania Assembly seemed about to succeed— this was in the spring of 1784—when the Bank of North America hastily offered to enlarge its capital and let them come in. It made the offer, which was accepted, because most subscribers to the proposed bank were tendering their payments in Bank of North America notes, and these were being presented for redemption in such volume that the bank was losing its specie. This experience convinced a good many people that it was impracticable to have two banks in a single community, the supply of specie being considered insufficient and raids on one another's reserves inevitable.[19]

V

Although the Bank of North America was helpful in the fiscal affairs of the confederated government as well as in the affairs of the business community, it could not make up for that government's characteristic weaknesses—one consequence of which was arrearages in the payment of soldiers of the Revolutionary Army now due to be mustered out and returned to their homes. In June 1783, when the bank was in its second year, about a hundred men of the Pennsylvania line mutinied at Lancaster for want of their pay and marched the sixty or seventy miles east to Philadelphia, which they entered on a hot summer day "with fixed bayonets and musick." They were joined by discontented troops in the local barracks, and three or four hundred in all put a cordon round Independence Hall, where the Pennsylvania Executive Council and the Continental Congress were sitting separately. While the leaders pressed their demands on the officials, the soldiers comforted themselves with spirituous drink served to them from the nearby tippling-houses, they uttered offensive words, and they wantonly pointed their muskets at the windows of the hall, where Elias Boudinot, James Madison, Alexander Hamilton, and other celebrities were scowling over the situation. They also threatened the bank, which was a little farther down the street. It was the agent of government, it had money, and money was what they wanted. It naturally mattered little

[19] Schwartz, *JPE*, LV (1947), 417ff.

to them that the bank facilitated commerce and the public finances, so long as they were unpaid themselves. But they faltered; after a few days they accepted furloughs and dispersed, as unpaid as ever but freshly promised. A really serious attack on the bank came two years later when the agrarians, with the help of persons unfriendly to the bank for private reasons, determined to repeal its charter.[20]

VI

It was in the spring of 1785, when the Bank of North America had been three years in business, that the effort to end its existence was undertaken by the agrarian majority in the Pennsylvania legislature. The first step, 16 March, was to authorize an issue of bills of credit by the state to pay its share of "the annual interest on the debts of the United States" and the interest on its own public debt. For this purpose an issue of £100,000 was authorized; £50,000 more was authorized to be lent by the state to private borrowers. This implied no love of the bills; but bad as they were the bank was worse, and their issue was a blow at it. Five days later, the 21st, a petition for repeal of the Bank of North America's charter was received by the Assembly. On 4 April, the state loan office at which the £50,000 was to be lent was authorized. The same day a bill to repeal the charter of the bank was introduced and ordered printed, counsel for the bank was refused a hearing, and the legislature adjourned, to take up the matter at the next session. A major controversy burst forth which was to preoccupy the community for two years.

The case of "the gentlemen from the country" against the bank included charges of usury, favoritism, "comity with commerce," interference with the state's prerogative of monetary issue, refusal to lend on the long terms thought necessary for honest borrowers, discrimination against husbandmen and mechanics, insistence upon punctuality in paying debts, admission of foreigners to investment in America, and other miscellaneous mischiefs. The case of "the gentlemen from the city" for it, aside from explanation of its usefulness, included the argument that repeal of the charter would be a breach of faith on the part of the state, an arbitrary invasion of property rights, and nugatory because the bank might continue anyway under the congressional ordinance of incorporation. Upon

[20] Hamilton (Lodge) I, 303, 314ff; Elliott v, 91-94; *Journals of Continental Congress* XXIV, 410, 412ff; *Pennsylvania Gazette*, 2 and 9 July 1783.

reconvening in August, the Assembly decided to grant the bank's plea to be heard in defense of its charter but made the point that the hearing was a matter of grace, not of right. It listened to the bank's spokesmen and also the spokesmen of the petitioners. Its mind remained unchanged, and an act repealing the charter was passed 13 September 1785.

Operations continued, but the loss of the charter was serious. There was little chance that the state courts would allow the bank any corporate rights or protect its shareholders from its creditors, and the charters got from Congress, from New York, and from Massachusetts were of little or no help. Public confidence shrank. The bank's stock dropped below par, its notes came home, and its cash fell off. When things were about at their worst, the bank was encouraged by the grant of a charter from Delaware in February 1786; but whether it would have been found practicable to move down the river into the friendlier jurisdiction is dubious. Meanwhile, however, the political complexion of the Pennsylvania Assembly was altered by the elections, in which the bank had been a leading issue, and an energetic effort was made to get the charter restored. More petitions were lodged with the Assembly, for and against the bank. A new committee considered the question, found evidence of prejudice and ignorance in the former committee's action, and recommended repeal of the former repeal. There ensued four days of lively and tense debate, from 29 March to 1 April 1786.

VII

The agrarian charges were numerous, as I have indicated, but their gravamen lay in the complaint that the bank was a monstrosity, an artificial creature endowed with powers not possessed by human beings and incompatible with the principles of a democratic social order. In the language of the Assembly report of 1785 recommending repeal, "the accumulation of enormous wealth in the hands of a society who claim perpetual duration will necessarily produce a degree of influence and power which can not be entrusted in the hands of any set of men whatsoever without endangering the public safety." And again: "We have nothing in our free and equal government capable of balancing the influence which the bank must create." William Findley, the influential agrarian leader who represented Westmoreland county, declared that "the government of Pennsylvania being a democracy, the bank is inconsistent with the bill of rights thereof, which says that government is not instituted for the emolument of any man, family, or set of men." Further, he said, "This institution, having no principle but that of avarice, which dries and shrivels up all the manly, all the generous feelings of the human soul, will never be varied in its object and if continued will accomplish its end, viz., to engross all the wealth, power and influence of the state." John Smilie, a representative from remote and mountainous Fayette county—whose farmers were to rebel ten years later against the taxing of their whiskey by the federal government—was incensed because the friends of the bank were said to include "the most respectable characters amongst us." It looked to him as if respectability meant riches. "This is holding out an aristocratical idea. 'An honest man's the noblest work of God.' A democratical government like ours admits of no superiority."[21]

These were considerations by which the bank would stand condemned even if no alternative to it existed. But the agrarians had an alternative in the state loan office. Robert Whitehill of Cumberland county complained that the bank's notes cramped the credit and circulation of the paper money of the state and that the bank, besides being incompatible with the public welfare in general, was of no help to the country people because "its loans are confined to forty-five days—a period which can never afford any opportunity for the country people to profit by it." It was an argument of John Smilie also that the bank's operations were a discouragement to agriculture—because it would lend for short term only—whereas the state's paper money had been of the utmost utility.[22]

There was far more interest in destroying the bank than in fostering the loan office, however, and Robert Morris, now a state Senator, twitted the few country gentlemen who professed such esteem for the state's paper money notwithstanding "it is notorious that they will not sell the produce of their farms for it." Nor did they all profess to like it. But they were one in their hatred of the corporate nature of the bank. When assured that "if this public bank be destroyed, private banks will arise out of its ruins till the demands of trade are satisfied," they were unmoved. Indeed Whitehill observed that if the bank had no charter, the "private circumstances" of the stockholders would then be liable for its debts. This seemed to him preferable. Findley also said the proprietors might still keep a private bank, as if that would be unobjectionable. The proprietors

21 Carey, 21, 52, 57, 65-66.   22 Carey, 15, 24, 61-62.

of a private bank would be merchants and members of an unloved class, but they would at least be individual human beings lifted by no artificial, aristocratical powers above the level of ordinary Americans. And they would not be alien. For one of the most exasperating peculiarities of incorporation was that it enabled foreigners to invest money in America. The agrarians could see no advantage in this but only the disadvantage that it led to the drain of profits back to Europe.[23]

VIII

In their rebuttal of the agrarian attack, the friends of the bank sought to establish two general facts. One was that the merchants of the community had a right to maintain a bank for their own convenience; the other was that the bank was useful as well to everyone else.

Before they had a bank, Robert Morris explained, the merchants had had to lend to one another. One who was shipping a cargo, to assemble which he had expended all or much of his ready cash, would draw a bill on the purchaser—a merchant in England or in Barbadoes, for example—to whom the goods were being shipped, and would sell the bill at a discount to a merchant who was at the time in funds. The latter would gain the amount of the discount for the use of funds that would otherwise have been temporarily idle in his hands, but he would soon have need of the funds for payments to be due on his own purchases. So he would willingly be a lender only for the intermediate period when he held cash for which he had no instant need, and he would wish to be as fully assured as possible that he would have his money returned to him punctually. By becoming stockholders in a bank, the merchants had pooled their cash to make it go further. But there were very few of them, Mr Morris said, "who do not stand in need of the whole of their money in the course of business, and when in need they borrow occasionally perhaps the whole amount or more." Further, "it is upon these principles the merchants generally remain stockholders—when one does not want his money, it is earning his share of the dividend from another; and by thus clubbing a capital together, as it were, the occasional wants of all are supplied." Why, he asked in substance, should not the merchants do collectively and conveniently what they had used to do severally and inconveniently?[24]

[23] Carey, 28, 62, 74, 80-81.   [24] Carey, 95.

The second point urged in favor of the bank was its provision of a ready and adequate means of payment which passed from the hands of the merchants who bought produce into the hands of the farmers who sold it and thence into the hands of others in the community. "The utmost that the country gentlemen can any ways contend for," declared Thomas Fitzsimons, another of the bank's friends, "is that they, living at a distance and wishing to be accommodated with loans of money for long periods, can not have them at the bank. But is that a reason that the inhabitants of the city and its vicinity shall not have the privilege of accommodating each other? Though the money is not lent to the farmer, yet, as it facilitates the purchase of his products and the procuring him ready money for them, he derives thereby a full share of the advantage."[25]

Suppose, Robert Morris again said, a ship arrives from the West Indies with a cargo of rum and sugars—is she to be detained because merchants can not procure money to purchase flour to load her? Morris recalled occasions when farmers had waited vainly with their loaded wagons in Market Street and at the end of the day had driven them home as full as they came, because there were no buyers; and there were no buyers because there was no cash. Produce in the market had been plenty, he said, and he himself had been eagerly bent on the purchase of it, but could not command the money for the purchase, although possessed of sufficient property. Now that there was a bank, money was always available, for the bank furnished its notes to the merchants in exchange for their obligations, and the notes served as money with which they paid for their purchases. At the same time, contrary to allegations, the community's cash was conserved. For, explained Thomas Fitzsimons, "where there are no banks every merchant or trader must at all times have money in his chest or in his drawer unemployed. . . . If he wants to make a purchase of any considerable value, he collects money for some time in order to enable him to make that purchase." The bank made these several hoards unnecessary. Moreover, the bank discriminated against loans that would lead to shipments of cash from the community. Formerly when a ship was put up for London, the remitters who wished to ship specie cast about to get it, and away it went if they succeeded; they now make application to the bank and "the directors being interested to obstruct the shipments of money and knowing those who want discounts for that purpose, they watch

[25] Carey, 104-05.

them as closely as a cat does a mouse and refuse such discounts until the ship is gone."[26]

The bank was also defended from the specific complaint that it obstructed the use of the state's bills of credit. It accepted them with the reservation that the liability incurred by doing so should not entail repayment in specie but in the equivalent of the bills received. This necessitated keeping double accounts—one set in specie and one set in Pennsylvania paper money; and these accounts showed, Robert Morris told the Assembly, that the whole amount of the emission, that for the loan office excepted, had passed through the bank the first year and been credited on its books.[27]

The bank's friends met the complaint that the bank had alien stockholders by explaining that Americans needed European investment and gained more from it than the Europeans did. When foreign capital entered the country in the form of goods bought on credit, Robert Morris explained, the price of the goods might be increased by as much as thirty per cent; when it came in the form of investment in bank stock it cost only the bank's dividend rate, which did not exceed eight per cent. It was better to finance domestic trade with a bank employing foreign capital than to finance it by going into debt to foreign merchants.[28]

"Did the first settlers of America bring capitals with them? Some few individuals might, but the generality certainly did not; if they could accomplish the bringing the necessary implements of husbandry, it was doing a great deal. The settlers that have continued to follow the first comers, from that time to this, were in the same way. Very few have brought capitals, and yet nearly all have grown rich.

"How did this happen? It has happened by the use of European capitals.

"How were these obtained for that use? Not by borrowing money; for they could not . . . obtain such loans. If they could, the country would have grown rich much faster. But they borrowed goods. America has risen to opulence by means of the credit she obtained in Europe. The goods so borrowed, or, in other words, bought upon credit, were not procured on the same easy terms on which money is usually lent. It would have been much better for the traders in America to borrow money at six, eight, ten per cent, or at any rate of dividend made by the bank, and to have purchased their goods

[26] Carey, 43, 51, 93-94, 104.   [27] Carey, 119.   [28] Carey, 55-56.

with the ready money so borrowed; for with ready money, those purchases might have been made ten, fifteen, twenty, and perhaps in some articles, thirty per cent cheaper than on credit.

"It is true that the merchants in England usually shipped goods on one year's credit, without charging interest for that year. But it has been always said and in some instances proved upon trials in the courts of law, that the year's interest is amply compensated by the advances put on the real cost of the goods, besides other benefices derived by the English merchant by means of drawbacks, discounts, etc., etc. And if the American importer can not pay at the expiration of the twelve months, an interest account commences and is continued in such manner that he pays at the rate of compound interest until the debt is discharged. Under these disadvantages, the credit obtained in Europe at a rate of interest equal to fifteen, twenty, or perhaps thirty per cent has been the foundation of that prosperity which we behold in America. That credit has been extended by the importer to the country shopkeeper; and through him to the farmer and mechanic, who being thereby enabled to pursue their labours, have drawn produce from the surface and bowels of the earth, which has not only defrayed the whole of the cost and charges but enriched the industrious.

"Must not then an institution which draws money from Europe for the use of our citizens at the rate of seven and three fourths or eight per cent be extremely beneficial? Could America by means of such institutions, or by any other means, obtain loans sufficient to enable her to purchase all the goods wanted from Europe with ready money, she would find a vast and lasting advantage in it."

Mr Morris, however, did not pretend that the bank offered all that the farmers required. On the contrary, he said that long-term credit as well as short-term was needed and that there should be institutions specializing in each. "A loan office," he said, "established on proper principles and on a solid foundation would promote and encourage the landed interest and operate as much in its favour as a bank does in favour of commerce." He had some share in the landed interest, he continued, having a quantity of lands within the state; and he was "willing to submit to a tax to be paid in hard money to establish a fund for the purpose of lending sums to farmers for the improvement of their lands." His offer accomplished nothing. The agrarians, still assured of a majority, simply held their thumbs down. They were not interested in collaboration or compromise. They had attacked the bank in order to destroy it—not supplement it or correct it. They insisted on having its head.[29]

IX

The Assembly room was crowded with auditors of the debate, a verbatim account of which, dedicated to Benjamin Franklin, was published by Mathew Carey within a few weeks. The bank was the subject of acrid public controversy, oral and written. Able pamphlets in its defense were produced by James Wilson, a distinguished lawyer and later an influential member of the convention that wrote the federal Constitution, and by Pelatiah Webster, a merchant, a stockholder, and an active writer. But the most effective participant on either side was Thomas Paine. The bank was produced, he said in his *Dissertations* in its defense, "by the distresses of the times and the enterprising spirit of patriotic individuals," a phrase that catches the substance of Hamilton's and Morris' arguments and puts in a nutshell the circumstances in which American banking had its origin. "Those individuals furnished and risked the money," he said, "and the aid which the government contributed was that incorporating them." The government had never made a better bargain and got so much for so little. The bank had done what the government could not. "The war being now ended and the bank having rendered the service expected, or rather hoped for from it, the principal public use of it at this time is for the promotion and extension of commerce. The whole community derives benefit from the operation of the bank. It facilitates the commerce of the country. It quickens the means of purchasing and paying for country produce and hastens on the exportation of it. The emolument, therefore, being to the community, it is the office and duty of government to give protection to the bank."[30]

As for the absurd condemnation of foreign investment in the bank's stock, Paine said the enemies of the bank "must have forgotten which side of the Atlantic they were on," for their arguments would be true if the situation were the other way round and Americans were putting their money in foreign banks. He also expatiated on the evils of paper money, which, since he had not come to America till 1774, he had never known in the form of colonial bills of credit but only as continentals. So he assumed that all paper money was

[29] Carey, 37-38.   [30] Paine (Conway) II, 153, 167; Paine (Foner) II, 431.

bad. It was bad because it was not convertible into specie, which was the only real money. He also implied that all paper money was legal tender and said that the punishment of a legislator who should so much as "move for such a law ought to be *death*."* The paper money authorized by the Assembly, he said, was driving out hard money and taking its place. "The farmer will not take it for produce, and he is right in refusing it. The money he takes for his year's produce must last him the year round; and the experience he has had of the instability of paper money has sufficiently instructed him that it is not worth a farmer's while to exchange the solid grain and produce of a farm for the paper of an Assembly whose politics are changing with every new election and who are here one year and gone another."[31]

In contrast to the Assembly's paper money, Mr Paine said that "bank notes are of a very different kind and produce a contrary effect. They are promissory notes payable on demand and may be taken to the bank and exchanged for gold or silver without the least ceremony or difficulty." The great difference, as he put it, was that bank notes were not issued "*as* money but as hostages to be exchanged for hard money." Every advantage lay with bank notes— so long, that is, as "the government do not borrow too much of the bank nor the bank lend more notes than it can redeem."[32]

Thomas Paine wrote of the agrarians' ideas with scorn. But commerce he praised. He was a business man himself, or sought to be, and his friends were business men. Enterprise had no better spokesman. He wrote a few years later in the *Rights of Man*: "In all my publications, where the matter would admit, I have been an advocate for commerce, because I am a friend to its effects. It is a pacific system, operating to cordialise mankind by rendering nations as well as individuals useful to each other. . . . If commerce were permitted to act to the universal extent it is capable, it would extirpate the system of war and produce a revolution in the uncivilised state of governments. The intention of commerce has arisen since those governments began and is the greatest approach towards universal

---

* The italics are Paine's. Death was the punishment customarily prescribed for counterfeiting. To recommend it for a legislator who should do no more than *move* a legal tender law was going pretty far.

[31] Paine (Conway) II, 171, 179-80; Paine (Foner) II, 427.
[32] Paine (Conway) II, 184-86.

civilisation that has yet been made by any means not immediately flowing from moral principles."[33]*

Thomas Paine evidently found it hard to believe that the agrarian opposition to the bank was honest, and he ascribed motives to it that were much too sophisticated. Thus he suspected that the representatives of the western counties of Pennsylvania, which were barred by the mountains from ready access to Philadelphia and made tributary instead to Baltimore, were attacking the bank in order to embarrass Philadelphia to the advantage of Baltimore. But he was probably right in the suspicion that the agrarians were encouraged in their course by wealthy enemies of the bank, who, he said, "view a public bank as standing in the way of their private interest." In succeeding years the efforts of rival business groups to break one another's banks recurred frequently; and so did the use of the agrarians as cat's-paws. Paine quoted a wealthy Philadelphian, George Emlen, as complaining that while the bank stood a monied man had no chance, that his money was not so valuable to him as before the bank was set up, and that "if the bank was demolished he could buy country produce for exportation cheaper." Gouverneur Morris said the usurers "never intermitted their efforts to destroy the bank"; and Robert Morris spoke to the same effect.[34] The confusion of alignments in this controversy, which was typical of others to come later, has testimony in the following words of a contemporary observer: "You might have seen the violent whig, the bitter tory, and the moderate man laying their heads together with the earnestness and freedom of friendship; the Constitutionalist and Republican were arm in arm; and the Quaker and Presbyterian forgot their religious antipathies in this coalition of interests. The ultra-radicals, however, never swallowed the idea of the bank in any form."**

X

At the end of the debate, 1 April 1786, the Assembly had again adjourned without undoing its repeal of the charter. But the agrar-

---

* Paine's emphasis was the reverse of Jefferson's, who in the conciliatory mood of his first inaugural recommended "encouragement of agriculture, and of commerce as its hand-maid."

** This is quoted by Robert L. Brunhouse in his *Counter-Revolution in Pennsylvania*, page 151, to show how "the bank issue crosscut party lines."

[33] Paine (Conway) II, 456.
[34] Paine (Foner) II, 424, 434-35, 1256; Sparks III, 443; Carey, 96.

ian cause had weakened, and the next elections shifted the membership closer to the bank. They also had the result of making Benjamin Franklin—who was a stockholder in the bank and whose son-in-law, Richard Bache, was a director—president of the state. During a period of more than a year in which it had got on without the charter, the bank had grown pretty certain of recovering it. The expectation was realised in March 1787, when a new one was enacted. The agrarians had attempted too much. One of their leaders, William Findley, said about thirty years later that repealing the charter instead of reducing the size of the bank had "changed the majority, and men of the greatest talents and influence in the state, who would not otherwise have served, were returned in favour of the bank. . . ."[35]

But the new charter was more explicit and restrictive than the old had been; it was good for only fourteen years and not forever, it reduced the "wealth" of the bank to two million dollars instead of ten, it forbade the bank to trade in merchandise and to hold more real estate than was needed for its place of business and to protect it from loss on loans, and it required that copies of the by-laws be deposited with the state authorities. In narrowing the scope of the original charter and keeping the corporation closely within the reach of the state, these limitations were prophetic of a tendency for corporate powers to be more narrowly defined at the same time that their effectiveness was to be increased.

For a short time, the relations of the Bank of North America to the confederated government were close, but Robert Morris, still Superintendent of Finance, sold the government's stock, as already said, being unable to complete the payment for it, and the bank itself became more and more absorbed in private business. It can scarcely be said ever to have been the "national bank" it was designed to be. Its directors wanted to make money, and they succeeded, for the annual dividend averaged close to ten per cent for the first forty years of its existence.[36] Long before that it had become merely the oldest of the country's banks and one of the more successful, with no other distinction, and it continued so under successive charters till 1929, when it was absorbed by one of its younger competitors, the Pennsylvania Company for Insurances on Lives

[35] Franklin x, 496; Lewis, 120; "William Findley," *PMHB*, v (1881), 444; Wilson, *PMHB*, LXVI (1942), 3.
[36] Lewis, 152.

and Granting Annuities, chartered in 1812. All that is of marked interest in the 147 years of its life occurred in the first five. But the conflict of principles and interests—economic, social, moral, and political—in that first lustrum was to recur often and far more momentously in the country's later history.

CHAPTER 3

The Start in New York, Boston, and Baltimore

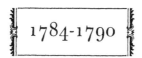

1784-1790

I. Banks in four cities — II. New and Old World banking — III. Merchant, agrarian, and speculator — IV. Banking practice — V. Deposits and other accounts — VI. Punctuality — VII. The solitary bank

I

OBSERVERS in other commercial centers were little deterred by the political difficulties of the bank in Philadelphia but much encouraged by its economic success. So it was not long before efforts were making elsewhere to set up banks. In New York rival groups set to work about the same time. One, comprising land-owners and led by Chancellor Livingston, sought to establish a "land bank," i.e., one whose capital was to be mainly in real estate mortgages, like a privately sponsored colonial loan office. Its projectors, Alexander Hamilton said sarcastically, considered it "the true philosopher's stone that was to turn all their rocks and trees into gold." There seem to have been two other groups, with which Colonel Hamilton was successively associated, which were mercantile and projected a "money bank," whose capital was to be wholly in specie. These two in the end were resolved into one. The land bank group and the money bank group each tried to get an exclusive charter and each frustrated the other. But the money bank was organized, nevertheless, and began business without immediate incorporation. This was the Bank of New York. From its opening, 9 June 1784, till 1791, when it was granted a corporate charter, it was conducted under a constitution drawn up by Alexander Hamilton. Before it opened, Hamilton arranged for its cashier, William Seton, to visit Philadelphia for a first hand study of the Bank of North America's operations.[1]

Meanwhile, in February 1784, the Massachusetts legislature

[1] Paine (Conway) II, 163; Domett, 4-6, 113; *New York Packet*, 12 and 23 February, 15 March, 1 May, 7 June 1784.

granted a charter to a group of Boston merchants incorporating the Massachusetts Bank. This bank began business, 5 July 1784, less than a month after the Bank of New York. Some of the Boston merchants were already shareholders in the Bank of North America in Philadelphia, and they sent a letter to its president, Thomas Willing, requesting information and advice. Banking was new to them, they said. Mr Willing replied that it had been new to him and his associates also. "When the bank was first opened here," he wrote, "the business was as much a novelty to us . . . as it can possibly be to you. It was a pathless wilderness, ground but little known to this side the Atlantick. No book then spoke of the interior arrangements or rules observed in Europe—accident alone threw in our way even the form of an English bank bill. All was to us a mystery."

"In this situation," he went on, "we adopted the only safe method to avoid confusion. Educated as merchants, we resolved to pursue the road we were best acquainted with. We established our books on a simple mercantile plan, and this mode . . . , pointed out by experience alone, has carried us through so far without a material loss or even mistake of any consequence." Mr Willing also sent copies of the Philadelphia bank's by-laws and regulations, which were adopted in Boston with little change. Samuel Osgood, who was a director of the Bank of North America, became cashier of the Massachusetts Bank, and another of the latter's officers visited the Bank of North America in order to study its methods of operation.[2]

In Baltimore, meanwhile, beginning in 1782, several attempts to form a bank had been stimulated by the success of the Bank of North America in Philadelphia, but according to Robert Morris the organizers could not muster sufficient subscriptions to carry through their project, and it was not realized for some years. By that time trade had been greatly stimulated by war in Europe following the French Revolution, subscribers had become more responsive, and in 1790 a charter was granted incorporating the Bank of Maryland, which opened the next year.[3]

By 1790, accordingly, eight years after organization of the Bank of North America, four banks were in business, or in train to be, in four leading cities—Philadelphia, New York, Boston, and Baltimore.* Three of the first four banks were long lived. The Bank of

* Attempts to set up banks had been made elsewhere—notably in Providence, Richmond, and Charleston—but had been abortive. A comprehensive

[2] Gras, 12-13, 28, 209-12. [3] Carey, 93.

North America continued in business from 1782 to 1929, as I have said. The Bank of New York has continued in business uninterruptedly since 1784; it was the second bank established in North America and is now the oldest. The Massachusetts Bank took a national charter in 1865 and was absorbed in 1903 by the First National Bank of Boston. The Bank of Maryland continued in business forty-four years and failed in 1834.

II

In 1790 each bank was a public bank; that is, it was distinctly more than a private institution. Though its active management was private, it was bound as well as enfranchised by governmental authority, and the state was as often as not a shareholder, or might be.* There were two ways of assessing the unique, public nature of "the Bank" in its community. The jaundiced view was that private interests had wormed their way into official favor and usurped privileges they should not have. The realistic view was that the community, whether shrewdly or not, had adapted private initiative and wealth to public purposes, granting privileges and exacting duties in return. Though banks grew numerous, there persisted a strong conviction that a charter was a covenant which the grant of other charters violated. But the conviction gave way, slowly and obstinately, and what overcame it was not logic but self-interest, and corruption. One group after another pleaded, cajoled, fought, and bribed its way to a bank of its own. Thus monopoly was slowly impaired. But the impairment was no more agreeable to the opposition which wanted no banks at all than to the banks themselves which had to encounter increased competition. To the agrarians, the multiplication of bank charters was an extension of privilege rather than a division of it.

---

account of the early establishments in various cities will be found in Joseph Stancliffe Davis, *Essays in the Earlier History of American Corporations,* II, chap. II.

* There were honorific as well as contractual evidences of the peculiar regard in which "the bank" in a community was held. In Philadelphia, in 1790, "the President of the Bank" (the Bank of North America, of course) with the President of the State, the Chief Justice, and others, was a pallbearer at the funeral of Benjamin Franklin. For years, at Cambridge, "the President of the Bank" (the Bank of Massachusetts) had as his right a seat on the rostrum at Harvard commencements.

Behind these current conceptions were the great public banks of issue in the Old World—the Bank of England, the Bank of Amsterdam, the Bank of Venice, and others. These were the models in everyone's mind, and especially in the minds of the moral opponents of banking for whom the fact that something derived from the Old World was reason enough for not wanting it. Moreover, despite the growth of banks, it was long before pluralities of them became everywhere common. Rather the situation in 1790, when the three states, Pennsylvania, Massachusetts, and Maryland, had each a sole incorporated bank, remained typical in one state or another for some time and enforced the conception of a bank as properly a unique institution. And it was still the habit of writers to discuss the advantages and disadvantages of "a bank," not using the plural "banks" or the generalization "banking." In fact everything that Alexander Hamilton, Thomas Paine, and other writers said in advocacy of banks was said, explicitly or implicitly, with a "public" bank in mind. Private banking received no attention till many years had passed.[4]

In setting up public banks of issue without first evolving a private banking system, the pioneer American bankers were in a way putting the cart before the horse. In Europe—particularly in Italy, the Low Countries, and England—banking had had a long, quiet, and gradual development; the liabilities of bankers in the form of deposits had for centuries supplemented the metallic monetary stock, and the public banks—nowadays called the central banks—came at a later stage. In America, on the other hand, banking arrived suddenly by transplantation and in public rather than private guise. Richard Hildreth wrote in 1840: "The whole system of banking in America has been formed upon the model afforded by the Bank of England—the system of private banking which prevails in Great Britain never having been introduced into this country and being even prohibited by statute in many of the states. . . ." What little native inheritance it had was from the loan office and no less governmental than what it got from abroad. The country became spotted with public banks and had no private ones, at least none of sufficient importance to leave evidence that they existed. By subsequent standards of free enterprise this was anomalous, but the anomaly became corrected by the speedy adaptation of the public banks to private interest, as illustrated by the Bank of North Amer-

4 Paine (Foner) II, 429ff.

ica. The process was attended by great growth in the number of banks, a growth which ineluctably broke down the unique association of the first few banks with the state and also with commerce. But in the process of becoming adapted to private enterprise, banks never lost all the birthmarks of their public origin, and those they ultimately did lose—such as note issue and unique association with the state—they lost only slowly.[5]

American banking differed also from Old World banking in that it originated in a want of capital, not in a surplus of it. For European economies were already mature when their first banks arose, and they possessed age-old accumulations of wealth upon which those banks could rest. In England, stores of coin and plate had been lodged with goldsmiths, and the goldsmiths had turned bankers to find a use for the treasure. Nothing of the sort happened in America, where wealth was in hope more than in possession, and the need of homely necessities was so great that stocks of gold and silver could rarely be retained even when they could be assembled. It was in dearth like this and not in abundance that American banking had its genesis. Needs were great, means were few, and men were resourceful. The impulsion to which they responded was that of demand, not supply, and their response was to club together their scanty funds, as Robert Morris said, and form institutions that should do for them collectively what they could not do so well severally.

This condition is reflected in a succinct description of banking that Alexander Hamilton gave President Washington in 1791. "For the simplest and most precise idea of a bank," Hamilton wrote, "is a deposit of coin or other property as a fund for *circulating a credit* upon it which is to answer the purpose of money." This description is still as sound as it was then, though no one would now think of putting it that way. Hamilton had earlier indicated the essential nature of banking, when he observed that the Pennsylvania Bank was making purchases with its assets and not with its liabilities.[6]

Yet despite the scantiness of means, and in fact because of it, enthusiasm for new banks was extravagant. Capital was often subscribed and heavily over-subscribed within a few hours of the opening of books; in Providence in 1791, when 450 shares were offered, 1,324 were subscribed; and next year in New York, $10,-

---

[5] Hildreth, *Banks, Banking, and Paper Currencies*, 118.
[6] Clarke and Hall, 106.

000,000 of new capital was subscribed in two hours when $1,000,000 only was offered.[7] The heavy subscriptions arose to some extent, doubtless, from the practice of bidding for much in order to make sure of getting some. They were feasible because payments in specie could be delayed and minimized. Banks lent on their own stock. Benjamin Franklin, for example, had gone into debt to the Bank of North America for the stock he purchased in it. So had the government of the United States. The bank was so hard put for cash that it had to have porters carry its specie busily to and from the cellar in order to give the customers a magnified notion of what it had; and some of its proprietors ostentatiously brought in deposits of gold and silver that had unostentatiously been carried out a little while before.* The bank can not reasonably be blamed for putting its best foot forward, but that sort of thing was to become mischievously frequent. For a century and a half America was to be straining beyond her means, growing in wealth, to be sure, but hypothecating her gains as fast as she made them in order that she might make more. In a mature economy the effort to do business with insufficient capital is contemptuously called working on a shoe string; in 18th and 19th century America it was a popular virtue decried by those who could not make it work. Eventually more was demanded of banks than they could perform, but till after 1800 their record was good; "there can be no question," Professor Joseph S. Davis says of the 18th century American banks, that they "were

---

* A hundred and twenty-five years later, in the panic of 1907, a rural bank in Iowa, of which I was assistant cashier, resorted to a similar stratagem. The cashier and I, who constituted the entire office force, fetched all our bags of coin from the vault and piled them where the customers could not help seeing them. Subsidiary coin was legal tender for only very small amounts in those days, and the value of the lot was inconsiderable—ten of the bags contained only 1,000 pennies each—but the display was impressive, and we kept our doors open. We found it still more effectual, however, to conceal our paper currency and offer payment to uneasy depositors in silver. Even the partisans of William Jennings Bryan balked at that; I remember a free-silver enthusiast, a Civil War veteran, who angrily refused ninety silver dollars, the amount of his quarterly pension, and stalked inconsistently and angrily from the bank with his check uncashed—which, of course, suited us exactly. It will be observed that we pretended, unlike the Bank of North America, to be worse off than we were in fact—concealing our relatively large amount of paper currency and displaying our relatively small amount of coin.

[7] J. S. Davis, *Earlier American Corporations* ii, 62, 81.

the most important and the most successful of the eighteenth century business corporations."[8]

Although the first American banks were new phenomena to both their friends and their enemies, almost everything about them, taken separately, was old and familiar. They were a rearrangement in special form of powers and functions that previously had been scattered and unformalized. The corporate form, which the first American banks took, was already known, especially for organizations of a public nature; and so, of course, was the practice of borrowing. The notes the banks issued were, in form if not in essence, just another variety of paper money, which had long been generally known. In substance the accounts of banks with their customers were like those that merchants had maintained with planters and farmers, especially in the southern colonies where great cash crops of tobacco, indigo, and rice were produced. In colonial Virginia and Maryland, for example, planters would consign shipments of tobacco to correspondents in England who would sell the tobacco and hold the proceeds for the planters' instructions. "It is a fact," wrote Thomas Jefferson as late as 1813, "that a farmer with a revenue of ten thousand dollars a year may obtain all his supplies from his merchant and liquidate them at the end of the year by the sale of his produce to him without the intervention of a single dollar of cash."[9] The planters' credit on the merchants' books would be very much like deposit credit on a bank's books: the credit might indeed be an advance or loan to finance goods ordered by the planter, in which case the merchant was essentially a banker. Banks, however, probably bore more likeness to the colonial loan offices than to anything else in American experience. For these were places where borrowers obtained credit upon security and whence they carried away notes to be passed into general circulation by payments from hand to hand. In all, consequently, the banks took up and continued not only practices known to merchants but practices familiar to others as well; and the novelty lay in having an institution, of semi-official aspect, which specialised in monetary transactions as distinguished from the transactions in real property to which they were ancillary.

III

The decade 1781 to 1791, which spanned the establishment of banks in Philadelphia, New York, Boston, and Baltimore, was fol-

[8] J. S. Davis, *Earlier American Corporations* II, 108.
[9] Jefferson (Ford) IX, 408n.

lowed by one in which the number grew so rapidly that contemporaries spoke of a rage for banks—a "bancomania." In 1792, alone,
a year of great speculation, eight banks were set up. This rapid
growth did not mean an unalloyed triumph for the principles upon
which the first four banks had been founded. Unlike the infant
Hercules, those four had merely scotched, not killed, the enemies
that beset them in their cradles. This was especially true of the
agrarian opposition, which grew side by side with banking itself.

But there also arose a speculative, easy-money opposition that
behaved very differently from the agrarian. It had no aversion to
banking *per se* but only to the strait-laced notions of the merchants
who then controlled banking. For there was more than one kind of
merchant; there were the impatient and risk-loving as well as the
cautious and conservative—men who were willing to turn land
speculator, as Robert Morris did, or to turn entrepreneur and build
canals, set up iron foundries, sail ships, spin silk, or venture anywhere else outside their warehouses in search of wealth. As speculators and entrepreneurs they needed credit on long term and could
not remain satisfied with the thirty- to ninety-day discounts that
sufficed for merchandising. Moreover, with increasing population,
markets, and demand, the speculators and entrepreneurs grew to be
the dominant users of credit. The typical merchants of 1790 became
an old-fashioned minority; in the commercial centers they might
still keep a few banks devoted to their interests, but they could not
hope for long to confine banking in general to their own needs. The
pressure of demand by other borrowers became too great.

Yet the cleavage between speculator and conservative produced
vigorous contention within the business world over the use of credit.
The conservative merchant clung to its use in the exchange of goods.
The speculator saw wealth in more things than trade and wanted
the use of credit broadened accordingly. The arguments were illustrated in a controversy in Baltimore newspapers several years before
there was a bank there. In November 1784 it was announced that a
group of merchants purposed establishing a Bank of Maryland like
the Bank of North America in Philadelphia, and that the legislature
would be asked to incorporate it, to penalize the counterfeiting of
its notes, to make its notes receivable for taxes, and to provide that
the state authorities might examine it and "at all times have access
to its books and papers." A week later came counter-proposals from
speculators who were indebted to the state on purchases of confis-

cated British property and wished the state to issue paper money which was to facilitate the payment both of debts owed by the state and of debts due to it. The first group advocated a bank "established after the example and long experience of other commercial countries, under the immediate observation of government, calculated to increase the medium of commerce and to induce punctuality among the trading part of the community." At such a bank, "every day and every hour of the day, the possessor of a bill may prove its value equal to gold and silver by making an exchange." A medium of payment would be provided by it which farmers as well as merchants could use: whether one borrowed at the bank himself or not, the circulation of its notes would make it possible for him to sell his goods. Paper money let out upon long credit, "which is a known destructive error," would never do. It was bound to depreciate.[10]

On the other hand, the speculators were equally positive. They said the merchants would have a bank where loans would "exceed not thirty or the most sixty days" and where the farmer, the planter, and the mechanic could therefore not expect to borrow. What the community needed was paper money "emitted upon the security of landed estate"; land was "fixed and immovable, not to be affected . . . by the precarious issue of commerce." Both sides coaxed the agrarians, arguments against the merchants' bank being signed "Planter" and arguments for it being signed "Farmer," and each side claiming to show where the agrarian interest truly lay.

One is aware of a difference between what is conservative in business and what is risky and of a like difference between a man who is conservative and one who is not. But there is no definition distinguishing the two clearly and *a priori*. One has to wait and see how things come out. Robert Morris was once among the conservatives and successful, he turned to land speculation, and he ended bankrupt; his partner, Thomas Willing, never deviated from conservatism and success. Toward the close of the 18th century, there was an interval when everything American—even a large part of agrarianism—seemed to merge homogeneously into speculation. As Professor Joseph Stancliffe Davis has said, "One gigantic speculation had been notably successful—the achieving of independence"; and it is no mere coincidence that participants in that achievement included a conspicuous number of energetic, imaginative men who

---

[10] *Maryland Journal and Baltimore Advertiser,* 7, 9, 17, 19, 26, and 30 November; 7, 14, and 19 December 1784; Bryan, 17-18.

were interested in making money and became creators of the succeeding age of enterprise. Land speculation came first; to Benjamin Franklin, George Washington, and Robert Morris it was one material expression of their confidence in America. When government obligations were made abundant by the Revolution, they too became an object of speculation, and that speculation also was an expression of confidence in America. Canals, bridges, toll-roads, banks, and manufactories lay in the path of what came to be called enterprise, and countless men of practical imagination turned in countless different ways to their erection with the vigor and the spirit that had characterized their efforts to erect a new nation. And for these projects of peace, which had a scope far beyond that of merchandising, credit was as essential as it was to political revolution.[11]

IV

"Discounts," said the rules of the Bank of New York in 1784, "will be done on Thursday in every week, and bills and notes brought for discount must be left at the bank on Wednesday morning, under a sealed cover, directed to William Seton, Cashier. The rate of discount is at present fixed at six per cent *per annum*; but no discount will be made for longer than thirty days, nor will any note or bill be discounted to pay a former one." This followed the practice in Philadelphia, where Thomas Willing said they discounted "only for thirty days"; though, according to Robert Morris, "sometimes through tenderness" a credit was prolonged. The rules of the Massachusetts Bank, which would "not be deviated from in the smallest instance nor on any pretence whatever," permitted discounts for thirty or sixty days only, depending on the security, with no privilege of renewal on any terms. The directors were convinced that the existence of the bank depended "on the Punctual payment of Discounts and all Monies at the Time they become due . . . ," and the names of delinquent debtors to the bank were posted conspicuously. That the strictness of these rules was a reality seems borne out by the circumstances. Lending was not left to bank officers, and it was not possible to walk into the bank, ask an officer for a loan, and get it. Lending was the responsibility of the directors, who were merchants advancing their own money, as they felt, to other merchants. The directors of the Massachusetts Bank met for discounts twice weekly, and each director in turn voted for or against each

11 J. S. Davis, *Earlier American Corporations* II, 7.

discount by dropping a white or a black ball in a box in a corner of the director's room. A single black ball was enough to reject a discount.[12]

Such rules, the first to govern banking in North America, constituted orthodoxy and retained prestige long after banking practice developed wide deviations. Orthodox doctrine has been that banks should lend only for short term and only to finance actual sales of commodities, a good banker, it was said, being one who knew the difference between a bill of lading and a real estate mortgage. It is notorious that this doctrine was professed long after it became otiose, but it does not follow that it was always otiose. So long as commerce has been a leading economic interest in any given center, there always have been banks specializing in short-term commercial credit. Philadelphia, New York, Boston, and Baltimore were more eminently merchant cities in the last two decades of the 18th century than they have been since, and their banks were more eminently mercantile. They could have lent on real estate mortgage security, but they would have lost thereby their utility to the merchants who organized them. "A bank," said Pelatiah Webster, "is a sort of mercantile institution or at least has such a close connexion with the whole mercantile interest that it will more naturally and properly fall under the direction of merchants than of any other sort of men less acquainted with its nature and principles and less interested in its success."[13]

This meant that the earning assets acquired by banks were obligations arising from the sale and purchase of merchandise at wholesale. Almost by definition bank credit was mercantile. From the nature of their business, merchants had among themselves both the readiest means of supplying credit and the most attractive uses for it. No other economic group possessed so much cash to lend or could repay borrowings with such certainty in so short a time. This condition of itself put them on the threshold of banking and made them the first to engage in it. Agriculture had a potential demand for credit but no comparable means of supplying it or of making competitive offers for what was obtainable; and the country was as yet without the manufactures, the transportation systems, and the manifold services that were later to diversify its economic activity and multiply the uses to which credit might be put. Hence banking germi-

[12] Domett, 19-20; Gras, 45-46, 210, 273-76.
[13] Pelatiah Webster, 439.

nated and rooted itself in the one place that at the time it could—in commerce.

In doing so it conformed to the most approved thought of the time. Of this conformity its sponsors were quite aware, being familiar with the writings of British economists, and their resolution was undoubtedly strengthened by their orthodoxy. But one can not help seeing that what really counted was the fact that the first American bankers were merchants seeking to advance their own interests by an improved means of providing the credit they needed and that they lent as bankers the way they had lent as merchants. That expedience had more to do with the credit practice than orthodoxy did is shown by the readiness to lend to the government and to nascent industrial enterprises. The government, whether municipal, state, or federal, was a notoriously slow debtor, but its right to bank credit was unquestioned. Providing capital for new industries was by modern judgment less compatible with orthodox mercantile credit practice than was lending to the state, but with industry a wholly new thing this could not have been recognized. The Bank of New York in 1792 made substantial long-term loans to the Society for Useful Manufactures, then preparing to go into operation at Paterson, New Jersey. According to Alexander Hamilton, banks, "within reasonable limits, ought to consider it as a principal object to promote beneficial public purposes." As fast as those "beneficial public purposes" multiplied, bank credit followed them, but so far its important use remained in commerce, for the merchants were still able to hold their own.[14]

Although the first American banks were mercantile, the earning assets they held do not seem to have comprised the bills, drafts, or acceptances of orthodoxy but simply the promissory notes of local merchants who borrowed at the bank to pay the bills drawn on them by the merchants who shipped to them from overseas. Not till about 1820 do American banks appear to have purchased on a large scale the obligations drawn against shipments of merchandise. The reason for their not buying such obligations at first is presumably that they had no chance to. When they were established in the '80's and '90's of the 18th century, trade with Britain and the Indies was already more than a century old and with it the procedure by which Old World merchants collected what was due them from the New. They drew on the latter, the drafts followed the cargoes, and

14 Domett, 48-49; Hamilton (Lodge) IX, 512.

the ship captains collected payment, in either goods, return bills, or specie. This was not changed in any one port, Philadelphia, New York, Boston, or Baltimore, the moment a bank was established there. British merchants selling to Americans probably preferred to collect what was due them through established means. The bank, consequently, performed its function by lending to the local merchant so that he could pay the drafts drawn on him. The bank indeed would undoubtedly prefer to lend to its local customers rather than buy claims on them from others. There might be no difference economically, but legally and in good will there might be considerable. Moreover by the purchase of drafts the bank would become debtor to a British creditor and obligated to effect payment in a fashion for which it was as yet unprepared, not having foreign balances. At the same time, the bank would probably eschew the purchase of bills drawn against exports because it had not the means of collection. It had rather lend to its local customer and let him make his collections through channels he was already using. Altogether, therefore, I am inclined to think that the first banks avoided the purchase of bills, especially in foreign trade, and confined their credit to local borrowers. In their circumstances, moreover, most trade that was not local was foreign—Charleston or Baltimore being quite as "foreign" to Boston, for example, as Bristol or Bordeaux. In New York the office of the Bank of the United States "sold to merchants foreign exchange resulting from government drafts on Amsterdam" in the Bank's favor, but this seems to have been exceptional till after 1800.[15]

V

The following is a balanced statement of the Bank of New York for 1 May 1791:*

Bills discounted	$845,940.20	Capital stock	$318,250.00
Due from Corporation	12,222.44	Notes outstanding	181,254.00
Cash	462,815.87	Due depositors	773,709.67
		Profit and loss	47,764.84
	$1,320,978.51		$1,320,978.51

* I have used the dollar sign, $, which is an anachronism. It did not come into use till twenty or twenty-five years later.

15 Redlich, 17.

This shows the bank's condition at the time it became a corporation, after seven years in business. It is known to have held government securities and these may be included among bills discounted, though the amount due from New York City, the "Corporation," is shown separately. The net cash, besides coin, may have included some notes of the banks in Philadelphia, Boston, and Baltimore. The capital stock was at the time not fully paid in, for it was supposed to be $500,000 before the charter was granted in 1791; under the charter the authorized capital became $1,000,000, of which $950,-000 was shortly paid in, the state subscribing $50,000. The amount due depositors is more than four times the amount due note-holders. It presumably included government funds.[16]

Bookkeeping was very different from what it has since become. At first, balanced statements do not seem to have been drawn up except for occasional, special purposes—certainly not daily. In 1791 the by-laws of the Bank of the United States required that the Bank's books and accounts "be regularly balanced on the first Mondays in January and July in each year, when the half-yearly dividends shall be declared. . . ."[17] Thomas Willing's letter to the Massachusetts Bank indicates that this was the practice of the Bank of North America, a practice taken over from mercantile bookkeeping. A running total of notes in circulation would be maintained, of necessity, but no corresponding total of deposits, though individual deposit accounts must have been kept current. Modern accounting methods and the requirements of supervisory authorities make a daily balancing of the books invariable now, but the first American banks had neither modern standards nor modern requirements—though they were very good banks. The Bank of North America, 24 September 1792, directed its bookkeepers to prepare balance sheets every Monday and Thursday, but how much the accounting varied from modern practice is indicated by the following general statement headings found in the collection of the bank's records held by the Historical Society of Pennsylvania: "State of the Bank and Inventory taken 31 December 1793"; "State of the Bank in the Spring," 1793; "State of the Bank founded partially but not fully on the account in the General and Particular Ledgers," 31 December 1800. The latter contains the two following items: "Balances due on Personal Accounts in 4 Particular Ledgers as struck and returned by

---

[16] Domett, 37; Knox, *History of Banking*, 393.
[17] Holdsworth, 133.

the bookkeepers, 788,115.20" dollars; and "Balances due on Personal Accounts in Ledger of Debts Payable and Receivable as returned by Bookkeepers, 22,807.25" dollars.

The two statements that follow are illustrative.*

State of the Bank on the Morning of the 3d of May 1802.

Bills discounted outstanding	$1,818,357.12
Foreign Notes	70,000
Specie	246,103
	$2,134,460.12
Stock	$742,800
Notes in Circulation	646,984
Balance due Bank of United States	84,289.09
Balance due Bank of Pennsylvania	18,078.57
Balance due Bank of New York	5,741.86
Discount	34,439.90
Deposit Money	602,126.70
	$2,134,460.12

State of the Bank on the Morning of the 4th of November 1802.

Bills discounted	$1,731,996.65
Specie	255,144
Foreign Notes	62,000
	$2,049,140.65
Stock	$742,800
Notes in Circulation	556,641
Balance due Bank of United States	84,691.31
Balance due Bank of Pennsylvania	32,628.35
Balance due Bank of New York	3,124.09
Discount	35,045.36
Deposit Money	594,210.54
	$2,049,140.65

Figures drawn up in balance, like the foregoing for the Bank of North America and those already shown for the Bank of New York

* These statements are taken from the books of the bank in the collection of the Historical Society of Pennsylvania. Again I add the dollar sign, not used in the original.

in 1791, have a deceptive definiteness and tempt one to unwarranted comparisons. Still they are informative. They indicate that almost no account had then the relative importance it has now, except the main body of earning assets. And these have changed radically in composition. They consisted then of short-term promissory notes almost wholly but now consist of all kinds of obligations and of government and corporation securities. On the liability side, the statements differ from those of to-day in that banks no longer have notes in circulation, their obligations to the public comprise deposits only, and their capital is relatively far smaller. Early American bank liabilities seldom seem to have been more than two or three times the capital, whereas to-day liabilities are commonly ten or fifteen times the capital. A bank's proprietors had then to supply a far larger portion of the funds upon which it operated; to-day they depend on the public for most of the funds and themselves supply a small fraction of them.

Because banking laws and public discussion in the 19th century were preoccupied with note issue, there has been a tendency in the States to think of note issue as *the* original banking function, superseded at a later stage by deposits. In fact the importance of deposits was not realized by most American economists, Professor Charles F. Dunbar being the distinguished pioneer and exception, till after 1900; and then there was a comfortable assumption that the object of so recent a discovery must itself have been recent. On the contrary, European banking was a matter of deposit credit and bills of exchange for centuries before note issue first became prominent, which was in England. English influence and American conditions worked together to make note issue prominent in America too, but never so predominant, I am convinced, as is generally thought. Deposits always have been important in American banking, but several things have tended to keep the emphasis off them. First was the mistaken notion that deposits represented only specie put in the bank "for safekeeping"—what was later called a "special deposit"— that they were therefore a book credit for money, and had importance only as its surrogate and as between the bank and the depositor. Second was the notion that the only money supplied or created by banks in the process of lending was their circulating notes. Third was the fact that because the country could not afford to accumulate specie enough for monetary purposes, bank notes made up the bulk of the circulation. Fourth was the fact that laws and public discussion fixed on circulation and continued to give it a factitious importance long after its quantitative importance had ceased to justify it. Fifth was the fact that most bankers thought note liabilities were more profitable than deposit liabilities and hence did all they could to extend their note circulation.[18]

But it is obvious that the first banks had deposit accounts and that borrowers at the banks had the proceeds of their loans credited to their accounts. In 1786 Pelatiah Webster, after explaining the advantages of a bank in terms of bank notes or bills, went on to say: "The advantage would be still greater if instead of bank bills the owner would take a bank credit and draw checks on the bank whenever he needed his money; this would enable him to pay any sum exactly without the trouble of making change; he would be able in any future time to prove his payments if he preserved his checks, which he received cancelled from the bank, as every man ought to do. . . . This practice is found by experience to be so very convenient that it is almost universally adopted by people who keep their cash in our present bank." According to Thomas Paine there were then about 600 such people maintaining deposit accounts with the Bank of North America.[19]

In 1790 Alexander Hamilton wrote: "Every loan which a bank makes is in its first shape a credit given to the borrower on its books, the amount of which it stands ready to pay either in its own notes or in gold or silver, at his option. But in a great number of cases no actual payment is made in either. The borrower frequently, by a check or order, transfers his credit to some other person, to whom he has a payment to make; who in his turn is as often content with a similar credit, because he is satisfied that he can, whenever he pleases, either convert it into cash or pass it to some other hand as an equivalent for it. And in this manner the credit keeps circulating, performing in every stage the office of money. . . . Thus large sums are lent and paid, frequently through a variety of hands, without the intervention of a single piece of coin." Hamilton knew this important fact first hand, for there is a letter among his papers in the Library of Congress in which William Seton, writing in New York, 3 February 1791, informs Mr Hamilton, in Philadelphia, that his promissory note had been received, discounted, and passed

18 Dunbar, 173, 179; Usher, passim; De Roover, passim.
19 Pelatiah Webster, 434; Paine (Foner) ii, 416, 432.

to his credit, and that his "present ballance in Bank including the discount is 2907 dollars and $\frac{44}{100}$s."[20]

The direct result of such transactions in volume would be an amount of deposit credit exceeding the bank's cash. And this is what the figures of the Bank of New York in 1791 show: $463,000 in cash and $774,000 due depositors. But not all this cash arose from deposits; most of it, in the current view, was capital. Moreover, the earning assets, $858,000, greatly exceeded the circulation, $181,-000, and must therefore have been offset by some other liability, which would naturally be deposits. But to show in figures the magnitude of deposits and circulation year by year for the period before 1834 is impossible, though statistical series might be developed from the scattered but abundant data that would be quite as good as those provided by the Treasury after 1834. There are few other statements contemporary with the 1791 statement of the Bank of New York, but there are many by 1800 or shortly thereafter. What I have seen indicate that deposits sometimes exceeded circulation and that circulation sometimes exceeded deposits. The variations are due as much to place as to time, apparently, and depend considerably on the presence or absence of government deposits. Some banks, especially in commercial centers and particularly in New York, seem to have preferred from a very early date to cultivate deposits while others preferred to cultivate note circulation. These tendencies developed by the 1830's and 1840's into marked specialization.

I imagine that so long as the banks were definitely commercial, their customers, being merchants, probably kept the bulk of their current funds in deposit balances. But after 1800 the greatest increase in the number of banks was outside the commercial centers, and note liabilities for banks in the aggregate outgrew deposit liabilities. This was the situation in 1834, when the Treasury began publishing comprehensive figures, such as they were. Yet even then notes exceeded deposits by about a fifth only, and the largest banks, at least in New York, had few or no circulating notes at all. Notes continued their excess uncertainly for about twenty years, and then were left far behind for good. The reason for the temporary excess of notes, I should say, is in part that the Jacksonian period, in which it occurred, was characterized by an intense popular expansion and democratization of business enterprise which required more

[20] ASP, Finance I, 68; Hamilton Papers 11, p. 1393.

money than had been needed in an agrarian economy. In these circumstances, people at first used more of the hand-to-hand currency to which they had been accustomed, and only as they became more sophisticated did they turn to demand deposits, which the older business classes had always preferred. A less theoretical reason is the hypertrophy of note circulation induced in the Jacksonian period by the energetic efforts of bankers to keep their notes from being redeemed. Notes were exchanged for that purpose. Banks in remote towns would do this systematically, each taking, for example, $10,000 of the other's notes, counting them as cash while still on hand, and offering them to customers in preference to their own notes, deposit credit, or drafts on other banks. Still another consideration is that the Bank of the United States ceased to be a regulator of the state bank note issues in 1834, just at the time the Treasury series began to be published. Finally, the Treasury series includes the most casual sort of data, and deposits would not, according to the prevailing sense of their importance, be reported so regularly as circulation would. These conditions would combine to exaggerate circulation and to minimize deposits.

Though some effort may have been made by the 18th century banks to segregate credit for deposits of specie from credit for amounts lent to borrowers, it is not reflected in any early bank statements. The banks did segregate credit for paper money, but that was because its convertibility into specie was uncertain, whereas transactions in their own liabilities were always on a specie basis. My supposition is that banks found it impracticable to maintain two specie accounts for a single customer and instead maintained one only for each, to which all credits and debits on a specie basis were entered regardless of the transaction, whether a loan or a deposit of cash. The combined account probably came to be called a "deposit" account because the bookkeeping process was the same in both cases and because the term "deposit" was natural for specie transactions and nothing equally good suggested itself for the others.

Secondly and more important, as soon as there were several banks, the book credit entered in favor of a borrower at one bank could become transferred to another bank by checks or by bank notes deposited therein exactly as coin might be deposited. When this stage was reached, the fact that a given deposit originated in a loan became obscured, because the loan was made at one bank and the credit was transferred to another. So, also, the more com-

prehensive fact that the bulk of "deposits" originated in loans—
that deposits were in fact mostly bank credit—also became obscured; for whereas a given loan was a single transaction, the
transfer of the funds lent from bank to bank as they served for a
succession of payments from person to person would result in a
series of deposit transactions not only divorced from the original
loan transaction but far more frequent. In these circumstances it
would cease to be obvious that deposits were a result of lending; if
anything, they would seem only to precede it. Moreover, since in
principle the checks and notes "deposited" were payable in specie, it
seemed reasonable to say the deposits represented specie, even
though it was known that the aggregate deposits of all banks exceeded the aggregate specie.

As soon as there was a plurality of banks in any community, it
became evident at once how indissolubly banks are bound to one
another with respect to lending and reserves. Every time it lent, a
bank in effect put its competitors in possession of claims against it
which enabled them to demand so much of its reserves. Banks
raided one another rapaciously. This was stupid, and after some
sixty years or so, when banks in Philadelphia tried to force the banks
of New York to close, it was given up. But it was associated with a
phenomenon never absent from banking and of essential significance
in the control of credit by the public authorities. This is the influence of bank reserves upon the power of banks to lend.

In 1792 William Seton of the Bank of New York wrote to Alexander Hamilton in great uneasiness about current withdrawals of
specie for shipment to India and asked the Treasury's help. In
1799 Robert Troup wrote to Rufus King that "late shipments of
specie to India and China have so drained the vaults of our banks
that at present we have a heavy pressure for money." And he added
that "this pressure is increased by a resolution of the Manhattan
Company lately announced to set up a new bank." In 1804 James
Cheetham of New York, after observing that "all banks, if prudently and ably managed, find it necessary to curtail their discounts
when their specie gets low," went on to say: "The truth of this
remark was sensibly felt in this city a few weeks ago when several
hundred thousand dollars were taken from it to satisfy the demands
of the English government under the British treaty. The discounts
usually done were instantly curtailed. There was a general complaint

of a want of bank accommodation, but the cause was not well understood."[21]

It seldom is. Instead it seems to be assumed that if banks curtail their loans, it is because they are seeking to coerce or punish their customers. This contention is one that demagogues have always thriven on. Banks are guilty of misdoing when they have lent too much, but the amount of ill-nature animating their curtailments is negligible. They are under a pressure to lend that is practically irresistible, unless the prospective borrower is of doubtful standing. The pressure is internal, for they want to make profits, and external, for their customers want to borrow. Save for intervals this is the constant condition under which they have operated since 1781. Only a cramping of their reserves can stop them.

If a bank lent out all its reserves till it had no money left on hand, it would clearly be in an awkward position. People with checks they wanted to cash would raise a hubbub. No bank lets itself get into such a state; but every loan a bank makes *tends* to push it in that direction. Accordingly the successful management of a bank keeps it between the two hypothetical extremes of lending nothing at all and lending everything it has; and when it finds its reserves inadequate or apprehends that they may become inadequate, it is impelled to curtail its lending. This sensitivity of the lending process to alterations in the volume of reserves—either of an individual bank or of banks collectively—is an invariable characteristic of banking and manifest whatever the form of lending, the form of liability, or the form of reserves. Thus in 1800, when lending was on promissory notes, when bank liabilities were partly in circulating notes and partly in deposits, and when reserves were wholly in specie, a shift of reserves from bank to bank—which would happen, say, when the government disbursed funds it had in one bank to persons who kept their funds in another bank—or a loss of reserves by the banks generally in the form of specie shipments to India, would at once affect the ability of banks to lend, as James Cheetham pointed out. Now, a century and a half later, the composition of earning assets is different, liabilities are in deposits only, and reserves are in the form of balances due from the Reserve Banks. Yet the sensitivity of the lending process to alterations in the volume of reserves—of the individual bank or collectively—is as real and as important as ever.

[21] Charles R. King, *Rufus King* III, 34-43; Cheetham, 22.

VI

In the judgment of practically every contemporary who had anything favorable to say about banks, one of the outstanding advantages derived from them was the establishment of punctuality in the payment of debts. How difficult it had been for debtors to be punctual, even assuming the honest disposition to keep promises made and accepted, can be imagined in a society where the supply of tender, legal or acceptable, was straitly limited and could be used only by those lucky enough or astute enough to lay hands on it first. The supply of specie was not elastic. It could not be expanded readily at seasons when a large number of due payments coincided, nor could it be fetched readily from where it might be to where the debtors needed it. This was the familiar situation that had led to colonial issues of paper money, which were often excessive, and were always a nuisance in their conflicting multiplicity.

The establishment of banks made punctuality easier. It did not make Americans any more honest than they had been nor did it introduce any more effective means of making them pay. Instead it simply created a new source and form of money, readily available upon agreement between borrower and banker. A debtor possessed of property who could not obtain silver or gold with which to make a payment that was due need not paw the air in fear that his property would be seized, but might borrow at the bank and with its notes or a check drawn on it pay what he owed. There were limitations on this procedure, of course; the banks would not and could not give every debtor all he wished, nor did they at first venture outside the field of commercial credit, where debt was a normal and productive means of anticipating payments and not the stagnant burden that long-term borrowers were apt to find it. But this second limitation was not so confining as it may sound. Credit released anywhere does not stop at the point of release any more than water, flowing from a tap, stands still where it falls. Credit, like the money of which it is a form, passes from one person to another, dissolving one obligation after another. In the business world every creditor is also a debtor, and what he receives he pays. Consequently, though the early commercial banks chose their own debtors within a limited business group, their benefits, as their apologists explained, ran far outside that group.

VII

As compared with the intricacy of 20th century inter-relation-ships, the 18th century setting was an uncomplicated one in which the banking function can be watched more plainly than when many banks are engaged in it. When there was one bank respectively in Philadelphia, New York, Boston, and Baltimore, each was organ-ically tantamount to a complete banking system, especially in the sense that each directly increased its deposits by lending. Notes of each and checks drawn on it would rarely go to any other bank; till transport improved and inter-city business grew, obligations of a bank in one city seldom appeared in another city, and one bank seldom gained funds from any of the others. So when one of the banks lent and credited its customer accordingly, its deposit liabili-ties were increased and remained so, as Alexander Hamilton ex-plained, till the credit was withdrawn in specie, which was less often than not, or till the loan was repaid. The amount borrowed would be transferred from one creditor of the bank to another and would be sometimes in the form of bank notes, but it would never leave the bank's books unless it went to a bank in another city. This simple condition could not have lasted long. Thus shortly after the opening of the Bank of Maryland, in Baltimore, the following letter was addressed to it, 2 June 1791, by Thomas Willing, president of the Bank of North America in Philadelphia:

"Your favor of the 19th of May last has this day been laid before our Board of Directors. The subject of it is of much importance as well to your institution as our own. I am therefore authorized to inform you that having the best disposition to support the credit and to promote the interest of the Bank of Maryland, we shall as we have hitherto done, receive your paper as far as it may be con-venient for us to do so and you will no doubt do the same by ours. But as to any stipulation respecting the quantity or the time we may continue to take each other's notes, we do not think it advisable at present to enter into it as a matter obligatory on either side. . . .

"We received the first of your notes, which appeared at our coun-ter, and in the whole have had about 15,000 dollars brought in, all of which except about 4,000 dollars has again been paid away to those who have been willing to take it as a remittance to Maryland, and we have the pleasure to say we have found no difficulty with it hitherto."[22]

[22] Redlich, 16; Bank of North America Papers, No. 2, Minutes and Letter Book, November 1781–January 1792.

In this letter, which also acknowledges specimen signatures of the Bank of Maryland's officers, the Bank of North America discourages the practice by which banks at a distance from each other exchanged notes in order that each might have its notes put in use far from home and therefore made apt to remain in circulation longer. But the letter also shows how commonly banks were already becoming holders of one another's cash obligations through the normal course of business. Thus in May 1795 President George Washington in Philadelphia sent a remittance of over $4,000 to Alexandria, Virginia, for the purchase, as it happens, of bank stock.[23] The remittance included $960 in notes of the Bank of the United States, Philadelphia, and these came into the possession of the Bank of Alexandria, which thereupon became creditor of the Bank of the United States in Philadelphia to the extent of $960. The multiplication of such transactions gradually knit the individual banks into the continental system they constitute to-day.*

But until inter-bank relationships arose, each bank was a virtually complete banking system. From 1781 to 1784, when it was sole, the Bank of North America was the equivalent statistically of the entire banking system of the United States. It was self-contained. So long as it had the community's confidence, its notes would not be presented for redemption but only, or almost only, for deposit credit or the payment of a debt due the bank. So in the 20th century, deposits of the American banking system are not usually reduced by withdrawals of currency but by repayment to the banks of what they have lent. Although aggregate deposits have, it is true, been reduced in the United States by currency withdrawals on several occasions—the last time in 1933—the thing is anomalous. For such demands spell, for the time being, a cessation of the banking function; that function subsists on public confidence, and with no confidence there can be no banking.

* ". . . by 1810 banks were already dependent on each other to such an extent that they had lost that freedom of action which, for instance, the Bank of North America, the Massachusetts Bank or the Bank of New York had had for about a decade, during which they possessed regional monopolies. This statement is but another way of saying that by 1810 American banks had become part and parcel of a banking system." Redlich, 23.

23 Washington (Fitzpatrick) xxxiv, 207-08.

CHAPTER 4

Money, Banking, and the Federal Constitution

1787-1791

I. Economic reasons for federal government — II. The monetary clauses of the Constitution — III. The contemporary demand for paper money — IV. The monetary clauses and acceptance of the Constitution — V. The Constitution and banks — VI. The monetary clauses in the courts

I

TILL 1789 the general government of the United States rested on the Articles of Confederation, adopted in 1781. It was the Congress of the Confederation that chartered the Bank of North America the last day of that year, and the dubiety that had clouded that act was characteristic of the Confederation's ineffectiveness in nearly everything it did and failed to do. It was weaker than its parts, which followed their thirteen, sovereign, jealous, and selfish courses to the rapid deterioration of common interests. Each prized its sovereignty before everything and sought to advance itself at the expense of its neighbors. Though united in name, the states were close to fulfilling a fear expressed by Alexander Hamilton during the war that the near future would bring his fellow Americans all the leisure and opportunity they wished to cut each other's throats.[1]

The persons most immediately injured in this situation were merchants and others concerned with inter-state business transactions. Besides imposts to be paid on the entry of goods into one state from another, there were more direct discriminations. States having no convenient ports for foreign commerce were in effect taxed by those through whose ports their commerce passed. James Madison said that "New Jersey, placed between Philadelphia and New York, was likened to a cask tapped at both ends; and North Carolina, between Virginia and South Carolina, to a patient bleeding at both arms." It is illustrative of the feelings engendered in this situation that New Jersey interfered with maintenance of the Sandy Hook lighthouse

---

[1] Hamilton (Lodge) I, 217.

marking the entrance to New York harbor. Moreover the monetary payments essential to commerce were subject to a variety of kinds of money of uncertain value and to laws which protected local debtors and disturbed contractual relationships. A merchant in Massachusetts or Connecticut, for example, was helpless in collecting amounts due him from Rhode Island, because Rhode Island money though depreciated was legal tender, and Rhode Island in her courts and laws sought to protect her citizens from oppression by "foreigners." The situation was as bad as before the Revolution, or rather it was worse. For then, though each colony had had its own monetary system, Parliament had sought to keep down the confusion; whereas now there was no central authority in Great Britain's place, and the states were even more intransigent and inconsiderate of one another, each being sovereign, than the colonies had been.[2]

But this state of affairs, though bad for merchants, was not disagreeable to most people. The rugged agrarian, who stayed decently by his own hearth, was not discontented by it. He lived his self-sufficient, homespun life with little dependence upon distant markets and suppliers and felt small dissatisfaction with the existing governmental organization. The ineffectiveness of the Confederation and the frowardness of the states toward each other was more apt to please than displease him. He had no sympathy with the commercial classes, and the governmental jealousies that for them meant interference with trade, for him meant freedom in his woods and fields.

The first step toward a new federation was taken in 1786, when Virginia, then the largest and wealthiest state, authorized commissioners to confer with like commissioners from other states on "the trade of the United States; to examine the relative situations and trade of the said states; to consider how far a uniform system in their commercial relations may be necessary to their common interest and their permanent harmony," and to report on means of attaining "this great object." Commissioners from only five states foregathered, but these, sitting in Annapolis, agreed unanimously upon a report, prepared by Alexander Hamilton, in which they quoted their instructions, observed that the object of their meeting was "the trade and commerce of the United States," and recommended that a meeting of representatives of all states and with larger powers be arranged; because "in the course of their reflections on the subject they have been induced to think that the power of regulating trade

2 Madison, *Writings* (Hunt) ii, 395, 405.

is of such comprehensive extent . . . that to give it efficacy . . . may require a correspondent adjustment of other parts of the federal system." This proposal led directly to the constitutional convention itself, which sat in Philadelphia during the summer of 1787 and composed the federal Constitution ordaining the present form of government of the United States. Both the document and the federation ordained by it owed little at the start to the agrarian majority of the population but much to merchants and men of property. It was the plight of commerce that thrust the reluctant states into a more perfect union.[3]

The commercial interest reflected in these prolegomena to the Constitution coincided with the convictions of Franklin, Washington, Hamilton, Madison, and others whose concerns were far more than commercial. These men believed that America had impending over it two possibilities, of which one was fission and chaos, the other ascendency into national power, welfare, and dignity. The end of their effort, naturally enough, turned out to be a political document, not merely a commercial one. Yet the commercial considerations were no less fundamental than the political; they became quite as explicit later in the *Federalist* essays which followed the Constitution and even more explicit in the administrative and legislative measures by which the Constitution, under the leadership of Hamilton and Washington, was bodied forth in the new federal government.

II

The monetary clauses of the Constitution are three; they deal respectively with coin, bills of credit, and the impairment of contracts. They are in the form of one authorization and four prohibitions: the authorization being for the federal government to coin money and regulate its value; the prohibitions being against the states' coining it, emitting bills of credit, making anything but gold and silver legal tender, and impairing contracts.

The authorization is in Article I, section 8, which says the Congress shall have power "To regulate Commerce with foreign Nations, and among the several States, and with the Indian Tribes; To establish an uniform Rule of Naturalization, and uniform Laws on the subject of Bankruptcies throughout the United States; To coin Money, regulate the Value thereof, and of foreign Coin, and fix the Standard of Weights and Measures. . . ." The prohibitions are in

[3] *Formation of the Union,* 38-42.

section 10 of the same Article, which says, "No State shall enter into any Treaty, Alliance, or Confederation; grant Letters of Marque and Reprisal; coin Money; emit Bills of Credit; make any Thing but gold and silver Coin a Tender in Payment of Debts; pass any Bill of Attainder, *ex post facto* Law, or Law impairing the Obligation of Contracts, or grant any Title of Nobility." The prohibition of laws impairing the obligation of contracts belongs amongst the monetary provisions, because, as James Madison put it later, "the violation of contracts had become familiar in the form of depreciated paper money made legal tender"; and this he mentioned as one of the important reasons for seeking to form a union in which such impediments to business might be prevented.

In simple terms the provisions may be put as follows: With respect to coin the Constitution authorized the federal government to issue it and forbade the states to do so. With respect to paper money it forbade the states to issue it but omitted to say what the federal government might do. Also with respect to legal tender and contractual obligations it forbade the states to interfere with either but omitted to say what the federal government might do.

Offhand this seems an asymmetrical and ambiguous treatment of the three topics. Why, it may be asked, was the power to coin money specifically granted the federal government and denied the states, whilst the power to issue paper, to make anything but gold and silver legal tender, and to impair contracts was merely denied the states? Was it intended that though the states might not issue paper money, establish other legal tender, and impair contracts, the federal government might do so? The question is not to be answered by the Supreme Court's subsequent decision that the federal government does have the power nor by the fact that the federal government has exercised the power. The question is historical and is not answered by jurisprudence or by subsequent practice. Was the power *intended*? The answer, according to the records of the convention, seems clear enough: it is no.

Under the Articles of Confederation the general government had the power to issue bills of credit, and a continuation of that power was in the draft of the Constitution submitted by the committee of detail, 6 August 1787; whence however the convention struck it out by a vote of nine to two. The discussion plainly showed that by striking it out the convention purposed prohibiting it. The aim was, in the words of various delegates, "to shut and bar the door against paper money"; it would have "a most salutary influence on the credit of the United States to remove the possibility of paper money"; the authorization for the federal government to emit it, "if not struck out, would be as alarming as the mark of the Beast in Revelations"; it would be better to "reject the whole plan than retain the three words 'and emit bills' "; "the monied interest will oppose the plan of government if paper emissions be not prohibited"; "if the United States had credit such bills would be unnecessary; if they had not, unjust and useless." Congress would be authorized to borrow but not in that way. James Madison asked if it might be enough to prohibit "the making of them a *tender*," but the others thought not.[4]

The only delegate who avowed himself "a friend to paper money" was John Mercer, a Maryland lawyer of considerable property, "though in the present state and temper of America, he should neither propose nor approve" its issue; he was merely "opposed to a prohibition of it altogether." His associate from Maryland, Luther Martin, later said they both had argued against the deletion, taking the ground that it would be "a novelty unprecedented" to establish a government without a power that well might be "absolutely necessary" in case of war. At most, these two friends of paper money made no case for it at all on monetary grounds and took no more loyal stand than its enemies, Mason and Randolph of Virginia, who also thought it inexpedient to tie the proposed government's hands, though Mason confessed his "mortal hatred to paper money," and Randolph his "antipathy" to it.[5]

It was generally understood at the time that the new federal government, being an artificial creation, was to have only those powers specifically granted it, whilst the states, being sovereign, retained all powers not specifically relinquished. Consequently, the federal government not being given the power did not possess it. This was the prevailing and orthodox view of the Constitution, which, as Madison said, "is not only a general grant out of which particular powers were excepted; it is a grant of particular powers, leaving the general mass in other hands"; and so it had been understood by its friends and by its foes. The most prominent of the latter, Luther Martin, just mentioned, bitterly assailed the Constitution for the tyranny it was setting up; but nevertheless he believed that this tyranny

[4] *Formation of the Union*, 475, 556-57; Farrand II, 308-10.
[5] *Formation of the Union*, 556-57; Farrand II, 309; III, 172ff, 205-06, 214-15.

would not have the power to issue bills of credit, though he thought its not having that power was anomalous. The principle involved was that subsequently expressed in the tenth amendment: "The powers not delegated to the United States by the Constitution nor prohibited by it to the states are reserved to the states respectively or the people." Hence the Constitution, in the general intent of its authors, forbade the issue of paper money by the federal government as well as by the individual states, though without saying so. "The provisions of the Constitution," Albert Gallatin said in 1831, "were universally considered as affording a complete security against the danger of paper money."[6]

Yet this understanding of the matter was not quite universal. David Ramsay, a member of South Carolina's ratifying convention, understood that though the states were forbidden to issue paper money, the federal government might do so. And Alexander Hamilton, for whom the Constitution was the point to start, not stop, implied to Congress in 1790, before the Constitution was two years old, that the federal government had the power to issue bills of credit, though of course he thought it should not do so. The emitting of paper money by the individual states was wisely prohibited, he said, and the spirit of that prohibition ought not to be disregarded by the federal government. There is no record that the convention discussed the provisions respecting coinage, or the ban on state laws authorizing bills of credit, making anything but gold and silver legal tender, or impairing the obligation of contracts. A clause forbidding Congress to pass laws impairing contractual obligations was moved but not seconded or discussed.[7]

Since bills of credit, though used as money, were primarily evidence of debt on the part of the government, the power to issue them was closely related to the power to borrow; in the Articles of Confederation the Congress had been authorized, in one breath, "to borrow money or emit bills on the credit of the United States." The Confederation, that is, might borrow either by open negotiation, as when it sold certificates (i.e., bonds) to willing buyers, or by giving its debtors payment in obligations which they accepted willy-nilly. It was the latter method of borrowing that the Constitution intended to stop. Borrowing by negotiation was unobjectionable. The states retained their power to do so, and the new federal government was

6 Clarke and Hall, 40; Gallatin III, 236, 330-31.
7 Ford, *Pamphlets*, 374; ASP, Finance I, 71; *Formation of the Union*, 728.

explicitly given it: "The Congress," says section 8, "shall have power . . . to borrow money on the credit of the United States. . . ." But not, as the authors of the Constitution conceived, by the issue of paper money that should be legal tender for the payment of debts and irredeemable in specie; though that is something the government has since done, nevertheless, with the sanction of the Supreme Court.

III

The recent memory of continental and other revolutionary bills certainly disposed the convention to want no more paper money, but what impelled its members was the still more recent issue of paper money in various of the states. These issues had been authorized under the pressure of two groups, viz., tax delinquents and speculators indebted to the states for the confiscated property of loyalists and British subjects. It was occasioned by the economic depression that followed the war. Payments to the state, for taxes and for purchases, had to be made in specie, but specie was painfully scarce. Alexander Hamilton had remarked in 1781 that the people in some of the states were "distressed to pay their taxes for want of money, with ample means otherwise"; in western Massachusetts the situation was especially bad. Albert Gallatin wrote that at that period the farmers in western Pennsylvania, where he had then lived, were dependent on barter in their exchange of goods and services and that failure to perform contracts in barter meant ruinous obligations to pay money, because money was not procurable. It was in this same period that Robert Morris, one of the wealthiest merchants in the principal city of the country, said currency was so scarce there that trading in the produce market stopped and farmers went home at the end of the day with their wagons full of unsold stuff. James Madison, 4 June 1786, commented to James Monroe on "the scarcity of money, which is really great," he said. "Our situation is truly embarrassing. It can not perhaps be affirmed that there is gold and silver enough in the country to pay the next tax. What then is to be done? Is there any other alternative but to emit paper or to postpone the collection?" In 1798, more than a decade later, Alexander Hamilton remarked "how difficult and oppressive is the collection even of taxes very moderate in their amount, if there be a defective circulation. According to all the phenomena which fall under my notice, this is our case in the interior parts of the country."[8]

[8] Hamilton (Lodge) III, 351-52; x, 316-17; Gallatin III, 315-16; Madison, *Writings* (Hunt) II, 245.

It was in 1786, when Madison mentioned the intense shortage of specie, and in Massachusetts, where Hamilton had mentioned its seriousness, that the Shays rebellion of tax delinquents, debtors, and miscellaneous malcontents broke out. Daniel Shays had been a captain in the revolutionary army, and he now found himself directing armed men whose first object was the avoidance of court judgments against them as tax delinquents and who bound themselves to prevent the sitting of any court that should attempt to take property by distress. But they had other objects too. They protested against extravagance, importations, wealth, and wasteful taxation. They wanted the legislature to meet elsewhere than in opulent Boston, and they wanted the state to issue paper money. There was plenty to reprobate in their behavior, which was less violently paralleled in Rhode Island and New Hampshire, but their protest against the loss of property in consequence of conditions they could not help was reasonable. No efforts of theirs could fetch in silver and gold with which to pay taxes and debts, and the dearth of legal tender was not a thing for which they should be punished. Their demand for it was excused by the consideration that if the state wanted taxes paid, it had some responsibility for providing a medium in which they could be paid. Moreover, since paper money was only one thing they wanted, it hardly does for this demand to be denigrated as a "craze for paper money" or an agitation to evade the payment of debts and taxes.[9]

For one thing, agrarians did not join generally in the demand, by any means. William Findley of Pennsylvania, who was one of the most prominent, had recognized the "amazing usefulness" of paper money in the colonial period and also that "congress money" had done essential service in the dark hours of the Revolution; but, he had asked, should it therefore be continued? His answer was no; it had become dangerous and its use should cease. It was like the army, which, when the war was over, should not be continued.[10]

For another thing, the notion that the demand arose from a low sense of honor is unjust and irrational—how much so is indicated by the roughly contemporary plea of one of the country's wealthiest business men for more of such money—the difference being that he wanted circulating notes issued by a public bank and not by government directly. This was William Bingham of Philadelphia, who wrote to Alexander Hamilton, newly appointed Secretary of the

[9] Minot, 34-35, 54-55.   [10] Carey, 70, 75.

Treasury, 25 November 1789, urging upon the Secretary the importance to the country of endeavoring "by all possible means to increase the quantity of circulating medium"; this he said, "may be effected by turning a great portion of the gold and silver of the country into an active and productive stock . . . by substituting paper. . . ." At present the only money was gold and silver "—and it costs the country a vast sum of productive labor to purchase the necessary quantity of this expensive medium to discharge the duties of circulation." The Shays rebels did not explain the problem so perspicuously or so patiently as Mr Bingham did, but they had the same condition in mind. The difference is that he wanted a circulating medium in the form of bank notes and they wanted a legal tender in the form of state bills of credit.[11]

The interest of speculators seeking protection of their gains was something very different from that of farmers seeking to prevent the loss of their homes; yet both inspired much the same demand for relief. While the farmer advocates of paper money in New England were using force of arms, the speculator advocates of it in Maryland and Virginia were advertising in the press the predicament in which debtors to the state for confiscated lands found themselves, there being no obtainable cash with which they might make the payments due. They would like to have the state authorize some paper money which they could borrow in order to pay their existing indebtedness to it. They would still be in debt but on more comfortable terms. According to a Baltimore newspaper of 1784, a number of gentlemen who were in debt to the state for confiscated property and who had also purchased certificates of the state had proposed that the state "emit as much paper currency . . . as would amount to the principal and interest of all her liquidated certificates; and that the holders of such certificates should be permitted to exchange them for the said paper currency." They could then use the currency to pay their debts to the state. In all likelihood they would also realize a profit on their certificates, having usually purchased them at a heavy discount.* The best known of the Maryland speculators was Samuel

---

* Of this propaganda, in which plans for a bank in Baltimore were involved, Alfred C. Bryan wrote: "The merchants of Baltimore favored it (i.e., the bank). The agricultural and speculative elements opposed it; the former . . . argued that it would draw capital from the country to the city

11 Wettereau, *JEBH*, III (1930-31), 681.

Chase, whose purchases of confiscated British property kept him in straits for several years and from 1785 to 1788 in particular, at which time he was a loud proponent of paper money to be emitted by the state on loan. Charles Ridgely and William Paca, prominent land-buyers of more substantial fortune, also wanted it.[12]

There was the same interest in Pennsylvania, evidently. "There are a set of men," Thomas Paine wrote of that state, "who go about making purchases upon credit, and buying estates they have not wherewithal to pay for; and having done this, their next step is to fill the newspapers with paragraphs of the scarcity of money and the necessity of a paper emission, then to have a legal tender under the pretence of supporting its credit, and when out, to depreciate it as fast as they can, get a deal of it for a little price, and cheat their creditors; and this is the concise history of paper money schemes." Like Robert Morris, Thomas Paine also saw that the speculators and the agrarians had considerable in common, though antithetic in economic, social, and political outlook. Both groups were in debt to the states and saw with equal clearness that the likeliest way to relieve the pressure on them was through issues of paper money by the states. Neither wanted bank notes—the agrarians because they wanted nothing to do with banks on any grounds and the speculators because they could not meet the rigorous thirty-day conditions on which the banks lent.[13]

Under the incongruous but effective demands of these two groups, several state legislatures had done what was demanded: they had authorized fresh issues of bills of credit at the state loan offices.* These bills did not depreciate in value as sadly as continental bills had done, but they did depreciate and to that extent confirmed the aversion already roused by the continentals. But they also did more. They plagued the country with a heterogeny of currencies that varied in value from time to time and were legal tender for the payment of debts in some places but not in others. Hence they were both

---

and thus check improvement and agriculture. The latter . . . the speculative class . . . preferred state issues." Bryan, 18.

* Some "loan offices" lent the state's bills of credit, and some "loan offices" borrowed for the state by selling certificates. Whether the same loan offices did both I do not know. Loan office certificates, like modern bonds, were not intended for use as money, but they did sometimes circulate, like bills.

12 Crowl, chaps. IV and V; *Maryland Journal and Baltimore Advertiser*, 26 November, 7 and 17 December 1784; Behrens, chap. VIII.
13 Paine (Conway) II, 178.

an impediment to trade and a source of inequity in contracts. Business was burdened with litigation, and the legal significance of money eclipsed the economic.

The agitation for paper money had been most intense on the eve of the federal convention. The Shays rebellion was quelled in February 1787, only two months before the delegates convened who were to write the Constitution. James Madison, a man of law and not of the business world, whose predilections were agrarian, had been incensed by the "itch" and the "general rage" for paper money in preceding months, though he acknowledged, as I have said, that the scarcity of money was really great. "Pennsylvania and North Carolina took the lead in this folly," he wrote Thomas Jefferson in Paris, 12 August 1786. "In the former the sum emitted was not considerable, the funds for sinking it were good, and it was not made a legal tender." (Not being legal tender, it might be more acceptable than if it were.) Of Pennsylvania's paper money, he continued, "It issued into circulation partly by way of loan to individuals on landed security, partly by way of payment to the public creditors. Its present depreciation is about ten or twelve per cent." In North Carolina, he said, the issues were larger and all were legal tender. In South Carolina they were not legal tender. "But land is there made a tender in case of suits. . . ." New York, he said, "is striking £200,000 (dollar at 8s) on the plan of loans to her citizens. It is made legal tender in case of suits only." He also reported on measures in New Jersey, Rhode Island, Massachusetts, Connecticut, New Hampshire, and Maryland. He was gratified a few weeks later when paper money was "rejected in emphatic terms by a majority vote of 84 vs. 17" in the Virginia Assembly, which called it "unjust, impolitic, destructive of public and private confidence, and of that virtue which is the basis of Republican Government." Paper money, he said, "by fostering luxury extends instead of curing scarcity of specie. The produce of the country will bring in specie if not laid out in superfluities. . . ." These views of Mr Madison were also those of Mr Jefferson, who spoke for agrarians more typically than any advocate of paper money did.[14]

IV

It is commonly said and perhaps still more commonly supposed that the people who tried to keep the Constitution from being ratified were moved by the craze of "debtor classes" for paper money. Of the

---

[14] Madison, *Writings* (Hunt) II, 259-60, 277.

opponents of ratification, Professor Orin G. Libby said: "The state system under the Articles of Confederation served as a shield for the debtor classes. Many of the motives behind the arguments for state sovereignty were not of a character to be urged in the debates. . . ." The statement is evidently intended to explain why the Constitution was objected to so little for its interdict against paper money and the impairment of contracts, the explanation being that the "debtor classes" were reluctant, perhaps ashamed, to acknowledge the reasons that moved them.

This, it seems to me, is to assume a condition contrary to fact and then to assume an explanation of its supposed existence. That there was some dislike of the proposed ban on paper money is obvious, but the reasons for it and the nature of it are not. The record of paper money at the time the Constitution awaited ratification was ambivalent. The experience in the colonial period had been good, that during the Revolution had been bad. Different people construed the evidence differently, according to their own experience, their principles, and their interest. The same man might favor paper money when it lightened his obligations and refuse it when asked to take it in payments due him. For political reasons, opponents of the Constitution might find it expedient to denounce it not so much because they wanted paper money as because the ban on it was a radical cut in state sovereignty. This alone might explain James Madison's statement to Thomas Jefferson, 17 October 1788, that "The articles relating to treaties, to paper money, and to contracts, created more enemies than all the errors in the system, positive and negative, put together." Madison's dislike of paper money is expressed with more than common frequency and feeling. It bothered him far more than it did Hamilton, I should say; and as one might expect, the defense of the Constitution's ban on it in the *Federalist* (XLIV) was written by Madison, not Hamilton.[15]

Luther Martin of Maryland was the only man of prominence whose disapproval of the Constitution's ban on paper money was outspoken and to the point. Yet he did no more than urge that it was a mistake for the states to abnegate the power to emit bills of credit; for Maryland and some others had "formerly received great benefit from paper emissions," and might in the future find it advantageous again, "if public and private credit should once more be restored." He also disapproved, for similar reasons, the ban

---

15 Libby, 2; Madison, *Writings* (Hunt) v, 271.

against legislation by the states impairing contracts, for it might on occasion be necessary "to prevent the wealthy creditor and monied man from totally destroying the poor though even industrious debtor." But his disapproval was tactical and minor. What he really opposed was the subjection of Maryland to a new and over-riding sovereignty—a subjection to which loss of the power to issue bills of credit and impair contracts was but incidental. It was the chains which had been forged for "his country," Maryland, that he adjured her to reject, and he neglected no consideration in support of his plea. His arguments *may* arise from some attachment to easy money for its own sake, but not necessarily, or for any evident reason. Patrick Henry of Virginia also opposed the Constitution, being sure the states would "sip sorrow" if it were ratified. But, though his attitude toward paper money varied from time to time, he now declared it would be the bane of the country; "I detest it," he said. He opposed the Constitution on other grounds. So did William Grayson, a colleague in the Virginia convention. Paper money, Grayson said, was an "engine of iniquity" so "universally reprobated" that no Constitution was needed to protect the people from it.[16]

This hostility to paper money seems to have prevailed in the Shenandoah valley. In 1786, the year before the Constitution was composed, a petition was got up in Botetourt county—"the most definitely frontier of the Valley counties"—in which paper money was denounced as "dishonest in principle and a menace to the morals of the people, because it robbed the industrious of the fruits of their labors." In 1787 and 1788 when ratification of the Constitution was pending, the newspapers of Winchester promised that "the new federal Constitution would be a death blow to the long-feared evil of paper money." Professor Freeman H. Hart, who reports the foregoing, was evidently impressed by the failure of the facts he encountered to support the generally repeated statement that agrarians wanted paper money, for he observes: "Thus the people of the Valley not only refused to join in the paper-money movement but vigorously opposed it, in spite of the fact that their debt problem was a serious one, in many cases more serious than in those areas that were demanding such currency. It is noteworthy that not a word approving a paper emission can be found in any Valley newspaper, in any collection of private papers, in any petition to the Assembly,

---

[16] Farrand III, 206, 214-15, 232; Elliott III, 156, 290-91.

or in any vote of a Valley member of the Assembly. On the contrary if such a remedy was mentioned, it was only in terms of spirited disapproval." This is far from the paper money agitations which Frederick Turner would lead one to look for in a frontier community.[17]

At the same time, a correspondent wrote to Thomas Jefferson in Paris that the opponents of the Constitution in Maryland and Virginia were persons who had debts to pay or fortunes to make and wished for "scrambling times" and "paper money speculations." It is far more likely that such dislike of the ban on paper money as arose was of this sort rather than agrarian. But opposition to the ban, whatever its source, was unimpressive. Instead, hostility to the Constitution rested on its erection of a super-government to which the sovereignty of the individual states was to be sacrificed. Not one amendment was aimed at the prohibition of paper money or at the prohibition of laws impairing the obligation of contracts. This is the observation of Professor A. C. McLaughlin, who says in his *Constitutional History of the United States*: "There must have been a good deal of opposition on this ground, though it did not come prominently to the fore."[18] One supposes that Professor McLaughlin also, though he continued to think the opposition "must have" existed, was impressed by the absence of evidence that it had.*

In Rhode Island, the last state to ratify, distrust of the Constitution was very strong and so was the demand for paper money. But it does not follow that the Constitution was objectionable mainly because of its paper-money clauses. Rhode Island had borne more

---

* Since this discussion of agrarian "crazes for paper money" was written, Professor Robert J. Taylor's *Western Massachusetts in the Revolution*, with its chapters on the Shays rebellion, has been published. Professor Taylor's account is unfortunately like others in making no analysis of "the debtors" to show who they were, what was the nature of their indebtedness, and how it was related to their advocacy of paper money. But he does show that the shortage of specie was acute, that the tax burden payable in specie was heavy, that the need of legal tender was realized, and that the rebels had important grievances other than monetary. He gives no support to the notion of a lax financial integrity and craze for paper money. And he notes (p. 172) that though opponents of the Constitution were strong in the Massachusetts ratifying convention, the record "contains no mention . . . of that part of the Constitution which forbids the states to issue paper money or make anything but gold and silver a tender for debts."

---

17 Hart, 127-30; Turner, *Frontier in American History*, 32.
18 Crowl, 133-35; McLaughlin, 222n.

than her share of the cost of war and had suffered relatively greater loss to her shipping. She had also been accustomed for a century and a half to greater liberties under her charter than other colonies possessed. Among such factors in her feelings about federal union, paper money was one but not dominant. Nor was she a frontier community, such as Frederick Turner found to be the typical home of paper-money advocacy, but an old, commercial one.[19]

The ban on bills, though relatively little was made of it by the enemies of the Constitution, had the utmost importance for its authors and supporters. James Wilson of Pennsylvania said that one need not look beyond the provisions regarding bills of credit and the impairment of contracts to find the whole Constitution justified. James Madison, in Number XLIV of the *Federalist*, confidently urged the desirability of those provisions: "The extension of the prohibition to bills of credit, must give pleasure to every citizen, in proportion to his love of justice, and his knowledge of the true springs of public prosperity. The loss which America has sustained since the peace from the pestilent effects of paper money on the necessary confidence between man and man, on the necessary confidence in the public councils, on the industry and morals of the people, and on the character of republican government, constitutes an enormous debt against the states chargeable with this unadvised measure, which must long remain unsatisfied; or rather an accumulation of guilt, which can be expiated no otherwise than by a voluntary sacrifice on the altar of justice, of the power which has been the instrument of it."

On the whole, the monetary clauses of the Constitution seem to have won exceptional favor, offering what was objectionable to the fewest people and what was commendable to the most.

V

There is nothing in the Constitution about banks and banking, though there might well have been, for the subject was already of both economic and political importance when the Constitution was being written. There were then three banks in the United States, and everybody knew about them. The Bank of North America was situated in the second block to the east on the opposite side of Chestnut Street from the State House, where the federal convention

---

[19] Bishop, *Rhode Island History* VIII (1949), 1-10.

was sitting.* The charter controversy, which had occupied the Assembly in the very hall where the convention met, had ended only two months before. The bank was around the corner from the Indian Queen Tavern, where the members of the convention met informally. Some of the delegates had attended the Congress that chartered the bank six years before; one, Robert Morris, had proposed it; another, James Madison, had declared it unconstitutional. There had been a bank in New York and a bank in Boston for three years and projects for banks had been considered in most other American cities. Banks had long been the subject of pamphleteering and of newspaper and legislative controversy. Among the delegates, George Washington, Benjamin Franklin, Robert Morris, Alexander Hamilton, Elbridge Gerry, and John Langdon were at the time or had been owners of bank stock. General Washington had owned stock in the Bank of England, acquired by marriage, for nearly twenty-six years, including the period of the Revolution; he had sold it in 1786, the year before the convention. Seven delegates at least were stockholders in the Bank of North America, and three of these, Robert Morris, Thomas Fitzsimons, and George Clymer, who were members of the Pennsylvania Assembly, had been champions of the bank in the charter controversy.[20] Many if not most members of the convention must have had bank notes in their pockets in the course of the meetings.**

Banks were mentioned in the convention incidentally to the question whether the federal government should be empowered to grant charters of incorporation, which was left open. Madison proposed that Congress be given specific but limited powers to grant charters of incorporation, and later held, since the powers were not given, that Congress did not possess them. Other advocates of the power held back from putting the question to a vote lest it be lost and the

* The Bank of North America was on the north side of Chestnut Street, between Third and Fourth. Independence Hall (the State House) is on the south side of Chestnut, between Fifth and Sixth.

** The seven members who were Bank of North America stockholders were Benjamin Franklin, Robert Morris, Gouverneur Morris, Thomas Fitzsimons, James Wilson, and George Clymer, all of Pennsylvania; and John Langdon of New Hampshire. Others, especially Gunning Bedford of Delaware, may have been stockholders. Benjamin Franklin's home in Franklin Court was in the center of the block almost directly behind the bank.

20 Beard, *Economic Origins*, 166-67; Washington (Fitzpatrick) II, 337; III, 221n; xxviii, 496-97; Washington (Ford) IV, 72; Lewis, 133-47; Domett, 132; Gras, 539.

record be definitely against it, whereas if not acted on it could be held, as in fact it was eventually, that the power existed. In the *Anas*, Jefferson says he was told in 1798 that Robert Morris had wished to propose that the Constitution authorize the chartering of a bank and that Gouverneur Morris had urged him not to do so, because the idea was so controversial that its mention would kill the chances of getting the Constitution ratified. This was understood to have been said in personal colloquy between a few delegates and not before the convention as a whole. William Findley, who like Jefferson had not been a member of the convention, said in 1794 that incorporated banks had been discussed in the convention frequently.[21]

But if the delegates were familiar with bank notes and the monetary use to which they were put, why did they not say something about them in the Constitution while occupied with its monetary clauses?

In all likelihood it was because the subject was too touchy. Within the convention, banks had more friends than enemies, but outside it was the other way round. Moreover, bank notes were not considered to be money but its surrogate. They owed their value to their convertibility into money. Bills of credit, on the contrary—at least those that had made most trouble—had been money itself, legally speaking, and not merely convertible into money. For at the time, and for a good many years later, bank notes had never failed to be converted, nor had they ever exceeded specie in volume.* It will be recalled that Thomas Paine, in whose opinion specie was the only real money, had emphasized the difference between Pennsylvania bills of credit and notes of the Bank of North America. "The Assembly's paper money," he had said, "serves directly to banish or crowd out the hard, because it is issued *as* money and put in the place of hard money. But bank notes are of a very different kind and produce a contrary effect. They are promissory notes payable on

---

* The amount of specie in the colonies before the Revolution was conjectured by Pelatiah Webster to be less than 12 million dollars, by Alexander Hamilton 8 million, by Noah Webster 10 million. It was undoubtedly more than 8 million in 1787, at which time the note issues of the three banks were probably less than 1 million. Though less concentrated in Philadelphia, New York, and Boston than the notes, specie probably exceeded the notes even there.

[21] *Formation of the Union*, 563-64, 724-25; Jefferson (Ford) I, 278; J. S. Davis, *Earlier American Corporations* II, 12-14.

demand and may be taken to the bank and exchanged for gold and silver without the least ceremony or difficulty." Years later, when their volume had grown excessive and their convertibility into specie had broken down, James Madison, the aged "father of the Constitution," was asked what he recalled the thought of the convention to have been with respect to the monetary function of banks; and he answered that the interference of bank notes with a sound medium (meaning coin), though since become a great evil, had not been foreseen by the convention. And even had it been foreseen, he added, it was questionable whether the convention, with so many obstacles to overcome, would have ventured to guard against it by an additional provision. Yet by 1811 the monetary function of banks had become so apparent to Senator William H. Crawford of Georgia that he held the power to incorporate them was embraced in the powers to coin money.[22]

VI

The imprecision of the monetary clauses of the federal Constitution has enabled succeeding generations to impute various meanings to them. When the Constitution was about fifty years old, the agrarian followers of Andrew Jackson, who construed it strictly and made up the only simon-pure hard-money party the United States has ever had, contended passionately that it meant there should be no money but silver and gold. When the Constitution was about a hundred years old, the agrarians then called Populists held as passionately to the opposite dogma that it authorized the issue of irredeemable paper and denounced the gold of the Jacksonians as the stuff the farmer and laborer were crucified on. From time to time a considerable number of persons have contended that the Constitution requires the federal government to vary the quantity and value of money so as to fix the price level. The future may be trusted to produce still other things it will be held to require.

In examining the monetary clauses of the Constitution earlier in this chapter, I considered them in the light of conditions and purposes coeval with their composition. But since the Constitution is the continuing basic law of the land, its meaning is a matter of jurisprudence; it means what the courts say it does, and the courts can not be merely historical when they pass judgment. I shall run forward summarily into later history in the following paragraphs in

22 Paine (Conway) II, 184; Clarke and Hall, 310, 441-43, 778.

order to indicate the later significance of the constitutional provisions I have been discussing.

The meaning of the term "bills of credit" came before the Supreme Court for the first time in *Craig* v. *Missouri*, 1830, when it had to be decided whether the Constitution permitted the issue of ·certificates" which the state of Missouri had been lending at loan offices similar to those of colonial days and which circulated as money; and the Court in an opinion written by Chief Justice John Marshall concluded that the certificates were bills of credit and therefore forbidden. Can it be maintained, asked Marshall, that "the Constitution, in one of its most important provisions, may be openly evaded by giving a new name to an old thing?" He thought not and was very positive about it. The opinion in this case, which exhibited less concern about the evil of paper money than about the evil of a state's interference in federal prerogative, was one of Marshall's strongest. It was generally understood to foreshadow a conclusion that the notes of banks chartered by the states must also be unconstitutional, because it seemed reasonable to suppose that the states could not legally do through their creatures what they could not do themselves. Yet when the question of bank notes came to be decided, after Chief Justice Marshall's death, the Supreme Court in *Briscoe* v. *Bank of Kentucky*, 1837, held that such notes were not bills of credit and therefore not forbidden. The decision, about as weak and timid as any the Court ever pronounced, was in effect nullified by Congress in 1865, when through the medium of a revenue law it imposed a prohibitive tax on the notes of state banks. Thus the issue of notes by state banks is in effect prohibited, whether contrary to the Constitution or not. Moreover, the prohibitive tax was found by the Supreme Court to be constitutional, the decision being given in 1869 in *Veazie Bank* v. *Fenno*. So the status of state bank notes is actually the same as if they had been declared bills of credit and therefore unconstitutional, save for the difference that the statutory ban may be changed more easily than one in the Constitution.[23]

The interdict against the states' emitting bills of credit has presented no problem beyond that of defining what bills are, nor has the interdict against laws impairing contracts, except outside the field of legal tender. But the silence with respect to corresponding

[23] *Craig* v. *Missouri*, 4 Peters 433 (US 1830); *Briscoe* v. *Bank of Kentucky*, 11 Peters 326 (US 1837); *Veazie Bank* v. *Fenno*, 8 Wallace 533 (US 1869).

action by the federal government, though intended to be preclusive, has become, with the Court's blessing, permissive. The federal government can and does issue bills of credit. Jurisprudential evolution has responded to economic and political change. Economic change in time made the use of paper money indispensable, and the Constitution had to be accommodated to that fact. Political change made the exercise of sovereign monetary powers by the federal government also indispensable, and the Constitution had to be accommodated to that fact too.

The few times before the Civil War that the Treasury issued notes which in fact circulated as money, it did so on the principle that it was engaged in borrowing, and the question of federal power to issue paper money as such did not then come before the Supreme Court. But in 1862, during the Civil War, the government resorted to the issue of notes for the same reasons that the Continental Congress had issued bills during the Revolution, and the question was raised whether the notes, which came to be called "greenbacks," were constitutional. For the law made them legal tender, which so far, under the federal Constitution, only silver and gold had been. This action ran counter to what had seemed impregnable tradition: Marshall's apodictic statement in *Sturges* v. *Crowninshield* that nothing but gold and silver could be legal tender had expressed the general conviction; as did Justice Field's later in *Juilliard* v. *Greenman*, when he said in his dissent: "If there be anything in the history of the Constitution which can be established with moral certainty, it is that the framers of that instrument intended to prohibit the issue of legal tender notes both by the general government and by the states; and thus prevent interference with the contracts of private parties." This interference was, of course, the immediate consequence of making the greenbacks legal tender. In the first suit resulting that came to the Supreme Court, the problem was that a certain Mrs Hepburn had contracted in 1862 to pay one Henry Griswold $11,500—meaning specie, of course—but offered in 1864 to pay him the amount in greenbacks, which meanwhile had also been made legal tender. Her offer was refused because the amount in greenbacks was worth only $4,500 or so in specie. The Supreme Court, in this first case, held with the traditional view that the Constitution was a hard-money document, and though the Court condoned the issue of the notes as a means of obtaining funds to wage war, it found their legal tender quality unnecessary, and unconstitutional as to debts previously contracted. The creditor did not have to accept the debtor's greenbacks. This was in 1869.[24]

Whether or not this decision reflected on the honor of one who sought to discharge her debt by repaying less than half what she had borrowed, it was certainly felt to reflect on the ability of the government to make its money worth what it said. And though the debtor had to be satisfied with the decision, the government itself did not. For meantime a newer and more puissant tradition had grown up— a tradition of nationalism fostered over a long period and now sanctified by the Civil War. The federal union of individual states was no longer the cabined product of a compact between sovereignties but sovereign itself. And being that, it could not be without the power to say what its money should be.

In compliance with this new extension of Hamiltonian principle, the Supreme Court reversed itself and in the *Legal Tender Cases*, 1870, found the greenbacks constitutional. Their issue was held to be an act of sovereignty. This might have surprised Alexander Hamilton, but I think it would not have shocked him. As for the impairment of contracts, the Court made assurance doubly sure by concluding both that payment in depreciated greenbacks of a debt contracted in specie values did not impair the contract and that it could be authorized by the federal government even if it did. It happened, however, that the decision in the 1870 cases turned on the issue of notes as a wartime measure and still implied, therefore, a substantial abatement of sovereign powers. In 1884 the Supreme Court decided in *Juilliard* v. *Greenman* that greenbacks could constitutionally be made legal tender even in time of peace. This victory for nationalism and easy money prepared the way in turn for the Gold Exchange Act of 1934, which forbade the domestic monetary use of gold and limited the circulation to paper, to silver dollars, and to minor coin. In 1935 the Supreme Court upheld that act in *Norman* v. *Baltimore and Ohio* and other gold clause cases. These decisions removed whatever constitutional inhibition ever existed upon the power of Congress to authorize anything it wishes as money. Thus in the course of 150 years, changes in monetary and business habits, in governmental responsibility, in statutes, and in jurisprudence have strengthened the Constitution's ban on issues of money by individual states but have nullified completely the original

[24] *Sturges* v. *Crowninshield*, 4 Wheaton 204 (US 1829); *Juilliard* v. *Greenman*, 110 US 451; *Hepburn* v. *Griswold*, 8 Wallace 625-26 (US 1869).

intent that the federal government should have no power to make anything but the precious metals legal tender.[25]

One can either consider the departure from the original intent a calamity or hold that the original intent, though wise at the time, could not possibly endure. Alexander Hamilton himself foreshadowed what would happen. In 1783 he said that authority to emit paper money was "a resource which though useful in the infancy of this country and indispensable in the commencement of the Revolution, ought not to continue a formal part of the Constitution, nor ever hereafter to be employed, being in its nature pregnant with abuses." Yet fifteen years later, 22 August 1798, in a letter to Oliver Wolcott, his successor as Secretary of the Treasury, he mentioned the difficulty and oppressiveness of collecting taxes, as I have already noted, "if there be a defective circulation"; and he continued: "For these and other reasons which I have thought well of, I have come to a conclusion that our Treasury ought to raise up a circulation of its own. I mean, by the issuing of Treasury-notes payable, some on demand, others at different periods from very short to pretty considerable—at first having but little time to run. This appears to me an expedient equally necessary to keep the circulation full and to facilitate the anticipations which government will certainly need. By beginning early, the public eye will be familiarized, and as emergencies press it will be easy to enlarge without hazard to credit. . . ."[26]

In substance, but not in the form he intended, Hamilton's words have been followed. The change from 1789, however, is more than a matter of putting paper alongside gold. In 1789, money was gold; in 1935, gold had become money. I mean that when it was sought in the 18th century to give substance and worth to the money to be issued by the new and untried government, it was stipulated that that money should comprise gold (and silver), so much were the precious metals esteemed above the word of political authority. But in the 20th century money is become a creature of government, political authority having supplanted, in the domestic sphere, the place the precious metals primitively held. In *Norman* v. *Baltimore and Ohio*, 1935, it was not even contended on behalf of gold that it was money—nay, the only money with which debtors discharged their obligations to creditors—but merely that it was a commodity transferred according to contract; and it was precisely because gold was held to be only one of various forms of money subject to selection or rejection by the state that the political authority could override contracts calling for payment in gold. Only as between economies, in the mid-20th century, does gold have anything like the importance it had within the economy in the 18th century. And even between economies its value has become relative, not absolute.

The radical change that has occurred in federal monetary powers since the Constitution was fresh has been determined in the first instance by the practical advantages of paper money over metallic and in the second by growing preponderance of federal authority—both of these, in turn, being products of fundamental economic change. Paper established its advantage by popular choice, without formality and against the might of law, which was biased in favor of the precious metals. Formally, however, the question to be decided by the courts has not been what kind of money the country should have but what the nature and scope of the issuing authority should be. And time after time the federal government has emerged from the question with amplified powers. In this development the monetary clauses of the Constitution have been invoked seldom and little. To be sure, it has been recognized long and repeatedly, both in court and outside, that since bank liabilities provide the bulk of the money supply, their control is relevant to the monetary powers of the federal government. John C. Calhoun, early in the 19th century, perspicuously related the federal government's authority over banking to its authority over the monetary system; his later contemporaries often did so; and the extinction of the Bank of the United States at the hands of Andrew Jackson was recognized at the time to be a repudiation by the federal government of responsibilities imposed upon it by the Constitution for the monetary system, since the Bank was regulator of the private bank issues that constituted the major part of the monetary supply.

But the point seems always to have been made almost fugitively. In 1824 Justice Johnson of the Supreme Court mentioned it in *Osborn* v. *Bank of the United States*; in 1837 Justice Story, dissenting in *Briscoe* v. *Bank of Kentucky*, said plainly that the issue of notes by banks under state charter was "subject always to the control of Congress, whose powers extend to the entire regulation of the currency of the country"; in *Veazie Bank* v. *Fenno*, 1869, the

Supreme Court affirmed that Congress, in execution of its monetary powers, could constitutionally authorize the circulation of certain banks' notes and forbid the circulation of others; and in the *Legal Tender Cases*, 1870, and in *Juilliard* v. *Greenman*, 1884, the incorporation of the Bank of the United States was recognized to have been an exercise of powers over the currency of the country.[27] Yet, these *obiter dicta* notwithstanding, the regulation of banking has not rested primarily on the federal government's monetary powers, though banking is primarily a monetary function. Even with respect to money *per se*, the courts have been indisposed to look for authority in the monetary clauses only. In *Norman* v. *Baltimore and Ohio*, the Supreme Court put it as follows: "The broad and comprehensive national authority over the subjects of revenue, finance, and currency is derived from the aggregate of the powers granted to the Congress, embracing the powers to lay and collect taxes, to borrow money, to regulate commerce with foreign nations and among the several States, to coin money, regulate the value thereof, and of foreign coin, and fix the standards of weights and measures, and the added express power 'to make all laws which shall be necessary and proper for carrying into execution' the other enumerated powers."[28]

More particularly, in dealing with questions of federal jurisdiction, the courts have relied more and more in recent years on the clause of the Constitution which allocates jurisdiction over interstate commerce. That clause amply covers the monetary function as well as the other functions of banks and offers therefore a single authority of adequate scope, which the monetary clause would not. Resort to the inter-state commerce clause avoids, for example, any awkward tendency to settle jurisdiction according to function, with banking proper falling under monetary powers and trusteeship falling under inter-state commerce powers. With these attendant activities of 20th century American banks—trusteeship, checking facilities apart from lending, safety box rental, etc.—this history is not concerned. These things are important to the proprietors and managers of banks because they are means of earning income and may be conveniently associated with the banking function proper. And they are not unlawful as, for example, the selling of merchandise

27 *Osborn* v. *Bank of the United States*, 9 Wheaton 871-73 (US 1824); *Briscoe* v. *Bank of Kentucky*, 11 Peters 349 (US 1837); *Veazie Bank* v. *Fenno*, 8 Wallace 533, 548-49 (US 1869); *Juilliard* v. *Greenman*, 110 US 445; *Legal Tender Cases*, 12 Wallace 537, 543-44 (US 1870).
28 *Norman* v. *Baltimore and Ohio*, 294 US 240-41.

or the provision of legal advice would be. But they have no more than a convenient connection—not an essential one—with the lending of credit for monetary purposes, which is the original and characteristic function of banks and was in the period of this history, with few exceptions, the only one. I observe a distinction, therefore, that the courts nowadays have little or no occasion to observe; though in respect to a constitutional problem of governmental organization affecting the monetary powers of the federal government it might be important. Yet as things are, one has the anomaly, in principle, of the monetary function being considered, for reasons of jurisprudence, with little attention to what the Constitution says about it but with attention chiefly to what the Constitution says about interstate commerce.[29]

[29] *Noble State Bank* v. *Haskell*, 219 US 104; *Doherty* v. *United States*, 94 Fed. (2nd) 495.

CHAPTER 5

The Bank of the United States

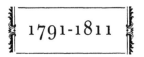

1791-1811

I. The Bank proposed — II. Hamilton versus Jefferson — III. Organization of the Bank — IV. A central bank — V. The Bank of England pattern — VI. The restriction on liabilities — VII. Capital and specie — VIII. The nature and status of "deposits" — IX. Hamilton's origination of fractional reserve requirements

I

ITS silence about banks notwithstanding, the Constitution became involved in the subject in its second year, when Alexander Hamilton in December 1790, during the third session of the first Congress, submitted his plan for a National Bank. The plan was embodied in the second of the several great reports prepared by him during the early years of his secretaryship of the Treasury, the others being on manufactures and on public credit. In these reports he outlined the major elements of a program for raising up a powerful and prosperous nation. The factors already given were immense material resources—utilized chiefly so far in agriculture and in maritime shipping—an energetic, multiplying population, and the private credit of individual men of wealth. The factors needed were manufactures and public credit. Hamilton's program combined magnitude and comprehensiveness, on the one hand, with, on the other, meticulousness in detail and a thorough understanding of all he was talking about. The reasonable convictions he had had in 1779 respecting the utility of a bank had been confirmed by the experience of the three banks that had been established since. He now wished to have one set up that should directly and adequately serve the needs of the federal government, which was to incorporate it and own a substantial share of its capital.

The proposed institution was not simply another commercial bank. Like the Bank of England, it would conduct commercial business but would also do far more. It would be an important aid to the new federal government in collecting taxes and in administering the public finances; it would be a source of loans to the Treasury. Subscriptions to its capital might be paid one-fourth in gold and silver coin and three-fourths in obligations of the federal government. This arrangement would provide sufficient capital to support an extensive circulation, but it would also enhance the current price of government obligations and thereby sustain the government's credit.

In the Senate, Hamilton's report was referred to a committee comprising Caleb Strong of Massachusetts, Robert Morris of Pennsylvania, Philip Schuyler of New York, Pierce Butler of South Carolina, and Oliver Ellsworth of Connecticut. All of these but General Schuyler had been members of the constitutional convention; all shared Hamilton's ideal of a strong federal government. At least three of them, Strong, Morris, and Ellsworth, were bank stockholders and interested in fiscal matters. Schuyler was Hamilton's father-in-law. The committee—presumably to no one's surprise—brought out a bill to incorporate a Bank of the United States in accordance with Hamilton's recommendation. The handling of the measure illustrates the important fact observed by Professor Beard that the first federal administration and Congress continued, developed, and applied, largely in the same hands, the principles established by the constitutional convention in order "to restore public credit, establish adequate revenues, create a nation-wide judicial system, pay the debt, strengthen the defences on land and sea, and afford adequate support to trade and commerce." Being for a "National Bank," Hamilton's proposal implied the purpose, familiar since the constitutional convention four years earlier, of subordinating the states to the new consolidated federal government. It roused vehement resistance.[1]

Opponents of the proposal objected that the Constitution conveyed no authority to form a bank or any other kind of corporation and that by chartering one the federal government would be disregarding the limitations of its powers and interfering with the rights of the states. James Madison, now a member of the House of Representatives, pointed out that the proposed institution "would interfere so as indirectly to defeat a state bank at the same place," and would "directly interfere with the rights of states to prohibit as well as to establish banks." The proposal for a national bank, he said, "was

[1] Beard, *Economic Origins*, 105-07.

condemned by the silence of the Constitution; was condemned by the rule of interpretation arising out of the Constitution; was condemned by its tendency to destroy the main characteristic of the Constitution; was condemned by the expositions of the friends of the Constitution whilst depending before the public; was condemned by the apparent intentions of the parties which ratified the Constitution; was condemned by the explanatory amendments proposed by Congress themselves to the Constitution; and he hoped it would receive its final condemnation by the vote of this House." For more than a bank was at stake; the constructions of the Constitution that had been maintained in the course of the arguments for it, Madison said, went "to the subversion of every power whatever in the several states."[2]

Secretary Hamilton's proposal was also subjected to an agrarian attack like that the Bank of North America had sustained in the Pennsylvania Assembly five years before. Banks, it was averred, were a corrupting influence and would destroy the free institutions of the New World. "What was it drove our forefathers to this country?" demanded an agrarian representative from Georgia, James Jackson. "Was it not the ecclesiastical corporations and perpetual monopolies of England and Scotland? Shall we suffer the same evils to exist in this country, instead of taking every possible method to encourage the increase of emigrants to settle among us? For, if we establish the precedent now before us, there is no saying where it shall stop." He said the bank was "calculated to benefit a small part of the United States—the mercantile interest only; the farmers, the yeomanry of the country, will derive no advantage from it." William B. Giles of Virginia presumed "that a law to punish with death those who counterfeit the paper emitted by the bank, will be consequent upon the existence of this act; hence a judicial decision will probably be had of the most serious and awful nature. The life of an individual at stake on one hand; an improvident act of the government on the other." Eventually at least one man was put to death for counterfeiting notes of the Bank; and this fact was urged twenty years later by another Virginian, Senator Brent, as one of the things that made the bank constitutional by practice and acquiescence.[3]

The Senate, whose discussions were not at that time recorded, passed the bill incorporating the Bank, 20 January 1791. The

---

[2] Clarke and Hall, 41, 44-45, 83.
[3] Clarke and Hall, 37, 55, 74, 402.

debates in the House ended 8 February 1791, after rousing more "warmth and passion" than James Madison liked; the votes for chartering the bank were 39 and those opposed 20. Most of the ayes—33 out of 39—were from New England, New York, New Jersey, and Pennsylvania; most of the nays—15 out of 20—were from Virginia, the Carolinas, and Georgia. One South Carolina vote was for the bill, one Massachusetts vote was against it. Eleven Republicans voted for the Bank, and six Federalists voted against it. The measure was sent for approval to President Washington, who took all the time permitted him by the Constitution, "in anxious and diligent inquiries into the constitutionality of the bill and in the consideration of his duty in relation to it." He referred it to the Secretary of State, Thomas Jefferson, and to the Attorney General, Edmund Randolph, for their opinion. Both agreed that the measure was contrary to the Constitution.[4]

Mr Jefferson, grudging even that the Bank might be a convenience, was positive that it was not a necessity. And, he asked, "Can it be thought that the Constitution intended that, for a shade or two of convenience, more or less, Congress should be authorized to break down the most ancient and fundamental laws of the several states, such as those against mortmain, the laws of alienage, the rules of descent, the acts of distribution, the laws of escheat and forfeiture, the laws of monopoly? Nothing but a necessity invincible by any other means can justify such a prostration of laws which constitute the pillars of our whole system of jurisprudence." Mr Jefferson could not abide considerations of administrative advantage which seemed to him to put an efficient working of the governmental machinery before the maintenance of a simple society composed as wholly as possible of individual human beings and as little as possible of institutions.[5]

Hamilton on his part could not abide what seemed to him Thomas Jefferson's visionary and anarchic metaphysics, which he believed "would be fatal to the just and indispensable authority of the United States." He declared that it was the purpose of the Constitution to set up a workable government and that to find it frustrating that purpose at the very outset was preposterous. He countered with a sweeping and audacious assertion of federal sovereignty: "Now, it appears to the Secretary of the Treasury

4 Clarke and Hall, 35-36, 82, 85-86, 298.
5 Clarke and Hall, 93-94.

that this general principle is inherent in the very definition of government and essential to every step of the progress to be made by that of the United States; namely, that every power vested in a government is in its nature *sovereign* and includes, by force of the term, a right to employ all the means requisite and fairly applicable to the attainment of the ends of such power and which are not precluded by restrictions and exceptions specified in the constitution, or not immoral, or not contrary to the essential ends of political society."[6] These words, which proved to have a potency for far more than establishment of the Bank, evidently satisfied the President; he did not use the veto he had asked Mr Madison to prepare but signed the act incorporating the Bank, 25 February 1791.[7]

II

It is obvious that in the beginning the political prominence of banking in the United States outstripped its economic importance. When there were still only three banks in the country, the subject engaged an inordinate amount of attention. The proposed National Bank became so much a political and constitutional issue that far more was said of it as such than is of record respecting its operations and economic significance.* It was its proposal, Professor Beard has said, "which first summoned to the political battle that high talent for analysis, deduction, reticulation, and speculative imagination which has characterized American constitutional conflicts from that day to this." John Marshall, whom Beard quotes, wrote in his *Life of Washington* that the systematic opposition of the Jeffersonians to the principles on which the Union was formed and administered had its origin in the issues raised by Hamilton's reports to the first Congress; and with respect to the bill to establish the Bank of the United States he said: "This measure made a deep impression on many members of the legislature; and contributed not inconsiderably to the complete organization of those distinct and visible parties, which in their long and dubious conflict for power have since shaken the United States to their centre."[8]

The people who were most eager for a strong central government

* The Bank's own records disappeared years later, probably as waste paper, after its liquidation was completed; those in the Treasury were probably destroyed by fire in 1833.

6 Clarke and Hall, 95.   7 McLaughlin, 245.
8 Beard, *Economic Origins*, 109, 157-58; Marshall II, 206-07.

and who wished to apply the Constitution constructively were the people who also wanted banks. They were the commercial and monied class. They were men of substance, they were creditors of the government, and they had a natural wish to recover what they had risked on American independence. This wish was identical with the wish that there be a strong and effective government to maintain that independence.

Their opponents were principally agrarians who had been mistrustful of the Constitution and were now mistrustful of the central government created by it. They were mistrustful of all business interests. Those in the Pennsylvania Assembly who in 1785 had almost annihilated the Bank of North America attempted two years later to keep Pennsylvania from ratifying the Constitution; and in Congress the same group maintained a consistent hostility not only to the Bank of the United States but to other Hamiltonian measures.* They, too, like the merchants had wanted political independence, but to them independence and a strong central government were incompatible. They saw in the latter the replacement of the British yoke with a Hamiltonian one.[9]

Hamilton's proposal of a federal Bank was a plain defiance of agrarian interests and of the view that the powers of the federal government were definitely limited. In their reception of it, Madison in Congress and Jefferson in his report to Washington both affirmed what shortly became embodied in the tenth amendment—that in effect the federal government possessed only the powers given it. Jefferson said that he considered "the foundation of the Constitution as laid on this ground." The ideas later developed and enunciated in the Kentucky and Virginia Resolutions of 1798, where the Constitution was asserted to be a compact between sovereign states and the general government to be one with special purpose and possessed of delegated, limited powers only, were already clearly present in Jefferson's and Madison's arguments against the Bank in 1791. On the other hand, it was in defense of his proposal for a federal Bank that Hamilton made to President Washington the statement of federal sovereignty I have quoted—a statement that has governed constitutional jurisprudence ever since.[10]

* William Findley, a conspicuous exception, had been prominent in the attack on the Bank of North America, but twenty-five years later, in Congress, he was equally prominent in defense of the Bank of the United States.

[9] Wilson, *PMHB*, LXVI (1942), 17.   [10] Clarke and Hall, 91.

Thus the principles appealed to in one constitutional issue after another and at last in the Civil War got their first and clearest statement in the dispute of 1791 over the Bank recommended by Alexander Hamilton. The controversy demonstrated at the very outset that the Constitution had not displaced rival principles or reconciled them but had become their dialectical arena. Although it was not a popular document, it became equally accepted by both sides as soon as it was ratified; and the original differences about its wisdom gave way to differences as to how it should be interpreted and applied. Alexander Hamilton had been disgusted because it did not abolish the individual states outright and consolidate them at once into a single new sovereignty; but he had furthered it with all his might, nevertheless, and purposed now to make it, deficient as it was, the start for the national government he thought necessary. Thomas Jefferson, on the other hand, purposed to make it a bulwark against encroachments by the central government upon the popular sovereignties of the states and the reserved liberties of the people. Mr Madison, its chief artificer, and the associate of Alexander Hamilton in the *Federalist* papers which had brilliantly advocated it, shrank from Hamilton's radical course and joined Jefferson in promoting the doctrine that the Constitution was a pact between sovereignties which had established a central government logically inferior to themselves and possessed of only those powers specifically delegated to it. Hamilton made the Constitution a plenary charter for a national government to which the states would be ineluctably subordinated. Jefferson and Madison made it a barrier against that development. To Hamilton, the Constitution was an open door; to Jefferson and Madison, it was one that had been shut.[11]

Among the framers of the Constitution, there were some, writes Dr Charles M. Wiltse, "who feared most the tendency of a weak government to degenerate into anarchy," and there were others who feared most "the tendency of a strong government to absorb all power to itself" and destroy freedom. The issue lay between those who trusted human nature in the mass more than government, which Jefferson did; and those who distrusted it more than government, which Hamilton did. Hamilton, a son of the 18th century, saw as had Jehovah before the flood that every imagination of the thoughts of men's hearts was only evil continually, and he shaped his ideas of government to accord with that observation. Jefferson, also a

11 McLaughlin, 234.

son of the 18th century, looked on man with more of Rousseau's indulgence and shaped his ideas of government on greater hopes for human nature. These contrasting attitudes became political traditions. But the distinction between them, an intellectual and moral one as conceived in the 18th century, became in the 19th century a crassly pragmatic one in which the comparative advantages of centralized powers and dispersed powers remained clear but the preference for one or the other changed with time and selfish interest. In recent years it has become the economic posterity of Alexander Hamilton that complains of centralized authority and, with an unacknowledged appeal to Jeffersonian principles of government, resists what it considers an unconstitutional interference with human rights—that is, property rights and business. And it is the professed posterity of Thomas Jefferson—now more industrial than agrarian —which fears the evil of a weak governmental authority and which, since 1913, when it set up a central bank system, has out-Hamiltoned Hamilton in elaborating the federal government's apparatus for the guidance of economic behavior.* There persist to-day, accordingly, two political groups with economic differences that are reminiscent of those that divided Americans in 1791, but the two, like Hamlet and Laertes, have switched weapons.[12]

Alexander Hamilton prepared America for an imperial future of wealth and power, mechanized beyond the handicraft stage of his day, and amply provided with credit to that end. Thomas Jefferson represented the yeomanry and designed for America a future of competence and simplicity, agrarian, and without the enticing subtleties of credit. Writing in Paris in 1785 to a correspondent in the Netherlands, he said that were he to indulge his own theory, he would wish the United States "to practice neither commerce nor navigation but to stand, with respect to Europe, precisely on the footing of China." All American citizens should be farmers, selling their sur-

---

* The change is reflected in decisions of the Supreme Court before and after 1936. In a series of cases in 1935, the Court, with strict, Jeffersonian interpretations, found unconstitutional the Railroad Retirement Act of 1934, the National Industrial Recovery Act of 1934, the Bituminous Coal Conservation Act of 1935, and other similar laws sponsored by the administration of Franklin D. Roosevelt. In 1937 a freshly constituted Court, with liberal Hamiltonian jurisprudence, found similar legislation constitutional, notably in the National Labor Relations cases of that year.

12 Wiltse, *From Compact to National State*, 155.

plus produce to those nations that should come to seek it. But this he acknowledged was theory only; Americans had a decided taste for navigation and commerce, which they took from their mother country, and their government was in duty bound to calculate all its measures accordingly. Yet in another letter, written at Monticello to John Adams in 1812, he said with satisfaction that in his part of the country every family was a manufactory within itself, producing with its own materials and labor all the stouter and middling stuffs for its own clothing and household use. "We consider a sheep for every person in the family as sufficient to clothe it, in addition to the cotton, hemp, and flax which we raise ourselves." And in a surge of the sanguine idealism he had professed to give up thirty years before, he went on: "The economy and thriftiness resulting from our household manufactures are such that they will never again be laid aside, and nothing more salutary for us has ever happened than the British obstructions to our demands for their manufactures." Now, it is clear that a man who at every opportunity turned passionately to the agrarian ideal, seeing in the agrarian way of life an advantageousness, a purity, and a humanity with which commerce and industrialization were incompatible, should hate banks. For banking presupposed a complex, specialized economy which found a flexible monetary supply indispensable and the notion of a sheep for every member of the family, to provide its stouter and middling stuffs, something to laugh at.* Americans still maintain a pharisaical reverence for Thomas Jefferson, but they have in reality little use for what he said and believed—save when, on occasion and out of context, it appears to be of political expediency. What they really admire is what Alexander Hamilton stood for, and his are the hopes they have fulfilled.[13]

III

A few days after the act incorporating the Bank of the United States was signed by President Washington, a supplementary measure was enacted directing that subscriptions not be opened earlier than 4 July so that prospective subscribers in remote parts

---

* The effect of "British obstructions" and the War of 1812 was the opposite of what Mr Jefferson expected. Instead of being revived, agrarian household manufacture was overwhelmed by the machine-driven industry that the war raised up.

13 Jefferson (Ford) IV, 105; IX, 333.

of the country would not be cramped for time. When the books were opened, the entire $8,000,000 available to the public was heavily oversubscribed within an hour. The subscribers, Professor Wettereau observed, besides merchants, professional men, and politicians, included "prominent speculators in public securities" who were active during the controversies over adoption of the Constitution and of Secretary Hamilton's funding system. Thirty members of Congress subscribed, this being more than a third of the whole membership and a half or more of the number that had voted for the Bank. Harvard College, the Massachusetts Bank, and the state of New York were subscribers. There was active speculation in the $25 subscription certificates almost at once, and in August they rose to a market price of $300 or more. This speculation, in the opinion of the Bank's friends, was merely incidental; in the opinion of its enemies, it was a main purpose and intent of the Bank's organizers.[14]

Though the authorized capital of the Bank was $10,000,000, of which $2,000,000 was to be paid in specie, the Bank was permitted to organize as soon as $400,000 had been received from the subscribers. Whether much more was ever got from them on successive installments is doubtful, though the Bank subsequently accumulated a treasure much in excess of what the stockholders were supposed to pay. Payment for the government's stock was accomplished under an authorization in the charter that was taken over almost intact from Hamilton's proposal and was presumably intended by him to give the appearance of a cash payment. In effect the Treasury drew for $2,000,000 on the United States commissioners engaged in selling government securities in Amsterdam, deposited the drafts with the Bank, and then drew against the deposit to pay for the stock. Technically this consummated the purchase of the stock with funds borrowed in Europe. But it was not desired to have the drafts go through and the specie shipped from Europe, because it would have had to be shipped back for other purposes. So the Treasury borrowed $2,000,000 from the Bank and used the amount to take up the drafts on the commissioners, with which the whole transaction had opened. The net effect was therefore to leave the government in possession of $2,000,000 of Bank stock and in debt to the Bank for $2,000,000, though technically the money owing to the Bank

14 Wettereau, *PMHB*, lxi (1937), 273-75; Clarke and Hall, 114.

had not been used to buy the stock but to "restore" the funds in Amsterdam which had been "used" for that purpose.*

This transaction and the failure to get the privately owned stock paid for with any less make-believe has fallen under the strictures of some historians, especially Professor W. G. Sumner, who strike me as unrealistic and inconsistent, unless they mean to deplore procedures generally followed in the growth of the American nation, both economic and political. The early Americans were short of capital, particularly capital in the form of gold and silver. If that dearth of gold and silver had been allowed to hold up their formation of banks, the circle would never have been broken; instead they resorted to arrangements which had the practical virtue of establishing the proper procedure in principle if not in fact. And in time, because the pretense worked, they accumulated the gold and silver and made the principle a reality. It is a case where a pious lifting of oneself by the bootstraps is preferable to cynical realism or conscientious passivity. And for the most part a saner and more honest practice in capitalization established itself as soon as a surplus of wealth made it possible. Without the initial act of faith, so to speak, the surplus would have been slower in coming. The Americans had declared their political independence before it was a reality, not after; and what they did in the matter of financial competence was much the same.[15]

But in many matters other than payment of early American bank capital, the question of what constitutes a specie or cash transaction is one of considerable subtlety. In a primitive sense there must be a handing over of actual cash, of course; but if A owes B $1,000 and B owes A $2,000, it is silly for them to hand $3,000 to and fro; instead B pays A the $1,000 difference, which settles the whole matter. Constructively such a transaction is a cash transaction. A large part of business payments in a modern economy is of this sort, being settled by offsets, and the residues or differences only being settled by cash. Cash payments also include those that *could* be in cash if either party wished, which is true of payments by check. On the supposition that bank notes and bank deposits were con-

* The account of the transaction which Hamilton submitted in response to the enquiry of a suspicious Congress was detailed, sarcastic, and calculated to overwhelm his inquisitors with particulars if not with light. ASP, Finance I, 193-94.

15 Sumner, *History of Banking*, 32-33.

vertible at will into specie, all payments in either form of bank liability were constructively specie or cash payments. Alexander Hamilton established this principle, and its importance in a monetary economy can scarcely be over-stressed. He ruled that a statute of 1789 requiring that import duties be paid in gold and silver meant that they might be paid in the equivalent of gold and silver, which by his dictum included bank credit but excluded inconvertible paper money. That distinction no longer holds, but it was then immensely important. To be sure, the inclusion of credit was easily abused, both by persons who understood it too well and by those who failed to understand it well enough. But the constructive monetary use of bank credits and various forms of liability, whether good or bad for humanity, is an outstanding feature of the modern economy, especially the American; and Hamilton's prompt and decisive establishment of bank credit as the major device of monetary settlement was a notable piece of economic statesmanship.[16]

At first, stock ownership of the Bank of the United States, aside from the government's, was mainly in Boston, New York, Philadelphia, Baltimore, and Charleston, though it soon gravitated overseas. In October 1791 the stockholders elected directors, the most prominent of whom were Thomas Willing, president of the Bank of North America but thereafter president of the Bank of the United States, and his son-in-law, William Bingham, one of the ablest business men in America and father-in-law, later, of Alexander Baring (Lord Ashburton) and of Henry Baring, the two Baring brothers marrying two Bingham sisters. The directors, 25 in all, were 9 from Pennsylvania, 7 from New York, 4 from Massachusetts, and 1 each from Connecticut, Maryland, Virginia, North Carolina, and South Carolina—a distribution between the commercial North and the landed South not very different from that of the votes in Congress authorizing the Bank. Thomas Willing was president from 1791 to 1807, when he resigned because of age and ill health and was succeeded by David Lennox, who was president the remaining four years of the Bank's existence.[17]

The Bank opened 12 December 1791 in Philadelphia, then the seat of the federal government. It first occupied Carpenters' Hall, on Chestnut between Third and Fourth Streets, but in 1797 moved round the corner to its new building on Third between Chestnut

16 ASP, Finance I, 49.
17 Wettereau, *PMHB*, LXI (1937), 269, 275.

and Walnut Streets, two streets east of Independence Hall. The building still stands, handsome and in use, though the business community in which it originally centered has moved westward. In architecture it was one of the early products of neo-classic fashion and set a trend to which American banks were long faithful. Its architect was Samuel Blodget, later the author of *Economica*, 1806, the first statistical and economic survey of the United States.[18]

The Bank's shareholders in other cities than Philadelphia were alert to have local offices established as soon as possible. Hamilton was known to be opposed to branches, lest they disrupt management and divide the Bank's strength; and there were others who thought the same: Pelatiah Webster, whom Professor Wettereau quotes, doubted the possibility of managing a bank "ramified through a continent of 1500 miles extent with that uniformity, prudence, or even integrity which the safety and success of it would absolutely require." But the majority were not deterred, and a branch program was decided on even before the Philadelphia office was opened. In this matter Secretary Hamilton was disregarded. He wrote, 25 November 1791, underscoring his words, that "the whole affair of branches was *begun, continued,* and *ended,* not only without my participation but *against my judgment.*" Indeed, he said, "I never was consulted; but . . . the steps taken were contrary to my private opinion of the course which ought to have been pursued." The local banks then in existence (December 1791) were four—the Bank of North America, the Bank of New York, the Massachusetts Bank, and the Maryland Bank—and there was considerable local disposition to turn these into branches of the Bank of the United States. In no place did that purpose prevail. But the division of choice in the matter is one of the earliest evidences of a tendency to question the Hamiltonian belief that the interests of business would be better served by the federal government than by the states. Business men generally supported federal union at the outset because they were dissatisfied with individual statehood and the looseness of confederation. But in early despair of this original federalist hope, Fisher Ames wrote prophetically to Hamilton, 31 July 1791, when the Bank of the United States was being organized, that he doubted if anything could "be done to destroy the state banks," though he hoped they would be absorbed by the Bank of

18 Blodget, 165.

the United States. "I have had my fears that the state banks will become unfriendly to that of the United States. Causes of hatred and rivalry will abound. The state banks . . . may become dangerous instruments in the hands of state partizans." Failure of the effort to turn the existing local banks into branches indicated the alignment of a good part of the business world on the side of the states and a drawing back from too much federalism. Branches of the Bank were opened in the spring of 1792 in Boston, New York, Baltimore, and Charleston; a branch was opened in Norfolk, Virginia, in 1800, in Washington and in Savannah in 1802, and in New Orleans in 1805. This made eight, the total the Bank ever had, though from time to time many other towns—Hartford, Alexandria, Richmond, Natchez, Louisville—sought unsuccessfully to become the homes of branch offices.[19]

Establishment of the office in Norfolk was preceded by a long and acrid controversy which was wholly political and in which the Bank itself tried passively to keep out of trouble while Hamilton tried to get an office established there and the Jeffersonians tried to prevent it. When one was at last opened, Hamilton had been out of the Treasury several years. The office in Washington was established at Albert Gallatin's request made shortly after Jefferson became President and he himself Secretary of the Treasury. From years of observation and discerning opposition, Mr Gallatin already knew the business of the Treasury well and the importance of the Bank to it. In June 1801, the month following his appointment, he asked that an office be opened in Washington, and flew thereby in the face of a cardinal Jeffersonian tenet. The Bank's directors, who might well have expected something less appreciative from Mr Jefferson's administration, complied with pleasure. The office in Savannah was opened apparently on the Bank's initiative, the volume of shipping in that port being attractive; but the action, though at first welcomed, produced considerable trouble in the end. The state levied a tax on the branch, payment was refused, and collection was enforced, the state's officers carrying off $2,004 in silver from the Savannah vaults. The Bank sued but lost. However, the case *Bank of the United States* v. *Deveaux* was determined by the Supreme Court as by the lower court on grounds of jurisdiction, the constitutional issues remaining untouched. These were identical

---

[19] Wettereau, *JEH*, ɪɪ, Supplement (1942), 72-73, 75, 79, 83, 88; Hamilton (Lodge) ɪx, 498; Hamilton Papers 11, pp. 1540, 1541.

with those involved some years later in *McCulloch* v. *Maryland* and *Osborn* v. *Bank of the United States*.[20]

IV

Subsequent evolution, not only in the United States but elsewhere, has made it much more evident than it was in 1800 what sort of institution the Bank of the United States was and how it differed from ordinary banks. In its own day it was called a "public bank" or "national bank" and distinguished as the Bank of England was by its services to the state. Essentially it belonged in the category of "central banks," a genus that had not then been clearly differentiated. For that reason the Bank of England itself was not then designated a central bank. In Britain every one knew that the Bank of England was in a class by itself, because, though the difference between it and other banks, both incorporated and unincorporated, might be hard to define, it was easy to recognize. The British banking system, in its institutional form at the end of the 18th century, was more than 100 years old, and either in law or in custom there were established privileges, responsibilities, limitations, and relationships. In America in 1791 there was almost nothing of the sort. When the Bank of the United States was incorporated in February 1791, there were only four banks in the country, each less than ten years old, and there was but one more by the time it was opened in December.*

Consequently there was as yet no place for the Bank of the United States corresponding to the place already occupied in the British banking system by the Bank of England. Much less was there a place like that occupied in the British banking system by the Bank of England since the mid-19th century, by the Federal Reserve Banks in the American banking system, or by the Bank of Canada in the Canadian banking system.

V

Alexander Hamilton's exemplar for the Bank of the United States had been the Bank of England. Those sections of the Act

* These were the Bank of North America, the Bank of New York, the Massachusetts Bank, the Bank of Maryland, and the Bank of Providence.

[20] Wettereau, *JEH*, ii, *Supplement* (1942), 76-78, 84; Warren i, 392; *Bank of the United States* v. *Deveaux*, 5 Cranch 61 (US 1809); *McCulloch* v. *Maryland*, 4 Wheaton 315 (US 1819); *Osborn* v. *Bank of the United States*, 9 Wheaton 737 (US 1824).

of 1694 which authorized establishment of the latter had influenced the measures which had already incorporated the Bank of North America, the Massachusetts Bank, and the Bank of Maryland, but to nowhere near the extent the act was to influence the charter of the Bank of the United States. When the Bank of North America was incorporated there were only three corporations with banking powers in the British Isles besides the Bank of England. These were the Bank of Scotland, the Royal Bank of Scotland, and the British Linen Company. The charters of the first two were very different from the Bank of England's and the third was not incorporated as a bank at all. The Bank of Ireland was chartered in 1783 on the pattern of the Bank of England and its charter was not used by the Americans as an independent source. The few American charters preceding that of the Bank of the United States had been couched in brief, general, and plenary terms, creating a body corporate and politic but stipulating little about structure and powers. The charter of the Bank of the United States was lengthy, detailed, restrictive, and conditioned to the banking functions which were to be performed. It was prepared by Secretary Hamilton on the basis of his proposal, or "report" to Congress. The manuscript draft of this report, which is in the Library of Congress, is full of deletions and insertions reflecting Hamilton's care for details as well as principles. In effect it takes over from the Bank of England's charter various provisions that have been fixed ever since in American and Canadian banking laws.*

One of the provisions adopted by Mr Hamilton was that in section XXVII of the Bank of England Act, which, to the intent that Their Britannic Majesties' subjects might not be oppressed by the Bank's "monopolizing or engrossing any Sort of Goods, Wares, or Merchandizes," forbade the Bank to deal or trade in commodities. The Bank of the United States was likewise forbidden to deal or trade in goods, and subsequent bank charters and banking laws, in the States and in Canada, have continued the prohibition. Another section of the British act, XXX, forbade the Bank of England to purchase lands or revenues from the Crown or make

* Establishment of the Bank of England was authorized by the Tunnage Act of 1694, the provisions of which relating to the Bank are now known, with their amendments, as the Bank of England Act. Paragraphs are not always numbered in old printings of the Act and in some the numbers vary by one from what I cite.

loans to Their Majesties without Parliament's consent. The Bank of the United States was likewise forbidden to purchase any public debt or lend to the United States or to individual states beyond a certain amount unless authorized by Congress. Similar restrictions became customary in subsequent banking measures and survive in a ban on the direct purchase of obligations from the United States Treasury by the Federal Reserve Banks, except within limits temporarily and jealously allowed by Congress.

A third provision, found in section XX of the Bank of England Act, made the Bank of England "able and capable in Law to have, purchase, receive, possess, enjoy, and retain to them and their Successors Lands, Rents, Tenements, and Hereditaments of what Kind, Nature, or Quality so ever. . . ." This authorization had already been taken over in the ordinance incorporating the Bank of North America, 31 December 1781, but with an important change which reversed it into a restriction. The change was to add the words, "to the amount of ten millions of Spanish silver milled dollars and no more." A like rendering was proposed by Hamilton for the Bank of the United States, and the charter accordingly authorized the Bank "to have, purchase, receive, possess, enjoy, and retain . . . lands, rents, tenements, hereditaments, goods, chattels, and effects . . . to an amount not exceeding the whole fifteen millions of dollars, including the amount of the capital stock . . ." (which was $10,000,000). The restriction is obscure, and appears to have been so to its contemporaries. The amount to which the Bank of North America was restricted was sometimes spoken of as the bank's capital, which it certainly was not, the capital, in our sense, being $400,000. Yet whatever it was taken to mean, the restriction continued to be standard in American and Canadian bank charters for a half century or so; it was perhaps the one charter condition that was universal. I have found no old charter from which it was omitted. It apparently reflected an older disposition to restrict assets rather than liabilities, for though it had not been in the act authorizing incorporation of the Bank of England—where the corresponding language granted a power without restricting it—it had been in other earlier British acts.[21] In Massachusetts bank charters, however, it took another turn, becoming in time a limitation on the amount a bank might have invested in the property it occupied. Thus, for example, the Bank of Gloucester, Massachusetts, 1800,

[21] Carr, passim.

was limited to $8,000 in "lands, rents, tenements, hereditaments, goods, chattels, and effects," and these were to be held for its occupancy only, whereas the Bank of North America had been limited to $10,000,000 without other conditions; but the capital of both banks was the same, $400,000.

VI

The most interesting restriction taken from the Bank of England Act was the following, in section XXVI, which stipulated that the Bank

". . . shall not borrow or give Security by Bill, Bond, Covenant, or Agreement under their common Seal for any more, further, or other Sum or Sums of Money exceeding in the whole the Sum of twelve hundred thousand Pounds, so that they shall not owe at any one Time more than the said Sum, unless it be by Act of Parliament. . . ."

The amount of the limitation, £1,200,000, was the amount of the Bank's capital.

In Hamilton's manuscript the restriction appears in the following form:

"VII. The totality of the debts of the company, whether by bond, bill, note, or other contract, shall never exceed the amount of its capital stock."[22]

Hamilton's version, though shorter, left the force of the British original unaltered. But in his report as submitted, the restriction was qualified with a parenthesis:

"6. The totality of the debts of the company, whether by bond, bill, note, or other contract (credits for deposits excepted) shall never exceed the amount of its capital stock."[23]

The restriction next appeared, in the charter as enacted, in the following form, which in wording runs back to the 17th century original but does include the exemption of deposits:

"The total amount of the debts which the said corporation shall at any time owe, whether by bond, bill, note, or other contract, shall not exceed the sum of ten millions of dollars over and above the monies then actually deposited in the bank for safe keeping, ..."

[22] Hamilton Papers 9, p. 1221.　　　　[23] ASP, Finance I, 74.

The amount of the limitation, $10,000,000, was the amount of the bank's capital, as in the case of the Bank of England.

This restriction on liabilities, adopted by Alexander Hamilton from the charter of the Bank of England, contained the germ of fractional reserve requirements, which have become of basic importance to American bank regulation. The beginning of the evolution is not apparent in the restriction on the Bank of the United States, however, for no ratio is explicit in it. A ratio is explicit, however, in the restriction embodied in the charter of the Bank of New York, which was enacted, 21 March 1791, less than four weeks after the charter of the Bank of the United States and closely paralleled it. In the Bank of New York charter the restriction was closer in form to what Hamilton had first proposed and clearer than in the federal Bank's version.

> "The total amount of the debts which the said corporation shall at any time owe, whether by bond, bill, note, or other contract, over and above the monies then actually deposited in the bank, shall not exceed three times the sum of the capital stock subscribed and actually paid into the bank. . . ."

The capital being paid in specie, this restriction of liabilities to treble the paid capital was the reciprocal, it is obvious, of a requirement that cash reserves be not less than one-third of liabilities. This became a familiar ratio of cash reserves; in the United States it was rivaled only by the ratio of one to four. The formula, with varying ratios, was included by 1800 in 19 out of 30 American charters then in force, and thereafter it became standard until it began to be replaced before the middle of the 19th century with new formulas, roughly the reciprocals of the old, requiring reserves in respect to liabilities. In 1822 it was embodied in the first Canadian bank charter, the Bank of Montreal's, in a form derived from both the Bank of the United States and Bank of New York charters, the ratio being one to three.* The restriction continued in Canadian legislation about fifty years, till after Confederation. It then disappeared until in the Bank of Canada Act, 1934, a nominal reserve

---

* The restriction in the Bank of Montreal charter read as follows:
"Ninth: The total amount of the Debts which the said Corporation shall at any time owe, whether by Bond, Bill, or Note, or other Contract whatsoever, shall not exceed treble the amount of the capital stock actually paid in (over and above a sum equal in amount to such money as may be deposited in the Bank for safe keeping)."

requirement, five per cent, was imposed on all the chartered banks with respect to their domestic deposit liabilities. This has since been raised.

Although, as said, there is no expressed ratio in the federal Bank formula, there is one implied. It is a ratio of one to five. It derives from the arrangement that in effect the capital of the Bank be paid one-fifth in specie and four-fifths in obligations of the government.*Liabilities equal to the Bank's gross capital would therefore be five times its specie capital. In this arrangement proposed by Secretary Hamilton and enacted by Congress, three major desiderata were established: one was a permissible expansion of bank credit in a ratio to specie that was within the range approved by British discussion and practice; the second was acquisition by the Bank of adequate specie; and the third was eligibility of the federal government's bonds as a substitute for specie in satisfaction of three-fourths of the amount due from subscribers, other than the government, to the Bank's capital.

Hamilton was aware that no one ratio of specie to liabilities held the field against all others. In his report he said that ratios of "two and three to one" were amongst those mentioned by authorities. But in his report he followed an explanation of the utility of banks which had been presented by Adam Smith in the *Wealth of Nations* and in which the ratio of one to five had been used. Adam Smith had also mentioned a ratio of one to four, but Mr Keith Horsefield in his studies of 18th century banking ratios in England has shown that there was no orthodoxy in the matter. Hamilton could choose what he thought reasonable within the range of what his authorities thought reasonable. His choice was probably the meeting point between the maximum amount of bonds that could be made eligible and the minimum amount of specie the Bank should hold. That was a matter of judgment. For the arrangement was one with a double objective, viz., enhancement of the federal credit and establishment of the Bank. The bonds of the new, unfledged government had to be made attractive to men with money and hard heads. Convertibility of the bonds into bank stock was one means of making them so. Hamilton said in his report to Congress that when the current price of the bonds was considered, and when it was further considered

---

* The capital was to be $10,000,000, of which the government would take $2,000,000, leaving $8,000,000 for public subscription, and of this, $2,000,000 was to be paid in specie and $6,000,000 in public debt.

how a rise in price would probably be accentuated by their convertibility, the advantage of the arrangement to the subscribers would "easily be discovered." And from the influence which that rise would have "on the general mass" of the public debt, he saw benefits accruing to all public credit and to the country at large. He gauged his proposals accordingly. He followed the Bank of England pattern in making "government stock," as bonds were then called, eligible for payment of the Bank's capital, but departed therefrom in making it eligible for payment of three-fifths only. Moreover, the British arrangement had incorporated the subscribers to new obligations, mainly; the American arrangement incorporated the holders of bonds already authorized and outstanding. The American arrangement was also that the federal government take a proprietary interest in the Bank, which the British government did not have in the Bank of England.[24]

VII

In calling a *restriction* of liabilities in respect to specie capital the reciprocal of a *requirement* of specie in respect to liabilities, I take specie and specie capital to mean the same thing. In the 20th century bank, capital means an account on the liability side of the balance sheet which represents a residue belonging to the stockholders after all other corporate liabilities have been satisfied. This meaning, which modern double-entry bookkeeping has imposed, is quite different from what capital means in economics and in common sense. There it means property, wealth, possessions, goods, money—depending on the context—and that is what it meant in 18th century usage. The capital of a bank was its basic assets, the gold and silver put in its coffers by its proprietors. Adam Smith in 1776 called a bank's capital the "treasure" which supported its circulation; Pelatiah Webster in 1786 had "the wealth" of the Bank of North America include its capital of "900,000 Mexican dollars"; Hamilton in 1784 prescribed, in the constitution of the Bank of New York, that "the capital stock shall consist of five hundred thousand dollars in gold and silver"; in his report of 1790 he spoke of banks circulating "a far greater sum than the actual quantum of their capital in gold and silver"; and of a bank's ability "to circulate a greater sum than its actual capital in coin." About the same time, Thomas Paine spoke of a bank's having "capital . . . equal to the redemption"

24 Horsefield, *JPE*, LVII (1949), 70; ASP, Finance I, 75.

of its notes and "capital . . . not equal to the demands" upon it, meaning of course the specie needed to support the circulation. The Massachusetts legislature in 1792 related the Massachusetts Bank's liabilities to its "capital stock in gold and silver actually deposited in the bank and held to answer the demands against the same." In 1808 an abortive measure introduced in the Quebec legislature to incorporate a Bank of Lower Canada contained an unusual version of the customary restriction that betrayed clearly the equivalence of capital and specie, for it rested the restriction directly on specie and thus anticipated, by thirty years, though it did not become law, the eventual requirement of specie reserves. It limited the liabilities to "treble the amount of the gold and silver actually in the bank, arising from their capital stock. . . ." There is no reason to think that the variation was one of substance and not merely form; it indicates what every one meant but usually said a different way.[25]

Specie and capital were the more readily identified because of the over-riding importance of specie. It was the one scarce ingredient in American banking. The 18th century American banks, particularly the first three or four whose initial experience was antecedent to the first banking laws, had to stand on their own bottoms. Being sole in their respective communities, they had no fellow banks to coerce or implore, no United States Treasury, no city correspondents, no Federal Reserve Banks, no liquid investment market, and no claim on any one but the debtors whose obligations they held. In this situation, specie was their only recourse. Without it their case was comparable to that of a modern bank without vault cash, without checks against other banks, without balances due from the Reserve Bank or from correspondents, and without marketable securities.

Hence it is not strange that some banks, at least, actually held specie to the full amount of their capital. From its establishment in 1784 to 1790, the Massachusetts Bank's specie regularly exceeded its capital; records are missing for the next decade or so, but the excess recurred from time to time in the early 19th century. The Bank of New York, 1 May 1791, had $463,000 in "cash," not including notes on hand, and capital of $318,000. The Bank of the United States, one-fifth of whose capital should have been held in specie, did not in fact hold that much, according to the records, till 1797, and after 1798 its specie was about half the amount of its total capital, more or less.

[25] Pelatiah Webster, 449; ASP, Finance i, 68; Paine (Conway) ii, 209, 221.

For a strangely long time, fifty years or more, it continued to be assumed in bank charters that capital would always be "paid capital" or "capital actually paid." But it was realized at length that payment of capital in coin could not be taken for granted; much less could retention of the coin. The law thereupon became more and more mandatory as banks and their proprietors became more and more delinquent, there being a universal unwillingness to see that the aggregate of authorized bank capital had become far larger than the amount of gold and silver which could be got together. The requirements of specie already exceeded the supply of specie. Still the requirement of a paid and retained capital was deemed possible for any one bank, and so legislation continued to impose it regardless of its absurdity in the aggregate. To run forward, for illustrations, into the future, the Massachusetts legislature in 1829 forbade new banks to begin business till they had at least half their capital paid in and the authorities had examined and counted it, "actually in the vaults," and ascertained that it was "intended to have it therein remain"; the bank commissioners of Alabama in 1838 told the legislature that banks should be "compelled to keep their whole capital in specie"; and the Parliament of Prince Edward Island in 1855 required that the "capital stock" of the Bank of Prince Edward Island, which it was then incorporating, "consist of current gold and silver coins of this Island. . . ." The specific testimony that comes nearest to being coeval with the stipulations, so far as I know, is the statement of Professor George Tucker of the University of Virginia in 1839, when restrictions originating with the Bank of the United States and the Bank of New York were still in force generally: "It seems not improbable that when the first charters were granted, the legislatures being then little familiar with the subject of banking and understanding from English writers that the Bank of England considered it a rule of safety to have in its vaults one-third as much specie as it had notes in circulation, they conceived that after having required the whole capital stock to be in specie they were adopting the same rule as the Bank of England in limiting the amount of circulation to three times the capital stock. . . ."[26]

It was in Virginia, Professor Tucker's state, that by an act of 22 March 1837 the effectual start was made toward replacing eventually the universal statutory *restriction* of bank liabilities in

[26] Tucker, 205.

ratio to capital with a universal statutory *requirement* of bank reserves in ratio to liabilities. Though restriction of a bank's "debts" was retained relative to the amount of "moneys deposited" and "capital stock actually paid in," it was also required

"That the total amount of the bills or notes of any bank in circulation shall not at any time exceed five times the amount of gold and silver coin . . . in the possession of the bank and held to pay the demands against it."

The force of this requirement, one sees, is practically identical with that proposed in Quebec three decades before, as I said a few paragraphs back; except that Quebec would have had a ratio higher than Virginia's and applicable to both deposits and note liabilities instead of the latter alone.

VIII

Since the restriction on the Bank of England's debts was confined to liabilities incurred under seal and said nothing of deposits, it is to be supposed that it applied to circulating notes only. Hamilton's specific exemption of "deposits" from the restriction was a departure from the British original, was not in the preliminary draft of his report, and seems to have come to him as an afterthought. But what he and his contemporaries intended to exempt seems to have been strictly deposits of specie and not deposit credit arising from loans. For to them deposits meant only specie. Indeed, the distinction between the liability for deposits of specie and the liability for amounts lent, which is no longer observed and has not been for 150 years or more, seems to have been sharply recognized in the 18th century. And the nature of the liability for amounts lent seems to have been better understood than the nature of the liability for specie. The latter was persistently confused with bailment. Considering the varieties of coin and bullion, their individual values, and the profit derived from trading in them as commodities, one can not wonder that depositors wished to draw out the same thing they had put in and thought of a bank as a warehouse which provided safe-keeping under earmark. The banks resisted this view of their liability but rather for practical than legal reasons. In 1784 the directors of the Massachusetts Bank ruled that "any person who shall deposit money in the bank shall have a right to take out the same kind of money as that which they deposited, . . . provided that such kind of money shall then be in the bank."[27] That banks for a while were accustomed to segregating liabilities in a way this ruling implies is certain. For several years after New York issued bills of credit in 1786, the Bank of New York segregated specie and paper accounts; and as late as 1816, 1817, and even later than that, resumption of specie payments was attended by segregation of accounts payable in specie from those payable in bank paper not redeemable on demand.

But it is evident that the nature of the liability for specie deposits, as distinct from the liability for funds lent, was unsettled. There was a twilight between practice and law, with the depositor prone to think of the specie as *his* specie lying in the bank for safekeeping and with the bank forced by the facts to consider it bank property, for which, however, the bank was in debt. The courts in time established bank ownership, and "deposits" became definitely a liability. But for long the question was beclouded. Thus Hamilton, in explaining the matter, said that specie deposited lies in a bank and "much oftener changes proprietors than place"; which plainly implies that he considered the specie was not the property of the bank but of its customers. That seems to have been the way he and his contemporaries thought of the gold in the Bank of Amsterdam: it belonged to the depositors, as if in earmark, and its hypothecation by the bank was not a use by the bank of its own property but a fraud. In America certainly, the matter, like others that confuse our own generation, simply had not yet been settled at the end of the 18th century.[28]

On the other hand, in the sentence before his explanation of specie deposits, Hamilton had made the observation that every loan which a bank makes is in the first instance a credit on its books in favor of the borrower and that, unless withdrawn in specie, it remains a liability of the bank till the loan is repaid. In these words he explained 20th century banking as well as 18th, and how bank lending creates bank deposits, with the difference that he did not call them "deposits" but reserved that term for specie transactions, distinguishing credit for specie from credit for the proceeds of loans. He did so because he observed banking in terms of the individual bank and not of many banks constituting a system. He was writing at a time when there were three banks only in America, each

---

[27] Gras, 245.   [28] ASP, Finance I, 68.

sole in its community. The effect each bank's lending had on its own position was in those circumstances direct and unobscured; its loans obviously increased what would now be called its deposits; for the checks drawn on it were not being deposited in other banks nor were the checks drawn on others being deposited in it. Each bank was a closed and separate system. Hamilton simply noted what in the then situation was plain and required no unusual discernment. The records of the Massachusetts Bank indicate how common it was at the very beginning to credit borrower's accounts with the amounts lent them; and the known figures of deposit liabilities are plainly too large to have arisen from specie alone. Such credits seem in practice to have been included with deposits proper but in discussion to have been kept distinct. A deposit was of something tangible, whether for safekeeping or to apply on a capital subscription. The liability for amounts lent was called credit or book credit, as by Hamilton in the passage in which he described the procedure.

Though exempting specie deposits from the restriction could scarcely have given a bank any more inducement than it already had to acquire specie, it doubtless seemed logical to Hamilton that the liability arising from deposits of specie be distinguished from the liability representing the proceeds of loans and that it be excepted from limitations on an expansion that could occur only when liabilities were assumed in excess of the specie held. The issuance of notes and the crediting of customers' accounts might and did entail the assumption of liabilities in excess of specie holdings, but not when the issuance or the credit resulted from a deposit of specie.

One may be tempted to consider whether Alexander Hamilton could have intended to restrict note issue only and leave deposit credit free to expand without limit, knowing its potential importance and wishing to make the Bank of the United States as powerful a credit agency as possible in the new American economy. It is unlikely. To be sure, the restriction was later thought to mean circulating note liabilities only, but that is because the 19th century became obsessed with circulation, forgot the 18th century distinction between credit for deposits of specie and credit for money lent, and lost all notion of the nature and importance of what it called deposits.* Hamilton understood the nature of book credit for loans,

---

* Although Albert Gallatin recognized the interchangeability and practical identity of notes and deposits, he thought note issue should be regulated and

but he no more foresaw its importance in the 20th century than in the 25th. Assuming that he did foresee it, one can not believe that he would have deemed a five-to-one ratio of expansion for deposits insufficient, much less that he would have deemed a total exemption of them desirable. He was no advocate of *laisser faire.* Nor, had he meant to exempt deposits (in our sense), would he have used a word reserved in his day for transactions in specie. I think that he meant to exempt merely the liability for deposits of the latter. It was his minor purpose to avoid even seeming to neglect any facilitation of specie accumulations and to avoid the vanity of restricting what could not occur, viz., a specie deposit liability in excess of specie deposits. At the same time, by exempting only the liability for specie deposited, he restricted just those liabilities whose expansibility required it, viz., note circulation and credit for amounts lent.

That the exemption then and for a long time after was understood to mean specie deposits only is indicated, I think, by the emphasis in phrases common in bank charters everywhere: "specie actually deposited," "the simple amount of all moneys actually deposited," and "moneys deposited for safekeeping." It is indicated particularly in the bill I have mentioned which was introduced in the House of Assembly, Quebec, 1808, to incorporate a Bank of Lower Canada, the liabilities restricted to be "exclusive of a sum equal in amount to that of the gold and silver actually in the bank arising from other sources" than payment for capital stock.

Paralleling such efforts to exempt specie deposits explicitly, there were other efforts to restrict book credit explicitly. The purpose of both was logically the same. As early as March 1792 the Massachusetts legislature had sought to curb the Massachusetts Bank's volume of discounting and accordingly amended its charter as follows:

> "The total amount of all the promissory notes of said Corporation, together with the money loaned by them by a credit on their books or otherwise, shall not at any one time exceed *double* the amount of their capital stock in gold and silver, actually deposited in the bank, and held to answer the demands against the same." (Italics in the original.)

---

deposits should not. See Professor Dunbar's admonition to economists about notes and deposits fifty years later. Dunbar, 173, 179.

Here both the bank's circulation and the book credit due customers for sums lent them are specifically limited. In January 1800 the Massachusetts legislature restricted the Gloucester Bank as follows:

"The total amount of all discounts made by the said Corporation and monies loaned by them by a credit on their books or otherwise shall not at any time exceed double the amount of their capital stock paid into the Bank, and held to answer the demands against the same; and the said Corporation shall not issue, or have in circulation at any time, bills, notes, or obligations to a greater amount than double their stock as aforesaid, in addition to the simple amount of all the specie deposited in said Bank for safe keeping."

In this case the legislature for the first time put the restriction on earning assets and on liabilities both, each being limited to twice the amount of paid capital. Unlike its 1792 predecessor, however, which had put book credit among the liabilities, the legislature of 1800 put it among the earning assets. There is nothing unusual about this inconsistency, for in the 18th century, even where banking was better understood than it was by legislators, accounts were not rigidly classified as they have come to be through a century and a half of accounting discipline. The practice then was less conventional than now, for then, taking advantage of the fact that every item on a bank's books has both an asset and a liability aspect, it might be called either; whereas now every item belongs rigidly on one side or the other. Thus deposits were sometimes what a bank held and sometimes what it owed; and circulation represented money lent as much as money owed. There is a modern parallel in the fact that bank credit may be measured either in assets or in liabilities, and though the statistical practice of measuring it in loans and investments is now well established, deposits are often taken informally as its measure, and the law provides for its control through the ratio of reserves to deposit liabilities.

There is a conceivable alternative to consider in exegesis of the phrase, "money lent by a credit on the books." It is that overdraft is meant, or credit on open account, as is customary in Britain and perhaps most of the world. Possibly that is the meaning. Overdraft certainly used to be known in American banking; the Suffolk Bank of Boston, for example, in the 1830's regularly called its claims on other New England banks overdrafts. But how common the practice was—as a *reputable* practice—I can not even guess. Nor have I any clear idea how the American aversion to overdraft is to be explained. It is perhaps associated with bank supervision, which is another American peculiarity; but if so, the aversion of supervision to overdraft would itself have to be explained. Perhaps it arises from the greater risks attendant on lending in the 19th century American economy and a resulting preference for signed documentary evidences of debt as against open account charges. But this is mere rationalization.

IX

Professor W. G. Sumner wrote sixty years ago of Alexander Hamilton's work: "The charter of the Bank of New York, which came from his hand, became the model on which numberless charters were afterwards constructed, and the charter of the Bank of the United States, which he now proceeded to make, was taken as a model by so many others that we must attribute to his opinions on banking a predominant influence in forming the banking institutions of this country." It is curious however that Hamilton's authorship of the New York charter seems much less clearly authenticated than his authorship of the federal charter. The draft of the federal charter is in the Hamilton papers in the Library of Congress, and it re-appears in altered form in the official report to Congress. But neither Hamilton's son, who included in Hamilton's writings the "constitution" under which the Bank of New York was conducted before it received its charter, nor John Cleaveland, who wrote in 1857 that the charter of the Bank of New York "was substantially the model upon which all the bank charters granted" in New York "were framed prior to 1825," nor H. W. Domett, historian of the bank, ascribes authorship of its charter to Hamilton.[29]

In Lodge's edition of Hamilton's writings, however, it is stated that "nothing has been omitted except a draft of a charter for the Bank of New York, 1786, and one of a charter for the Merchants' Bank of New York, 1803, which throw no light on Hamilton's opinions or on the development of the principles which were by his efforts embodied in legislation."

Though the texts of the two charters vary, as they should because of the great differences in the circumstances in which they were pre-

[29] Sumner, *History of Banking*, 22.

pared, the attention to details and the general approach to the problem satisfy me that Hamilton prepared both. The important matter of the ratio of liabilities to capital is convincing by itself. In both he modifies the Bank of England's restriction on debts with a multiple ratio between liabilities and capital, which introduced into American banking laws the principle of fractional reserves. Some one else may have had the same idea he had, but I doubt it.

I do not pretend, to be sure, that in originating the legal concept of fractional reserves by limiting liabilities to five and three times specie capital, he entertained any notion of the regulatory function to be achieved by reserve requirements. He merely, for the purpose in hand, devised an arrangement that should restrict the expansion of bank liabilities, and though it turned out to be ineffective in practice—because it did not include deposit liabilities—it opened the evolutionary path to arrangements that are effective.

CHAPTER 6

Politics and the Growth of Banking

1791-1816

I. The number of banks in 1800 — II. Political and economic changes — III. New York—the Manhattan Company — IV. New York—the Merchants Bank — V. New York—the Bank of America — VI. Banks elsewhere — VII. Money banks, state banks, combination banks

I

THE following list shows 29 banks in business in 1800. It is evident that banking soon spread outside the main commercial centers, although every town included was something of a port in the sense that it could accommodate the light-draft vessels of that day. Banking was still ancillary to commerce, and commerce was still waterborne and an affair of foreign trade.

Char-tered*	Opened*	Name	Place	Authorized Capital about 1800
1781	1782	Bank of North America	Philadelphia	$ 2,000,000
1791	1784	Bank of New York	New York	950,000
1784	1784	Massachusetts Bank	Boston	1,600,000
1790	1790-1	Bank of Maryland	Baltimore	300,000
1791	1791	Providence Bank	Providence, R.I.	400,000
1791	1791	Bank of United States	Philadelphia	10,000,000
1792	1792	New Hampshire Bank	Portsmouth	100,000
1792	1792	Union Bank	New London, Conn.	500,000
1792	1792	Hartford Bank	Hartford, Conn.	930,000
1792	1792	New Haven Bank	New Haven, Conn.	400,000
1792	1792	Union Bank	Boston	1,200,000
1799	1792	Essex Bank	Salem, Mass.	300,000
1801	1792	Bank of South Carolina	Charleston	640,000
1792	1792	Bank of Albany	Albany, N.Y.	260,000
1793	1793	Bank of Columbia	Hudson, N.Y.	160,000
1793	1793	Bank of Alexandria	Alexandria, Va.	500,000
1793	1793	Bank of Pennsylvania	Philadelphia	3,000,000
1793	1793	Bank of Columbia	**Washington, D.C.	500,000
1795	1795-6	Bank of Baltimore	Baltimore	1,200,000

Char- tered*	Opened*	Name	Place	Authorized Capi- tal about 1800
1795	1795	Bank of Nantucket	Nantucket, Mass.	100,000
1795	1795	Merrimack Bank	Newburyport, Mass.	
1795	1795	Bank of Rhode Island	Newport	400,000
1796	1795	Bank of Delaware	Wilmington	110,000
1796	1796	Bank of Norwich	Norwich, Conn.	200,000
1799	1799	Manhattan Company	New York	2,000,000
1799	1799	Portland Bank	**Portland, Maine	300,000
1800	1800	Gloucester Bank	Gloucester, Mass.	100,000
1800	1800	Bank of Bristol	Bristol, R.I.	120,000
1800	1800	Washington Bank	Westerly, R.I.	50,000

* Dates are often uncertain. Incorporation sometimes preceded the opening for business, sometimes followed. In making this list I have followed principally J. S. Davis, *18th Century Corporations*, ɪɪ, chap. ɪɪ; Gouge ɪɪ, 42; and Blodget, *Economica*, 159. The figures for capital, mainly taken from Gouge, indicate ambitions rather than actualities and relate to 1800, not the year of founding.

** In 1793 the city of Washington, D.C., was not in existence, but the Bank of Columbia may have arisen in the woods as one of the capital's first harbingers. In 1799 Portland, Maine, still belonged to Massachusetts.

II

In 1791, when the Bank of the United States was chartered, the Federalists, a monied minority of the population, were in control of the government, and there were three banks in operation. In 1811, when the Bank of the United States was let die, the Federalists were disintegrated, the Jeffersonians had long been in power, and banks, which were one of that party's principal traditionary aversions, had multiplied from three to ninety. In the next five years the number increased to nearly 250; by 1820 it exceeded 300—an increase of more than a hundred-fold in the first thirty years of the federal union. It is hard to imagine how banking could have been propagated more under its sponsors than it was under its "enemies."

That banking flourished with the decline of Hamilton's party and the ascendancy of Jefferson's connotes the fact that business was becoming democratic. It was no longer a select and innumerous aristocracy—business opportunities were falling open to everyone. The result was an alignment of the new generation of business men with the genuine agrarians, whose rugged individualism constituted the Jeffersonian democracy's professed faith and required very little alteration to fit enterprise as well. The success of the Republican party in retaining the loyalty of the older agrarians while it recruited among the newer entrepreneurial masses was possible, Professor Beard has explained, because Jefferson's academic views pleased the one group and his practical politics propitiated the other. It was also because equality of opportunity in business and the principle of *laisser faire* could be advocated with a Jeffersonian vocabulary.[1]

The number of banks grew from 6 to 246 in the twenty-five years between establishment of the Bank of the United States in 1791 and establishment of a new Bank of the United States in 1816. This growth was not the multiplication of something familiar, like houses or ships or carriages, but a multiplication of something unfamiliar or even mysterious. Had banks been thought to be merely depositories where savings were tucked away—as came to be thought in time—there would have been nothing remarkable about their increase. But they were known to do more than receive money. They were known to create it. For each dollar paid in by the stockholders, the banks lent two, three, four, or five. The more sanguine part of the people were happy to have it so, no matter if they did not understand how it could be. The more conservative, like John Adams, thought it a cheat. Since the Republican party had both its agrarian wing and its speculative-entrepreneurial wing, it came to include both the conspicuous opponents of banking and the conspicuous advocates of it.*

The Jeffersonian impetus in banking may well have begun in reaction to the Federalist character of the first banks, all of which were conceived and defended as monopolies. The surest procedure for any new group that wished to obtain a bank charter from a Jeffersonian state legislature was to cry out against monopoly in general and in particular against that of the Federalist bankers who would lend nothing, it was alleged, to good Republicans. The argument was persuasive. Jeffersonians, if they could not extirpate monopoly, could at least reduce its inequities by seizing a share of its rewards. So Jefferson himself seems to have thought. "I am decidedly in favor of making all the banks Republican," he wrote Gallatin in July 1803, "by sharing deposits among them in propor-

---

* The Republican party of Thomas Jefferson became in time the Democratic party of Andrew Jackson, though Jackson himself seems never to have abandoned the original name Republican, obsolescent in his day. The later Republican party, to which Abraham Lincoln belonged, has no connection with the original Republican party.

[1] Beard, *Economic Origins*, 467.

tion to the dispositions they show." Dr Benjamin Rush wrote to John Adams in 1810 that though Federalist and Democratic principles were ostensibly at issue between the parties, "the true objects of strife are a 'mercantile bank' by the former and a 'mechanics bank' by the latter party." The State Bank of Boston solicited federal deposits in 1812, following the demise of the Bank of the United States, with the assurance to the Republican administration that the State Bank was "the property of sixteen hundred freemen of the respectable state of Massachusetts, all of them advocates of the then existing federal administration, associated not solely for the purpose of advancing their pecuniary interests but for the more noble purpose of cherishing Republican men and Republican measures against the wiles and machinations" of the rival political party. The same course could be followed by any sort of special interest—geographic, economic, or what not—which wanted credit and was dissatisfied with the existing banks. So the number grew. Each borrowing interest wanted a bank of its own. Soon, as Dr Rush said, banks were serving not only merchants but "mechanics," on whose skills the Industrial Revolution was progressing, and farmers. The charter of the Washington Bank, Westerly, Rhode Island, June 1800, solicited both interests. It recited that "added to those common arguments in favour of bank institutions, such as promoting punctuality in discharge of contracts, . . . and extending commerce by accumulating the means of carrying it on, there are also arguments in favour of such establishments, as promoting the agricultural and mechanical interest of our country." It declared that "those banks which at present are established in this state are too remote or too confined in their operations to diffuse their benefits so generally to the country as could be wished." It mentioned the embarrassments into which "the farmer is frequently drove for the want of means of stocking his farm at those seasons of the year when money is obtained with the greatest difficulty"; and it expressed the belief that "in a place peculiarly fitted by nature to encourage the industry and ingenuity of the mechanic by holding out the sure prospects of a profitable return for his enterprise, nothing is wanting but those little assistances from time to time which banks only can give."[2]

The next step beyond making banks ancillary to agriculture and industry was to make them ancillary to public improvements of large scale. In 1809 it was proposed in Congress that the Bank

[2] Gallatin I, 129; Rush, *Letters* II, 1069, 1078; Redlich, 22, 23; Stetson, 19.

of the United States be replaced by "a general national establishment of banks throughout the United States" whose profits should be devoted to public roads, canals, and schools. In the individual states such proposals were put into effect. Sometimes banking was the real object of the incorporators, and the enterprise or "public improvement" was merely a blind or an excuse; sometimes banking was really subordinate, or at any rate not the sole object.[3]

In 1791 American business had been concerned mainly with foreign commerce; by 1816 it was concerned mainly with a greatly diversified internal economy. The change had been impelled chiefly by the abundance of native resources to be developed, but it was hastened and intensified by the Napoleonic wars, which for two decades or so kept Britain and France at one another's throats and involved all Europe besides, driving Britain to strike at France's trade with the United States and France to strike at Britain's. American seaborne commerce was battered from both sides. War with either or both belligerents overhung the country for years and broke out at last, with Britain, in 1812. It ended in 1814. By then the dominant interests of American business had been turned decisively toward the domestic field; and the potential demand for bank credit had been enlarged both in volume and in variety.

Before the turn of the century, politics had been roiled by the Jay Treaty, the X Y Z affair, the Alien and Sedition Acts, and the Kentucky and Virginia Resolutions. After the turn of the century, the Embargo of 1807, the Non-Intercourse Act of 1809, and war in 1812 made matters still worse. Disunion itself came within speaking distance. There was extreme economic and social instability: expansion, migration, and realignment of interests. The population, which in 1790 had been 3,900,000, became 9,600,000 by 1810; and by 1812 the original thirteen states had become eighteen. Through migration and settlement all the territory east of the Mississippi had become American—save Florida, which was shortly, in 1819, to be picked up—and in the Louisiana Purchase, 1803, half the territory beyond the Mississippi had been acquired. In 1793 the cotton gin had been invented and the way cleared for Cotton to become King and the leading means of payment for the goods required from Europe for the building up of American industry. The steamship *Clermont* made her pristine passage up and down the Hudson in 1807. By 1810, manufacturing with water power had suddenly

[3] Clarke and Hall, 120.

become common; the number of cotton mills in 1807 was fifteen and of spindles 8,000, but in 1811 those numbers had grown to eighty-seven and 80,000. These and other profound changes that were going on with violent rapidity and literally changing the face of the earth with roads, canals, factories, and cities, did not yet shake agriculture from its basic place in the economy; they did, however, raise up mechanical industry and inland transportation to rival and in time surpass foreign commerce, which had originally shared with agriculture the country's economic activity.

It is obvious that this immense expansion of business could not be the work of an established, limited group of capitalists. It was the work of immigrants and of native Americans born on farms—self-made men with energy, ingenuity, and an outstanding need of money with which to finance their enterprises. Most of them did not become millionaires, but they were business men, nevertheless.

III

The relative importance of New York and Philadelphia was becoming very different at the end of the 18th century from what it had been a half-century before. Benjamin Franklin had been drawn to Philadelphia; Alexander Hamilton and Aaron Burr had since been drawn to New York. Philadelphia was a city of great wealth, but New York was a city of enterprise. A newer and more aggressive spirit, in both politics and business, flourished there, and though Philadelphia was to remain till about 1840 the financial center of America, one can see by 1800 not only the natural advantages New York possessed, but a characteristic energy and ingenuity that seem to explain her triumphant exploitation of them.

In New York City, from 1784 to 1791 there was no bank but the Bank of New York, and from 1791 to 1799 there was no other but the local office of the Bank of the United States. Both were Federalist. During those fifteen years, though business growth was substantial, the establishment of other banks was obstructed partly by Federalist protection of the two banks already established and partly by conservative opposition, largely agrarian, to banking in general. But in 1799, through a skilful stratagem of Aaron Burr's, a corporate charter was obtained under which a new bank was set up, the Bank of the Manhattan Company, of far greater size than the Bank of New York, of much wider proprietorship, and Jeffersonian in its political ties. Its establishment was an important event in both economic and political history.*

Colonel Burr was provided an opportunity for his stratagem by the pestilence of yellow fever in New York the previous summer. A joint committee of the Common Council and other local bodies reported the following winter that amongst "the means of removing the causes of pestilential diseases" it considered "a plentiful supply of fresh water as one of the most powerful," and it earnestly recommended "that some plan for its introduction into this city be carried into execution as soon as possible." New York was then dependent upon ponds, wells, cisterns, and the carting of water in from the country for sale. In accordance with the joint committee's report, bills authorizing various hygienic measures and in particular the construction of water works by the city were introduced in the legislature at Albany. They failed to receive attention. Late in February 1799, Mayor Varick of New York City informed the Common Council of a visit he had just received from a group of six gentlemen, prominent residents of the city, who were concerned about the status of the bills. They were Aaron Burr, one of the city's Republican representatives in the state legislature, which was still Federalist; Alexander Hamilton, now engaged in private legal practice; John Murray, a wealthy Quaker merchant, then president of the Chamber of Commerce and formerly a director of the Bank of New York; Gulian Verplanck, Federalist, president of the Bank of New York;** Peter Wendover, Republican, president of the Mechanics Society; and John Broome, Republican, formerly president of the Chamber of Commerce. Their concern as reported by Colonel Burr was lest the legislators reject the proposed bills, there being discontent with the plan to enlarge the Council's powers, even to protect the city's health. He thought it "problematical whether those bills would pass in the form proposed" and suggested that the Council request the legislature, if the bills were not deemed proper in the form proposed, to "make such provisions on the several subjects thereof as to them should appear most eligible." Fresh proposals to this end were then suggested by Alexander Hamilton.

* Since my account was written, the Manhattan has merged with the Chase National Bank; it is now the Chase Manhattan Bank but still under the original corporate charter of 1799.

** The Minutes of the Common Council call Mr Verplanck, erroneously, "President of the Office of Discount and Deposit of the Bank of the United States in this City." (II, 514.)

These were that the Council, instead of seeking authority to build and operate the water works itself, favor incorporating a business company for the purpose.[4]

The Council, when the views of Burr and Hamilton were reported to them by the Mayor and the Recorder, was impressed. But it resolved, before proceeding, that the new proposals ought to be signed by their sponsors and that more should be explained about the legislature's attitude. It directed that its resolution "be communicated to Mr Burr and Major General Hamilton without delay," and that since the matter was of "great importance to the welfare of the city," a special meeting of the Council be called as soon as their reply was received. General Hamilton responded the next day, and on the 28th his letter and enclosure were laid before the Council. In these he stated that the action of the group had been informal and merely that of private individuals offering information which they thought might be useful to the city. "Specific propositions in writing were requested from, not proposed by, them." But, he said, "Having been digested by me, as the sum of a previous conversation among ourselves, I have no objection to authenticate them by my signature—and I freely add that the changes in the plan of the corporation which they suggest have the full concurrence of my opinion." With respect to the pending measures for financing and constructing water works, he thought it doubtful if the legislature would or could grant the city a source of revenue which would be adequate "if the business be done on a scale sufficiently extensive." He proposed therefore that a business company be incorporated for the purpose with a capital of $1,000,000, the city to own a third and the City Recorder to be a director.

The Council responded wholeheartedly. The legislature was apprised by resolution of what had occurred and of the Council's realization that by the terms of the bills then pending its cares and duties would be considerably extended and its members "subjected to great additional trouble without any emolument to themselves." The Council also mentioned the possibility "that a company would be best adapted to the business of supplying the city with water"; although in public and official opinion till then city ownership of the water works had been preferred to private. It emphasized its anxiety that measures for the water supply and the city's health be authorized, disclaimed any attachment to the pending bills, and

4 New York City, *Minutes* II, 494-98, 500-08, 514-20.

assured the legislature of its acquiescence in whatever the legislators should decide was best.

This action by the Council "seems to have removed the chief
obstacle to the success of Mr Burr's plan." In Albany he now introduced a bill entitled "An act for supplying the city of New-York
with pure and wholesome water." Its preamble stated that since
"Daniel Ludlow and John B. Church together with sundry other
citizens" had associated for the purpose of providing a water supply
for the city and had obtained subscriptions of capital to that end,
they should be given a corporate charter to encourage "their laudable undertaking, which promises under the blessing of God to be
conducive to the future health and safety of the inhabitants of the
said city." Daniel Ludlow and John B. Church were business men
whose names lent just such credit to the project as those of
Alexander Hamilton, John Murray, and Gulian Verplanck had lent
it already. Daniel Ludlow, a Tory during the Revolution, was now
a proprietor of the largest importing and mercantile business in
New York. John B. Church was Alexander Hamilton's brother-in-
law and friend, an astute speculator, and a Federalist.

The bill designated the corporation the "President and Directors
of the Manhattan Company" and authorized a capital of $2,000,-
000, which was twice what Mr Hamilton had mentioned, and the
city was to own a tenth and not a third. The bill also designated
the first directors; the majority, including Mr Burr, were Republicans, but Federalists had some prominence of place. Further, after
giving the corporation the necessary power to erect dams, divert
streams, lay pipes, etc., etc., the bill provided in Section 8 "That it
shall and may be lawful for the said company to employ all such
surplus capital as may belong or accrue to the said company in
the purchase of public or other stock or in any other monied transactions or operations not inconsistent with the constitution and laws
of this state or of the United States, for the sole benefit of the
said company."

The bill passed the lower house apparently without question.
Since there were Federalists outside the legislature willing to put
money in the project, it is not strange that there were Federalists
inside willing to vote for it. But in a committee of the upper house
one senator wished to have the plenary clause I have just quoted
stricken out. "Mr Burr," according to Matthew L. Davis, his
friend and biographer, "promptly and frankly informed the honour-

able member that it not only did authorize but that it was intended the directors should use the surplus capital in any way they thought expedient and proper. That they might have a bank, an East India Company, or anything else that they deemed profitable. That the mere supplying the city with water would not of itself remunerate the stockholders. Colonel Burr added that the senator was at liberty to communicate this explanation to other members and that he had no secrecy on the subject." Because of this explanation, probably, and not in spite of it, the bill was passed. Its real object, according to the conservatives, was "to furnish new projects and means for speculation."[5]

It then went to the Council of Revision, where the monied powers were again questioned—this time by Chief Justice John Lansing, a Republican, not a Federalist—who observed that the company was "vested with the unusual power to divert its surplus capital to the purchase of public or other stock or any other monied transactions" and so might use its funds in trade or any way it chose. Even at this late date it was trade and not banking that he foresaw, which indicates that the latter had not yet been mentioned prominently as the likely aim of the company's monied powers. He thought the grant of such powers a "novel experiment" and that they "should be of limited instead of perpetual duration." Even this mild amendment, which would merely have given the plenary powers a period, was over-ruled. The measure became law, 2 April 1799. Less than a fortnight later the company began negotiations with the Council about the water supply.[6]

It also got under way with its plans for a bank. Robert Troup, a conservative and Federalist, reported to his friend Rufus King, 19 April 1799: "It is given out that we are to have a new bank established by the Company and that they will also embark deeply in the East India Trade and perhaps turn their attention to marine insurance." He said that "The most respectable mercantile and monied interests are opposed to the measure; and they attach much blame as well to the Council of Revision as to the Assembly and Senate. I have no doubt that if the company carry their schemes into effect, they will contribute powerfully to increase the bloated state of credit which has of late essentially injured us by repeated and heavy bankruptcies." A few weeks later, 5 June, he mentions

[5] M. L. Davis, *Aaron Burr* I, 414; Charles R. King, *Rufus King* II, 597.
[6] Pomerantz, 189; M. L. Davis, *Aaron Burr* I, 415-17.

"a resolution of the Manhattan Company lately announced to set up a new bank." Less than a year later the Manhattan advertised its readiness to insure lives and arrange annuities. Its main interest, however, was its banking business, which its aggressive management and close association with the rising Jeffersonian or Republican party developed rapidly into the largest in the city and the state. The city owned a tenth of its stock and was represented on its board of directors; the state also acquired stock and made the bank its fiscal agent. The charter was perpetual and subjected the company to no restrictions or requirements such as the Bank of New York or other, later competitors were under. In 1832, the attorney general of New York having brought suit against the company on the ground that its charter was invalid and that it was carrying on banking operations without authority, the state Supreme Court upheld the company. Its opinion rested not alone on the original charter, but also on subsequent and repeated recognitions by the state of the company's being engaged in banking.[7]

It was later alleged by the Federalists, for political reasons, that Aaron Burr used the water works merely as a blind to be dropped as soon as his charter was granted. On the contrary, the company set about the business of the water supply at once—it is an evidence of their having got to work that before the year was out they had a freshly dug well in the Lispenard Meadows into which some one threw the dead body of a young woman of easy virtue.* Nevertheless, and not because of the unfortunate young woman only, the Manhattan Company never made as much of its water works as of its bank. It seems to have continued selling water through most of the 19th century and to have continued pumping it after it could no longer be sold, because to have stopped might have been construed a violation of its charter. But this does not signify that Aaron Burr was not in earnest about the water works, even though, as his friend Matthew L. Davis said, "his object was a bank." He probably intended to have both. By contemporary standards there was nothing

---

* Looked back upon, it is an oddity of current relationships that the young man accused of throwing her in had as counsel Aaron Burr and Alexander Hamilton, who defended him successfully. The mystery of her death had the city immensely excited. Pomerantz, 300-01; Wandell and Minnigerode I, 134-45.

[7] Charles R. King, *Rufus King* II, 597-98; III, 34-35; J. S. Davis, *Earlier American Corporations* II, 232; *People* v. *Manhattan Company*, 9 Wendell 351.

grotesque in the union of a water works with a bank: in 1774 a water system had been undertaken in New York, and circulating notes, like bank notes, had been issued to finance it; and this arrangement, which Burr perhaps recalled, was to be repeated in the 19th century scores of times in the establishment of banks to build turn-pikes, canals, railways, and what not. But as subsequent experience was to prove repeatedly, banking could not be successfully combined with other projects. In later cases the banks were broken by the attempt at combination. The Manhattan Company fostered its bank and let the water works go.[8]

Alexander Hamilton, Gulian Verplanck, and John Murray would not knowingly have helped Aaron Burr to get a banking charter more valuable than the Bank of New York's. But that they would help one of the city's legislative representatives in a business-like effort to get the city a fit water supply was to be expected. They were public-spirited, normally susceptible to flattery, and doubtless glad to join magnanimously with political opponents for the city's good and the furtherance of enterprise. Aaron Burr knew how to value, to obtain, and to use their assistance. No better means of obscuring and furthering his purpose can be thought of than his having with him at the start three men so closely associated with the banks to which his own would be a powerful rival. At the same time, what he asked could be done earnestly and in the best faith. Hamilton need only express himself as a citizen of New York and in accordance with conventional views respecting the spheres of government and enterprise. Yet one can readily imagine Colonel Burr's feeling a pleasure not too apparent on the surface as his distinguished political opponent and fellow member of the bar so competently and wholeheartedly raked chestnuts for him from the fire.

And when Mr Hamilton, Federalist leader and sponsor of both the Bank of New York and the Bank of the United States, realized a little later what had really been afoot, he must have ground his teeth. But there would be nothing he could say without advertising Burr's success in taking him in, and the memory of the public disclosure he had been forced to by the Reynolds blackmailing two years before must have doubly deterred him from acknowledging— this time to no purpose whatever—that he had been tricked again,

---

[8] Charles King, *Croton Aqueduct*, 85-88, 95-99, 105, 107, 109; Pomerantz, 285; Harlow, 127.

though less painfully. The episode doubtless contributed, however, to the judgment expressed in his letter to James A. Bayard, 16 January 1801, limning the characters of Mr Jefferson and Colonel Burr and concluding that Mr Jefferson would be the less dangerous of the two as President of the United States. Therein he observed incidentally of Aaron Burr that he "talked perfect Godwinism" and applauded the French Revolution for "unshackling the mind." Further, "I have been present when he had contended against banking systems with earnestness and with the same arguments that Jefferson would use"; and in a footnote he added: "Yet he has lately, by a trick, established a bank—a perfect monster in its principles but a very convenient instrument of *profit* and *influence*."[9]

Aaron Burr's ruse was more than just a trick. It was a minor revolution, economic and political. It illustrates the larger revolution which in the country as a whole was changing the disciplined and restricted economy of the 18th century into the dynamic, complex, *laisser faire* economy of the 19th century. It illustrates the repressive hold that the Federalists, who ten years before had established the central government, were trying to maintain on business and that was driving the party's less patient adherents into the rebellious Republican fold. For the city of New York to have gone on much longer with only the Bank of New York and the office of the Bank of the United States was out of the question. The energy and ambition of its business community were too great. The Federalists had brilliantly advanced business enterprise but could not long dominate it. The party was to linger on, monied and ineffective, while its young men flocked incongruously into Mr Jefferson's Republican ranks and later into General Andrew Jackson's Democratic ones; where they made it part of the destiny of those two popular leaders and enemies of privilege to clear the way for a new, larger, and more powerful class of money-makers than could have existed before enterprise became democratic.

According to Matthew L. Davis, Colonel Burr was "lauded by the Democratic party for his address and they rejoiced in his success."[10] For now they too had a bank and a bigger one than the Federalists. But their rejoicing was impaired, for the Federalists used the Colonel's success to produce his defeat in the elections that followed shortly. They made out the whole thing to have been a

[9] Hamilton (Lodge) x, 415.
[10] M. L. Davis, *Aaron Burr* I, 417.

monstrous deception: a shameful advantage had been drawn from public suffering and a bank chartered under guise of a water works. This overstated the matter far worse than Aaron Burr had understated it. He had gulled Alexander Hamilton and some other Federalists, hurting, however, only their pride. The others he had led pleasantly into temptation. The crucial clause in the water bill was not inconspicuous. It was not buried in a sheltering context but stood out solitarily in its own paragraph. It did not advertise a bank to be sure, but it did indicate something valuable. Colonel Burr wished it to be seen, by the discerning. He had something to sell. Without attracting opposition, it was to his interest to attract subscribers, and Federalists were welcome. He was the promoter, skillfully taking advantage of the city's need of a water supply, of the disposition to think that a business corporation could provide one better than the city government could, of the demand for a Republican bank, and of the growing pressure of wealth for investment in corporate enterprise, whether Republican or Federalist. It happened that his ruse misdirected and delayed development of the city's water supply. But that he could not have intended; he thought, as others did, that banking could be successfully united with public improvements and other enterprises—an idea that continued to be respected among Americans for forty costly years.

But it was not Federalists alone that defeated Burr. They persuaded the Republicans to reject him. "In the city of New York," wrote Jabez Hammond, a contemporary and upstate Republican himself, "it is probable that in 1799 many Republicans voted the Federal ticket in consequence of their dissatisfaction with the manner in which the law granting banking powers to the Manhattan Company had been smuggled through the legislature and for the reason that Colonel Burr, who was confessedly the contriver and the agent who effected that extraordinary measure, was then a candidate." But this ungrateful view did not persist. In 1800 the Republicans triumphed, and Burr became their candidate for Vice President. For, Jabez Hammond explains, the bank was now in operation; instead of being odious and an object to be dreaded, it had "the power of conferring favors and was an object to be courted...."[11] Indeed, the prevailing view of New York Republicans was the following, expressed by James Cheetham in 1804: "It is well known that previous to the incorporation of the Manhattan Com-

[11] Jabez Hammond I, 135.

pany, the Branch Bank and the New York Bank, governed by *federal* gentlemen, were employed in a great measure as *political engines*. A close system of exclusion against those who differed from them on political subjects was adopted and pursued. There were but few active and useful Republicans that could obtain from those banks discount accommodations. . . . The incorporation of the Manhattan Company corrected the evil. All parties are now accommodated."[12]

IV

In 1803 Alexander Hamilton helped organize the fourth bank in New York City, the Merchants Bank—perhaps with some thought of vengeance for his hoodwinking in the matter of the Manhattan. The Republicans now had a majority in the Assembly and on behalf of their Bank of the Manhattan Company refused the Merchants a charter. Hamilton drew up articles of association for the new bank, as he had done for the Bank of New York twenty years before, and as the latter had done, the new one began business without incorporation. Among its organizers were Oliver Wolcott, former Secretary of the Treasury, who became its president, and Isaac Bronson, who was both banker and writer on banking. In order to limit the bank's liability to its "joint stock or property," as if it were a corporation, the articles of agreement made it a condition that no person who should deal with the bank or become its creditor should "on any pretense whatever have recourse against the separate property of any present or future" stockholder. How effective this device might have been I have no idea, but it did not allay the desire of the bank for a corporate charter. The Manhattan Company, however, sought to prevent not its being chartered only but its being left alive. It "would be injurious to the Republican party" because its proprietors were "Federalists and tories." Though a charter was denied the Merchants Bank, accordingly, one was granted the same year, 1803, to the Republican sponsors of the New York State Bank, Albany, which was in a sort of alliance with the Manhattan, and sought its charter on the ground that the Bank of Albany, chartered in 1792, was Federalist and the city needed a Republican bank. The State Bank people also asked for exclusive rights to exploit the salt springs in New York, promising to sell salt for not more than five shillings a bushel. But though

12 Cheetham, 33-34.

they offered to pay for the right, the profits in prospect seemed so exorbitant—the cost of getting the salt out being a tenth of what might be asked for it—that the monopoly was refused, even to such earnest Jeffersonians.[13]

Meanwhile, in New York City, the Manhattan continued pressing for extinction of the Merchants. "At a very numerous and respectable meeting of merchants, traders, and other citizens," 15 March 1804, resolutions were adopted in which the "mischievous tendency" of the Merchants Bank was denounced and its "emitting bills of credit" without the consent of the legislature was declared to be a "dangerous innovation repugnant to the principles of every well regulated state." It was resolved that the bank, "being entirely self-created, is hostile to the security of property." The resolutions were signed by Daniel Ludlow, president of the Manhattan, and by John B. Church, among others. The published list of signers also included Herman Le Roy, president of the Bank of New York, and several others who stated publicly later that they were not at the meeting or consulted about the use of their names. The following month, 11 April 1804, the legislature enacted the restraining law which forbade unincorporated banks to issue notes or to lend. This was the measure enacted in Massachusetts in 1799, which in turn was based on the act of Parliament of 1741 extending the Bubble Act of 1720 to the American colonies.* That extension had sought to prevent *all* paper money issues and like projects of bodies politic inimical to the public welfare; the present enactments sought to prevent issues inimical to the monopoly of the banks already incorporated. The purposes were antithetic, but the statutory vehicle was in substance the same. And its last purpose—that of shielding monopoly—happened to be the same as that the Bubble Act itself seems to have had originally. The suppression of irresponsible note issue was, of course, in the public interest, though that was not its sole motive.[14]

The war on the Merchants Bank was bitter and was bitterly repulsed, both in New York City and in Albany. One judge knocked another down in the state senate. But the bank survived and in 1805 it got a corporate charter, with bribery on its side and despite brib-

---

* One recognizes the old form still—forbidding unauthorized persons to do what corporations are authorized to do—and the old confused effort to establish a clear line between natural persons and artificial persons.

[13] Hubert, 1-5; Jabez Hammond I, 328-29, 332-33.   [14] Hubert, 58-59.

ery on the other.* The Merchants Bank continued in business from 1803 to 1920, having meanwhile surrendered its original charter in 1865 for a national one. In 1920 it was absorbed by the Bank of the Manhattan Company. So the Manhattan, after more than a century, put an end to the Merchants, though in more amiable fashion than at first attempted.[15]

The attack on the Merchants Bank was fairly typical of the way the forces of enterprise dragged the government into their competition and mixed politics with business. James Cheetham, uninhibited newspaper editor, political enemy of Aaron Burr, but now the Manhattan's champion, without a blush called on the legislature to stop the unlawful operations of the Merchants Bank and "protect the chartered banks," particularly the Manhattan. And it is evidence of contemporary feelings if not facts that a friend of the Merchants alleged that a friend of the Manhattan had declared to a committee of the Legislature "that he believed the Merchants Bank to be a political institution which ought to be suppressed; that he was authorized by the Manhattan Company to offer terms more advantageous than any the Merchants Bank had offered or could offer to the State; that he accordingly offered the State 500,000 dollars of Manhattan stock at par, which at a certain advance mentioned by him would, he said be a *douceur* of 150,000 dollars, provided the State would suppress the Merchants Bank; that it was in contemplation to unite the Manhattan Company with the State Bank (Albany) in order to connect the Republican monied interest throughout the State; that the Manhattan Company deserved the countenance of Government and had strong claims to patronage, because it had contributed greatly to the late changes in public affairs and because it was owing to the Manhattan Company that Mr Jefferson had been elevated to the Presidential Chair."[16]

This last statement was presumably suggested by the fact that the Bank of the Manhattan Company had helped substantially to put the Republicans in power in New York in 1800. And by this victory, Jabez Hammond observed, the situation in the other states being balanced, the choice of "electors in favor of Mr Jefferson was

---

* Bribes were effected by arranging for legislators to acquire stock at a low price and then have it taken off their hands at a premium.

15 Dillistin, 50-51.
16 Cheetham, 34; "Spectator" (Woolny), *Concise View*, 11-12.

rendered certain and his election to the Presidency was equally certain." Down in Virginia too, John Taylor of Caroline said the press mentioned the possibility that Jefferson's election might have been determined by the Manhattan. Moreover, as it happens, one of Mr Jefferson's first federal appointments, when he became President in 1801, was to make the Manhattan's president, Daniel Ludlow, navy agent in New York, though a capitalist, a banker, and a Tory.[17]

The efforts of the Manhattan Bank to get the Merchants Bank suppressed, which were themselves skirmishes in a greater and longer-lived conflict of interests respectively Hamiltonian and Jeffersonian, were still going on in July 1804 when Alexander Hamilton was killed in his duel with Aaron Burr.

V

In 1810 to 1811—the charter of the Bank of the United States being about to expire—the New York legislature chartered six banks, and in 1812 it chartered four more; which, however, relative to what other states were doing was conservative. One of the charters of 1811 was enacted for the Mechanics and Farmers Bank of Albany and required that a majority of the directors be "practical mechanics." The next year the charter "incorporating the New York Manufacturing Company with banking privileges" recited the following considerations: "Anthony Post, John L. Van Kleeck, Samuel Whittemore and Isaac Marquend, together with other citizens . . . have associated together for the laudable purpose of establishing and perfecting the manufacturing of iron and brass wire and of cotton and wool cards . . . and have presented a petition setting forth the importance of such establishment, . . . the difficulty of inducing persons to invest their money in untried enterprizes, however important to the general welfare, and the necessity of allowing them the privilege of annexing a banking institution to their establishment, to enable them to carry the same into effect." Accordingly these enterprising makers of iron and brass wire and cotton and wool cards were made a body corporate, with power to open a banking office and to employ part of their capital "not exceeding $700,000 in the whole, in the ordinary business of banking." Five years later, their banking business was acquired by the Phoenix Bank, which also had been chartered in 1812.

[17] Jabez Hammond I, 134; Pomerantz, 92; Taylor of Caroline, *Principles and Policy*, 316.

One of the three other banks incorporated in 1812 was organized by the New York stockholders of the Bank of the United States, who, wishing to obtain a charter under which the business of the Bank's New York office might be continued, applied for incorporation as the Bank of America. The capital would be $6,000,000, including $5,000,000 of Bank of the United States stock. It would be the largest bank in the States and a gain for New York over Philadelphia in the financial and commercial rivalry that had arisen between them. Being mainly Federalist and possessed of so much capital, the bank was sure to be opposed both by the Republicans, who had a legislative majority, and by the existing banks in New York. Accordingly an expert and influential lobby was organized in its behalf, its managers being David Thomas, recently ousted state treasurer, and Solomon Southwick, state printer, president of the Mechanics and Farmers Bank of Albany, and publisher of the Albany *Register*. Both men were Republican but of the more pliable sort. They took on a staff of workers, mostly "low and worthless fellows," including an Irish preacher named John Martin, who were to work upon the legislators. In the same tenor, the charter engaged the bank to pay the state a bonus of $600,000, of which $400,000 was for the use and encouragement of common schools, $100,000 for roads and navigation, and $100,000 for the encouragement of literature. The bank was also to lend "the people of the state" $2,000,000, "to be repaid as provided by law."[18]

The Governor, Daniel D. Tompkins, was an orthodox Republican, and addressing the legislature in January 1812, he had urgently protested against establishment of more banks. With those now proposed, he said, bank notes "to the enormous sum of $94,000,-000—a sum at least sixteen times greater than the whole specie capital of the state"—might be issued; "a failure to discharge such a debt will produce universal bankruptcy and ruin."[19]

But the bank's friends were strong and determined. They obstructed other legislation and deliberately held up a nomination of DeWitt Clinton, the Lieutenant Governor, for the Presidency of the United States. They got the bank measure through the lower house, in the midst of charges of bribery, and it went on to the Senate, where passage was already assured, when Governor Tompkins, 27 March 1812, prorogued the legislature till 21 May, prac-

[18] Jabez Hammond I, 290-91, 299-301, 306-09.
[19] New York State, *Messages from the Governors* II, 696.

tically the maximum period for which he had authority. He recalled, in communicating his order to the legislature, that at a previous session it had been "ascertained beyond any reasonable doubt that corrupt inducements were held out to members of the legislature" to vote for a bank charter (he may have meant the Merchants Bank); that at the latest session, according to "very general public opinion," there had been similar attempts on behalf of the Jersey Bank of New York City; and that now, "It appears, by the journals of the Assembly that attempts have been made to corrupt by bribes four members of that body . . . ; and it also appears by the journals of the Senate that an improper attempt has been made to influence one of the senators." On these grounds, because "the morals, the honor, and the dignity of the state require it," and in order "that time may be afforded for reflection," the sitting was prorogued. The Governor also expatiated upon the evils of banking in general and upon the particular evil that the stockholders of the Bank of America would include many foreign investors.[20]

When the message of prorogation was read in the Assembly, "a scene of confusion and uproar ensued and, for a few moments, outrage and violence." The power to prorogue, under the state constitution of 1777, which was still in force, "had been considered as a remnant of royal prerogative" held over from the colonial régime— when the British Governors represented the King and their frequent prorogations had been an exasperating incident of the friction between colonies and mother country—and hence unsuitable in American government.[21]

But despite the Governor's drastic effort, the charter was enacted when the sitting resumed. Both leaders of the bank's lobby, David Thomas and Solomon Southwick, were indicted and tried for bribery but acquitted. Their humbler assistant, John Martin, the preacher, was sent to the penitentiary. The bank itself flourished; its first president was Oliver Wolcott, former Secretary of the Treasury and more lately president of the Merchants Bank. For a century or more the Bank of America was among the leading banks of New York; about 1928 it passed into the control of Mr A. P. Giannini of San Francisco; in 1931 it was absorbed by the National City Bank.*

* Since this writing the National City, by merger with the First National, has become the First National City Bank.

[20] Jabez Hammond I, 309-10; New York State, *Messages from the Governors* II, 708-12.
[21] Jabez Hammond I, 309.

The latter also, now one of Wall Street's oldest and largest banks, was incorporated in 1812 a fortnight before the Bank of America but with no great forensic to-do. The immense stir over the Bank of America seems to have been caused basically by its large size and its being the local successor to the Bank of the United States, which was "Federalist and British." The last was especially bad because war with Britain was brewing—it was declared later in the same month the Bank of America was chartered, June 1812.

VI

I have narrated at length what happened in New York City because the developments there were of unusual importance, in both a political and an economic sense. The New York City business community, as I have said, was already foremost in the country in energy, originality, and aggressiveness. Its political ties within the state were powerful and were becoming so in Washington. It still had much to win from its rivals, especially Philadelphia, but it was on its way. Moreover what happened in New York displays the forces and interests that were at work throughout the economy. The resources of America that for three centuries had lain in desuetude for lack of industrial techniques were now acquiring values that filled men with excitement. To exploit them money was needed, and to provide money there must be banks. So banks there were, everywhere.

In the following paragraphs, I attempt brief indications of the early establishment of banks in other states than New York. They are based meagrely on doubtfully accurate information; but I think they have nevertheless some illustrative use. The general authorities on the subject are Sumner and Knox. I have departed from their inaccuracies where access to more adequate accounts made it possible to do so; but still my record is a compromise between the need of some general attention to origins and the practical impediments to my making—and presenting—fresh reviews of the subject in state after state.

In Pennsylvania the Bank of North America and the Bank of the United States had been alone till 1793, when largely through the efforts of Albert Gallatin, then a Republican member of the legislature from the mountainous southwestern part of the state, the Bank of Pennsylvania had been established. It followed the model of the Bank of the United States. A third of its capital was owned by the state, and in time it had offices in Harrisburg, Reading, Easton, Lancaster, and Pittsburgh, besides Philadelphia. It was the largest bank in the country under state charter. Gallatin said that this and similar investments later enabled the state "to defray out of the dividends all the expenses of government without any direct tax during the forty ensuing years and till the adoption of the system of internal improvement, which required new resources."[22]

In 1803 the Philadelphia Bank was organized "on a plan nearly similar to the Merchants Bank in New York," its articles of association being identical with those prepared for the latter by Alexander Hamilton. It was also involved at once in a feud with the Bank of Pennsylvania like that in New York between the Merchants and the Manhattan. The following year, 1804, after customary hostilities in and out of the legislature, it was given a corporate charter. The Farmers and Mechanics Bank was next incorporated, in 1809, with a charter, significant of the times, stipulating that a majority of the directors be "farmers, mechanics, and manufacturers actually employed in their respective professions." The state took stock in both these banks. In 1811 the legislature refused a charter for the expiring Bank of the United States, and Stephen Girard set up as a banker in the latter's place without one. In 1813 the legislature passed a bill authorizing incorporation of twenty-five new banks, and then after the Governor vetoed it, passed another in 1814, over a second veto, authorizing incorporation of forty-one. This would mean a seven-fold increase at one stroke, there being six chartered banks already. Within two years, thirty-five of the forty-one were already in business. In 1819 the inflation that arose impelled a committee of the Pennsylvania Senate to aver that the act of 1814 authorizing this multiplication of banks had inflicted a more disastrous evil than the commonwealth had ever experienced before— a judgment that the Governor had anticipated in his veto and that Gallatin much later confirmed.[23]

In Massachusetts the Bank of Massachusetts had the field to itself from 1784 to 1792, when the Union Bank was chartered and the Boston office of the Bank of the United States was established. One-third of the Union Bank's capital was subscribed by the state government, which was also authorized to take stock in several banks subsequently organized, particularly the Boston Bank, 1803,

[22] Henry Adams, *Gallatin*, 86; J. S. Davis, *Earlier American Corporations* II, 95.
[23] Gallatin III, 292; Wainwright, 6-13.

and the State Bank, 1811. The latter purchased and occupied the Boston quarters of the Bank of the United States upon expiration of the latter's charter in that year. Its attachment to the principles of Mr Jefferson and the administration of Mr Madison has been mentioned. The three older banks were in the hands of Federalists, who used them, the State Bank's president told Secretary Gallatin, "to check the growth of Republicanism and thus indirectly to weaken the constituted authorities of the nation." The State Bank's establishment stirred up a local war such as already had followed establishment of the Merchants Bank, New York, and the Philadelphia Bank. It was another of the victories the newer set of business men, working through the party of Jefferson, were winning over the conservatives who had not yet left the dying Federalist party.[24]

In 1806 the Vermont legislature incorporated the Vermont State Bank, which was owned wholly by the state and was apparently without specific capital. Earlier efforts to enact bank charters had been resisted by the hard-money conservatives, but when they had to yield because their jurisdiction became over-run with notes of banks in other states, they determined to supersede private enterprise by putting Vermont itself into banking. The bank received all the funds of the state on deposit, and the state was fully pledged to redeem the bank's obligations to other depositors. The directors were chosen by the legislature and were required to report to it annually. The bank's officers had power to issue executions directly on the property of delinquent debtors, and the constitutionality of this power was later affirmed by the state's Supreme Court. The bank had offices in Burlington, Westminster, Woodstock, and Middlebury. Despite its legal powers, which were virtually those of the state itself, the bank's losses were so great and its credit was so much impaired that it had to close about 1812; it cost the state about $200,000 to discharge its obligation to other creditors, who were understood to have been paid in full. Vermont was an agrarian community and its bank, which unlike most of its contemporaries at the time of its establishment in 1806 was not mercantile, seems to have been a prototype of the bank monopolies that flourished later in the agrarian West.[25]

In Rhode Island the officers of the Providence Bank, 1791, had

24 Stetson, 19.
25 25th Congress, 2d Session, HR 79, 108-10; Knox, *History of Banking*, 354-55.

a power over the property of delinquent debtors similar to that granted officers of the Vermont State Bank, but instead of issuing executions themselves they called on the clerks of courts to issue them. In Virginia in 1793 the Bank of Alexandria was authorized in somewhat the same spirit to sue delinquent debtors on ten days' notice, and the debtor was allowed no appeal from a judgment rendered against him. The quasi-governmental nature of banking was also recognized in Delaware, where in 1807 the Farmers Bank of the State of Delaware was established. This bank is still in business. It is perhaps the oldest in the States still operating under its original charter and with only minor changes in form of organization. Its charter follows closely that of the Bank of the United States. The legislature made it "a bank for the state of Delaware," which became permanently its most important stockholder. It established offices in Dover, where its headquarters were, and in New Castle, Georgetown, and eventually Wilmington, all of which but the New Castle office are still in operation, with others of more recent establishment. According to a practice then common, separate capital was allocated to each branch, and each branch manager was designated a president. The state legislature appointed—as it still does—three of the directors of the principal board of the bank and three directors of each branch board. During its first half century the Farmers Bank of Delaware had few competitors. Although banks have become more numerous in the state, all have been incorporated by special legislative act as in the early days of the republic; banking legislation has been little changed from what it was over a century ago and there is no general banking law.[26]

In Maryland banking was represented in 1792 by the Bank of Maryland and an office of the Bank of the United States, both in Baltimore. In 1795, in lieu of enlarging the capital of the Bank of Maryland, the legislature chartered the Bank of Baltimore, of which the Bank of Maryland became a stockholder. In 1804 the Union Bank, in Baltimore, and the Farmers Bank, in Annapolis, with offices later in Easton and Frederick, were both chartered. The two had been formed as unincorporated banking institutions and had to unite their forces against those of the two older banks before they could obtain charters. The state was authorized by law to hold stock in practically all banks and was in fact a stockholder in several, all, however, established before 1811. In 1804 the Farmers

[26] Knox, *History of Banking*, 371, 527; *Munroe*, 145-46.

Bank began paying interest on deposits—four per cent on time and three per cent on demand; since it lent chiefly to farmers, its practice belonged in the category of savings banking and illustrates the growing tendency of incorporated banks to do other than commercial lending. There were four banks in Baltimore and two elsewhere in Maryland by 1810, at which time the number in Baltimore was doubled and one was set up in Elkton—the Bank of the United States having been marked for death and the Maryland delegation in Congress being one of the most hostile to it. Baltimore then had twice as many banks as any other city in the country, but the increase stopped in 1813 with assurance from the Maryland legislature that for twenty years no more would be incorporated. In return the favored banks furnished the money to complete a turnpike to Cumberland in western Maryland.[27]

In 1792 the Bank of South Carolina was organized, but it was not chartered till 1801; in 1802 the State Bank of South Carolina was chartered; and in 1812, to augment the confusion, the Bank of the State of South Carolina, the faith of the state being pledged to support it and make good all its liabilities. Assets were transferred to it by the state, it became the state's depository and fiscal agent, and "its profits were employed in paying the interest and in reducing the principal of the public debt." It was in fact the state itself engaged in banking. It appears to have had no branches. In 1809 and 1810, respectively, the Union Bank and the Planters and Mechanics Bank were incorporated. For more than twenty years there were these five banks in South Carolina, not counting the Charleston office of the Bank of the United States, which was taken over in 1835 by the Bank of Charleston, newly organized.* All had their head offices in Charleston. South Carolina had no serious banking difficulties and no bank failures till the collapse of the Confederate authority in 1865.[28]

In 1802 incorporated banking made its first appearance beyond the Alleghenies, almost at the heels of the retreating red man.

---

* The Charleston office of the first Bank of the United States became the Charleston City Hall. The office of the second Bank is now the head office of the South Carolina National Bank; with its furnishings of the 1820's and '30's, it is probably the oldest banking office in the United States still in active use as such.

[27] Bryan, 20-25, 30, 38; Knox, *History of Banking*, 469ff, 481-84; ASP, Finance II, 838.
[28] Knox, *History of Banking*, 563-65.

Hitherto it had belonged to the cities of the seaboard. But even in the West it was commerce still that instigated it. The new bank was set up in Lexington, Kentucky, then the principal town beyond the mountains. Though Lexington had a population of less than 1,800 in the year 1800, it was larger nevertheless than Pittsburgh or Cincinnati, and other cities that now surpass it did not even exist. But the people of Kentucky being agrarian, it was evidently apprehended by the monied aristocrats of the community that a charter for a bank would be too hard to get. So incorporation was requested for the Kentucky Insurance Company instead, with a charter in which mention of a bank or of banking was omitted, though language otherwise common to American bank charters and as old as the Bank of England's occurred in it, including the authorization to lend and to issue notes. The charter was approved, 16 December 1802, and the company, which was supposed only to insure river boats and cargoes, began also to do an open and profitable discount business. Its notes came into general use and its first year's dividend was almost twenty per cent. Anyone who read the charter with half an eye open could not help seeing that it authorized banking in effect, whether or not in word; the purpose was more transparent than it had been in Aaron Burr's Manhattan charter three years before back in New York. Yet an outcry arose which indicated that the promoters had not been mistaken in assuming that Kentuckians disliked banks. Felix Grundy, then an ambitious young frontier politician, at once made capital of the legislative trick, though he had participated in it; and by thundering against it and against banks in general, he got re-elected to the legislature. Henry Clay, his political rival, also young and ambitious, was at the same time re-elected as a champion of the bank, in which he was a stockholder. Both men were vociferous Jeffersonians. In order to cut the ground from under their enemies' feet, the bank's friends proposed an amendment to its charter which should limit its issues of notes. Felix Grundy fought the amendment too, for he had promised to kill the bank, not domesticate it, and he and Clay went through an oratorical performance that quite enchanted their frontier constituencies. Clay won the first draw but lost the second, at the next session, 1805, when Grundy moved to repeal the charter on the familiar agrarian grounds that the bank was monopolistic, aristocratic, privileged, and thoroughly inimical to free institutions. He and Clay harangued for two days, and then the charter was repealed by a heavy majority. But the Governor vetoed the repeal, quite unexpectedly, and Henry Clay by an ingenious counter-measure divided his opponents and contrived to keep the veto from being overridden.[29]

The dust of this combat had barely settled when the legislature was confronted at the same session by a bill to incorporate a State Bank of Kentucky, in which the state was to own half the stock. This measure Felix Grundy supported and Henry Clay attacked, to the confusion of other legislators and the populace. It failed to pass at first, but at a later session, December 1806, it was enacted; Henry Clay, notwithstanding his earlier stand, became one of the bank's directors; and five years later, as a United States Senator, he became a major agent in ending the career of the Bank of the United States. The Bank of Kentucky appears to have obtained a monopoly of Kentucky banking, which it held till January 1818, when the state, in one act, incorporated forty new banks.

Meanwhile during the furor over the Kentucky Insurance Company and about four months after its incorporation, the Miami Exporting Company of Cincinnati had been chartered by the Ohio legislature in April 1803, ostensibly for the transport of farm products to New Orleans. Like the Manhattan Company in New York, it had a charter which made no mention of banking, but did authorize the corporation's president and directors to "establish such correspondences, make such shipments, and dispose of the funds of the company in such manner as they shall judge most advantageous to the stockholders." The president and directors needed no more authority than that to go into banking, which they did at once, as their neighbor, the Kentucky Insurance Company, had done. Thereafter banks were established as banks, and by 1812 there were about eight in the state.

VII

Three classes of banks are discernible in the period so far covered. One is the "money bank" of the commercial centers where capital could be paid in specie and assets comprised short-term loans to merchants. One was the bank established in communities where agricultural interests predominated, where specie capital was sparse, and where in consequence the credit of the state was the bank's principal or only capital. Such were the Bank of Vermont and the

29 Mayo, 54, 158ff; Parks, 21ff.

Bank of the State of South Carolina. A third class of bank combined banking and some other activity, either to conceal the banking function from hostile legislators who were being asked for a charter, or because the combination was expected to be profitable, or for both reasons. Concealment very soon proved unnecessary. It was resorted to only in the brief period around 1800 when the opposition was strong but could easily be taken in; thereafter it was either unnecessary or futile. Belief in the usefulness of combinations increased, however. A factory, or canal, or some years later a railway, if combined with a bank, could be financed by the money created by the latter; construction was paid for by the notes of the bank and the notes were backed by the works constructed.

Banks of this sort proved to be impracticable. Banks owned or controlled by states sometimes succeeded and sometimes not. The fact of governmental interest too often meant inefficiency, unsoundness, and failure, as in the case of the Bank of Vermont; but no less often, as in the case of the Bank of the State of South Carolina, such banks were ably managed, successful, and long-lived. Commercial banks, too, might be good or bad, depending on the honesty, ability, and strength of the owners and managers. But in the long run it was this class of bank that predominated in American banking, the role of government becoming supervisory rather than proprietary.

CHAPTER 7

Failures and Restraints

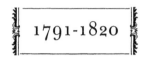

1791-1820

I. The Farmers Exchange Bank of Rhode Island — II. Redemption — III. Restraints — IV. *Laisser faire* — V. Reserve requirements — VI. Functions — VII. Friends and enemies

I

TILL 1809 no failures had occurred among American banks, which were better managed, on the whole, than their intercourse with the powers of political darkness from time to time would lead one to expect. But in the early spring of 1809, the failure of the Farmers Exchange Bank, Glocester, Rhode Island, made up for all the respectability American banks had displayed. Glocester, a wooded township in northwestern Rhode Island, has now about 2,500 inhabitants. In 1800 it had some 4,000.

The Farmers Exchange Bank was incorporated in February 1804, with an authorized capital of $100,000, and from the first, according to a legislative report of 1809, it was conducted, "as the perplexed and confused state of the books sufficiently evinces, negligently and unskillfully."* It was a sort of musical comedy bank. The directors got the use of some specie, left it in the bank for a few days in deference to the expectation that they pay for their shares of the bank's capital with real money, and then replaced it with their promissory notes. This was not unusual. Objectively it was what the federal government had done when it paid for its shares in the Bank of the United States. The directors later acquired more shares from owners who had given the bank promissory notes for them, and they paid for these acquisitions by returning the notes to the makers. In April 1805 they authorized one of their number, Daniel Tourtillot, to take out of the bank the sum of

* My account is condensed from the Rhode Island Assembly's committee Report, March 1809, especially pages 8, 30-39; for access to it I am particularly obliged to Miss Grace M. Sherwood, librarian, the Rhode Island State Library, Providence.

$2,500—he actually took $2,875—and carry the same to Hartford and lay it out in corn and rye to be fetched to some market in Rhode Island and sold for the profit of the directors in common. The directors never declared any certain dividend of the profits of the bank but once a year paid interest to the stockholders at the rate generally of eight per cent on the amount of the latter's stock; and the residue, amounting in some years to $130 each, they divided amongst themselves. In March 1808 they had notes circulating to the amount of $22,514 and specie on hand of $380.50.

Their bank had greater possibilities than this, however, and attracted the interest of an imaginative financier of Boston, Andrew Dexter, jun., formerly of Providence. Dexter was the proprietor of the Boston Exchange Office, incorporated in 1804. Its original purpose, which was to buy out-of-town bank notes at a discount and demand payment of them at face value, was very useful, for it tended to restrain inflation and check the depreciation of circulating notes. Andrew Dexter's scheme was to reverse the machinery, using it to delay, not expedite, the collection of notes. He got the Glocester Bank by arranging that the eleven directors whose shares he acquired be paid by a distribution to them of assets of the bank, including the promissory notes with which they had themselves "paid" for their stock. For him to buy the bank with the bank's own assets presumably seemed proper on the ground that since the bank was his what it owned was his too. On like terms he became also the bank's chief debtor. He "was furnished with as much money as he thought proper to demand and prescribed his own terms as to the security he gave, the rate of interest, and the time and manner of payment." According to the written terms on which he borrowed, he should "not be called upon to make payment until he thinks proper, he being the principal stockholder and best knowing when it will be proper to pay." He took with him to Boston the dies with which the bank's notes were imprinted and thereafter kept them, having notes struck off as he pleased by printers in Newburyport. The only brake upon his operation was the necessity of sending the notes to Glocester to be signed, which took time. But as soon as he received them thence, he sold them for what he could. There were speculators always looking for cheap money either to retail or pick up bargains with, and mostly he exchanged what he had for other banks' notes. Cultivating a practice that became more and more common, he sought to send the notes of his own bank as far as possible, so that they could not be returned by their recipients for redemption; and to this end he seems to have controlled also the Berkshire Bank in Pittsfield, Massachusetts, sending Pittsfield notes to Glocester and Glocester notes to Pittsfield. Toward the end he was achieving a still better arrangement which enabled him to exchange notes with a bank in Marietta, Ohio. Noteholders who found their way to Glocester and demanded redemption were given drafts on him in Boston, payable weeks hence, or otherwise put off, in the manner described in the following letter of instructions, 21 May 1808, to William Colwell, the bank's cashier:

"I take the liberty to mention some ideas which myself and friends have respecting the manner of managing the concerns of the bank. The general rule should undoubtedly be to pay punctually; but to this there are important exceptions, such as when we are run upon by brokers or any persons whatever merely for the purpose of making a profit out of the injury and loss of the bank. These ought to be paid only by drafts on the Exchange Office, at forty days sight. The Providence banks should, in my opinion, be plagued as much as possible, by detaining them as long as it will naturally take to count out all kinds of specie change, intermixed, in the most deliberate manner. The change is very important and ought to be husbanded as much as possible. I hope you will have the goodness to remember never to pay it away except where the intention is to plague or delay the person."

Colwell, a long-suffering Quaker, was paid a salary of $400 a year. His chief labor was the signing of bank notes, which were of small denominations, because small notes stayed out longest, and the smaller they were, the more he had to prepare. They were signed mostly at night in order that no one might see the excessively large number of them. "I wish you to employ yourself constantly in signing bills," Dexter wrote him, "except during the time you are naturally in the bank. I should conceive you might write in the day time as well as night, provided you shut yourself up between the bank hours in your private chamber, letting no one know or suspect your business." The poor man evidently reached the point of breakdown from having to spend his nights signing notes and his days evading payment of them but promised to "bear my heavy load without murmur." The president of the bank, Judge John Harris, helped when he could, but his court duties seem to have taken too much time. Colwell wrote as follows 12 December 1808: "Thy letter

with bills, etc., I have this moment received. The president will be
in Boston to-day. The bills I shall sign as fast as I can, but I think
it will be best at present to do it as privately as possible, mostly in
the evening. I believe I can finish fifty thousand a week. Thou wilt
have a full opportunity to discourse with Judge Harris and Fair-
banks on the subject; and be assured I shall be ready to do whatever shall be thought most beneficial to our institution."

Dexter was dissatisfied. "I am sorry you have signed no more
bills," he wrote from Boston a week later, "and beg you to sign at
least twice as many more during the next week. I wish you would
work day and night so as to sign if possible $20,000 a day. Have the
goodness to mention it to the president that he may do the same."
Dexter himself was busy making Glocester and Pittsfield hold each
other up. Pittsfield would be kept alive for a time with transfusions
of Glocester's bills and then transfusions from Pittsfield would be
needed to resuscitate Glocester. When it was the latter's turn to be
saved, Dexter wrote to his miserable cashier not to lose courage but
sign more bills. "Merchants are advertising to take Glocester bills
at par for goods," he assured him. "Many persons of property and
respectability have offered to assist in every way possible to defeat
the villainous combination of men who are considered to be perfectly contemptible in their manner and character"—these villains
being bill-holders who demanded specie. But with more bills, Dexter
said, "I can be certain, through means of one or two banks and my
friends to raise (I trust) immense funds. The greater part of the
bills I have heretofore received were sent to distant parts and disposed of in such manner that they can not return to injure the
bank." But he must know "what hour" the bills will be ready; "what
hour," he repeats and again repeats. How faithfully his cashier
worked, the fate of banks hanging on his quill, was reported by a
stockholder in the bank, who deposed as follows for the legislature's
committee of enquiry: "That the deponent's son lives in the house
where the bank was kept and keeps a store there, in which the
deponent is interested; that the deponent was there the greater part
of the time the winter passed and lodged in said house about one
half the time; that the room in which the deponent slept was adjoining the room in which the business of the bank was transacted; that
persons were frequently in the bank in the night time and there
continued until the deponent went to sleep; that they sometimes
came into the bank as early as two o'clock in the morning and very
often at four o'clock."

But nothing of all this availed. "Our situation becomes every day more disagreeable," the exhausted Mr Colwell wrote. "The discontent and irritation among the people is very great. We have been sued to-day, and our bank is the common topick of conversation through the country. . . . Our specie is now reduced to less than $200. . . . I do not think it will be the least injury to the bank to shut it up for a day or two." Again he was bid not to lose heart, but it was too late. He and a director removed the bank's books, note portfolio, and cash, amounting to $86.46, lest they be seized by the officers of the law; and when the legislative committee arrived, the bank itself was gone.

The misfortune was reported in the Providence *Gazette*, 25 March 1809; and in the same issue some lands in Glocester were advertised for sale with the sardonic suggestion that they were "extremely eligible for speculators, especially in bank stock." But to many persons, perhaps most, the episode was not funny, nor were the operations of Andrew Dexter, jun., less portentous than those of John Law. America now had a bubble of her own to match the Mississippi and the South Sea with. The *Gazette* averred that the directors and managers of the bank "have practiced a system of fraud beyond which the ingenuity and dishonesty of man can not go." In Congress during the debates of the next year or so on rechartering the Bank of the United States, Representative William A. Burwell of Virginia told how the Rhode Island bank had "issued notes to the amount of $800,000 upon a capital of $45." Representative Joseph Desha of Kentucky put it less delicately: the bank, he said, "when it was ripped up, had but some odds of forty dollars in its vaults." The episode was typical of banking, people believed, and twenty-five years later William Gouge in his widely read denunciation of banks retold the story as awful evidence of what cunning men could do when they had a corporate charter. It exhibited the corporation as a convenient *alter ego* which multiplied human capacities for mischief. One wonders not that such conclusions were drawn but that the corporation survived them.[1]

One evening in Paris in 1813, Albert Gallatin, then American Minister to France, took occasion to counsel his sixteen-year-old son, James, who served as his secretary, about his future. The son set down his father's counsel in his diary as follows: "To-day, after all correspondence was terminated, father began to talk to me. He

[1] Clarke and Hall, 144, 185; Gouge, Part II, 50; Mackenzie, *Butler and Hoyt*, 15-24.

warned me as to my future life—that is, if I decided to remain in America—never, above all things, to forget my birth and the duties that birth brings—never to do anything to dishonor a name which for centuries had never borne a stain—always to remember that true nobility was simplicity—always to be civil, particularly to those who were not my equal—to guard against the horde of adventurers who were certain to swarm to America—that the country was so vast that the hidden wealth in minerals, etc., etc., must be enormous—adventurers would come with the lust of gold—men without scruples or conscience or education—that there would be terrible corruption—never to mix myself with any man who did not carry on his business or speculations in an honest manner— far better to die poor and honoured than to sully my name—that the country would suffer for years from corruption—immense fortunes would be made and lost and men of evil repute would, on account of the power of their money, keep corruption and dishonesty afloat."[2]

No one could judge his adopted country better than Albert Gallatin, who knew its wildernesses and its cities, and its rich and its poor, its farmers, speculators, merchants, politicians, and statesmen. He had come to it in youth, with ardors raised by Rousseau and perceptions refined by Voltaire. He now had behind him a noble public career. And he must long before have abandoned whatever dreams he may have cherished of a Jeffersonian paradise in America. Like Mr Gallatin, most sensitive and thoughtful men were shocked by the harshness of the Industrial Revolution and the fierce spirit of enterprise begot by it. That spirit often merged into cupidity and chicane; in their judgment it usually did. But the good banks and the good business men made little noise. The rash, the ignorant, the rapacious, and the vicious made much. Sound bankers threaded their honest, conservative way through the tumult of expansion, speculation, and misbehavior. In Wall Street, for twenty years more, Mr Gallatin himself was to do it. There is concrete evidence of honesty and conservatism in the number of banks that survived not only the difficulties of that period but those of all subsequent ones to the present and established the striking fact of continuity in an economy of dynamism and vicissitude.

Professor Sumner was less indulgent than I am. Speaking of this early period, up to 1812, which seems to me to be characterized by

---

[2] James Gallatin, *Diary*, 5-6.

an admirable banking practice, the Glocester episode being unique, Professor Sumner acknowledged that some earlier writers had referred to "the period before the second war as one in which there had been some sound, honorable, and high principled banking"; and then he sourly declared, "Investigation does not verify this . . . these earlier bankers invented nearly all the later abuses, and they set about the exploitation of them with less reserve than their successors." This seems to me an extraordinary judgment, particularly in its anachronism and its neglect of the tentative and experimental nature of evolution.[3]

II

In June 1809, a matter of two or three months after the Dexter affair, the Massachusetts legislature imposed a penalty of two per cent a month on notes that debtor banks failed or refused to redeem. The law was upheld by the courts, which in March 1812 found it "equitable and wise"; the failure of banks to be punctual in meeting demands "now that bank bills form almost exclusively the circulating medium of the country is a public inconvenience of great extent and introductive of much mischief." Mr Gallatin considered the Massachusetts law one of the most efficient in restraining improvident issues. Daniel Webster, when a representative from Massachusetts, got a similar penalty included in 1816 in the charter of the new Bank of the United States, where it applied to payment of deposits as well as notes. The same month, April 1816, New York began, with the Bank of Niagara and the Bank of Jefferson County, to include in all charters a stipulation that the charters would be forfeited upon failure of the banks to redeem their notes. Pennsylvania and Maryland began enacting similar conditions early in 1819. But such stipulations were not effective.[4]

According to William Gouge, the Bank of Darien, Georgia, set up as a barrier to payment of its obligations the requirement that each person presenting its notes for redemption swear, at the bank, before a justice of the peace, in the presence of five directors and the cashier, that he was owner of the notes and not agent for another, besides which he had to pay a charge of $1.37½; and this had to be done separately as to each note presented.[5]

[3] Sumner, *History of Banking*, 37.
[4] Gallatin III, 318; *Brown* v. *Penobscot Bank*, 8 Massachusetts Reports 449; Knox, *History of Banking*, 398, 448, 488; Clarke and Hall, 673-74.
[5] Gouge, Part II, 141.

Individual creditors who sued to recover on unredeemed notes as on any unpaid debt seldom if ever gained anything. Stephen Girard's bank was sued in 1814 for refusing to redeem its notes during general suspension, but the plaintiffs seem to have sought to harass Mr Girard rather than obtain payment—the amounts were small, one claimant, an umbrella-maker, suing for $25—and to have been discouraged by the firmness of his defense. Isaac Bronson, president of the Bank of Bridgeport, Connecticut, and a prominent capitalist in his day, sued in 1815, also during general suspension, for payment of notes of New York banks that he held. He seems to have got no satisfaction, but he got some prolix and extravagant abuse in the New York press for a course that was "unjust, impolitic, and odious." It was said in the New York *National Advocate*, 1 November 1815, that "any attempt at present or during the approaching winter to curtail discounts with a view to the payment of specie is fraught with misery and ruin to every class of society who depend upon their enterprise and industry for their prosperity in life."[6]

In Windsor County, Vermont, in 1808 an indictment was sought against a man who held notes of the Vermont State Bank and demanded specie for them. It alleged that Jireh Durkee, of Boston, "being an evil-disposed person and not minding to get his living by truth and honest labor but contriving how he might injuriously obtain . . . money to support his idle and profligate way of life and diminish and destroy the resources of the state of Vermont and rendering it difficult and impossible for the good citizens thereof to obtain money," had presented $9,000 of the bank's notes at the Woodstock office and obliged the bank to pay them. The effect of such action, which would enable Durkee "to realize a filthy gain," said the complaint, was to prevent the bank from making loans to "good citizens."[7]

Bank note redemption under pressure presented a dilemma that was long unsolved. The issue of notes was an exercise of the common law right to borrow and go into debt. It was the undisputed expectation, therefore, that bank notes, like other promissory notes, would be paid. That was the view in the courts and out. A bank note was not money but a promise to pay money; payment was redemption of the promise. It was also perceived that if the notes were not paid

6 McMaster, *Girard* II, 281-84; "Aurelius," New York *National Advocate*, 26 October 1815; Venit, *JEH*, V (1945), 202.

7 25th Congress, 2d Session, HR 79, 111.

they depreciated in value as circulating media. So there were two important reasons why they should be paid.

But on the other hand a bank's payment of its notes involved a loss of specie reserves and an impairment of its power to lend. Local borrowers could readily see that—especially if the payment had to be made to strangers who came into town with valises full of notes, which had been acquired systematically at a discount, and who purposed carrying away a corresponding amount of gold and silver. That sort of thing was deflationary. It would frustrate local enterprise.

Public opinion wavered in confusion before the two evils, finding each in turn the worse. Should bank notes be kept at par or should bank credit be restricted? Few people could be consistent in all circumstances, for the two things seemed hopelessly incompatible. Sometimes it was dear money that troubled them and sometimes it was cheap money. The Maryland legislature, 15 February 1819, enacted a law against banks that refused to redeem their notes. Two days later, 17 February 1819, it enacted another against persons who demanded that they redeem them. The first was entitled an act "to compel . . . banks to pay specie for their notes, or forfeit their charters"; the second, an act "to relieve the people of this state, as far as practicable, from the evil arising from the demands made on the banks of this state for gold and silver by brokers"—it forbade traffic in notes for less than their nominal value. Pennsylvania in a similar law, March 1819, made banks liable to forfeiture of their charters upon refusal to redeem their notes—except for brokers or dealers "habitually in the practice of receiving or buying notes at less than nominal values." The distinction the legislators had in mind is easy to recognize, but it was hard to define and establish.

The way out followed from the practical conclusion, enforced by usage, that the obligations of banks were not ordinary debts but money; and that a public interest was at stake in them which overrode that of any particular debtor and creditor. But that conclusion was reached slowly and with uncertainty.

Meanwhile banks themselves made the problem worse by their raids on one another. Loammi Baldwin, subsequently a well-known engineer, wrote in 1809 that a most important difficulty for banks arose from their imprudent jealousy in "running" upon each other for gold and silver in order to impair one another's credit and improve their own positions. If they would stop this, he said, and mutually aid and support each other "there would be little danger of failures." It was undoubtedly difficult or impossible to tell in many cases whether demands by some banks upon others were legitimate or greedy and malicious. John C. Calhoun in March 1816, doubting the wisdom of Daniel Webster's amendment penalizing the Bank of the United States two per cent a month for any failure to redeem its obligations, said that too severe a penalty might produce combinations against it, and "be dangerous to the institution by inviting a run on it and thereby producing a suspension of payment." Actually, banks resorted to two extremes, both of them often. Sometimes they raided one another ruthlessly, which was strictly legal, though lethal. At other times they agreed to evade redemption and sustained one another's notes, which if not illegal was at least contrary to the law's intent and public interest though otherwise rather sensible. Proper practice, which combined the principle of both extremes, was maintained all the time by many banks, perhaps most, but not for a century was it generally achieved.[8]

In Massachusetts, conservative efforts to enforce payment of bank notes seem to have had better support than elsewhere. And it was bankers themselves, not legislators, who were responsible for them. In 1803 the Massachusetts Bank, the Union Bank, and the Boston office of the Bank of the United States united in systematically collecting out-of-town bank notes, and in 1804, as I have already said, the Boston Exchange Office was organized to specialize in such collections. It did so till Andrew Dexter got control and used it to delay rather than expedite note redemption. In 1809 sixty-four merchants and firms in Boston announced the following collective action against banks that evaded redemption of their notes:

"The subscribers, merchants and traders in the town of Boston, from a disposition to afford every facility and convenience to their country customers, have been in the habit, since the establishment of country banks, of receiving the bills issued by them in payment for goods or debts at par,—and which they were for a good while enabled again to circulate without loss.

"Within the last two years, however, many country banks have unwarrantably abused this confidence placed in their bills by refus-

8 Baldwin, 46-47; Clarke and Hall, 674, 809.

ing payment of them when presented or by opposing every obstacle which chicanery and artifice could invent to delay or evade it. The obvious consequences have followed, the public confidence has been shaken, their faith in written promises of institutions avowedly established as *patterns of punctuality* no longer exists. Country bank paper has depreciated and can not be negotiated without a discount which varies from two to four per cent. We have, however, in hopes this unwarrantable conduct would be abandoned, continued to receive this paper at par and borne the loss of the discount till our patience is exhausted and our suffering interest calls loudly for a change of measures. We have therefore found ourselves compelled to send the bills home for payment and in case of refusal shall proceed to the collection by due course of law. We beg you will communicate this letter to the President and Directors of ———Bank and hope that by a prompt payment of their bills they will save us from the disagreeable necessity of resorting to the legal alternative."[9]

In 1814 the New England Bank, Boston, incorporated the year before, arranged to receive the notes of out-of-town banks and charge the depositors only the actual cost of collection. Something promptly occurred which shows that resistance to note redemption was not merely a provincial affair. The bank had sent its agent to New York with about $140,000 of notes of New York banks. Silver coin in that amount had been collected in payment by the agent, had been loaded in three wagons, and had started on its way to Boston. The wagons had not gone far when they were halted by order of the federal Collector of Customs for New York; and the money was carried back by force and placed in the vaults of the Bank of the Manhattan Company, of which the Collector was a director. The action was protested by the New England Bank's agent, but the Collector declined to alter his purpose, alleging a suspicion that the coin was on its way to Canada, with which, since it was British, the States were then at war. In Boston, however, it was believed that his behavior "was chiefly actuated by dislike to the frequency with which the New England Bank dispatched large sums of the New York bills, which flooded Massachusetts, to be redeemed." The Massachusetts authorities laid the matter before the President of the United States, James Madison, "with the expression of their judgment that the collector had committed an

---

[9] Gras, 75; Massachusetts Historical Society, *Proceedings* xi (1870), 307.

outrage on one of their corporations, ought to relinquish the deposit, and be dismissed from his office." Their effort "so far succeeded as to have the money restored."[10]

The argument that redemption of notes was disadvantageous to borrowers, because it reduced the power of banks to lend, soon gave birth to the further argument that there were positive advantages in prolonged or even permanent suspension, because it augmented the power of banks to lend. To exclude or limit the use of bank credit was to confine the volume of money to small compass—gold and silver only—and deny the public the means adequate for an ever-expanding volume of monetary transactions. If banks were released from having to redeem their notes, they could lend more freely and every one would be better off. In November 1814, Samuel D. Ingham of Pennsylvania, who fifteen years later was Secretary of the Treasury under President Jackson, expressed himself in Congress on the subject of suspension in this wise: "I do not apprehend any serious consequence will result from the temporary suspension of specie payments. The experiment was tried many years ago in England and has been continued up to this time, without injury to the commercial interests and with essential benefit to the nation at large." It had been demonstrated, he said, that but a small quantity of specie was sufficient when the public had faith in a bank; accordingly, since suspension made it impossible to get any specie at all, "necessity would become an auxiliary to faith and business would go on as usual." This happy conclusion was not unknown by any means in Britain, where, as Mr Ingham said, the Bank of England's suspension of payments had been long continued. And the sarcastic comment upon it of Thomas Love Peacock, novelist and officer of the East India Company, was that "promises to pay ought not to be kept; the essence of a safe and economical currency being an interminable series of broken promises."[11]

In America too the conclusion that a circulating medium merely required faith, and no specie, seemed preposterous to the conservatives, both capitalist and agrarian. But the conservatives were becoming a minority. Though law-making and practice had now and then their nervous swings, the secular trend was toward easy money and expanding credit. Of the two evils, Americans in the long run stuck to the lesser: too much money was better than not enough.

10 Felt, 218.   11 Clarke and Hall, 501-02.

III

It was in this period beginning around 1800 and on the complaint of chartered banks that the issue of notes by their unincorporated competitors began anew to be prohibited. The complaint was reasonable, for one of the purposes of incorporation was to establish limited and controllable privileges in the general interest; and if these privileges were of any use they should be protected. The earlier intent of these laws, however, had been to complete the ban on note issue, which they forbade for unincorporated banks and which was impossible for incorporated banks so long as the legislature incorporated none. But once some banks were incorporated and thereby authorized to issue notes, the prohibition became a means of protecting those banks.

It was an inadequate protection, however, for it bore on unincorporated banks and bankers only, but not on canal companies, academies, blacksmiths, etc., outside the field of banking, whether incorporated or not. These found that they could go into debt profitably by issuing notes which looked like money and circulated as money. The problem of the law-maker was to distinguish between notes which should be allowed to circulate as money and notes that should not. It was like the problem of distinguishing practically and equitably between creditors who should be allowed to demand payment of bank notes and those who should not. Restraining laws were tried in one version after another as the various state legislatures sought the verbal formula that would accomplish what they purposed. Massachusetts in June 1809 enacted a second statute outlawing notes of banks not incorporated in Massachusetts. In March 1810, Pennsylvania forbade unincorporated banking companies either to receive deposits or to issue notes, but also declared that nothing in the act should interfere with others "in such manner and for such purpose as hath been hitherto usual and may be legally done." In the general act regulating banks, March 1814, sections XIII and XIV restated the prohibition against note issue by others than chartered banks "in the manner or nature of bank notes." Still another prohibition was enacted in Pennsylvania in March 1817, because "notes and tickets in the nature of bank notes" had been issued "as well by individuals as by corporations not established for the purpose of banking." Virginia again enacted a restraining act in February 1816 and New York in 1816 and 1818. Other states adopted like restraints.[12]

[12] Chitty, 425ff.

These restraints favored corporations at the expense of private individuals, and considering the prejudices both popular and official against the corporate form of business organization, it is remarkable that they were enacted at all. But they were supported by dissatisfaction with a monetary medium comprising the personal obligations of any Tom, Dick, and Harry. The restraints accordingly marked stages in the evolution of the business corporation and also in the evolution of the concept of money, which was expanding to include bank liabilities as well as coin. "Previous to the restraining acts," said the courts, "there was no power possessed by a bank not allowed to individuals and private associations. They could in common issue notes, discount notes, and receive deposits." Now it was different; the banking function, to the extent that it involved the *creation* of money (as distinct from the mere safekeeping of it) was reserved to corporations authorized by the state for that purpose. The common law right to borrow was being distinguished from the right to borrow by the issue of obligations intended to circulate as money. The latter was being more and more positively reserved to chartered banks.[13]

This distinction between the legalistic and realistic concept of bank obligations had already been made years before in the courts of Great Britain, where the public had been making monetary use of such obligations for a much longer time than in America and where there had never been the abuse of them that Americans had experienced with their bills of credit. In *Miller* v. *Race*, January 1758, Lord Mansfield had rejected the fallacy, as he called it, of likening bank notes "to goods, or to securities, or documents for debts. Now, they are not goods," he said, "not securities, nor documents for debts, nor are so esteemed; but are treated as *money*, as *cash*, in the ordinary course and transaction of business, by the general consent of mankind; which gives them the credit and currency of money, to *all* intents and purposes. They are as much money as guineas themselves are, or any other current coin that is used in common payments, as money or cash."[14]

IV

The early years of the republic are often spoken of as if the era were one of *laisser faire* in which governmental authority refrained from interference in business and benevolently left it a free field. Nothing of the sort was true of banking. Legislators hesitated about

13 *New York Firemen Ins. Co.* v. *Ely*, 2 Cowan 710.
14 *Miller* v. *Race*, 1 Burrows 457.

the kind of conditions under which banking should be permitted but never about the propriety and need of imposing conditions. To begin with, Hamilton and the Federalists closely restricted banking as a quasi-state monopoly at a time when the opposition would have permitted no banking at all. The issue was between prohibition and state control, with no thought of free enterprise. The developments and reactions from these original party positions were various, but in all of them the state was a jealous and dominant figure. In between the later extremes of state monopoly and prohibition the state tried all degrees and types of control involving proprietary interest or not but always involving restrictions and regulations. To be sure, all these laws were charters of incorporation, and an incorporated bank had no rights other than those given it by its legislative creator. It stood in a very different position from a natural person; but even the latter, if he undertook banking, might find his common law right to borrow prescinded so as not to interfere with the issue of notes by corporate banks. The impression was general that the exercise of the banking function without express authorization from the sovereign power was improper, if not impracticable, and that legislatures had the obligation to legislate for it with all the detail they chose. Their readiness to do so arose in part from recurring evidence of bad banking but also from the more fundamental consideration that banks, being by nature imbued with monetary powers, were in a peculiar sense responsible to the state.

One of the commonest restraints on banking was the restriction or prohibition of bank notes of small denomination. In March and November 1792, which was pretty early in bank legislation, Massachusetts and Virginia respectively forbade the issue of notes in denominations less than five dollars, but the ban was not consistently maintained. Maryland did the same in 1795. In 1810 North Carolina forbade notes for less than one dollar and New Jersey, in January 1812, notes for less than three dollars. Similar restraints were adopted generally in other states. The objection to small notes was that they stayed in circulation, seldom being presented for redemption, became disgustingly dirty, and encouraged counterfeiting. All this signified a demand for them. It is true that banks profited from their issue, because they seldom had to be redeemed, but prohibiting their issue was of doubtful wisdom so long as the public demand for them was real: they took the place now filled by minor coins and met a need that the country was not yet ready or able to meet in a more satisfactory but expensive way.[15]

One of the commonest requirements was that banks submit reports of their condition to public officials. It was imposed on banks almost from the beginning. The charter of the Bank of the United States, 1791, required that it report regularly to the Treasury, and in 1792 Massachusetts in March and Virginia in November required the Massachusetts Bank and the Bank of Alexandria, respectively, to submit information regularly to the state authorities. The former was to furnish the Governor and Council "once in six months, at least, and as much oftener as they may require" with statements of the amount of capital, the debts due the bank, the deposits, the notes in circulation, and the cash on hand. The Bank of Alexandria was to report "the situation of the bank and its funds" to the Governor and Council annually, and the statements submitted are still on file in Richmond. The charter of the Union Bank of Boston, June 1792, also stipulated that the bank be examined from time to time by the legislature. In June 1803, in chartering the Plymouth Bank, Massachusetts began a regular requirement of twice-yearly reports. In December 1806 the Bank of Kentucky was required to submit weekly reports to the Governor and annual reports to the legislature. In March 1809, Rhode Island required that reports be not only submitted but published. Such requirements were soon universal, and enforcement of them became more and more effective as state officials were designated to receive them and authorized to act upon the information obtained.[16]

The conditions imposed on banks by the various state legislatures began a regulatory procedure that has run continuously to the present. But not all the conditions set were wise by any means. In Massachusetts from 1802 to 1816 nearly every bank charter issued required that a certain amount of loans be agricultural, be secured by mortgage, and run for at least a year. In 1807 Connecticut began prescribing that banks "at all times" accept subscriptions to their capital by schools, churches, and charitable institutions, the stock not to be transferable but to be redeemed for the subscribers on six months' notice; in 1809 the legislature refused to repeal the requirement and it continued for fifty years or more. In December 1812, Maryland made the renewal of certain charters conditional upon

---

[15] Knox, *History of Banking*, 360, 433, 476, 546; Gallatin III, 301; Gras, 217-18.
[16] Gras, 218-19; Walsh, 26, 37-39.

investment by the banks in a company formed to construct a turn-pike westward to Cumberland. In 1814 Pennsylvania required the forty-one banks to lend one-fifth of their capital "for one year, to the farmers, mechanics, and manufacturers" of their districts. In February 1816 when some Massachusetts banks declined to lend to the state, an act was passed requiring them to do so, on penalty of two per cent a month of the sum the state wished to borrow. Throughout the country, banks were under specific requirements to lend to their state governments on special terms, and before 1820 the practice of exacting bonuses for the enactment or renewal of charters had become established; though like other impositions on banks these requirements did not reach their worst extremes till later.

V

The restriction on bank liabilities in ratio to paid capital which Alexander Hamilton had adapted from the act incorporating the Bank of England and which was embodied in different forms in most American bank charters beginning with the Bank of the United States and the Bank of New York in 1791, became by the end of the century still more general. Restrictions on the loans of banks in ratio to paid capital also became frequent. The ratios varied. In New York it continued to be one to three between specie capital and liabilities, in Massachusetts one to two. In Connecticut and other New England states it was reduced still lower; in Virginia it was one to four. Although verbally applicable to all but a very limited class of liabilities, it was in practice taken as applicable only to note circulation. On such terms it seems to have been nugatory, because nowhere did note issues approach the limit, except perhaps in New England, where the limit was lowest.

Since that time bank liabilities have come to be about ten times capital. That in the early 19th century, they should have equaled scarcely more than half of capital, seems anomalous, the demand for credit being what it was. But the explanation seems to be that, in the first place, deposit liabilities approximately equaled note liabilities, and that, in the second place, bank capital was largely fictitious, in the sense that it was legally supposed to be wholly in specie and in fact was not. In 1815 there were 208 banks reporting $82,000,000 of capital and $17,000,000 of specie. Their circulation was $45,000,000, which I believe implies deposit and note liabilities combined of $90,000,000 or so, and a ratio between them and specie of five to one.[17]

The failure of note circulation to reach a higher ratio with capital was often noted but not explained. Samuel Ingham of Pennsylvania declared in Congress in 1814 that "No bank conducted with integrity ever did issue notes to the amount of its capital; and no bank that has any regard to its reputation will ever dare to do it." Further, he said, "It is, I believe, unusual for the large state banks to issue, in paper, more than one-third or at most one-half the amount of their capital, although they often lend or discount to the whole amount." In 1816 Representative Henry St George Tucker of Virginia remarked in Congress that the loans and investments of the Philadelphia banks were "nearly three times as great as their notes in circulation." He found the same true of banks in the District of Columbia, though individual banks varied greatly.[18]

The truth was, obviously, that about half or more of bank loans went into bank deposits and not into circulation. But this was beyond the apprehension of most observers, or if apprehended it was a fact that no one knew how to use. For thought was dominated by the misleading term "deposits"—and even "deposits for safe-keeping"—which seemed of necessity to imply the receipt and possession of equivalent specie and to exclude anything so volatile as book credit in evidence of what the banks had lent but had not parted from. At the same time circulating notes were in fact used in extraordinary volume; Alexander Baring told a Commons committee in 1819 that "the system of a paper currency has been carried to a greater extent in America than in any other part of the world," a condition which relates itself to that which had taken its place a century later when the use of checks drawn on deposit balances had become more extensive in America than anywhere else in the world. In the early 19th century the prominence of notes, being great, seemed still greater. Note liabilities obscured the existence of deposit liabilities and banking was discussed as if they were the only liabilities—the more so because they were easy to understand, while deposit liabilities, even if noticed at all, were not. The superficial and temporary prominence of notes has kept its dead hand on banking discussion and banking laws for generations. In 1887, more than half a century after the period under consideration, Professor Charles Dunbar had to reprove his colleagues in the study

[17] Trotter, 376.   [18] Clarke and Hall, 500, 644-45.

of money and banking for continuing to think and speak as if bank notes were the most important part of the monetary supply, or even the whole of it, and as if deposits did not exist, though by then they had for several decades represented the bulk of bank credit and of the money in use.[19]

In the figures quoted a little way back for 1815, specie ($17,000,-000) was about a fifth of what I conjecture notes and deposits combined to have been ($90,000,000). In 1811 some reckonings of Senator James Lloyd of Massachusetts show it to have been a fifth of "circulation bottomed on bank paper and bank credits," whatever that may mean. Counting only the Bank of the United States with specie of $5,000,000 and twenty banks in Boston, New York, Philadelphia, and Baltimore with an average of $150,000 each, making $3,000,000 in all, and adding $2,000,000 supposed to be in circulation outside the banks, he got aggregate specie of $10,000,-000. "The circulation of our country," he said, "is at present emphatically a paper circulation; very little specie passes in exchange between individuals. It is a circulation . . . amounting perhaps to $50,000,000. And on what, sir, does this circulation rest? It rests upon the $10,000,000, if that be the amount of specie in the country, and upon public confidence." The Senator probably got his $50,000,000 by reading in Adam Smith of what circulation could be maintained on a given specie base and obediently multiplying his specie by five. But besides that, even allowing for the great fluctuations such as then occurred, his magnitudes were mostly wrong. A later and better source reports eighty-nine banks, for January 1811, the month preceding, with specie of $15,400,000, capital of $52,600,000, and circulation of $28,100,000; which makes specie a little less than half the note circulation and circuitously supports my conjecture that deposits were at least equal to circulation. In December 1814 a communication to the Treasury from the banks in Manhattan stated that the note circulation of the Bank of the United States had never been more than $6,000,000 and that they themselves, with aggregate capital of $15,000,000, had a circulation of "not upon an average" more than $5,000,000.[20]

A contemporary, finding in such figures that circulation was less than half the amount of nominal capital and less than twice the amount of specie, must have thought that on the whole the showings

[19] British Parliament, *Expediency of Resuming Cash Payments*, 182; Dunbar, 172ff.
[20] Clarke and Hall, 321-22; Trotter, 376; ASP, Finance II, 876.

probably satisfied the laws. A modern student can only feel certain that the standards of statistical reporting in 1811 were not those of a period a century and a half later, look skeptically on all compilations of the time, and yet feel pretty sure that deposits were more important than was realized.

Massachusetts in 1792 had restricted the loans rather than liabilities of the Massachusetts Bank to twice its paid capital. In 1800, with the Gloucester Bank, the restriction was applied both to loans and liabilities and was typical thereafter of Massachusetts charters. In January 1812, New Jersey restricted both loans and circulation to twice the paid capital in chartering a number of banks. Later, *e.g.*, in New York in 1827, the restriction on both assets and liabilities became more common, but it never became so general as the restriction on liabilities alone (meaning, contemporaneously, *note* liabilities).

VI

Though the first American banks were patterned directly on the Bank of England, and though, as Professor Sumner observed fifty years ago, they were established with "the notion of a national bank for each state," the pattern was soon diversified. It arose from the unusual if not unique status of the first banks, which though public and expected or intended to be the only banks in their respective jurisdictions, were partly governmental and partly private. Since their status fell in no familiar category, it was liable to misunderstanding and political distortion. It was liable to be pushed toward the un-Hamiltonian extremes of either much greater governmental control or much less. Some states—*e.g.*, Vermont, South Carolina, and Kentucky—went in time to the first extreme and set up bank monopolies that in each case were an arm of the state government itself. This type of institution—which reverted to the principle of the colonial loan office—was most prominent in the South and West, where in some jurisdictions it persisted till the middle of the 19th century. Elsewhere the deviation was to the other extreme of dissociating banks and the state as much as possible, and though this trend progressed more slowly, it became dominant at length over all American banking. It began with a division of the state's proprietary interest among two or more banks and advanced with the increase in the number of banks till the interest was wholly abandoned.[21]

[21] Sumner, *History of Banking*, 20.

Concomitant with the political status of the first American banks, there had been a specialization in the credit needs of merchants, by whom and for whose purposes they had been founded. Those banks had imposed on themselves two cardinal conditions: the holding of specie reserves adequate to maintain the circulation of notes in ratios of one dollar in specie to two or more dollars in notes; and the holding of short-term earning assets that turned over six to twelve times a year and produced, at least in theory, a constant inflow of specie. But the disruption of commerce resulting from Napoleon's wars, the Industrial Revolution, and the startling diversification and intensification of business enterprise which attended the advent of the 19th century were immediately manifest in modifications of banking practice. Farmers began to want bank credit, the state wanted it, and manufacturers and carriers, who had not existed before, wanted it too.

Alexander Hamilton and his associates had already advocated the extension of credit to the state and industry but had held back from its extension to agriculture. This was because their banks were formed largely for governmental purposes and because industry in the 18th century was something small, new, and specially deserving. It was not expected that government and industrial loans would in time put banks as deeply into long-term credit as agriculture would have done. The most obvious evidence of the changing practice was the lengthening maturities of loans. A few banks, favorably situated and straitly managed, continued to confine their credits to thirty- and sixty-day maturities, or said they did; but by 1800 probably, the majority had begun to lend for longer periods. Three-month, four-month, and six-month maturities increased. Moreover, it was no longer a firm expectation, as it had originally been, that promissory notes would actually be paid at maturity, for renewals were becoming a matter of course. In spite of these essential changes in credit practice, the tradition of short-term credit continued to be held in pious respect and bankers liked to pretend that they were faithful to it.[22]

The place that banks were taking in the economy can be made clearer by contrast with three other types of credit institution which were becoming important in this same period. These were unincorporated banking houses, mutual savings banks, and insurance companies. The unincorporated banking firms were called "private

[22] Dewey, *State Banking*, 182-86; Bray Hammond, *QJE*, XLIX (1934), 79ff.

banks," in contradistinction to incorporated banks, which, in the beginning were "public." In a very short time, however, the incorporated banks began to be as private in practice as any, save that they were subject to special statutory conditions; and at the same time private business very generally adopted the corporate form. Yet unincorporated banks continued to be called "private." In the 18th and 19th centuries, unchartered banks were mainly in commercial and trading centers, they developed typically out of merchandising, and they were frequently affiliated with British merchant banking houses. The most important of them was the bank of Stephen Girard in Philadelphia, which because of the scale and nature of its business, was classed with the incorporated banks. Such resemblance very often invited adverse legislation, as I have already said, and the more successful and long-lived private banking houses avoided looking and acting like incorporated banks. In particular they eschewed note issue. An outstanding example was the house of Alexander Brown and Sons in Baltimore, which was set up in 1800. Alexander Brown began as an importer of linens principally, but transactions in foreign exchange and commercial credit soon outweighed the other business of the firm and affiliated houses subsequently established in Liverpool, Philadelphia, New York, London, and Boston. "From the beginning, . . . the firm besides being importers on their own account, dealers in sterling exchange, and ship owners, issued credits for the importation of goods by others and were known as merchant bankers. . . ."[23]

In Charleston, Philadelphia, New York, and Boston similar banking houses were very important, though as a class much less is known of them than of incorporated banks. They avoided the political publicity that enveloped the latter, and since they were not subject to regulation, their affairs did not become a matter of public record. They differed from the incorporated banks in that their liabilities were not so widely held by the public but were usually concentrated in the hands of fewer and selected creditors with whom they had intimate relations. Their assets were typically of a sort that had a quick turnover. Although these conditions did not embrace all advantages by any means or avoid all risks, they tended to give the unincorporated banking houses a compact business in contrast to which the business of the incorporated banks sprawled, especially when their control was political. The banking houses

[23] J. C. Brown, 21.

were usually more versatile and flexible than the incorporated banks and were managed by individualistic proprietors who probably felt a repugnance for the political interest that a corporate charter implied.

At the other end of the scale from the unincorporated banking houses were the mutual savings banks and the insurance companies, both of which specialized in long-term assets and long-term liabilities, i.e., savings. The first of the mutuals were the Provident Institution for Savings, Boston, and the Philadelphia Savings Fund Society, both of which began their long careers in 1816. The mutual savings banks became strong in the northern Atlantic states, and ten that were in existence by 1820 are still active.* Elsewhere they got no important foothold. They were intended to encourage thrift and industry among the poor and did not call themselves banks at first, but "funds," "institutions," and "societies." They have always been distinct from commercial banks, both in corporate structure and function. They are without capital and without stockholders, being owned by their depositors. Though they have come to be called "banks," they are not banks in the proper sense because their liabilities do not expand with their acquisition of earning assets and are not used as a customary means of payment. The obvious distinction between them and commercial banks is that demand deposits subject to check are maintained with the latter and not with savings institutions. But other institutions than mutual savings banks also have savings deposit liabilities. Commercial banks themselves do; they began to invite savings and pay interest shortly after 1800. But their savings business is no more related in principle to the essential banking function—which is the creation of credit to be

---

* These ten are the following:

Massachusetts	1816	The Provident Institution for Savings in the Town of Boston
Pennsylvania	1816	The Philadelphia Saving Fund Society
Maryland	1818	The Savings Bank of Baltimore
Massachusetts	1818	Salem Savings Bank
Rhode Island	1819	Providence Institution for Savings
Rhode Island	1819	The Savings Bank of Newport
New York	1819	The Bank for Savings in the City of New York
Connecticut	1819	Society for Savings, Hartford
New York	1820	The Albany Savings Bank
Massachusetts	1820	Institution for Savings in Newburyport and Its Vicinity

transferred by check and to serve as money—than their letting of safe deposit boxes or their managing of trust funds. These latter are important to banks as sources of income, but they are quite distinct from banking proper.

In the same early period, insurance companies also had a swift and widespread beginning. Insurance business and banking were frequently combined. The first bank in Kentucky was an insurance company; and one of the largest banks in Philadelphia to-day, the First Pennsylvania Banking and Trust Company, was established in 1809 and incorporated in 1812, as the Pennsylvania Company for Insurances on Lives and Granting Annuities. It retained this formidable name till 1947, though it had long before given up the insurance of risks and confined itself to trusts and banking, under amendments to its charter.

VII

In the period 1791-1816 American banking went through an adolescence. One sees it experimenting energetically in untried directions, sometimes brash and expansive where it was most wrong and sometimes hesitant and unsure where it was on safe ground. In some respects, the law, parent-like, could not keep up with the banks but followed them with ineffective commandments and prohibitions. In other respects the banks leaned irresolutely on the law and besought sanctions for what they were to do. Some of the experiments turned out to be very bad. Bank credit was to Americans a new source of energy, like steam, and it was not to be known in advance of experience under what conditions it would work well or ill.

Meanwhile both the friends and the enemies of banks were fortified in their convictions by experience. How much the friends were encouraged is shown by the number of new banks incorporated. How much the enemies were dismayed is indicated by the letters of Thomas Jefferson, who demonstrated with logarithms in 1813 that the country could not afford banks. "My original disapprobation of banks circulating paper is not unknown, nor have I since observed any effects either on the morals or fortunes of our citizens which are any counter balance for the public evils produced." Banks debased the currency, in his opinion, and made a mockery of men's promises. "He who lent his money to the public or to an individual before the institution of the United States Bank of twenty years ago," he said, "when wheat was well sold at a dollar the bushel and receives now his nominal sum when it sells at two dollars, is cheated of half his fortune; and by whom? By the banks, which, since that, have thrown into circulation ten dollars of their nominal money where was one at that time." Considering the paper money issued by Congress in the Revolution and the paper money since issued by banks, he averred: "The object of the former was a holy one; for if ever there was a holy war, it was that which saved our liberties and gave us independence. The object of the latter is to enrich swindlers at the expense of the honest and industrious part of the nation." John Adams was of the same opinion. "Every dollar of a bank bill that is issued beyond the quantity of gold and silver in the vaults represents nothing and is therefore a cheat upon somebody," he said in 1809, with either a blind or defiant indifference to earning assets.[24]

Among the less doctrinaire critics of banking, including its discriminating friends, there was no thought of extirpating the banks nor was there faith in laws as the only means of regulating them. There was a mounting realization that banks performed an organic operation amounting to something more than the sum of its parts, and that the regulatory influence of a central bank upon the system was necessary. But, as recounted in the next chapter, that realization did not avail against the combined but incongruous enmity toward the Bank of the United States of those persons who wanted no banks and those who wanted banks with no restraint upon them.

[24] Jefferson (Ford) ix, 394, 399-401n, 402n, 416n; John Adams, *Works* ix, 610.

CHAPTER 8

The Federal Bank in Operation and Extinction

| 1791-1811 |

I. Central banking — II. Relations with the Executive —
III. The Bank's enemies and friends — IV. Constitutionality
and realism — V. The end of the Bank

I

IN 1791, when the Bank of the United States was established, there
was still no one American banking system. Instead there were four
little isolated banking systems situated in Boston, New York, Philadelphia, and Baltimore. These, however, before many years, grew
and coalesced into a single system comprising many banks which
regularly received one another's obligations and maintained continuous debtor-creditor relations with one another. For the population had grown, the means of transportation and communication
had improved, and business had increased in variety and volume.
The notes and checks of the several banks accompanied the movement of travelers and goods from one community to another. Banks
in different cities collected payments from and for one another.
They had settlements to make with one another and payments on
behalf of their respective customers, in consequence of which they
found it convenient to open reciprocal accounts. For example, the
president of the Bank of North America in Philadelphia was
instructed by his directors, 14 April 1794, to arrange with the
Bank of New York a mutual credit of $40,000 "for the accommoda-
tion of the respective customers of both banks in remitting monies
between New York and Philadelphia." When the Philadelphia Bank
was established in 1803, it arranged for like accounts with the
Merchants Bank in New York.[1]

Above all, as banks became numerous, each was affected by the
credit practice of others. When some enlarged their loans, the funds
they lent would turn up in other banks, and be lent again by them,
with the result that the credit expansion initiated by one or some

[1] Schwartz, *JPE*, LV (1947), 422; Wainwright, 27.

would be accelerated by others. Contrariwise, a contraction of credit was equally contagious. The demand for credit which any one bank refused to satisfy tended at once to press on other banks. So, even more, would the efforts of particular banks to reduce their loans; the liquidation tended to drain other banks of their funds to the same degree that expansion had filled them up. These phenomena, as I have said before, were generally more visible and understandable when banking was observed in terms of note issue than they are now when bank liabilities are all in deposits. For the movement of bank notes into circulation in consequence of lending went on tangibly before one's eyes, but the increase of deposits, which is the consequence nowadays, does not. Individual banks, despite an illusion of independence in times of expansion, became painfully aware of one another's pressure in times of contraction; as when a given bank, having discounted heavily for its customers and entered deposit credit on its books in their favor, finds itself confronted by the demands of other banks expecting payment of the checks drawn by the borrowers against their borrowed funds and deposited by the recipients in other banks. In normal happy times, when all banks are lending readily, the rising tide washes everything with an abundance of funds, and the claims on any one bank are less apt to be embarrassing; but the possibility that some day some banks will not have enough to meet the others' claims is always real.[2]

The Bank of the United States, like all the local banks, was both debtor and creditor to the others. From time to time, the course of business, and Treasury disbursements especially, would make the Bank a greater debtor to some local banks than creditor; but this was exceptional. Being the main government depository and having offices in the principal commercial cities, the Bank was the general creditor of the other banks. It had the account of the largest single transactor in the economy—the federal government—and the receipts of the government being mostly in the notes of state banks and these notes being deposited in the Bank, it could not help being their creditor. By pressing them for payment of the notes and checks received against them, the Bank automatically exercised a general restraint upon the banking system. The more any bank lent, the more it went into debt. The larger the volume of notes and checks outstanding against it, the greater the pressure to which it became subjected.

2 Hamilton, *Reminiscences*, 255.

This restraint upon bank lending came later to be designated central bank control of credit. Neither Alexander Hamilton nor any one else had foreseen it. The Bank of England was performing a similar function in Britain, but it operated on the demand for credit, whereas the Bank of the United States operated on the supply. That is, in the States, with the private banking system engaged in furnishing credit expansively and liberally, the task of the central bank was performed by pressing the private banks for redemption of their notes and checks and thereby restraining their extension of credit. In Britain, the private banks were more dependent on the central bank for the means with which to expand their credit, and the task of the central bank was performed by granting or denying the demands upon it for funds. In the States the corollary to restraint upon lending banks was lenity toward them. The advance of funds to ease their position seems to have been exceptional; but in 1810 in its memorial to Congress on recharter, the Bank reported that grants of credit to local banks amounted generally to a tenth of its capital, or $1,000,000. In a statement which Mr Gallatin gave Congress in 1809, the amount was $800,000. In another, given in 1811, just before its dissolution, the Bank was owed $1,287,500 by state banks and its balances in their favor were $634,000. Typically, the Bank was creditor of the private banks, on balance; to-day it would be debtor, holding their reserves as the Federal Reserve Banks now do.[3]

The attitude of state banks toward credit control by the Bank of the United States varied. The conservative ones that expected to pay their debts and were always prepared to do so acknowledged the wisdom of central bank restraint. They recognized the advantages to the economy of a governor and a central reserve. The reckless and speculative bankers resented it, whatever their private convictions, if any, as to constitutionality and federal powers.

While it was regulator of the local banks, the Bank of the United States was also their competitor. But it was a competitor on a higher plane. Modern central banks generally do not compete with the banks they regulate, though they may do so on the principle that the competition is itself regulatory and makes the banking system more widely and thoroughly serviceable.* The Bank of England

* For example—an unusual one—the Banco Nacional de la Republica

[3] ASP, Finance II, 352, 452, 469-70; William Hamilton, *Debates*, 27.

still has some private business, but in 1800, like the Bank of the United States, it had so much that its public function was to many persons quite unapparent except as usurpation and privilege.

It was later said, on very poor authority, that the Bank of the United States instead of improving the circulating medium "did much to injure it" by being too conservative. "A system of permanent loans was adopted towards individuals and likewise to banks." This statement was made to the Secretary of the Treasury in 1817, by James McCulloch, cashier of the Baltimore branch of the second Bank of the United States. No doubt the first Bank had some slow loans, and it might not have been spotlessly impartial toward its debtors, being a human institution. Nevertheless McCulloch's statement is unsupported by other evidence of the Bank's policy, and probably reflects nothing more than his wish to make the United States Treasury think that the second Bank was better managed than the first.[4]

Although constant receipt of the notes and checks of local banks made the Bank of the United States the constant regulator of the latter, the Treasury also played the same role. The Bank was situated right in the path of the function, so to speak, where performance of it was most natural, but the Treasury had a prominence, a political interest, and an operating interest which often drew it into performance of the function. Neither Hamilton, nor Wolcott, nor Gallatin refrained in the Treasury from assuming major responsibility for central bank assistance in special cases, though the routine performance of the function, as effected through current collection of balances due from the local banks, was left to the federal Bank.

Late in 1796 the Bank of New York lent the Treasury $200,000, and gave it deposit credit for that amount. Since the Treasury itself wished to have the funds in its account with the Bank of the United States, or others to whom it gave checks drawn against the credit wished to have them there, the New York office of the Bank of the United States received the checks the Treasury drew, became thereby creditor of the Bank of New York, and wanted payment

---

Oriental del Uruguay, Montevideo, not only conducts the customary central banking functions but has also a large pawn shop, which by competing with private shops regulates their practice.

[4] ASP, Finance IV, 774.

accordingly. It asked to be paid in specie. The Bank of New York requested Alexander Hamilton's intercession. He accordingly wrote Secretary Wolcott, once his subordinate, that the New York Bank's "large accommodations to the government" had produced a balance against it in favor of the New York office of the Bank of the United States, "which has lately called for $100,000 in specie and it is apprehended may speedily call for more." Mr Wolcott replied promptly. Since the Bank of the United States was having to go easy on the Bank of New York, it was really the Bank of the United States that was making the loan, he said, for quite evidently the Bank of New York was in a position to make it only so long as the Bank of the United States was forbearing. Why, he might have asked, had the Bank of New York contracted to lend the money if it could not produce it without borrowing it elsewhere? What he did say discloses the systematic nature of banking operations and their need of central bank governance: he assured the Bank of New York "of as full and cordial assistance in any pressure of their affairs" as should be in his power; "I think, however, that they must principally rely on sales of stock, and in my opinion, any sacrifice ought to be preferred to a continuance of temporary expedients." The Secretary was talking like a central banker: a bank had lent too much and exposed itself to pressure from its inter-bank settlements; it turned to a recognized source of relief; it was scolded, told to sell some securities in the market, and assured that if worse came it would be helped further; for the structure can not be allowed to collapse merely that one bank be made to suffer for its mistake. But as usual it is more than one. "These institutions have all been mismanaged," the Secretary writes; "I look upon them with terror. They are at present the curse, and I fear they will prove the ruin of the government. Immense operations depend on a trifling capital fluctuating between the coffers of the different banks." The Secretary of the Treasury does not shed the central bank responsibility upon the central bank, where it belongs; he worries with it in the Treasury. So did his successor, Albert Gallatin, whom the Bank of Pennsylvania, in 1802, asked for relief because "they fall regularly $100,000 per week in debt to the Bank of the United States" in consequence of the Treasury's deposits in the latter. Mr Gallatin responded partly through Treasury action and partly through action which he asked the federal Bank to take. His doing so was typical. The central banking responsibility was left to the central bank only in part.[5]

It is necessary for a proper discharge of the central bank's functions that it hold large reserves, for what it holds are the ultimate reserves of the banking system. They are a concentration of the banking system's strength, and enable the central bank to meet and prevent weaknesses that arise in any quarter. It is the banking system's lender of last resort. The approach to this end by the Bank of the United States is signalized by its very large specie holdings. According to Secretary Gallatin's figures, these were more than $15,000,000 in 1809, which was an amount half again as large as the Bank's capital and roughly equivalent to the aggregate specie reported to be held by all eighty-nine other banks in the United States two years later on the eve of the Bank's demise.

The claims of a central bank to be governor of the banking system, holder of its ultimate reserves, and lender of last resort, do not include a monopoly of loans to the government, though it may be the lender to which the Treasury has special and preferential access. "It is very much the policy of the Treasury not to be exclusively dependent on one institution," Hamilton said. And Gallatin, conscious though he always was of the importance of recourse to the Bank of the United States for loans, did not rely on it alone.[6]

The functions of the Bank and its relations to the Treasury and the banking system are illustrated in the following letter from Albert Gallatin, in the Treasury, 4 February 1805, to Thomas Willing, president of the Bank. The letter was occasioned by the hostilities, described in a preceding chapter, between the Merchants Bank, New York, and its competitors, especially the Bank of the Manhattan Company. The Merchants was a final stronghold of the New York Federalists, and its president was Oliver Wolcott, Mr Hamilton's successor in the Treasury. The Manhattan was Jeffersonian, and naturally the administration was on its side. Yet Mr Gallatin was clearly depending on the assistance of the Bank of the United States, supposedly Federalist like the Merchants. The Bank of the United States, however, being managed in Philadelphia, was perhaps neutral in New York's domestic rivalries.

"I have within these two days," Mr Gallatin wrote, "received information from several quarters, intimating that the actual scar-

[5] Hamilton (J. C. Hamilton) vi, 175-76, 184; Gallatin i, 80.
[6] Hamilton (J. C. Hamilton) vi, 185.

202

city of specie in New York, combined with the conduct of the directors of the Merchants Bank, might be attended with some danger, as it has already with great inconvenience, to the commercial interest of that city generally, and to the Manhattan company particularly. You must be sensible that a very sudden and great diminution of discounts by any of the considerable Banks might cause distress and ruin to many; and it is possible that even that resource might not be sufficient to ward off the danger. Of the effect of a suspension of payments on private and public credit as well as on the revenue, you are too well aware, to render it necessary for me to add anything.

"Under those impressions I have negotiated with the Manhattan company for a remittance to London on the first of January next, which, as I pay them now, will place in fact a deposit of near 200,000 dollars in their hands for about six months. In payment I have given them a draft of 110,000 dollars on the Bank of the United States, and the balance on those of Pennsylvania and Rhode Island. This resource may, however, to them prove insufficient, and I have to request that, in the measures which you may take for the purpose of affording relief to New York, you will, so far as is consistent with the safety of the Bank of the United States, support also the Manhattan and New York Banks. This I might effect by making actual deposits with them; but I think that the object will be obtained in a safer and easier way by leaving it under your management. I do not wish you, however, to make any greater advance to the Manhattan company, on your own account, than you may think eligible, and will, from time to time, if you chose it, convert such advances into deposits of public monies by giving them drafts on you. Nor is it my intention that you should, even in that way, make them advances to an amount dangerous to yourselves. The safety of your Bank must, at all times, be the primary object; but in a critical moment, every assistance consistent with that, should be afforded to the other Banks.

"The important question, however, is, how present relief shall be given to New York generally. I perceive that you sent them last week two hundred thousand dollars; and, on looking at the returns from the several offices, I think that you might, without any risk, draw as much from Baltimore, and at least one hundred thousand dollars from Boston. The other offices are perhaps too distant to afford any immediate assistance.

"In aid of this, it may be eligible, as it will relieve to a certain degree the distress arising from the necessary diminution of discounts, to transfer to New York the purchase of a greater portion of bills on Holland; and with that object I will direct Mr Simpson in Philadelphia and Mr Dalton in Boston to suspend their purchases for Government, until they shall hear from me, and request you, in the mean while, to give me your opinion on the subject.

"So far as relates to the pressure from the Merchants Bank, it appears to me, that, whilst its directors persist in their attack, it becomes necessary, in self defense, not to increase their means by either discounting for them or purchasing their bills. And, as it respects the revenue, permit me to request that you will give particular instructions to the directors of your office in New York, to assist, whenever the parties deserve credit, persons indebted for revenue bonds in discharging them.

"Although it may be hoped, from the low price of dollars in England, from the present rate of exchange with that country, and from the probability of a war between them and Spain, that the scarcity of specie is momentary, yet I apprehend the effect of the payment of the £200,000 sterling due by Government to Great Britain on the 15th of July next. I am not permitted by law to pay it in Europe, nor have I any certainty that the British Government would accept it there. Yet I would try to remove some of the difficulties and run the risk of the others, provided that the Bank of the United States shall think it an object of sufficient importance to themselves to prevent that exportation of specie, by undertaking to make the payment in Europe. They may now obtain that amount at par, and perhaps below par; and it seems to me that it would be their interest to effect the payment in Europe by the purchase of remittances, even if they incurred some loss, rather than that the specie should be exported. If they shall consider the subject in that point of view, it will be necessary that it should be communicated to me without delay, as no time should be lost, in that case, to purchase the bills and make the other necessary arrangements. But if they do not think it eligible to undertake the operation, every previous precaution must be used, that the exportation be not attended with any serious inconvenience.

. . . .

"P.S. The subject of the public deposits in the Bank of the United States having lately caused some excitement and being now before Congress, it is probable that I will be obliged to make shortly a report upon it. I will thank you, on that account, to transmit to me a statement of every dividend made by the Bank on their stock since their first establishment; as I intend to show therefrom that the profits arising to the Bank from those deposits have been much exaggerated."*

II

The first six years of the Bank's existence were passed with its creators and friends, the Federalists, in power, with President Washington at the head of the government, and with Alexander Hamilton and Oliver Wolcott at the head of the Treasury. The next four years were spent with the Federalists still in power, with Oliver Wolcott still head of the Treasury, and with President John Adams neutral toward the federal Bank though still abhorring all banks. The remaining ten years were spent with the party in power that had resisted the Bank's establishment and under the administration of two Presidents, Thomas Jefferson and James Madison, who had led that resistance.

Mr Jefferson never abated his dislike of the federal Bank and had more chance than Mr Adams had to act as he wished; yet he deferred to Albert Gallatin and withheld his hand.** Mr Gallatin had no prejudice against banks. When a member of the Pennsylvania legislature in 1793, he had successfully proposed that the state set up the Bank of Pennsylvania, to be related to it much as Hamilton had related the federal Bank to the federal government, and when he became head of the Treasury he altered little that he had found, notwithstanding the eagerness of his party to glory in disclosures of Hamiltonian turpitude and to repudiate Hamiltonian accomplishments.[7]

Mr Gallatin showed his appreciation of the Bank especially in his patient effort to get an office of it established in New Orleans after

* The text of this letter and passages from others later are presented with the kind permission of the Historical Society of Pennsylvania. Etting Papers, Bank of the United States, vol. 1, p. 73.

** I often take the liberty of calling the Bank of the United States the "federal Bank" for short. This is anachronistic, for in its own day it was called a "national Bank." But since the Bank was federal, since it resembles the present Federal Reserve Banks, and since it was quite unlike the national banks of to-day, I choose the anachronism as the lesser evil.

[7] Walters, *PMHB*, LXX (1946), 265-66.

the States acquired the Louisiana territory from France in 1803. The Bank was unwilling to establish the office, and President Jefferson was even more unwilling to have it asked to do so. Jefferson had tacitly acquiesced in the matter of the Washington office, but now his aversion was not to be so easily subdued. The Bank, he wrote Secretary Gallatin, was "of the most deadly hostility existing against the principles and form of our Constitution." He deemed "no government safe which is under the vassalage of any self-constituted authorities or any other authority than that of the nation or its regular functionaries." To speak as if the nation were "under the vassalage" of the Bank was evidence of considerable excitement, but the Bank was the largest corporation in the country, its stockholders included Congressmen and other public officials, and its offices, opulently housed in several leading cities, were evidences of a ubiquitous power scarcely less palpable to the President than that of an army quartered upon the people. The Bank, he said, "penetrating by its branches every part of the Union, acting by command and in phalanx, may, in a critical moment, upset the government." He adjured Mr Gallatin: "Now, while we are strong, it is the greatest duty we owe to the safety of our Constitution to bring this powerful enemy to a perfect subordination under its authorities." Later, in the *Anas*, he explained his fears of the Bank more clearly. "While the government remained at Philadelphia," he said, "a selection of members of both Houses were constantly kept as directors who on every question interesting to that institution or to the views of the federal head, voted at the will of that head; and together with the stockholding members could always make the federal vote that of the majority. By this combination legislative expositions were given to the Constitution and all the administrative laws were shaped on the model of England and so passed. And from this influence we were not relieved until the removal from the precincts of the bank to Washington."[8]

Mr Gallatin discreetly skirted his chief's adjuration and dwelt concretely on the Bank's usefulness. The great advantages derived from banks, he said, and especially from the Bank of the United States were:

"1st. A safe place of deposit for the public moneys.

"2nd. The instantaneous transmission of such moneys from any one part of the continent to another, the Bank giving us immediately

[8] Jefferson (Ford) I, 164-65; VIII, 284-85.

credit at New York, if we want it, for any sum we may have at Savannah or any other of their offices, and *vice versa*.

"3ʳᵈ· The great facility which an increased circulation and discounts give to the collection of the revenue."

For these reasons, the Secretary said, he was "extremely anxious" to have an office set up in New Orleans; and against that he found "none but political objections," which he ignored. He wished to have the New Orleans office as much as Mr Hamilton had wished to have a Virginia office and worked as sedulously for it. But this time the conflict was within the party and no motive governed Mr Gallatin but that of the Treasury's convenience. Gallatin did not mention loans to the government, presumably because the New Orleans office would not affect them. On other occasions he gave due weight to the importance of government borrowings.[9]

Jefferson gave way to Gallatin in the matter and even signed the bill authorizing the Bank to establish the New Orleans office, though he did not refrain from doubting the Bank's constitutionality. Mr Gallatin had then to prevail on the Bank, which was very cold toward the New Orleans project. The exertions he put himself to for almost two years in cajoling and prodding the President, the Congress, and the Bank in order to get the New Orleans branch is cogent evidence of the Bank's importance to the Treasury, especially because Mr Gallatin had not been in any way committed to the Bank from the beginning.

The Bank's governmental relationships had begun with the government's proprietary interest, out of which arose a debt to the Bank of $2,000,000 repayable in ten annual installments. Instead of receiving payment, the Bank had to lend the government even more because Congress neglected to provide revenue. Though the government had an income from the shares, it was eventually forced by the pusillanimity of Congress to sell them. By January 1797— at the end of General Washington's administration—2,160 shares had been sold at a premium of 25 per cent; and in July 1797, John Adams now being President, the government sold 620 more shares, part at a premium of 20 per cent and part at a premium of 25 per cent. The remaining 2,220 shares were sold to the Barings in 1802, during Mr Jefferson's administration, at a premium of 45 per cent. The government's profit on all the sales was $672,000 or 30 per cent, and the dividends it received while shareholder were $1,100,000.[10]

---

9 Wettereau, *JEH*, ii (1942), Supplement, 86-87.　　　10 Holdsworth, 48-49.

The Bank acted as fiscal agent of the Treasury: it effected payments of interest on the public debt, at home and abroad; it received subscriptions to new issues of government securities; it effected payment of the salaries of government officials, including Thomas Jefferson himself and the numerous Congressmen who believed it to be unconstitutional; "it facilitated the incessant and complicated foreign exchange operations of the Treasury"; it moderated the outflow of specie; and it supplied bullion and foreign coins to the Mint. It helped collect customs bonds, which was a very important part of its business; as Albert Gallatin explained to President Jefferson, the Bank discounted very largely for importers. Presumably this included direct discounts to them and also discounts for the Treasury of the bonds given by them—due by installments in usually a year or less—for the duties they had to pay. These duties comprised the bulk of the government's income. The Bank's notes provided a uniform part of the circulating medium, receivable for all payments due the government. The Bank was the principal depository of government funds, which it transmitted without charge at the Treasury's request, and, in accordance with the act incorporating it, submitted weekly reports of its condition to the Secretary of the Treasury. The following is a statement of the Bank's condition reported to the Senate by Secretary Gallatin, 3 March 1809, of which "some minor items," he said, "arising from accidental circumstances are omitted for the sake of perspicuity," and I have condensed it still further:[11]

I.	Earning assets		
	Government securities		$ 2,200,000
	Loans to individuals, consisting chiefly of discounted notes, payable at sixty days		15,000,000
	Due from state banks		800,000
II.	Specie in the vaults		5,000,000
			$23,000,000

I.	Capital		$10,000,000
II.	Monies deposited, viz:		
	"Credits on the bank books, commonly called deposits," both of the government and of individuals	$8,500,000	
	Bank notes in circulation	4,500,000	13,000,000
			$23,000,000

[11] ASP, Finance II, 351-52.

With respect to the restriction of the Bank's note liabilities to the amount of its capital, it is to be noted that they were less than half what they might have been and less even than the amount of the Bank's specie, and that note and deposit liabilities combined, $13,000,000, were less than five times its specie, which was the ratio of expansion Alexander Hamilton had had in mind. But these figures, Mr Gallatin said, were taken "on a medium" for specie and "monies deposited, including both the credits on the bank's books, commonly called deposits, and the bank notes in circulation." According to Professor Wettereau the specie was calculated to be actually, at the time, in excess of $15,000,000 and the deposits in excess of $17,000,000; and it is Professor Wettereau's conjecture that Mr Gallatin feared the actual figures would show the Bank in too strong a position for its political good. It is also possible that his "medium" was closer to normal, from the under side, than the figures of a given date.

III

The excellent record of the Bank of the United States and the friends it won did it insufficient good politically. In January 1808, three years before expiry of the charter, the stockholders sent a memorial to Congress, deeming it "a duty to the Government and to the commercial world as well as to themselves to submit . . . the expediency of protracting the duration of their charter." The Bank's action evidently seemed premature to Mr Gallatin, for he had written to Thomas Willing, its president, the previous November, that he wished the question of renewal to be "fairly discussed and not blended with or affected by any extraneous political considerations." For that reason, he said, he preferred "that the subject should be decided by Congress after the Presidential election, that is to say, at the next rather than during this session." He tried still to achieve the delay, apparently. The Senate referred the Bank's memorial to him in April 1808 with the request that he submit a report on it "at the next session of Congress," but the report, which urged renewal of the charter, was not submitted till 3 March 1809, the day before the close of President Jefferson's term. Professor Wettereau says that Gallatin evidently feared Jefferson's hostility to the Bank and, when he received the memorial from the Senate, delayed his report until it was too late for action to be taken before Jefferson's term expired. Congress then neglected the matter till January 1810, when the House considered it desultorily for a few weeks and in April dropped it. In January 1811 it was taken up and debated actively in both chambers. It was postponed "indefinitely," that is, for good, in the House 24 January by a vote of 65 to 64. Meanwhile, in the Senate, no consideration having been given Gallatin's report of 3 March 1809, he was asked for another, which he submitted 30 January 1811. Thereupon, 5 February 1811, a bill to amend and renew the original act of incorporation was introduced. It was debated in the Senate for ten days and defeated the 20th by a vote of 18 to 17, there being a tie on the floor and the deciding vote against the Bank being cast by the Vice President, George Clinton of New York.[12]

The alignment in Congress for and against the Bank in 1791 had not been without incongruities, some northerners and some Federalists voting against it and some southerners and some anti-Federalists for it; and to some extent the same had been true in Pennsylvania in 1786 when the Bank of North America's charter was controverted; but the incongruities had become since then much more striking. The Jeffersonian or Republican party now in power had been the minority opposed to incorporating the Bank twenty years before, but the administration wing now supported renewal of the charter. President Jefferson had repeatedly acquiesced in the Bank's existence, though with truculent personal reservations. President Madison, the Bank's first formal opponent, now approved its continuance, on the ground, he said later, admitting "expediency and almost necessity," of "deliberate and reiterated precedents." The act originally establishing the Bank, he said, "had been carried into execution throughout a period of twenty years with annual legislative recognitions; in one instance, indeed, with a positive ramification of it into a new state; and with the entire acquiescence of all the local authorities as well as the nation at large." Madison was encouraged in his tolerance, as Jefferson had been, by Albert Gallatin, who was still Secretary of the Treasury and the leading advocate of recharter. In the Senate, William Crawford of Georgia, an upland planter and Jeffersonian, led for the Bank, and another Jeffersonian, William Findley of Pennsylvania, did so in the House —the same agrarian William Findley who had joined in attacking the Bank of North America twenty-five years earlier in the Penn-

12 ASP, Finance II, 301; Clarke and Hall, 115, 274, 300, 446; Wettereau, *JEH*, II (1942), Supplement, 83; Albert Gallatin to Thomas Willing, 25 November 1807, Gratz Collection, Historical Society of Pennsylvania.

sylvania legislature.* Another Jeffersonian was John Taylor of South Carolina, who spoke energetically for the Bank in the House of Representatives in 1810 and in the Senate in 1811. Still other Jeffersonians who vigorously supported renewal were Senator Richard Brent and Representative David S. Garland of Virginia, Senator John Pope and Representative Samuel McKee of Kentucky, and Representative Willis Alston of North Carolina—all from the South and West.[13]

On the other hand, the Jeffersonians who opposed the Bank despite the administration's advocacy of it were of two kinds. The first comprised unreconstructed agrarians, of whom the most prominent was Senator W. B. Giles of Virginia. He was a veteran opponent of the Bank and of Alexander Hamilton. As a representative he had voted with James Madison against the charter twenty years before, he had advocated an amendment to the Constitution forbidding anyone holding any office in the Bank of the United States to be a member of either house of Congress, he was the author of resolutions calling Hamilton severely to task for his conduct as Secretary, and he would gladly have had the Bank's charter repealed. Others were Representatives J. W. Eppes (Thomas Jefferson's son-in-law) and W. A. Bunnell of Virginia; Representatives Joseph Desha and R. M. Johnson of Kentucky, Robert Wright of Maryland, and John Rhea of Tennessee; Senator Michael Leib and Representatives John Smilie (who with William Findley had fought the Bank of North America in the Pennsylvania legislature) and William Crawford of Pennsylvania.

The other group of Republicans opposed to the Bank represented business. The principal of these were Senator Henry Clay of Kentucky, not a business man himself but closely associated with business men and interested in two Kentucky banks, and General Samuel Smith of Baltimore, a rich banker, merchant, and Senator from Maryland. There were also Representative Isaac McKim of Baltimore, a wealthy merchant, and Representative P. B. Butler of New York, an enterprising business man interested in transportation in the Niagara Falls region. Representative Andrew Gregg of Penn-

---

* William Findley wrote in 1814 that he had not advocated repeal of the Bank of North America's charter in 1786, though he voted for it in preference to continuing a perpetual monopoly, "but I was in favour of substituting a smaller bank in its place." *PMHB*, v (1881), 444.

[13] Clarke and Hall, 780.

sylvania voted against the Bank, though he seems to have made no speech; and upon leaving Congress shortly thereafter, he became president of a state bank in Pennsylvania. Samuel Taggart, a Federalist representative from rural Massachusetts, remarked at the time, "It is a matter of astonishment that every representative of the great commercial towns, with the exception of Mr Quincy and Mr Pickman of Massachusetts, voted for the indefinite postponement"—that is, to kill the Bank. Taking into account the way representatives of business enterprise worked against the Bank, and the way numerous agrarians worked for it, one finds it hard to ascribe the Bank's discontinuance to agrarian opposition.[14]

The conventional view is that the business world was for the bank and the agrarian world was against it. The exact opposite is not true but nearly so. The evidence for the conventional view is its repeated assertion. There is also a specious reasonableness about it, if one assume that a bank is never anything but a bank, that the business world is never divided, and that economic groups always act homogeneously. Professor Holdsworth, for example, says that "in general, the banks and trade organizations of the country favored renewal" of the charter; but his evidence does not indicate that they did. On the other hand, some historians, including those contemporary with the events, have plainly and repeatedly recognized the agency of state banks in the cutting off of the Bank of the United States.[15]

Outside the government, unofficial advocates of the Bank were few and fettered by its reticence. Matthew Carey, a prominent Jeffersonian, and Condy Raguet, another, complained of the dearth of information on which to establish a cogent case. Other Philadelphians and the four state banks in the city petitioned Congress to renew the charter, urging the Bank's usefulness and importance—which, to Philadelphia at least, they must have realized keenly since its headquarters were there and still supported the city's financial primacy. The Bank of New York also memorialized Congress for renewal of the federal Bank's charter. These five state banks—only one of them outside Philadelphia—seem to have been the only ones which cared or bestirred themselves to speak in its behalf. And the president and directors of the Bank of New York expressed in their memorial the public interest as clearly as their own: "They view the

14 American Antiquarian Society, *Proceedings* xxxiii (1923), 352-53.
15 Holdsworth, 83; Mayo, 375.

institution of the Bank of the United States as highly useful to the state banks. From the extent of its capital, its numerous branches, and above all from the protection of the Government, it is enabled to facilitate remittances to every part of the United States, to equalize the balance of specie capital among the different cities, and in cases of any sudden pressure upon the merchants to step forward to their aid in a degree which the state banks are unable to do. It is also able to assist any state institution which from peculiar circumstances may require it."[16]

The advocates of the Bank were temperate and uninspiring. The opponents, on the other hand, outdid one another. A memorial signed by eighty Pittsburghers, 4 February 1811, declared that the Bank "held in bondage thousands of our citizens who dared not to act according to their consciences from fear of offending the British stockholders and Federal directors." The legislatures of several states, Massachusetts, Pennsylvania, Maryland, Virginia, and Kentucky, "instructed" their respective Senators to vote against recharter because the Bank was unconstitutional and encroached dangerously on the sovereignty of the states. There were also influential private citizens of great wealth who were not at all inhibited by so-called class interests from helping to kill the Bank. John Jacob Astor of New York was furious because the Bank had closed his account and refused him further credit; he published his correspondence with it and determined to compass its death. So he informed Secretary Gallatin, a personal friend whom he highly esteemed, that if the Bank's existence were ended, as he hoped it would be, he and associates of his would have $2,000,000 ready for the Treasury's use in order to spare it inconvenience.[17] Mr Astor was an investor in state bank stock and of course had ready alternatives to dealing with the Bank of the United States.*

* The authorities in British North America (Canada now) regularly drew bills of exchange on London and sold them in New York for specie with which to meet administrative and military expenses. In the fall of 1810 Mr Astor purchased £50,000 sterling of such bills and drew $200,000 in specie from the New York office of the federal Bank to be sent north. Something he did or failed to do in obtaining the specie angered the Bank's directors, and they closed his account. This in turn angered him and he resolved to close the Bank. Porter ii, 957-58.

[16] ASP, Finance ii, 453, 460, 470; Holdsworth, 83; Henry Adams, *History* v, 327-37; Wettereau, *PMHB*, lxi (1937), 263-85.
[17] ASP, Finance ii, 470, 479; Porter ii, 957-58.

Jacob Barker, a New York speculator and banker, was also offended at the Bank. He told his story to the Philadelphia *Aurora*, a Republican newspaper that was venomous toward Secretary Gallatin, and, as Barker said himself, helped get its columns filled with denunciations of the Bank. He also went to Washington, "urged on members of Congress the objection to the Bank, and supplied the *Public Advertiser* of New York with editorial articles, not ceasing his exertions until the fate of the Bank was sealed." His half brother, Gideon Gardner of Nantucket, Congressman from Massachusetts, voted against the Bank; and on the whole, Barker thought it "not unreasonable to conclude that he had some influence in overthrowing the first United States Bank." He did not give agrarians any credit for the victory or even mention them.[18]

IV

But personal and business considerations such as I have described were subordinated, in public discussion, to general arguments. The favorite contention was that the Bank of the United States was unconstitutional. This was a line of attack that had a lofty and disinterested sound, that could be taken up by anyone, no matter how little he knew of banking, money, or the government's fiscal affairs, and that sustained endless discourse. In Clarke and Hall's *Legislative History of the Bank of the United States*, some thirty-nine speeches on renewal of the charter are recorded, not counting arguments on parliamentary procedure and incidental issues, and thirty-five of these dealt with constitutionality. It is entirely credible that some of the speakers were sincerely concerned about constitutionality, but one feels some skepticism when arguments that had been made by James Madison twenty years before were now offered with great earnestness by General Samuel Smith and P. B. Porter, enterprising business men of Baltimore and Buffalo respectively; or when, as Professor Dorfman observes, Senator Henry Clay used arguments against the Bank—this "splendid association of favoured individuals invested with exemptions and surrounded by immunities and privileges"—that had already been used by his political opponents against one of his banks in Kentucky.[19]

Second to constitutionality in emphasis was the question of the state banks. Everyone considered it and recognized its practical importance. The agrarian friends of the Bank of the United States

---

[18] Barker, 32.   [19] Dorfman, 341; Parks, 21ff; Mayo, 163ff.

found fault with the state banks, denied they were adequate or suitable for what the government needed, and declared they had to have the discipline of the Bank of the United States. The business friends of the Bank of the United States were not so hostile to the state banks but denied their adequacy and suitability. The agrarian enemies of the Bank of the United States were forced at least to tolerate the state banks; its business enemies lauded them enthusiastically. Representative R. M. Johnson of Kentucky, an ardent Jeffersonian, complained that the Bank of the United States would interfere with state banks and in particular "would contract very much the circulation of the state bank notes and would in many other respects come in collision with state rights."[20]

At two points the state banks and constitutionality impinged on each other. Advocates of the Bank argued that it was "necessary" and consequently constitutional because section 8 of the Constitution empowers Congress "to make all laws which shall be necessary and proper" for executing certain specified functions; e.g., collecting taxes, paying debts, providing for the general welfare. The enemies of the Bank declared in reply that it was unnecessary because it did nothing for the federal government that state banks could not do; whereupon the advocates of the Bank declared in their turn that this was an admission of necessity and consequently of constitutionality, since if it were necessary to have any kind of bank, it was constitutional for Congress to provide the kind it thought best. The other point, now made apparently for the first time, but not the last, and originating with Senators Taylor of South Carolina and Crawford of Georgia, both Jeffersonian and agrarian, was that the state banks were unconstitutional because they were issuing bank notes, which were bills of credit, and thereby, though creatures of the states, were doing something that the states themselves had not the right to do.[21]

But for the most part the state banks roused questions of expediency and wisdom only. Senator Crawford asked rhetorically what had induced certain "great states" to instruct members of the Congress to vote against the United States Bank.* "Their avarice," he replied. "They have erected banks, in many of which they hold

---

* In the smaller and newer states of the South and West there was considerable jealousy of the "great states," Virginia and others to the North, which were the most populous and wealthy.

[20] Clarke and Hall, 232.　　　　[21] Clarke and Hall, 309-10, 441-42, 459.

stock to a considerable amount, and they wish to compel the United States to use their banks as places of deposit for their public monies, by which they expect to increase their dividends. And in the banks in which they hold no stock, many of the individual members of their legislatures are stockholders and no doubt were influenced to give instructions by motives of sheer avarice." Senator Taylor of South Carolina boasted that his state, though a very large stockholder in some of her banks, had not been governed by the selfish policy which he implied had governed other states in advising their delegations to vote against the Bank of the United States. He denounced vigorously the proposal that the federal government depend on state banks, which he identified with "the city influence, the London and Paris influence," against which stood "the nation, the great agricultural interest, the solid yeomanry of the country." The Bank of the United States was on the side of the latter and against it were "the great capitalists, monopolists of state banks." This, of course, was traditional agrarian language, but with the tables turned. Senator Taylor had described himself as "of that class of the community, by some called clod hoppers." He stood for their interests and wished that the Bank of the United States charter be extended, being "desirous, in that way, to paralyze the speculation now standing, like the pike, ready to snap at the bait." He stated that he had never owned bank stock or borrowed a cent from any bank.[22]

Senator Pope of Kentucky said that no matter how the question of renewing the charter were disguised, "still it will clearly appear to be a contest between a few importing states and the people of the United States." He mentioned the instructions of the two largest states, Pennsylvania and Virginia, "in substance requiring Congress to give up to the state banks the collection of the national revenue." If, he said, the object of the opposition were "to eradicate the banking system from the country, I might, in obedience to my former prejudices, be more disposed to join them." But this was not even pretended. The sole object in killing off the federal Bank, he said, "is to generate more of these vipers. . . ." Like Senator Taylor of South Carolina, he regarded the Bank of the United States as helpful to the newer and less commercial states. "If we relinquish entirely our power over the monied capital," by ending the career of the Bank of the United States, "will not the influence of the interior states be diminished and that of the commercial states

22 Clarke and Hall, 310, 410-11, 418, 449, 458, 462.

increased?" Then the great commercial states would have the monied capital, and the greater part of the federal deposits would be in their banks.[23]

Representative Samuel McKee of Kentucky was another who averred that refusal to renew the Bank's charter would enhance the power of certain states. The federal revenue would then be collected and deposited in state banks. About a third of it would be deposited in Pennsylvania banks; and those banks, he said, as related to the federal government, are "entirely foreign banks," over which the federal government had "no control whatsoever." By failure to renew the Bank's charter, public funds would be wrested from the people's hands, "not for the public service or public good but for the express purpose of putting it into the pockets of the wealthy capitalists of Pennsylvania! the state bank stockholders of Massachusetts, Maryland, and Virginia!" He asked if the state banks were not as dangerous to political liberties as the Bank of the United States and warned his party that with them "you have all the evils of the United States Bank without any of the advantages."[24]

I have cited so far only southern and western advocates of the Bank of the United States as against the local banks, but there were northerners with the same ideas. Representative John Nicholson, Republican, of up-state New York, said he perfectly understood that "this preposterous plan of substituting state banks has been suggested and in some measure urged through the influence of some of those banks," and it seemed incredible to him that "this miserable quackery" should succeed. Thomas R. Gold, also from up-state New York, but a Federalist, spoke more picturesquely of "the new and gladdening reign of state banks" that the demise of the Bank of the United States would introduce. "Preparations are in forwardness for celebrating the nuptials of these state-damsels, who with little modesty, attend in the ante-chamber, eager to rush into the arms of patronage in the Treasury." The state bank interest was plain. "Are the policy, the cooperation, and active movements of the state banks not seen? While the United States Bank is going down, do you not observe the wreckers hovering on the coast?" The states were ready to fill up, with new banks, any room left by the Bank of the United States.[25]

Besides such observations on the replacement of the government

---

[23] Clarke and Hall, 361, 371.   [24] Clarke and Hall, 209, 297-98.
[25] Clarke and Hall, 225-26, 261.

Bank's services with those of the state banks, there was pointed recognition that the Bank of the United States regulated the state banks. Senator Crawford of Georgia assured those who believed banking to be injurious that its injurious effects were diminished by the federal Bank. The state banks, "whose credibility in this case is unquestionable," had acknowledged that the influence of the Bank upon them was good; "that it prevents excessive discounts and emissions of paper, which but for this check would inevitably take place." He declared that this was far more effective restraint than could be imposed by legislation. Willis Alston of North Carolina declared that the Bank of the United States "serves as a controlling power, keeps the state banks in proper bounds, and prevents them from issuing a vast quantity of paper, which would inundate the country." Jonathan Fisk, an up-state New York Republican, stated that the Bank of the United States had "confined the discounts of other banks to certain limits and compelled them to observe some proportion between their loans and actual funds. And in this way it has served as a barometer to ascertain the credit of other banks—as a regulator to keep them within such bounds as might be safe to the community." John Stanly of North Carolina declared that it was "from the state banks that danger is to be apprehended." They had over-issued in the past, "and such again may be the case, if we remove the check, the restraining influence, which the large and solid capital of the Bank of the United States, and its prudent direction, has enabled it to exercise over the state banks—these 'mushrooms', as the gentleman has called them, which like Jonah's gourd have sprung up in one night and withered in the next."[26]

There was also repetition by the Bank's opponents of the juvenile idea that foreign investment in its stock imposed a burdensome and degrading tribute on the country. And this notion, too, was answered by no one more effectually than by some of the agrarians. The veteran William Findley of Pennsylvania said that foreign capital had been of "great advantage to the United States," for from its use "our own commercial capital has been created and our country improved." He observed that, according to the Barings, American merchants "were always indebted to British merchants and manufacturers upwards of £2,000,000 sterling, for which they had a credit of eighteen months"; and he asked why, if foreign investment

[26] Clarke and Hall, 158, 191, 290, 314.

in America were dangerous, this commercial indebtedness were not equally so. "No man," said Senator Taylor of South Carolina, "who has attentively considered the rise, progress, and growth of these States, from their first colonization to the present period, can deny that foreign capital, ay, British capital, has been the pap on which we first fed—the strong aliment which supported and stimulated our exertions and industry, even to the present day. . . ." Yet he affirmed that southerners, though they sold to Britain and bought from her, were "not the less Republican, nor the less independent in their politics, nor the less free from foreign partialities." Samuel McKee of Kentucky also defended foreign capital, and observed that Mr Jefferson himself must have approved it, else how could his administration have sold the government's stock in the Bank "directly to Englishmen?" And if it were bad for stock of the federal Bank to be owned abroad, the argument was equally good against the state banks and proved the necessity for their destruction also.[27]

I have again emphasized southern and western advocacy of the Bank in order to question the idea that political alignment on renewal of the charter was capitalist and agrarian. In 1791 the northern business interest which had voted for the Bank had been strongly Federalist; it was no longer so. The Bank of the United States had been favored by that interest's need of the federal government to protect and foster trade. Since then the states too had proved to be useful instruments of business expansion, and the number of state banks had multiplied from three to ninety. Multifarious economic enterprise of a modern sort was taking the place of the predominantly mercantile business activity of the eighteenth century. The Industrial Revolution had become more than a barely palpable force. The rifts between the agrarian world and the business world, and between the North and South, were as sharp as ever, but the attitude of each toward government had altered. The debates on renewal of the charter show business sheering toward closer association with the separate state governments, and the agrarians sheering toward a closer association with the federal government.

But this mutual interchange of policies between the two groups was not complete and clear-cut. The Republican party—Jefferson's party—was no longer overwhelmingly agrarian. It now comprised

[27] Clarke and Hall, 209, 417, 465.

both a business wing and an agrarian wing. The business wing was against the Bank; the agrarian wing was divided for and against it. Which was orthodox and which schismatic can not be said. President Madison and Secretary Gallatin were for the Bank, and with them were enlightened agrarians who recognized that the federal Bank was a curb on the state banks. The die-hards who were against anything called a bank, no matter what its purpose and effects, were against the federal Bank with a stubborn consistency which aligned them with the more aggressive business and state bank interests. The latter included Senator Henry Clay of Kentucky and Senator Samuel Smith of Maryland in Congress, and outside they included many banks which united political and business interests in powerful local or regional institutions, such as the Bank of Kentucky. These interests controlled newspapers and made them in this campaign against the Bank of the United States a clamorous and abusive instrument of faction. Their banks were inflationary, political, and avid of public business. The Bank of the United States stood in their path both as government depository and as regulator of the currency. They by no means constituted the whole, for there were some conservative institutions, the venerable Bank of New York among them, which recognized the value of the central bank's regulatory powers and supported it. But far from being the recognized leader of the business interests, the Bank of the United States had the more enterprising part of the business world sticking knives in its back while its forensic enemies damned it verbosely in the public councils for being unconstitutional. The prophecy of Fisher Ames twenty years before that causes of hatred and rivalry would abound and make the state banks unfriendly to the Bank of the United States was quite fulfilled.

In urging the usefulness of the Bank and the wisdom of continuing it, the administration Republicans were, of course, reversing the party's original stand with respect to the Bank and inviting the repeated charge of apostasy. They were impelled, to that extent, to construe the Constitution liberally, taking into account the repeated acquiescence in the Bank's status by all three branches of the federal government and by the states severally and the implied confirmation of its legality in supplementary laws. Senator Brent of Virginia, a Jeffersonian, urged this argument at length, and in the course of it asked, if the Bank were unconstitutional, what of the legislators, courts, jurors, and officers by whose will at least one man had been hanged for counterfeiting the Bank's notes? "Are they not murderers?" For death had been inflicted in support of an institution which it was now declared "Congress had no right to create and for the violation of laws the constitution prohibits."* Senator Brent's argument that this "vibrating constitutional doctrine, to-day one thing, to-morrow another," would reduce the Constitution to nothing, was put by Senator Crawford still more forcibly. "Suppose, sir, you now decide that it is unconstitutional for Congress to incorporate a bank; this will not settle the constitutional question. . . . You say you have not the right to incorporate a bank. Ten years hence other men come into power and say they have the right and exercise that right for twenty years. The bank then will have been constitutional for twenty years, unconstitutional for ten years, and constitutional for twenty more. Are we to go on in this unsettled, miserable, halting manner?" His views of the Constitution were of no orthodox narrowness. "The original powers granted to the Government by the Constitution," he had already said, "can never change with the varying circumstances of the country; but the means by which those powers are to be carried into effect must necessarily vary with the varying state and circumstances of the nation. . . . The Constitution, in relation to the means by which its powers are to be executed, is one eternal now."[28]

Both reconstructed and unreconstructed Jeffersonians were involved in departure from the true Jeffersonian hostility to all banking—the former by their support of the national Bank and the latter, including Jefferson himself, by siding with the state banks—but the former group found it easier to reconcile their support of the Bank with agrarian tradition than did the latter group their tolerance of the state banks. For the former could say, and did, that the federal Bank was an institution over which the government had some control, that it was very different from the local banks, and that it minimized the evils of the latter. The wing of the party that continued its hostility to the Bank had, on the other hand, to

---

* In 1791, it will be recalled, Giles of Virginia had presented this possibility as an argument against the Bank.

In 1845 the defense of a counterfeiter in New York was that the statute authorizing the establishment of the bank whose notes he had counterfeited was unconstitutional, that the bank itself had therefore no legal existence, and that he therefore had committed no crime. The courts upheld him. *DeBow* v. *The People*, 1 Denio 9.

[28] Clarke and Hall, 309, 402, 445.

reconcile itself with the state banks and to pretend that they were somehow less injurious to society than was the Bank of the United States.* This was difficult, particularly since the notorious behavior of the Farmers Exchange Bank of Glocester, Rhode Island; whereas the worst to be alleged of the federal Bank was that King George might get control of it and thereby regain America. "Sir," was the response of Senator John Taylor of South Carolina to this argument, "if the sky were to fall, we should catch larks."[29]

V

Neither group of the Bank's enemies could have killed it alone; the vote against it had in each house a margin of one only. In its own behalf, the Bank did little but stand in proud silence on its record. But merit was not enough. Professor Wettereau observes that though the affairs of the Bank had been, in Gallatin's words, "wisely and skilfully managed," the directors manifested political ineptitude. This implies that they tried something and failed. I doubt if they cared much to try; they had a lobbyist in Washington, but he was worthless. The Bank, though profitable, was a public rather than a private institution, the directors themselves were not politicians, and they did not choose to demean themselves in order to gain public appreciation. For years they had been the objects of calumny and legislative threats. They could make more money other ways and live happier lives. So they must have been either very stubborn or excessively patriotic to have had their hearts set on continuing the Bank. Aside from all this, the directors may have been discouraged by the threats of interference with the Bank's branches by the states. The Bank lost the suit over Georgia's taxation of the Savannah branch, *Bank of the United States* v. *Deveaux*, just a year before expiry of the charter and when it already seemed

* Respecting the alleged political influence of the Bank of the United States, Samuel McKee of Kentucky reminded Congress that Rhode Island, Connecticut, and Delaware were the only states represented in both houses exclusively by Federalists; yet there never was a branch of the Bank of the United States in any of them. There were branches, however, in Georgia, South Carolina, Virginia, Maryland, New York, and Massachusetts, and the head office in Pennsylvania. "The two first are exclusively republican states, and those parts of all the others, except Massachusetts, where those banks are seated, are represented on this floor by Republicans. . . ." Clarke and Hall, 205.

29 Clarke and Hall, 459.

likely that hostility to the Bank in Congress would prevail.* But
even if it did not, the directors could scarcely have seen much that
was attractive in the prospect of operating branches more at the
government's convenience than at the Bank's own, in states alive
with hostile legislators, officials who burst into the Bank's vaults,
and jealous courts.[30]

The government, accordingly, showed more concern to have the
charter renewed than did the Bank's directors; the stockholders,
being largely foreign, had little to say in the matter. And the
government's concern was Secretary Gallatin's. Discontinuance of
the Bank meant for the Treasury a reorganization of procedures
followed for twenty years and the devising of new agencies and
arrangements. He naturally would seek to avoid such disruption.
The speeches in Congress in advocacy of the Bank seem to reflect
his patient and skillful coaching. Yet personal animosity to him in
Congress was a main impediment to recharter, as he seemed to think.
"In 1810 the weight of the administration was in favor of a renewal,
Mr Madison having made his opinion known that he considered the
question as settled by precedent, and myself an open and strenuous
advocate. We had the powerful support of Mr Crawford in the
Senate and no formidable opponent in either House but Mr Clay,
a majority of political friends in both Houses, and almost all the
Federal votes on that question; with no other untoward circumstance
but the *personal* opposition to Mr Madison or myself of the Clintons,
the Maryland Smiths, Leib, and Giles. The banking system had not
yet penetrated through the country, extending its ramifications
through every hamlet, and the opposition due to the jealousy or
selfishness of rival institutions was confined to a few cities; yet the
question was lost." Mr Gallatin evidently considered the state banks
much less influential in 1810 and 1811 than at the time he made
his statement, 1830.[31]

Another retrospect of interest is that of Erastus Root, Republican
representative from Otsego and Delaware counties in New York,
who about thirty-five years after the event recalled the controversy
in Congress over recharter of the Bank in the following paragraphs:
"When the charter of the Bank was about to expire and the

* The Bank lost on a question of jurisdiction, the merits of her suit not
being touched.

[30] *Bank of the United States* v. *Deveaux*, 5 Cranch 61 (US 1809); Warren i, 389-
92; Wettereau, *PMHB*, lxi (1937), 284.
[31] Gallatin ii, 435.

question of its renewal began to agitate the public mind, this country was in the midst of its difficulties which resulted in war. Great Britain had vexed us by the impressment of our seamen and by her orders in council blockading all the northern coast of continental Europe. France, too, under the pretense of retaliating the British orders in council, visited our commerce with the destructive influence of her Berlin and Milan decrees. The Federalists, although they did not undertake entirely to exculpate, evidently took sides with, Great Britain as against France, if not their own country. They cast the heaviest censure upon France and were opposed to a war with Great Britain. The Republicans, on the other hand, threw the greatest blame upon Great Britain as having led the way in depredation. At this time a large portion of the stock of the Bank of the United States was owned in England. It was not originally subscribed by Englishmen but had been remitted there in payment of debts. The prejudice of the Republicans was very strong against Great Britain and everything British or in any wise connected with her. The Bank was called a British bank, and its supposed influence in this country was dreaded. A majority of its directors were Federalists, and this circumstance, added to their British predilections, induced the whole Federal party to favor its recharter. Under such circumstances it is not wonderful that the great mass of the Republican party were opposed to the Bank.

"Nought but a sense of a strong necessity of a national Bank could induce any Republican to give it his support. I remember well how often I attempted to reason my political friends into a belief that a national Bank was so necessary to a sound currency and a safe management of the Treasury that we ought not to hazard the timely creation of a new one. I attempted to repel the notion of a supposed British influence in this country through the English stockholders. I urged that the influence, if any, would be the other way—America operating upon England. As the English stockholders could have no agency—not even remote—in the management of the affairs of the Bank, they could have none of that influence which the disposition of pecuniary favors may be supposed to give; but, on the contrary, the stockholders, deriving their income from funds managed by American directors, liable to sequestration by the American Government, dependent as to its amount in a great measure upon the peaceful and prosperous condition of this country, and in the event of a war its receipt entirely cut off—at least for a time—would have every inducement which interest can prompt to influence their government to forbear. All this reasoning was of no avail with the Republicans of Otsego and Delaware. With them it was a Federal Bank, a British Bank, which would keep us under Federal and British influence. They were my constituents, for I was their Representative in Congress. I was unwilling to displease my constituents and therefore stepped aside when the vote was taken on rechartering the Bank. I fled the question—a trick I have seldom performed and of which I never was proud."[32]

The legislative record shows that Mr Root was one of eleven members absent on this vote, of whom seven were out of town and four, including him, "were absent from indisposition and other causes."[33]

When it was settled that the charter was not to be renewed, the Bank asked for two years' extension in which to liquidate, but it was refused. Senator Henry Clay's committee, to which the request was referred and which included only one friend of the Bank, Senator James A. Bayard of Delaware, reported that since the charter was unconstitutional, extension of it would also be unconstitutional. Furthermore it observed with insolence that "the paper of the Bank of the United States is rapidly returning and that of other banks is taking its place"; that the ability of the state banks to lend was being enhanced; "and when it shall be further increased by a removal into their vaults of those deposits which are in the possession of the Bank of the United States, the injurious effects of a dissolution of the corporation will be found to consist in an accelerated disclosure of the actual condition of those . . . whose insolvent or tottering situation, known to the Bank, has been concealed from the public at large." As if banks did not, customarily and properly, "conceal from the public at large" the private affairs of their customers! But the long-winded malice of the committee's remark never found the predicted support in facts. There were no such losses. There was no accelerated disclosure of tottering situations. The branches were sold to the organizers of new local banks. Liquidation of its affairs was not completed for many years, the final dividend being paid in 1852 and bringing total payments to 109 per cent of the capital; 100 per cent, however, had already been returned to the stockholders by the year 1815. Therefore they lost only interest and prospective profits. The real losers by the Bank's dissolution were the govern-

[32] Jabez Hammond I, 578.   [33] Clarke and Hall, 275.

ment and the economy as a whole—except that the government as stockholder lost nothing but instead made a good profit.[34]

The Philadelphia business was acquired and continued by Stephen Girard, who when the charter expired was the Bank's largest stockholder, though not wholly as a matter of his free choice. Mr Girard had had upwards of $1,000,000 of his funds in Europe, which about 1810, in alarm at the way Bonaparte's empire was expanding, he began transferring from the continent to England and thence, concerned about Britain's ability to withstand Bonaparte, to the United States. So large a flight of capital had to be accomplished by such means as availed, and these were in bonds of the states, in stock of the Bank, and in merchandise. About half the total amount, more than $600,000, Mr Girard brought over in goods, and the remainder he exchanged through the Barings for bonds and stocks then held abroad. He acquired thus nearly $400,000 of Bank stock. While this was going forward it had become plain that the Bank's federal charter would not be renewed and that neither could a charter be obtained from Pennsylvania. Mr Girard was evidently uneasy about his growing investment in the Bank, but after some hesitancy and consultation with the Bank's directors and officers he continued his acquisitions. By December 1811 he seems to have decided to transform his investment into a local bank of his own, and in May 1812 he bought the Philadelphia office of the Bank of the United States virtually on the hoof, acquiring all at once the staff, including particularly the cashier, George Simpson, and the building, but only part of the assets.* The new concern was the Bank of Stephen Girard, wholly owned by him and unincorporated. Yet visually it was the old Bank of the United States unchanged: customers found themselves in the same handsome room and dealing with the same staff. The chagrined enemies of the Bank within the state had the same impression and kept their enmity trained on what seemed practically the same object as before. "Girard was opposed by both the conservative and radical financial interests of the state."** His bank had about the same amount of capital as he had fetched from Europe.

* Most of the assets, it appears, were liquidated, not sold.

** Kenneth L. Brown, "Stephen Girard's Bank," *Pennsylvania Magazine of History and Biography*, LXVI (1942), 29-55. I am indebted to Mr Brown's essay for the details of this paragraph.

34 Clarke and Hall, 448; Holdsworth, 107-08.

CHAPTER 9

War, Suspension, and Resumption

1812-1816

I. Trade and the Treasury — II. A new federal Bank — III. Arguments for and against it — IV. The new charter — V. Organization of the new federal Bank — VI. Resumption by the state banks

I

"The creation of new state banks . . . ," wrote Albert Gallatin, "was a natural consequence of the dissolution of the Bank of the United States. And, as is usual under such circumstances, the expectation of great profits gave birth to a much greater number than was wanted. . . . That increase took place on the eve of and during a war which did nearly annihilate the exports and both the foreign and coasting trade. And, as the salutary regulating power of the Bank of the United States no longer existed, the issues were accordingly increased much beyond what the other circumstances already mentioned rendered necessary."[1]

Mr Gallatin reckoned that between 1811 and 1816 bank note circulation increased from $28,000,000 to $68,000,000; and this increase implied an even greater increase in loans. The regulator of bank credit had been removed, the need of bank credit had diminished, and the supply of it was expanding. This made the weakness of the banking system grave at the best, and circumstances were not of the best. When the British raided Washington in August 1814 and threatened Baltimore, the alarm induced runs on the banks for specie and they had to stop paying it out. The runs spread from Baltimore to Philadelphia and New York. The banks in New England did not suspend, but otherwise suspension was general throughout the country.[2]

General bank suspension was a new thing for Americans, but in effect it was like the earlier failures to redeem governmental paper money. The principal novelty lay in the proof that a banking sys-

---

[1] Gallatin III, 285.   [2] Gallatin III, 286-87.

tem as well as a government could issue obligations beyond its means. Yet a general suspension was not in 1814, nor for years later, the violently disturbing matter it became subsequently, and worst of all, over a century later, in 1933. In 1814, suspensions simply meant that banks could not or would not pay specie to their creditors. They remained open, however, and otherwise transacted business as usual, as the Bank of England had been doing since 1797. Their notes and the checks drawn on them continued as media of monetary payment. The condition resembled the modern suspension of gold payments by government, which ends the use of gold for monetary purposes within the economy but by no means impedes internal monetary payments otherwise. The suspension, consequently, was no hardship to the banks. It was like a man's going to bed when he has a fever; he is certainly more comfortable that way, and he may even be reluctant to get up again. So it was with the banks. Their obligations ceased to worry them, and therefore they could worry less about the obligations of their debtors. As Daniel Webster and others repeatedly observed in Congress, their profits during suspension were "extravagant."

General suspensions were regarded as if they were merely the aggregate of individual failures; yet in fact they differed qualitatively, in *Gestalt* fashion. Legislative and regulatory action by the states had some effect against individual suspensions, but it was quite futile against general suspension. Federal action only could be effectual there, and federal action, by failure to recharter the Bank of the United States, was outlawed. Consequently a problem that was organic to the whole economy—to the whole nation—was left in the laps of the several states, which as parts and segments of the whole, dealt with it, or not, as if the Constitution had never been written; and as many solutions might be attempted as the several sovereignties, whose numbers were increasing, might or might not decide.

One consequence of the suspension was that bank notes at once began to sink under discounts varying "not only from time to time but at the same time from state to state and in the same state from place to place." According to Mr Gallatin, the currency was worth 100 cents on the dollar in New England, 93 cents on the dollar in New York and Charleston, 85 cents in Philadelphia, 75 to 80 cents in Baltimore and Washington, "with every other possible variation in other places and states." This was the money the government had to accept if it were to collect the taxes and imposts due it, for there was none other. But what was more serious, the revenue itself had shrunk. Duties on foreign trade were the principal source of federal income; that trade had been disrupted, and no other sources had been found.[3]

Before the Bank of the United States closed, March 1811, Secretary Gallatin had arranged for state banks to take on the Treasury's business, but they were a poor substitute at best, and in the existing circumstances they were nearly useless. The Treasury now had no one responsible place to turn for quick loans, but must negotiate here, there, and everywhere, encountering varying dispositions and abilities. Its funds were no longer available where it needed them, as the Bank's branch organization had made possible, but must be transported by such means as could be found. Besides these external difficulties, the Treasury, upon Mr Gallatin's departure in May 1813, fell into the weak hands of William Jones and then of George W. Campbell. In October 1814 Alexander J. Dallas of Philadelphia became Secretary. Although Mr Dallas was a very competent person and eventually left things better than he found them, he had at first a pathetic time.

On bond issues of $61,000,000 authorized by Congress from 1812 to 1814, only $45,000,000 had been sold and less than $8,000,000 of that was sold at par. Most was sold at discounts ranging from twelve to twenty per cent. In 1814 an offering of $25,000,000 produced only $10,000,000. A congressional committee in 1830 calculated that indebtedness of more than $80,000,000 incurred by the government from 1812 to 1816 had yielded in specie values only $34,000,000. Soon after Secretary Dallas took office, he reported that nearly $2,000,000 of Treasury obligations were past due and unpaid in Philadelphia, New York, and Boston, and the Treasury had no funds in New England for payment of the interest on the public debt held there. He reported that the Secretary of War, needing money to pay the militia who had marched from Tennessee against the Creek Indians, obtained a loan in bank notes for that purpose from the Bank of Chillicothe, Ohio. Some of these notes had since been offered in payment of taxes to the collectors of internal duties in the state of Tennessee. "But as the banks of Tennessee (where the money collected for taxes is required to be deposited) refuse to receive them as cash deposits, the collectors in

[3] Gallatin III, 331-32; Dewey, *Financial History*, 122-23.

their turn refuse to receive them as cash for taxes." So the government was borrowing more than it was getting, and was paying the soldiers depreciated money that it would not itself accept. Repeating a few days later that interest on the public debt had not been paid punctually, and that a large amount of Treasury notes had already been dishonored, Secretary Dallas said that "the hope of preventing further injury and reproach in transacting the business of the Treasury is too visionary to afford a moment's consolation."[4]

As if these painful admissions were not enough, the Federalist opposition rubbed salt in the sores. Representative Alexander C. Hanson of Maryland scornfully described the local credit standing of the Treasury in the District of Columbia in these words: "So completely empty was the Treasury and destitute of credit that funds could not be obtained to defray the current ordinary expenses of the different Departments. Disgraceful, humiliating, as the fact was, it ought not to be concealed from the nation and he felt it his duty to state to the House that the Department of State was so bare of money as to be unable to pay even its stationery bill. The government was subsisting upon the drainings of unchartered banks in the District. . . . Yes, it was well known to the citizens of the District that the Treasury was obliged to borrow pitiful sums which it would disgrace a merchant in tolerable credit to ask for. . . . In short it was difficult to conceive a situation more critical and perilous than that of the government at this moment, without money, without credit, and destitute of the means of defending the country."[5]

II

With affairs in this posture, the Treasury had a livelier need than ever of a central bank—not merely to lend it money but to marshal the banking system back onto a specie basis and restore a fairly decent currency. Yet according to the venerable agrarian, William Findley of Pennsylvania, now at the close of his long career in Congress, "the erection of a Bank was not so desirable on account of the government as for the general convenience of the country." Though the Treasury should have been taking the initiative, it seems to have done less at first than outsiders were doing. Already

---

[4] Catterall, 2-3; 21st Congress, 1st Session, HR 358, pp. 9, 12 (McDuffie Report, 13 April 1830); Congress, *Annals*, III, 652-53, 717-18, 767-69; Clarke and Hall, 536.

[5] Congress, *Annals*, III, 656-57.

in January 1814, months before the suspension, the petition of "a hundred and fifty inhabitants of the city of New York" praying that a new "National Bank" be incorporated with a capital of $30,000,-000 had been submitted to Congress.[6]

This petition may have been instigated by John Jacob Astor of New York and Stephen Girard of Philadelphia, with whom was associated David Parish, a business man from Hamburg, of Scottish ancestry, who seems to have made money with equal ease on both sides of the Atlantic. Their interest rose from a large investment in bonds of the federal government, for they were the principal individual purchasers of the Sixteen Millions Loan of 1813. Stephen Girard's active promotion of the Bank may also have been influenced by resentment at the attitude of chartered banks toward his own, which was unchartered. The other Philadelphia banks had been very unfriendly, refusing to accept his notes and draining down his specie. Girard, Parish, and Astor developed their plan early in 1814, while Congress was giving the request of the New York petitioners desultory attention. Their purpose was the same as Alexander Hamilton's in 1790, viz., to enhance the value of government bonds by making them exchangeable for stock in a new federal Bank. During the spring David Parish had repaired to Washington, and there, besides members of Congress, he had interviewed President Madison and Secretary Campbell. But their plans miscarried. In August Washington had been raided by the British, Baltimore had been attacked, and it was then, under pressure of the public excitement and fear, that the banks had stopped redeeming their notes. The government was back in Washington shortly, and within a fortnight of his arrival there in October, Secretary Dallas—who presumably knew the plans of Astor, Girard, and Parish and may have owed his appointment to their intercession—responded to an inquiry from Congress with the outline of a plan for a new Bank. But it was a plan too much influenced by the Treasury's need of a place to borrow. Besides having $44,000,000 of its capital invested in government obligations, the proposed Bank was to lend the government $30,000,000. Congress refused to entertain the proposal. In the House a committee measure was prepared in its stead by John C. Calhoun of South Carolina. It too failed.[7]

In January 1815 the two houses agreed upon a new measure,

[6] Clarke and Hall, 475.
[7] McMaster, *Girard* II, 245; K. L. Brown, *JEH*, II (1942), 126-27.

which, however, President Madison vetoed, 30 January 1815. The objection of Congress to the administration's original plan had been that the Bank had too much of the government in it. President Madison's objection was that in the Bank proposed by Congress the government was left out. His objections were wholly practical. He said the capital proposed for the Bank was insufficient to enhance the public credit by giving a lift to the market price of government bonds. The Bank would be "free from all legal obligation to cooperate with the public measures." Moreover, it could not be relied on "to provide a circulating medium," without which, he said, taxes could not be collected, "nor to furnish loans, or anticipations of the public revenue." The President wanted a Bank but not this one; and Congress, he hoped, would "hasten to substitute a more commensurate and certain provision for the public exigencies."[8]

Congress had the subject before it a fortnight and was so close to enactment of a charter conformed to President Madison's views that Jacob Barker, who boasted of his part in annihilating the former federal Bank, got together $100,000 with which to buy shares in the new one. He says he had to pay a premium of twenty-three per cent—that is, $100,000 in specie cost him $123,000 in New York bank notes. He expected a handsome profit, but, he says, "unfortunately news of peace travelled too soon." The treaty ending the war with Great Britain was signed at Ghent, 24 December 1814, but news of the signing did not reach America for several weeks. On 11 February, according to Barker, the new charter was on the table ready for the question, pending concurrence on some last-minute changes in language, "when an express on its way to Alexandria for a speculation in flour passed through Washington with the news of peace, which so elated Congress that the members left their seats without waiting for an adjournment, and they could not again be induced to consider the question of a national Bank during that session." John C. Calhoun confirms this. The bill was brought up again but killed by indefinite postponement, 17 February, the vote being 74 to 73.[9]

Ten months later, when Congress convened in December 1815, President Madison again, in his annual message, emphasized the need of doing something about the currency. The country was now

---

[8] Clarke and Hall, 564, 594-95.

[9] Barker, 123; Clarke and Hall, 606-08; Congress, *Register of Debates* xiv, Part 1, 483.

at peace, and it was true that the government's fiscal needs were lightened; but the banks were still not redeeming their notes. "The benefits of an uniform national currency," said the President, "should be restored to the community." In the absence of the precious metals, a substitute should be devised, and he implied that Congress must choose between the notes of state banks, the notes of a national bank, or the notes of the government. At the same time Secretary Dallas, in his annual report, reviewed the problem and said that a national bank would be "the best and perhaps the only adequate resource to relieve the country and the government from the present embarrassments." The state banks he considered necessary and useful but not adequate without a central bank; the government had the power to issue "a paper medium of exchange" but not the occasion. Upon the whole, he recommended "that a national Bank be established at the city of Philadelphia, having power to erect branches elsewhere, and that the capital of the Bank (being of a competent amount) consist three-fourths of the public stock and one-fourth of gold and silver."[10]

At this stage John C. Calhoun took the congressional leadership on the question, doing so at the urging of Henry Clay of Kentucky, now Speaker of the House. This was despite the fact that it was Calhoun's bill that the President had vetoed a year before. After further consultation with Secretary Dallas, Mr Calhoun, 8 January 1816, introduced a new bill. It was intensively debated, for though the Republicans had got over the worst of their factiousness, the Federalists were uncompromising. It passed the House, 14 March 1816. In the Senate, after like discussion, it passed, 3 April, with amendments; in these the House, on the 5th, concurred. The act was approved by President Madison 10 April 1816.[11]

III

The question of constitutionality, which had so much sincere prominence in 1791 and so much insincere prominence in 1811, had none at all in these debates of 1814, 1815, and 1816. President Madison put the matter clearly and magnanimously when he waived the question of a national Bank's constitutionality, which he had been the first to press twenty-five years before. He waived it "as being precluded . . . by repeated recognitions, under varied cir-

10 Clarke and Hall, 609, 612-13.
11 Catterall, 18-21; Clarke and Hall, 681-82, 706, 713.

cumstances, of the validity of such an institution, in acts of the legislative, executive, and judicial branches of the government, accompanied by indications in different modes of a concurrence of the general will of the nation. . . ." This view of the matter seemed to prevail, save for a few die-hards who said little and were attended to still less. Clarke and Hall's *Legislative History of the Bank of the United States* records only two discourses on constitutionality in these debates. Representative Robert Wright of Maryland, who had opposed recharter in 1811, now concluded that the Supreme Court had decided on the Bank's constitutionality "by often recognizing it"; the question was settled. He might have bowed to the same fact, of course, in 1811. But the real animosities, personal, social, and partisan, that killed the old Bank were now satisfied, and the Republicans were ready to restore what they had destroyed, especially since the government they still controlled was in a sad state. Accordingly, the debates had turned on practical questions: whether the proposed Bank should have its headquarters in Philadelphia, New York, Baltimore, or Washington, the amount of capital, the proportions of specie and government obligations therein, the kind of government obligations, and the nature and extent of the government's interest. The administration wished to make the capital $50,000,000; the opposition contended that this was too much and that it included too little specie. The opposition also found fault with political control of the Bank, and appointment of its president by the administration. *Laisser faire*, the balance of trade, the money market, and the issue of Treasury notes—sophisticated concepts which had not long been in congressional vocabularies—had begun by now to occupy some of the time formerly devoted to constitutional analysis and deduction.[12]

The outstanding discourse on the subject was John C. Calhoun's, which centered attention for the first time upon the monetary questions involved rather than the legal. Speaking, 26 February 1816, for the measure that was enacted a few weeks later, he took it for granted that a national Bank would be helpful in the administration of governmental finances and addressed himself rather to "the cause and state of the disorders of the national currency and the question whether it was in the power of Congress, by establishing a national Bank, to remove those disorders." This emphasis was novel, perspicuous, and realistic. The state of the currency, he said, "was a

---

[12] Clarke and Hall, 594, 709.

stain on the public and private credit and injurious to the morals of the community." It was also opposed to the principles of the federal Constitution. Mr Calhoun's argument was reported as follows:

"The power was given to Congress by that instrument, in express terms, to regulate the currency of the United States. In point of fact, he said, that power, though given to Congress, is not in their hands. The power is exercised by banking institutions, no longer responsible for the correctness with which they manage it. Gold and silver have disappeared entirely. There is no money but paper money; and that money is beyond the control of Congress. No one, he said, who referred to the Constitution, could doubt that the money of the United States was intended to be placed entirely under the control of Congress. The only object the framers of the Constitution could have had in view, in giving to Congress the power to coin money, regulate the value thereof, and of foreign coins, must have been to give a steadiness and fixed value to the currency of the United States. The state of things at the time of the adoption of the Constitution afforded Mr Calhoun an argument in support of his construction. There then existed, he said, a depreciated paper currency, which could only be regulated and made uniform by giving a power for that purpose to the General Government. The states could not do it. He argued, therefore, taking into view the prohibition against the states issuing bills of credit, that there was a strong presumption this power was intended to be exclusively given to Congress. . . ."

With respect to banks, Mr Calhoun said, "No man . . . in the convention, as much talent and wisdom as it contained, could possibly have foreseen the course of these institutions; that they would have multiplied from one to two hundred and sixty; from a capital of four hundred thousand dollars to one of eighty millions; from being consistent with the provisions of the Constitution and the exclusive right of Congress to regulate the currency, that they would be directly opposed to it; that, so far from their credit depending on their punctuality in redeeming their bills with specie, they might go on *ad infinitum* in violation of their contract, without a dollar in their vaults. There had, indeed, Mr Calhoun said, been an extraordinary revolution in the currency of the country. By a sort of under-current, the power of Congress to regulate the money of the country had caved in, and upon its ruins had sprung up those institutions which now exercised the right of making money for and in the United States. For gold and silver are not now the only money; whatever is the medium of purchase and sale must take their place; and as bank paper alone was now employed for this purpose, it had become the money of the country. A change, great and wonderful, has taken place, said he, which divests you of your rights, and turns you back to the condition of the Revolutionary war, in which every state issued bills of credit, which were made a legal tender and were of various values."

This was not merely a legal condition, in Mr Calhoun's judgment; it was a practical and moral one. In five years or so the amount of paper in circulation had increased from eighty or ninety to two hundred million dollars. The banks had been too prodigal of their engagements, issuing more paper than they could possibly redeem. "This excess was visible to the eye, and almost audible to the ear; so familiar was the fact, that this paper was emphatically called *trash*, or *rags.* . . . In what manner, he asked, were the public contracts fulfilled? In gold and silver, in which the Government had stipulated the pay? No; in paper issued by these institutions; in paper greatly depreciated; in paper depreciated from five to twenty per cent below the currency in which the Government had contracted to pay, &c. He added another argument—the inequality of taxation in consequence of the state of the circulating medium, which, notwithstanding the taxes were laid with strict regard to the constitutional provision for their equality, made the people in one section of the union pay perhaps one-fifth more of the same tax, than those in another. The Constitution having given Congress the power to remedy these evils, they were, he contended, deeply responsible for their continuance." Mr Calhoun believed that a national bank would be able to correct the condition of the currency, both by influence and by example. For one of its first rules "would be to take the notes of no bank which did not pay in gold and silver." If this failed to bring the state banks into line, "Congress must resort to measures of a deeper tone which they had in their power."[13]

It is interesting that this constitutional argument for the federal government's responsibility in monetary matters—and hence in banking—and against the state's unconstitutional interference therewith through the agency of the state banks, should have come from that corner where, not many years later, states' rights and

[13] Calhoun, *Works* II, 155-57, 158, 161, 162; Clarke and Hall, 630-34.

nullification of federal powers were to be most boldly and ably advocated. It was the South Carolinian John Taylor who in 1810 first questioned in Congress the encroachment of state banks upon federal prerogatives, and the Georgian William H. Crawford who developed the theme. Now John C. Calhoun propounded it more forcibly; and Crawford's successor, Senator William W. Bibb of Georgia, joined him, denouncing "that species of swindling by which the important necessary power of sovereignty, the regulation of the currency of the country, was taken from the government." Senator James Barbour of Virginia spoke in the same key: "The power intended by the Constitution to have been lodged in the hands of the general government, was, by the failure of the government to make use of it, exercised by every state in the union. . . . Hence arose an excess of paper issues, causing depreciation to an extent which could scarcely be estimated—an evil which called for a remedy in a language not to be misunderstood." And Henry Clay, who in 1811, in the Senate, had been one of the deadliest of the former Bank's enemies, now, as an earnest sponsor of the new one, capably exploited the same theme as Mr Calhoun. Had he foreseen in 1811 what had since come to pass, he said, "he should have voted for the renewal" of the earlier charter. Provisions of the Constitution too little considered in 1811 now seemed to him to make it the duty of Congress to restore the money of the country to soundness. The Constitution "confers upon Congress the power to coin money . . . ; and the states are prohibited to coin money, to emit bills of credit, or to make anything but gold and silver coin a tender in payment of debts. The plain inference is that the subject of the general currency was intended to be submitted exclusively to the general government. In point of fact, however, the regulation of the general currency is in the hands of the state governments, or, which is the same thing, of the banks created by them. Their paper has every quality of money except that of being made a tender, and even this is imparted to it by some states in the law by which a creditor must receive it or submit to a ruinous suspension of the payment of his debt." He believed it "incumbent upon Congress to recover the control, which it had lost, over the general currency." For Congress to attempt direct and drastic action upon the banks he thought impracticable; an effectual remedy, but indirect and milder, could be got through a national Bank. Another Kentuckian, Representative William P. Duval, had been bold and ingenious enough to derive the constitutional power of Congress to establish a national Bank from its power to issue bills of credit—a power, as I said in an earlier chapter, not originally intended, not yet recognized, but eventually affirmed by the Supreme Court.[14]

It is also interesting that Thomas Jefferson should have reasoned as Crawford, Calhoun, and Clay did with respect to the constitutionality of state bank notes, though he shied from coercing the states. He had proposed instead that they be *asked* "to transfer the right of issuing circulating paper to Congress exclusively"; he thought they would do it. Then, when they had, Congress could forbid the further issue of bank notes. It was in a letter to his son-in-law, John W. Eppes, written 24 June 1813, before the debates on the new charter, that he had recommended this means of recovering at once the constitutional control of the currency that the issue of notes by the state banks had destroyed. His remedy was an odd one, but his diagnosis was that of a stalwart array of authorities, whom Daniel Webster also was soon to join. In the matter of constitutionality Andrew Jackson had the same opinion.[15]

Although the argument for centralizing monetary powers in the federal government and denying them to the states had logic and cogency, it is not to be overlooked that it was pressed in Congress by War Hawk leaders committed at the moment to nationalism and a general defense of federal powers. This doubtless made them the readier to defend national monetary powers in particular.

The Federalist opposition to their proposals, led by Daniel Webster, Representative from Massachusetts, had involved no question of the utility of banks or of the constitutional power of Congress to establish one, such as the agrarians had urged when the former Bank was being controverted. The Federalists had not changed from the stand on banking they had taken in 1791. But they had found the proposed new Bank a very weak and unpromising contraption, desperately conceived as a means of pulling the Treasury out of the hole. "To look to a Bank," Webster had said in January 1815, "as a source capable not only of affording a circulating medium to the country but also of supplying the ways and means of carrying on the war—especially at a time when the country is without commerce—is to expect much more than ever will be obtained." Banks were useful, he said; "but they are not sources of

14 Clarke and Hall, 485, 671-72, 685, 687-88.
15 Jefferson (Ford) ix, 393.

national income." Moreover what was proposed "looks less like a Bank than a department of government. . . . Its capital is government debts; the amount of its issues will depend on government necessities. . . . This is, indeed, a wonderful scheme of finance. The government is to grow rich because it is to borrow without the obligation of repaying and is to borrow of a Bank which issues paper without liability to redeem it. . . . Other institutions, setting out perhaps on honest principles, have fallen into discredit through mismanagement or misfortune. But this Bank is to begin with insolvency. It is to issue its bills to the amount of thirty millions, when everybody knows it can not pay them. It is to commence its existence in dishonor. It is to draw its first breath in disgrace."[16]

This was not all hyperbole by any means. The bill that Mr Webster's sarcasm was directed against had been opposed also by Mr Calhoun and rejected by the House. The vote had been so close that it was decided by the Speaker, Langdon Cheves of South Carolina, subsequently a very able president of the Bank that was eventually agreed upon. In voting against it, he had declared his conviction that a Bank as authorized in the measure would fail "to resuscitate public credit; to establish a circulating medium; and to afford the ways and means for the support of government." Like Calhoun and like Webster he apparently wished to have a Bank established but not this one.[17]

But a year later, February 1816, though a new measure on the pattern of the Federalist act of 1791 had been brought in, Mr Webster had still opposed it. His attitude seems captious, and governed at the moment by partisanship rather than principle. But so it was all around. Senator Rufus King of New York, Alexander Hamilton's old friend, who had supported the Federalist Bank and been one of its directors, stood out against a Republican one. The Bank now, as in 1791, was incidental to a party program and was favored or disfavored accordingly. Alexander Hamilton and the Federalists had advocated it then, James Madison and the anti-Federalists, now the Republicans, had opposed it. But Jeffersonian policy had got into a position where a national Bank was as essential to it as it had been to the Federalists twenty-five years before. So now the Federalists, no longer constrained by principle so far as the Bank itself was concerned, but consistent still in opposition to anti-

16 Clarke and Hall, 563-67.
17 Clarke and Hall, 571.

British, pro-war, Jeffersonian Republicanism, were against the new Bank. This alignment, with allowance for some individualistic Jeffersonians who were against the Bank on principle and some individualistic Federalists who were for it on principle, had been reflected in the final vote.[18]

The division of votes on the final act to incorporate the Bank had been geographically like that of 1791, with the sentiments of both sides reversed. In 1791 with the Federalists in power, the North had established the Bank, and the South had opposed it. Now, in 1816, with the Republicans in power, it was the South and West that reestablished the Bank, and the North that opposed it. In the House of Representatives the votes of New England and of the four middle states, New York, New Jersey, Pennsylvania, and Delaware, were 45 to 35 against the Bank.* In the nine southern and western states they were 45 to 26 for it. The Senate went for the Bank more heartily than the House, the vote being 22 to 12, and more than half the votes for the Bank coming from the South and West. If the votes of the two houses be combined, New England and the four middle states gave 44 votes for the Bank and 53 against it; and the southern and western states gave 58 for it and 30 against. Virginia was the only one of the latter whose delegation gave a majority against the Bank; it was a majority of one, Virginia's vote being 11 against the Bank and 10 for it. In the North, of nine states, only Rhode Island, New York, and New Jersey gave majorities for the Bank. The vote in 1816 was more clearly regional than either the vote in 1791 on chartering the old Bank or the vote in 1811 on renewal.[19]

Jabez Hammond, of New York, a member of Congress at the time, summarizes the action of 1816 in these words: "The Bank of the United States was chartered during this session. The bill for its charter was reported by Mr Calhoun, chairman of the Finance Committee. It was supported generally by the Republican members of Congress, and among its supporters Clay, Calhoun, Forsyth, Ingham, Lowndes, and J. W. Taylor were the most influential and

---

* This was the House vote, 14 March 1816, which first passed the measure. The House concurrence in the Senate's amendments came later. There was also a House vote, preceding concurrence, to postpone indefinitely; it failed 91 to 67, which was more decisive for the Bank than the vote, 80 to 71, by which the act first passed.

[18] Clarke and Hall, 683-85.   [19] Clarke and Hall, 681-82, 706, 712-13.

efficient.* It was opposed by the Federalists as a party, at the head of whom in the House of Representatives was Mr Webster. They were joined by some of the southern and a few other Democratic members. By the aid of these, Mr Webster entertained sanguine hopes of resisting successfully the passage of the bill, but his expectations were disappointed by a defection in his own ranks, which he did not anticipate and which he perceived with surprise and mortification. Mr Grosvenor from this state and Mr Hulbert from Massachusetts, before the close of the discussion, declared themselves in favor of the Bank, and eventually about fifteen other Federalists voted with them in favor of the bill."[20]

IV

The relation of the new federal Bank with the state banks was, as before, a matter frequently mentioned in the Congressional debates. At the very outset, 17 November 1814, Representative Jared Ingersoll of Pennsylvania said that "the most powerful, pervading, and indefatigable hostility out of doors will be organized by the innumerable state banking institutions; which comprehend within the sphere of their influence almost every man of property in the country, who may apprehend that a Bank of the United States would tend to curtail, to cripple, or to destroy their resources." Mr Ingersoll was somewhat mistaken, since two men of the greatest property, Girard and Astor, found it to their interest to advance the cause of a new federal Bank. Yet a week after he spoke he was confirmed by a memorial presented to Congress "on behalf of five banks in the city of New York" remonstrating against the proposed Bank of the United States and contending, contrary to the sound money principles of which bankers are supposed to be the guardians, that Treasury notes would be preferable to the notes of a federal Bank. John C. Calhoun deplored the great control which the state banks had over public opinion and over the press, declaring "that the present wretched state of the circulating medium had scarcely been denounced by a single paper within the United States." In general,

---

* I.e., Henry Clay, Kentucky; John C. Calhoun, South Carolina; John Forsyth, Georgia; S. D. Ingham, Pennsylvania; William Lowndes, South Carolina; John W. Taylor, New York. "Democratic" and "Republican" meant the same thing to Jabez Hammond and his contemporaries.

[20] Jabez Hammond I, 572-73.

however, the banks seemed to be in a more tractable mood than in 1811, and though their critics in Congress were plain-spoken about them, their friends there were now agreeable to the new project. Criticism of them came chiefly from Mr Calhoun and others who aspersed their constitutionality. Secretary Dallas was more conciliatory. He said in his letter to Chairman Calhoun of the House currency committee, 24 December 1815: "Sinister combinations to defeat the operations of a national Bank ought not to be presumed and need not be feared. It is true that the influence of the state banks is extensively diffused; but the state banks and the patrons of the state banks partake of the existing evils; they must be conscious of the inadequacy of state institutions to restore and maintain the national currency; . . . and, upon the whole, they will be ready to act upon the impulse of a common duty and a common interest." Mr Calhoun was less trustful. The banks were solvent, he believed, and could again redeem their notes were they not indisposed to do so by the "vast profits" which suspension brought them and the twelve to twenty per cent dividends they were paying. "Those who believed that the present state of things would ever cure itself must believe what is impossible; banks must change their nature, lay aside their instinct, before they will aid in doing what it is not their interest to do." He concluded that "it rested with Congress to make them return to specie payments. . . ." John Randolph of Virginia was more skeptical. "It was unpleasant, he said, to put one's self in array against a great leading interest in a community, be they a knot of land-speculators, paper-jobbers, or what not; but, he said, every man you meet, in this House or out of it, with some rare exceptions which only served to prove the rule, was either a stockholder, president, cashier, clerk, doorkeeper, runner, engraver, paper maker, or mechanic, in some way or other to a bank." The state banks, "with their $170,000,000 of paper on $82,000,000 of capital," were only too able to hold their own. "However great the evil of their conduct might be, . . . who was to bell the cat? who was to take the bull by the horns? You might as well attack Gibraltar with a pocket pistol as to attempt to punish them." Representative John Forsyth of Georgia had the same views. "When you threaten the state banks," he said, "they laugh at your threats; when you menace them, they menace you in turn." Such remarks about the state banks were sometimes arguments against the proposed federal Bank, on the ground that it would be no better, and sometimes they were arguments for it.[21]

But the state banks still had their friends. Representative Alney McLean of Kentucky was concerned lest some injury be done to "states extensively interested in their own banks, by forcing a branch of the national Bank upon them. This was the case in Kentucky, where the state owned a great portion of the stock of the state bank, which was very prosperous and its stocks very profitable." McLean was unwilling to put it in the power of any group "to impose upon that state, without its consent, an institution which might be extremely prejudicial to its interests." Samuel Smith of Maryland, who as a Senator in 1811 had seen the state banks able to do all that the Bank of the United States might do, was now as a Representative converted to the need of a federal Bank. He agreed that it "would contribute better than any other measure to the restoration of a general medium of circulation of uniform value; he was afraid, he said, that it was the only remedy." But he was not disposed to be harsh about the state banks. He thought it might be prudent for Congress "to let down these institutions as gently as they could." The banks had lent unwisely and on too long terms, he admitted, and their notes had thence depreciated; but they should not be censured for this. Their loans had aided the country; they had reduced themselves by serving the public. In other words, he seemed to think that though it was bad of banks not to pay what they owed, it was good of them to lend, and it was as liberal lenders that they should be judged. Yet General Smith agreed that it was the duty of the banks to resume specie payments, "so soon as it was possible to do it without loss. . . . If they did not do it, they ought to be compelled to do it; and through the instrumentality of a Bank of the United States, the government might be able to coerce them." He was not wholly satisfied with the plan of the Bank but believed a suitable modification could be achieved. "He could find but few gentlemen, he said, who in conversation did not appear favorable to the establishment of a Bank."[22]

V

The new charter now in effect differed from the old mainly in verbosity, being about treble the length. The changes of themselves

---

[21] Clarke and Hall, 507, 531, 617, 633-34, 655, 663.
[22] Clarke and Hall, 636-38, 678.

did not require a new statute but might readily have been effected in the old one by amendment. In every sense the new Bank was what the old one might have been. For this and other reasons, I think the corporate distinction between the first and second federal Banks has been too much emphasized and the identity of their function neglected. They were separate legal entities, to be sure, but that is less significant than their likeness and continuity, for they served the same needs in the same way for forty of the forty-five years from 1791 to 1836.

The old Bank had had a capital of $10,000,000; the new had $35,000,000. The old shares had a par of $400—the new a par of $100. The government had owned, for a while, $2,000,000, or one-fifth, of the stock of the old Bank; it had $7,000,000, or one-fifth, in the new Bank's stock and was to receive a bonus of $1,500,000 payable in three installments during the first few years of operation. The new Bank, like the old, had its head office in Philadelphia and was authorized to establish branches wheresoever its directors saw fit; under certain conditions it might be required, unlike the old Bank, to establish at least one in each state. As in the case of the old Bank, the charter was to run twenty years. The new Bank, like the old, was to be the principal depository of the United States Treasury,* it was to report to the Treasury, and it was subject to Treasury inspection. There was to be the same number of directors, twenty-five, but in the new Bank five of these were to be appointed by the President of the United States, with approval of the Senate.**

The new Bank's liabilities were restricted to the amount of the capital, as had been those of the old Bank; and, also as in the case of the old, the specie capital of the Bank was to be at least one-fifth of the gross capital. So in effect the same ratio as before between specie and liabilities, one to five, was authorized.

On 1 May 1816, about three weeks after approval of the charter by President Madison, the five commissioners designated by him to superintend subscription to the new federal Bank's stock met at Mr Girard's bank in Philadelphia to formulate their plans; and on the 4 July subscriptions began to be received. The charter prescribed that lists be opened for subscribers in Portland, Maine; Portsmouth,

---

* The old Bank had been depository in fact, though the statute had not said specifically that it should be.

** The two charters are compared in detail in Dewey, *The Second United States Bank*, 164ff.

New Hampshire; Boston; Providence; Middletown, Connecticut; Burlington, Vermont; New York; New Brunswick, New Jersey; Philadelphia; Wilmington, Delaware; Baltimore; Richmond; Lexington, Kentucky; Cincinnati; Raleigh; Nashville; Charleston; Augusta, Georgia; New Orleans; and Washington, D.C. This and an elaborate procedure to be followed by the five commissioners in Philadelphia and the three in each of the other cities were familiar practice in the establishment of state banks. Their purpose was to give every one a fair chance to acquire stock. For it was characteristic of the mounting democratic tendency that opportunity to become a capitalist should be thrown as widely open as possible. Mr Calhoun said it was the boast of his party, the Republicans, that it had "the yeomanry, the substantial part of our population," on its side and could "present the opportunity to every capitalist, however inconsiderable, to share in the capital of the Bank."* To the same purpose, no shareholder, no matter how many his shares, had more than thirty votes—a vain limitation, which was evaded by persons who got themselves designated as nominees or attorneys to vote any number of proxies.

But the opportunity was not too inviting, and contrary to the familiar experience of having new issues of bank stock riotously over-subscribed in a matter of hours, subscriptions to the federal Bank came in slowly. When the twenty-day period which the charter stipulated closed, the subscriptions were about $3,000,000 short of the $28,000,000 to be taken by the public. Accordingly the lists were reopened in Philadelphia, as prescribed, at Mr Girard's bank, and the entire $3,000,000 wanting was at once subscribed by Mr Girard himself, to the general astonishment and vexation of would-be subscribers who were not so quick or so flush. Girard did not keep it all, however; he transferred the greater part to others, including his associate, John Jacob Astor. The purpose of this omnivorous subscription, according to Mr Girard's own statement later, was two-fold. He wished to insure that the Bank be established; and he wished to prevent further "increase of a multiplicity of proxies" by his speculative rivals.[23]

Following Thomas Jefferson's fruitful idea that banks be made Republican—if there must be banks—President Madison chose

* It makes no difference that Mr Calhoun said this in 1814 of an earlier version of the charter than the one finally enacted. Clarke and Hall, 528.

23 Biddle Papers 4, Folio 792; McMaster, *Girard* ii, 314.

Stephen Girard and four other Republicans to be the government directors; and he and Secretary Dallas successfully supported another, William Jones, to be the Bank's president. The public stockholders chose their directors 29 October 1816, ten of them Republicans and ten Federalists. The head office opened in Philadelphia, 7 January 1817, the first ten months of the charter's duration having elapsed before the Bank began to transact any business.[24]

VI

Even before the organization of the Bank was completed, preparations had to be undertaken to end the general suspension of specie payments. This was the more exigent because Congress had passed a resolution requiring that after 20 February—barely six weeks later—payments to the United States should be either in specie, in Treasury notes, in the federal Bank's notes, or in state bank notes that would be redeemed on demand. Accordingly the last-named had to be rehabilitated promptly. Unless an arrangement were made by which the notes of the state banks would become redeemable, wrote Secretary Crawford, there would be no medium on and after 20 February in which dues to the United States could be paid.

Congress was peremptory because it was generally believed that the banks, besides prospering from the moratorium they maintained in their own favor, had accumulated adequate specie and could redeem their notes if they only would. It was a "well known fact," wrote William Jones to Secretary Crawford, 9 January 1817, just before the Bank opened, that "the principal banks whose paper is thus degraded are not only solvent but rich in surplus funds and resources." Jones was repeating what was generally believed. It had been Daniel Webster's contention for some time that the federal Bank was not needed, since the state banks could redeem their notes and only awaited compulsion. And it was he who had introduced the joint resolution, April 1816, which was now about to go into effect.[25]

Secretary Dallas himself, even before enactment of the charter, had sought, but in vain, to get the state banks' consent to resumption. Again, fortified by the charter and by the Webster resolution, he had tried in July to get them to resume redemption of notes for less than $5. They would not. In October Mr Dallas had resigned and was succeeded by William H. Crawford of Georgia, who as

24 Catterall, 22.　25 ASP, Finance iv, 764-65; Catterall, 23.

senator had championed recharter of the old Bank of the United States, and since then had been Minister to France and latterly Secretary of War. In December he made the Treasury's third proposal, and it too was refused, though it was now only two months till the date when unredeemable notes could no longer be accepted by the Treasury.[26]

"The situation," in the words of Professor Catterall, "was extremely critical for both the government and the Bank." Without the consent of the state banks the government could not collect its revenues after 20 February, because it was constrained by the Webster resolution, "and yet that resolution would be of no effect in securing specie or specie-paying paper." The Bank, for its part, was in danger of losing its own specie to the state banks if it redeemed its notes and they did not redeem theirs. Not all the banks were intransigent, however; the more responsible in the money centers wished to resume redemption, and on 1 February 1817 terms were agreed upon by a convention of representatives of the Bank of the United States and the chartered banks of Philadelphia, New York, Baltimore, and Richmond. The terms were mainly as follows:

The incorporated banks of New York, Philadelphia, Baltimore, and Richmond engaged, "on the 20th instant, to commence and thenceforth to continue specie payments for all demands upon them." This would make it possible for the Treasury to accept their notes and checks for payments due the government.

The Bank of the United States agreed to give debtor banks credit for checks on other banks that were parties to the agreement. Thus a bank, in Richmond say, which owed the federal Bank for notes and checks received by the Treasury and deposited by it in the Bank could pay the amount due by drawing on banks, say in Philadelphia or New York, where the Richmond bank had funds. Practically, this avoided the transport of specie (and in a pedantic sense an actual payment in specie).

The Bank of the United States assumed the state banks' deposit liabilities to the Treasury but allowed the state banks till the July following to transfer the funds. The federal Bank thereby virtually lent the state banks what they owed the Treasury and enabled them to pay the Treasury at once.

The Bank of the United States agreed not to demand current payment of other balances due it from the state banks till it had

26 ASP, Finance IV, 266, 283, 496-97.

itself lent $2,000,000 in New York, $2,000,000 in Philadelphia, $1,500,000 in Baltimore, and $500,000 in Virginia, assuming there was demand for credit to such amounts. This assured funds for the local money markets to help them meet the balances that might be due from them to other markets.

The federal Bank and the state banks would settle their note balances with one another daily. "The Bank of the United States and the incorporated banks of New York, Philadelphia, Baltimore, and Virginia will interchange pledges of good faith and friendly offices, and upon any emergency which may menace the credit of the aforesaid banks or the branches of the United States Bank will cheerfully contribute their resources to any reasonable extent in support thereof—the Bank of the United States confiding in the justice and discretion of the state banks respectively to circumscribe their affairs within the just limit indicated by their respective capitals as soon as the interest and convenience of the community will admit."

Finally the agreement was to "be obligatory upon all the contracting parties" if approved by the Secretary of the Treasury.[27]

Under this arrangement, specie payments were resumed, with substantial shortcomings. Apparently the situation was better than it had been, and a pretense was maintained of its being better than it was. But redemption was not certain and universal; there was still a premium on specie and still a discount on bank notes, with considerable variation in both from place to place. Three years later, February 1820, Secretary Crawford reported to Congress that during the greater part of the time that had elapsed since the resumption of specie payments, the convertibility of bank notes into specie had been nominal rather than real in the largest portion of the Union. On the part of the banks, he said, mutual weakness has produced mutual forbearance. Bank stockholders and bank borrowers, who were numerous, also forbore to make demands that would be contrary to their own interests; for "every dollar in specie drawn out of the banks, especially for exportation, induced the necessity of curtailments." Yet the Secretary was sanguine; the convertibility of bank notes into specie was "becoming real wherever it is ostensible"; and, he warned, "If public opinion does not correct the evil in those states where this convertibility is not even ostensible, it will be the imperious duty of those who are invested with the power of correction to apply the appropriate remedy." The Secre-

[27] Catterall, 24-25; ASP, Finance IV, 769.

tary's last sentence thunders in the index loudly but vaguely, and it is doubtful what he meant. Presumably, though, he was thinking of that power over the banks which he believed was included in the constitutional authority of Congress over the circulating medium, and what he meant was that Congress should outlaw the state banks' notes—which is what it did do forty-five years later.[28]

Though imperfect and incomplete, resumption was an achievement and the Secretary's own. The Bank supplied the machinery, the Secretary supplied the brains. He tutored, corrected, and prodded the Bank's president. Central banking policy was more intelligently developed in the Treasury than in the central bank itself. Mr Crawford had also to mediate between the state banks and the federal Bank, for each feared the other. He assured the Pennsylvania, Delaware, and Maryland banks in a general letter, 28 January 1817, that the Bank of the United States would not be hard on them. "The deep interest," he said, "which that institution must feel for the credit of the paper system and its intimate connexion with the government are considered sufficient guarantees for the intelligent and disinterested manner in which this operation will be effected, independent of the power of the Treasury Department to control its proceeding at any moment by changing the deposits to the state banks." He then impressed upon the federal Bank the need of conciliating the state banks. Writing to its president, William Jones, 7 February 1817, and urging that it concede a certain point, he said: "If the state banks can be brought, by a concession of this nature, to move harmoniously with each other and with the Bank of the United States, the beneficial consequences resulting from it will be cheaply attained by such a concession." He had also to deal with bankers who presumed to condition the right of the Treasury to its own funds; he was apprised on 1 January 1817 by the State Bank in Boston—that stalwart Republican bank whose noble interest in more than pecuniary gain was mentioned earlier—that it had been induced and even obliged by the intense call for money "since the peace" to discount freely to the mercantile interest, to manufacturers, and to other business borrowers and that it would "be extremely injurious to be obliged to call suddenly on those persons" in order to meet the Treasury's demands. For this and other reasons, the bank's president said without the slightest embarrassment, "we request of you, sir, an

28 ASP, Finance III, 496; Catterall, 37-38.

assurance . . . that you will not draw from us over $30,000 a month. . . ." It was in the face of such self-interest that Secretary Crawford, with the help of responsible bankers who were more sensitive about their obligations, got the central bank to working and redemption of a sort restored.[29]

The performance was disappointing but not a failure. Nor was the central banking function itself at fault. The difficulty was one of having not merely to replace a necessary institution that had been wantonly abandoned but of undoing the unnecessary mischief that arose from its abandonment. America was resourceful and energetic enough to recover from such gross and reckless errors, but they were errors and grossly expensive nevertheless.

[29] ASP, Finance IV, "Correspondence Relative to the Public Deposits," 495-99, 974-1077 passim.

CHAPTER 10

The New Federal Bank

1816-1822

I

The year 1817 was a year of false promise. The Bank of the United States was established anew, and its constitutionality was little questioned. Prominent political leaders who had formerly opposed it were now its friends. The private banks had recognized its place in the economy, and the Treasury relied on its special services. The general suspension had been ended, nominally at least. The same year the first permanent bank in Canada had been established—the Bank of Montreal—and being patterned after Alexander Hamilton's proposals, it seemed to confirm the correctness of the American precedent. The champions of the Bank of the United States had been justified by the miserable experience consequent on the dissolution of 1811. With the restraints of the old Bank out of the way, private banks had rushed into business, extended too much credit, and suspended *en masse* when trouble came. Continuance of the Bank would not have prevented the suspension, perhaps; but the suspension made the Bank's discontinuance harder to defend. Its opponents were chastened, and many had been converted.

Yet a new peril threatened the federal Bank in the grip on it that speculators and politicians got while it was still in the process of organization. Captain William Jones, an unfortunate Philadelphia merchant and politician, was made president of the Bank, though he had recently gone through bankruptcy. Neither that interesting circumstance nor his recently having been Secretary of the Navy and acting Secretary of the Treasury in Mr Madison's cabinet would seem to have qualified him for so important a responsibility. According to Prime, Ward, and King, correspondents of the Barings and New York's leading merchant bankers, Congress, in setting up the Bank, "levied a tax which by our monied men was thought too oppressive, and a considerable proportion of the stock, with the power of governing the institution, fell into the hands of speculators." Stephen Girard tried to stop this development but failed. Of the meeting of stockholders in Philadelphia, 28 October 1816, he wrote that "Intrigue and corruption had formed a ticket for twenty directors of the Bank of the United States who I am sorry to say appear to have been selected for the purpose of securing the presidency for Mr Jones. . . . Although Mr Jacob Astor of New York and I have obtained . . . that the names of Thomas M. Willing of this city and Mr James Lloyd of Boston should be inserted in the ticket of directors now elected, yet there are still several persons whose occupations, moral characters, or pecuniary situation will not inspire that indispensable confidence which is absolutely necessary to establish and consolidate the credit of that institution." The day the Bank opened for business, 7 January 1817, Mr Girard wrote: "If I live twelve months more I intend to use all my activity, means, and influence to change and replace the majority of directors with honest and independent men. . . ." But his activity, means, and influence taken alone were inadequate.[1]

This is not what might be supposed would happen. Girard had promoted the Bank earnestly, he was the largest and most prominent stockholder, his friends and associates were wealthy, he was one of the commissioners appointed by the President of the United States to supervise subscriptions, he was a government director, his banking offices had been the headquarters at which elections and organization had been determined, and his bank had been the agent in subscription payments and other preliminary transactions. He was astute and powerful. He might have been expected to wrap the Bank around his little finger. On the contrary, he was frozen out from the first, and his wishes were realized only after his participation had relaxed and the force of circumstances had taken over. The explanation, I think, is that he belonged to the 18th century, and his conservatism was uncongenial to the new and democratic enterprisers who were filling the business world with such numbers, such

[1] Redlich 104, 182; W. B. Smith, 99; Baring Papers, OC, 30 June 1821; McMaster, *Girard* II, 314-15; K. L. Brown, *JEH*, II (1942), 138-43; Walters, *JPE*, LIII (1945), 115ff.

diversity, such commotion, such free-for-all aggressiveness, such sanguine irresponsibility, such readiness for sleights-of-hand, and such contempt for established codes and old-fashioned honesty, that though his money might be useful, his example was too slow and unambitious. In the past it had meant something that ships of his had been named for French philosophers—the *Voltaire*, the *Helvétius*, the *Montesquieu*—but he was left now among a generation who knew only enough of philosophers to distinguish one from a stock-jobber. The sober pace of 18th century business was giving way, on the wave of *laisser faire* and the Industrial Revolution, to a democratic passion to get rich quick—an ambition which America seemed designed by Providence to promote. And it was men imbued with this passion and the unscrupulousness appropriate to it who had snatched control of the Bank of the United States.[2]

Captain Jones and his crew struck out at once on their new courses. He wrote Secretary Crawford in July 1817 that he was "not at all disposed to take the late Bank of the United States as an exemplar in practice; because I think its operations were circumscribed by a policy less enlarged, liberal, and useful than its powers and resources would have justified." And about the same time, February 1817, James W. McCulloch, cashier of the Baltimore office, who nearly ruined it a little later, wrote of the old Bank to the Secretary that, "Instead of extending its operations so as to embrace every real demand of commerce; instead of expanding its views as the country and its trade grew, it pursued a timid and faltering course." He and his associates meant to do otherwise.[3]

II

Even before the federal Bank was opened, the management had made a revealing decision in the basic matter of payment on subscriptions to the Bank's capital. The charter authorized payment of one-fourth in specie, and three-fourths in government securities or specie, the expectation being that no one would pay more than the fourth in specie. But several conditions combined to upset this expectation. One was a premium of 8 per cent on specie, which meant of course—values being expressed in terms of state bank paper, notes or checks—that it took $108 worth of bank credit to obtain $100 in coin. Naturally, for the subscribers this was tantamount to a requirement that on one-fourth of their subscription

[2] McMaster, *Girard* II, 317-18.   [3] ASP, Finance IV, 774, 807.

they pay $108 for each $100 subscribed. At the same time, the credit of the government had so much improved that government stock was also at a premium. The result of these two conditions was that the stockholders found it harder to pay their subscription than they had expected. They turned to the Bank itself for help, and the Bank was indulgent. It accepted their promissory notes in payment, secured by the Bank's own stock valued at a premium of 25 per cent.[4]

Legally it could not do this, and directly it did not. Instead, it "lent" its notes and these were "accepted" as specie on the principle that the notes of a bank that redeemed its obligations in specie were the equivalent of specie. This was another convenient consequence of Alexander Hamilton's having established the principle in 1790 that the notes of specie-paying banks were the equivalent of specie. For Hamilton's purposes—the payment of sums due the government—and for current monetary settlements the principle was a reasonable and useful one. But here it was different, for it evaded the basic need of putting silver and gold in the Bank's coffers. Its consequence, in fact, was that the Bank got neither the specie it should nor the government stock it should; for if specie notes were "specie," it was easier to pay the whole subscription in them than in either the precious metals or government stock. So the Bank did not begin operations in the intrinsically strong position its responsibilities required. It should have received from its private stockholders $7,000,000 in coin at least and $21,000,000 in government securities at most. According to Professor Dewey it received $2,000,000 in specie from them, $14,000,000 in government securities, and $12,000,000 in personal notes. The calculation is uncertain, however, because the capital was not paid all in one operation or before the Bank opened. Instead the subscribers paid in three installments, six months apart, and the Bank began operations when the first installment was made. Since the Bank's specie and government portfolio began to turn over in the course of operations, and since much "specie" was fictitious, I do not see how the exact amounts received from stockholders could be distinguished even nominally, much less in fact. This was the Bank's own view.[5]

The Bank did acquire more specie, however, through its own

---

[4] ASP, Finance III, 340-42; Catterall, 41.

[5] ASP, Finance I, 49; III, 288; Dewey, *Financial History*, 151; Dewey, *Second United States Bank*, 175-80; W. B. Smith, 100-01.

efforts. In December 1816 it sent John Sergeant, a prominent Philadelphia attorney, to Europe to negotiate for as much as $5,-000,000. Although it was folly to advertise the quest and so increase its hazards, the Bank's management with its characteristic pretentiousness must have told the newspapers, because they reported how the Bank was going to get specie and had already been offered $10,000,000 from London some weeks before John Sergeant's departure. Sergeant's arrival abroad was advertised in London also. This fanfare contrasted grimly with the difficulties actually encountered. The Barings rejected the business promptly, and other firms demanded too much for undertaking it. But in time Mr Sergeant got an offer which he could accept, though he still demurred for better terms. It was a contract with Baring Brothers, and Reid, Irving, and Company for $3,195,000 in silver to be paid for within some twenty months, the loan to bear 5 per cent interest. Immediately the price of the metal rose in the European markets, and the firms were hard put to meet their obligations. The Barings eventually did, but the other firm seems to have done nothing. The newspapers in the States, however, published vague, inspiring reports of "specie pouring in from all quarters." From the summer of 1817 to the end of 1818 the Bank imported $7,300,000, of which $675,-000 was gold from Lisbon and London, and the rest was silver from France and Jamaica mainly.[6]

Since the $7,300,000 was more than the amount due from the private shareholders under the law, the Bank may be said to have done in effect what was required of it. A requirement that capital be *paid* in specie did not require a bank to retain the specie, and in practice a relatively small amount of specie going in and out in enough successive transactions in the course of enough time could amount to any sum conceivable. So a literal compliance with the law, which in this respect was the same as state laws, could be achieved easily. On the other hand, it was impossible in any practical sense for $7,000,000 of specie to be amassed in any one spot in America in 1817. What the law said, therefore, can not be taken as a dependable register of what a bank could do. In getting the Bank of the United States organized with an adequate stock of specie, the shareholders and managers of the Bank did nothing to strike posterity with admiration, but neither did they do anything

[6] ASP, Finance III, 338; Boyd, *PMHB*, LVIII (1934), 213; Hidy, 70-71.

so much worse than posterity would do that their clumsiness and evasion can be reprobated.

Meanwhile, branch offices were being set up. Their organization had been undertaken early, and by the end of 1817 there were eighteen of them, after which the Bank established no more till 1826. In the next four years it established seven. Two were discontinued, and the maximum number at one time, 1830, was twenty-five. The offices, including Philadelphia, were established as follows:

1817 Philadelphia, Pennsylvania	1817 New York, New York
1817 Augusta, Georgia (discontinued 1817)	1817 Norfolk, Virginia
	1817 Pittsburgh, Pennsylvania
1817 Baltimore, Maryland	1817 Portsmouth, New Hampshire
1817 Boston, Massachusetts	1817 Providence, Rhode Island
1817 Charleston, South Carolina	1817 Richmond, Virginia
1817 Chillicothe, Ohio (discontinued 1825)	1817 Savannah, Georgia
	1817 Washington, District of Columbia
1817 Cincinnati, Ohio (discontinued 1820; re-established 1825)	1826 Mobile, Alabama
1817 Fayetteville, North Carolina	1827 Nashville, Tennessee
1817 Hartford, Connecticut (opened at Middletown but moved to Hartford, 1824)	1828 Portland, Maine
	1829 Buffalo, New York
	1829 St. Louis, Missouri
1817 Lexington, Kentucky	1830 Burlington, Vermont
1817 Louisville, Kentucky	1830 Utica, New York
1817 New Orleans, Louisiana	1830 Natchez, Mississippi[7]

Contemporarily, the branches were known and designated as "offices of discount and deposit," which was what they were called in the law. They were in twenty states and the District of Columbia. The old charter had merely permitted the Bank to have branches at the directors' discretion. The new charter plainly presupposed their establishment and in some conditions made it obligatory, doubtless because of the reluctance of the old Bank on occasion to establish branches as the government wished. From the point of view of a responsible management, branches were a hazard, for it was impossible to maintain close control over them. Local and regional interests were apt to take things in their own hands and commit the Bank seriously before the headquarters in Philadelphia, in the absence of modern communication, knew what was happening or could make their will known and effective. But on top of that the branches seem to have been under no individual limitation during the first two years or so; each was allowed to lend as if it were the whole institution and not a fraction thereof only.[8]

[7] ASP, Finance IV, 820; Catterall, 376ff.   [8] Catterall, 33.

The Bank began business in the midst of temptations on every hand to over-extend itself. Trade was active and prices were high in its first two years, 1817 and 1818. Economic recovery after the war was intensified by the diversion of enterprise from foreign trade to the domestic field, by the exploitation of new territory, and by the Industrial Revolution, which with machines was multiplying the efficiency of human effort miraculously. In the vast business parade that was forming, banks had a prominent place. They provided money, quintessential in what was being undertaken, and offered little resistance to the pressure upon them to lend. Very few men specialized in banking sufficiently to make it a conservative force in the general play of enterprise. Bankers were themselves imbued with the prevailing enthusiasm.[9]

In such a situation the restraining powers of a central bank were spurned. All that was wanted was more steam. The Bank yielded. It yielded first to its own greedy stockholders, by helping them get their stock the easiest way possible. It yielded to borrowers in general, living up to the open-handed philosophy which its president and its Baltimore manager expressed in the passages already quoted from them; though by doing so it enlarged its liabilities and exposed its specie to withdrawal. It yielded to the state banks, which sought to frustrate its pressure upon them for the current redemption of their notes. Unreasonable and preposterous though the private banks' position was, the federal Bank itself, in this period, was scarcely better.

III

Stephen Girard resigned as a government director, 31 December 1817, when the Bank had been working not quite a year. He was still the largest single stockholder, but that gave him no direct weight, since the charter allowed no stockholder more than thirty votes, no matter how much stock he had. The insiders against whom he and his minority were ranged had got around this restriction by spreading a given ownership over many names. The extreme case was in Baltimore, where George Williams, a director of the Bank, owned 1,172 shares but registered them under 1,172 different names with himself as attorney for all. So he had thirty-nine times the maximum number of votes the charter allowed any one stockholder. Mr Girard, dissatisfied with such things, aroused other stockholders,

[9] ASP, Finance iii, 496.

especially those in Charleston. "Although I would strongly recommend that the stockholders endeavor to effect a total change of its direction at the next election," he said, "I do not think they will accomplish it, but it may help to obtain competent men in 1820." The Charleston stockholders made opposition open by nominating Langdon Cheves of South Carolina for president of the Bank and by appointing a committee of correspondence to communicate with stockholders elsewhere in furtherance of a change in management.[10]

The changes purposed by the minority were expedited by a panic and recession which swept the country in 1818 and shook the Bank severely. In July with demand liabilities outstanding in excess of $22,370,000, it had specie of only $2,360,000; this was a ratio of a little more than one to ten, whereas the statute presupposed a ratio of one to five. Its situation was still much the same in October when the Treasury called for $2,000,000 in specie to pay off obligations incurred by the purchase of the Louisiana territory. This was nearly all the specie the Bank had, and it settled for drafts on London instead.[11]

Meanwhile the directors had begun tardily to give their duties serious heed. They initiated curtailments of credit and imports of specie, but just at the time that the Bank's slow-earning assets were least collectible and specie hardest to get. The Bank was forced in self-preservation to do exactly the opposite of what a central bank should do: it should check expansion and ease contraction. As lender of last resort and keeper of ultimate reserves, it should have those reserves in readiness before trouble comes, and not be driven to scurry for them vainly when the need for them is already at hand. Instead, the Bank had stimulated the expansion and now must intensify the contraction, having by its first course committed itself to the second.

In October 1818 a House committee under the chairmanship of John C. Spencer of New York was instructed to investigate the Bank; in January 1819 it reported that the charter had been violated in several particulars, but it recommended no drastic action to be taken, because "the Secretary of the Treasury has full power to apply a prompt and adequate remedy"—meaning evidently the power to remove the government deposits from the Bank. There were active demands, meanwhile, that the charter be repealed, but

---

10 ASP, Finance III, 314; Catterall, 39; K. L. Brown, *JEH*, II (1942), 146-47.
11 Catterall, 51.

Congress took the judicious view that the conduct of the Bank though bad was not incorrigible. The first correction was effected when William Jones resigned, only a fortnight after his re-election; his resignation was followed immediately by an advance in the price of the Bank stock, which had been offered at 93 but after he resigned could not be bought at 98 and in a matter of days was selling at 101 and kept on rising. The second correction occurred when Langdon Cheves was chosen president.[12]

It was moot whether the Bank was still worth saving, but the more responsible stockholders decided that it should be saved, and that was the conclusion in Congress; for the House, by heavy majorities, in February 1819, rejected proposals to repeal the charter. The Bank had, of course, as great potential usefulness as ever, if it were able to recover public confidence. That, as things turned out, it was unable fully to do. A popular hatred of it based on the grim efforts made to collect or secure what was receivable, subsided but was never extinguished. "The Bank was saved," wrote William Gouge, "and the people were ruined." Its violent efforts at recovery created a popular conviction of its power, when in fact they were impelled by a convulsive weakness. Twelve years later, Senator Thomas Hart Benton of Missouri dilated on the consequences of those efforts. "All the flourishing cities of the West," he exclaimed with oratorical fancy, "are mortgaged to this money power. They may be devoured by it at any moment. They are in the jaws of the monster! A lump of butter in the mouth of a dog! One gulp, one swallow, and all is gone!" In these chilling words he pictured the Bank, like the dog, in absolute control of the situation. On the contrary, in 1820, when the mortgages were taken, the Bank was as nearly gone as the butter. Its survival damned it worse than failure would have done. John Quincy Adams thought, as others did, that "the government is the party most interested in the continuance of the Bank and that the interest of the stockholders would be to surrender their charter." But at the moment, as usual in such crises, salvage seemed to the persons concerned an imperative duty, to be achieved at any cost.[13]

[12] Clarke and Hall, 732; McMaster, *Girard* ii, 355.

[13] Clarke and Hall, 734; Gouge, Part ii, 110; Congress, *Register of Debates* viii, Part 1, 1003; J. Q. Adams, *Memoirs* v, 38-39.

IV

But behind these embarrassments, something still worse had been hatching in Baltimore, where James A. Buchanan was president of the branch and James W. McCulloch was cashier. Baltimore had sought to be headquarters of the Bank, and perhaps the same ambition led the officers there to make it the biggest office if not the dominant one. From the outset the volume of its business expanded excessively. Baltimore was the newest of the important commercial cities, an active export center, and also an active distributor of northern products. "There is not a city in the Union," John Quincy Adams wrote, "which has had so much apparent prosperity or within which there has been such complication of profligacy."[14] Taking advantage of the demand of its merchants for funds to remit to their suppliers, the Baltimore office discounted profusely and furnished drafts on the Boston, New York, and Philadelphia offices of the Bank. The Baltimore office, had it been an independent bank, would have had to send the other branches funds in some form to enable them to pay the drafts, and even as a branch it should have recognized a corresponding duty. But the Philadelphia directors, at the instance of William Jones, the president, who was under the thumb of the Baltimore people, carried to an extreme the meritorious principle that the Bank with its branches constituted one integral and universal organization, each part of which must honor the obligations of every other part. So, for example, notes issued by the office in Charleston could turn up in Portsmouth or Chillicothe and pass current there because the Portsmouth and Chillicothe offices were expected to redeem them in coin if asked to. This was admirable as an ideal, but it assumed that every office was able in fact to honor the notes or other obligations of every other office. That ability depended on the possession of the necessary means, and the possession of the necessary means depended basically on the exchange of commodities. If Baltimore sent just as many dollars' worth of tobacco to New York as New York sent her in dry goods and if trade otherwise kept each city's bank supplied with currency, then the federal Bank's branches in each city would be able to honor one another's obligations readily. In fact, however, such perfect balances of trade and balances of payments between centers, regions, and countries are never found. There is always some disparity, and in consequence it is always harder to maintain the flow of cash pay-

---

[14] J. Q. Adams, *Memoirs* IV, 383.

ments in some directions than in others. The United States has become so nearly homogeneous now in the middle of the 20th century—partly from general productivity, partly from means of transport and communication, partly from banking operations, partly from large scale corporate enterprise, and partly from the maintenance of wide-spread governmental activities—that the flow of payments is practically equalized. In 1820 the homogeneity was far less than it is now; inter-regional payments were constantly and irregularly out of balance. Hence the Bank was operating on a basis of inter-regional parity that did not exist. Yet Baltimore, and other southern and western offices to a less extent, drew persistently on the offices in the North and East without the means to pay, and the headquarters in Philadelphia tolerated their action in the name of unity.

As I said, it was a Baltimore director, George Williams, who registered 1,172 shares of stock in 1,172 different names, with himself as attorney voting them all; and his example, though extreme, was not unique. The Baltimore people borrowed from the Bank to buy stock and systematically engrossed voting power. They made loans on the Bank's stock without informing the directors and then made more with no collateral at all. They made these loans mostly to themselves, they overdrew their accounts, and they deceived associates not in their own circle. Their chicane, said Nicholas Biddle, "created that solecism—a monied institution governed by those who had no money; it reduced the Bank at Philadelphia to a mere colony of the Baltimore adventurers."[15]

George Williams was a director both at Baltimore and at Philadelphia. James Buchanan, the president of the Baltimore office, was a partner of Samuel Smith, now a member of the House of Representatives but a Senator in 1811 when he opposed Albert Gallatin and renewal of the 1791 charter. The house of Smith and Buchanan had been for the past thirty years, according to John Quincy Adams, "one of the greatest commercial establishments in the United States" and notably an "exporter of specie to India by the half million at a time." All of Buchanan's transactions with the Bank were in the firm name, S. Smith and Buchanan. James McCulloch, the Baltimore cashier, had no means of his own, but he lent himself more than a half million dollars. The three, Buchanan, Williams, and McCulloch, composed a company for their carryings-

[15] Biddle Papers 5, Folio 1015.

on and paralleled Williams's device by holding 1,000 shares of the Bank's stock in 1,000 different names. Their dealings began as speculations, grew into frauds, and involved about $3,000,000 when the affair burst open. The net loss in the end exceeded $1,500,000. The straits the Bank was in on other scores had generated a vigilance which the conspirators could not elude, especially since their own difficulties were magnified by the recession. In January William Jones had resigned, in March and April they disclosed their dealings. It was one of the first things to confront Langdon Cheves when he became the Bank's president.[16]

James McCulloch was removed from his cashiership, and "for a day or two there was great blustering in the Baltimore newspapers, as if the grossest injustice had been done" him; "but the mine was blown up." At the moment, however, the most striking aspect of the affair seems to have been the failure of S. Smith and Buchanan. The house broke, John Quincy Adams said, "with a crash which staggered the whole city of Baltimore." It well might. "The moral, political, and commercial character of this city of Baltimore has for twenty-five years been formed, controlled, and modified almost entirely by this house of Smith and Buchanan, their connections and dependents." Samuel Smith was rich, and active in public life. He had the rank of general from a military career; he had been a prominent and influential member of the Congress for twenty-six years; he was a generous public benefactor, a person of distinguished mien, and husband of an aunt, by a marriage since annulled, to the younger brother of the *ci-devant* Emperor Napoleon Bonaparte. Yet he was but mortal. "General Smith," wrote Mr Adams, "is reported to have gone distracted and to be confined dangerously ill in bed."[17]

V

Langdon Cheves (whose name was pronounced Chivis) was a South Carolina attorney who had been a Republican member of Congress and Speaker of the House. He took the presidency of the Bank with some reluctance, for he might instead have been appointed by President Monroe to the Supreme Court—he had five years before refused the secretaryship of the Treasury relinquished by

16 J. Q. Adams, *Memoirs* IV, 325, 382; ASP, Finance III, 372-73, 375-77; Niles XXIII (1822), 91; Catterall, 47-49.
17 J. Q. Adams, *Memoirs* IV, 382-83.

Albert Gallatin. When he went to Philadelphia he was already "satisfied that there was a great want of financial talent" in the Bank's management. "But I had not the faintest idea that its power had been so completely prostrated or that it had been thus unfortunately managed or grossly defrauded. I never imagined that when it had at so much expense and loss imported so many millions of specie, they had been entirely exhausted and were not yet paid for; nor that the Bank was on the point of stopping payment."[18]

He began his administration March 1819 with a thousand things to be done at once, though the directors had already undertaken the changes required by the Bank's condition. He made drastic retrenchments in salaries and other expenses. He initiated investigations, dismissals, and prosecutions; for there were defaulters, though more modest ones, elsewhere than in Baltimore. He procured the appointment of new officers and directors and made the conservative minority dominant. His changes in policy began with curtailment of business at the southern and western offices. The government was persuaded to be accommodating and allow the Bank time to arrange transfers of public funds. A loan of $2,000,000 obtained from Baring Brothers and Hope and Company was taken largely in specie. The funds of the Bank were shifted into government securities. Definite limitations were put on the business of the various offices by allocation of capital to them. No branch was to draw on any other branch without having the funds to draw against.[19]

These measures took time; and meanwhile there were difficulties with the state governments and the state banks. Here too Maryland was a seat of trouble, for in February 1818 the Assembly had passed a law which imposed a tax of $15,000 a year on all banks or branches thereof in the state of Maryland not chartered by the legislature. The Baltimore office of the Bank of the United States refused to pay and was sued in the name of J. W. McCulloch, the Baltimore cashier, for the amount claimed by the state. This was some months before McCulloch's speculations became known. The Bank lost in the state courts and appealed to the federal Supreme Court.

The case, *McCulloch* v. *Maryland*, was of recognized importance, for other states besides Maryland—Tennessee, Georgia, North Carolina, Kentucky, and Ohio—were adopting practically annihilatory taxes on the Bank, and still others were considering it. When the former Bank, some ten years before, had appealed to the Supreme

[18] Haskell, 361-71; Niles xxIII (1822), 91.   [19] Hidy, 71-72; Catterall, 70-73.

Court against similar action by Georgia, the question became one of jurisdiction and the Bank lost without any decision on the constitutional issue. This was *Bank of the United States* v. *Deveaux*, February 1809. But now the constitutional issue was foremost. If the Maryland law stood, the individual states had it in their power to put the federal Bank out of business forthwith, and the federal government had not the power to form corporations or go in other directions beyond the letter of the Constitution.[20]

The Bank's position was one of irony. It came before the Supreme Court suing for its legality when its solvency was in doubt. It was a half-sunk creditor, harassed and harassing. Its position was even more desperate than was known, for while its plea was being made to the Court in the name of James W. McCulloch, he was helping himself, with his two colleagues, to its funds. It had barely got rid of Captain Jones, and Langdon Cheves had not taken charge. According to some people, it would be best for the stockholders if the charter were surrendered and the Bank liquidated; according to many more, the public interest demanded that this be done. In Congress efforts to that end were making.

VI

The chief counsel for Maryland before the Supreme Court was Luther Martin, Attorney General of the state, who thirty years before had been one of the most outspoken and active opponents of the federal Constitution. Counsel for the Bank were William Wirt, Attorney General of the United States, William Pinkney, and Daniel Webster. These were all among the greatest lawyers in the land. In preparation for the hearing, which opened 22 February 1819, Chief Justice Marshall sold the seventeen shares of federal Bank stock standing in his name; and he never afterward owned stock in the Bank. The hearing occupied nine days; its height was reached in the argument of William Pinkney, who spoke for three days.[21]

Mr Pinkney's argument was Hamiltonian: a government could not be effective unless it possessed the powers it needed for the performance of its functions. Federal responsibilities under the Constitution are large and federal powers are correspondingly so. Yet now it is being doubted, he said, "whether a government invested with

[20] Catterall, 64-65; Warren I, 389ff; *Bank of the United States* v. *Deveaux*, 5 Cranch 61 (US 1809); Wettereau, *JEH*, II (1942), Supplement, 84.
[21] Warren I, 499-511; Biddle, *Correspondence*, 285-90.

such immense powers has authority to erect a corporation within the sphere of its general objects and in order to accomplish some of these objects."* From this protasis of federal power, the apodosis was that Maryland had no countervailing power. It was absurd to suppose that if the union of states needed the Bank, an individual state could deny it the Bank. "There is a manifest repugnancy," Mr Pinkney averred, "between the power of Maryland to tax, and the power of Congress to preserve, this institution. A power to build up what another may pull down at pleasure is a power which may provoke a smile but can do nothing else."[22]

The court's decision, which was unanimous, was delivered by Chief Justice Marshall, 7 March 1819, the day after Langdon Cheves took office. It pursued William Pinkney's argument but derived more explicitly from that submitted by Alexander Hamilton to President Washington in 1791 in support of the Bank's constitutionality. It affirmed that Congress had power to incorporate and control a bank, and that the states had no power to interfere by taxation or otherwise. The import of the decision, as expected, went far beyond the status of the Bank itself and broadened the base of federal authority, confirming thereby the general identification of the Bank with strengthened federal powers. "Let the end be legitimate, let it be within the scope of the Constitution, and all means which are appropriate, which are plainly adapted to that end, which are not prohibited but consist with the letter and spirit of the Constitution, are constitutional." The court took no account of the Bank as a monetary agency, but it may have omitted purposely to do so, recognizing that to establish the Bank's constitutionality on narrow, specific grounds would fail to give the sweeping affirmation of federal powers from which the decision derived its importance. The federal government, the Court declared in effect, did not have to look closely in the Constitution for language which exactly or even approximately foreshadowed any particular means it wished to employ; it was assured by the Court that whatever its purpose, if constitutional, it had command of the means appropriate to that purpose. A further consideration is that since the Bank in 1818 or 1819 had signally failed in its monetary duties, a justification of

* Friends of the Bank saw it embraced *within* the framework of governmental powers and incident to them; enemies of the Bank saw it a monstrosity essentially *without* that framework but penetrating it.

[22] *McCulloch* v. *Maryland*, 4 Wheaton 382, 391 (US 1819).

the Bank on the ground of those duties would have been morally weak. As it was, the decision had far greater significance for the development of federal powers in general than for the development of federal powers with respect to money and banking.[23]

The partisans of the federal government and of the Bank were comforted by the Supreme Court's decision; the partisans of states' rights, the private banks, and the enemies of the Bank were angered and alarmed. The state banks had to pay state taxes; the federal Bank, though conducting its business within the states, did not. The federal government was "invading" the states. If it could "create a monied institution in the very bosom of the states, paramount to their laws, then indeed is state sovereignty a mere name." In the South and in the West, where states' rights were most cherished, the decision was attacked and efforts were made to defend the state authority from it. It was a sardonic coincidence, giving the unpopular decision a still worse flavor, that the Baltimore officer in whose name the Bank had sued, was disclosed a week later to have been an embezzler beyond the dreams of most contemporaries' avarice.[24]

Feeling was especially bitter in Ohio, where the Bank's earlier extensions of credit had been excessive and where it had now a host of debtors reviling it. Much Ohio real estate, especially in the city of Cincinnati, was coming into the Bank's hands on foreclosure. In the setting created by this condition, the Ohio legislature, 8 February 1819, had imposed a tax of $50,000 on each branch of the Bank in the state—there was then one in Chillicothe and one in Cincinnati—doing so on the rather remarkable legal grounds that since the Bank was transacting business at these two offices "in violation of the laws of this state," it was "just and necessary that such unlawful banking while continued should be subject to the payment of a tax for the support of the government." The statute also authorized the state Auditor in collecting the tax to enter every room, vault, and other place in the branch office and open every chest and receptacle. This was just a month before the Supreme Court heard *McCulloch* v. *Maryland*. When the decision in that case was announced, the Ohio officials were reluctant to undertake collection of the tax, but public and legislative opinion was for action. And especially, when the goings-on in the Baltimore office came out a week later, it was contended that the *McCulloch* case

23 *McCulloch* v. *Maryland*, 4 Wheaton 420 (US 1819).
24 Warren I, 511ff, 532ff.

was factitious, that it had been arranged in order to bolster up the federal Bank when it was about to collapse from internal vices, that it had been heard as a test case by agreement between Maryland and the Bank, and that Ohio should not be bound by the collusive action of others. The state Auditor, Ralph Osborn, concluded that he had no choice but carry out the state law. Anticipating what was going to be done, the Bank sought protection from a federal court, but the court's orders were construed not to have the force of an injunction, and in September 1819 Osborn bade his deputy collect the amount due from the Chillicothe office. The cashier of the office reported to the Secretary of the Treasury, 17 September 1819, that the warrant of the state Auditor was executed at noon that day "by John L. Harper (late of Philadelphia, deputed for the purpose), accompanied by two others, who without any previous notice whatever suddenly entered the office, and in a ruffian-like manner jumped over the counter, took and held forcible possession of the vault, while the said Harper in like manner intruded himself behind the counter, and as I was proceeding to turn the others from the vault demanded to know if I was prepared to pay the said tax; to which I answered in the negative and made an ineffectual exertion to obtain possession of the vault, when they were repeatedly forewarned against touching any part of the property, and admonished in the presence of several citizens of said injunction, which was shown and read to them but for which he declared his disregard; and, after another fruitless effort on my part to dispossess them of the vault, proceeded to remove therefrom and from the drawer, a quantity of specie and bank notes, amounting to $120,425, including $7,930 in Muskingum Bank notes, the special deposit on account of the Treasury; all which were taken to and received by the cashier of the Bank of Chillicothe." Harper, however, withheld $2,000 as his fee.[25]

The Bank obtained an order from the federal Circuit Court requiring the state Treasurer to restore the money. The Treasurer refused to obey the order and was lodged in prison. Federal commissioners appointed by the Court seized his keys and got the money, or what they could find of it, from the state Treasury themselves. The Ohio officials then appealed to the Supreme Court, a step which the radicals deplored, for they were unwilling to acknowledge the Court's jurisdiction. The state, they contended, was sovereign. They

[25] Warren I, 528ff; ASP, Finance IV, 903-06; Bogart, *AHR*, XVII (1912), 312ff.

pictured the affair as an encroachment by the federal government, particularly by the federal Court. "Ohio has to complain of the imprisonment of the treasurer, the taking from his pockets the keys of the treasury whilst so imprisoned, and the entry into the treasury and violent seizure of monies therein contained, the property of the state!!!" This view was shared by the legislature.* A committee recommended in January 1821 that the Bank of the United States be outlawed in the state courts and left "exclusively to the protection of the federal government." This action was not taken, but the Ohio Assembly did resolve in respect to the relative powers of the states and the Union to "recognize and approve" the Virginia and Kentucky Resolutions of 1798 and 1799, which, it will be recalled, had been inspired largely by the constitutional implications first raised by Alexander Hamilton's proposal in 1790 that the federal Bank be established.[26]

The furor, though intense, was brief. The Supreme Court's decision in *McCulloch* v. *Maryland* stood, and no change in its position was to be expected. By the time the Ohio case was heard in 1824, the Bank's affairs were in better condition and emotions had subsided. The decision, *Osborn* v. *Bank of the United States*, reaffirmed the principles and conclusions pronounced in *McCulloch* v. *Maryland*. Whatever course the enemies of the Bank might take against it in future would have to be legislative or executive rather than judicial.

VII

Concurrently, in the Maryland courts, the cases of the Baltimore speculators—Buchanan, McCulloch, and Williams—had been working their way through the anfractuosities of the law. So open was the misbehavior of the culprits, in old legal language called the Traversers, that little formality would seem required to have opened the jail door and thrust them in. It proved otherwise. New business and financial procedures attending the transformation of the country from an agrarian to a free enterprise economy made novel

* Ohio's governor and many others felt otherwise. Of the Chillicothe affair he said, "I view the transaction in the most odious light, and from my very soul I detest it. . . . I am ashamed it has happened in Ohio." ASP, Finance IV, 906.

[26] Warren I, 535; Niles XIX (1821), 339-40; *Osborn* v. *Bank of the United States*, 9 Wheaton 737 (US 1824).

misdeeds possible for which the laws were unprepared. The simpler forms of cheating and stealing were well enough known but the more complicated dishonesty of distinguished-looking persons who sat at their desks month after month in plain view while appropriating other people's funds to their own use through bookkeeping entries, false reports or no reports, substitutions, and euphemisms— all this was beyond the simplicities of the common law and was something with which legislators had still to cope. So from the first it had been doubted whether criminal indictments could be sustained, and the cases were prosecuted in the hope that if the mischief-makers could not be punished, the legislators would at least learn how the defect in the laws might be remedied.[27]

In other words, embezzlement, which involves misappropriating something entrusted to one and is now a familiar statutory crime, was not a crime to the common law, as larceny was. The theft of something *not* in the thief's possession occurred every day; but the theft of something already in his possession was rare in simpler times than ours and incongruous with the rule that possession was evidence of ownership. The novelty is clearly implied in the following statute of 1799 making embezzlement a crime in the United Kingdom:

"Whereas bankers, merchants, and others are in the course of their dealings and transactions frequently obliged to entrust their servants, clerks, and persons employed by them in like capacity with receiving, paying, negotiating, exchanging, or transferring money, goods, bonds, bills, notes, bankers' drafts, and other valuable effects and securities:

"And whereas doubts have been entertained whether the embezzling of the same by such servants, clerks, and others . . . amounts to felony by the law of England, and it is expedient that such offences should be punished in the same manner in both parts of the United Kingdom;

"Be it enacted and declared by the King's Most Excellent Majesty . . . that if any servant or clerk or any person employed . . . shall, by virtue of such employment, receive or take into his possession any money, goods, bond, bill, note, banker's draft, or other valuable security or effects for or in the name or on the account of his . . . employer . . . and shall fraudulently embezzle, secret, or

[27] Harper, pp. VI-VII.

make way with the same, . . . every such offender shall be deemed to have feloniously stolen the same. . . ."[28]

Maryland as yet had no such law. In its absence the charge was "conspiracy," a vague but ancient and fairly comprehensive tort. The Traversers made no denial of their deeds but only the excuse that they had intended no wrong and were sufferers for what others had done. "The conduct of the Traversers was indiscreet," their counsel granted; "they relied too strongly upon the hopes and calculations in which the whole community indulged; but the failure of their stock speculations was rather to be pitied as a misfortune than condemned as a crime." In fact, counsel averred, the fault was really that of France; for France at quite the wrong time for the defendants had borrowed money from England which would otherwise have been invested in the Bank's stock but going to France instead had left the stock "a drug on the market." The Traversers were the victims of this miscarriage. Moreover, the Bank itself was to blame because it was badly managed. "Its strange administration was an *incubus* upon it," and depreciated its stock. By this depreciation the Traversers' speculations were ruined; "so that in fact the Bank itself occasioned the losses" upon which the charges rested. But for its clumsiness, prices presumably might have advanced forever. And if the stock could have risen instead of falling, then the Traversers "would have been looked upon as nobles, as the architects of their fortunes, by the very men who now prosecuted them, and lauded to the skies as possessing spirits fraught with enterprise."[29]

The court was impressed with this persiflage and took the same indulgent view. In the words of one of the three judges, the Traversers "had charged themselves with the loans in the books of the Bank," they had at the time a prospect of repaying them, and "it appeared that they did then intend to repay" them. "Their subsequent disappointment by the failure of their speculation and their consequent ruin could not convert that into a crime which was not one at the time of doing it"; and the later measures to which they resorted for concealment "could make no difference in the case, since the act was to be judged of by the views and intentions with which it was done and not by anything which subsequently took place." The court's decision was accordingly "not guilty in law or in fact."[30]

But at another point, whose relation to the first is confused in

[28] 39 George III, c. 85 (1799, Statutes at Large, 1800).
[29] Harper, 113, 170.   [30] Harper, 232, 246.

the record, the court stated that the question before it was "simply, whether or not the acts charged amount to an indictable conspiracy at common law." It held that the principles upon which the indictments rested were "not sufficiently intelligible" and that its duty was to protect the people of Maryland "from punishment for any act which it is not *perfectly satisfied* is forbidden by the laws." The Traversers had also demurred that the state court had no jurisdiction, since the Bank was a federal corporation; but this the decision dismissed on the prior ground that the offense alleged was not indictable.*

The case had been heard first in 1820 before the Harford County Court, Bel Air, Maryland, whither it had been transferred lest "a fair and impartial trial could not be had" in Baltimore. The case then came before the Maryland Court of Appeals, in the December term 1821, where counsel for the state was joined by William Wirt, Attorney General of the United States, and counsel for the Traversers by William Pinkney.** The Appeals Court unanimously reversed the lower court's judgment and remanded the cases for retrial "on the facts." Yet upon retrial at Bel Air in March and April 1823, the original judgment was reaffirmed, two judges concurring and the third dissenting as before. To the dissident the case still presented this simple aspect: "The Traversers, in violation of a sacred trust and under false representations calculated to deceive those who were interested in the due execution of the trust, have taken from the funds of the office a large sum of money, which they converted to their own use, and have failed to return to the Bank a cent of their spoil." But this was not the view that prevailed.[31]

* Harper's *Report of the Conspiracy Cases*, Appendix 1, pp. 2, 30, 35. This authority is so blindly arranged and wanting in dates and other identification that at many points the proper order and relationships are quite uncertain.

** Luther Martin had led the state's defense against the Bank in *McCulloch v. Maryland*, and William Pinkney and William Wirt had been counsel for the Bank. Now in the *Conspiracy Cases*, with the state and the Bank joined against the Traversers, Wirt and Pinkney were opposed. Maryland and the Bank were partners in one case and opponents in the other; and counsel for both sides, particularly Martin, Pinkney and Wirt, were associated one time and opposed another. How Maryland could accept an associate which in its eyes was unconstitutional and without legal existence is not clear.

[31] *The State* v. *Buchanan,* 5 Harris and Johnson (Maryland Reports), 317; Harper, pp. vii, 278.

Though the Maryland laws were evidently wanting, it is probable that the court would have found the defendants guilty had the injured party not been the federal Bank. It joined instead the popular clamor and found the Bank guilty. The Bank was an alien in Maryland, unworthy to have its privileges sustained by the Free State against her erring, over-sanguine citizens—the Supreme Court of the United States in *McCulloch* v. *Maryland* to the contrary notwithstanding.

VIII

Meanwhile, the federal Bank was being watchfully flouted and resisted by a large portion of the state banks. As depository of the United States Treasury, it received their notes from the public in payment of taxes, and it credited the notes to the Treasury's balance, giving the Treasury immediate use of its funds. The natural expectation would be that the state banks would promptly redeem their notes and reimburse the government Bank. Some did, and some did not. In 1818 the Pittsburgh office asked payment of $10,920 of notes issued by the Commercial Bank of Lake Erie, in Cleveland, Ohio, and the latter in seeming compliance took the notes and boxed up the specie to redeem them; but when the wagons drew up to get the boxes, the bank's president refused either to deliver the specie or to return the notes. He offered instead a post-note due in twenty days and the Bank could take "that or nothing." He explained publicly that he considered the federal Treasury and the federal Bank "the same thing; that the Bank of the United States had converted their offices into broker's shops; and that he considered it a duty that he owed to society to resist their encroachments; that he would publish to the world the reasons for his refusal to pay and call on the other banks to act in the same manner and to form a coalition against the Bank of the United States."[32]

The Planters Bank and the Bank of the State of Georgia, both in Savannah, went still further. Instead of paying their debit balances promptly, they temporized, and the Bank had to allow its holdings of their notes to accumulate. In 1820 their indebtedness to it ran as high as $500,000, on which they paid no interest. The Bank offered to carry them for $100,000, without interest, but required that notes in excess of this amount be redeemed punctually. The state banks declared this preposterous. Their committee said: "The

[32] ASP, Finance IV, 855-56, 859-60, 927ff, 933-38, 957-58, 1054-56, 1068-69.

requisition by the office of the United States Bank for a *daily cash settlement* from the local banks has been resisted, not only as unnecessary and totally without example in the intercourse of the banks in this quarter of the Union, who have always acted towards each other with unlimited and distinguished confidence, but as otherwise objectionable." The Bank yielded to the extent of weekly settlements instead of daily, interest to be paid at 6 per cent on balances due it in excess of $100,000, and agreed to accept drafts on northern banks in place of specie. The local banks haltingly acquiesced in this arrangement but stuck to it less than six months. It interfered with their lending what they wished. So the Planters Bank, seconded by the Bank of the State of Georgia, annulled the agreement and advised the federal Bank not to accept any of its notes because it would not pay them: "we wish you to refuse our paper hereafter," the Planters president stated, "and I am instructed to request that . . . it may not be received at your office in any shape"; for the Planters was resolved "on refusing to pay its bills accumulated by the Bank of the United States unless their intercourse can be conducted on the liberal and friendly footing which prevails among the state institutions."[33]

Thus spoke men, in Savannah as in Baltimore and in Cleveland, "possessing spirits fraught with enterprise." One is uncertain which to admire the more, their effrontery or their enthusiasm. They believed in America as a place to get rich, and they recognized the magic possibilities of inflating the supply of money by avoiding cash settlements. Let every one honor every one else's promises, nor threaten the beautiful structure of unlimited credit by deflationary demands that the promises be redeemed. Let the economy float off the ground in a trance of mutual confidence. It was a monetary burlesque of Pauline theology, faith taking the place of works. The menace to this speculators' paradise was the federal Bank's insistence that it be paid promptly what was owing it; for in paying it the lending banks had to reduce their specie reserves and thereby inhibit their ability to lend. So contrary to the money-making interest were the Bank's restraints felt to be that resistance to them of any sort seemed warranted; and when the Bank sued the Georgia banks for payment, they fought it all the way to the Supreme Court, where in March 1824 they lost.[34]

[33] Catterall, 86-89.
[34] *Bank of the United States* v. *Planters Bank*, 9 Wheaton 904 (US 1824).

IX

In these court actions that I have been describing—*McCulloch* v. *Maryland*, 1819; the *Baltimore Conspiracy Cases*, 1819-1823; *Osborn* v. *the Bank of the United States*, 1824; and *the Bank of the United States* v. *Planters Bank*, 1824—there was a mesh of moral, economic, and constitutional problems which were profoundly disturbing to the American people. They arose from basic changes produced in the economy by the Industrial Revolution, the attendant diversification of economic effort, the expanding utilization of credit, and the spread of the spirit of enterprise. These were shaking to pieces the simpler economy of 18th century America and undercutting the moralities that had subsisted among a people who were mostly agrarian and whose minor commercial pursuits, by comparison with the free-for-all of 19th century democratic enterprise, were a cult as much as a business. The business world in a mere two or three decades had expanded enormously, absorbing thousands who had never known the traditionary discipline of 18th century commerce; and now, transactors in a new *milieu*, they were scheming, promoting, inventing, stock-jobbing, and scrambling on a scale and in fashions wholly novel to most of them. Speculators were replacing conservative merchants, and embezzlement had made mere cheating and larceny contemptible. In the business world were a minority, the most successful as well as the most honest, who maintained as fine a morality as tradition had inculcated: Stephen Girard, Prime, Ward and King, and Alexander Brown were leaders among them. But the majority were green, brash, and irresponsible. They were cunning rather than sagacious, and ignorance more than turpitude made a large proportion of them corrupt.

For enterprise had placed such subtle instrumentalities as credit, accounting, and the corporate forms of organization at the disposal of people unaccustomed to such things. The conventions of a monetary economy were coming swiftly into use and sweeping the unsophisticated off their feet. An economy in which barter had been important and financial transactions had been wholly subordinate to the exchange of goods was giving way to an economy concerned more and more with obligations, contracts, negotiable instruments, equities, and such invisible abstractions. Money *per se* was giving way to promises to pay money, most of which were never performed, in a primitive sense, but were canceled by bookkeepers in the increasingly frequent offset of liabilities; and specie was dissolving into obligations to pay specie in a volume greatly exceeding the total that existed. These devices yielded fortunes and so had validity, but they were as unsettling to society as were in their way the Newtonian physics, the sentiments of the French Revolution, romanticism, or machinery driven by steam. In the absence of enough experience, the point at which the proper use of a convention became an abuse was unperceived. If a promise was as good as a deed in some instances, it was unapparent why everything might not be left to promise. If things were worth what people thought they were worth, why was deception not preferable to reality? It was a principle stated by Adam Smith and other respected economists that a bank could virtuously put into circulation promises to pay equal in amount to five times the gold and silver it had to pay them with; to John Adams, as honest and intelligent a man as there was in the States, such a thing seemed a monstrous cheat. To Thomas Jefferson it was a swindle. So it continued to seem to perhaps the majority of Americans, though many of them, seeing how well it worked, calmed their consciences and made what they could of it. I doubt if one banker in four clearly understood what he was doing and what made it sound and proper. The others could not intelligently explain what they were doing and therefore could not intelligently justify it. To a certain extent, therefore, they literally could not tell the difference between right and wrong; for if they could owe five times what they could pay, why not a hundred? Or why not slip along with no means at all? If insolvency could be concealed, why not be insolvent?

Another novelty, inexplicable but momentous, was that by forming a corporation men could escape the obligation to pay their debts. Or so it seemed. And probably the majority who profited from the arrangement did not understand it and could not justify themselves. Nor could they convincingly deny the harsh judgment that as a corporate group men would do things that shame would keep them from doing individually. But incorporation was a form of collective effort that greatly augmented the efficiency of capital, and it throve in spite of moral misgivings.

So sudden and wide-spread was the recruitment into enterprise of men unprepared for its responsibilities that a lowering of moral standards was bound to occur. The more conservative, whether commercial or agrarian, were appalled by it. In that they were alike. But the agrarian majority were not very discriminating; they inclined instead to decry all business and enterprise. They were un-aware of the difference between a Langdon Cheves and a William Jones. They longed for the sturdy virtues of colonial and revolutionary times. In the austere light of their native ideals, corruption and business were one and the same thing. John Quincy Adams, who was not agrarian and who saw things very differently from his father, noted "the wide-spread corruption of the numberless state banks." A hundred honest bankers made less impression on these staunch moralists than one Andrew Dexter wrecking his bank in Glocester, or the three pickers and stealers in the Baltimore office of the Bank of the United States, with a number of smaller fry defaulting and embezzling here and there between.[35]

Moreover it was futile to consider the problem merely a moral one, as if a whole generation of men had all at once been born dishonest. The problem was the practical one that old disciplines had broken down in new circumstances. The bankers in particular were like boys with racing cars—the first ever built. What they needed was precisely what they would not have—an operating restraint such as the Bank of the United States automatically imposed, being so constituted, as Isaac Bronson said years later, that its own existence depended on its exercise of a controlling influence over the state banks. That restraint remained, so long as the Bank continued to have the deposit account of the largest transactor in the economy. But it was a restraint which the Bank in its current condition could not modify and direct with wisdom, as a central bank should.[36]

X

It was not long before the Bank's successes in the Supreme Court were paralleled by its improved operating condition. Langdon Cheves, with the indispensable support of the Bank's more responsible stockholders and directors, Stephen Girard, Nicholas Biddle, Alexander Brown, and others, had saved it. His achievement was the sort that gains a man no popularity; even many of his stockholders, whose investment he had preserved, were disgruntled because he was niggardly with dividends. There would be a decided opposition to him, Secretary Crawford wrote to Mr Gallatin in May 1822. In July Mr Cheves informed the stockholders that he would

---

[35] J. Q. Adams, *Memoirs* IV, 325.
[36] Raguet, *Financial Register* II, 12.

resign at the end of the year. "It was my desire to have done so," he said, "very soon after I entered upon the duties of the office." Albert Gallatin in October was asked to succeed him but refused. Late in November delegates representing stockholders in several seaboard states met to select a candidate and agreed upon Nicholas Biddle. "This gentleman is highly commended by some and much objected to by others," Niles' *Register* reported; but he was elected president of the Bank, 6 January 1823, without marked dissent.[37]

Mr Gallatin would have been a better choice, ideally. He was experienced, firm, sagacious; and no one else in public life equaled him in character and intellect. He was also quite without fancy or egotism. Neither he nor Langdon Cheves would have let himself be demoralized by the Jacksonians. They would have withdrawn in dignity, and let Andrew Jackson have his blundering way. But, as things were, I doubt if either would have managed the central bank better than Nicholas Biddle did before the Jacksonian attack. Mr Gallatin and Mr Cheves were both too conservative to last. In an expanding economy, with a powerful demand for credit, the central banker is called on mostly to be negative. He must resist and say no. He must endure the revilings of the optimistic, the speculative, and the enterprising, who will denounce him for holding back progress and enslaving mankind to the monetary system. Both Albert Gallatin and Langdon Cheves were contemptuous of such cant and would scarcely have survived the first collision. Nicholas Biddle also had the brains to see through it, but he had the resilience to maintain control. So long as the problem was mainly economic rather than political he made the central bank work as it should. It was his success that made the issue political. When it became political, he failed. The others would have failed too but sooner and less painfully.

Though Mr Cheves may have wished sincerely to resign, it is evident that he resented the readiness of the Bank to let him do so. He blamed Mr Biddle for what happened, and it seems likely that with the latter's support he might have stayed, the dissatisfied stockholders notwithstanding. For Mr Biddle put off increasing the dividends and in that respect pleased the stockholders no better. Both remained very reticent about their differences. They met and corresponded on rare occasions, but their courtesy to one another was punctilious and cool—Cheves because he would have it so, Biddle

[37] Kent, 86ff, 93-95; Niles xxii (1822), 291; xxiii (1822-23), 113, 209, 290; Gallatin ii, 244; James Gallatin, *Diary*, 197, 201.

because he could not be friends alone. Mr Cheves, proud, sensitive, and conscious of having been given the really dirty work to do and then let go, was aggrieved. So would any one have been, though few would have been so gentlemanly about it. But a quite objective decision as to policy had to be made and that, not personalities, was the ground of differences.

Fifteen years later, in 1837, when the charter of the Bank had expired and Mr Cheves was sixty-one years old, his fellow Carolinian, Dr Thomas Cooper, mildly criticized "the very harsh but really salutary exercise of his arduous office" and highly praised Nicholas Biddle. This stung Mr Cheves to an interesting and moving *apologia*: he described the scandalous situation of the Bank in 1819, the ordeal of making its debtors pay, and the snobbish resentment of Philadelphians at having a stranger running the Bank. "The office was one for which I had no particular predilection, independent of the peculiar difficulties which attended it, of which I had scarcely any idea when I agreed to accept it. . . . I know no earthly misery greater than to live in perpetual strife, and seeing this to be my probable fate, I determined in a few weeks after I entered the Bank to leave it" as soon as the task was finished. "I have . . . almost as little ambition to be considered an eminently skilful banker as an eminently skilful physician. . . ." Of his successor he said: "I have always borne testimony to Mr Biddle's talents and general fitness for his station. Our fate was to encounter very different circumstances. . . . I am very sure, however, that he has made larger profits for the stockholders than I should have done. . . . I have always been of opinion that a Bank of the United States neither ought, nor ought to be permitted, to conduct its business with a view to the largest possible profits, and therefore I should probably have done a more limited business. . . . If in the struggles of the Bank to be rechartered, my opinion was against it (as in fact it was), I nevertheless was silent. The relations in which I had stood to it forbade me to manifest opposition to it, in any way or in any degree. It is now no more, and I am free to declare that I am opposed to a national bank in any shape. I always believed it to be unconstitutional, and my experience and observation have satisfied me that it is inexpedient, unnecessary, and dangerous."[38]

This final and surprising declaration, which is unsupported by Mr Cheves' earlier record, if not indeed contradicted by it, seems to

[38] Niles LIII (1837), 8-9.

reflect the extreme position to which he advanced toward the end of his life in assertion of states' rights and limited federal powers. But there is no reason to doubt that he was correct in thinking that he would have managed the Bank more conservatively than Mr Biddle. He would probably have managed it too conservatively and roused even more quickly than Mr Biddle did the outcry of "oppression" against it.

For the Bank by nature and purpose conflicted with the dominant wishes of Americans. They wanted to exploit their resources, and to do that they wanted all the money they could get. An institution designed to curb the supply of credit could scarcely perform what Mr. Gallatin called its "unpopular duty" without becoming not merely unpopular but intolerable—and the more conservative it was the more intolerable.[39] The business world since the days of Thomas Paine's and Alexander Hamilton's identification of business enterprise with free government had been hurrying on with every encouragement, practical and philosophic, to the logical extremes of *laisser faire* and would brook no restraints upon its liberty to borrow.*

XI

Although the hostility most responsible in the end for destruction of the Bank of the United States was that of the state banks and of allied business interests requiring credit—and more particularly of those in New York—the chief hostility in the beginning had been agrarian and strongest in the Ohio valley. In the conventional accounts, this agrarian hostility still remains the real force that destroyed the Bank. One gets a picture of the Bank as a Shylock lending to distressed farmers, then exacting its pound of flesh from them, but in the end having its exactions frustrated by Andrew Jackson. The picture is fanciful. The Bank did not wish to lend to farmers, and farmers did not wish to borrow from it. It lent chiefly to merchants and other business men, most of whom owned some land—as everyone did who owned anything—and when in a period

---

* I have incidentally paraphrased Professor Joseph Dorfman, who in reference to Thomas Paine speaks of "that expansion of business enterprise that he and the enlightened men of his generation almost completely identified with free government." *The Economic Mind in American Civilisation,* 459.

[39] Gallatin III, 334-35.

of depression it had to take possession of its debtors' property, it found itself in possession of land. This did not make its debtors agrarians. The Bank acquired, for example, a large part of the city of Cincinnati; but no one supposes that Cincinnati property was farm property.

The farmers of the Ohio valley, however, as of most frontiers, had been in debt and in distress, though not to the Bank of the United States. They had been in debt to those from whom they had purchased their land; their principal single creditor was the government of the United States. The basic cause of their distress was the universal tendency to under-estimate the cost of bringing undeveloped land into profitable cultivation. That cost had always been high in terms of labor, but now it had become high in terms of cash, largely because land alone had lost in economic adequacy but must be supplemented more and more by stock and equipment. In the 17th and 18th centuries a farmer's needs had been supplied almost wholly from his labor and his land, for with these and with a few tools and weapons he could shelter, clothe, and feed his family. He had timber for fuel and shelter, and from hunting, fishing, and tillage he had food and apparel. There was little relatively that he needed to buy. But with increased settlement, the game disappeared, tillage became more important, equipment and live stock were needed in larger amounts. With these changes, the relative importance of land shrank, that of equipment and stock increased, and so did that of cash; till now in the 20th century, land is but a fraction of the farmer's total investment, its former relation to stock and equipment having become reversed.* The turn came early in the 19th century, coincidentally with the Industrial Revolution, which indeed was largely responsible for it. For the Industrial Revolution provided new occupations alternative to farming, it provided implements and supplies which were indispensable but cost money, and it stimulated farm production, though at the same time subjecting it to the rough pressure of change.

* This subject is discussed by Professor C. H. Danhoff in his "Farm Making Costs and the 'Safety Valve,' 1850-1860," *Journal of Political Economy*, June 1941. I have had the privilege also of reading additional manuscript material on the subject by Professor Danhoff. At the same time that farm land has been a steadily diminishing proportion of farm property, farm property has been a steadily diminishing proportion of all property. This subject is discussed by Professor F. W. Schultz, "The Declining Importance of Farm Land," *Economic Journal*, December 1951.

The fact and the import of these changes were seldom recognized. Men continued thinking and trying to farm as if they were still in 18th century America, and they emigrated in their thousands across the Appalachians to the valley of the Ohio, where land was accounted rich, abundant, and cheap, in the supposition that with the acquisition of such land their economic difficulties would disappear. But the conditions long taken for granted no longer held, and this land though rich and abundant was not cheap, though it appeared so. The settler, to make his initial payments, transport his family, provide himself with the necessary housing, tools, and animals, sustain his family while awaiting returns from the soil, and survive his errors and misfortunes, required capital in amounts of which he mostly never even dreamed. Wanting such capital, many and probably most immigrants contributed their labor gratuitously to the clearing of land, to its rudimentary improvement, and to the testing of its adaptabilities; and they got nothing but bare subsistence in return. All the gains were realized by their successors.

Later generations that contemplate an America which is miraculously productive in a myriad of ways, from sea to sea, can understand only with an effort the terrible cost to their progenitors of settling and improving it. Amos Kendall, who arrived in Kentucky in 1814 from New England and who became fifteen years later one of Andrew Jackson's closest advisers, describes in his autobiography the situation in which in 1809 he had found his older brother and sister, who were pioneering in northern Vermont, where they had purchased tracts of wild land on credit, built small log cabins, and made clearings. Kendall was satisfied "that they could never meet the payments for their land and were making improvements upon it for the benefit of others." So it turned out. "In the winter of 1813, his brother Zebedee abandoned his place, giving up all his improvements, and returned to his father's with little else than a wife and five children. In August of the same year his sister, having also five children, arrived at her father's. . . . Her husband, finding himself in painful pecuniary straits, had enlisted in the army of the United States and left her."[40] The cost of pioneering was borne by all generations. My great-grandfather, leaving the Eastern Shore of Maryland about 1800, was one of the thousands crossing into Kentucky, where about fifteen years later he was one of the thousands who moved on into Indiana, whence his son moved on to Iowa, whence

40 Kendall, *Autobiography*, 41.

in turn his grandson, some eighty years after the removal from the Eastern Shore, went on to California. There this grandson, my father, cultivating oranges on land which hitherto had produced only sage brush, helped to determine the important fact that the land he had purchased was not good for oranges. He lost, in this bit of economic exploration, all he had accumulated. Since then, race horses have been bred there, but with no advantage to him, or me.

On all frontiers the cost of pioneering—in effort, in spirit, and in cash—tended to exceed expectations tragically, though the situation was different in the South where the large scale production of cash crops prevailed and where slave labor had made a large capital investment other than in land long customary. The dearth of capital was worst where the illusion of cheap land prevailed; it made relief for agrarian distress a dominant issue for years in the politics of Ohio, Kentucky, Tennessee, and other parts of the West in the early decades of the 19th century. Settlers on land eventually rich found themselves unable to complete their payments, and abandoning what they had held and labored over, tried their dismal luck further on in still greater primitivity. Some, unable or unwilling to move, sought by political action to halt the surrender of their property to their creditors, and laws were passed staying executions and otherwise protecting the equity of debtors. This threw the burden on creditors, who were mostly no better able to bear it than their debtors were, for they also were debtors themselves. These included banks, forty of which had been set up in Kentucky alone in 1818 and failed in 1819. So in 1820 that state tried a new institution, the Bank of the Commonwealth of Kentucky, which added still more bank credit to too much bank credit. The notes of the forty banks set up two years before were already "redeemable" in notes of the Bank of Kentucky, established in 1806; and now there were also the notes of the new Bank of the Commonwealth of Kentucky, a corporation without real capital and merely a pathetic aspect of the state of Kentucky, which elected its directors and paid the salaries of its staff but could provide it no real substance.

Banking had been defined for George Washington by Alexander Hamilton as a means of supplying a large circulating medium on a relatively small base of specie: Hamilton had considered a ratio between specie and circulation of as much as one to five. Kentucky was stretching it toward a ratio of nothing to infinity. And this was being done by an agrarian community. After virtuously eschewing credit while the commercial world was thriving on it and while its own lot was retrogressing, these Kentucky agrarians had turned at length, desperately and emulously, to grasp the heady elixir, and had carried to ruinous absurdity the very power wherein Thomas Jefferson had discerned the danger of banking lay. They were resorting deliberately and officially to measures whose consequences were the same as those that agrarians had denounced for generations in John Law's projects, in the South Sea Bubble, and latterly in Andrew Dexter and his Farmers Exchange Bank of Glocester.*

The confusion of the agrarian community was painful. It had sought to relieve its distress by legislation, it had disobeyed its traditions in the process, its distress was worse than before. But in this snarl of principles, possibilities, realities, and exigencies, psychological escape was found in blaming the federal government and the federal Bank for everything. The solution, for which the state banks and the politicians were responsible, was a perfect one: it gave the suffering farmers sympathy and it gave the politicians fresh ground to stand on. In 1825 Governor Desha of Kentucky, a veteran enemy of the federal Bank, deplored "the insecurity now felt by numberless cultivators of our soil," which he considered "the chief cause of that extensive emigration which is now thinning the population of some of the finest sections of our state. . . ." "At every term of the federal court," said the Governor, "numerous judgments and decrees are obtained against our peaceful citizens for the lands and houses which they have honestly purchased, built, and improved, and orders given for their execution contrary to our laws. . . . And thus does this commonwealth suffer those who have improved, supported, and defended her, to be stripped of the proceeds of their life's labor and made the unpitied victims of heartless speculation and assumed power."[41]

The federal Bank preyed on the state banks, and the federal courts defended it. It received the notes of the state banks and

* The Shays rebels in New England a generation earlier had suffered from a dearth of money; the distressed settlers in the Ohio valley were now drowning in a superfluity of it. The difference in the two situations was, I imagine, that western Massachusetts in 1786 was a well-developed farming community with an inadequate legal tender; whereas the Ohio valley in 1820 was undeveloped with an inadequacy of everything but raw land and an unprepared population.

41 Niles xxix (1825), 220.

demanded redemption. It made the state banks pay, when what they wanted to do was lend. To the state bankers, most of whom were politicians themselves, this was oppression, and they readily convinced their fellow citizens that it was these measures of the federal Bank that drained wealth from the West and prevented them from being as generous as they wished. The Bank was an alien corporation which entered the individual states against their will and went about in them scot-free.* When the states sought to oust the monstrosity from their soil, Chief Justice Marshall and his coterie of soulless old Federalists on the Supreme Court affirmed its inviolability, and the federal courts within the states truckled to him, upholding the usurpation and rendering the regional sovereignties impotent to deal with their paramount problems. "How," asked Amos Kendall, "shall the states resist the consolidating tendency of our national government, which the decisions of the federal courts are annually making more apparent?" The states found no political or legislative answer. Even their own people denounced laws which sacrificed creditors to debtors. To General Andrew Jackson, for example, a Tennessee relief measure was "wicked, and pernicious, . . . profligate, and unconstitutional, . . . a law that will disgrace the state, destroy all credit abroad, and all confidence at home."[42]

So, bitter as was the western feeling, it did not become fatal to the Bank. The farm products of the western states—the most important being cotton—began to reach foreign markets with the extension of river haulage to New Orleans. The region grew economically more comfortable, the Bank's management improved, and the bitterness subsided. Later, when the assault arose that proved fatal to the Bank, it came from New York, and only its instrument was western. An advantage of the Bank in the West but its disadvantage in the East was that it engaged in the same type of lending and exchange dealings as the state banks. In the West this was advantageous because there was less good banking service there than the region required. In the East it was disadvantageous because the state banks felt that they were adequate and resented its competition. In the 20th century the central bank is not typically a

---

* "In Ohio and Kentucky," Nicholas Biddle wrote later to Mr Gallatin, "the complaints I believe were that the Bank having lent much would not lend more and that the state laws to violate the rights of creditors could not easily be made to reach the Bank." PLB, iii, p. 305, 29 July 1830.

[42] Kendall, *Autobiography*, 253; Sumner, *Jackson*, 157-58.

competitor of the commercial banks. The Federal Reserve Banks are not, though many commercial bankers mistakenly think they are. But in the early 19th century no central bank anywhere in the world confined itself to central banking exclusively. The Bank of the United States was typical of the stage of central banking evolution so far achieved.

CHAPTER 11

Nicholas Biddle

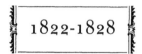

1822-1828

I. The federal Bank and the Jacksonians — II. Nicholas Biddle's earlier career — III. His personality and interests — IV. The Greek temple on Chestnut Street — V. Central banking — VI. Nicholas Biddle's policies — VII. Examples of the Bank's operations — VIII. The success of Nicholas Biddle's central banking practice

I

WE HAVE now come to one of the most controverted episodes of American history, the assault on the Bank of the United States by the Jacksonians and the aftermath thereof. Some readers may think that the attention I give the episode is inordinate, considering the merits of Professor Catterall's history of the Bank, and of Professor Walter B. Smith's recent account. But neither of these studies meets my purpose. Professor Smith's study is economic, whereas my interest is political, and Professor Catterall's, though also political, antedates a concept, relatively new, which gives the Bank a different significance from what it formerly had. This is the concept of central banking, a concept that distinguishes the regulation of bank credit as a function of critical importance in the economy. It is the function performed by the Federal Reserve Banks in the United States, by the Bank of Canada in Canada, by the Bank of England in Great Britain, and by the other central banks in their respective countries. Typically the central bank is unique in each economy, it is the government bank, and it is the regulator of private bank lending. Its work is conditioned by two peculiarly modern factors; viz., the overwhelming fiscal needs of modern governments with their immensely enlarged responsibilities, and the dependence of modern economies upon bank deposits, readily expansible by bank lending, for the bulk of the monetary supply.

A century ago the volume of the government debt and the volume of bank deposits were not nearly so great as they have since become. In the smaller and simpler economy of that period the central banking function was undeveloped and tentative. It was in an evolutionary state whose significance takes on a fresh aspect in the light of what has subsequently occurred.

This does not mean that Nicholas Biddle and the Bank of the United States were without defense until it was discerned over a century later that they had been engaged in an early exercise of central banking. Quite to the contrary, they were explicitly defended by historians from Gallatin through Catterall in the light of concepts then recognized and of facts then taken into account. Even so, defense of the dead is not the main purpose of historical writing; its greater purpose is to make the past known and understood in the most meaningful terms provided by subsequent experience. New concepts and new information call for new narratives. It is now clear that the Bank of the United States was a pioneer institution, of a significance in the light of twentieth century conditions which it did not possess for its contemporaries, either friendly or unfriendly. And not the Bank alone but its adversaries need a fresh presentation.

In popular accounts the Bank of the United States is most often presented as an embodiment of the "money power," a vague but immense evil, overcome by Andrew Jackson and his agrarian followers. It would be truer to say that it was a victim of the "money power," which used Andrew Jackson, states' rights, and agrarian sentiment to destroy it. The Bank was a federal institution which stood too much in the way of credit expansion to suit popular interests, and which kept the financial center of the country in Philadelphia long after it should have moved to Wall Street. Its effective adversaries were not farmers but business men. The events themselves made a crisis in the economic and political history of the country. They were not merely a conflict between Nicholas Biddle and Andrew Jackson but a conflict of deep meaning for the subsequent course the American economy was to take.

II

Nicholas Biddle, who succeeded Langdon Cheves as president of the Bank of the United States, belonged to a prominent Philadelphia family. He was born, 8 January 1786, with a superfluity of social and economic advantages. He was named for his father's brother, a naval hero of the Revolutionary War, whose career was brief but brilliant. His father, Charles Biddle, was a merchant who had also served in the Revolution and been vice president of Pennsylvania when Benjamin Franklin was president.

Nicholas Biddle finished his course at the University of Pennsylvania when he was thirteen—whatever that can mean—but was refused a degree because of his youth. He went to Princeton, where he was graduated two years later at the head of his class. He then studied law, was admitted to the bar, but did not follow the profession. He gave his time to literature and when seventeen or eighteen became a contributor to Joseph Dennie's *Port Folio*. This magazine, published in Philadelphia, was the most ambitious literary periodical in America. In 1804, when he was eighteen, Nicholas Biddle went to Paris as secretary to General John Armstrong, the American Minister, and had a hand in transactions following the Louisiana Purchase. He attended the coronation in Notre Dame of Napoleon Bonaparte as Emperor, December 1804. In 1806 he visited Italy and then went to Greece, at the time under Turkish rule and to the western world *terra incognita*. He was the first American imbued with a sense of classic glories to visit the unhappy land; and very few English and French travelers had preceded him. Five years before, in 1801, Lord Elgin had got the Turks' permission to remove the marbles of the Parthenon to England, and it was eighteen years later that Lord Byron arrived at Missolonghi. The young Mr Biddle enthusiastically copied inscriptions, measured monuments, identified ruins, and interviewed whom he could; at Delphi he found what he was sure must be the sacred fount of Castalia, crowded with washer-women curious at his curiosity. Later in England he had occasion to describe differences between modern and ancient Greek to scholars at Cambridge who knew only the latter; and gratified the American Minister, James Monroe, by his ability to achieve an "American triumph" of a sort that was rare.[1]

In London, Nicholas Biddle was secretary to Mr Monroe. The next year, 1807, he returned to Philadelphia. He became an editor of the *Port Folio* as well as a contributor. He also undertook the task of writing the story of the Lewis and Clark expedition, sent out by President Jefferson in 1804 to explore the Northwest beyond the Mississippi. Copious records had been made by the expedition, and these had to be condensed and prepared for publication. The final part of the task was done by Paul Allen, who called himself "the editor" and Nicholas Biddle, "the writer." Thomas Jefferson

[1] W. N. Bates, *Nicholas Biddle's Journey to Greece*; Charles Biddle, 415.

wrote the introduction to the work and sent it to Biddle with the following letter, 20 August 1813:

"In a letter from Mr Paul Allen of Philadelphia, I was informed that other business had obliged you to turn over to him the publication of Governor Lewis's journal of his Western expedition; and he requested me to furnish him with any materials I could for writing a sketch of his life. I now inclose him such as I have been able to procure, to be used with any other information he may have recieved [sic] or alone, if he has no other, or in any way you and he shall think proper. The part you have been so good as to take in digesting the work entitles you to decide on whatever may be proposed to go out under it's [sic] auspices; and on this ground I take the liberty of putting under cover to you and for your perusal my letter to Mr Allen, which I will request you to seal and hand on to him. I am happy in this occasion of expressing my portion of the thanks all will owe you for the trouble you have taken with this interesting narrative and the assurance of my sentiments of high esteem and respect."[2]

Mr Jefferson's thanks and Mr Biddle's trouble were justified in the product, which for more than a century was the standard account of the expedition. "It was Nicholas Biddle's version," writes Mr Van Wyck Brooks in his *World of Washington Irving*, "a first-rate narrative digest, that revealed to the people the travels of Lewis and Clark; and Americans could begin to imagine the nation of the future, stretching three thousand miles from sea to sea." According to the *Literary History of the United States*, by Spiller, Thorp, Johnson, and Canby: "The book prepared by Nicholas Biddle of Philadelphia from the manuscript journals is one of the great travel narratives of the world." Reuben Gold Thwaites, an authority on western exploration, wrote a half century ago: "So skillfully is the work done that probably few readers have realized that they had not before them the veritable journals of the explorers themselves, written upon the spot. The result will always remain one of the best digested and most interesting books of American travel."* By Biddle's arrangement the work was published without his name.[3]

* Since this was written, a new account, condensed by Mr Bernard De Voto from the original documents, has been published.

2 Biddle Papers 2, Folios 291, 314, 405; Biddle, *Lewis and Clark Expedition* (Elliott Coues, ed., 1893), p. xvi note.

3 Brooks, 132; Spiller, Thorp, Johnson, and Canby II, 763; Thwaites, 105-29; Biddle, *Lewis and Clark Expedition* (Paul Allen, ed., 1814), Preface.

In 1810 Biddle was elected to the lower house of the Pennsylvania legislature. At the same time his father, Charles Biddle, was elected to the state Senate. The father inclined to be Federalist, apparently, but the son was Republican. Thomas Jefferson in response to a letter from William Short had written, 6 September 1808, "Biddle we know and have formed an excellent opinion of him"; his travels and experience "must have given him advantages."[4]

In the session of 1811 the most important business, according to Charles Biddle's *Autobiography*, was the application of the Bank of the United States for a state charter, renewal of the federal charter having been refused by Congress. "Although," he wrote, "I had some doubt whether giving them a charter would not be a disadvantage to the Bank of Pennsylvania, of which I was, and had been ever since it was first instituted, a director, I thought it would be of advantage to the state and therefore voted and used what interest I had for it. My son in the House of Representatives made a speech in favor of it that was much admired." Among the admirers, the father said, was Chief Justice Marshall. The position taken in the argument was that of the Madison administration, for which Albert Gallatin was responsible, but it reflects also the original argument of Alexander Hamilton, to which the Chief Justice himself adhered a few years later in *McCulloch* v. *Maryland*. The speech was an able one—not merely for so young a man, saying to his fellow legislators unfriendly to the federal Bank that since the "first virtues are frankness and candour . . . I mean to tell you plainly and simply that you are wrong," but because it showed an unusual understanding of how the Bank of the United States worked.[5]

Young Mr Biddle was also interested in legislative measures for the improvement of agriculture and education; and in 1814, now a member of the state Senate, he prepared the reply of Pennsylvania to the address issued by the Hartford Convention. In 1817 he withdrew from the legislature and occupied himself for the next several years with development of the estate, Andalusia, that had come to him through his marriage, in 1811, to the daughter and heiress of one of Philadelphia's wealthiest men, John Craig. He was nominated for United States Senator from Pennsylvania, and he ran for Congress, but was defeated by Federalists both times. In the fall of 1818 President James Monroe wished to make him Secretary

---

[4] Charles Biddle, 330; Jefferson (Lipscomb and Bergh) xii, 159.
[5] Charles Biddle, 331, 415; William Hamilton, *Debates*, 27.

of the Navy, but feared if he did it would be accounted favoritism. Biddle was told by his friend John Forsyth of Georgia, later Andrew Jackson's Secretary of State: "You are a great favorite with the Chief magistrate. I mean personally. He has a sort of parental affection for you." President Monroe was wont to speak of Mr Biddle "in terms of the warmest affection both as to the qualities of his head and heart." In 1818, when the federal Bank's difficulties began to be known, Biddle was preparing for the State Department a digest of the laws of various countries affecting the trade of the United States. In January 1819, on President Monroe's nomination, confirmed by the Senate, he was made one of the five government directors of the federal Bank.[6]

This occurred amidst disclosures of the Bank's precarious condition but before Captain Jones' replacement by Langdon Cheves and before the Baltimore scandal came out. As a stockholder and as an unofficial participant in public affairs, Nicholas Biddle had been concerned about the Bank's difficulties, which were then absorbing every one's attention. He had assisted the Spencer committee, which investigated the Bank in December 1818, John Spencer, the committee's chairman, having sought and effusively acknowledged his counsel. The Biddle correspondence indicates that he was interested not only in the Bank of the United States but in banks generally; and this interest was less in banking as a means of making money than as a function of the economy. Nevertheless the duties of government director seem not to have been welcomed. The Bank was in a state that seemed to worsen every day, and the new director's cares, especially considering his attachment to President Monroe, might be heavy and disagreeable. His life, as things were, was the pleasantest possible, and he spoke agreeably of his "usual habits of literary and laborious indolence." Four years later, January 1823, he assumed the presidency of the Bank as successor to Langdon Cheves, but did so with none of the reluctance that had attended his appointment as government director. The Bank was to absorb him for sixteen years till his retirement in 1839.[7]

III

Nicholas Biddle was barely thirty-seven years old when he became the Bank's president; he was junior to his predecessors in the office

[6] Charles Biddle, 415-16; Conrad, passim; Biddle Papers 5, Folios 984, 989; 7, Folio 1340; 8, Folio 1467; Biddle, *Correspondence*, 14-26.

[7] Biddle Papers 5, Folios 888, 1011, 1023.

and to most of his associates of comparable responsibility. He had had no apprenticeship. The Bank was the largest corporation in America, and one of the largest in the whole world. Mr Biddle was not oppressed by his responsibilities, though he took them seriously, and did not deaden himself to other civic interests. In 1827 he addressed the American Philosophical Society in honor of its late president, Thomas Jefferson; and as chairman of the trustees of Girard College he was active in giving effect to the philanthropic provisions of Stephen Girard's will. He also remained incorrigibly jaunty and pagan, with none of the Puritanism traditionary in the Anglo-Saxon world of practical affairs. He had been at the Bank less than a year when he was asked by a young lady for something to put in her album and complied with verses describing his shift from literature to finance. Now, he said:

> "I prefer my last letter from Barings or Hope
> To the finest epistles of Pliny or Pope;
> My 'much-esteemed favors' from Paris, to those
> Which brought on poor Helen an Iliad of woes;
> One lot of good bills from Prime, Bell, or the Biddles,
> To whole volumes of epics or satires or Idyls;
> Nay, two lines of plain prose with a good name upon it
> To the tenderest fourteen ever squeezed in a sonnet.
> Why, I would not accept—not for Hebe's account—
> The very best draft from Helicon's fount,
> Nor give—this it grieves me to say to their faces—
> More than three days of grace to all the three Graces.
> Then their music of spheres! can it thrill through the soul
> Like kegs of new dollars as inward they roll?
> And Cecilia herself, though her lyre was divine,
> Never gave to the world notes equal to mine."[8]

Little of this sort of thing seems to have been done at the Barings', at Mr Gallatin's, or at Prime, Ward, and King's. Instead, Mr Samuel Ward, the head of the latter firm and the country's foremost banker, sponsored a more practical and edifying literary work, the Reverend Thomas P. Hunt's learned *"Book of Wealth,* in which it is proved from the Bible that it is the Duty of every man to BECOME RICH." Samuel Ward was a real banker.*

---

* I shall often mention Samuel Ward, his firm—Prime, Ward, and King— and his friend Thomas Wren Ward of Boston, merchant and American agent

[8] Biddle, *Ode to Bogle,* 13.

As a man of letters Nicholas Biddle came far at the end of a tradition—the urbane, Addisonian tradition in which the man of affairs and the man of letters were one, the tradition to which Benjamin Franklin, Thomas Paine, and Joel Barlow had belonged. These men had felt none of that repugnance to money-making which animated the younger generation of Nicholas Biddle's literary contemporaries—Emerson, Hawthorne, Thoreau—estranged them from the dominant mood of America, and made their work fugitive, romantic, subjective, and rebellious. But the Age of Reason was past. Literature and affairs had parted company, and a man was supposed henceforth to belong to one or the other. Nicholas Biddle belonged to both, and his example is not encouraging.

Yet enterprise in its fashion was imaginative and even poetic. It made of Emerson's remark about mouse traps a slogan of American inventiveness. It found his individualism nicely congruous with *laisser faire.* It also produced sentimental evocations of its own, inspired by dreams of the nation's manifest destiny, political and economic. How such things, in business terms, could excite imaginations quite unlike Hawthorne's is illustrated by the following passage from the report of a committee of the federal Bank's directors in 1817, when there were as yet fewer than 10,000,000 persons in America, and no railways, no petroleum, no electricity, no California. The report was addressed to the question whether the Bank should undertake dealing in bills of exchange on a large scale—a question which by no means suffocated the aesthetic susceptibilities of the committeemen: "In the course of their reflections on this important subject, your committee could not refrain from casting their eyes over the map of the United States and indulging themselves in the most pleasing anticipations. They see before them a country including within its bounds an extent of surface and a fertility of soil affording ample space and presenting a certain reward for the labor of almost innumerable inhabitants; cities increasing in magnitude, in number, wealth, and magnificence; the ample surplus of the varied productions of almost every climate on the globe flowing into those cities to be consumed or transported to countries abroad, producing an internal and external commerce

---

of Baring Brothers. Samuel Ward was the father of four unusual children, the best known being Julia Ward Howe. Thomas Wren Ward, whose name recurs more frequently in this narrative, is interestingly described in Professor Hidy's *House of Baring.*

which will keep millions of money on the wing between contiguous and distant cities, sections, and divisions of this great country."[9]

To the majority of Americans such sentiments, repeated to the end of the 19th century and beyond, were a comfortable substitute for the less comprehensible reflections of Thoreau in *Walden*, of Whitman in *Leaves of Grass*, or of Melville in *Moby Dick*. Nicholas Biddle might have appreciated the latter, but the effusions of the committee on bills of exchange would accord more with his interests. Magnificent, continental prospects, no doubt, had been impressed upon him by the Louisiana Purchase and the travels of Lewis and Clark—two Jeffersonian projects whose influence diverted multitudes of Americans away from Jeffersonian ideals. Their influence diverted Nicholas Biddle the more readily because nothing in his experience disposed him to 19th century romanticism and because the rational, social sort of taste he accepted from the 18th century did not lead him away from the arena of economic enterprise but into the thick of it—again as with Benjamin Franklin, Thomas Paine, and Joel Barlow. There, like the majority of his countrymen, leaving aside only the Transcendentalists and genuine agrarians, he could enjoy himself, as he facetiously told his young lady,

> "And renouncing illusions, find peace and content
> In that simplest, sublimest of truths—six per cent."

Yet this, in fact, he could not do. He was never a business man, and it is doubtful if he ever had the warm confidence of the business world, even when he had its admiration. He was called "clumsy" in Wall Street, as early as 1835. "His financial management has been little less than a series of blunders," it was said. A man who could not earn better than four per cent "ought to relinquish all claim to the character of financier." He had plenty of intelligence, but he lacked the hard, practical instincts that govern business men as they govern bees and keep their decisions within the limits of proper risk. It was by the most astute and substantial part of the business world that in the end he was most reasonably condemned. Business is, in the old sense, a mystery or cult, and it requires devotion. Mr Biddle had too irreverent a mind for it. He was too fond of playing a role and acting like a banker instead of being one. This was a fault not of vanity so much as intelligence. He understood too well how the whole thing worked, and he lacked in consequence the awe which, as his ancient Greeks knew, saves one from *hubris* and

[9] ASP, Finance III, 332.

impiety. Men of lesser understanding in business respected the mysteries with which they were engaged and kept secure. Nicholas Biddle, knowing he dealt with conventions, ventured to deal with them rationally. The consequences were deplorable.[10]

Mr Biddle took account of his deficiencies but made a merit of them, for in a letter of 29 October 1822 in which he seems to have been looking in the mirror to see who the next president of the federal Bank should be, he had set down three qualifications that officer should have: he should have "a talent for business," he should stand well with the government, and he should be a Philadelphian. "I say *talent* for business rather than being what is commonly called a man of business, for without meaning at all to disparage the knowledge of details which men of business are presumed to possess, I am quite satisfied from what I have myself seen at the Bank that the mere men of business are by no means the most efficient in the administration. The fact is that the misfortunes of the Bank, which grew principally out of the injudicious extension of the western branches, were actually occasioned by the men of business, and their errors were precisely the faults into which the men of business were most likely to fall. They trusted the western people with money and they trusted them with goods and suffered themselves to be deluded by the visions of equalizing exchanges and currencies more liberal habits of thinking would have easily dispelled."[11]

The criticism was sound, but the conclusion that the Bank would be better administered by someone with little business experience was not. Mr Biddle had what experience alone could never give, but he lacked what it could give. There had been nothing in his singularly happy, protected, and productive career to develop defenses against the non-intelligent or provide him with the earthy faculty of give and take. He had had no practical administrative experience of any sort, he had never known reverses or disfavor or the discipline of an organization, he had struggled for nothing that he possessed. He had not had to 'put up with superiors who were his inferiors. He had not learned to share responsibilities with others. He liked being irresistible. He had been admired by friends and untroubled by enemies. He was governed by consideration and reason and had the untempered intellectual's preference for what ought to be over what is. For the world of affairs, he was too naive

---

[10] New York *Evening Post*, 2 September 1835, quoting New York *Journal of Commerce*.

[11] Biddle Papers 8, Folio 1497.

and his air was too gay. His virtues were the open ones—candor, amiability, sincerity, and humor—but his character had little of ruggedness. "His countenance," a contemporary wrote of him at the height of his career, "does not wear the ascetic caste generally contracted by long continued and severe mental exertion, but is frank and cheerful, expressive of amiable and generous feeling." He brought to his difficult responsibilities as head of the central bank in a period of revolutionary economic expansion everything he needed except what he needed most. Even so his talents and virtues might have sufficed had it not been his extraordinary misfortune to have General Andrew Jackson cross his path. The General understood about banking too, for he had read about the South Sea Bubble. He was now an old man and a hero. He had thrust his way bodily through wilds such as Nicholas Biddle had made careful notes about in manuscript. He liked to annihilate whom he disapproved; and he had been fighting the British, the Indians, and his personal enemies while the young and golden Mr Biddle was reading books in Philadelphia, attending the opera, and writing light verses for pretty women.[12]

For contrast with the rugged and simple honesty glorified in Andrew Jackson, Nicholas Biddle has been given by the neo-Jacksonians a reputation for stratagem, intrigue, and deviousness which he did not have among his contemporaries and left no evidence of deserving. On the contrary, that sort of skill is something he conspicuously lacked. Among people who esteemed him, he was charming and influential, but with those who disliked him he was tactless and maladroit. Mr Van Buren, who was himself a master at working in the dark, did not notice any adeptness or power of deception in Nicholas Biddle, though he did, for example, in Daniel Webster; and in the same paragraph of his autobiography where he calls Mr Webster "wily" he speaks, referring to Mr Biddle, of "the off-hand frankness of his character." He calls Nicholas Biddle "spirited but reckless" and mentions "his excitable nature." He says that although Mr Biddle's "official conduct as president of the Bank . . . has been and always will continue to be with me the subject of unqualified condemnation, . . . his private and personal character has never to my knowledge been successfully impeached. I knew him from an early period of my life, had considerable intercourse with him which was not even interrupted by our political differences but was always

12 Conrad, 18.

agreeable and, I have no reason to doubt, on both sides—politics apart—sincerely friendly." He was incapable, in Martin Van Buren's opinion, of taking "illicit gains."[13]

The "off-hand frankness" and "excitable nature" seem to me eminently true of Nicholas Biddle; his feelings never got the better of his manners but often marred his judgment. He was sanguine, unsuspecting, and naive as one to whom the world has been singularly kind may be. He had faith in reason and truth, and the propaganda he distributed on the Bank's behalf comprised the soundest, clearest, and best material obtainable and that alone. At the beginning of his public career, when he was aged twenty-five, he had told his elders in the Pennsylvania Assembly frankly and plainly that they were mistaken; and he had suffered no ill consequences. But it was different in 1829 when he wrote the Secretary of the Treasury, frankly and plainly, that the Bank's directors "acknowledge not the slightest responsibility of any description whatsoever to the Secretary of the Treasury touching the political opinions and conduct of their officers—that being a subject on which they never consult and never desire to know the views of any administration." Mr Biddle's sentiment seems to me admirable, but I think his choice of language was not suitable for the ears of an administration whose bosom was the repository of civic virtue. The Secretary showed the sentence to the President and the President made a memorandum of it, *verbatim.*[14]

An example of Mr Biddle's egregious *naïveté* was his written answer to a Senate committee in 1832 when asked if the federal Bank ever oppressed the state banks. His reply was, "Never," which covered the ground adequately. But he continued with perhaps the most profound descent into indiscretion he ever made: "There are very few banks," he said, "which might not have been destroyed by an exertion of the power of the Bank. None have ever been injured. Many have been saved. And more have been, and are, constantly relieved when it is found that they are solvent but are suffering under temporary difficulty." This, as Senator Thomas Hart Benton observed, "was proving entirely too much." Had Mr Biddle flourished a pistol in the Senators' faces but assured them that he did not intend to shoot, he could scarcely have produced a worse impression than he did with these well-meant words. His

13 Van Buren, 634, 650-51, 663, 682.
14 22nd Congress, 1st Session, HR 460, p. 452; Jackson, *Correspondence* iv, 84-85.

enemies pounced on his statement and never let it be forgotten. Chief Justice Taney, when he was on the Supreme Court bench, twenty-seven years later, wrote that the statement ought "to have been of itself sufficient to prevent the renewal of the charter." It had disclosed a plan to destroy not only "the whole of the state banks," but "the hundreds of millions of property vested" in their stocks, "and the notes they had issued." The Chief Justice did not detail the means by which the Bank would accomplish this feat; "But," he went on, "I believed as soon as I read Mr Biddle's letter and believe now that it would gradually have compelled every state bank in the Union to wind up. His statement shows that the matter had been thought of and that the manner in which it could be done was well understood." In public life, to let one's frankness arm one's adversaries and fire their imaginations is a fault that comes closer to political ineptitude than to political skill.

A few years later, 1837, Dr Thomas Cooper of Charleston thought Nicholas Biddle should be run for President of the United States, but he found no encouragement. "Strange to say," he wrote Biddle, "I hear no objection to your talents or your integrity among those whom I have cautiously sounded, but they all object to you as being in want of the necessary knowledge and experience as a party politician." It is evidence of this general deficiency in Biddle's practical judgments that he was merely contemptuous of the writings of William Gouge, which he considered shallow, flashy, and journalistic—as they were. But they were not merely that, for they had astonishing popularity and influence. They did the Bank a hundred times more hurt than Nicholas Biddle's informed and thoughtful efforts did it good.[15]

IV

The new Bank of the United States, like the old, had opened in Carpenters' Hall and had occupied that building its first several years. About 1821 it moved out onto Chestnut Street into quarters occupied till 1824, when its new and final home, on the south side of Chestnut between Fourth and Fifth Streets, was completed. Here the banking house is still standing with distinction, a block east of Independence Hall, in a neighborhood of historic structures now in the care of the National Park Service.

[15] 21st Congress, 1st Session, SR 104, p. 6; Taney Papers, *Bank War* MS, 15-16 (also in Swisher, 168-69); Benton I, 159; Biddle, *Correspondence*, 297; W. B. Smith, 13.

"In this edifice," said the directors of the Bank in 1818 when announcing an award for the design to be selected, "the directors are desirous of exhibiting a chaste imitation of Grecian architecture in its simplest and least expensive form." The design they chose, prepared by William Strickland, was patterned after the Parthenon and produced a structure in white marble that is notable in American architecture. Classic taste was strong in Philadelphia; the first Bank of the United States, erected in 1797, was in that general style, and the Bank of Pennsylvania, 1798, razed many years ago, was a beautiful structure that established a definitely Greek influence. With the new Bank of the United States, that influence rose to a new level. The building had an international reputation, and was famous at home, especially among persons who disliked what was in it, as "the Greek temple in Chestnut Street." The more favorable view was that expressed by Philip Hone of New York on a visit to Philadelphia, 14 February 1838: "The portico of this glorious edifice, the sight of which always repays me for coming to Philadelphia, appeared more beautiful to me this evening than usual, from the effect of the gas-light. Each of the fluted columns had a jet of light from the inner side so placed as not to be seen from the street but casting a strong light upon the front of the building, the softness of which, with its flickering from the wind, produced an effect strikingly beautiful. How strange it is that in all the inventions of modern times architecture alone seems to admit of no improvement—every departure from the classical models of antiquity in this science is a departure from grace and beauty."[16]

Nicholas Biddle was not a director when William Strickland's design was selected, but he had become one and a member of the building committee by the time the corner stone was laid, 19 April 1819. Yet being "a vivid and consequential" person, writes Mr Talbot Hamlin in his *Greek Revival Architecture in America*, Mr Biddle "was a leader in Philadelphia, and it is probably largely owing to his enthusiasm and example that, once started, the Greek movement in Philadelphia grew by leaps and bounds, in large measure anticipating the taste of the rest of the country by at least a decade."[17] The residence he built, Andalusia, was in the same style and impressive though less beautiful; but as chairman of the trustees of Girard College he participated in producing in the College

[16] Kimball, *Architectural Record* LVIII (1925), 581; Gilchrist, 4; Hone, 302.
[17] Hamlin, 70-71.

building another masterpiece, though according to Mr Hamlin his influence on the architect, Thomas Walter, was more positive than good.*

Offices of the Bank erected in various cities reflected the style cultivated in Philadelphia. In Louisville, Kentucky, the city directory of 1832 stated in a description of the local branch then building that the proportions of its portico "are those of the temple of Bacchus at Teos," in Asia Minor. Under a like influence all the branches of the Bank of Indiana were Greek, but Corinthian, and presented from town to town in that state the same façade. If not Greek in pattern, bank architecture was at least classic. The Wall Street office of the Bank of the United States, designed by Martin Thompson and erected in 1822, was "a polished and knowing piece of dignified classic work, well detailed and beautifully executed"; its façade, preserved when the building was razed, is now the south façade of the American wing of the Metropolitan Museum of Art.[18]

V

Nicholas Biddle's career falls into two periods, preceding and succeeding President Andrew Jackson's first assault on the federal Bank in December 1829. The partition between the two periods is not definite, for the attack was slow in developing. But roughly speaking the seven years from 1823 to 1830 were a period of central banking, and the six years following, 1830 to 1836, were a period of central banking frustrated by politics. After 1836, when the federal charter expired and the Bank of the United States was succeeded by a Pennsylvania corporation of the same name, there was a third period of three years in which Mr Biddle displayed his brilliance and originality at their height but with a sudden and humiliating lapse into fatuousness from which he never recovered.

* In 1838, when the present Treasury building in Washington was under construction and Thomas Walter was continuing on the north, south, and west sides the original work done by Robert Mills on the east, he privately consulted Nicholas Biddle, "his literary confessor," about the plans and the presentation of them before a congressional committee. The Jacksonians were then occupying Washington, and Nicholas Biddle was under their curse. They would be startled, Mr Biddle remarked with amusement, to find him "even in the bricks and mortar of the Treasury." Biddle Papers, Nicholas Biddle to John Sergeant, 6 April 1838, PLB, 393.

18 Duke, 23; Hamlin, 135-36.

The central banking function was conducted by the Bank of the United States in two ways, of which one was self-acting and one was discretionary. Controls were self-acting when the Bank, as it received the notes of state banks in the deposits of government collectors and otherwise, required payment of them by the state banks. Save when the state banks would not or could not meet their obligations, this regulatory function proceeded in routine fashion; and its restraint upon the lending power of the state banks was comprehensive and effectual. It could be readily modified by the Bank's abstaining from the demand for payment and allowing the state banks to run into debt to it. This was discretionary and qualified the automaticity of the function. Discretionary procedure extended much further than that, however, in response to those general conditions over which individual banks had no control. Thus heavy imports in excess of exports entailed an adverse balance of payments which drew specie from the country as a whole. Poor crops or late ones meant that a given region and the banks situated therein would be called on to pay out more cash than they received. Large disbursements of funds by the federal government put pressure on some regions and banks to furnish the cash for transfer elsewhere. What the central bank should do and could do to counter-balance or mitigate the drift of money to and from the economy, from region to region within it, and from bank to bank, depended on circumstances and the resourcefulness of the management. It constituted the discretionary part of central banking.

Biddle's understanding of the art had first been indicated in his address on behalf of the old Bank in the Pennsylvania legislature in 1811. In 1819, in response to an enquiry from Representative John C. Spencer of New York, chairman of the House committee investigating the new Bank, he had made a more mature statement on the subject. His reply was written, 27 January 1819, a few days before President Monroe named him government director. "I think," he had written, "that experience has demonstrated the vital importance of such an institution to the fiscal concerns of this country and that the government, which is so jealous of the exclusive privilege of stamping its eagles on a few dollars, should be much more tenacious of its rights over the more universal currency, and never again abandon its finances to the mercy of four or five hundred banks, independent, irresponsible, and precarious."[19]

[19] Biddle Papers 5, Folio 1016.

In January 1821, being then a government director, Biddle had found himself at odds with other directors respecting loans by the Bank on its own stock. In the inchoate investment market of the time, where already demand outran supply, stock of the Bank was extremely important, not only for long-term investment but for the temporary employment of funds.* In lending on its own stock in those circumstances, the Bank was not providing itself a fictitious capital but was serving the money market by lending on a leading investment security; and most of the Bank's directors seem to have concluded that now, after two years of Mr Cheves' purgatives, the capital was restored and loans should be made on the stock of the Bank at par. Mr Biddle first of all doubted if it were a fact that the capital was already restored. He had various objections besides, the "most decisive" of which was that "By a public and voluntary assurance that its stock is whole and a public offer to lend upon it at par, the Bank . . . presents such an invitation to purchase its stock and such facilities to purchase without paying for it, as can not fail to render it the object of active speculation, to raise its price beyond its value, and ultimately to revive that unfortunate spirit from which the Bank and the country have already too deeply suffered." This was probably Langdon Cheves' opinion too, but the other directors refused to receive Biddle's protest; whereupon he reported the matter as government director, 29 January 1821, to Jonathan Roberts, Senator from Pennsylvania; to William H. Crawford, Secretary of the Treasury; and to President Monroe, who noted by endorsement Mr Biddle's fears that the directors' action would renew the speculations "which have caused heretofore so much misery and difficulty."[20]

When he became president of the Bank, Mr Biddle at once prosecuted the two measures respecting which he and Mr Cheves had quietly but sharply differed. One of these measures enlarged the Bank's circulation; the other, by the sale of stock forfeited as collateral, restored its capital. Mr Cheves had opposed both. As to the first, he had contended that because the Bank's notes were by law receivable in payments to the government and would be used for

---

* "Considerable investments [in the Bank's stock] have also been made by capitalists in the absence of active employment for their means. . . ." Baring Papers, Prime, Ward, and King to Baring Brothers, 30 June 1821.

[20] Biddle Papers 7, Folios 1355-58; Monroe Papers 30, Folio 5461.

that purpose, they would in consequence be returned to the Bank for redemption *pari passu* with their issue; wherefore the Bank should refrain from enlarging the volume of them in circulation lest it become embarrassed by the burden of redeeming them. The logic Cheves followed was simple: an increase of the Bank's circulation was an increase of the Bank's indebtedness, and indebtedness must be paid. Therefore the tendency of the circulation to increase must be resisted. What Cheves failed to see but Biddle did see is that the debts of a bank are in an exceptional and peculiar category because they have a monetary use which the obligations of other debtors do not have. In consequence they are not sought to be "paid," i.e., converted into coin. If a merchant or farmer received bank notes in payment for something he had sold, why should he rush to the bank and exchange them for coin? He accepted the notes, as Biddle had told the Pennsylvania legislators in 1811, not because they could be exchanged for gold but because they could be used to make purchases. It was only when they fell to a discount or proved otherwise to be less valuable than they were supposed to be that they would be returned to the issuing bank for redemption. Whatever rendered them more useful and convenient as money tended to reduce the demand for their retirement. That was the effect of the government's acceptance of them. It increased their use and the Bank's liabilities, as Mr Cheves feared, but it did not increase the demand upon the Bank for their redemption. To the contrary, it decreased that demand, as Mr Biddle expected. His policy of enlarging the Bank's circulation and replacing that of the state banks led steadily, whether with full intent or not, toward the Bank's becoming the sole bank of issue, with the state banks providing deposit liabilities only—a consummation, in the Bank's short career, never attained.

Respecting restoration of the Bank's capital by re-marketing the stock it held as forfeited collateral, Mr Cheves held that the capital should instead be reduced by permanent retirement of the stock. I think he was right. The Bank's capital of $35,000,000 was unnecessarily large, and a reduction would have been wholesome. Yet the restoration of the capital, though not so conservative as a reduction would have been, was conservatively managed. And it was still within the definition of central banking, which has both its expansive and its restrictive phases. The forfeited stock was sold at profit which went to surplus, and profits from operations were also retained.* "In January 1823," Mr Biddle wrote, "we began without one dollar in our pockets, and we have been trying ever since to accumulate a fund in reserve." Dividends were stabilized at six per cent from 1826 to 1828, and then at seven per cent, where they remained. This by contemporary standards was low and the stockholders were not satisfied; Nicholas Biddle might be more liberal than Langdon Cheves, but he was not liberal enough. In June 1828 a stockholder in Baltimore, where the most appetent seemed still to be, protested still—in effect he complained not merely of low dividends but of Mr Biddle's adherence to central banking responsibilities. Mr Biddle was doubtless aware, his complainant said, of the opposition to him in Philadelphia, New York, and elsewhere; the stockholders believing "that your object is to keep in check the state banks and to regulate the currency of the country *at their cost*. This, they say, may not be inconvenient to you, while you receive the salary of president of the Bank, but it does not suit them."[21]**

That the stockholders, or many of them, should resist a policy from within that the state banks resisted from without is natural because the stockholders in the early years of the Bank were as a whole no more conservative than the business world generally. In time, however, Mr Biddle subdued them; or rather he got rid of the troublesome ones when the Bank's stock became a good investment and shifted from the hands of speculators into those of investors, largely abroad.

Meanwhile Mr Biddle's conduct of the Bank was very careful. Nothing impressed him more than the delicacy and complexity of the economy; and whatever stimulation or pressure was required should be administered with care and lenity. The words "gentle" and "gently" were always coming from his quill. But to enterprise and speculation, whatever did not stimulate oppressed. The Bank, Albert Gallatin said, conducted "under the control of the general government," had "effectually checked excessive issues on the part of the state banks." He considered the first and principal advantage de-

---

* In selling the stock Biddle used the services of Reuben M. Whitney, and Prime, Ward, and King of New York. 22nd Congress, 1st Session, HR 460, pp. 112-156, 506, 433.

** The salary was $8,000 a year in 1836; in 1828 it was probably not so much. 29th Congress, 1st Session, House Document 226, p. 524.

21 Biddle Papers 12, Folio 2444; Biddle, *Correspondence*, 51.

rived from it to be its "securing with certainty" a uniform currency. He said this in 1831 when he was himself president of a state bank in New York but stood among the conservatives who recognized the need of restraint upon credit. The complaints of the state banks, he said, "that they are checked and controlled" by the federal Bank, "that, to use a common expression, it operates as a screw, is the best evidence that its general operation is such as had been intended. It was for that very purpose that the Bank was established." Mr Gallatin was not aware that a single solvent bank had been injured by the federal Bank, though many had been restrained more than they liked. "This is certainly inconvenient to some of the banks but in its general effects is a public benefit." In 1839 Professor George Tucker said in his *Theory of Money and Banks*: "The late Bank of the United States in this way was a curb on the state banks which they all felt and which, indeed, was the foundation of a jealousy that contributed to its overthrow. It was impossible that any state bank situated in the same town as one of the branches of the national Bank could much distend its issues without most of the excess finding its way into the latter in its collections of the public revenue; and as it was their established practice to exchange notes with the neighboring banks once a week and for the creditor bank to receive the difference in specie, they were thus effectually prevented from enlarging their issues much beyond the limits of prudence."[22]

Mr Gallatin and Professor Tucker were stating something that since 1810 and earlier had been recognized more and more yet not enough—that the primary purpose, real and avowed, of the federal Bank was regulatory.* It was that of central banking. That term, a

* Among other references to the central banking function the following are typical. Speaking of the currency in 1829 Condy Raguet said, "There is no man of intelligence in the least connected with our pecuniary concerns who does not perceive that the purity of that currency depends mainly on the Bank of the United States, without whose agency the whole circulating medium would be endangered." *Free Trade Advocate*, 23 May 1829, p. 325. In 1834 Governor Davis of Massachusetts observed that the federal Bank "has imposed a restraint upon the immoderate issues of paper by other banks and tended strongly to keep that paper up to the metallic standard of value." And in 1839 J. B. Felt, speaking in his *Historical Account of Massachusetts Currency* about conditions in 1816 after dissolution of the earlier federal Bank, said that "the monied machinery of the whole land, which had been kept in order by the checks and balances of the

22 Gallatin III, 333-35, 345; Tucker, 276-77; Biddle Papers, 1 PLB (1836), 204-05.

20th century locution, was not used, but the thing itself, in every essential, stood out. And Nicholas Biddle came close even to the modern term when he wrote, 13 June 1837, that experience had shown "the necessity of a large central controlling institution."*

VI

The Biddle Papers in the Library of Congress disclose constant preoccupation with these problems. The papers comprise the President's Letter Books, which hold the retained copies of letters, mainly administrative, routine, and official, to the branch offices, the Treasury, and others; and general files, which hold the incoming letters and also some drafts or copies of outgoing correspondence. The papers do not include routine cash and collection letters, etc., etc.; they seem to comprise only communications which had the attention of the president.

In a letter of 27 April 1826 addressed to Peter Paul Francis Degrand of Boston, who was preparing an essay on the Bank and had asked for some ideas, Biddle reviewed the Bank's policy under his administration. His review covers expansion of the Bank's note issue, retention of its capital, enlargement of its portfolio of business paper rather than government bonds, and development of domestic and foreign exchange dealings. He describes the Bank's control of the banking system and its "mild and gentle" nature. He describes also the sensitiveness of the banking system to an excess of imports—the effect of which is a withdrawal of specie from the country, and hence a diminution of bank reserves—and the successful measures taken by the Bank to prevent or compensate that diminution. He compares the prompt and preventive measures of the Bank of the United States in the stringency of 1825 with the tardy and inadequate measures taken by the Bank of England. His letter in part was as follows:

"The country had come out of the war with a currency debased

---

chief regulator, was alarmingly disarranged and worked to great disadvantage because that was removed." Felt, 220, 227.

* Already the French traveller, Michel Chevalier, had used the term "banque centrale," when writing from Philadelphia in 1834 about the Bank of the United States; and the corresponding term "central bank" was used in the translation of his letters published five years later. Chevalier, *Lettres sur l'Amérique du Nord* I, 96, 226; Chevalier, *Society, Manners, and Politics in the United States*, 77, 149.

by over issues, the natural consequence of the suspension of specie payments and the total absence of all control over the banking institutions. The Bank of the United States was established for the purpose of restoring the currency. It went into operation amidst a great number of institutions whose movements it was necessary to control and often to restrict, and it has succeeded in keeping in check many institutions which might otherwise have been tempted into extravagant and ruinous excesses. This necessary and salutary control could never be completely established until the Bank carried into complete execution the system of issuing only its own notes and receiving from the community the notes of other solvent banks. This system is now universal, and the general scheme of administering the Bank is to preserve a mild and gentle but efficient control over the monied institutions of the United States so as rather to warn than to force them into a scale of business commensurate with their real means.

"There is one part of this preservation system which is peculiarly interesting. Whenever the exchanges between the United States and foreign countries become adverse so as to force the rate beyond the expense of sending specie to the creditor country, there is an immediate shipment of the coin. . . . This is . . . a harsh corrective, because any great and sudden reduction of the circulating medium reacts throughout the community with a force inconvenient and often oppressive and unless managed with great delicacy may bring in its train the most disastrous consequences.

"To lessen the force of these results by preparing for them, by controlling as far as possible the exchanges so as not to let them long remain beyond the rates which induce large shipments of coin and where a reduction of issues must take place to render it as gradual as possible and not greater than the occasion may require: these are among the functions and the benefits of the Bank. They have been often employed with signal benefit. . . . It is difficult and perhaps presumptuous to say how far the disasters of England might have been prevented, but it may perhaps be safely asserted that the aid of £3,500,000 sterling to the sufferers which was extended in the month of March by the Bank of England might, had it been given in the month of December, have prevented some of the evils which it became necessary to remedy. A course of anticipation and prevention was pursued by the Bank of the United States in the autumn of last year by which there can be no doubt that much inconvenience and distress was averted."[23]

The following, 19 April 1825, to John White, cashier of the Baltimore office, is typical not alone of the problems the Bank dealt with but of Nicholas Biddle's habit of spelling things out to his subordinates. The letter concerns notes of Baltimore banks—presumably checks on them too—received in Philadelphia and sent to the Baltimore office. It also illustrates the Bank's method of easing the money market, with characteristic emphasis on lenity, by holding the notes of the state banks instead of demanding instant payment—a procedure followed, like present day open market purchases, at the Bank's initiative.

"You remark that in consequence of the receipt of the funds sent to you, you had drawn on the state banks for fifty thousand dollars. I am inclined to think that in the present state of our relations with the other institutions, it would be good policy not to be too rigid in our drafts on them. . . . I have found in practice that when we have been a little pressed, the best plan is to turn the demand gently over to the state banks, who can absorb it while they felt that they would not be urged for payment in specie; and thus in a little time our debt to them became reduced and the balances gradually turned in our favor, when we became again at our ease. My apprehension is that, as we are collecting Baltimore funds to send to you, if as you receive them they are followed by immediate demands, the state banks may become uneasy at these collections and in their own defense may diminish their business so as to react on the Office; whereas if the demands were forborne, they would see their balances turn in our favor without anxiety. And for our purposes the balances are as good as the specie."[24]

To the foregoing there was added a post-script in which Biddle said pleasantly but apodictically that the general administration of the Bank should control the specie held at the individual offices. The latter should not sell it. This was an important limitation on branch autonomy aimed at centralizing, in effect, the country's specie reserves—particularly that portion thereof most useful in making international payments.

Three days later, 22 April 1825, the following letter directed toward a different aspect of the current situation was addressed to

23 Biddle Papers 14, Folios 2826-27, 2842; 2 PLB (1825), 442.
24 Biddle Papers, 2 PLB (1825), 15.

Isaac Lawrence, cashier of the New York office: "Allow me again to invite your attention to the subject of turning the balances with the state banks in your favor by bringing your discounts within your income. In the midst of the speculations which are abroad, combined with the demands for specie, prudence requires that we should keep within reasonable limits, and that under all circumstances and at all hazards the Bank should keep itself secure and strong. Since the 18th of March when I wrote to you on the subject of your ability to do business paper falling due on or about the 1st of July, your discounts have increased about $700,000, a fair addition to your business which would be attended with no inconvenience did not an extraordinary demand for specie which has since arisen render the extension more hazardous by exposing you to calls for specie against which every consideration of prudence requires you to guard. It is no doubt very unpleasant and even painful to decline good business paper, but you have already by so large an increase of your discounts contributed your full share to the public accommodation—and beyond a certain limit the convenience of the customers of the Bank, however desirable it may be to promote it, is only a secondary consideration. . . . In the present state of the Office the true course I think is, to turn over as quietly as possible to the other banks, any demand which you can not supply—to let the diminution of your discounts, and the public revenue as it accumulates, turn the scale in your favor with the other banks, and then not to make sudden or very rigid demands on them for specie when you feel satisfied that you can claim your balances the moment they are wanted. By pursuing such a system you will I hope soon be able to regain your ascendency over the state institutions without risk or inconvenience."[25]

The following, on the same situation, was addressed to the New York cashier, 9 May 1825: "I am very glad to perceive that your Board have the firmness to decline doing so much paper and endeavour to keep your discounts within their present amount. At this moment the Bank has very little surplus means and if it had, whilst the spirit of speculation is abroad and the demand for dollars unsatisfied, every consideration of prudence warns us to be cautious. The Office at Boston is in much want of funds, and it is much better that any surplus beyond our indispensable wants should go there. By taking Boston funds, you ease the community and you reduce the

[25] Biddle Papers, 2 PLB (1825), 18-19 (also in Biddle, *Correspondence*, 34-36).

state banks' debt to you, which keeps them easy. Let me request you therefore to persevere in your present course and the pressure will soon be over.

"The Calcutta shippers have begun to-day to draw upon us for American half dollars. It is not easy to estimate the precise amount of the demand from that quarter, but we must be careful not to expose ourselves to hazard from it."[26]

The three foregoing letters preceded the crisis of 1825, which was reviewed by Biddle in 1832 for the Clayton committee. In October of that year the Bank had had to effect for the government a payment of seven millions on the public debt. This, which was the largest it had ever been called on to make, threw the Bank heavily into debt to the state banks at a time when it needed control of all its resources. By steady sales in New York, Boston, and Philadelphia from its holdings of government bonds, it rectified its position in four weeks and could then consider enlarging its portfolio of discounts. Mr Biddle asked the New York office to consider "whether it might now safely venture to set the example of a more free use of its credits." New York replied that its directors, after attentively considering the advice from Philadelphia, had "concluded to extend our discounts about $50,000 beyond our receipts." The $50,000 sounds like little even for the Wall Street of 1825, but it was not the total lent—it was the amount by which the total lent *exceeded* the total collected. Moreover, since its effect was to give the private banks claims upon the central bank for $50,000 of specie and to increase their reserves accordingly, it enabled them in turn to lend several times the amount obtained.[27]

The Bank's relations with the Treasury are illustrated by the following letter from Nicholas Biddle to William H. Crawford, Secretary of the Treasury, 20 November 1823: "The effort made under the act of Congress of the 20th of April 1822 to convert the six and seven per cents into fives failed. It failed, however, as you remark in your communication to Congress of the 23rd of December 1822 on account of the 'increased demand for capital for the prosecution of commercial enterprises' during that year. That demand has now ceased, and the capital of the country, contracted within a narrower circle of employment, is content with smaller profits, as may be perceived in all the objects of investment. . . . I incline to

26 Biddle Papers, 2 PLB (1825), 21.
27 22nd Congress, 1st Session, HR 460, pp. 434-37.

think therefore, from the present rates of these stocks, from the general abundance of unemployed capital in this country and in England, and from what passes within my own observation as to the disposition of stockholders, that if the act of Congress were revived, the government might be enabled to make a very advantageous conversion of any portion of the present loans into one at a lower rate of interest. How long this state of things may continue depends on general considerations of which you can best judge. My only purpose is to convey to you my own impression that the present would be a favorable moment for resuming the operation attempted last year."[28]

During the administrations of James Monroe and John Quincy Adams, relations with the Treasury continued close, and the Bank's services were valued. In 1827 the Bank was awarded a government loan at par, though private banks had offered a premium for it; and the consideration at the Treasury seems to have been only in part that the government as owner of one-fifth of the Bank's capital was a beneficiary in substantial part of the Bank's profits. It seems to have been also that the services of the Bank as the Treasury's fiscal agent meant so much to it in economy and convenience that to disregard the agent's interest was to disregard the principal's. No Secretary, familiar with the work of the Treasury, wished to have his department undertake the toting of government monies up and down the country. Biddle pointed out in 1828 that the Bank was making good the loss of $20,000 of pension funds recently embezzled at Albany and that in paying pensions alone the Bank provided the services of more than forty officers without charge to the government. He also observed to the Secretary of the Treasury, Richard Rush, that all the Bank's services for the government were performed without charge, "while in England the Government pay more than a million of dollars annually for the management of its debt by the Bank of England."[29]

The central bank and fiscal agency duties of the Bank dovetailed in the handling of the public debt. Biddle remarked in one of his frequent, almost routine, letters to Edward Jones, chief clerk of the Treasury, 4 October 1826, that "it is always an object of great solicitude with me to obtain the earliest information . . . in order

28 Biddle Papers, 1 PLB (1823), 70.

29 Biddle Papers, 2 PLB (1828), 391; Biddle, *Correspondence*, 57; Leonard D. White, chap. xxiv, 459-79.

to shape our business in such a way as may enable the Bank to pay off a considerable amount for the Government without diminishing the facilities which it is accustomed to give to the community." In a matter of forty years the federal government had become the largest single transactor in the whole economy—the largest recipient and disburser of funds, the largest employer, the largest purchaser, and the largest borrower. Its financial transactions were a principal factor in the money market and in the words of William Gouge, who was an enemy of the Bank, "so large as usually to derange the regular train of mercantile operations."[30] One of Nicholas Biddle's vigilant concerns was to offset the effect of government debt operations and prevent their disturbance of the money market. This concern reached even to the individual investor, as indicated by a letter, 14 April 1828, to Charles Goldsborough of Cambridge, the Eastern Shore of Maryland, listed with the Bank as a large holder of government bonds soon to be retired.

"When large payments of this description are made," Biddle wrote, "the Bank in order to break the force of a very heavy demand on a given day is in the habit of discounting on the collateral security of that stock for some time previous to the day of payment, and also of disposing of some part of its own stocks to those who wish to re-invest at that time. The object of this is to keep the monied concerns of the community easy by preventing the diminution of discounts of the Bank until the day of payment arrives and then suddenly throwing into the market large sums seeking immediate investment; by which means violent fluctuations in the money market are avoided. To the stockholders themselves this is a great advantage. If the whole is paid off at a given day, there is a great demand for reinvestment, and of course the reinvestment is made on unfavorable terms. But on the plan proposed the stockholder is enabled to look out for reinvestment before the press begins. . . ."[31]

Without as well as within the field of central banking, the Biddle papers show the Bank's president intimately and indefatigably engaged in all its affairs, an alert, intelligent, and conscientious executive. A strikingly large volume of correspondence had to do with administration of the branches and particularly with the discount and exchange policy of individual offices, which had to be related to the credit needs and economic character of the regions in which

[30] Biddle Papers, 2 PLB (1826), 188; Gouge, Part II, 177.
[31] Biddle Papers, 2 PLB (1828), 372.

the offices were respectively situated and harmonized with those of other offices and of the Bank and the country as a whole. Each office tended to be governed by its own interest, the more so because Philadelphia was far away and communication slow. But considerable was done to further central control by putting the branch cashiers under the Philadelphia headquarters. Said Mr Biddle: "My own theory of the administration of the Bank and my uniform practice is to consider the Cashier of an Office as the confidential officer of this Board, to rely on him, and to hold him responsible for the execution of their orders." The arrangement was made more effective by selecting cashiers for the branch offices from the Philadelphia staff. But the branch directors and presidents were pretty independent, and Biddle had to rely on reasoning with them. He evidently believed that if the correct policy were clearly and courteously explained, it would be faithfully followed, even when it entailed some sacrifice of local interests. His sanguine reliance on the general good as a governing motive was a matter of temperament, but had he chosen otherwise there was little he could have done, central control being so much impeded by distance and slowness of communication. Circumstances still supported Alexander Hamilton's misgivings of forty years before lest branches be fatally independent. This independence was only in part an evil that railways and telegraphs, when there were any, might cure; it was much more a matter of local pride and self-interest on the part of merchants and business men. The same psychological and political forces that kept opposition to the Bank alive made branch directors drag their feet in carrying out general directives which did not accord with local interest or predilection. They are reflected in the dealings of the Bank's enemies with its local offices—even by Andrew Jackson and Roger Taney when their assault on the Bank was bitterest. They are also reflected in the eventual conversion of the offices into independent local banks.[32]

Consequently, Biddle had always before him the problem of finding suitable directors and officers. Officers were seldom if ever dismissed for any cause but dishonesty, which however was impressively frequent, the Americans' level of business morality being in the early 19th century no matter of national pride. Directors served for only three years and had constantly to be replaced. To find business men who were honest, independent, reputable, and amenable

to unified policy for the direction of fifteen or twenty offices throughout the country was not easy. The greatest difficulty was to choose
directors who were not borrowers. "Enlargement of the direction,"
Biddle remarked, "is too often an increase of borrowers"; and again,
"large and habitual borrowers are not the best administrators of the
fund to be lent." The consideration prominently absent from his
correspondence about the choice of directors is party affiliation.[33]

Correspondence about business and credit conditions was considerable. Much of it was invited, rather more was volunteered. But
everyone who writes the Bank, Nicholas Biddle said, should have a
reply. He was asked for money, for his endorsement, and for advice.
"I have a few thousand dollars," wrote an old gentleman in Hagers-
town, Maryland, in 1826, "that I wish to place in your hands, and
as I am entirely ignorant of business, you must excuse me when I
say that I am told that money laid out in the United States Bank
stock and sold out again may double. . . . On the other hand, I am
told that the United States Bank is tottering to its foundation. Write
to me, my dear sir, and tell me the exact state of things, for altho' I
am independent I have not one cent to spare." In response to an
inquiry from the Commission of Public Buildings in Washington,
Mr Biddle sends detailed information about experience in heating
the banking rooms in Philadelphia and praises the ingenuity of one
of the Bank's officers who had so improved matters that one furnace
was doing what two furnaces and four fireplaces had been expected
to do, besides heating Mr Biddle's own office adequately if the door
from it to the banking room were left open. In answer to a perplexed
correspondent in Mississippi who has heard "foreign stockholders
and loans from foreigners" denounced, Mr Biddle explains at some
length in simple language that "it is the very best thing for a people
who are industrious but have not got much money" to obtain the
use of foreign capital, and he describes how interest and dividends
are paid to foreign investors by the export of American cotton. "I
have written this to you because, although I do not know you and
shall probably never see you, I consider you as a fellow citizen asking
information on an interesting subject, and I think that every true
American ought to set his face against these mean prejudices against
foreign capital and the paltry schemes which have been published
for defrauding foreigners who have trusted us." Messrs Brown
Brothers of Baltimore having just opened offices in New York, Mr

[33] Biddle Papers, 1 PLB (1825), 105, 209.

Biddle writes to Isaac Lawrence, president of the New York office of the Bank, to recommend the credit of the firm, known to him through its Baltimore and Philadelphia partners: "These gentlemen we know to be persons of great capital and prudence, of the most undoubted credit, and their operations are of a nature which renders them perfectly safe. I mention these circumstances as a matter of information only, without of course the most distant wish to interfere in the slightest degree with the distribution of the discounts of the office." When Mr Biddle notices a discrepancy in figures of public receipts and expenditures presented in the President's annual message, he politely mentions it to the Secretary of the Treasury. When he is away from his desk in Philadelphia, he is kept informed in detail day by day of what is going on; for, wrote William McIlvaine, the cashier, "I know your heart is with your treasure."[34]

VII

In an earlier chapter I mentioned the practice of the first American banks in lending by the discount of promissory notes instead of drafts and bills of exchange; and I ascribed this practice, which is a reversal of what banks seem to have done in Europe, to the American merchants' having already means of collecting their bills through their own shipmasters and the correspondents they had in commercial centers everywhere. The banks could perform no such service unless and until they got a network of correspondents superior to what the merchants had. So they were confined to simple lending. But by 1820, banks generally had correspondents, and hence could themselves effect collections; consequently the discount of bills and drafts then became attractive. In 1817 a committee of federal Bank directors, from whose report I quoted earlier in this chapter, recommended that the Bank undertake such business, to which its branch organization was naturally adapted. Its immediate recommendation was that domestic bills only be taken, the discounting of export bills to be deferred till after the domestic business had proved feasible. By 1830 the discount of bills and the sale of exchange seem to have become more important for banks in general—and the Bank of the United States—than simple lending. This is apparently because of the relatively high economic specialization by regions and of the relatively simple exchange of products between

[34] Biddle Papers 13, Folio 2667; 2 PLB (1826), 46, 103; 14, Folios 2785, 2931; 1 PLB (1837), 225-26.

regions. The South and West had no industry to speak of and what they did have served local consumers only. The northeastern seaboard had become much industrialized and its farming, like the West's industry, served local markets. There was a massive movement of meat, timber, and other such products down the Ohio and Mississippi to New Orleans, and of cotton also to New Orleans and other southern ports, whence these products were moved to the Indies, to Europe, and to the Northeast. In compensation there was a movement of manufactured goods from the Northeast and from Europe. So characteristic were given products of given regions that the inter-regional exchange was far more obvious than it has become in the 20th century. The Ohio valley and other internal regions then used the words "exports" and "imports" of the products exchanged with other parts of the United States, as the terms are used now only of international trade. For the same reasons the income and outgo of given regions were far more seasonal as well as inter-regional than they have since become. As at the fairs in Europe centuries before, every commodities market became an exchange market, for buyers of goods made their purchases with drafts, and the sellers wished to turn these drafts into cash, and the bankers enabled them to do it.[35]

In illustration of this to the Clayton committee in 1832, Mr Biddle quoted from a report by Congressman Churchill C. Cambreleng on western New York, where "all the banks . . . do a large and profitable business by discounting drafts on New York at sixty days and longer terms at the rate of seven per cent per annum, for the use of those who purchase produce for the New York market." One bank in Utica sent some $100,000 to $150,000 of such drafts monthly to its New York correspondent; on the other hand the same bank sold to the local merchants drafts on New York to pay for their purchases of goods there. So the bank financed the sale of western New York products in the New York City market and the purchase there of manufactured and imported goods by western New York. A bank in Rochester discounted drafts drawn against flour milled there and sold in New York to the amount of $100,000 monthly, and against the proceeds of these it sold drafts to local merchants for their purchases. These banks received a discount on the drafts purchased and a premium on those sold.[36]

[35] ASP, Finance III, 332-33; 22nd Congress, 1st Session, HR 460, pp. 316-17, 357.
[36] 22nd Congress, 1st Session, HR 460, p. 357.

"It has been deemed by the Bank," Mr Biddle wrote in 1832, "that next to the preservation of the currency the most important service it could render would be to facilitate the internal exchanges of the produce and labor of the citizens of every part of the Union. . . . The great object, therefore, to which the Bank has for many years directed its anxious attention, has been to identify itself thoroughly with the real business of the country and . . . to bring down these exchanges to the lowest cost. . . . By such an effort the Bank has thought that it assumed its true and federal character as the great channel for the intercommunication for the business of the Union; and that leaving to local institutions as much as they desired or could accomplish of the local business in every section of the Union, its more appropriate sphere was the general communication between them all." But taking into account the relatively larger development of private banking in the northern and middle states, the Bank of the United States sought to employ its funds primarily, Mr Biddle said, "in those sections of the Union where there is less banking capital and where the productions of the great staples of the country seem to require most assistance in bringing them into the commercial market." This governed loans as well as bill purchases. The observation applied especially to New Orleans, where the Bank had a larger volume of business in loans and in bills than at either Philadelphia or New York. For New Orleans was "the centre and the depository of all the trade of the Mississippi and its tributaries." Mr Biddle continued: "The course of the western business is to send the produce to New Orleans and to draw bills on the proceeds, which bills are purchased at the several branches and remitted to the branch at New Orleans. When the notes issued by the several branches find their way in the course of trade to the Atlantic branches, the western branches pay the Atlantic branches by drafts on their funds accumulated at the branch in New Orleans, which there pay the Atlantic branches by bills growing out of the purchases made in New Orleans on account of the northern merchants or manufacturers, thus completing the circle of the operations." At this time, it was pointed out, over $10,000,000 of bills, or half the amount held by the Bank, arose from the regional exports of the Mississippi valley; and the amounts payable, within an average period probably of sixty days, was $4,000,000 at New York and about $4,400,000 at Baltimore, Philadelphia, Providence, and Boston.[37]

37 22nd Congress, 1st Session, HR 460, pp. 316-18.

Against the proceeds of these bills, drafts were sold in many places without charge and elsewhere at low charges. "We may indeed repeat with confidence," Mr Biddle wrote, "what is said by a most competent judge, Mr Gallatin, that 'there is not, it is believed, a single country where the community is, in that respect, served with less risk or expense.' " Yet, it was reported in 1832, this "whole business of dealing in domestic bills of exchange, so essential to the internal commerce of the country, has been almost entirely brought about within the last eight years. In June 1819 the Bank did not own a single dollar of domestic bills; and in December 1824 it owned only to the amount of $2,378,980; whereas it now owns to the amount of $23,052,972." Its loans, however, were still twice that amount.[38]

After 1825 the Bank also dealt heavily and profitably in foreign exchange. The South's great production of staples for export, especially cotton, was the source of this exchange, which the Bank purchased chiefly at its offices in Charleston and New Orleans, in the form of bills drawn by the sellers on the buyers in England; and which it sold in the North, where manufactured imports were received, either in the form of the bills themselves or in the form of drafts against balances in London maintained by the proceeds of the bills collected abroad. Besides being profitable, the Bank's handling of the business steadied the foreign exchange market to the advantage of both southern exporters and northern importers. "When in the southern states," Mr Biddle said, "the crops are shipped to the northern states, their transmission is rendered easy on the part of the Bank by purchasing the bills drawn on the North to accompany them. If the same parties, instead of shipping their produce to the North, ship it to Europe, there is no reason why the Bank should not afford them the same facility by the purchase of their bills on Europe. While in the South, the presence of a large and constant purchaser thus gives greater steadiness and uniformity to the demand for bills on which the profit of the southern merchant and planter depends, the appearance in the North of the same purchaser as a large seller gives equal advantage to those who have remittances to make to Europe."[39]

The Bank's London balances to which the proceeds of purchased bills were credited and against which the bills it sold were drawn were kept first and mainly with the Barings. Mr Biddle seems to

[38] 22nd Congress, 1st Session, HR 460, pp. 312, 318.
[39] 22nd Congress, 1st Session, HR 460, p. 322.

have abused the arrangement, in their eyes, and the Barings repeatedly found it unsatisfactory. The balance fluctuated the wrong way. They complained that "by the large amount of funds left in our hands when everybody's hands are full of money, we are almost forced into speculations and investments in order to make some part of the interest which we are obliged to pay, and that too at a time when the abundance of money makes all prices high. . . ." But "then when money is really valuable, we have tremendous pulls upon our cash. . . ." When they sought to reduce the Bank's demands, Biddle annoyed them by opening a second London account instead of curtailing his business. Then, among other differences, the Barings considered that the Bank had use of their funds as soon as they received advice that it had drawn on them, whereas the Bank contended that the funds were not in its use till the drafts were payable. It was in such matters that Mr Biddle betrayed his lack of apprenticeship in business and his insufficient respect for its conventions, most of which, though they might appear illogical, had a basis in practical experience. He was too ready to invent new rules and get everything changed for something better.[40]

A basic condition of dealings in foreign exchange was that the balance of payments was customarily adverse, because the States, being an underdeveloped country in a process of intensive growth and exploitation, customarily imported more from Europe than they exported thence, with the result that the demand for European exchange regularly exceeded the supply. The deficiency was made up by the shipment of specie received from Mexico, by the Old World's loans to America, and by its investments in American securities. Immigration had the effect of moderating the deficiency, because immigrants always brought some money with them; but once arrived and having spent the little they brought, their numbers and their industry intensified the general growth which occasioned the economy's demand for capital from abroad. The European investments that supplied most of this capital were in bonds of the states and federal government and in stock of the Bank of the United States. In such transactions, involving the payment of interest and dividends to foreign investors, and sales, exchanges, and redemptions of securities, the federal Bank had an important part. But aside from dealings in the Bank's own stock and in federal bonds, private merchant

40 Hidy, 97, 114-15.

banking houses seem still to have had advantages, as they did in foreign exchange dealings proper.

How the operations of the Bank for the government and in the domestic and foreign field enmeshed is illustrated by a typical letter, 24 December 1831, from the cashier in Philadelphia to the cashier in New Orleans, in which it was recounted briefly that the Bank, as fiscal agent of the Treasury, would be called on to pay off $1,700,-000 of the public debt in the coming three months, and that Treasury balances would be low besides. Foreign holders could not be expected to take other securities in payment of the maturing securities they held but would want cash; which meant that the Bank must have balances in London to cover unusually heavy drafts. Accordingly New Orleans was asked to provide large amounts of bills against cotton shipments to Britain. "On every account, we should from present appearances desire to be re-inforced by all the means which you can throw into our hands." Philadelphia recommended, therefore, that local discounts in New Orleans "be prudently and gradually reduced" and that purchases of exchange should be extended "in a corresponding degree."[41]

These exchange transactions eventually shrank in importance as the country became more homogeneous and self-sufficient and the relative importance of its foreign trade diminished. But in the early 19th century the States were still economically colonial, and the importance to Americans of foreign immigrants, foreign investors, foreign suppliers, and foreign consumers was everywhere conspicuous.

Canada was prominent in these foreign relationships. Through her a part of the precious metals moving into New Orleans from Spanish America was converted into British exchange. For the expenses, military and administrative, of the provincial governments were met with specie that moved from New Orleans to New York and there was sold for provincial drafts on London, the demand in the United States for means of remittance to Europe making it profitable for Canada to sell bills on London in the New York market. Canada's supply of bills for sale was enlarged by her excess of exports over imports. By virtue of her abstinence from importation and consumption of goods and from internal development on the scale characteristic of the States, she had funds to sell which made her a factor of greater weight in the American

41 22nd Congress, 1st Session, HR 460, p. 516.

320

money market than her size and wealth relative to the States would lead one to expect. Canada and the American South constituted, indeed, parallel though disparate sources of the exchange needed by the American North to pay for the goods used in its industrial development. Both had British exchange to sell, Canada's arising from Britain's payment of her provincial expenses and the South's arising from Britain's purchases of her cotton. The North paid Canada in goods and specie, she paid the South in goods, and with the exchange acquired from these two sources on her left and right respectively she paid British suppliers for the goods needed in her own multifarious economic development. Compared with this development in the northern states, Canada and the American South had much less to show.

Since the transactions by which the British North American authorities obtained funds for governmental expenses focused themselves on the New York money market, the withdrawals of specie thence for use in the Provinces were frequently embarrassing to the Wall Street banks; and, to ease the pressure, efforts were made to employ the services of the Bank of the United States. The bills drawn by the provincial authorities on the British Treasury found their way to New York, in the words of Professor Adam Shortt, "partly through the medium of the banks or their agents, partly through the hands of merchants and their correspondents, and partly by direct messenger from the Commissariat. A considerable portion of the exchange was disposed of for specie, which was transferred to Canada," thence trickled back through countless channels of trade into the States, and in time had to be transferred in mass to the Provinces again. These large withdrawals recurringly tightened the New York money market, besides being expensive for the British North American authorities. Through the Barings, Mr Biddle in 1827 urged the advantage of direct transactions with the Bank of the United States. "His proposal was that the agents of the British Treasury in Canada should dispose of their exchanges directly to the Bank of the United States in New York, the Bank undertaking to supply the Government with specie as it might need it. This would insure the Government a better price for its bills and enable the Bank to supply its needs without any shock to the money market."[42]

"Such an arrangement would no doubt have resulted in considerable economy to the British Government." But it was rejected for

[42] Shortt, *JCBA*, viii (1900), 10.

a plan by which the Bank of England, with less chance of success, would be called on to perform much the same service. However, Professor Shortt believed that Mr Biddle's proposal would have caused a storm of protest in Canada. "It was a strong popular belief and a standing grievance against the banks that the scarcity of money and the high price of exchanges were due to the unpatriotic custom of selling Canadian bills on Britain to the Americans." Short-sighted people, in Canada as elsewhere, will cheerfully submit to disadvantages themselves rather than allow mutual advantages to strangers.

Without the excuse of patriotism, precisely the same objections to exchange operations by the Bank of the United States were felt in the States as in the Provinces. The more unsatisfactory the currency and the means of effecting payments at a distance, the more golden were the profits of dealers in currency, specie, and exchange. Many banks specialized in such transactions rather than in lending. The Bank of the United States was so placed that it could effect inter-regional payments for business men no less advantageously than for the government—except that transfers were made for the government without charge. But the advantages to the economy as a whole of the federal Bank's more efficient services were purchased at a sacrifice of the profits of banks and dealers already engaged in providing such services inefficiently. These banks and dealers naturally resented their loss and complained with asperity that the Bank of the United States was putting them out of business. So it was. If now in the 20th century the Americans should abolish the Inter-District Settlement Fund of the Federal Reserve Banks, which in the quiet, efficient, and unfailing performance of an immense task is unsurpassed, there might arise a fabulous volume of business for carriers hauling money over the country to effect payments between persons and corporations distant from each other. No one would say that their gain justified every one else's loss, but if the arrangement were already in existence, it would be hard to end.

The active concern of the federal Bank in the trade of the country made Nicholas Biddle disclaim interference. "The Bank," he said, "deems it an especial duty to abstain from all agency in regulating or influencing importations; . . . the encouragement to be given to the introduction of foreign merchandise is the province of Congress; and it would be equally a violation of their duty and a most dangerous exertion of power if the directors of the Bank, acting upon their own views of general policy, should assume to judge when the importations were sufficient, at what point they should be checked, and thus apply their power to stimulate, to discourage, or to prevent them. . . . It is the duty of the Bank to take the state of the country as the country has chosen to make it; to deal with the existing condition of things, but not to assume upon itself the charge of regulating the domestic industry and the foreign trade of the Union." This is an interesting statement. Mr Biddle was addressing Congressmen, some friendly, some unfriendly, some understanding, some ignorant. His disclaimer, though true in its spirit, disclaimed too much. The Bank, by lending or not lending, by charging less or charging more, could not help influencing the volume and movement of trade. But the influence was incidental and not governed by any general policy of restriction or stimulation. The Bank could not sensibly retard the ineluctable course of enterprise and internal development. In fact it scarcely tried to; its influence was generally, but for the most part moderately, on the side of expansion. It met demands, and so long as it did that, it could only be expansive. But to suit popular enterprise, it could not be expansive enough.[43]

VIII

In this earlier, unpolitical part of Nicholas Biddle's career, though he was without a day's prior experience in banking or any other business, he displayed a thorough command of his responsibilities in terms both of understanding and of leadership. His competence was acknowledged universally. There were people who failed to be charmed by him, and there were people who differed from him in judgment, but there was no doubt of his ability.

On the part of the Bank, correspondingly, one is impressed in this period by its performance of a rounded and complete central banking function. It acted, in the words of one of Nicholas Biddle's friends, as the balance wheel of the banking system. It regulated the supply of money; restrained the expansion of bank credit; governed the exchanges; safeguarded the investment market; protected the money market from the disturbing force of Treasury operations and of payments on balance, inter-regional and international; and facilitated Treasury operation *vis-à-vis* the rest of the economy. It

[43] 22nd Congress, 1st Session, HR 460, p. 319.

was in train to become the sole bank of issue and repository of the country's specie reserves. It even approximated, especially in the development of exchange transactions, the constructive rather than merely regulatory role of modern central banks; though in 19th century America there was precious little need of artificial stimulus to enterprise. Moreover the Bank performed these functions deliberately and avowedly—with a consciousness of quasi-governmental responsibility and of the need to subordinate profit and private interest to that responsibility. Its management, unlike the Bank of England's at the same time, did not seek to avoid acknowledgment of its principal purposes and *raison d'être* or pretend that its accomplishments in the public interest were incidental to the conduct of its private business. "From about 1800 to about 1860," in the opinion of Professor Jacob Viner, "the Bank of England almost continuously displayed an inexcusable degree of incompetence or unwillingness to fulfill the requirements which could reasonably be demanded of a central bank." Perhaps the Bank of England owed its survival somewhat to its shirking the responsibility and to its reticence, for the interests that wished to annihilate it differed little from their American counterparts; and certainly Mr Biddle's explicit acceptance and efficient discharge of the regulatory function of the Bank of the United States provoked the forces of speculation and enterprise to seek its destruction.* Be that as it may, the central banking function was apparently as clearly recognized and as successfully performed in the United States by the year 1825 as anywhere in the world—and more clearly and more successfully, I should say, than it was performed there a century later. The rise of the function in the expansive conditions governing the 19th century American economy is the more interesting because it was not stumbled upon as in England and because its principles and procedures were perspicuously and emphatically stated by the man most responsible for them and disposed to take the responsibility.[44]

In view of these two things—the central banking performance of the Bank of the United States and Nicholas Biddle's lucid run-

* In contrast to Nicholas Biddle's ready acceptance of central bank responsibilities, J. Horsley Palmer said in 1837 that for the Bank of England to have acted "in anticipation of events likely to occur would have been in direct violation of that principle upon which the Bank proposed to be guided and which Parliament had tacitly sanctioned." Palmer, *Causes and Consequences*, 36.

[44] Viner, 254.

ning commentary thereon—it is remarkable how Americans have abstained from considering any experience of their own in central banking prior to establishment of the Federal Reserve Banks and any comment of their early central banker about it. But the disasters which overtook Mr Biddle after President Jackson's assault upon the Bank diverted attention from what had gone before and from the bigotry and self-interest of that assault.* Furthermore the apostles of business enterprise who urged President Jackson to destroy the Bank had for the most part long and successful careers in which they affirmed and exemplified the advantages of *laisser faire*. Amos Kendall, one of the most intimate and influential of President Jackson's advisers, subsequently the founder and organizer of the commercial telegraph system in America, and a wealthy, self-made captain of industry, looked back with gratification on his part in destroying the Bank of the United States. "Experience has shown," he wrote years later, "how fallacious is the idea of regulating the currency by means of a National Bank"—or, as we should say, a central bank. "Indeed, the scheme of sustaining a paper currency of uniform value throughout a country so commercial and extensive as the United States is an absurdity. . . . Most absurd is the attempt to establish such a currency in a country full of local banks." After much painful experience, the achievements of the Jacksonians in the banking field were repudiated in the administrations of Abraham Lincoln, Woodrow Wilson, and Franklin Roosevelt, and the monetary order they destroyed was in principle restored. In reflecting on the stupidity, self-interest, and cost of the Jacksonian blunder, one may well remember how intelligently Nicholas Biddle played his responsible part in that order and how loyally, though not so intelligently, he tried to prevent its destruction.[45]

* Dr Fritz Redlich in his *The Molding of American Banking* has pioneered in the study of Nicholas Biddle as central banker. In other historical accounts of banking and central banking theory Biddle is scarcely mentioned, though ample attention is given his less important contemporaries.

[45] Kendall, *Autobiography*, 199-200.

CHAPTER 12

The Jacksonians

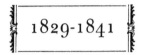

1829-1841

I. The background of the assault on the federal Bank — II.
The Bank's major Jacksonian enemies — III. Its other
Jacksonian enemies — IV. Andrew Jackson — V. Wall Street
versus Chestnut — VI. Speculation versus regulation — VII.
Jacksonian inconsistencies — VIII. The anti-Jacksonians

I

DURING the half century that ended with General Jackson's election, America underwent changes perhaps the most radical and sweeping it has ever undergone in so short a time. It passed the climacteric separating a modern industrial economy from an older one of handicraft; it passed from colonial weakness through bare independence to actual power and from an unjostled rural culture to the complexities of populousness, sectionalism, urban slums, mechanized industry, and monetary credit. Men who had spent their childhood in a thin line of sea-board colonies, close even in their little cities to the edge of the westward continental wilderness, spent their late years in a tamed and wealthy land spread already to the Missouri and about to extend beyond it. They lived to ride on railways and steamships, to use the products of steam-driven machinery, to dwell in metropolitan centers, and to feel within their grasp and the grasp of their sons more potential and accessible wealth than had ever before excited the enterprise of man.

An outstanding factor in the changes that came about was the flow of immigration from Europe. Between 1790 and 1840 the population grew from 4,000,000 to 17,000,000. In the latter year an average of 230 immigrants entered the country daily. Ten years later it was over 1,000 daily. The area of settlement and exploitation expanded swiftly under the pressure of this movement. While General Jackson was President the federal union came to include twice as many states as it had begun with and held territory that recently had belonged to Spain and France. It was shortly to add regions in the South and West taken from Mexico and regions in the Northwest that Great Britain claimed. Its expansion seemed irresistible.

The changes in social outlook were profound. Steam was generating conceptions of life, liberty, and the pursuit of happiness that were quite alien to Thomas Jefferson's; and the newcomers pushing into the country from Europe had more impatient economic motives than their 18th century predecessors. People were led as they had not been before by visions of money-making. Liberty became transformed into *laisser faire*. A violent, aggressive, economic individualism became established. The democracy became greedy, intolerant, imperialistic, and lawless. It opened economic advantages to those who had not previously had them; yet it allowed wealth to be concentrated in new hands only somewhat more numerous than before, less responsible, and less disciplined. There were unenterprising and unpropertied thousands who missed entirely the economic opportunities with which America was thick. There was poverty in the eastern cities and poverty on the frontier. Those who failed to hold their own in the struggle were set down as unfit.

Wealth was won and lost, lost and won. Patient accumulation was contemned. People believed it was not what they saved but what they made that counted. Jay Cooke, one of America's future millionaires, who was scarcely born poor on a farm but primitively at least, in a frontier settlement, was already on his way to fortune in a private banking firm before the age of twenty and writing home about his work with enthusiasm. This was in the winter of 1839-1840. "My bosses are making money fast," he said. "This business is always good, and those who follow it in time become rich. . . . Among our customers are men of every age and every position in society, from the hoary miser to the dashing buck who lives upon his thousands. Through all grades I see the same all-pervading, all-engrossing anxiety to grow rich." Something of the same sort, to be sure, was taking place in western Europe and especially in Great Britain. Half the people and most of the money for America's transformation came from there. But though industrial and technological revolution occurred also in the Old World, in the New, where vast resources awaited exploitation, it produced a dazzling, democratic expansion experienced nowhere else. The situation was such that the rallying cry, "*Laissez nous faire!*" expressed the views of Americans perfectly, when translated.

Socially, the Jacksonian revolution signified that a nation of democrats was tired of being governed, however well, by gentlemen from Virginia and Massachusetts. As Professor Sumner observed, what seems to have enchanted people with General Jackson when he became a candidate for President was not any principles or policies he advocated but his breaches of decorum, real or alleged.[1] Economically, the revolution signified that a nation of potential money-makers could not abide traditionary, conservative limitations on business enterprise, particularly by capitalists in Philadelphia. The Jacksonian revolution was a consequence of the Industrial Revolution and of a farm-born people's realization that now anyone in America could get rich and through his own efforts, if he had a fair chance. A conception of earned wealth arose which rendered the self-made man as superior morally to the hereditary well-to-do as the agrarian had been. It was like the conception which led Theodoric the Great to boast that he held Italy solely by right of conquest and without the shadow of legal, that is, hereditary right. The humbly born and rugged individualists who were gaining fortunes by their own toil and sweat, or wits, were still simple Americans, Jeffersonian, anti-monopolistic, anti-governmental, but fraught with the spirit of enterprise and fired with a sense of what soon would be called manifest destiny. They envied the social and economic advantages of the established urban capitalists, mercantile and financial; and they fought these aristocrats with far more zeal and ingenuity than the agrarians ever had. They resented the federal Bank's interference with expansion of the monetary supply. They found it bestriding the path of enterprise, and with Apollyon's brag but Christian's better luck they were resolved to spill its soul. They democratized business under a great show of agrarian idealism and made the age of Jackson a festival of *laisser faire* prelusive to the age of Grant and the robber barons.

In their attack on the Bank of the United States, the Jacksonians still employed the vocabulary of their agrarian backgrounds. The phraseology of idealism was adapted to money-making, the creed of an earlier generation becoming the cant of its successor. Their terms of abuse were "oppression," "tyranny," "monied power," "aristocracy," "wealth," "privilege," "monopoly"; their terms of praise were "the humble," "the poor," "the simple," "the honest and industrious." Though their cause was a sophisticated one of enterpriser against capitalist, of banker against regulation, and of Wall Street

---

[1] Oberholtzer I, 57-58; Sumner, *Jackson*, 179.

against Chestnut, the language was the same as if they were all back on the farm. Neither the President, nor his advisers, nor their followers saw any discrepancy between the concept of freedom in an age of agrarianism and the concept of freedom in one of enterprise. Only the poets and philosophers were really aware that a discrepancy existed and though troubled by it their vision was far from clear. Notwithstanding their language, therefore, the Jacksonians' destruction of the Bank of the United States was in no sense a blow at capitalism or property or the "money power." It was a blow at an older set of capitalists by a newer, more numerous set. It was incident to the democratization of business, the diffusion of enterprise among the mass of people, and the transfer of economic primacy from an old and conservative merchant class to a newer, more aggressive, and more numerous body of business men and speculators of all sorts.

The Jacksonians were unconventional and skillful in politics. In their assault on the Bank they united five important elements, which, incongruities notwithstanding, comprised an effective combination. These were Wall Street's jealousy of Chestnut Street, the business man's dislike of the federal Bank's restraint upon bank credit, the politician's resentment at the Bank's interference with states' rights, popular identification of the Bank with the aristocracy of business, and the direction of agrarian antipathy away from banks in general to the federal Bank in particular. Destruction of the Bank ended federal regulation of bank credit and shifted the money center of the country from Chestnut Street to Wall Street. It left the poor agrarian as poor as he had been before and it left the money power possessed of more money and more power than ever.

II

By the term "Jacksonian" I mean not merely the President's Democratic supporters, whom he still called Republican, but in particular his closest advisers and sharers in responsibility. These included most of his "Kitchen Cabinet," some of his official Cabinet, and a number of others. Those most responsible for the destruction of the Bank, without whose urgency and help it might not have been undertaken or achieved, were all either business men or closely concerned with the business world. Named in the approximate order of their appearance, they were Duff Green, Samuel Ingham, Isaac Hill, Martin Van Buren, Amos Kendall, Francis Preston Blair,

Churchill C. Cambreleng, Roger B. Taney, and David Henshaw—all but Taney being or becoming men of wealth. They did not include Major William B. Lewis, a Tennessee planter, one of the General's oldest friends and the only one of his intimates not openly hostile to the Bank. Others of importance were Thomas Hart Benton, James K. Polk, Levi Woodbury, Benjamin F. Butler, Jacob Barker, Reuben M. Whitney, William Gouge, and James A. Hamilton.

Duff Green was born in Kentucky but as a young man he went on to Missouri, where he became a land speculator and merchant, with a substantial business centering in St Louis. By the time he left there a decade later, he says: "I had established the first line of stages west of the Mississippi. I had a profitable contract for carrying the mail. I had placed the line under the charge of trustworthy partners, who paid me a large fixed income. I had a valuable business as an attorney. I was the editor and proprietor of a leading paper, giving me considerable profit, and I was investing my income in and adjoining the city of St Louis." He moved to Washington in 1825, where he owned the *United States Telegraph* and edited it in support of Andrew Jackson for President and in denunciation of the Bank of the United States. Newspaper publishing was apparently a simpler, less specialized, and perhaps more generally profitable form of business then than it has since become. He at first belonged to the Kitchen Cabinet, but before long he was thrust out because he was a friend of John C. Calhoun. Though Duff Green borrowed from the Bank, he approved its destruction. But his dislike of it was offset by his dislike of Amos Kendall and other Jacksonians and by his ties of family and friendship with Mr Calhoun. He continued a long, successful career in business enterprise, being banker, railway-builder, manufacturer, and promoter in divers fields.[2]

Andrew Jackson's first Secretary of the Treasury was Samuel Ingham of Pennsylvania, farm-born but apprenticed to a papermaker. He remained active in farming while engaged mainly in paper-manufacturing, coal-mining, railways, and eventually banking. Though primarily a business man he was always active in politics. As Secretary of the Treasury he opened the official assault on the federal Bank.

An assistant of his in the Treasury who instigated the attack was Isaac Hill of New Hampshire, also an appointee of General Jack-

2 Green, 27, 80-81; Washington *Telegraph*, 11 July 1832.

son's. He was frail and lame, an abusive editorial-writer, an acrid partisan, a publisher, a bank director, a bank president, and a substantial man of business. He too was a member of the Kitchen Cabinet. He failed to be confirmed in his Treasury appointment by the Senate, but promptly got elected a member thereof. As an editor, in Professor Sumner's words, "His main 'principle' was that things were in the hands of an 'aristocracy' and that he ought to organize the 'honest yeomanry' in order to oust that aristocracy from power. . . . He had the rancorous malignity of those men who have been in a contest with persons who have treated them from above downwards." When a candidate for Governor of New Hampshire in 1835 he had to be defended from the "grave reproach" of being wealthy. But if wealthy, it was urged, he had not always been so; "Isaac Hill was born of poor but respectable parentage." He was a self-made man and not one of "those sons of fortune who have been from their very cradle nursed in the lap of luxury, who have never known what it is to grapple with adversity, who have found every wish anticipated and every want supplied almost before it was experienced." Such "may thank their God that they are not as this mechanic," but they "will generally be found, in their race through life, . . . outstripped by those whose experience and whose training have prepared them by their very severity for a certain victory."[3]

Martin Van Buren, President Jackson's first Secretary of State, later Vice President with him, and his successor in the Presidency, was probably the most influential of the President's advisers and highest in his esteem. His father had been a farmer and tavern-keeper of very modest estate, and he himself was without formal education. He achieved polish, eminence, and wealth. In his early career he was an associate of Jacob Barker, a Wall Street banker of more enterprise than substance. He left the bar at the age of forty-six, when he became Governor of New York, "with a competence fairly earned, which his prudence and skill made grow into an ample fortune." Baring Brothers were informed by a New York correspondent, the banker Jonathan Goodhue, 16 March 1837, respecting the new President, that "Mr Van Buren is a very rich man," with an understanding of business "vastly better" than General Jackson's.[4] The Albany Regency, the New York political oligarchy of which he was the creative spirit, maintained banks and

---

[3] Sumner, *Jackson*, 186; Bradley, 1, 141-44.
[4] Shepard, 30; Baring Papers OC, 16 March 1837.

politics in the most intimate union. Mr Van Buren sponsored, as Governor, a law enacted in 1829 authorizing a system of state banks under a Safety Fund. He was always an efficient promoter of New York's economic interests. He did not openly oppose the Bank of the United States till late, or even then conspicuously, and Nicholas Biddle long refused to believe he was not the friend he had seemed to be. Mr Van Buren's tact was extraordinary; he had superlative skill in political manipulation and the advancement of his own interest without friction or apparent effort. Though self-made, like most of the men on whom General Jackson relied, Mr Van Buren differed from the others in performing his task with modesty and grace; he was without rancor, without assertiveness, and without the psychotic sense of insecurity and inferiority that seemed to torment many of his Jacksonian associates.

Francis Preston Blair replaced Duff Green as journalist spokesman of the Jacksonians. The new journal set up for him was the *Globe*. Amos Kendall said the *Globe* was originated by "those friends of General Jackson who regarded measures more than men and desired his re-election for another four years, not so much for his own sake, as to effect reforms in the government which no other man was capable of bringing about." Chief of these reforms, Mr Kendall said, was an end to the Bank. Blair, the *Globe*'s proprietor, had been president of the Commonwealth Bank of Kentucky and co-editor with Amos Kendall of the *Argus of Western America*. He was "heavily indebted" to the Bank of the United States—the amount exceeded $20,000—but the difficulty was got around by a settlement at about ten cents on the dollar, and he was fetched to Washington, where he began publication of the *Globe* in December 1830.[5] The paper was very profitable and with the government printing made Blair a rich man.*

Amos Kendall was a native of New England, the son of a typically

---

* Blair's indebtedness was to one of the Kentucky offices of the federal Bank. As already said, branches of the Bank, though legally offensive because of their subordination to Philadelphia, seem generally to have been well regarded as local or regional institutions in spirit. In 1836 Mr Blair occupied the handsome Washington residence since known as the Blair House, which remained in his family a century or more till acquired by the government to be maintained as an adjunct to the White House for the lodging of visitors of state.

[5] Catterall, 171; Biddle Papers 28, Folio 5730; 4 PLB, 220; Mackenzie, *Butler and Hoyt*, 87-88; Kendall, *Autobiography*, 372, 374.

poor but independent Massachusetts farmer of a typically puritan background. He was educated at Dartmouth. In 1814 he emigrated to Kentucky, where in time he became proprietor and editor in Frankfort of the *Argus of Western America.* Although scarcely a personal acquaintance before they came to Washington, Mr Kendall became invaluable to President Jackson directly thereafter. He was foremost in the Kitchen Cabinet. He held the office of Fourth Auditor of the Treasury but was far beyond his official superiors in influence. It was said that "whatever Kendall went for he fetched." He was known to the generality in Washington as an invincible, sallow, white-haired, unhealthy creature, but seldom seen. Harriet Martineau was fortunate enough to catch a glimpse of him once, and a Congressman who saw him at the same time told her that "he had watched through four sessions for a sight of Kendall and had never obtained it till now." The "invisible Amos Kendall," she reported, was "one of the most remarkable men in America, . . . supposed to be the moving spring of the whole administration; the thinker, planner, and doer; but it is all in the dark." His were the terse and commanding words repeated daily in the Jacksonian press: "The world is governed too much." Being made Postmaster General in 1835, he showed signal administrative ability in reforming the postal service. In 1845 he became associated with Samuel F. B. Morse in the commercial development of the telegraph. He had found Mr Morse "endeavoring, with little prospect of success, to get an appropriation from Congress to extend a line of his telegraph from Baltimore to New York; it being already in operation between Washington and Baltimore." He asked Mr Morse "whether he had no project to render his telegraph profitable as a private enterprise." Out of his enquiry an agreement arose which "vested Mr Kendall with full power to manage and dispose of Morse's interest in his patent-right, according to his discretion." And from this in turn came the erection of telegraph lines everywhere in the country, determined suits in defense of patents, the formation of numerous separate companies, and their eventual consolidation into a nation-wide system. One could not imagine a more explicit example of entrepreneurial behavior. Mr Kendall fought his way to such wealth and success that in time he had to defend himself from the charge, echoing one he had so often made against the Bank of the United States, that he and his business associates were "autocrats of the telegraph" and that "a more infamous monopoly than the American Telegraph Company" never existed. With Mr Van Buren, whose talents were of a different order, he was the ablest of the Jacksonians and an outstanding figure in American business enterprise.[6]

Mr Kendall's progress was a consistent one. As early as 1820 he was denying that labor was a source of value. He had always taken a harsh, puritanical view of things and scorned governmental relief in the days of western distress. He had favored "some degree of relief" but condemned Kentucky's interference with foreclosures. "Things will take their course in the moral as well as in the natural world," he had written. Legislatures could not relieve man of his responsibilities. "The people must pay their own debts at last." He had considered the Bank of the United States an artificial monopoly poisonous to individualism and its annihilation the paramount aim of "the Democracy." Speaking years later of "reforms in the government" in which he had participated, he said that "chief of these was its severance from the banking power organized and exercised under the charter of the Bank of the United States." It was his belief that Congress should "be content to let currency and private business alone." He never abandoned this view. He was an apostle and exemplar of *laisser faire*. Government, he said, "cannot make the people rich but may make them poor." Americans, in his opinion, were demanding "that their governments shall content themselves with protecting their persons and property, leaving them to direct their labor and capital as they please, within the moral law; getting rich or remaining poor as may result from their own management or fortune."[7] Mr Kendall turned to religion and philanthropy in his later years; he was a founder and benefactor of what is now Gallaudet College, for the deaf, Kendall Green, Washington, D.C. It was the only such college in the world, and he was its first president.*

* In 1813, while still at Dartmouth, Amos Kendall had submitted some poetry he had written to the *Port Folio* in Philadelphia, whose editors had offered a prize. He failed even of mention. He was naturally peevish about it; he thought the winning pieces were miserable. So do I, but they were not worse than his. If he later recognized in the president of the Bank of the United States the editor who had rejected his work, I can imagine it spurred the politician to avenge the poet; and in the end the smiling, insufferable aristocrat in Philadelphia who lorded it over borrowers and lenders got punished also for lording it over poor versifiers. Kendall, *Autobiography*, 82.

6 Martineau I, 257-59; Kendall, *Autobiography*, 372, 527; Kendall, *Circular*.
7 Kendall, *Autobiography*, 228, 229, 246, 374, 504-05, 510-13, 559.

Churchill C. Cambreleng, member of Congress from New York City, was a close associate of Martin Van Buren and an administration leader in the lower house, where he was known as New York's "commercial representative." He was a self-made man of modest North Carolina origins who had become a confidential agent and friend of John Jacob Astor. He had been friendly to the Bank of the United States before Jackson's election. About 1825 he had visited western New York at the request of the Bank, and for a fee, to study the relative advantages of Rochester, Utica, and Buffalo for a new branch office to be established in that region. He understood the operations of the Bank fully; Nicholas Biddle said it would be "difficult to describe more accurately the plan of circulation of the Bank" than he had done. Like Martin Van Buren, Mr Cambreleng was an efficient promoter of New York's interests, both political and economic. He was tireless and highly capable in his congressional leadership against the Bank.[8]

Roger B. Taney (pronounced Tawney) was President Jackson's second Attorney General and his fourth Treasury Secretary. He shared first place with Kendall and Cambreleng among the President's advisers in relentless, aggressive, resourceful enmity for the Bank of the United States. He was a Baltimore attorney and member of a family belonging to the landed aristocracy of southern Maryland, where he was reared. He was a shareholder in the Union Bank of Baltimore, its counsel, and an intimate friend of its president, Thomas Ellicott. This bank was one to which federal funds were transferred when he and President Jackson removed them from the federal Bank. Mr Taney had been interested previously in three other banks and a director of two. In an influential letter to President Jackson, 27 June 1832, he denied the constitutionality and expediency of the Bank on the ground that it bestowed privileges on some and refused them to others. He ignored the regulatory duties of the government and of the Bank, except as an "absolute dominance over the circulating medium of the country," and confined the Bank's usefulness to its safekeeping and transport of federal funds. As he disingenuously put it, "the simple question of selecting the most appropriate agent for conveying the public revenues from place to place has excited as much heat and passion as even the great question of the tariff." The question was not the simple one he said it was, and the regulation of banking and money

[8] 22nd Congress, 1st Session, HR 460, p. 357-58; Mackenzie, *Van Buren*, 101n; *Butler and Hoyt*, 104-06.

is no less important than the tariff. He dwelt on the unfairness to the state banks of chartering a federal Bank, exempt from state taxation, on "the burthens now borne by the state banks," and on the "heavy impositions" invidiously put on "the property of individuals in the state banks." For, he said, "the stockholders in the state banks, who are generally men in moderate circumstances, are subject to the weight of unlimited war taxation whenever the public exigency may require it—why should the stock in the Bank of the United States, which is generally held by the most opulent monied men, many of them wealthy foreigners, be entirely free from the additional taxation which war or any other calamity may bring upon the rest of the community? . . . The money of the citizens employed in the state banks is to be diminished in value by new burthens whenever the wants of the country require it, while the money of the opulent citizen and of the wealthy foreigner . . . is not to be allowed to feel the pressure. . . ." This was false. No such line could be drawn between the wealth of the federal Bank's stockholders and that of state bank stockholders, nor had the federal Bank any immunity from taxation, save by the states.[9]

Mr Taney was eventually appointed Chief Justice of the Supreme Court by President Jackson, where his decisions regularly favored free enterprise and competition—and typically so in the Charles River Bridge case, 1837. In this major decision he denied that rights had been vested in one toll-bridge corporation which must be allowed to obstruct the erection of other bridges needed by the community. The rights of the first, the Charles River Bridge, ran back by succession almost two centuries to a legislative grant to Harvard College for a ferry between Cambridge and Boston. The income from tolls on the bridge that replaced the ferry made it a very profitable investment. But one bridge in time proved not to be enough; and the new bridge that was built being eventually passable without toll, to the loss of income and investment by the Charles River Bridge's proprietors, the latter sued in the Supreme Court for redress. Their suit was rejected. The State, according to Taney's opinion, could not be supposed to have surrendered "its power of improvement and public accommodation in a great and important line of travel along which a vast number of its citizens must daily pass." For though the rights of property are to be "sacredly guarded, we must not forget that the community also have rights and that the happiness

[9] Swisher, 190-93; Jackson Papers 81, Folio 15985, 16008, 16011.

and well being of every citizen depends on their faithful preservation." Especially "in a country like ours," declared Chief Justice Taney, "free, active, and enterprising, continually advancing in numbers and wealth, new channels of communication are daily found necessary, both for travel and trade, and are essential to the comfort, convenience, and prosperity of the people."[10]

It does not derogate from the propriety of this opinion to point out that though it is compatible with agrarian doctrine its real affinity is with *laisser faire*. It favored free enterprise, and at the same time it contributed to a new concept of the corporation. Though it seemed at the moment a blow at corporate rights in the sense that it refused to preserve a monopoly of bridge traffic anciently conferred, its beneficiary was not an individual or several individuals but a new and rival corporation competing with the old. It therefore further familiarized people with corporate competition as well as corporate monopoly and definitely helped the corporation replace the individual as an agent of free enterprise in the economy. Mr Taney, I am sure, intended no such eventuality. Nor, I am sure, did Justice Story and Daniel Webster, by insisting on the preservation of the rights long vested in the original bridge company, intend that future material progress be shackled to 17th century grants appropriate to 17th century life. But Taney just as surely was on the side of *laisser faire* and rampant business individualism as Story and Webster were on the side of economic and technical conservatism. He was not attacking vested rights *per se*, or corporate rights, or property rights, or wealth, or capitalism, but propounding a new democratic concept that within his own lifetime was to be more typical of capitalism than was the clumsy, antediluvian monopoly that he refused to sanction.

And so of his interposition in banking—to say that it was agrarian and anti-capitalistic is absurd. By siding with the state banks against the federal Bank, he simply contributed to a new and democratic concept then current, which in New York in 1838 achieved what at the time seemed one of the notable glories of the age of Jackson—the authorization of "free banking." Yet even if *laisser faire* be deemed beneficent on the whole, it does not follow that it was properly applicable to the monetary function or warranted Taney's advocacy, in Horace Binney's words, of "an unregulated, uncontrolled, state bank paper currency." The monetary

---

[10] *Charles River Bridge* v. *Warren Bridge*, 11 Peters 419, 546.

function is within the province of governmental responsibility, and though Mr Taney and the other Jacksonians did not deny it, they did deny, to their own stultification, that banking was a monetary function. Instead they were interested in banking for the good, earthy reason that it was a fine way to make money. As Secretary of the Treasury in the Cabinet of a President who believed banks to be unconstitutional as well as morally evil, Mr Taney said publicly and officially that "there is perhaps no business which yields a profit so certain and liberal as the business of banking and exchange; and it is proper that it should be open as far as practicable to the most free competition and its advantages shared by all classes of society." Mr Taney made little money himself but both in administrative office and on the bench he propounded the philosophy of competitive enterprise with remarkable success. And such was his command of the arts of sycophancy and misrepresentation—always, however, in furtherance of democratic rights—that he readily got the old hero he served to face the opposite way from his real convictions and knife his own agrarian cause.[11]

David Henshaw, one of the most important business men who helped in the assault on the federal Bank, was a poor farmer boy who became a banker, a railway-builder, newspaper-publisher, business-promoter generally, Collector of the Port of Boston, and Jacksonian political boss of Massachusetts. "Though a wealthy man," Professor Arthur M. Schlesinger, Jr., observes, "Henshaw had many of the prejudices of his humble origin. His personal rancor toward the aristocracy which had snubbed him was not unlike that of his good friend, Isaac Hill." Professor Arthur B. Darling says of Henshaw and his associates that "in order to develop political influence over the poorer classes, they themselves made capital of their hostility toward the wealthy." Henshaw's *Remarks upon the Bank of the United States*, 1831, and his proposal in 1832 for a new bank with $50,000,000 of Jacksonian capital which should replace the aristocratic monster in Philadelphia that had a capital of only $35,000,000, were echoed in the message President Jackson sent to Congress when he vetoed the federal Bank's charter in 1832. His arguments were echoed again in the reasons given to Congress by Secretary Taney in 1833 for having ceased to deposit the public funds in the public Bank. "Even if it be expedient to grant a Bank

11 Congress, *Register of Debates* x, Part 2, 2322; Treasury Department, Secretary, *Reports on Finances, 1789-1849* III, 457.

upon the same plan," Henshaw said, "it ought not to be exclusively to the present stockholders. . . . The whole community should be offered the opportunity to have an interest in the institution on equal terms." This argument, though false in its implication, impressed the President. Henshaw in 1830 had deposited in his own bank the public funds he took in as Collector of the Port of Boston, thus pioneering in the action that Jackson and Taney took three years later in removing the federal funds from the federal depository and putting them in pet state banks.[12]

David Henshaw's views on vested rights received still more formidable confirmation. Having had land to sell in South Boston to which free access must be provided, he and his associates had built a bridge, given it to the state, and sold the land profitably. Later Henshaw championed the new Warren Bridge against the old Charles River Bridge in the controversy to which I have just referred in speaking of Roger B. Taney. He was scorned by the more intellectual and idealistic Jacksonians, but the irrefragable arguments he offered in the Boston press against the sanctity of charter grants and in favor of free bridges and free enterprise can be found again in the learned opinion which Chief Justice Taney rendered in the Charles River Bridge case.*

From among the foregoing Jacksonians, Major William B. Lewis is missing. He was one of Andrew Jackson's oldest and closest friends, a neighbor in Tennessee, Second Auditor of the Treasury, and a resident with the General at the White House. He was an expert politician, adept in the manipulation and creation of "public opinion," but seems to have had no economic interest other than that of southern planter. He was the only cultivator of the soil, the only real agrarian, the President kept close to him in Washington, and he was of the well-to-do sort, not the horny-handed. He was also the only one of the President's closest associates to befriend the Bank of the United States. He seems to have thought it more

* Since writing this, I find that Professor Darling has also compared Jackson's veto with Henshaw's compositions and noticed "that Jackson was familiar with Henshaw's arguments." More than familiar, I should say; and so was Taney. It was sensible of Jackson and Taney to heed Henshaw's advice, which for their purposes was invaluable, and Henshaw deserves credit that he has never got for his help in achieving Jacksonian aims. Darling, 136, note 13.

[12] Schlesinger, 147; Darling, 7; Henshaw, 36; New England Historical and Genealogical Society, *Memorial Biographies* I, 491.

sensible to make the Bank Jacksonian than to destroy it. His was the sole agrarian element in the administration's relations with the Bank, and it was not hostile.

III

Of these leading participants in the attack on the Bank of the United States, the most important were Van Buren, Cambreleng, Kendall, Henshaw, and Taney—the first being the least conspicuous, the last the most, and the others, resourceful and indefatigable, in between. But close after them came Senator Thomas Hart Benton, "a fantastic senator from Missouri," as Miss Martineau called him. He was one of the most loyal agents of the attack, though he joined in it after it had begun. He always rode loose in the saddle, Theodore Roosevelt said. He had been a stockholder in the Bank of St Louis, which closed in 1819 with heavy losses, and a director of the Bank of Missouri. The latter closed in 1821 because of pressure on it— according to Duff Green—by the Louisville office of the federal Bank to make it redeem its notes. In the Senate, one of Benton's first and most vaunted efforts was to have the federal system of fur trade factories abolished. In the words of Kenneth W. Porter, biographer of John Jacob Astor: "The factories were government trading houses, first established in 1796, supplied with the usual types of Indian goods and selling to the natives at cost, with the intention of protecting the Indians against the exorbitant charges and raw alcohol of the private trader and of attaching them by ties both of commerce and of friendship to the government of the United States." President George Washington had been largely responsible for establishment of the system. "Its only chance for success, however, lay in making the fur trade a government monopoly, and against this the capitalists interested in the extravagant profits of that trade were able to put up a completely successful resistance." The principal of these capitalists was John Jacob Astor, whose interests were incorporated as the American Fur Company. "The experience of the Indian factory system," Senator Benton wrote, "is an illustration of the unfitness of the federal government to carry on any system of trade. . . ." He knew its inside working was "entirely contrary to the benevolent designs of its projectors." By his diligence and determination he got a law enacted "to abolish the factories and throw open the fur trade to individual enterprise. . . ." Individual enterprise meant John Jacob Astor and his

American Fur Company. The Senator became counsel for the company, with whose officers he had been associated already; and one of these officers, congratulating him on the success of his attack on the federal fur factory system, told him he deserved "the unqualified thanks of the community for destroying the pious monster." Benton had entered the Senate about the same time that Cambreleng, John Jacob Astor's associate, entered the House.[13]

There is clear consistency, of course, between Senator Benton's successful effort to destroy the federal government's regulation of the Indian fur trade and his successful effort to destroy the federal government's regulation of the currency and bank credit. Both efforts were in the interest of private enterprise and consonant with *laisser faire*. And it is interesting to find the federal system of Indian trading posts called the same thing that the federal Bank was called—a "monster." Senator Benton also contended that silver and gold were the only proper money and the only money of the Constitution. He accordingly opposed all paper currency, including bank notes, and advocated an exclusively metallic circulation. His opposition to bank notes had no effect upon state banks but only upon the federal Bank, and his advocacy of a metallic circulation was incidentally to the interest of the gold-producers of the Carolinas and Georgia. He took a more direct interest in bringing about the surrender of federally owned lead mines in Missouri to private ownership. "He fought well for the spirit of Enterprise," writes his most recent biographer, Professor William N. Chambers, "and for particular enterprises."[14]

James K. Polk, later President of the United States, was one of General Jackson's closest and oldest friends. And of them all, he was certainly the most statesmanlike. He was a successful lawyer, of agrarian origin and predilection, but spent most of his short life in public office. He was a skillful parliamentarian and very able in his conduct of the administration's course in the House of Representatives—particularly in pressing for investigation of the Bank and in defense of Taney and the President for having moved the government deposits. His allegations about the Bank were specious and unfair but those of convinced Jeffersonian mixed with trained advocate. Like Andrew Jackson he stifled his agrarian dislike for all banks in order to concentrate his energies on the federal Bank.

13 Martineau I, 246; Porter II, 710-11, 713; Benton I, 20-21.
14 Hepburn, 58; Chambers, 88, 110-11.

But he, at least, came close enough to consistency to get the state banks themselves abjured when he became President. He and Major Lewis alone of General Jackson's close advisers seem to have been wholly without business interests.[15]

Roger Taney's successor as Secretary of the Treasury was Levi Woodbury of New Hampshire, a lawyer of modest beginnings, who with Isaac Hill and Samuel Ingham, initiated the first official Jacksonian attack on the Bank, apparently more with the idea of getting into it than doing away with it. Already a member of the Cabinet when removal of the federal deposits from the federal Bank was being arranged and effected, he was a stockholder in the Bank of the Metropolis, Washington, which for a time was intended to be made a sort of head of the pet banks.[16]

Benjamin F. Butler of New York had succeeded Roger Taney as Attorney General. Though not a leader in the attack on the Bank of the United States, he warmly seconded it. He had been a law partner of Martin Van Buren and before that manager of the Bank of Washington and Warren, Sandy Hill, New York. This bank, which suspended in 1825, belonged to Jacob Barker, who had used it in conjunction with his Exchange Bank in Wall Street to float circulating notes in remote spots in order to make their redemption difficult. This, of course, was the kind of thing the federal Bank impeded. When the bank in Sandy Hill was in trouble in 1819, Butler explained in the press that "the bank is able to pay and intends to pay its notes, but it supposes that the honest yeomanry, who compose the bone and gristle of the land are entitled to every accommodation in preference to greedy speculators and arrogant monied aristocracies." In his later years, according to the *Dictionary of American Biography*, Mr Butler was concerned with the law alone and particularly with "the management of a small group of corporation cases involving very large sums of money. . . . In politics he was a staunch Jacksonian Democrat."[17]

Jacob Barker, the owner of Butler's bank, was the same Jacob Barker I have already mentioned for his boast that he had killed the original Bank of the United States in 1811. In 1818 he alone was given three years of grace by a Democratic New York legislature in the restraining law of that year forbidding note issue by all

---

[15] Congress, *Register of Debates* x, Part 2, 2248, 2289; viii, Part 2, 1901; 22nd Congress, 2nd Session, HR 121, pp. 7ff; 23rd Congress, 1st Session, HR 263.
[16] 23rd Congress, 1st Session, SD 16, p. 262.
[17] Mackenzie, *Butler and Hoyt*, 19.

other unincorporated bankers in the state. In 1825 he and his associates were reported to have got control of several banks and insurance companies in New York, including the City Bank, and the Bank of the United States was alarmed lest he raid it also for control. He was convicted of fraud in 1826 and the verdict was twice sustained on appeals, but he avoided imprisonment. Mr Van Buren in his autobiography spoke loyally of him as "a great banker in New York, afterwards a lawyer in New Orleans, and everywhere and in every situation an extraordinary man and always my personal friend." He was not a personal adviser of President Jackson but a typical Jacksonian business man.[18]

Another picturesque character, more directly associated in the Jacksonian assault on the federal Bank, was Reuben M. Whitney, a former director. He had been in business in Canada for several years including the period of the war. He was a director of the Bank in 1822, 1823, and 1824. In 1824 he had very successfully managed the sale in New York of the Bank's forfeited stock and had then been on very good terms with Nicholas Biddle. In 1825 he had failed in business. In 1829 he had joined Condy Raguet, William Gouge, and others in a so-called workingmen's protest against the granting of more bank charters. In 1832 Whitney appeared before Judge Clayton's congressional committee and made grave charges of dishonesty against Nicholas Biddle. But he erred in making them circumstantial and easy to refute. John Quincy Adams, a member of the committee, said he had "scarcely dared to indulge the expectation that this desperate lunge against a citizen of unsullied honor could have met so immediate and so total a discomfiture." Though Whitney's charges were formally repudiated by the committee, he was retained by the Jackson administration as an aide in the attack upon the Bank and as an agent of the Treasury.[19]

William M. Gouge, of Philadelphia, was also an accomplished and effectual enemy of the Bank of the United States, though not among Andrew Jackson's personal advisers. He was well informed about banking in a journalistic way and wrote very readably. In 1829 he signed the protest of Condy Raguet's workingmen's committee in Philadelphia against incorporating any more banks. His lively *History of Paper Money and Banking*, 1833, was extremely

[18] Mackenzie, *Butler and Hoyt*, 28-31; Cleaveland, 237-38; Biddle Papers 12, Folio 2422; Van Buren, 75; Walters *JPE*, LIII (1945), 118.
[19] Raguet, *Free Trade Advocate* I, 298; 22nd Congress, 1st Session, HR 460, pp. 112-56, 306-08, 384-91, 426-27, 432-33.

popular. An edition of it was published in London by William Cobbett, whose hostility to the Bank of England resembled Jacksonian hostility to the Bank of the United States. Of the *History* Condy Raguet wrote that it "exposes . . . the mischiefs resulting from incorporating people to do what ought to be left to individuals to accomplish upon their personal responsibility." In 1835 Gouge was given a position in the Treasury in Washington. Although his earlier work was comprehensively inimical to all incorporated banks, he became—after destruction of the Bank of the United States—a friendly, vigorous exponent of orthodox commercial banking practice. He published a short-lived *Journal of Banking* and like the more influential Jacksonians, Kendall, Taney, and others, advocated in effect a private banking system without regulation.[20]

I have described the men who were the more active and influential in the assault on the Bank; but the interests of others close to Jackson also indicate the administration's tie with business enterprise. The most prominent of these was Colonel James A. Hamilton, the son of Alexander Hamilton, New York lawyer, member of Tammany, and speculator. He describes his business interests at this time as follows in his *Reminiscences*, published in 1869: "From 1825, when I purchased eighty lots of ground, . . . I devoted my attention to making money by dealing in real estate in New York and Brooklyn and building houses, with very marked success. I purchased a block of ground bounded by four streets, near the Navy Yard, Brooklyn, with a dwelling house, at public auction, which I divided into lots and sold at over one hundred per cent advance. I purchased lots in Jackson Street, built four two-story brick houses, and sold them at a considerable advance. In association with Mr C. H. Hall, I built a Bull's Head tavern, corner of Twenty-fourth Street and Third Avenue, and laid out proper yards between that and Twenty-third Street. I also built two brick dwellings north of Twenty-fourth Street and Third Avenue. I sold the Bull's Head property and the two houses for forty thousand dollars. I built a three-story brick house in Laight Street and one in Varick Street, where I lived for several years. I purchased a large square on Broadway, where the New York Hotel now stands, for fifty-two thousand dollars. After holding it for three or four years, I sold it in parcels at a very great advance."

[20] Raguet, *Free Trade Advocate* i, 298; Gouge, *Journal of Banking* i, 5; Gouge, *Hunt's Merchants' Magazine* viii (1843), 313ff.

Colonel Hamilton was Acting Secretary of State till Martin Van Buren could assume the office, and he sojourned at the White House from time to time thereafter, helping the President with correspondence and documents. For some reason President Jackson seemed to like him very much, and admired his father. Once he said to the son: "Colonel, your father was not in favor of the Bank of the United States." The Colonel was so much astonished he could make no reply.[21]

Three other important Jacksonians who do not fit into the foregoing groups are Louis McLane of Delaware, Edward Livingston of New York and New Orleans, and John Forsyth of Georgia. Mr McLane, one of the many former Federalists who supported Jackson, was an able, ambitious lawyer and a staunch advocate of the Bank in the same circumstances that Albert Gallatin had been one. He was Jackson's Secretary of the Treasury from 1831 to 1833 and Secretary of State from 1833 to 1834. Edward Livingston was a penologist, codifier of statutes, and "the first legal genius of modern times," according to Sir Henry Maine. He came from a distinguished and wealthy New York family. He and John Forsyth, a Georgia lawyer of Virginian background, both served as Secretaries of State, Mr Livingston from 1831 to 1833 and Mr Forsyth from 1834 to the end of Van Buren's administration in 1841. Livingston, like McLane, earnestly but ineffectively opposed the Jacksonian course against the Bank; Forsyth, in earlier years an intimate friend and correspondent of Nicholas Biddle, took no active part in that course beyond definitely supporting it. McLane, Livingston, and Forsyth were all three accomplished men of the world like Nicholas Biddle and as unlike the grim, uneasy Kendall and Taney as day from night.

With the business interests and objectives of the Jacksonians I have no quarrel save for the cant which made the conflict over the Bank of the United States appear to be one of idealism against lucre and of human rights against property rights. The Jacksonians were no less drawn by lucre than the so-called conservatives, but rather more. They had no greater concern for human rights than the people who had what they were trying to get. The millionaires created by the so-called Jacksonian revolution of "agrarians" against "capitalists"—of the democracy against the money-power —were richer than those they dispossessed, they were more nu-

[21] J. A. Hamilton, *Reminiscences*, 66, 69, 87, 150, 151, 154, 279-80; Jackson, *Correspondence* v, 189, 208.

merous, they were quite as ruthless; and *laisser faire*, after destroying the monopolies and vested rights the Jacksonians decried, produced far greater ones. There was nothing sacred about the federal Bank. The defense of it is simply that it was very useful and if not perfect it could have been improved, had its enemies felt any interest in improving it. The Jacksonians paid no heed to its merits but canted virtuously about the rich and the poor, hydras, and other irrelevancies. This was good politics. But it cannot conceal the envy and acquisitiveness that were their real motives. What the Jacksonians decided on, they directed their propaganda toward, and got. What they went for, they fetched, like Amos Kendall. An unusual number of them were not only business men but journalists, and gained both profit and influence through the press—notably Duff Green, Amos Kendall, Francis Preston Blair, Isaac Hill, and David Henshaw. They told the world it was governed too much. They vied with their great contemporary James Gordon Bennett in a glib and vigorous style. The Washington *Globe*, the organ of the administration, was attractively printed on good paper, every active Jacksonian had to take it, and, its contents aside, even the best people could feel satisfied to have it lying on the parlor table. It relied otherwise on unashamed, repetitious adulation of Andrew Jackson and defamation of his enemies. It presented matters in black and white, Bank and President, hydra and hero. "Many a time," Amos Kendall is made to say in John Pendleton Kennedy's satire, *Quodlibet*, "have I riveted by diligent hammering, a politic and necessary fabrication upon the credulity of the people—so fast that no art of my adversary could tear it away to make room for the truth. Therefore, I say to you and our democratic friends—hammer without ceasing."[22]

IV

Andrew Jackson himself had been lawyer, legislator, jurist, merchant, and land speculator, but principally planter and soldier. His origin was humble and agrarian. He was a self-made man. He belonged to an aristocracy of a frontier sort peculiar to the Southwest of his day—landed, proud, individualistic, slave-owning, and more bound by the cruder conventions than the politer ones. Cockfighting, betting, horse-racing, and the punctilio of the duel seem to have satisfied its cultural needs. It was without the education and discipline of the older aristocracies of the sea-board. It possessed

[22] Kennedy, 178.

more of the aristocrat's assertive and obnoxious vices than his gentler, liberal virtues and stood on property and pretension rather than birth and breeding. In a quarrel General Jackson would resort to the field of honor if his enemy were a "gentleman" but merely beat him with a stick on sight if he were not. Such distinctions seem to have been lost on Albert Gallatin, an aristocrat of a different water, in whose fastidious judgment President Jackson was "a pugnacious animal."[23]

Yet the distinction and courtesy of the General's manners took by surprise those who knew him first as President; he was by then unwell, grieving over the death of his wife, and softened besides by what age will sometimes do to men. He was not now the brawler in taverns and at racetracks. "I was agreeably disappointed and pleased," wrote William Lyon Mackenzie of Upper Canada in 1829—a man of considerable violence himself in word and deed— "to find in General Jackson great gentleness and benevolence of manner, accompanied by that good natured affability of address which will enable persons who wait upon him to feel at ease in his presence. . . ." When he chose, however, the General still could storm outrageously enough. He could simulate bursts of passion that terrified strangers, who shrank from having the President of the United States burst a blood vessel on their account, even though they were not fond of him. But his tongue seldom slipped. No one profited from blunders of his. What mistakes he made arose from a child-like trust in his friends and not from carelessness with his adversaries.[24]

He was exceptionally susceptible to the flattery and suggestion of his friends. This did not impair his maintaining a forceful, determined leadership. He listened to his advisers individually and chose his plan of action himself. His native views were agrarian and Jeffersonian, though of Jefferson himself he could entertain very low opinions, and no one—not Alexander Hamilton himself—ever went further from the constitutional principles of Jefferson than Jackson did in his nullification proclamation of December 1832. With him, moreover, as with other self-made men of his time, agrarian and Jeffersonian views faded into *laisser faire*. He was a rugged individualist in all directions. He was no friend to the shiftless and indigent who got into debt and then could not get out. He paid his

[23] Marquis James, 109; Henry Adams, *Gallatin*, 651.
[24] Mackenzie, *Sketches*, 46-47.

own debts, no matter how hard he found it to do so, and he expected others to pay theirs.

"Andrew Jackson was on the side of the capitalists," writes Mr Marquis James of his earlier career. "His first case in Nashville in 1788 had landed him as champion of the creditors against the debtors. Jackson desired wealth." He had been opposed to western relief measures taken on behalf of debtors in the ten years preceding his election to the Presidency. They were wicked, pernicious, profligate, and unconstitutional. Opinions like this put him logically on the side of the Bank of the United States, which was the pivotal creditor, and opposed him to the banks made of paper, such as the Bank of the Commonwealth of Kentucky, over which his kitchen adviser, Francis Preston Blair, had presided. But solecisms embarrassed the General very little. On the frontier more than elsewhere, the modification of an agrarian economy into an industrial and financial one was such, in William Lyon Mackenzie's words, as to "make speculation as extensive as life, and transform a Jeffersonian democracy into a nation of gamesters and our land into one great gaming house where all are forced to play, while but few can understand the game." General Jackson's prejudices were stronger than his convictions, and he was himself among the least consistent and stable of the Jacksonians. "Not only was Jackson not a consistent politician," says Professor Thomas P. Abernethy, "he was not even a real leader of democracy. He had no part whatever in the promotion of the liberal movement which was progressing in his own state. . . . He was a self-made man . . . he always believed in making the public serve the ends of the politician. Democracy was good talk with which to win the favor of the people and thereby accomplish ulterior objectives. Jackson never really championed the cause of the people; he only invited them to champion his. He was not consciously hypocritical in this. It was merely the usual way of doing business in these primitive and ingenuous times." Of his election to the Presidency Professor Richard Hofstadter writes that it was not "a mandate for economic reform; no financial changes, no crusades against the national Bank, were promised. . . . Up to the time of his inauguration Jackson had contributed neither a thought nor a deed to the democratic movement, and he was elected without a platform."[25]

What counts is that Jackson was popular. He was a picturesque

[25] Marquis James, 89; Mackenzie, *Butler and Hoyt*, 105n; Abernethy, 248-49; Hofstadter, 54.

folk character, and it does his memory an injustice to make him out a statesman. "All the remodelling and recoloring of Andrew Jackson," says Professor Abernethy, "has not created a character half so fascinating as he was in reality." To the dissatisfied, whether through distress or ambition, Andrew Jackson offered a distinct and attractive change from the old school of leaders the country had had—and not the least by his want of real ideas. He became the champion of the common man, even though the latter might be no longer either frontiersman or farmer but speculator, capitalist, or entrepreneur of a new, democratic sort, who in every village and township was beginning to profit by the Industrial Revolution, the growth of population, and the expanding supply of bank credit. This new common man was manufacturer, banker, builder, carrier, and promoter. He belonged to the "active and enterprising," in the luminous contrast put by Churchill C. Cambreleng, as against the "wealthier classes." And his conflict was not the traditionary one between the static rich and the static poor but a dynamic, revolutionary one between those who were already rich and those who sought to become rich.[26]

General Jackson was an excellent leader in the revolt of enterprise against the regulation of credit by the federal Bank. Though the inferior of his associates in knowledge, he was extraordinarily effective in combat. And as a popular leader he combined the simple agrarian principles of political economy absorbed at his mother's knee with the most up-to-date doctrine of *laisser faire*. Along with several of the best constitutional authorities of his day—but not Mr Taney—General Jackson believed that the notes issued by state banks were unconstitutional. In 1820 he wrote to his friend Major Lewis: "You know my opinion as to the banks, that is, that the constitution of our state as well as the Constitution of the United States prohibited the establishment of banks in any state. Sir, the tenth section of the first article of the federal Constitution is positive and explicit, and when you read the debates in the convention you will find it was introduced to prevent a state legislature from passing such bills." Seventeen years later, in 1837, he wrote to Senator Benton: "My position now is and has ever been since I have been able to form an opinion on this subject that Congress has no power to charter a Bank and that the states are prohibited from issuing bills of credit or granting a charter by which such bills can be issued

---

[26] Abernethy, 124; 22nd Congress, 1st Session, HR 460, p. 333.

by any corporation or order." Yet in effect he did as much as could be done to augment the issue of state bank notes and was proud of what he did. Most statesmen would feel some embarrassment in such a performance.[27]

The Jacksonians were anything but rash. Once decided that they should fight the Bank rather than wed with it, they developed their attack patiently, experimentally, shrewdly, probing the aristocratic victim and teasing public interest into action. The President himself took no unnecessary chances, but those he had to take he took without fear. He was a man of "sagacious temerity," in the words of one of his contemporaries. His attack on the Bank was like his careful slaying of Charles Dickinson in a duel thirty years before. His opponent had been formidable—much younger than he and an expert marksman, which he himself was not. Each was to have one shot. Jackson and his second had gone over the prospects carefully and decided it would be best to wait for Dickinson to fire first. For though Jackson would probably be hit, "he counted on the resource of his will to sustain him until he could aim deliberately and shoot to kill, if it were the last act of his life." So he awaited his adversary's fire and, as he had expected, he was hit. But his coat, buttoned loosely over his breast, as was his wont, had presented a deceptive silhouette, and the ball had missed his heart. He concealed his hurt and concentrated on his helpless enemy, whose life he now could take. "He stood glowering at him for an instant, and then his long pistol arm came slowly to a horizontal position." He aimed carefully and pulled the trigger. But the hammer stopped at half-cock. The seconds consulted while the principals stood, and Jackson was allowed to try again. Once more he took deliberate aim, his victim waiting in evident horror, and fired. Dickinson fell, mortally hurt. "I should have hit him," Jackson asserted later, "if he had shot me through the brain." The same mystical will power, the same canny and studious appraisal of probabilities and of relative advantages, weighed in the conflict with the Bank. The President tantalized the frank and impatient Mr Biddle, he waited for him to make the appropriate mistakes, and then with care and effectiveness he struck. His adversaries' weaknesses were no less at his command than his own skill.[28]

27 New York Public Library, *Bulletin* IV (1900), 190; Jackson, *Correspondence* IV, 446; Bassett II, 590.

28 Ingersoll, 264; Marquis James, 116-18; Bassett, 63-64.

V

Andrew Jackson, a westerner, was not elected by the West alone; New York, where the Republican party had been strong ever since Aaron Burr had contrived to get a bank established that could serve its interests, was an important factor in his election and even more important in his administration. In both houses of Congress the New York delegations included some of his ablest supporters; James A. Hamilton and Martin Van Buren were among his most influential advisers—the former less and less important to him as time went on, the latter more and more. Mr Van Buren's judgment, skill, and charm gave him remarkable influence over the President personally and over his administration as a whole.

Economically as well as politically New York had gained greatly in importance as compared with Massachusetts, Pennsylvania, and Virginia in the forty years of the Republic's existence. New York City had had at first no decisive natural advantages over Philadelphia, long the country's metropolis, except perhaps her more central position on the coastline of the northern states. But the greater commodiousness of her harbor became of decisive importance after the volume of commerce and the tonnage of ships had grown to sufficient magnitudes. By 1820 she surpassed Philadelphia in population. The Erie Canal, completed in 1825, was an audacious and costly exploitation of the state's topographic advantages. It brought New York City an immense and growing western trade and determined her commercial primacy over Philadelphia. Projects of equal importance were impracticable for Pennsylvania, and till railways were constructed Philadelphia's commerce depended on natural conditions. Moreover, Philadelphia, seated between New York and Baltimore, had two rivals for western trade, whereas New York had none but Philadelphia herself. For such reasons opportunity tended to be better for the man of enterprise in New York than in Philadelphia, and a democratic, dynamic, and competitive expansion of business became characteristic of that city and of the state too. The Albany Regency, perhaps the most efficient party machine in American history, was not parasitical on business, as most political organizations are, but constructive and energizing. Under the quiet, self-effacing, but electric leadership of Martin Van Buren, it devised a symbiosis between business and party in which both prospered.

In 1828 Martin Van Buren, then senator from New York, was elected Governor when Andrew Jackson was elected President. He kept the office only a few weeks and resigning went to Washington to take the office being held for him at the head of Jackson's Cabinet. During his brief Governorship he obtained enactment of a law establishing a Safety Fund system for the insurance of the liabilities of New York banks. This measure, though drawn in very careless form, was of great practical and political importance. It made the banks of the state a system not only strong and worthy of public trust but congenial to the Albany Regency. It gave the people of New York a source of credit which usefully supplemented the Erie Canal as a source of wealth. Both projects were typical of Mr Van Buren's public policy and both animated it. The Canal, which New York built by herself, rebuked the clamor of poorer and less enterprising states in the West and South for federal aid in such projects. The banking system, centering in Wall Street, cast doubt on the wisdom of maintaining a federal Bank in Philadelphia. Mr Van Buren's opposition to what he thought misuse of federal powers in both these directions achieved success in two famous vetoes by President Jackson. The first was the veto in 1830 of a measure authorizing the use of federal funds to build a turnpike between Maysville and Lexington, Kentucky. The second was the veto in 1832 of a measure renewing the charter of the federal Bank. Mr Van Buren's responsibility for the first was direct and clear; his responsibility for the second was indirect, the forces involved running far beyond his instigation.

Van Buren's policy with respect to federal aid and the federal Bank both reflected his consistent obedience to the constitutional principles of Thomas Jefferson and James Madison. In both, Van Buren opposed Hamiltonian "consolidation" of federal power. He defended states' rights less vocally than John C. Calhoun but not less effectively. Both men had the material interests of their states at heart but both harmonized their championship of those interests with a doctrine that had more than mere expediency to justify it. The federal funds spent on canals and roads elsewhere might diminish New York's particular advantages, which Mr Van Buren would not brook, but even if they failed to do that they magnified the influence of the federal government, which also, on general grounds, he would not brook.

The Maysville veto was intended to prevent the rise of an abuse; the federal Bank veto was intended to end one already established. The Bank of the United States was not merely another product of unconstitutionally aggrandized federal powers, but, in Van Buren's words, "the great pioneer of constitutional encroachments," the evil growth of federal expansion having begun with Alexander Hamilton's proposals in 1790 for a national Bank. It was the pioneer, but it was also the foremost current exemplar, of federal encroachments. And besides that it was a material block in the way of New York's interests. Through the state's efforts and those of her leading city, the latter had become a national market for money and commodities and the nerve center of national enterprise. No other community gained from the country's growth as she did or was more prominently identified with its prosperity.[29]

Yet in the federal Bank Philadelphia retained an impressive stronghold of her former primacy. It was the Bank in Philadelphia in whose Wall Street office the revenues of the port of New York were received on deposit. Those revenues, paid by New York business men, were larger than those of all other American ports together, but they passed into the control of directors who were mostly Philadelphians. New York's jealousy in this matter was no empty question of first place in an honorific sense but a lively question of whose pockets the profits were going into. It was the Bank in Chestnut Street whose constant regulatory action restrained the freedom of Wall Street's banks to lend what they considered to be their own money and also the freedom of their customers to borrow it. With General Jackson in the White House and the Safety Fund banks under way, a point was reached where something could be done to end the financial subordination of Wall Street to Philadelphia and to the Bank there, whose charter would expire in seven years. Nothing, it would seem, was more deserving Mr Van Buren's care, on grounds of his personal convictions and the material interests of his state, than that renewal of the federal Bank's charter be prevented.

In his *Autobiography* Mr Van Buren ascribed "the highest and most enduring honors" won by the Jackson administration to four leading lines of policy. One of these was the refusal of federal aid for internal improvements; another was the refusal to continue "the existing National Bank" or "any other equally unauthorized by the federal Constitution and to substitute . . . an agency which . . . would promise greater safety and greater success" in management of the government's fiscal affairs. When he wrote these words, in retrospect, he probably had in mind the independent Treasury

[29] Van Buren, 184.

system. But twenty years earlier with equally characteristic ambiguity, he might have used them of some one of the Jacksonian projects for a new bank as big as the Bank of the United States or bigger and *not* in Philadelphia.[30]

It is vain of course to look for an open avowal of Mr Van Buren's purpose. He seldom committed himself and then only in terms as equivocal and disarming as possible. He was a lamb who led lions. Moreover, among the particular and general reasons for ending the Bank of the United States, it was inexpedient to advertise any but the general. An attempt to whip up a country-wide passion for the relief of Wall Street from the tyranny of Chestnut was quite unnecessary and if made would fail. The assault on the Bank must take the conventional form of a popular revolt against privilege—a struggle of the "people" against the "money power"—and a democratic checking of federal encroachments on the constitutional rights of the states. This was managed without too much difficulty and few persons suspected that more was involved than what they heard shouted—especially since capitalists are supposed to stick together, whether in New York or Philadelphia, and to cut the throats of the poor only, not one another's.

Nicholas Biddle himself was taken in. It was an egregiously long time before he recognized the conflict of interest with New York, though he had been familiar with New York's "want of disposition to promote the interests of the Bank of the United States," as a correspondent of his put it. He got advice of New York's purpose, 10 December 1828, the month after General Jackson's election, when Richard Rush of Philadelphia, Secretary of the Treasury in the Cabinet of John Quincy Adams, wrote him: "You have probably as much, or more, to fear for the Bank from New York as from Virginia and with even less excuse. In Virginia there are still constitutional scruples. In New York none. But the frog of Wall Street puffs himself into the ox of Lombard Street and will not have you abuse him. *Hinc illae lachrymae.*" A year later, just after President Jackson's first public slurs on the Bank had taken Biddle by surprise, Alexander Hamilton, jr., of New York, Colonel James A. Hamilton's brother, warned Biddle to "have no confidence in Van Buren; as an aspirant for the Chief Magistracy, he is without principle and totally destitute of sincerity." Five months later Mr Biddle was advised, 21 May 1830, by a New York admirer of

[30] Van Buren, 275.

Martin Van Buren and a director of the State Bank at Albany, that establishment of Safety Fund banks, which had been actively proceeding, had given Mr Van Buren occasion to have "some agency" in the President's derogatory references to the Bank. The following month, 14 June 1830, Henry Clay wrote Biddle of a report he had just had from "one of the most intelligent citizens of Virginia" that a plan to undertake destruction of the federal Bank had been decided on at Richmond the previous autumn during a visit there by Martin Van Buren. "The message of the President, and other indications, are the supposed consequences of that plan." This Richmond arrangement evidently coupled the Bank and John C. Calhoun, the destruction of both being to the interest of New York and Martin Van Buren. The Richmond meeting was also attended by Felix Grundy, according to his letter to President Jackson, 22 October 1829, about a new concern to supersede the existing Bank of the United States. Henry Clay wrote again, 11 September 1830, that "a strong party headed by Mr Van Buren, some Virginia politicians, and the Richmond Enquirer, intend, if practicable, to make the Bank question the basis of the next Presidential election. I now entertain no doubt of that purpose."[31]

Two years later, in February and March 1832, Erastus Root, a Jacksonian Congressman from up-state New York, broke with his party and in Congress publicly and explicitly imputed the attack on the federal Bank to the schemes of Martin Van Buren and the New York banks. A few weeks later, May 1832, John Quincy Adams wrote in a minority committee report: "In every state in the Union there is a large capital . . . invested in stocks of multiplied state banks. Most of these are rivals in business with the Bank of the United States, and they have all boards of directors and most of them are colleagued with newspapers, all eager for the destruction of the Bank of the United States—an institution doubly obnoxious to the system of Safety Fund banks in the state of New York. . . . It is therefore not surprising that in the city and even in the state of New York, that animosity against the Bank of the United States of almost all the local banks should have been so great as even to spread its influence into the legislature of the state. . . . The same operation is active under feebler excitements in many other states."[32]

[31] Biddle, *Correspondence*, 60, 89, 101-02, 105, 111; Jackson, *Correspondence* IV, 83-84.

[32] 22nd Congress, 1st Session, HR 460, pp. 379-80.

"The state banks," Amos Kendall wrote the year following, "dared not" lend, because if they did their notes would come into the possession of the federal Bank "and the next day constitute a demand against them for specie. . . . It was on all hands conceded that the power of the Bank over the money market in New York arises almost exclusively from its being the collector and depository of the immense revenue received there." Michel Chevalier, the French visitor, writing from Philadelphia in January 1834, observed that the Vice President, "whom his opponents call the cunning Van Buren" and who aspired to become President, wanted the seat of the Bank transferred to New York and was "too enlightened seriously to wish the destruction of an institution fraught with so much good to the country." Again in April, writing from Washington, M Chevalier could not believe that Jackson and Van Buren were really as much opposed to a national Bank as they had the air of being. He thought a combination of circumstances possible, he said, which would reconcile its existence with the views and interests of Mr Van Buren—such as "the creation of a Bank of which the seat should be New York instead of Philadelphia."[33]

Major William B. Lewis, writing to James A. Hamilton in New York, 30 March 1834, said "the strongest ground to take" in support of the party was that since the President's removal of the government funds to state banks, all the federal revenue collected at the New York Custom House was deposited in New York City's banks "instead of being transferred to a neighboring rival city." He said that "our friends should ring the changes upon this view of the case in every quarter" of New York. Finally Nicholas Biddle himself recognized New York's hostility, long after every one else on the Bank's side. "It is a mere contest," he wrote in May 1833, "between Mr Van Buren's government bank and the present institution—between Chestnut Street and Wall Street—between a Faro Bank and a National Bank." Some years later Jabez Hammond, a contemporary and admirer of both Mr Van Buren and General Jackson, who himself thought the Bank's activities "nefarious," recorded in his history of New York's political parties the fact that the attack on the Bank of the United States had the support of the banks in the different states and of the Safety Fund banks in New York especially. He said:

[33] 23rd Congress, 1st Session, HR 17, p. 15; Chevalier, *Society, Manners, and Politics,* 66, 91-92.

"More than two-thirds of the revenue of the United States, amounting to many millions annually, was paid into the United States Branch Bank and when there was under the absolute control of the mother Bank at Philadelphia. The state banks believed that if the United States Bank should be annihilated, these immense deposits would be made in their own vaults, and hence all the benefits arising from deposits and also the whole profits of the very great circulation of United States Bank notes would be transferred from the United States to the state banks—without compelling them to increase their own capital to the amount of a single dollar. . . .

"Although probably a majority of the stock of the banks of the state of New York was held by citizens politically opposed to General Jackson, nearly all of those citizens either directly or indirectly supported him in his opposition to the re-charter of the Bank. . . . All intelligent New Yorkers agreed that this charter enabled a corporation located in Philadelphia, a majority of whose acting directors resided in that city, to exercise a dangerous power over the monied and mercantile operations of the great city of New York."[34]

Finally there is evidence in a statement by Martin Van Buren to which Dr Fritz Redlich has called attention. In his *Autobiography*, written years after these events, Mr Van Buren says that at first President Jackson "went no further than to announce objections to the Bank under its existing charter, but Mr Biddle was too sagacious and too well acquainted with the ways of the world not to find in them evidence of a strong and in all likelihood an unyielding opposition to any national bank of the description desired by him and his associates. Having made this discovery and being himself a man of resolute and persistent spirit," Mr Van Buren continues, "he dismissed on the instant all hopes of assistance from the President" and prepared to fight. These words, as Dr Redlich has said, unmistakably imply the early determination of the Jackson administration to destroy the Bank; and they affirm Mr Biddle's sagacity in recognizing that determination. They do not say that Nicholas Biddle surmised or supposed or imagined what the Jacksonian policy was or that he was mistaken; instead they blandly confirm his "discovery." In taking it for granted that the Jacksonian policy was discerned by a man so intelligent as Mr Biddle, Mr Van Buren acknowledges that the policy was already formed, long before Mr

[34] J. A. Hamilton, *Reminiscences*, 282; Biddle, *Correspondence*, 209-10, 242, 306; Jabez Hammond II, 350-51; de Tocqueville I, 409.

Biddle was provoked to do what was alleged afterwards to warrant the Bank's destruction. Mr Van Buren's acknowledgment of a determination is on sure ground, because it involves something in which he had part, but his imputation of "discovery" to Mr Biddle, though flattering to the latter, is completely mistaken. Mr Biddle, as the events show, was childishly hopeful of an accord with the administration, remained persuaded that the only difficulty was the President's uninformed prejudice against banks, which he was sure could be removed, and became reprehensibly willing to let the President do anything he chose to the charter if only he would consent to its renewal. But what the Jacksonians wanted was not the existing Bank under any conceivable modification; they wanted something wholly their own, not in Philadelphia, with new ownership and management.[35]

To renew the Bank's charter, Roger B. Taney advised the President, was tantamount to giving "Nicholas Biddle, the president of the Bank, his executors, administrators, and assigns . . . all the powers, privileges, and immunities now intended to be conferred on the individuals who happen to be the stockholders in the existing Bank. . . . What is called renewing this charter is in fact and in law nothing more nor less than granting a new charter to certain favored and designated persons instead of leaving the privileges it confers equally open to the competition of all and giving to every citizen an equal opportunity of sharing in the advantages which the government is about to sell."[36]

The Jacksonians were probably much better agreed about destruction of the existing Bank than about the sequel to it. Some, as will appear, wanted a new Bank as large or larger in New York. Some wanted it in Boston. Andrew Jackson himself apparently would have had it in Washington. Others were interested chiefly in the advantages to be spread among existing banks and new local banks everywhere. In the end the latter view prevailed. No one big new bank was needed in New York to realize the advantages to be gained over Philadelphia, and the preference for local institutions was general.

VI

Despite the fact of a strong and determined rebellion within the business world against the Bank of the United States, the fiction that the attack on the Bank was on behalf of agrarians against

[35] Van Buren, 619-20; Redlich, 150.   [36] Jackson Papers 81, Folios 16000-02.

capitalists, of humanity against property, of the poor against the rich, and of "the people" against "the money power," has persisted. There was, to be sure, an extremely respectable minority comprising the more conservative and thoughtful men of business, Mr Gallatin, for example, and Nathan Appleton, who defended the Bank till near the end, but it will scarcely do to say that they represented the business world while C. C. Cambreleng, David Henshaw, and Reuben Whitney did not.

It is obvious that New York, besides gaining most from a successful attack on the Bank, risked the least; for it did not need, as the South and West did, the capital brought in by the Bank's branches. The West's aversion for the federal Bank was like the nationalistic resentment in a 20th century under-developed economy which wants and needs imported capital but growls at the "imperialism" of the country that is expected to provide it. The western enemies of the Bank were moved by complex psychological and political considerations—including past distress and present dependence—while its New York enemies were moved, much more simply, by covetousness and rivalry. This was the decisive new ingredient provided in the Jacksonian attack. The agrarian prejudice had been alive since 1791 and most dangerous to the Bank a few years past during its critical days and the distress in the Ohio valley. The state bank opposition was almost as old as the agrarian. And the relative importance of the two varied with the decline of agrarianism and the growth of enterprise. New York, now the center of enterprise, added to the long-lived antagonism a hearty and acute self-interest. That Andrew Jackson proved to be the instrument of her interest was the happy result of Mr Van Buren's skill and devotion.

It goes without saying that Andrew Jackson himself did not understand what was happening. He had started with a vague, agrarian prejudice against banking which on occasion cropped up throughout his life but never led him to deny himself the service of banks or the friendship and support of bankers.* It was no great task for his advisers to arouse this dormant distrust, nourished on what he had read about the South Sea Bubble, and focus it upon the Bank in Philadelphia, a city whence he had suffered years be-

* He did not cease transacting personal and family business with the Nashville office of the Bank of the United States, which he presumably dissociated from the main office in Philadelphia. The view was reasonable. Gravitation of the branches toward independence was a perennial source of weakness to the Bank; and eventually they became local banks in fact.

fore, at the hands of a bankrupt merchant and speculator, a harsh financial misfortune. Nor was an elaborate plot required to be agreed upon among conspirators. The first harassment of the Bank from the administration group was evidently spontaneous and simply aimed at making the Bank Jacksonian. Some time elapsed before it got under directed control. Even then there is no reason to suppose that the program was not mainly opportunistic. In the early stages the object need have been only to make sure that the charter be not renewed. To this end the General's mind must be fixed against the Bank, and the proper improvement of opportunities could be left to the discretion of those in whose path the opportunities appeared. The adviser who influenced the General most directly or who perhaps left the best record of what he did was Roger B. Taney, though he joined the Jacksonian circle late. He succeeded in filling the General's mind with a vindictiveness that Martin Van Buren or Amos Kendall would probably not have produced. They too would have killed the Bank but with less emotion and less cant. "When a great monied institution," Mr Taney told the General, "attempts to overawe the President in the discharge of his high constitutional duties, it is conclusive evidence that it is conscious of possessing vast political power which it supposes the President can be made to feel." The Taney reasoning is sound, but the premises are misrepresented, and the effect was to fill the President with bitter suspicion of the Bank; though the alleged "attempts to overawe the President"— this was written in June 1832—were the reasonable attempts of Mr Biddle to gain support for the Bank, find out what the scowls and rumblings from Washington signified, and remove the doubts that he thought were troubling the President.[37]

But thanks to the sort of thing Mr Taney kept telling him, the President by now had few doubts such as Mr Biddle imagined. He was merely considering how best to proceed against the Bank. Replacement, he realized, was necessary, and for a long time he was fumbling over unintelligible projects to that end. One of these projects, which may be intelligible to those whose understanding has not been corrupted by some knowledge and experience of the subject, was described to James A. Hamilton, 3 June 1830. The President had in mind "a national bank chartered upon the principles of the checks and balances of our federal government, with a branch in each state, the capital apportioned agreeably to representation and

[37] Jackson Papers 81, Folio 16006.

to be attached to and be made subject to supervision of the Secretary of the Treasury." He recalls having shown Mr Hamilton "my ideas on a bank project, both of deposit (which I think the only national bank that the government ought to be connected with) and one of discount and deposit, which from the success of the State Bank of South Carolina I have no doubt could be wielded profitably to our government with less demoralizing effects upon our citizens than the Bank that now exists. But a *national* Bank, entirely *national* Bank of deposit is all we ought to have: but I repeat a national Bank of discount and deposit may be established upon our revenue and national faith pledged and carried on by salaried officers, as our revenue is now collected, with less injury to the morals of our citizens and to the destruction of our liberty than the present hydra of corruption and all the emoluments accrue to the nation as part of the revenue." But these ruminations belonged merely to a period of waiting. As soon as a promising arrangement offered, the President acted. He ordered the federal funds removed from the Bank and put in the banks of his friends.[38]

Besides contributing mainly, by this course, to a shift of the money market from Chestnut Street to Wall Street, the General contributed to the inflation, the speculation, and the various monetary evils which, with a persistent agrarian bias, he blamed on banks and paper money. There were plenty of men in his own party, among them better agrarians than himself, who would have cleared his vision and tried to, but the old gentleman preferred the sycophantic advisers who stimulated his suspicions and prejudices, blinded him to facts, confused him about the nature of the federal Bank's usefulness, diverted his attention from the possibility that it be amended and corrected instead of being destroyed, and allowed him to declaim the most ignorant but popular clap-trap.[39]

VII

Although the Bank was by no means the only thing that occupied the Jacksonians, its destruction was apparently esteemed by many of them their finest accomplishment. It rumpled and demoralized the aristocrats they envied. It redistributed vested rights. It established *laisser faire*. It freed banks from federal credit regulation. It reduced the government's monetary powers by more than half. It

---

[38] J. A. Hamilton, *Reminiscences*, 167-68.
[39] [J. R. McCulloch], *Edinburgh Review* lxv (1837), 227-28.

stimulated business. It furthered the interests of New York City, Boston, and Baltimore at the expense of Philadelphia. In all this there was abundant satisfaction for Van Buren, Kendall, Henshaw, Cambreleng, Taney, and others who were like-minded.

There were many dissidents among the Jacksonians, however, who deplored the materialism of the Democracy. To the intellectuals prominent in the party, and especially to George Bancroft, David Henshaw was an abomination. The *Pennsylvanian* of Philadelphia, itself Jacksonian, felt the presence in the party of too many "Wall Street gamblers." Erastus Root, the up-state New York agrarian in Congress, defended the federal Bank from Martin Van Buren's Albany Regency and the New York banks and got purged for it. When the New York *Evening Post* protested in 1835 at Amos Kendall's order forbidding the use of the mails for abolitionist literature, it was excommunicated by the administration's mouthpiece in Washington: "The *Evening Post* has on various occasions shown a disposition to fly off from the Democratick Party by running into extremes. . . . The spirit of agrarianism was perceivable in all the political views of the editor, and it seemed as if he was inclined to legislate altogether upon abstraction and allow the business of the world and the state of society to have nothing to do with it." A writer in the *Democratic Review* in December 1838 distinguished Democrats by trade from Democrats in principle, ironically disparaging the latter in favor of the more sensible Democrat by trade, who "got a snug slice of the public deposits" for his bank.[40]

From a very different viewpoint, the Canadian patriot, William Lyon Mackenzie, whose great-grandson a century later was Canada's premier, had much to say of the Jacksonians. He had contrasted the economic and political backwardness of the Provinces under British rule with the progress and prosperity of the States and had tried to make both the British government and his fellow subjects learn something from American experience. But in his own province of Upper Canada, and in the others, authority had remained unyielding, with Family Compact, Church, and Seigneury. So, like George Washington and his compatriots sixty years before, Mr Mackenzie had been driven to conclude that armed rebellion was necessary. With the sentiments of the American Declaration of Independence in mind, he had "engaged at last," he said, "in a

[40] Niles xlv (1833), 39; Congress, *Register of Debates* viii, Part 2, 2036ff, 2069ff; New York *Evening Post*, 24 September 1835; *Democratic Review* iii (1838), 368.

desperate though for the time an unsuccessful attempt to transplant the same institutions" into Canada. He had failed and fled to the States, where, expecting to remain, for there was a price on his head in the Provinces and some of his associates had been hanged, he supported the Jacksonians. He was a journalist. In singular circumstances he came in possession of the private correspondence of prominent New York Jacksonians—Van Buren, Cambreleng, and others.[41] Reading it, he asked himself, "Is this, can it be, free, enlightened, democratic America? The America of my early dreams it surely is not." No idea, he thought, "can be more erroneous than that men of humble origin are more friendly to the class among whom they were reared than the dwellers in palaces and among the opulent of the land."*

Popular propaganda has acquired more general and familiar use since the age of Jackson, but none more skillful. With the exception of a few persons who, with John Pendleton Kennedy, could appreciate the art of Amos Kendall and his associates, Americans were hypnotized by the Jacksonian propaganda, and Andrew Jackson himself—its main object—got guidance and inspiration from it. That many historians still follow the Jacksonian formula points to its effectiveness. In the words of one, for example, "The poor men of the East and of the West were asserting the power of their mass strength and, putting Andrew Jackson in the presidency, were smashing that symbol of financial autocracy, the great Bank of the United States." I take this quotation not as the isolated judgment of one historian but as typical of the view that seems in recent years to have gained in conventional favor, despite the record of the conspicuous business interests of the leading Jacksonians, of the accomplishments of the federal Bank, and of the disposition of the

---

* He published the correspondence he had found, and it was never repudiated. To Mr Van Buren, however, he was "that somewhat notorious person" who found an old trunk, rifled it of its contents, and published them —a "pitiful enterprise." Upon the grant of amnesty in 1849, Mr Mackenzie, his mind completely changed about America, returned to Canada, where the efforts in which he had risked hanging had already borne fruit in Lord Durham's brilliant report and in the achievement of responsible government for the Provinces through the further efforts of Robert Baldwin and Louis H. La Fontaine. Van Buren, *Autobiography*, 536-69; Lindsey, 458, 470ff.

[41] Mackenzie, *Van Buren*, 16, 90n; *Butler and Hoyt*, 140n.

state banking interests toward it, especially in New York and Boston.[42]

The words of another historian are equally typical. "By doing away with paper money," he says, Jacksonian policy "proposed to restrict the steady transfer of wealth from the farmer and laborer to the business community. By limiting banks to commercial credit and denying them control over the currency, it proposed to lessen their influence and power. By reducing the proportion of paper money, it proposed to moderate the business cycle, and order the economy to the advantage of the worker rather than the speculator."[43]

These statements seem to me fallacious, individually and collectively. For one thing I do not believe that Van Buren, Kendall, Cambreleng, Henshaw, and Taney ever purposed restricting the transfer of wealth from the farmer and laborer to the business community, or lessening the influence and power of banks, or moderating the business cycle, or ordering the economy to the advantage of the worker. The passage reflects the Jacksonians' views neither of men nor of money. The two latter aims they never thought of, in modern terms, and the two former were nearer the opposite of what they sought. And if Van Buren, Kendall, Cambreleng, Henshaw, and Taney ever supposed that any of these aims could be achieved by getting rid of paper money and limiting banks to commercial credit, then I shall have to acknowledge that they were less bright than I supposed. They probably understood the equivalence of note and deposit liabilities as well as Albert Gallatin did, and they certainly knew that a greater volume of business payments could be made by check more conveniently than by bank notes, if not already so made. Their attack on banking powers, except as exercised by the federal Bank, was pretense. But it was pretense conveniently obscured by the current confusion as to what comprised banking powers. So long as most people identified banking with note issue, an attack on note issue seemed deadly to bankers and the money power. Instead, it would be bad for bankers in the backwoods, for whom note issue was still important, but the bankers in Wall Street it would never touch.

But, of course, the notion that even the note issue function of banks was seriously threatened was not entertained by any sophisticated Jacksonian. Senator Thomas Hart Benton, it is true, seems to have entertained it, for when in 1837 he saw banks and bank issues

[42] Gabriel, *American Democratic Thought*, 44. [43] Schlesinger, 125.

increasing, he showed signs of real surprise. "I did not join in putting down the Bank of the United States," he said, "to put up a wilderness of local banks. I did not join in putting down the paper currency of a national bank to put up a national paper currency of a thousand local banks." It is doubtful if many Jacksonian leaders shared his *naïveté*. They may rather have been amused at Old Bullion's primitive ideas.[44]

That the party should have been so largely a party of business enterprise and that its leaders should have been men so devoted to the principle of *laisser faire* is not in itself to be reprehended, of course. Even the critics of that principle can excuse the Jacksonians for being impressed by it. In a sense *laisser faire* was idealistic in that it assumed human nature to be good and governments, save at their simplest, evil. But the preoccupations of *laisser faire* were in fact materialistic. It was the device of men who wished to make money. They clothed their new aspirations in the familiar, idealistic language of the religious and agrarian traditions in which they had been reared. There was no other period in American history, one would hope, when language was more idealistic, endeavor more materialistic, and the tone of public life more hypocritical than during the Jacksonian revolution.

On the Bank itself, of course, the party was divided, though the close associates of the President who befriended it, William B. Lewis, Louis McLane, and Edward Livingston, were exceptional. On the tariff, which rivaled the Bank in importance, the division was far more confusing; though the party was professedly for low tariffs, it was responsible for schedules that provoked the doctrine of nullification. Logically, free trade should have been deduced as directly from Amos Kendall's dictum, "the world is governed too much," as was the quashing of currency and credit regulation, and a substantial number of Jacksonians contended consistently for both, as Cambreleng did. But others, including Jackson himself, and the country as a whole, chose governmental interposition in the form of protective tariffs and rejected it in the form of credit restriction. These were choices that followed the higher logic of what was most profitable: government should boost business but should not bother it —becoming at its best Hamiltonian in one direction and Jeffersonian in the other. Party-wise, and reduced to the simplest terms, the Jacksonian aims—that is, Mr Van Buren's—were to end Philadel-

[44] Congress, *Register of Debates* XIII (1837), Part 1, 610.

phia's rivalry of New York as financial center and Mr Calhoun's rivalry of Mr Van Buren himself as successor to Andrew Jackson in the presidency. Both aims were achieved, at the sacrifice of monetary regulation on the one hand and of low tariffs on the other.*

VIII

Nicholas Biddle, who seems to have been a Jacksonian himself to the extent of having voted for the General in place of his old friend John Quincy Adams, had no such band of helpers to defend the Bank of the United States as General Jackson had to attack it. The older, more conservative, non-political part of the business world supported the Bank with enough decorum but too little energy. Those who defended it the loudest did so because they disliked Andrew Jackson. Henry Clay and Daniel Webster, though they were committed to the Bank on principle, were far more committed to anything that would thwart the General.[45]

Henry Clay was himself a very popular westerner, skillful in politics, ambitious, and able. He too had been a poor boy but singularly fortunate in winning important friends to ease his rise. Except for farming and cattle-breeding, statecraft absorbed him. His policy of fostering American industry with protective tariffs was much approved in the North, though it conflicted in principle and even in practice with *laisser faire*. Clay's policy ultimately prevailed and was of immense consequence to business enterprise, but he was not himself a successful money-maker.

Neither was Daniel Webster. The impracticality and improvidence in business matters of these two brilliant men contrasts interestingly with the shrewd acquisitiveness of their Jacksonian opponents, who knew how to make money and hold on to it. For Henry Clay and Daniel Webster, champions of the "money power," of "monopoly," and of "privilege," were always going beyond their means, floundering in debt, and dependent on their friends to keep them on their feet. Thomas Wren Ward, of Boston, a business man of the foremost ability and character, reported to his principals, the Barings, that

* My analysis is the same in substance as Mr Wiltse's in his biography of Calhoun: "Opposition to internal improvements and opposition to the Bank were the basic economic interests of New York and were therefore the corner stones of Van Buren's policy." Charles M. Wiltse, *John C. Calhoun, Nullifier*, 40; also chap. 10.

45 Biddle, *Correspondence*, 55-56.

he considered Mr Webster "by far the greatest man we have," and "in bringing power on a given point . . . probably greater than any man now living." Yet, he also said, "great as Mr Webster unquestionably is, and sound as are his views generally, and able as he is on great occasions in defending the true principles of the Constitution and upholding the rights of property, still I do not give him my esteem and confidence." This was because, in Mr Ward's opinion, he showed "a disregard to his moral obligations and a recklessness in pecuniary matters." Mr Ward depicts Mr Webster as living largely by passing the hat among wealthy men, who lent him money because of his public importance and scarcely expected him to repay it; in England he would try to do the same. "It will be easy to have him in your books if you desire it, but whatever he may owe you, I think you will be very safe in writing off to profit and loss."[46]

The two best aides Mr Biddle had were Horace Binney and John Sergeant, Philadelphia lawyers of great competence. The latter was a personal friend of Nicholas Biddle from the literary days of the *Port Folio*. Neither Binney nor Sergeant had had so golden a social and economic background as Nicholas Biddle, but neither could they be called poor farm boys and self-made men. They were the best of Mr Biddle's aides in the inadequate sense that they were highly intelligent, judicious, and reputable gentlemen; which, of course, made them no match whatever for President Jackson's array of experts. Unlike Henry Clay and Daniel Webster, they had something of the sincere, understanding loyalty to the Bank that Nicholas Biddle had. They knew its purpose and value as he did. Mr Webster knew its purpose and value long enough to make a speech; I doubt if Mr Clay ever bothered to go beyond the simple generalization that the Bank was an important institution which Andrew Jackson did not like.

Politics also kept John C. Calhoun from helping the Bank as he might have done. More than anyone else, he could claim the chartering of the Bank in 1816 as his work, and he understood the Bank's operations better than anyone else in Washington. But just at the time when the assault on the Bank was most critical—in 1832 and 1833—Mr Calhoun was wholly absorbed in resistance to the tariff. In January 1834, however, he passed a scathing and accurate judgment on removal of the public deposits from the government Bank and on the reasons offered to Congress by Secretary Taney for this

46 Baring Papers, T. W. Ward to Baring Brothers, 29 April 1839.

removal. In this address and in another in March, no less brilliant, he discussed the functions of the Bank clearly and objectively. His thorough understanding of its functions in the economy was based, as Nicholas Biddle's had originally been, on intelligent study and not at all on experience. Yet even more forcefully than the Bank had ever done he rested his argument where it belonged—on the constitutional responsibility of the government for the currency. He was distinguished among American statesmen in his realization that banking is a monetary function, that regulation of all the circulating medium is the duty of the federal government, and that the duty is to be exercised through a central bank; not for more than a century was such understanding of the subject to be expressed again in Congress. Daniel Webster in particular had never asserted the positive and proper defense of the Bank of the United States as Mr Calhoun had. His arguments were merely legal, not economic. According to Webster, the Bank was authorized by the Constitution if necessary to the government's operations. This fell far short of seeing in the Bank the one effective means of meeting the federal government's responsibility, under the Constitution, for the circulating medium. Further, Daniel Webster leaned on the jejune defense of vested rights, an obsolescent contention which weakened the Bank's case by the antagonisms it raised and failed entirely to take it off the ground prepared for it by its selfish enemies. Mr Calhoun's argument, practically alone, put the case on the high, affirmative, responsible ground of monetary powers, where it belonged. But politically it had no effect. The idea that the federal Bank regulated the monetary supply in accordance with the Constitution's assignment of powers made no appeal to people who did not see that bank credit was part of the monetary supply, or, if they did see, were unwilling to have it regulated.

CHAPTER 13

The Assault on the Federal Bank

1829-1832

I. The 1829 message — II. The 1830 message — III. The Bank's application to Congress — IV. The Jacksonian counter-play — V. The Clayton report — VI. The branch drafts

I

IN THE two preceding chapters I have described the issues and the participants in the conflict over the Bank of the United States; the conflict itself and its sequel are next to be narrated.

The first Jacksonian feints at the Bank, as already said, implied less desire to destroy it than to fetch it within the party pale as spoils of victory. In January 1829, before Jackson's first inauguration, proposals came to Philadelphia from Kentucky that directors be chosen from both parties, the names of eligible Democrats being furnished therewith. Mr Biddle refused to let party membership influence selections either way and accepted reports that the politicians named were unsuitable regardless of their politics. The following summer, complaints of the partisanship of Jeremiah Mason of the office in Portsmouth, New Hampshire, came to Biddle about the same time from Samuel D. Ingham, President Jackson's Secretary of the Treasury, from Senator Woodbury of New Hampshire, and indirectly from Isaac Hill in the Kitchen Cabinet, also of New Hampshire. A tart exchange of letters ensued between Mr Biddle and his fellow Pennsylvanian, Secretary Ingham. In it a sharp and disturbing difference of principle was˷ disclosed—a difference so serious that to some men in Mr Biddle's position it would have been a signal to resign.*

Beyond that interchange, at the moment, Mr Biddle seems to

* This correspondence was included by John Quincy Adams in his minority report, 14 May 1832, and will be found in House Report 460, 22nd Congress, 1st Session, pp. 438-79; it is discussed by Mr Adams on page 393 of the foregoing and by Professor Catterall, *Second Bank of the United States*, 172-79.

have faced no more than the routine effort of certain presidential aides to capture the Bank for the party. But this course was soon superseded by the more ambitious plan to replace the Bank with something entirely new and not in Philadelphia. The President himself always denied that he had ever entertained the idea of continuing the Bank. "The charge made," he said later, "of my being friendly to the Bank of the United States until I found it could not be used for my political purposes, when I turned against it, is one of the foulest and basest calumnies ever uttered. . . . I have always been opposed to it upon constitutional grounds as well as expediency and policy." He also affirmed that he had wished to speak out against it so early as in his inaugural but had been dissuaded: every one knew, he said, that he always had been opposed to the Bank of the United States, "nay all banks." In May and October following his inauguration in March 1829 he was in fact already in correspondence with Senator Felix Grundy about a wholly new "national bank" to replace the existing federal Bank.[1]

This does not mean that the General went into the White House girded up to exterminate the federal Bank. The evidence, the circumstances, the personalities, and the relevant interest suggest something far less simple. The General, I think, had entered the White House with nothing more definite than, as he said, a traditionary aversion to all banks and constitutional scruples about them. His feelings had not kept him from dealing with banks, however, or in particular with the Nashville office of the federal Bank, where he had his account. He may nevertheless have looked forward to preventing a renewal of the federal charter, which would expire within his administration if he were to serve two terms. Before any such program became formulated, however, certain of his subordinates were moving in on the federal Bank as into all departments of the federal government. This and presumably nothing more was what Isaac Hill and Secretary Ingham purposed in opening their initial skirmish with the Bank's president.

When these routine steps in the party interest were begun Mr Van Buren was still in Albany, fostering his Safety Fund bank bill; but after the bill was enacted and he had joined General Jackson in Washington, Mr Van Buren must have had no difficulty in supplanting the Treasury's unimaginative scheme with his own more radical one. He could simply suggest to the President a pro-

[1] Jackson, *Correspondence* IV, 37, 83-84, 445; V, 236; Catterall, 182-85.

cedure for bringing to an end the offensive and unconstitutional Bank in Philadelphia. No emphasis whatever need be given the benefits to New York. The course Mr Van Buren wanted seems to have been agreed upon at Richmond in October 1829 and to have made destruction of the federal Bank, "as at present constituted," the definite purpose of the President and his intimates.

The Richmond meeting is the one of which reports, confirmed by Senator Felix Grundy's correspondence with the President, were made to Nicholas Biddle from various quarters that its purpose was to commit the party to attack the Bank. Major Lewis alone seems to have dissented from its decision and to have continued cultivating the Bank in good faith; and, though Secretary Ingham, as a self-made business man, may have relished laying down the rules for the aristocratic banker Nicholas Biddle, still, being a Pennsylvanian himself, he may have shrunk from proceeding too far against Pennsylvania's principal institution.

The plan to end the Bank called for care and caution. There was not now the popular hatred of it that there had been five years before. From General Jackson's inauguration in March 1829 the charter had almost seven years to run. At the moment the Jacksonians had to recognize that the Bank's standing in public esteem was high; it was as good as it ever had been, or better. Five years had elapsed since the Supreme Court had last denied the right of an individual state to interfere with it, and prosperity had lessened the occasion for interference. The Bank was resented by the state banks, but nothing more had occurred to arouse ill will. If the Bank were to be done away with, a case against it must be worked up.

Nicholas Biddle, meanwhile, though without very explicit assurances from the administration of its good will, had been led to hope for the best. Major Lewis, 16 October 1829, only a week or so before the Richmond meeting, had written him from the White House to acknowledge a conciliatory letter about political influences on branch office appointments. The President was gratified, the Major said, and requested him to say that he had too much confidence in Mr Biddle to believe for a moment that he would knowingly tolerate the conduct in the branch offices of which the Jacksonians complained. "The President thinks," he said, "as you do, that the Bank of the United States should recognize *no* party; and that in all its operations it should have an eye *single* to the interest of the stockholders and the good of the country. . . ." A few days later, 21

October 1829, one of the Bank's directors, from Philadelphia, Matthew L. Bevan, wrote to Mr Biddle as follows after calling on the President in Washington: ". . . I cannot withhold a moment the pleasure it gives me in saying the result of my visit is most satisfactory, inasmuch as the President expressed himself in the most clear and decided manner friendly to the Bank—'that it was a blessing to the country administered as it was, diffusing a healthful circulation, sustaining the general credit without partiality or political bias'—that he entertained a high regard for its excellent President (I use his own words), who with the Board of the parent Bank possessed his entire confidence. . . ."[2]

A few days later, 26 October 1829, Samuel Jaudon, the Bank's cashier, wrote Mr Biddle that he had called on the President, who had said, *inter alia*, "that in reference to yourself particularly he had the most unbounded confidence in the purity of your intentions; that the support which you had given to the financial operations of the Government was of the most gratifying as well as effectual kind. . . . Throughout our interview, which lasted for an hour, the tone and manner of the President were of the most mild and friendly character. . . ." Major Lewis, 9 November 1829, wrote a fellow Jacksonian in Philadelphia: "Say to Mr Biddle the President is much gratified with the report I have made him upon the subject of his Bank; all things with regard to it will be well."[3]

About this time Mr Biddle sent Major Lewis a plan for retirement of the public debt, respecting which the Major sent him word, 11 November 1829: "I will submit it to the General. I think we will find the *old fellow* will do justice to the Bank in his message for the handsome manner in which it assisted the Government in paying the last instalment of the national debt."[4]

About a week later Mr Biddle was himself in Washington and had a cordial interview with the President. According to an undated, informal memorandum in Biddle's papers, the President thanked him for his plan of paying off the national debt and told him he would have no difficulty in recommending it to Congress. "But," the President had said, according to the memorandum, "I think it right to be perfectly frank with you—I do not think that the power of

2 Biddle Papers 21, Folio 4219 (also in Biddle, *Correspondence*, 79-80, 81-82).

3 Biddle Papers 21, Folios 4232-33 (also in Biddle, *Correspondence*, 84).

4 Biddle Papers 21, Folio 4249, in Biddle's own hand as an extract from correspondence of W. B. Lewis with Henry Toland (also in Biddle, *Correspondence*, 85).

Congress extends to charter a Bank out of the ten mile square.*
I do not dislike your Bank any more than all banks. But ever since
I read the history of the South Sea Bubble I have been afraid of
banks. I have read the opinion of John Marshall, who I believe was
a great and pure mind—and could not agree with him. . . . I feel
very sensibly the services rendered by the Bank at the last payment
of the national debt and shall take an opportunity of declaring it
publicly in my message to Congress." Mr Biddle told him that he
was "very much gratified at this frank explanation" and that "we
shall all be proud of any kind mention in the message—for we
should feel like soldiers after an action commended by their
General"; to which the President replied, "Sir, it would be only an
act of justice to mention it."[5]

However, a week later, Nicholas Biddle was warned by Alexander
Hamilton, jr., 27 November 1829, that the President would speak
against the Bank in his message: "I have long had an anxious solicitude for the permanency of the Bank of the United States," he
wrote, "and it is consequently a source of deep regret that I understood the renewal of its charter is to be unfavourably noticed in the
President's message." Mr Biddle refused to believe the warning. He
replied the next day: "The rumor to which you allude," he said,
"I have not heard from any other quarter, and I believe it is entirely
without foundation. My reason for thinking so is that during a
recent visit to Washington from which I returned on Thursday
last, I had much conversation of a very full and frank character with
the President about the Bank, in all which he never intimated any
such purpose. On the contrary he spoke in terms the most kind and
gratifying towards the institution—expressed his thanks for the
services it had rendered the Government since his connection with
it, and I look to the message with expectations of the most satisfactory kind."[6]**

He also wrote in his draft of a letter to Hamilton four days later

* That is, the federal District of Columbia, then ten miles square, in which
the city of Washington is situated.

** Alexander Hamilton, jr., was a supporter of John C. Calhoun—his
brother James A. Hamilton, a supporter of Andrew Jackson. But it is a
reasonable conjecture that the first brother got from the second the news
of which he warned Nicholas Biddle.

5 Biddle Papers 21, Folio 4248 (also in Biddle, *Correspondence*, 93-94); Bassett ɪɪ,
599-600.
6 Biddle Papers, 3 PLB (1829), 98.

that "the administration of the Bank is on the best footing with the President and his particular friends," but he scratched out those words to say instead—alluding to a certain Jacksonian editor—that "abuse of the Bank does him no service in the opinion of the President and his best friends."[7] In this comfortable mood, Mr Biddle was confronted almost immediately by the unexpected words of the President's message to Congress. The Bank's charter, the President said, would expire in 1836 and it was not too soon to begin considering if it should be renewed. "Both the constitutionality and the expediency of the law creating this Bank are well questioned by a large portion of our fellow citizens; and it must be admitted by all that it has failed in the great end of establishing a uniform and sound currency."[8]

That the constitutionality and expediency of the Bank were questioned is one thing—that they were "well questioned" is another. Thirty-eight years had elapsed since establishment of the first Bank, and it or its successor had served the administrations of all six of Jackson's predecessors. One of its original opponents, Thomas Jefferson, had as President acknowledged its constitutionality by acquiescence, and another, James Madison—the foremost authority on the Constitution—had specifically abandoned his former objections to the Bank, had recommended re-establishment, and had approved the act effecting it. The Supreme Court had twice affirmed the Bank's constitutionality. Indeed, after 1791 nobody of comparable authority with its original opponents—Jefferson and Madison—ever attacked the Bank on constitutional grounds.

The President's second assertion—that the Bank had failed to establish a sound and uniform currency—was preposterous. When Mr Gallatin asked him what he meant, he got no intelligible reply. Half a century later Professor Sumner wrote that the currency had never before been so good as when President Jackson spoke, and that it had never been so good since. "The proceedings," he wrote, "of which the paragraph in the message of 1829 was the first warning, threw the currency and banking of the country into confusion and uncertainty . . . and they have never yet recovered. . . ." Subsequent studies have confirmed Professor Sumner's judgment. "Probably never since 1789," writes Professor Walter B. Smith, "had the

[7] Biddle Papers 21, Folio 4298.
[8] Biddle Papers 21, Folios 4308, 4311; Richardson III, 1025.

United States had a dollar which was sounder or more stable" than in the period—1826 to 1832—of General Jackson's assertion.[9]

Besides slurring the Bank, in one part of the message, the President commended it in another, as he had told Mr Biddle he would. "The payment on account of public debt made on the 1st of July last was $8,715,462.87," he said. And he continued in words obviously prepared by the Treasury: "It was apprehended that the sudden withdrawal of so large a sum from the banks in which it was deposited, at a time of unusual pressure in the money market, might cause much injury to the interests dependent on bank accommodations. But this evil was wholly averted by an early anticipation of it at the Treasury, aided by the judicious arrangements of the officers of the Bank of the United States." This fulfilled the President's promise, and was probably all that Nicholas Biddle expected.[10] The part that he had not expected came later in the message.*

But he was now aware that Alexander Hamilton, jr., had been correct after all. "You will see," he wrote briefly, 9 December, "that you were better informed than I was. The result I see with surprise and regret and I write now merely to say that when I recollect all that I saw and heard in Washington my surprise at the contents of the message increases every moment." This expresses scant sophistication. Mr Hamilton replied at once, saying that if there had been time and if "you had not appeared quite so confident in your conclusions, I should have endeavoured to prove that you were under a delusion." But now that the President had spoken, Mr Hamilton thought it "only remains for you to make the best of an unpromising cause. . . . I would suggest the propriety of abstaining from the expression of any opinion intimating a want of fairness and integrity in the President; I am satisfied he feels no personal hostility, and consequently no conduct of the Bank ought to create

* James A. Hamilton says that he was called on to help President Jackson with this message and that in the draft already written the Bank "was attacked at great length in a loose, newspaper, slashing style." He says he advised that the subject be omitted, but the President declared himself to be "pledged against the Bank." He says the President told him a little later that in attacking the Bank he disliked to act contrary to the opinion of a majority of his Cabinet but could not shirk his duty. At the same time, Hamilton says he was asked to work out the details of Jackson's "proposed National Bank," which was to be "attached" to the Treasury and to have the "Customhouse a branch." Hamilton, *Reminiscences*, 151.

[9] Sumner, Jackson, 281-82; W. B. Smith, 76.   [10] Richardson III, 1014.

such a feeling." Mr Biddle replied at once, 12 December, that Mr Hamilton's views were "quite sound and correspond exactly" with those entertained at the Bank. "My impression," he said, "is that these opinions expressed by the President are entirely and exclusively his own, and that they should be treated as the honest though erroneous notions of one who intends well."[11]

But Mr Biddle could not fondly dream for long that these disturbing opinions of the President's were exclusively his own; for less than a month later he was informed by Roswell L. Colt that Congressman Cambreleng had advised a mutual friend in New York "three months ago . . . to sell out his Bank shares—for that the administration were hostile to the Bank . . . and that its charter would not be renewed and that the government would create a new Bank, a national one, to be located at Washington with branches only in such states as should pass a law authorizing it, and made use of very similar objections to the Bank as those introduced into the message—from which he infers that Van Buren was consulted on that part of the message. . . ."[12]

II

In both houses of Congress the President's questions about the Bank were referred to committees, and both committees upheld the Bank forcefully. The chairman of the Senate committee was General Samuel Smith of Baltimore, who had been a leader of the old Bank's enemies in preventing renewal of the first charter and in driving Mr Gallatin from office, and who later had been prostrated physically and financially by the devastation of the Bank's Baltimore office at the hands of his partner, James A. Buchanan. Perhaps that experience had chastened him. At any rate his report, submitted 29 March 1830, was a brief, lucid, and cogent discussion of the Bank's responsibility for the country; it followed in great part what Nicholas Biddle had supplied, word for word. It concluded: "On the whole the committee are of opinion that the present state of the currency is safe for the community and eminently useful to the Government; that for some years past it has been improving by the infusion into the circulating medium of a larger portion of coin and the substitution of the paper of more solvent banks in lieu of those of inferior credit; and that if left to the progress of existing

[11] Biddle, *Correspondence*, 88-91; Biddle Papers, 3 PLB (1829), 103.
[12] Biddle, *Correspondence*, 66-67. This letter was misdated 7 January 1829; it should be 7 January 1830.

laws and institutions, the partial inconveniences which still remain of the paper currency of the last war will be wholly and insensibly remedied. Under these circumstances they deem it prudent to abstain from all legislation, to abide by the practical good which the country enjoys, and to put nothing to hazard by doubtful experiments."[13]

The House committee, whose chairman was George McDuffie of South Carolina, produced a lengthier and more comprehensive report, addressed more directly to the two questions raised by the President. Respecting the first, it emphasized the approval of the Bank's constitutionality by both parties; the acquiescence of Mr Jefferson, the reversal by Mr Madison and Mr Clay of their original opinions, and the unanimous decision of the Supreme Court; and it repeated the query of Mr Dallas fifteen years before whether the question of constitutionality could not be deemed "forever settled and at rest."[14]

The committee then passed from the passive question whether the Constitution *permitted* a federal Bank to the constructive question whether in the circumstances the Constitution did not *require* it, taking substantially the position that Mr Calhoun had stated in 1816. It observed that the power to coin money and fix the value thereof was "expressly and exclusively vested in Congress," that "this grant was evidently intended to invest Congress with the power of regulating the circulating medium," coin being regarded "at the period of framing the Constitution as synonymous with 'currency,'" and that the states were prohibited from "coining money or emitting bills of credit," with the net effect that the regulation of the circulating medium, "whether consisting of coin or paper," was taken from the states and vested in Congress—"the only depository in which it could be placed consistently with the obvious design of having a common measure of value throughout the Union." When the Bank was incorporated in 1816, the committee said, a state of things had existed which "furnished a most pregnant commentary" on these clauses of the Constitution; "the currency of the country consisted of the paper of local banks variously depreciated." Congress "not only had the power, but . . . were under the most solemn constitutional obligations, to restore the disordered currency; and the Bank of the United States was not only an appropriate means for the accomplishment of that work but . . . the only safe

[13] Clarke and Hall, 776.   [14] Clarke and Hall, 735-38.

and effectual means." This, the committee remarked, had been President Madison's view.[15]

The report then adverted to the President's second question, or rather his assertion, that the Bank had "failed in the great end of establishing a uniform and sound currency." From this opinion, after giving it "all the consideration to which it is so justly entitled from the eminent station and high character of the citizen by whom it is entertained," the committee were "constrained to express their respectful but decided dissent." They stated on the basis of clear evidence that the Bank had furnished a circulating medium more uniform than specie, "a currency of absolutely uniform value in all places." It explained that the salutary agency of the Bank in furnishing a sound and uniform currency was not confined to that part thereof comprising its own bills but the greater part comprising the bills of the state banks. "One of the most important purposes which the Bank was designed to accomplish and which, it is confidently believed, no other human agency could have effected under our federative system of government, was the enforcement of specie payments on the part of numerous local banks, deriving their charters from the several states and whose paper irredeemable in specie and illimitable in its quantity constituted the almost entire currency of the country. Amidst a combination of the greatest difficulties, the Bank has almost completely succeeded in the performance of this arduous, delicate, and painful duty."[16]

These reports were submitted in March and April 1830. They disposed of the President's remarks so positively that Nicholas Biddle was anxious lest the President "feel vexed at being thus contradicted." As Professor Catterall says, if this anxiety implied an impulse to conciliate, Mr Biddle "adopted a curious method of conciliation." For he had the reports reprinted and distributed, at the Bank's expense. This tactless performance vexed the President more than the reports themselves and enabled the Bank's enemies to denounce its political efforts.[17]

Meanwhile the evidences of official policy were conflicting and perplexing. Most of the official Cabinet opposed an attack on the Bank. Working relations with the Treasury continued normal and Mr Biddle was himself renominated government director by the President. Major Lewis of the Kitchen Cabinet kept the door open,

15 Clarke and Hall, 631, 739-40.   16 Clarke and Hall, 745-49.
17 Biddle Papers, 3 PLB (1830), 227; Catterall, 199.

exchanged friendly letters, and proposed Jackson supporters for branch appointments, Judge Overton, "a particular friend of the President," among them. "The President is well," he said in closing such a letter, 3 May 1830, "and desires me to present his respects to you." But the same day, 3 May 1830, the President himself sent Colonel James A. Hamilton in New York a copy of the McDuffie report on the Bank with these words: "I presume it to be a joint effort and the best that can be made in its support, and *it is feeble.* This is intended, no doubt, as the first shot; it will pass without moving me." A month later, 3 June 1830, he wrote Colonel Hamilton again, calling the Bank three times a "hydra of corruption"; it is "dangerous to our liberties by its corrupting influences everywhere and not the least in the Congress of the Union"; it has "demoralizing effects upon our citizens. . . ." And later that same month, 26 June 1830, he wrote to Major Lewis a complaint that Duff Green could not be trusted with the attack on the Bank.[18] "The truth is, he has professed to me to be heart and soul against the Bank," but Calhoun "controls him as the shewman does his puppets, and we must get another organ to announce the policy. . . ."*

A month before, however, 25 May, Major Lewis had again written Mr Biddle, marking his letter "confidential": "Before closing this letter permit me to say one word in reference to a subject mentioned in your last letter to me—I mean the information you received of the President's having declared that if Congress should pass a law renewing the charter of the United States Bank, he would put his veto on it. I told you in Philadelphia when you first mentioned the thing to me, that there must be some mistake, because the report was at variance with what *I* had heard him say upon the subject. In conversing with him a few days ago upon the subject, he still entertained the opinion that a *National* Bank might be established that would be preferable to the present United States Bank; but that, if Congress thought differently and it was deemed necessary to have such a Bank as the present, with certain modifications, he should not object to it. If the President finds that his

---

* Duff Green was Vice President Calhoun's devoted supporter. His daughter married Calhoun's son. Calhoun was Van Buren's rival for the Presidency, succeeding Jackson's.

[18] Biddle, *Correspondence*, 99; J. A. Hamilton, *Reminiscences*, 164, 167; Jackson, *Correspondence* IV, 156.

scheme is not likely to take, I do not believe he will be opposed altogether to the present Bank."[19]

Two months later Mr Biddle received a letter from Josiah Nichol, 20 July 1830, president of the Nashville office and a friend of President Jackson, reporting conversations with the latter, who had just been for some two days a guest in his home and of whom he said: "He appears to be well satisfied with the facilities that the Bank have given to government and individuals in transferring their funds from one point to another and acknowledges that a Bank such as the present only can do so. He appears to be generally pleased with the management of the Bank of the United States and branches —and particularly so with this office. I have taken considerable pains and gave him all the information I consistently could on banking subjects—and believe have convinced him that the present Bank and branches could not be dispensed with without manifest injury to the country and particularly so to this western country, as no other currency could be substituted. . . . The only objection he appears to have to the present Bank is that a great part of the stock is held by foreigners, consequently the interest is taken from the country. He is well satisfied that politics have no influence in the Bank or in the choice of directors, and I am well convinced that he will not interfere with Congress on the subject of renewing the charter of the Bank—although on this subject he keeps his opinion to himself. He speaks of you in the most exalted terms and says there is no gentleman that can be found would manage the Bank better or do the Bank and country more justice."[20]

So while the General privately breathed animosity for the hydra of corruption, Mr Biddle was let think by the General's friends that all was well. It was about this time that word came to him from New York and also from Kentucky conveying fresh reports that the real enemy of the Bank was Martin Van Buren. He was also reminded of President Jackson's ill will. Mr Gallatin wrote him, 14 August 1830, recognizing the "ability and success" with which he had managed the Bank but calling his "early attention to the imminent danger there is that the renewal of the charter may not be obtained on any terms and to the absolute necessity of the sacrifices which will, at all events, be requisite in order to succeed." Mr Gallatin recalled the failure to renew the old charter in 1811, when the Bank had had a majority

[19] Biddle Papers 22, Folio 4624 (also in Biddle, *Correspondence*, 103-04).
[20] Biddle Papers 23, Folio 4721 (also in Biddle, *Correspondence*, 106-07).

of political friends in both Houses, and when "the banking system had not yet penetrated through the country . . . and the opposition due to the jealousy or selfishness of rival institutions was confined to a few cities; yet the question was lost." Now, he believed, the situation was worse. "Opposition arising from interested motives pervades the whole country; in this state [New York], for instance, . . . the country banking interest is all-powerful on all questions connected with that subject; with a sect of politicians throughout the Union 'state rights' has become a watchword; worst of all, the President has prematurely and gratuitously declared himself and given the signal of attack to his adherents." A month later, 11 September 1830, Henry Clay mentioned to Mr Biddle the increased animosity of administration papers toward the Bank, and in November Mr Biddle was himself asking about the revived story of "a combination between certain politicians of Richmond and the Secretary of State against the Bank."[21]

In his second annual message, December 1830, the President disparaged the Bank somewhat more harshly, saying that nothing had occurred that lessened "the dangers which many of our citizens apprehend from that institution as at present organized." He asked if it would not be possible to have a bank in its place that should be a branch of the Treasury, "based on the public and individual deposits, without power to make loans or purchase property," and that should remit the funds of the government, its expenses to be met by the sale of exchange. "Not being a corporate body, having no stockholders, debtors, or property, and but few officers, it would not be obnoxious to the constitutional objections which are urged against the present bank." The President also expressed the belief, in a passage which indirectly acknowledges the federal Bank's regulatory function, that "the states would be strengthened by having in their hands the means of furnishing the local paper currency through their own banks, while the Bank of the United States, though issuing no paper, would check the issues of the state banks by taking their notes in deposit and for exchange only so long as they continue to be redeemed with specie." Presumably the proposed Bank would have no liabilities, and would be no more than a name over a door in the Treasury. It sounds much like the hollow political affairs, set up in several western states, that exemplified banking at

---

[21] Biddle, *Correspondence*, 101, 105, 111; Biddle Papers, 3 PLB (1830), 398-99; Gallatin ii, 431-32, 435.

about its worst. It also sounds like the proposals of the Boston promoter and political boss David Henshaw, published three months later. Thus to avoid the federal government's continuing to violate the Constitution through the national Bank, the states were to continue violating it through the banks chartered by them to issue notes.[22]

III

Baffled by the Jacksonian behavior, Mr Biddle continued month after month plucking petals from daisies. The Bank had ample majority in both houses of Congress to enact a new charter but not majority enough to over-ride a veto of it by the President. For practical as well as sentimental reasons, Mr Biddle preferred that charter be an administrative measure, as in the past it had been. The language of the administration newspapers seemed to reflect a settled animosity toward the Bank, but the administration itself seemed by no means so unfriendly. In March 1831 Mr Biddle said that he heard such various opinions that he ended by knowing nothing.[23]

He was left in uncertainty in part because though General Jackson's more intimate advisers were committed against the Bank, some were unready, and several official advisers were not committed at all. Mr Calhoun, the Vice President, had first to be removed from Mr Van Buren's path to the Presidency, and the Bank must wait its turn to have its head taken off. And just then, as it happened, attention became diverted from the Bank still more by the ladies of official Washington, who refused to recognize one of their number, Peggy Eaton, the Secretary of War's wife, whom they considered a hussy. This was in defiance of the President, who gallantly and venerably championed her. He had known her long. She was a witty, pretty, saucy creature; he had been touched years before by the way she sang hymns of an evening to her aged mother, and her new husband was an old and dear friend of his. The affair seems for months to have absorbed more of the President's attention than he gave to business of state. At length Mr Van Buren resolved the problem by his proposal that the Cabinet be wholly reconstituted. This was done, and by accident the change in favor of Mrs Eaton produced a membership better disposed also to the Bank, including particularly a new Secretary of State, Edward Livingston of New

---

[22] Richardson III, 1091-92; Henshaw, 38ff; J. A. Hamilton, *Reminiscences*, 167-68.
[23] Catterall, 207; Biddle Papers, 3 PLB (1831), 496.

Orleans, and a new Secretary of the Treasury, Louis McLane of Delaware. Both were in favor of continuing the Bank and let the President know it, frankly and earnestly.[24]

This seems not to have annoyed the President, whose wish now was that the question of the Bank be deferred till after next year's election. For if it came up at once, the charter would pass Congress, and he would be confronted with the choice of approving or disapproving it. Approval would offend his party in some states, including New York; disapproval would offend his party in others, including Pennsylvania. If the matter could be postponed till after 1832, the election would be in less jeopardy.

On the Bank's side of the question, there was no want of time, in a sense, because the present charter would not expire till 1836, four years after next year's election. Had the President been well disposed, the question of recharter could certainly have been postponed; had the President been in doubt, the question might still have been postponed. Actually there seems now to have been no doubt in his mind about the Bank but only about the way to kill it off.

Affairs standing thus, with the President wishing to postpone the question of the charter and Mr Biddle wishing to be in less uncertainty, Secretaries Livingston and McLane consulted the President and Mr Biddle in search of a compromise. In the fall, 1831, a tentative understanding was worked out, the administration to be assured of postponement, the Bank to be assured of recharter. Professor Catterall says: "At last the Bank seemed to be nearing the goal it had long striven to reach—a re-charter with the assent of the President. Biddle, Livingston, McLane, and Jackson now acted under a sort of informal compact: the secretaries to work for recharter, Jackson to remain quiescent for the present but to sign a bill in the long run if his wishes were met, and the Bank on its part to wait until after the election before presenting its petition for a charter and to accept the modifications desired by the President."[25]

Yet this was all upset in early December 1831, when the President's annual message and the Secretary of the Treasury's report were delivered. The President was so far subdued that he merely affirmed his adherence to the opinions he had already expressed about the Bank, "as at present organized," and left the question "to the investigations of an enlightened people and their representatives." Secretary McLane, however, praised the Bank's services at

[24] Parton III, 184; Jackson, *Correspondence* III, 218.   [25] Catterall, 210.

length in his report and recommended recharter; taking into account particularly the "multiplicity of state banks" which could not in any other manner be controlled in their issuance of paper money than through the Bank of the United States.

The Bank's enemies were shocked at the weakness of their hero's words and the assurance of his Secretary's. When the intended message was read to the Cabinet, the Attorney General, now Roger Taney, had protested at what had been written for the President, and in consequence the language had been altered though not enough to suit Taney. His apprehension was correct: it was widely believed by the Bank's enemies that the President had suffered himself to be duped. Mr Biddle, however, had no such belief. He was disappointed, for the President did not say what he had been led to expect would be said. Or rather he said more. From the conversations with Secretary McLane, Mr Biddle had expected the President would be milder and less reminiscent of past pronouncements than he was. He too was right. The President would have been milder had not Mr Taney interposed and got him to reaffirm his dislike of the Bank. This was not the first time that Mr Biddle had got one impression privately of what the President would say and a quite different one from what he did say.

What precisely was in the President's mind one can not tell. He wrote Colonel James A. Hamilton in New York, 12 December 1831, a week after the message: "Mr McLane and myself understand each other and have not the slightest disagreement about the principles which will be a *sine qua non* in my assent to a bill rechartering the Bank." This sounds like as definite a commitment as there could be to approve recharter. Since the President communicated it to a friend of the Bank, one would suppose he realized that Mr Biddle might hear of it. But very different testimony was to come later from Mr Taney; he said that the doubts he had felt at the moment lest the President, "under the influence of his new advisers, . . . be persuaded to consent to re-charter of the Bank with some plausible but unsubstantial restrictions on its power," proved to be groundless. For, he said, "I did not then know General Jackson as well as I afterwards knew him. If I had, these doubts would never have been entertained." Presumably, Mr Taney came to believe that the President had never intended to spare the Bank, though Messrs Livingston and McLane thought he intended to and his words to Colonel Hamilton indicate it. Nor did Congressman Cambreleng of New York seem to fear that the Bank would be spared. Secretary McLane's Treasury report, he wrote, 29 December 1831, "is as bad as it possibly can be—a new version of Alexander Hamilton's two reports on a national bank and manufactures and totally unsuited to this age of democracy and reform." However, he continued emphatically, "the battle . . . will go like wildfire when we commence our war against the Lords and Bishops."[26]

Not all these things were known to Mr Biddle, of course, but enough was known to have beaten away at his confidence severely. In the August preceding, his younger brother, Major Thomas Biddle, a director of the St Louis office, had been killed in a duel incidental to attacks in Missouri on the Bank. Jacksonian politicians, it was alleged, had brought the duel about; this the Jacksonians denied, but Nicholas Biddle could not have helped being embittered, especially because the duel had been provoked by slurs on his own integrity.* Moreover, there were plans afoot among the Jacksonians in the East for a new bank, on the scale of the Bank of the United States, to be set up in New York, and for all Mr Biddle knew the President might decide not to approve a new charter unless it made New York the headquarters. And the Jacksonian press, perhaps in fear lest the President be weakening, was more venomous toward the Bank after the message than before.

At the same time, the opponents of President Jackson had coalesced in a new party, the National Republicans, and nominated Henry Clay for President and John Sergeant, counsel for the Bank and one of Biddle's closest advisers, for Vice President. This was later the Whig party. Its leaders were almost importunate that the Bank apply at once for recharter, not because they loved it so much but because they believed the President would be fatally embarrassed if he were confronted with a new charter before election and had to choose between approval of it and veto. John Sergeant and Daniel Webster were both convinced of this. So was Henry Clay. So were many others. It was not Nicholas Biddle's idea, but he did fall in with it—less perhaps because he believed it would work than because he had found the arrangement with the President would not.

---

* This duel was fought on an island in the Mississippi. The two men stood five feet apart, their pistols nearly touching, and each killed the other. (St Louis *Beacon*, 1 September 1831, 22 September 1831; Niles XLI (17 September 1831), 37; Hone I, 36.

26 J. A. Hamilton, *Reminiscences*, 234; Taney Papers, *Bank War* MS, 87 (also in Swisher, 178); Mackenzie, *Van Buren*, 230.

Accordingly, 6 January 1832, a month after the message had re-awakened his misgivings, he asked that the Bank's application for recharter be laid before Congress; which was done.

This decision to put the matter before Congress was come to thoughtfully and with the concurrence of able politicians, though not the ablest. The Bank had every right to apply directly to Congress but had sought the administration's approval first as a matter of common sense and courtesy. For three years the administration had been blowing hot and cold by way of answer. Charles Jared Ingersoll, while he was still a friend of the Bank, which he later sided against, said that Secretary Livingston acknowledged to him that the President's various messages in effect invited reference of the question to Congress for action. However the request to Congress has generally been called a mistake. It was one, certainly, if to resist Andrew Jackson were sacrilege. And it was one, certainly, in the sense that it failed to achieve recharter. But no one supposes that the Bank would have been rechartered had the question been left to the President's convenience. He was determined to kill the Bank; behind him were his select advisers and lieutenants—Amos Kendall, Roger Taney, Churchill Cambreleng, Thomas Hart Benton, and, most inscrutable of all, Martin Van Buren—who were determined to kill it. And behind them were the state banks and state politicians determined to kill it. All that Mr Biddle could do was make the end come a little harder or a little less hard, a little sooner or a little later.[27]

This is not to say positively that the influence of McLane, Livingston, and Lewis—especially in the absence of Van Buren at the Court of St James—was negligible, and that it must have failed even had Biddle refrained from asking Congress for recharter. Yet it seems to me that this was practically the case. I find Jackson so much committed by his own prejudices to the program of Taney, Kendall, and Cambreleng that he could not have been persuaded in any probable circumstances by McLane, Livingston, and Lewis; and I think he listened to the latter partly out of politeness to old friends but mainly for the tactical purpose of confusing and deceiving the enemy. He was in combat.

IV

On 26 January 1832, the federal Bank's petition being before Congress, Senator William L. Marcy of New York, author of the

27 Biddle, *Correspondence*, 178.

celebrated Jacksonian aphorism, "to the victors belong the spoils," presented the request of certain citizens of Massachusetts for a federal charter incorporating a new national bank with a capital of $50,000,000 to supersede the wicked Philadelphia mammoth that had a capital of $35,000,000. The sponsor of the scheme was David Henshaw, the Jacksonian political boss of Massachusetts, banker, capitalist, newspaper publisher, and promoter. He already was interested in three banks. His proposed $50,000,000 bank was to have "powers and obligations similar to those" of the Bank of the United States in Philadelphia, which the petition said was "chiefly in the hands of foreigners and a few wealthy American citizens." It was to pay the federal government an annual "bonus" and an additional "bonus" to each state in which it had a branch office. Less than a fortnight later, 6 February, John Anderson of Portland, Maine, a Jacksonian Congressman, later Collector of that port, presented a like petition in the House.* The day before, Congressman Cambreleng had urged Jesse Hoyt of New York, his friend and Mr Van Buren's, that the Working Men's Party "be up and doing on the United States Bank question"; for they were "democrats in principle." A week later, 12 February, he acknowledged what he called the "very good" plan of another friend, Elisha Tibbets, a New York speculator, for a bank of $35,000,000 to be set up in Wall Street to take the place of the Bank in Philadelphia. This "splendid new bank," as it was advertised in the press, was to have a New York charter but was to be a federal depository and have branches in all the states, with their consent. It was generously expected to "save Congress the trouble of rechartering the present Bank of the United States."[28]

The Tibbets plan evidently did not seem so good to others as to Cambreleng, and a few days later he advised his friend Hoyt that it be deferred to Henshaw's for the present, lest the Pennsylvanians make embarrassing use of it. In the same letter Mr Cambreleng mentions arrangements then making with President Jackson for an investigation of the federal Bank. He implies the President's privity to the scheme, which, as disclosed later, was to interpose an

---

* This probably represented also Senator Isaac Hill of New Hampshire, David Henshaw's friend and the original instigator of trouble for the Bank of the United States from the Jackson administration.

[28] Congress, *Register of Debates* VIII, Part 1, 180; Part 2, 1752; Mackenzie, *Van Buren*, 231, 232; *Butler and Hoyt*, 100, 101; 22nd Congress, 1st Session, HR 95, p. 1-5; New York *Advertiser*, 11 and 18 February 1832.

inquiry by a committee hostile to the Bank and so work up the case against renewal of the charter. The letter, dated Washington, 16 February 1832, follows:

"I return you the letter—Judge Clayton of Georgia has a resolution prepared and will offer it as soon as he can—it will cover the object in view—I shall see the President to-night—who has a confidential director on the spot. You need not fear but what we shall take care of the Mammoth in some way or other.

"I think on reflection that it would be well enough to let the plan Mr Tibbets had in view alone for the present. Let them follow the Bostonians and Portland people in asking for a new bank from the federal government—but on the plan they propose—this is on the whole better than to set up for ourselves, which might be made use of by the Pennsylvanians against us, here and elsewhere—We can bring forward a state bank next year—mention this to Mr Tibbets."[29]

The resolution that, according to Mr Cambreleng's letter, was to be offered by Judge Clayton, a Representative from Georgia, had been prepared by Senator Benton of Missouri, the Senator's tactical opinion being that if the investigation of the Bank were denied, "it would be guilt shrinking from detection," and if it were ordered, "it was well known that misconduct would be found." In other words, the purpose of the inquiry was not to obtain information but to propagate convictions already held. That widely advertised honesty of the Jacksonians which insured their not taking property out of other people's pockets did not operate so powerfully when it was a matter of putting notions in other people's heads. "Our course of action," said Senator Benton, "became obvious, which was to attack incessantly, assail at all points, display the evil of the institution, rouse the people, and prepare them to sustain the veto." In the middle of February, while the issue was up, Cambreleng wrote his friend Hoyt, "the more we discuss it, the stronger we shall get"; and a month later he wrote that if a new charter were enacted, "public duty" would compel the President to veto it.[30]

But at the same time that President Jackson was privy to this scheme which aimed at preventing recharter, he was also negotiating again with Secretary Livingston, who was obtaining the

29 Mackenzie, *Butler and Hoyt*, 101; *Van Buren*, 233.
30 Benton I, 235-37; Mackenzie, *Butler and Hoyt*, 101-02.

conditions upon which recharter would be agreeable. The Bank's representative, C. J. Ingersoll, had seen the President 1 February, not yet broaching the question of the Bank but preparing to do so. A few days later, 5 February, S. E. Burrows, a New York speculator, wrote Mr Biddle that he had just spent three days with President Jackson—"dined, supped, and remained as one of his family"—and doubted if he would veto a new charter. The day following, the 6th, Mr Biddle had written both Mr Ingersoll and Horace Binney in Washington, outlining a new approach to the President. The moment, he thought, was a crisis for General Jackson and for the Bank which afforded the Pennsylvania delegation, and eminently Senator Dallas, an opportunity of doing great good. "Let them go forward and mediate between the President and the Bank—make him name his modifications, make the Bank agree to them, make the re-charter an administration measure. You see at a glance all this. Do put them up to it; make Mr Livingston and Mr McLane stir in it. It is a real *coup d'état*. Try if you can not bring it about, without loss of time." The issue he depicted was between Philadelphia and New York, between the political ambitions of Senator Dallas and Mr Van Buren.[31]

Mr Biddle's miscalculation of New York's strength, and his wild surmise that Van Buren could be crowded out by Dallas, may be left aside. But why he should be willing to renew discussion just after affronting the President by laying his petition before Congress is not hard to see; he still preferred recharter as a peaceful, administration measure. He also may have supposed that putting the question before Congress had impelled the President to be reasonable rather than face the dilemma of having either to approve a new charter or to veto it. The President, for the moment, was willing perhaps to have such a thing supposed. Certainly Mr Ingersoll in Washington encountered nothing adverse from him, and he pursued the plan with energy. Mr Biddle, heartened, appreciative, naive, and hortatory, wrote again the week following, 13 February 1832: "You know that I care nothing about the election. I care only for the interests confided to my care, and so far from having the least ill will towards the President, so far from wishing to embarrass his administration, I will do everything consistent with my duty to relieve it from trouble and will go nine tenths of the way to meet him in conciliation. . . . For instance, the President wishes some

[31] Biddle, *Correspondence*, 170-74; Biddle Papers, 3 PLB (1832), 247-50; Biddle Papers 31, Folio 6388.

modifications in the charter. Well, let him take the charter and make any changes he likes, let him write the whole charter with his own hands, I am sure that we would agree to his modifications; and then let him and his friends pass it. It will then be his work. He will then disarm his adversaries, he will gratify his friends, and remove one of the most uncomfortable and vexatious public questions that can be stirred."[32]

This was written in Philadelphia on the 13th. It was three days later, 16 February, in Washington, that Mr Cambreleng said he expected to see the President that night on the proposed Clayton resolution and that, in the same letter, he counseled going softly on the Tibbets banking scheme.* Five days after that, 21 February 1832, Mr Ingersoll was jubilant. Secretary Livingston seemed to think the publication of Tibbets' scheme for a splendid new bank in Wall Street was going to help; he was "anxious to be the author of the President's conversion, who, he says, ought to be fixed if anything can fix him by Tibbets' scheme." The Secretary even hoped to convert Attorney General Taney and Amos Kendall, of whom Mr Ingersoll and Major Lewis also did not despair. But two days later, the 23d, Judge Clayton introduced his resolution for an inquiry and supported it with a long series of charges. The same day Mr Ingersoll reported to Mr Biddle the stipulations upon which the President and all his Cabinet, save Mr Taney alone, agreed. They were, in the main, that the government hold no stock in the Bank, that the President appoint one or more directors at each branch, that the states might tax branches, and that the President appoint annually the president of the Bank from among two or three persons nominated by the directors. Mr Biddle accepted all these stipulations, the last one tacitly. He was delighted. Two years before he would have shot himself. Yet his fears were not wholly quiet. He still doubted the President, too much aware that the Bank had still no unequivocal, direct commitment. "If it

* New York's care to avoid monopoly of the assault on the federal Bank is reflected in Mr Cambreleng's advice to his friends to follow Boston and Portland in asking the federal government for a new banking charter. It is further reflected in a remark two years later, 3 January 1834, by Senator Silas Wright, also of New York, that it was become "too late to fear any effect from the allegation that our state leads" in attacks on the federal Bank in Philadelphia. Mackenzie, *Van Buren*, 101 note; *Butler and Hoyt*, 102, 104-105.

[32] Biddle Papers, 4 PLB (1832), 167 (also in Biddle, *Correspondence*, 182).

pleases," he said, "the next thing is to obtain some overt act, some decisive committal—for the extreme mobility of the principal person in our drama makes me anxious to see him fixed—irretrievably committed."[33]

His anxiety was better grounded than he knew. For in the House, 28 February 1832, Mr Cambreleng, who was there considered the President's spokesman, openly intimated in support of the Clayton resolution for an inquiry that if a new charter were enacted, it would be vetoed. Mr Cambreleng practically hoped one would be enacted, in order that the President "might send it back to us with his veto—an enduring monument of his fame." But the next day Secretary Livingston gave Mr Ingersoll the assurance that the President had nothing to do with the Clayton resolution. "Not at all"; the President wished the business ended. If a bill goes to him that is acceptable, "he will sign it without hesitation." This was a very large "if," and the Secretary came to realize it. Less than a week later, after assuring Mr Ingersoll again that "the President would sign such a bill as you and I have arranged," he immediately added: "I have never heard him say so. But I have good reason to rely on it."[34]

Meanwhile the most interesting incident of the debates on the proposal that the Bank be investigated was the refusal of Erastus Root, the up-state New York Jacksonian, to go along with his fellow New Yorkers. I have quoted already in an earlier chapter General Root's important account of the difficult position in which he was put by his favorable judgment of the first federal Bank. In 1811 he had had his predial constituents to resist; he now in 1832 had Tammany and the Albany Regency. Speaking in the House, 7 March 1832, he urged that the Bank of the United States be continued with the government's interest in it augmented. He refused to be bound by the instructions of the New York legislature to oppose the Bank and declared those instructions to be the will of New York's banks but not of its people. More specifically he ascribed them to the Safety Fund banks, organized and insured under the act of 1829 which Mr Van Buren had sponsored during his brief Governorship. Most of the country banks under this law, having a common interest in politics as in operations, transacted their business with what General Root said might be called the mother

[33] Biddle, *Correspondence*, 183-87.

[34] Congress, *Register of Debates* VIII, Part 2, 1911; Biddle, *Correspondence*, 187, 189.

bank of the system—the Farmers and Mechanics Bank in Albany. They had a deep interest, he said, in the prostration of the federal Bank. It arose first from local competition with the Bank's branch offices in New York City, Utica, and Buffalo, which lent at six per cent, being limited to that rate by the charter, while the Safety Fund banks might legally charge seven per cent. Naturally they resented competition which kept them from charging what the state law allowed. There was a hue and cry, General Root said, to pull down the Bank of the United States and everything else that stood in the way till all the banks in the state should be "collected under one mighty influence," that being the Safety Fund system and the Albany Regency. Most New York City banks antedated the system, and the Regency wanted them to join it, for their capital was more than double that of all the country banks put together. President Jackson's mention of the federal Bank in his 1829 message, General Root said, had presented the desired opportunity. "Seizing upon this expression of the President as one of hostility to the Bank, . . . the city banks were encouraged to enter into the combination and contribute their share to the fund—now hoping and expecting that the Bank of the United States would be put down and that they would have not only the great emporium of commerce but in addition all the deposits of the government and thus become the arbiters of the fiscal affairs of the nation. . . . The immense revenue collected in New York, amounting to about three-quarters of that of the whole nation, must be paid into the state banks. . . . The city of New York would become the money market of the nation." For, he said, "the general place of deposit of the revenues of government must become the headquarters of the money market. . . ." So the people were being told that "a national Bank is a formidable monster capable of doing mischief on a gigantic scale, while the state banks are so many lambs and can hurt nobody." Applications for new charters, Mr Root said, had been made at the rate of one a day in New York during the two months just passed. Mr Tibbets' splendid scheme for a big new bank in New York to replace the aristocratic mammoth in Philadelphia also got some of General Root's sarcasm. "Are gentlemen belonging to different and distant quarters of the Union," he asked, "willing to become fiscal tributaries to the city of New York?"[35]

General Root affirmed his loyalty to President Jackson though refusing to join in the assault on the federal Bank. For several days

[35] Congress, *Register of Debates* VIII, Part 2, 2040-41, 2074-75.

he had the wrath of his colleagues poured on his head, "because he does not swear fealty to the Regency and acknowledge the supremacy of the Safety Fund system of New York." Before the debate ended, Mr Cambreleng had to excommunicate him. Yet what the General said was merely decried by the others, not denied, and he was sanctimoniously left to settle his accounts "with his conscience and his God."[36]

John Taylor of South Carolina, William Findley of Pennsylvania, and Erastus Root of New York were three unconfused agrarians who saw the difference between the federal Bank and the private banks and that the federal Bank's restraints upon bank credit and business expansion were in accord with agrarian principles.* General Root's firmness in the matter is remarkable at a time when in the course of twenty years the more distinguished politicians had vibrated from side to side of the question. In the pleasant simplicities of Delaware and Otsego counties, far from the financial world, and governed by nothing more sophisticated than the intelligent use of his faculties, he had observed the performance of the first federal Bank, the *melée* following its end, and the performance of the second. His conclusions stood.

V

Judge Clayton's resolution was adopted 14 March 1832—not wholly from opposition to the Bank by any means, for the House majority favored the Bank, but because Mr. McDuffie, who had the bill to recharter in charge, wished it deferred and the tariff brought up first. He was a friend to the Bank but a son to South Carolina. So the Bank was thrown to the wolves for a few weeks, in order that the tariff might be considered. The debate on the resolution had mainly concerned the character of the inquiry, which Judge Clayton and Mr Cambreleng contended should be entrusted to the enemies of the Bank. It was silly and useless, they argued, and contrary to parliamentary usage, to have an inquiry conducted by persons who wanted no inquiry made. It was outrageous, the Bank's friends argued, to have an inquiry conducted by persons already committed to the findings to be arrived at. For Judge Clayton, when moving the

---

* John Taylor of South Carolina was not, of course, his more famous contemporary John Taylor of Caroline, who was a Virginian and always vehemently against the federal Bank.

[36] New York *Advertiser*, 11 March 1832; Congress, *Register of Debates* VIII, Part 2, 2036ff, 2069ff, 2113, 2119ff, 2040-41, 2150ff; Mackenzie, *Van Buren*, 234.

resolution for an inquiry, had frankly outlined the charges against the Bank, and these, in fact, reappeared in substance later as the committee's conclusions. Sittings in Philadelphia and Washington lasted about a month, after which the committee hastily produced a majority report damning the Bank as had been proposed. Then came a report from the minority defending it and last of all one supplementary thereto by Mr John Quincy Adams, who was indignant at the unfairness and demagogy of the majority with respect to Nicholas Biddle. "To vindicate the honor of injured worth" was, in Mr. Adams' opinion, "among the first of moral obligations," and he prepared his report accordingly. Mr Biddle's management of the Bank seemed to him "marked with all the character of sound judgment, of liberal spirit, of benevolent feeling, and of irreproachable integrity."[37]

The report of the majority concluded that the investigations, "imperfect as they were, fully justify the committee in saying that the Bank ought not, at present, to be rechartered." It averred that the Bank was not useful and that its management was unintelligent and dishonest. Colonel R. M. Johnson of Kentucky, however, subsequently Vice President of the United States, dissociated himself on the floor of the House from this latter charge, though he had signed the report. "I did not expect," he said, "to see in the affairs of the Bank perfection on the one hand, nor did I expect to find swindling and peculation on the other. I expected to see an institution with great power to do good and to do evil and under the guidance of honorable and upright and wise men, subject to error in the management of its concerns. What I expected to see, I have seen, and no more." And he reported that "as respects the integrity and honor of the president and directors of the Bank," nothing "had transpired to shake my favorable opinion of them." This was in consequence the opinion of the majority of the committee members, as the minority report observed, for the committee had divided four to three and with Colonel Johnson the minority would have been a majority. Mr Cambreleng himself, the last day of February, had disclaimed "all charges of corruption" against the Bank. "The well known honor and integrity of the president of the Bank" were, for him, "sufficient guaranty of the purity of conduct of its officers."[38]

[37] Congress, *Register of Debates* VIII, Part 2, 1875; 22nd Congress, 1st Session, HR 460, pp. 403, 408, 410.
[38] 22nd Congress, 1st Session, HR 460, p. 29; Congress, *Register of Debates* VIII, Part 2, 1907, 2670-71.

A perusal of the majority report must correct any supposition that only in the 20th century have legislative committees devoted their powers to bigotry and demagogy. In the scornful words of John Quincy Adams, "a spirit of predetermined hostility" informed the majority report, "prying for flaws and hunting for exceptions." Its arrogant pages were pervaded from beginning to end with "consciousness of authoritative power," unmingled with courtesy. Batches of questions, about 160 in all, many of them defamatory in their drift, ranging over the entire history of the Bank and the entire monetary field, domestic and international, abstract and particular, were presented to Biddle by the committee, and then published in the report without his answers. The explanation was that he had "not been able, from the press of his other indispensable duties, to answer."[39] The implication was that he had feared or refused to do so. His answers were appended later to the minority report.*

The majority of the committee, satisfied of the two basic evils of the Bank, viz., its unconstitutionality and its antagonism to free enterprise, stopped at nothing in its denigration. As Mr Adams said, they found the Bank's managers wrong whatever they did. "If they enlarge their discounts and accommodations, they supply temptations to over-trading and bring the Bank to the verge of ruin. If they contract their issues, they produce unheard of distress in the trading community." One would suppose from some passages of the report that the management of the Bank was stupid, from others that it was malignly intelligent. The committee considered at length a cock-and-bull story of favors by Mr Biddle to his relatives, and though it formally concluded that the charge, which had been made by Reuben Whitney, was "without foundation," the majority nevertheless detailed the story through forty-four pages and did not mention their having concluded that the charge was groundless. They considered at length an allegation of usury resting on a controverted

---

* The reply to one set of questions is missing, perhaps because the information is included elsewhere in the testimony.

In answer to one of Cambreleng's questions, Biddle observed that "the existence of the fact itself is some evidence of its possibility." According to Hezekiah Niles, there was a toast to Biddle in Washington for fixing "a fool's cap upon the head of New York's commercial representative." Niles XLII (11 August 1832), 423.

[39] 22nd Congress, 1st Session, HR 460, pp. 29, 360, 362, 372, 384, 403.

loan of depreciated state bank notes ten years before, respecting which the Bank had already made restitution and for which the present administration of the Bank was not responsible. These and other matters that had been "subjects of imputation against the Bank," the committee considered and submitted "without expressing any opinion." Instead one was insinuated.[40]

The committee ignored the Bank's quasi-governmental nature, speaking of it as if it were merely a bank like any other and as if it had somehow wormed itself into a parasitical relationship with the government. The Bank knew or it ought to know, it said, that when it received government funds it had to repay them. It said, regardless of the President's own statement to the contrary in his 1829 message, that it could not see that the government required any aid in its fiscal operations or that the economy was affected by them; and in particular that it could not "discover in what manner the operations of commerce could have been disturbed or the value of pecuniary investments have been affected by the payment of the public debt by the government." Nor could it discover that the Bank was of any use to the government. These professions of ignorance were probably those of Judge Clayton, who could make them honestly, as Mr Cambreleng could not. Judge Clayton, who publicly declared the Bank was "broke" because its specie holdings were less than the amount of its notes, was responsible for a similar but more obscure allegation in the report. Mr Cambreleng could not help knowing the allegation was false. The procedure, however, seems to have been for the experts to thrust forward an ignoramus to say with a ring of sincerity the disturbing things which counted most politically. Meanwhile President Jackson kept his personal checking account with the Bank.[41]

In the opinion of Hezekiah Niles, the zeal of the majority recoiled upon them and made their report ridiculous. He said in his *Weekly Register*, 12 May 1832: "We are no partizans of the Bank. We have yielded our constitutional objections . . . but would not have the present Bank rechartered with its present power—not because that we are prepared to make any charge against the Bank of recent abuses of that power but for the reason that the Bank has more power than we would grant to any set of men, unless responsible to

---

[40] 22nd Congress, 1st Session, HR 460, pp. 2, 112-56, 401-02, 433.
[41] 22nd Congress, 1st Session, HR 460, pp. 22-23; Congress, *Register of Debates* viii, Part 2, 1880, 2660; Jackson Papers 81, Folio 15980.

the people, as members of Congress are. But we regard this 'report' as the strangest mixture of *water gruel and vinegar*, the most awkward and clumsy and exaggerated *ex parte* production that we ever read. . . . Never did a man more mistake himself than Mr Clayton, when he thought himself capable of grappling a subject like this; but Mr Cambreleng (who manufactured more than eight millions of tons of coasting vessels for England) is fitted to attempt anything— the other gentleman seems only to have said yes and no."*

VI

A favorite and much cultivated charge of the Jacksonians, which came out in the Clayton report as in most attacks, was that the Bank's branch drafts were illegal and violated the charter. Because the charge was so prominently made and because it touches the main purposes of the Bank so closely, it requires consideration. The branch drafts were obligations issued in the form of circulating notes and in small denominations. Their purpose was to supplement the circulating notes proper. The reason for issuing them was that the charter was interpreted to require that the Bank's notes all be signed by its president and cashier, although this had become impossible. The charter did not make the direct requirement that the notes be so signed, but merely assumed that they would be, the language being descriptive, not prescriptive. Specific requirements were made respecting the issue of notes, but they included none respecting official signatures. The relevant language of the charter ("Paragraph Twelfth of Section 11") was part of the standard verbiage left over from the evolution of negotiable instruments. It had been common in American bank charters ever since Alexander Hamilton's day. Its purpose was to affirm the negotiability of the Bank's obligations, whether issued under seal, which was reserved for obligations of $5,000 or more, or on order of the Bank and signed by its two principal officers. The charter gave the Bank's obligations the same negotiability that was possessed under the law merchant by the obligations of natural persons.

The provision belonged to a period when the corporate form of business was becoming more and more important but had not yet

---

* Mr Niles' reference to Mr Cambreleng's manufacture of British tonnage is not to be taken literally. It alludes sarcastically to an error in some of Mr Cambreleng's statistics. Niles XLII (31 March 1832), 75, 92, 209. Cambreleng was a free trader, Niles a protectionist.

got its legal status clarified and established. The courts, which had been occupied for centuries in evolving principles and procedures appropriate to private property in the form of obligations of natural persons, had now the task of applying those principles and procedures to the obligations of artificial persons. It had also the task of differentiating the responsibilities of these artificial persons—or corporations—from the responsibilities of the natural persons who were their proprietors or their agents. The statute, as drawn by Alexander Hamilton, made the nature of the corporate obligation clear: whether it bore the seal of the Bank or the signature of its officer it was an obligation of the Bank, not of the officer signing it. It was "binding and obligatory" upon the Bank "in like manner and with like force and effect as upon any private person or persons, if issued by him, her, or them, in his, her, or their private capacity . . . ," and it was "assignable and negotiable in like manner as if . . . issued by such private person or persons." That is, if payable to order, the obligations were "assignable by endorsement" and if payable to bearer they were "assignable and negotiable by delivery only." This was the force of the paragraph in which signature was mentioned; there was no requirement of signature and no penalty for the issue of notes without signature. Such a requirement would certainly have seemed otiose, since the Bank would have had its notes signed as a means of self-protection whether required or not.

In 1791 the provision had had only the significance I have indicated, the president and cashier being able to sign easily all the notes required for circulation. But the practice of having all notes signed by those two officers, combined with the incidental assumption in the law that they would be so signed, established in time the loose conclusion that they must be so signed.

Yet the growth of the country, of its business, and of the need of currency in commensurate volume was such that two men could not possibly sign all the notes that were needed. It was scarcely possible to sign enough to replace what were worn out; to have signed all that were required would have compelled the two responsible officers of the Bank to neglect all other duties. At one time Mr Biddle reckoned that 400,000 notes were needed; which if it were possible to scrawl as many as 150 signatures an hour for 10 hours a day would take the entire working time of the two officers for nearly a year. "The almost constant manual labor of signing notes," a committee of Congress had said in 1823, "must too much exhaust the two principal officers of the Bank and in a greater or less degree disqualify them from a due application of their minds to the extensive, critical, and important concerns of the Bank."[42] The Bank of England, according to Mr Biddle, then had ten officers who were authorized to sign notes.*

Between 1818 and 1823 the Bank had asked Congress four times for a suitable amendment to the charter, but the reasonable request was never granted. The refusal arose in part from inertia and in part from the readiness of the Bank's enemies to trammel it all they could. This was directly in the interest of the state banks. The fewer the notes issued by the government Bank, the more the state banks could issue and the less effective currency regulation would become; because the government Bank would have to pay the state bank notes back into circulation instead of replacing them. It was also in the interest of brokers and note-shavers, who throve on an unregulated currency, specializing in the varying values of the notes in circulation and profiting by public ignorance of those values and inability to collect payment on notes of distant banks. The federal Bank's notes and drafts, being universally known and accepted, diminished their business.[43]

Since change had made the language of the charter archaic, it would have been preferable if Congress had altered it to accord with the realities to which it applied. But since Congress would do nothing, the Bank's management did the best it could with the charter as it was. It decided to issue the needed obligations as "drafts," notes not being the only obligations it had authority to issue. The drafts were like cashiers' checks, being drawn by the branch managers on the Bank itself; they were endorsed to bearer, were similar in form to the Bank's statutory notes, and served the purpose of the latter. In effect they made it possible for the branch

---

* The Bank of England, from whose charter Alexander Hamilton had adapted the paragraph under discussion, had had a similar problem. The Bank of England's notes, which in terms of the charter were issued at first only under corporate seal, had been limited to the amount of the Bank's capital; and when that restriction became impracticable with growth in the use of the Bank's notes, the device was resorted to of issuing notes without the seal but signed by Bank officers.

[42] Biddle, *Correspondence*, 38-39; Biddle Papers, 2 PLB (1826), 122-26; Congress, *Annals*, 17th Congress, 2nd Session, 1134.
[43] 22nd Congress, 1st Session, HR 460, pp. 2-4, 48-57.

managers to share the task of signing the necessary instruments. In form and appearance they so closely resembled "notes" that the difference was unapparent—a result which reflected the fact that in practice there was no difference. The one was exactly as good as the other, though the Bank's enemies made it appear that the drafts were inferior—"payable nowhere," as Mr Cambreleng liked to say.

The Bank had advice of the legality of the proposed drafts from Horace Binney, Daniel Webster, and Attorney General William Wirt, whose opinions were subsequently corroborated in the federal courts. In *United States* v. *Shellmire*, 1831, a case which arose from the counterfeiting of a branch draft and in which the question was presented whether the drafts were illegal, the court affirmed their legality under section 18 of the charter, which explicitly contemplated the Bank's issue of "checks or orders" and authorized penalties for counterfeiting them. The court found "no prohibition direct or indirect against issuing this kind of paper . . . or any word or expression by which Congress has excluded it" from the Bank's powers; nor "anything in its nature which would justify such inference." The Bank was "free to contract debts by any other mode than by their promissory note," and no authorization for branch drafts by name was needed. Their issue was "an act indispensable to the transaction" of the Bank's ordinary business. The question if "notes" might be issued without the signatures of the president and cashier was not presented, and no opinion about it was expressed.[44]

This approval by the court made the drafts no more tolerable to the Bank's enemies, however. Senator Thomas Hart Benton even denied the validity of the court decision. His eloquence was moving: "It is this illegal, irresponsible currency which has enabled the Bank to fill the Union with debtors in chains, who scream incessantly for the life and glory of their Juggernaut and attack with the fury of wild beasts every public man who will not square his public conduct by the devouring miseries of their own private condition and the remorseless cravings of their insatiate idol." Even if things had been as bad as this, the branch drafts could not have been the cause. In 1832, about the time Senator Benton's ears were ringing with the

---

[44] 22nd Congress, 1st Session, SD 78; *United States* v. *Shellmire*, 1 Baldwin 370; *United States* v. *Shellmire*, 27 Fed. Cas. No. 16,271, pp. 1052-53 (ED, Pa. 1831); Congress, *Register of Debates* VIII, Part 1, 139.

screams of the Bank's victims, the drafts were less than a quarter of its circulating liabilities. Their use lay in providing bills of small denomination for the public, not in providing the Bank its earning assets. Their issue was creditable to the management of the Bank and an intelligent implementation of the law establishing it. They made the law work as it was intended to work. The Bank's enemies would have made the law stand in the way of its own purpose, which if it could be done was the next best thing to repealing it. For it is to be emphasized that there was no intrinsic virtue whatsoever ascribed to the so-called requirement of the president's and cashier's signatures. Other official signatures would have done as well. The refusal of Congress to change the presumed requirement implied no merit in the requirement. The only reason for seeking to limit the Bank's issues to notes signed by the president and cashier was that it would impede the Bank's work greatly enough to frustrate the main purposes of its existence.

Professor Catterall, in his monograph on the Bank, disposed of the branch draft arguments of Colonel Benton, and also of Professor Sumner, whose understanding of the banking function was unfortunately less impressive than his distinction in other fields would lead one to expect. But since Professor Catterall's day, strictures on the drafts by Chief Justice Taney have come to light. They appear in manuscript form among the Taney papers in the Library of Congress. The document embodies a retrospective account of the Jacksonian conflict with the Bank written by the Chief Justice in 1849, never completed apparently and never published save for representative excerpts quoted by Professor Carl B. Swisher in his life of Taney. In it the issuance of the branch drafts is unequivocally condemned as a palpable evasion of the statute, whereby the Bank contrived to increase its power over the circulating medium and over the state banks. "The Bank itself," the Chief Justice said, as if the branch offices were not integral parts of the corporation, "was not a party" to the drafts "and neither drew, nor accepted, nor promised to pay them." Yet the Bank "had influence enough to obtain an order from the Treasury Department directing them to be received in all cases as money in payment for government dues. . . . And it is no small proof of the power which the Bank had acquired that it was able to circulate as money these issues, obviously in fraud of the law to which it owed its existence and for the payment of which it was difficult to say who was responsible or where the holder had a right to apply."[45]

The Chief Justice's implication that "the Bank itself," "the corporation," existed only in Philadelphia and that the branches were not indissoluble parts of it but distinct entities for which it was doubtfully responsible in law, is odd, to put it politely. The drafts were bills obligatory of the Bank, and it is hard to believe that had the question come before the Chief Justice himself in a suit at law, he would have hesitated one little moment to find the Bank liable. As it was, he ignored the absence from the charter of any explicit requirement of the president's and cashier's signatures; he ignored the context, derivation, and substance of what was construed as such requirement; he ignored the provision of the charter under authority of which the drafts were issued; he ignored the competent legal opinion obtained by the Bank respecting the drafts; he ignored the court decision affirming their legality; and he ascribed approval of the procedure by Treasury Department officials not to their judgment and their heed of what he passed over but to the corrupting influence of the Bank. He did not simply call the drafts illegal and disagree with the authorities who had approved them; he called their issue "obviously in fraud of the law," though undertaken on legal advice as good as his own and approved by a court from whose decision no appeal had been made. As it happens, incidentally, issuance of the drafts had first been proposed by John Forsyth, also a lawyer, who was later Secretary of State in President Jackson's cabinet when Mr Taney was Secretary of the Treasury.

Since I think Mr Taney's conduct toward the Bank fanatic and deserving little respect, it is the more needful that I stress the informal character of the remarks which occasion my criticism. The document in which they appear embodies not a legal opinion but a reminiscence. According to Professor Swisher, "it never reached the stage of a polished draft."[46] Accordingly it need not be taken very seriously in its bearing on either the Chief Justice's legal ability or the Bank's misconduct; though one would scarcely have supposed that so much which was outstanding and essential would be left out of account in even a rough draft of a statement about events in which one had had so important a part, prepared only some fifteen

[45] Taney Papers, *Bank War* ms, 23-24 (also in Swisher, 170-71).
[46] Swisher, 165-72, 462-63.

years after the events occurred, by one who was still to preside over the Supreme Court for many years with unimpaired mentality.*

But despite Mr Chief Justice Taney's great merits as a witness, I should like to turn from his testimony to that of Albert Gallatin, never a lawyer or jurist, but a Jeffersonian, a scholar, diplomat, financier, statesman, and no less interested in banking than Mr Taney himself. "Five dollar drafts," he wrote in 1831, "drawn by the branches of the Bank of the United States on the Bank, circulate at this moment in common with the usual five dollar notes. Similar drafts, varying in amount to suit the convenience of purchasers, are daily drawn by the Bank on its offices, and by those offices on each other, or on the Bank. . . . The holders of those bills have the same recourse against the Bank as the holders of bank notes. Those bills are of the same character, depend on the same security, and in case of failure would share the same fate with bank notes."[47]

The Bank's issue of the drafts, appraised as a practical matter, makes it clear that an evolution was already under way by which the Bank of the United States would become the sole bank of issue, as the Bank of England was soon to be and as the Federal Reserve Banks and the Bank of Canada have since become. Had the federal Bank survived, the state banks would have been impelled the sooner to become banks of deposit only—which they now are—and which the orthodox hard-money Jacksonians, including Andrew Jackson himself, were always demanding that they be. The Bank of the United States would have retired gradually from major competition with the private banks to occupy precisely the place in the economy that the Bank of England, the Bank of Canada, and the Federal Reserve Banks now do, except that its stock would probably have remained in the private investment market. It was already the principal repository of bank reserves and the readiest source of additional reserves, which it had always furnished the state banks by refraining from demands upon their specie and which it was beginning to furnish by outright lending. An arbitrary limit upon the Bank's power to provide a circulating medium, which the Jacksonians

---

* I share Dr Fritz Redlich's regret that Professor Swisher, the general tone of whose biography of Taney I admire, fails to see "Taney's glaringly incorrect factual statements, for instance, about branch drafts or the policy of the Bank. . . ." Redlich, 290, note 84.

[47] Gallatin III, 265.

tried to set by finding the branch drafts illegal, would have impeded the Bank's fulfillment of its original purpose and the normal evolution of the banking system as a whole. When the Bank surmounted the impediment, the Jacksonians set down its success among its major crimes.[48]

There was at this time in Illinois a young man—Abraham Lincoln—who was to become an active Whig opponent of the Jacksonians. Speaking in Springfield in 1839, when he could himself recall what seemed to him the prosperous conditions prevailing prior to the war on the Bank, he said his party did not pretend that the United States Bank could have established and maintained a sound and uniform currency "in *spite* of" the government in Washington; "but," he said, "we do say that it has established and maintained such a currency and can do so again by the *aid* of that government; and we further say that no duty is more imperative on that government than the duty it owes the people of furnishing them a sound and uniform currency." He was to say practically the same again in 1863 when as President of the United States he urged adoption by Congress of the national bank act as a measure necessary in defense of the Union. But in 1832 the hour was not yet his; it was Andrew Jackson's.[49]

[48] Biddle, *Correspondence*, 228.
[49] *Collected Works of Abraham Lincoln*, Roy P. Basler, editor, I, 164, 210, 226.

CHAPTER 14

The Federal Bank Destroyed

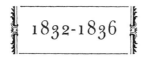

1832-1836

I. Veto of the new charter — II. Impairment of the Bank's condition — III. Removal of the government funds — IV. Official reasons for the removal — V. Consequences of the removal — VI. Contemporary comment — VII. Significance of the federal Bank's destruction — VIII. Contrast with the Bank of England

I

THE tariff and the Clayton report out of the way, Congress passed the new charter early in July 1832. The President, 10 July, vetoed it.

The message accompanying the veto is a famous state paper. It is legalistic, demagogic, and full of sham. Its economic reasoning was said by Professor Catterall, over fifty years ago, to be beneath contempt. Its level is now no higher. The message was prepared by Amos Kendall, who made the first draft, and by Roger Taney, who put it in final form, with the assistance of the President's secretary, Andrew Donelson. Taney wrote later: "I passed three days in this employment, the President frequently coming in, listening to the reading of different portions of it from time to time as it was drawn up and to the observations and suggestions of Mr Donelson and myself, and giving his own directions as to what should be inserted or omitted." This procedure doubtless produced the conflicts and inconsistencies in the message, Taney from his long interest in banks having very different ideas from Jackson's on the subject. The part of the message which dealt with the constitutionality of the Bank reaffirmed the Jacksonian tenderness for states' rights and anxiety at the aggrandizement of federal powers. The part which dealt with economic matters was an unctuous mixture of agrarianism and *laisser faire*. The message asserted that the federal government's "true strength lies in leaving individuals and states as much as possible to themselves." It conformed to Amos Kendall's axiom that the world is governed too much. It ignored the public nature of the

Bank and repudiated its regulatory responsibilities: all that monetary regulation required was a mint and an occasional act of Congress. The message rested heavily on an identification of the Bank with the rich, by whom it was used to oppress the poor.[1]

"It is to be regretted that the rich and powerful too often bend the acts of government to their selfish purposes," the President said. "Many of our rich men have not been content with equal protection and equal benefits but have besought us to make them richer by act of Congress." The government should not be prostituted "to the advancement of the few at the expense of the many." The charter was objectionable not only because it favored the rich but also because it stood in the way of the better proposition offered by citizens "whose aggregate wealth is believed to be equal to all the private stock in the existing bank." The question, apparently, was not one of wealth but of whose wealth. That a bank "competent to all the duties which may be required by the government" might be so organized as to avoid constitutional objections, the President did "not entertain a doubt"; and had he been called on to furnish a better project, "the duty would have been cheerfully performed." This implies that he had to be called on—though he himself had raised the issue and it had been a burning one for many months. The President's correspondence indicates that he had no project of his own; and of those advertised by Jacksonian politicians in Boston and New York, he had condemned none, and one he mentioned with favor in the veto message.

It is typical of the legalistic bias of the message that the alleged enrichment of the rich was ascribed wholly to the value of the charter and not at all to the Bank's operations. There would be a premium on the shares of stock, and this premium would in some metaphysical fashion be money transferred by act of Congress to rich men in Philadelphia from poor men everywhere else. "The powers, privileges, and favors bestowed" upon the Bank, "by increasing the value of the stock far above its par value operated as a gratuity of many millions to the stockholders." This "gratuity," "present," "bounty," or other equivalent comes up paragraph after paragraph. Presumably the stock of a Jacksonian bank would not rise to a premium. "It appears that more than a fourth part of the stock is held by foreigners and the residue is held by a few hundred

[1] Taney Papers, *Bank War* MS, 126 (also in Swisher, 194); Richardson III, 1139, 1153.

of our own citizens, chiefly of the richest class"—and it was to them that the charter would "make a present of some millions of dollars." That a fifth of the shares were owned by the United States government was not mentioned.

It was frequently implied in the message that foreign investments in America were objectionable. The Jacksonians, however, did not discourage foreign borrowing as a matter of general policy. With the possible exception of President Jackson himself, they knew as well as any one that a new country eagerly bent on a rapid exploitation of its resources procures abroad all the capital it can. Their objecting to the Bank's foreign shareholders could only have been intended to impress the ignorant, who were numerous. To this end, the message made its way solemnly into the absurd. If the Bank came to be mainly owned abroad, it was said, and if the owners were of a country with which war arose, what would be the condition of the United States? "Of the course which would be pursued by a bank almost wholly owned by the subjects of a foreign power and managed by those whose interests if not affections would run in the same direction there can be no doubt. . . . Controlling our currency, receiving our public moneys, and holding thousands of our citizens in dependence, it would be more formidable and dangerous than the naval and military power of the enemy." The Bank, that is, though situated across the ocean from its "owners" and in the jurisdiction of a government possessing police powers of its own, was pictured as able nevertheless to defy that government. Yet it was recognized that the charter denied foreign shareholders any part in control of the Bank; for paragraphs earlier in the message, the argument had been that since foreign shareholders had no vote, any increase in their holdings would have the effect of throwing control of the Bank into the laps of a diminishing proportion of domestic shareholders. The message had things both ways. The foreign stockholders were on the one hand a menace because they might control the Bank; they were also a menace because they could not.

The professed belief of President Jackson was that banking created fictitious capital in the place of specie; yet the President was made to contend that foreign capital was not only dangerous but superfluous. For domestic capital was "so abundant . . . that competition in subscribing for the stock of local banks has recently led almost to riots." Indeed, he declared, "subscriptions for $200,-000,000 could be readily obtained." He was doubtless right; but they could be obtained only in the fictitious capital that in other paragraphs incensed him. By the hard-money standards he really cherished, not one-tenth of $200,000,000 existed in the country altogether. But this fact did not impress the legalistic Mr Taney, nor, through the veil of Mr Taney's cant, did it impress the General.

There was the same casuistry in identifying the Bank with the rich as with foreigners. Of its total capital of $35,000,000, the government owned $7,000,000 and foreign shareholders $8,000,000, which left $20,000,000 to be owned by Americans. Though a substantial part of this was held by stockholders in Philadelphia, the shares were widely distributed and actively traded. The stockholders at any given moment, including the permanent and impermanent, represented a great deal of wealth but by no means *the* wealth or *the* rich. There were many wealthy men who owned little or none. Relatively little was owned in New York, though by now there was probably more wealth there than in Philadelphia. Prime, Ward, and King, the wealthiest firm in New York or the whole country, owned none. The attack on the Bank was not an attack on the rich men of the country but on some rich men and in the interest of some other rich men. These were Mr Taney's "poor and oppressed."[2]

David Henshaw, banker and promoter, was one of the most influential of these poor and oppressed Jacksonians. A year before the veto, in his *Remarks upon the Bank of the United States*, he had confuted Mr Gallatin's argument that the Constitution vested in Congress exclusively the control over the monetary system and that the federal Bank was established and operated in implementation of that power. He denounced the federal Bank's "right to destroy the state banks," which he found implied in Mr Gallatin's thesis. He decried "this stupendous power claimed for Congress—a power to destroy the main branch of the great credit system of the country— that system which to the trading world is more valuable than the water loom to the manufacturer or the steam engine to the navigator." As things were, he said, "The trading community who deal in foreign commerce and in fact all borrowers at home thus stand at the mercy of a corporation of monied monopolists, an oligarchy of Shylocks, who would desolate a whole state to add a farthing to their gains." And in a contention which re-appeared in the President's veto message, he wrote: "Even if it be expedient to grant a

---

[2] Baring Papers, OC, Prime, Ward, and King to Baring Brothers, 7 December 1832.

bank upon the same plan, it ought not to be exclusively to the present stockholders. . . . The whole community should be offered the opportunity to have an interest in the institution on equal terms." He illustrated his argument with the impudent supposition that the same men had always owned the Bank, and that if they had got its stock when they were twenty-one, they were now forty-one and had had it long enough. He advocated the President's suggestion of a bank founded on the credit of the government. The President's plan, he said, "strikes at the root of the monied influence" and would "transfer the immense profits resulting from the bank monopoly, from the monied aristocracy into the public coffers." Though the proposed bank would have no private capital, Henshaw evidently hoped to have a say in its management and to be a borrower from it.* Later he wants a $50,000,000 bank with half the stock owned privately; and this may be the project mentioned favorably by Jackson in the veto message. Both Jackson and Taney seem to have been impressed by his ideas, among which were the following: "The Nation therefore owes a new debt of gratitude to its venerable Head for bringing this subject to its notice thus early, thus fearlessly and directly. It has called down upon him the vindictive hatred of a **MONIED OLIGARCHY**; but the people will sustain him. And if in his second official term he can exterminate this aristocratic monster—this bank hydra—and rear upon its ruins a people's bank, an institution of which the people can reap the profits, . . . they will give greater lustre to his character as a statesman than the battle of New Orleans to his fame as a warrior."[3]

The veto message also gives echoes of a South Carolina publication of the year before, 1831—viz., the report of the president of the Bank of the State of South Carolina to the legislature—though the echoes do not suggest direct borrowing so much as common draughts from the ever-living fountains of Jacksonian cant. The South Carolinian bank president says that if the Bank of the United States were "purely a national institution—if the profits of it went

---

* Banks in Boston, he says, "are generally under the direction of active young business men who have themselves but a small pecuniary interest in the banks they manage. . . . They are generally money borrowers and are compensated for managing the affairs of the bank in the facilities afforded them in their mercantile pursuits by loans from the banks they manage." He was an active young business man of forty himself and might see much to gain in helping run Jackson's bank. Henshaw, 42-43, 44-45.

[3] Redlich, 176-77; Henshaw, 18, 33, 36, 46-47.

into the coffers of the general government," patriotism might induce the state banks to submit. "But when it is recollected that it is in fact the establishment of a *monied Aristocracy*; that a few individuals reap the greater part of the profit and direct its operation; that they can and do control the money concerns of the country and the acts of all who are engaged in them; it should excite the indignation of every genuine lover of liberty and call forth the united opposition of the people of the different states." About the same time the Comptroller General of South Carolina also attacked the federal Bank: "The supposition that this institution is useful because it keeps all other banks in check by controlling their issues and thereby preserving a sound currency, concedes at once its absolute power. . . . It possesses the power of destroying the state banks, without regard to their solvency."[4]

The veto message was prodigiously popular. Its critics replied to it feebly. They could not reply effectively because they could get down to no fundamental disagreement with the materialistic, *laissez nous faire*, everybody-get-rich philosophy of the message. The purposes and services of the Bank were forgotten even by its friends in a childish outburst of resentment at Jackson's interference. Henry Clay and Daniel Webster had never appreciated or understood the Bank except as a source of fees or as a fine, big bone to fight the other party over; and for them the issue now was simply one between ins and outs. Nicholas Biddle did not forget the Bank's purposes and services, but he did forget that they alone were the grounds for a defense of the Bank—whether successful or not. He, with the others, in effect, let the administration choose grounds and procedures that gave Andrew Jackson every advantage in combat. They took the defensive on his terms. "It is difficult," said the Washington *Globe*, 12 July 1832, "to describe in adequate language the sublimity of the moral spectacle now presented to the American people in the person of Andrew Jackson." The General's political opponents were so sodden in the same earthy clap-trap as the Jacksonians themselves that they could not give the American people a penetrating view of the "moral spectacle" presented to them. But a quiet gentleman in Concord, Ralph Waldo Emerson, saw the matter more clearly. "We shall all feel dirty," he feared, "if Jackson is re-elected."[5]

[4] South Carolina Legislature, 413-14, 682 (italics in the original); *Southern Review*, November 1831, p. 14.
[5] Emerson II, 528.

II

The President himself had raised the issue of continuing the Bank of the United States and then, ruminating on the 1832 elections, he had evidently preferred to postpone it. But his enemies had not. They had thrust the issue into the foreground—and wholly to his advantage, as it turned out; for the assault on the Bank, though undertaken in unpromising circumstances, proved to be excellent politics. Henry Clay was defeated resoundingly and with him the Bank. President Jackson could have longed for no greater victory.

The Bank's management never recovered its poise and judgment after being distracted from internal affairs to politics. This was the time, Mr Gallatin said, when it ceased to be an effective regulator of the currency. He, Isaac Bronson, Nathan Appleton, and other business conservatives who had supported it, began now to fall away—not in the least attracted by the Jacksonians but repelled by Nicholas Biddle's bad judgment. The Bank's condition was sometimes very good, as Thomas Wren Ward reported to the Barings in 1833, and sometimes not so good. At the time the Clayton inquiry was proceeding, Biddle had learned that in three months the government would pay off $6,500,000 of bonds. The notice was unaccountably short, and the Bank was unprepared. Its portfolio was full, its circulation was large, its reserves were low—about twenty-two per cent. Mr Biddle was forced to take measures and endure embarrassments that were unbecoming in a central banker.* He first failed to arrange a solution at home and then had to send an agent to London, a large portion of the bonds being held abroad, to negotiate one with the Barings. The arrangements made there turned out to contravene the charter and had to be disavowed. The burden was assumed by the Barings, who borrowed to see things through, but was lightened by the Bank's own tardy exertions and particularly by its facilitating a $7,000,000 loan which the Barings had undertaken for the Union Bank of Louisiana.[6]

* Professor Hidy, who is very informative in his *House of Baring* about dealings with the Bank of the United States, covers in pages 117 to 120 the episode of the bonds (the three per cents) to be retired in 1832. Professor Catterall (pp. 268-73) and Professor Walter B. Smith (pp. 157-59) recount the episode from the viewpoint of the Bank.

[6] Catterall, 145-47; Congress, *Register of Debates* x, Part 2, 2380-81; Hidy, 117-20; W. B. Smith, 157-59.

Nicholas Biddle's responsibility for such things is extenuated by the unrelenting harassment to which he was subjected by the Jacksonians. The government owned a fifth of the Bank's capital, but the administration was quite uninhibited by this fact from doing all it could to impair the value of the stock. The government directors, chosen by the President, used their powers to obtain information to be handed to the Bank's enemies, with the natural result that the Bank's management instead of confiding in the board of directors, concealed all it could from them. The task of managing so extensive and important an institution was exacting at the best, and it could not be supposed that it would be wisely discharged by men feverish with combat. The blame deserved by Nicholas Biddle is less for the errors and oversights from which the Bank suffered in these circumstances than for his persistence in a situation where such things were inevitable. So long as he was confronting solely economic problems and could deal with them objectively, he had succeeded. But his success had confronted him with a political problem, because business enterprise would not brook his control of bank credit and resorted to political means of frustrating him. When confronted with the political problem, he went to pieces.

III

President Jackson, gratified by the immense popular support which the 1832 election gave the course he had taken, did not purpose letting the hydra spend its four final years fading away in peace. In his annual message to Congress, about a month after the election, he recommended sale of the government's stock in the Bank and inquiry by Congress whether the government's deposits should not be removed from it. The House of Representatives rejected both suggestions. The Treasury requested a report on the deposits from Henry Toland, a Democrat and former director of the Bank, and was advised by him that they might be left safely where they were. Despite what was preparing in Washington, the federal Bank's stock was a market favorite, and there was comment in the press that speculators who had been selling it short, "on the strength of Mr Cambreleng's operations in Washington and Wall Street," would wish they had been bulls instead of bears.[7]

The President and his advisers determined that the deposits should not be left where they were. But the state banks, though

7 W. B. Smith, 170.

they still wanted the deposits as much as ever, grew suddenly shy of Andrew Jackson with the bit in his teeth and were afraid to touch them. In any event the terms of transfer had to be attractive to the banks and a disruption of the money market had to be avoided. J. A. Hamilton had taken up the matter in New York at President Jackson's request but had got nowhere, partly because he lacked confidence in the arrangements he was supposed to make and partly because the banks themselves had got alarmed. Hamilton reported that they were adverse, as the two leading bankers in New York, Mr Gallatin and Mr Bronson, certainly were. There was some doubt if the administration could make the change legally without the approval of Congress; and more doubt if an arrangement effected hastily under no pressure of need could be wise. Even if the federal Bank gave up submissively, the transaction would be difficult because as its deposit liabilities shrank it would have to reduce its assets—that is, it would have to make its debtors pay their loans. That would throw a demand for credit onto the private banks. Both enemies and friends knew this was inevitable, and the enemies expected the Bank to make things as bad as possible. The more sagacious, though still in favor of robbing the victim, thought that instead of leaving him alive and vengeful it would be better to let him die first and then strip the corpse in security. Mr Van Buren might have preferred that patient, sensible course, but it was not the way Andrew Jackson liked to do things; nor did it suit Taney, Kendall, and Henshaw.[8]

But obstacles to the President's purpose also arose in his Cabinet. The charter authorized the Secretary of the Treasury to remove the deposits from the Bank, though if he did so, he must tell Congress why. Secretary McLane was opposed to removing them. No predecessor of his had ever done so, in his own judgment there was no good reason for their removal, and Congress was opposed to its being done. This difficulty was got around by another Cabinet shift, which made Mr McLane Secretary of State and William J. Duane his successor at the Treasury. Mr Duane was one of Philadelphia's leading lawyers, counsel for Stephen Girard, and son of the most violent journalistic enemy of the old Bank.* His appointment seems

---

* One recalls that Mr Duane's father, William Duane, editor of the *Aurora*, had been both a prominent and influential enemy of the earlier Bank of the United States and a particular friend of the Philadelphia Bank, chartered by the state. Wainwright, 13, 14.

[8] Benton I, 385; J. A. Hamilton, *Reminiscences*, 253-58.

to have been extraordinarily casual, little being known of him by the people in Washington or by him of them. No promise that he would order the deposits removed was asked and no expectation that he would do so was mentioned. The day he took office in Washington, he was called on by Reuben M. Whitney, who being now employed at the Treasury was one of his subordinates, and apprised for the first time that the President intended removal of the deposits. "On the next evening (Sunday)," Mr Duane said, "Mr Whitney again called on me in company with a stranger whom he introduced as Mr Amos Kendall, a gentleman in the President's confidence, who would give me any further explanations that I might desire as to what was meditated in relation to the United States Bank." Mortified at this way of doing things, Amos Kendall being another of his subordinates, Duane refused to discuss the subject with them. They in turn were annoyed with him. So was General Jackson, when he had to confirm what Whitney and Kendall had said and when he learned that Duane was not minded to do what his subordinates at the Treasury had told him he was expected to do. After some firm argument, however, Duane told the President he would resign if in the end he found himself still unable to comply with the President's wishes. He clearly expected the President to bring up the question again.[9]

Meanwhile Amos Kendall, Roger Taney, and the President, dissatisfied with the approach that Colonel Hamilton had made to the state banks, arranged something better. They had the assistance of Thomas Ellicott, president of the Union Bank of Baltimore, in which Attorney General Taney was a stockholder. Ellicott in April 1833 found that Taney and Kendall "entertained some fears" lest trouble arise from shifting the federal funds to the private banks and assured them that he apprehended no embarrassment to either the Treasury or the public. He also sent President Jackson encouraging suggestions and advice on the proposed change and offered to help the administration "in the adjustment of these regulations and execution of any plan" that might be undertaken. It was arranged that Kendall call on the banks in Baltimore, Philadelphia, New York, and Boston to determine through interviews what prospects there were of their accepting the government funds. Secretary Duane was not informed of the course that was being arranged but was asked by the President to prepare instructions for such an

---

[9] Parton, *Jackson* III, 512-13; Kendall, *Autobiography*, 377; Niles XLV (1833), 237ff.

errand. He did so and submitted them to the President, who sent them to Kendall—the Secretary's subordinate—who told the President they were unsatisfactory. The President told him to change them, which he did, and upon their return to him sent them to the Secretary, who accepted the changes as the President's and sent them to Kendall. So the latter set out, self-instructed, in July 1833. He had already had some experience in missions apparently, for three months before, Thomas Ellicott had written him as follows from Baltimore: "I now send to thee a letter to Lynde Catlin, Esq., President of the Merchants Bank of New York, which thee will either use or not as thee may find expedient when thee gets there. He is a gentleman with a clear head and will understand the whole subject at once, but there may be reasons which I am not apprised of, why he ought not to be conferred with on the subject. The Vice President, I presume, knows well the characters and dispositions of the different banks and their officers in New York and can indicate those which will be most likely to meet in a satisfactory way the wishes of the Government." It may be supposed from this that the modest Mr Van Buren was not out of touch with what was going on.[10]

Amos Kendall's first object was simply to learn what banks would signify that "they were desirous of performing the service now rendered by the United States Bank to the government, should it be deemed necessary or expedient to employ another agent." Those that signified an interest, which were most of the banks in Baltimore, Philadelphia, and New York, but only two of the thirty in Boston, were then informed of the conditions on which it was proposed that the government's business be transferred to them. In New York it was Mr Kendall's odd experience to find that the two leading Jacksonian banks still hung back while the leading bank of the opposition was acquiescent. The latter was the Bank of America, which had originated in the New York office of the old Bank of the United States in 1811 and "every director" of which "was a Whig and opposed to General Jackson's administration." The other two were the Mechanics Bank and the Manhattan, a majority of whose boards "were Jackson men," Kendall said. "Yet the Bank of America was foremost in yielding its support to the proposed measure of the government. The president, George Newbold, was a gentleman of comprehensive views, who did not accept the dogma of his

[10] Taney Papers, Ellicott to the President, 6 April 1833; Ellicott to Kendall, 13 April 1833.

party that a national bank was a necessary financial agent of the government; and he fully appreciated the wrong done to New York in depriving her of her natural advantages by the legislation of Congress, which undertook to make Philadelphia the financial centre of the Union." Mr Newbold also saw profits in the proposed arrangement. "Little difficulty, therefore, was experienced in making acceptable terms with his bank." Then the two Jacksonian banks, on further consideration, decided also to accept the proposed arrangements. Stopping in Philadelphia and Baltimore again, Kendall returned to Washington, having concluded tentative agreements and "accomplished his object in a most satisfactory manner."[11]

It is clear that Amos Kendall knew how to talk to the bankers and gain their confidence. Their shyness was overcome, and as the conviction spread that the President was determined to distribute the deposits, every one wished to get his share. It was Jabez Hammond's observation, with New York particularly in mind, that "the local state banks, anxious to enjoy the golden harvest growing out of the use of the national deposits, could not wait patiently the death of their great rival for the fruition of their hopes, but availed themselves of the indignant feelings of General Jackson towards Mr Biddle and the managers of the national Bank, and goaded him on forthwith to cause a transfer of the Treasury funds from that Bank to their own vaults. Their zeal was sharpened from the knowledge which the shrewd and keen-sighted directors of these institutions possessed of the surplus revenue which they foresaw was soon to accumulate in the Treasury and which, as they imagined, would for an indefinite period remain in the vaults of the banks and be subject to their use." It was very evident to New Yorkers in general, Mr Hammond said, that transfer of the revenues "to our own banks would greatly increase the wealth of our own citizens and would facilitate bank accommodations to business men and speculators." There were fresh stories of a big new Jacksonian Bank in Wall Street with as much as $50,000,000 of capital; and T. W. Ward mentioned anonymously a banker, "shrewd and influential and cunning," who in his opinion "had more to do with removing the deposits and in the hostility to the Bank in this city than any other person."[12]

[11] Kendall, *Autobiography*, 378-81.
[12] Jabez Hammond II, 434-35; *United States Telegraph*, Washington, 13 August 1833; Baring Papers, OC, T. W. Ward to Baring Brothers, 31 December 1833.

The President was gratified by the results of Mr Kendall's effective presentation, and learning that "the state banks were not only not afraid" but would give the government "the same services on substantially the same terms as the Bank of the United States," he "determined that the change should be made before Congress met." Since Congress would not approve, it should not be consulted. He had a paper prepared by Mr Taney in which he stated his intention to have the deposits removed, taking the responsibility on himself, and his reasons for the action. This he read to his Cabinet and then published in the *Globe*, 20 September 1833. The Cabinet was again divided, and Secretary Duane was incensed. He declared that the President had violated their understanding by not discussing the matter with him again before coming to a decision and that now he would neither order the deposits removed nor resign. The President gave him two days to think things over and then dismissed him without further frittering. The Jacksonians thought Duane's conduct contemptible and incomprehensible. Why should a man interpose with his "broken pledges to protect a corrupt institution against the honest old patriot whose only object was to rescue his country from its demoralizing influences?" Why indeed, if those were the facts?[13]

Mr Duane's own account of this episode indicates that the President was guided wholly by his more sycophantic advisers, Taney, Kendall, and Whitney, and that he himself, the Secretary of the Treasury, was treated by his own subordinates, with the President's concurrence, as if he were a mere dummy to be pushed into position and manipulated as they chose. Mr Duane was indeed much more consistent than President Jackson, for being opposed to all banks, as the President also professed to be, he could not subscribe to a preference for the great mass of them—over which the government had no control—as against the one institution over which it had control. "I refuse to carry your directions into effect," he wrote the President, ". . . not because I desire to favor the Bank of the United States, to which I have been, am, and always shall be opposed," but for reasons of which the following are the more significant: The House of Representatives had "pronounced the public money in the Bank of the United States safe." If the Bank had "abused or perverted its powers, the judiciary are able and willing to punish." He believed that "a change to local and irresponsible banks will tend

---

[13] Kendall, *Autobiography*, 384-86; Parton, *Jackson* III, 514ff.

to shake public confidence and promote doubt and mischief in the operations of society." And he said that it was "not prudent to confide, in the crude way proposed by your agent, in local banks when on an average of all the banks dependent in great degree upon each other, one dollar in silver can not be paid for six dollars of the paper in circulation."* This last was intelligent criticism of the contemporary banking situation. The condition it described was the one any real agrarian should have been concerned about. It had aroused Thomas Jefferson over forty years earlier when the ratio was merely one to one and a half. Mr Duane's criticism touched the mounting weakness that was to bring disaster in less than four years and that Mr Biddle, for all his intelligence, seems not to have seen, viz., the excessive expansion of bank credit, which from nothing forty years before had swollen to six-fold counting circulation alone, and to twelve-fold counting deposit liabilities also—the latter being almost, if not quite, the equal of the former. This is twice the ratio of liabilities to reserves long maintained by the American banking system at the middle of the twentieth century. However angry and obstinate Mr Duane may have been, the reasons he gave for his refusal were themselves sound and sufficient. It is very likely that he was indebted for some of them to his fellow townsman and Girard trustee, Nicholas Biddle.[14]

Removal of the public funds would force the Bank of the United States to reduce her assets commensurately with what she owed the government; and to reduce her assets she would have to refuse loans and collect some already made. Besides the loss of the government balances, she had to expect some withdrawals by individual depositors alarmed by her situation. The contraction of credit required by the removal could not occur without pain and inconvenience, as if nothing had happened. The funds formerly in the federal Bank would thenceforth be in state banks, but it did not follow that credit would be available exactly as before. Trouble was

* Horace Binney, a few months later, made a similar estimate. "We have from 80 to 100 millions of bank notes with a metallic circulation . . . not greater perhaps than as 1 to 7. We have, it may be, 140 to 150 millions of bank notes and bank deposits . . . with about the same proportion of specie in the banks to sustain it." In England, he said, specie was one-half, in France nine-tenths. Congress, *Register of Debates* x, Part 2, p. 2321, 7 January 1834.

[14] Niles xlv (1833), 237; Biddle, *Correspondence*, 212, 215; Leonard D. White, 33-38.

in the circumstances inevitable; and Mr Biddle very naturally refused to "venture on the Quixotism of preventing all inconveniences to the public for the measures intended to destroy" the Bank. In August 1833, when Amos Kendall was arranging with the metropolitan banks to take over the government balances, the Bank began to prepare itself for the change. It first took pains to avoid increasing its discounts, and it shortened maturities.[15]

It was now September 1833. In Mr Duane's place at the head of the Treasury, the President installed his faithful Attorney General, Roger B. Taney. Three days later, 26 September, the new Secretary announced that beginning the first of October, deposits to the credit of the government would no longer be made in the Bank of the United States but in the following private banks: the Girard in Philadelphia; the Commonwealth and the Merchants in Boston; the Bank of the Manhattan Company, the Mechanics, and the Bank of America in New York; and the Union Bank of Maryland in Baltimore. All seven selected banks were Jacksonian, save only the Bank of America in New York.* One, the Commonwealth Bank in Boston, was an interest of David Henshaw, the fertile source of many valuable Jacksonian ideas. Another, the Union Bank in Baltimore, was an interest of Secretary Taney, who being one of its stockholders knew that it was a good bank; and its president, Thomas Ellicott, had also been a fertile source of Jacksonian ideas. Some fourteen years earlier, when the Supreme Court had been about to hear the case *McCulloch* v. *Maryland*, and determine the constitutionality of the Bank of the United States, Chief Justice Marshall had sold his holdings of Bank stock. Mr Taney acted more thriftily. While arranging for the federal deposits to be shifted into private banks he not only retained his state bank stock but bought a little more, though as nominee for his sisters and sister-in-law. He delicately refrained, however, from himself selecting his own bank as a depository; the President did it for him.** The exalted spirit in which

---

* In President Jackson's Cabinet, according to Amos Kendall, there was some opposition "on political grounds" to making the Bank of America a depository; "but," he says, "it was promptly withdrawn when he stated the particulars of his negotiation in New York." Kendall, *Autobiography*, 387.

** It is significant of the odd views taken of speculation and investment that Taney was criticized for selling his bank stock at an advance, which he had not done, but was not criticized for continuing to hold it. Swisher, 241, 269.

15 Biddle, *Correspondence*, 234.

the shift of funds into the "pet banks" was achieved is reflected in Colonel Benton's statement that he "felt an emotion of the moral sublime at beholding such an instance of moral heroism."[16]

The same exalted spirit is present in Secretary Taney's inflationary advice to his seven selected banks. To the president of each he said: "In selecting your institution as one of the fiscal agents of the government, I not only rely on its solidity and established character, . . . but I confide also in its disposition to adopt the most liberal course which circumstances will admit towards other monied institutions generally. . . . The deposits of the public money will enable you to afford increased facilities to commerce and to extend your accommodation to individuals. And as the duties which are payable to the government arise from the business and enterprise of the merchants engaged in foreign trade, it is but reasonable that they should be preferred, . . . whenever it can be done without injustice to the claims of other classes of the community."[17]

The funds in the Bank of the United States were not to be withdrawn outright but were to run off, i.e., to be disbursed gradually without replacement. Only current receipts would be put in the new depositories. This sensible arrangement was decided on in order to deprive the Bank of an excuse for contracting credit and "notwithstanding," said Mr Kendall, "some pressure from the state banks, who desired to have at once possession of all the public deposits." The number of "pet banks" selected by the Secretary was to be considerably increased, for, as Taney explained, in contending against one monopoly it was not his desire to create others; but he very soon found himself in trouble.* The pets had expressed fear lest the federal Bank avenge herself by accumulating their notes and suddenly demanding payment of specie in excessive amounts, and Mr Taney, to protect them, secretly gave them large drafts on the Bank which they were to hold and use "only as a measure of defense." Drafts of $500,000 each, payable respectively to the Bank of America, the Manhattan, and the Mechanics, were sent to George Newbold in New York, president of the first, to be held by him for all three.

---

* There were ninety-one pet banks by the end of 1836. (Taus, 268.) The Treasury had always made some use of state banks as limited and special depositories, but the new arrangement differed from precedent both in degree and in kind.

16 Taney Papers, Taney to Ellicott, 5 May 1833; Benton I, 379.
17 23rd Congress, 1st Session, SD 2, pp. 21, 33-34.

The Girard in Philadelphia was sent a draft for $500,000; and the Union in Baltimore $300,000.[18]

The President thought Mr Taney was very smart in this "check-mating" of the Bank, but that he was not so smart soon became apparent. Encouraged by Taney's express invitation to use the funds already deposited with them—"the deposits of the public money will enable you to afford increased facilities to commerce," he had said, "and to extend your accommodation to individuals"— and having the drafts also in their possession, the pet banks began to increase their loans on the basis of both deposits and drafts. This tended to put them in debt to the Bank of the United States, because as borrowers drew on their borrowed funds, the volume of notes and checks outstanding against the banks that lent increased and more of them came into the federal Bank's possession. Thus the increased discounts of the pets tended to make it necessary for the federal Bank to take the action which would give the pets occasion to use the drafts Taney had sent them. His own bank in Baltimore was the worst of all. Its president, Thomas Ellicott, had promised Taney upon receipt of his drafts to use them only as planned, but the next day he cashed two of them. The Secretary was "extremely annoyed" and scolded Ellicott, who however professed some misunderstanding. Taney summoned him to Washington, where, according to Amos Kendall, who was present at the interview, Ellicott made a "stammering, incoherent statement" about transactions in Tennessee for which he had had to use the money. The Girard Bank of Philadelphia,* as soon as it received its draft for $500,000, expanded its loans and was soon owing the federal Bank so much that its draft had to be used within a month.[19]

Meanwhile the New York banks had fallen nearly $1,000,000 in debt to it. They informed Taney, 7 November 1833, that the drafts he had given them would not be enough. Two days later they wrote suggesting that they cash the drafts at once. On the 14th he wrote that he should "prefer having them returned to be cancelled" and cautioned the banks "not to extend their discounts too far." The same day they said again they thought they "should act immediately

---

* The Girard Bank was not the original institution owned by Stephen Girard, who had died two years before, but its successor, under state charter.

[18] Swisher, 238, 240; Kendall, *Autobiography*, 387; 23rd Congress, 1st Session, SD 16, pp. 321, 337, 343-44; Catterall, 302-05.

[19] Swisher, 239-43; 23rd Congress, 1st Session, SD 16, pp. 321, 324, 327-28, 333; Kendall, *Autobiography*, 389.

and present the checks." On the 16th he wrote them that he hoped they would not. He warned them again not to lend to excess. He thought it "neither your interest nor that of the community of New York to use the drafts," but he assured them again that if it should become necessary they would "immediately be furnished with the means of repelling every act of aggression on the part of the Bank of the United States." This was certainly an egregious situation: the Secretary of the Treasury, moved by the aggression of the pets, was promising to save them from the "aggression" of the federal Bank. On the 18th the Manhattan Company cashed its draft for $500,000. Mr Newbold wrote that "viewing the question in the abstract" they agreed in New York that the other two drafts should not be cashed, "and yet as affairs are now situated" they would probably have to be. Taney "approved" what had been done, but relied on their discretion not to use the other drafts unless it were made necessary by the Bank of the United States. On the 21st one draft was returned to him. On the 29th he wrote that what he saw in the press indicated that the Bank of the United States was seeking to produce a panic, dismay, and ruin. This would justify use of the last remaining draft, and he was "prepared to reinforce it immediately," if the pet banks "deem it necessary." The remaining draft was not used, however, and seems to have been returned later.[20]

When the federal Bank learned of the drafts, it had protested to the Secretary at his disregard of established practice. In reply he did not give the real reason for his action but said the drafts were not of the usual sort drawn for Treasury disbursements and therefore did not call for the usual notice. On the contrary, one would suppose that the less usual the drafts, the greater the occasion for notice. Horace Binney in a scornful discussion of Taney's conduct properly said that the lists of drawings furnished the Bank by the Treasury "became instruments of deception and gave false information to the Bank of the . . . Treasury demand." In simpler terms, if Taney expected "aggression" by the Bank, he should have warned it plainly that he was going to protect the state banks. If he thought that not sufficient he might still have issued the drafts and told the Bank he had done so. This would have been honest, effective, and befitting administrative responsibility. But Taney seems to have been inspired by ignorant, legalistic fear and by the desire to make things as difficult as he could for the Bank without creating too

---

[20] 23rd Congress, 1st Session, SD 16, pp. 340-63; J. Q. Adams, *Memoirs* ix, 41.

direct and obvious trouble for the Treasury and the business world. So, far from informing the Bank where and when he would withdraw funds, he kept it in the dark. This doubtless gratified his emotions, but it forced the Bank to measures otherwise unnecessary and contrary to the public interest. The Bank, as Professor Walter B. Smith observes, was in a very uncertain situation. "It could not really predict what the Treasury would do, and there was always the possibility of a run by individual depositors. . . . The spotty character of the Treasury's drafts on its balance was an important factor. . . . On some of the branches the demands were heavy and on some they were light. The Bank was fighting a defensive war and could not perfectly anticipate where the enemy would strike."[21]

IV

In December the President reported in his annual message that the removal of the public funds from the federal Bank had been successfully accomplished. "The state banks are found fully adequate . . . ," he said. "They have maintained themselves and discharged all these duties while the Bank of the United States was still powerful and in the field as an open enemy, and it is not possible to conceive that they will find greater difficulties in their operations when that enemy shall cease to exist."[22]

About the same time, Mr Taney gave Congress his reasons for shifting the deposits. He put first the need of impelling the Bank to begin liquidating its business at once. He had indeed impelled the Bank in that direction, and then he had deplored what the Bank was doing under that impulsion. He felt an unwillingness to believe, he said, "that such an institution as the Bank of the United States could bring itself . . . to bring general distress on the people." Consistency would require that these words be taken as sarcasm, but their context makes them sound more like sanctimony. The Secretary of the Treasury, in Horace Binney's words, "says the design of removing the deposits was to compel reduction, and he censures her because she reduces." But it was equally bad, in Mr Taney's opinion, for the Bank to have expanded its loans and discounts earlier—from $42,000,000 to $63,000,000 in the year 1831 and then to $70,000,000 the first half of 1832—while renewal was pending. This was one of the more important reasons why the Bank

---

[21] Congress, *Register of Debates* x, Part 2, 2327; W. B. Smith, 162.
[22] Richardson iii, 1330-31.

had "justly forfeited the confidence of the government." It was something "without example in the history of banking institutions"; and it demonstrated, the Secretary averred, that the Bank "was using its money for the purpose of obtaining a hold upon the people of this country in order to operate upon their fears and to induce them, by the apprehension of ruin, to vote against the candidate whom it desired to defeat." In Mr Taney's legalistic mind there was no room for economic considerations, and fluctuations in the Bank's balance sheet had only a political significance. If she lent, it was merely to corrupt and enslave the people; if she did not lend, it was merely to starve them.[23]

One of Secretary Taney's preposterous assertions was the following: "It is well understood that the superior credit heretofore enjoyed by the notes of the Bank of the United States was not founded on any particular confidence in its management or solidity. It was occasioned altogether by the agreement on behalf of the public, in the act of incorporation, to receive them in all payments to the United States; and it was this pledge on the part of the government which gave general currency to the notes payable at remote branches." The legal tender quality of the Bank's notes in respect to payments due the government was important, of course, but contrary to what the Secretary said it was not a fact, nor was it "understood" to be one, that the notes were acceptable to the public "altogether" because they were acceptable to the government. As Mr Gallatin's committee said, contradicting Mr Taney, the credit the Bank's notes had was due principally to general confidence in the Bank's management and strength; and this confidence gave its notes greater value even than those of some local specie-paying banks. Though important, the legal status of the notes was not essential. There were state banks and even private bankers whose obligations "enjoyed superior credit" without unique legal status, and those of the federal Bank's successor, the United States Bank chartered by Pennsylvania, attained perhaps even greater credit than those issued under the federal charter.[24]

Prominent among the Bank's sins in Mr Taney's opinion were its loans to editors and Congressmen. Yet these were not below the practices of the time, and even by the Jacksonians were denounced less for their immorality than for the effectiveness imputed to them.

[23] 23rd Congress, 1st Session, SD 2, pp. 12, 15; SD 16, p. 343; Congress, *Register of Debates* x, Part 2, 2352.
[24] 23rd Congress, 1st Session, SD 2, p. 5; Union Committee, *Report*, 10.

The borrowers were not friends of the Bank exclusively nor were the loans made with stipulations and understandings. The borrowers included Jacksonians, some of whom were the Bank's most virulent enemies: Duff Green, $15,600; Francis Blair, $20,000; Amos Kendall, $5,375; Isaac Hill, $3,800; John H. Eaton, $9,000; W. B. Lewis, $10,765; John Forsyth, $20,000; and R. M. Johnson, $10,-820. Duff Green, whose Washington *Telegraph* had initiated the Jacksonian attack on the Bank, in negotiating his loan had written: "It may be proper to add that no accommodation given by the Bank will induce me to alter in any respect the course which my paper has pursued in relation to it." Some so-called loans by the Bank to men on the federal payroll were merely routine salary advances, the Bank being the government's paymaster, and signified no borrowing whatever in the ordinary sense. This applies to none of those just listed, however. Most of those listed and other such were loans made by branch offices and not by Philadelphia. As I have said, politicians usually did not include the branch offices in their attacks upon the Bank but treated them as local institutions. Only when it was expedient to damn the Philadelphia management and the Bank as a whole were its operations through the branches denounced. Had there been any sincere rather than political objection to the Bank's lending to Congressmen and government officials, General Jackson might have recommended that it be forbidden by law. The Jacksonians were more disposed to denounce it than prevent it. As to corruption, Professor William G. Sumner wrote over seventy years ago: "It is not proved that the deposits were ever used by the Bank of the United States for any political purpose whatever. It is conclusively proved that the deposits were used by Jackson's administration, through Whitney's agency, to reward adherents and to win supporters." Twenty years later Professor Catterall said "there never has been any evidence produced to show that the Bank . . . ever spent a dollar corruptly"; but the accusation was repeated so much, he said, that there has been an inclination "to accept as proved what was only vehemently asserted."[25]

The Bank had also engaged in self-defense, and here Secretary Taney passed to what emphasis would indicate to be the most flagitious of the Bank's sins—its publication and distribution of material expounding its own case. Nothing the Bank did incensed the Jack-

[25] Biddle, *Correspondence*, 124, 357-59; Sumner, *Jackson*, 358-59; Catterall, 243; 22nd Congress, 1st Session, HR 460, pp. 109-10.

sonians more, as if its first moral duty were to keep still while its enemies said what they pleased. Their sentiments were those of the old French song:

"Cet animal est très méchant—
Quand on l'attaque, il se défend."

Both the mode and the fact of its action were beyond the pale. The mode was such, Taney declared, "that the whole capital of the Bank is, in effect, placed at the disposition of the president." This was his way of saying that the directors had authorized Mr Biddle "to cause to be prepared and circulated such documents and papers as may communicate to the people information in regard to the nature and operations of the Bank." Since there was no limit set by the directors, Mr Taney observes that the entire capital of the Bank might be consumed, as if such expenditures would be made from capital funds and as if the use of $35,000,000 for publications were within practical possibility. The expenditures to which he adverted, for "stationery and printing," somewhat exceeded a total of $80,000 for the two years 1831 and 1832. Since the account was not detailed, possibly having been withheld from the government directors on whom the Secretary depended for his information, it is not apparent how much of the $80,000 was for supplies required in the Bank's operations. These would certainly amount to considerable; yet it is implied that the expenditure was wholly for what would be called propaganda.[26]

But even if propaganda, it was of a commendable sort, comprising mostly public documents, whose distribution the Bank merely facilitated. It included specifically copies of congressional committee reports on the Bank, both *pro* and *con*, speeches in Congress on it, Mr Gallatin's classic essay of 1831 (prepared at the request of the Bank and with its assistance but without remuneration to the author), an essay on banking by Professor George Tucker of the University of Virginia, Clarke and Hall's *Legislative History of the Bank of the United States* (a compilation prepared at the direction of Congress), and copies of editorials and articles from the press. The latter seem to have included reviews of a speech by Senator Benton and of the veto message, which were presumably what Mr Taney called attacks upon officers of the government. Mr Taney

[26] 23rd Congress, 1st Session, SD 2, pp. 16, 30-31.

did not mention the Bank's reprinting and distributing copies of the veto message itself—but, in a surge of sincerity, he may have included the message among the attacks, in agreement with Mr Biddle that it was self-damaging.* Of the general character of the material there is indication in Nicholas Biddle's private instructions on one occasion that it was to be "explanatory of the operations and conduct of the Bank" and "confined to that object exclusively"; and on another that "the only way in which we can hope to dissipate the ignorance and the prejudice that in many places prevail on the subject of the Bank is by the publication of judicious explanations of its operations." Senator John C. Calhoun, no passionate partisan of the Bank, was moved to say "that, assailed as it was by the Executive, it would have been unfaithful to its trust, both to the stockholders and to the public, had it not resorted to every proper means in its power to defend its conduct, and, among others, the free circulation of able and judicious publications." With the principal exception of Jackson's veto message, the material was objective, informative, and well done; there is nothing better in early American economic writing than what the Bank made available.[27]

Although Mr Taney was a lawyer, and counsel for corporations, he said in effect that since the government owned one-fifth of the Bank, one-fifth of what the Bank spent was the government's money —and that the Bank had as much right to charge such expenses to the government's account as it had to incur them at all. He also said: "So far as the nation is concerned in the character of the Bank, the people, through their own representatives in Congress, can take care of their own rights and vindicate the character of the Bank if they think it unjustly assailed. And they do not need the aid of persons employed and paid by the Bank to learn whether its charter be constitutional or not; nor whether the public interest requires it to be renewed; nor have they authorized the president and directors of that institution to expend the public money to enlighten them on this subject."[28]

* Later, in 1835, the Bank distributed at its own expense a speech by Senator John Tyler of Virginia denouncing it for distributing speeches at its own expense; but it did so because the Senator asked it to. Catterall, 267, notes 2, 3.

[27] 23rd Congress, 2nd Session, SD 17, p. 322; Biddle Papers, 3 PLB (1832), 296; Kendall, *Autobiography*, 385.
[28] 23rd Congress, 1st Session, SD 2, p. 17.

The Secretary's reasons for the change in depository were dealt with in two outstanding addresses in Congress. Horace Binney, counsel for the Bank, one of its directors, and a surviving trustee of the former federal Bank, spoke in the House, 7 January 1834, and John C. Calhoun in the Senate a few days later. Horace Binney went again over the regulatory function of the Bank and condemned the Secretary's "doctrine of an unregulated, uncontrolled, state bank paper currency." He recognized the existence of a banking *system*; he spoke realistically of the inter-related forces at work in the economy and of the Bank's adaptation of its services to general rather than special interests, observing that the Bank's enemies disregarded what was actual and important to dwell on details and magnify improbable evils. Mr Binney's discourse was factual and intelligent, but he was surpassed by John C. Calhoun, who, after Henry Clay and Thomas Hart Benton had each harangued in the Senate for three days, said all that needed to be said in a brilliant address of little more than an hour. Still hot from the nullification crisis of the year before and staunch in his defense of states' rights as conceived in the tradition of Thomas Jefferson and the Kentucky and Virginia Resolutions of 1798, he nevertheless affirmed anew, as he had first in 1816, that the Bank of the United States was the means by which Congress discharged the responsibility put upon it by the federal Constitution to regulate the currency. "So long," he said, "as the question is one between a Bank of the United States incorporated by Congress and that system of banks which has been created by the will of the Executive, it is an insult to the understanding to discourse on the pernicious tendency and unconstitutionality of the Bank of the United States." The Secretary, he said, might privately entertain an opinion of the Bank's constitutionality, "but that he, acting in his official character and performing official acts under the charter of the Bank, should undertake to determine that the institution was unconstitutional and that those who granted the charter and bestowed on him his power to act under it had violated the Constitution, is an assumption of power of a nature which I will not undertake to characterize, as I wish not to be personal." If the charter were unconstitutional, he asked, what authority had the Secretary to act under it? Senator Calhoun insisted that the Secretary of the Treasury, practically speaking, had no proper authority to move the public monies from the depository provided by Congress, unless he found them unsafe—which was not even pretended.* Did anyone think, he asked, that the deposits could be insured at a lower rate, now that they had been removed from that depository? He condemned the Secretary's argument that, in effect, "the letter ought to prevail over the clear and manifest intention of the act" which incorporated the Bank, and ridiculed the "awkward and disreputable position in which his own arguments have placed him."[29]

V

Removal of the deposits from the Bank of the United States, according to David Henshaw's *Morning Post*, Boston, 28 September 1833, was going to be an excellent thing for most people. "Heretofore," it said, "scarcely anyone received discounts from the branch in this city but the great capitalists—the millionists—the Appletons, the Lawrences, etc."—a statement that conflicts with the testimony of other Jacksonians that the Bank's loans had got the masses in its grip. But, the *Morning Post* went on, "when the deposits are transferred to the state banks"—three of which in Boston, the Commonwealth, the Franklin, and the Market, belonged to those Jacksonian millionists, David Henshaw and his associates—then "men of smaller business and capital will stand as good chance to receive discounts from them as the 'big bugs'. . . . The drain of money to Philadelphia will cease."[30]

But as apprehended by the conservative part of the business world, more trouble arose than Henshaw would lead one to expect. Whatever the President's intention, according to a contemporary writer in the *American Quarterly Review*, the net result was the same as if he were "using the whole energies of the government for the exclusive benefit of stockjobbers and lenders of money at usurious interest." When their measures produced, as would be expected, a tightness in the money market, the Jacksonians at first pooh-poohed it. The President wrote Colonel Hamilton of New York, February 1834: "There is no real general distress. It is only with those who live by borrowing, trade on loans, and the gamblers in stocks. It

---

* A month before, 12 December 1833, Mr Cambreleng had said that the shift of the deposits was not motivated by fears for their security—the Bank of the United States, he had said, "was a safe place for the public money"—but by "great public considerations." Congress, *Register of Debates*, x, Part 2, 2172; 23rd Congress, 1st Session, SD 2.

[29] Congress, *Register of Debates* x, Part 2, 2322; Calhoun II, 313-14, 318-19, 335-36.
[30] Darling, 137.

would be a godsend to society if all such were put down. This will leave capital to be employed by individuals either combined or otherwise without the sanction of government, and leave all to trade on their own credit and capital without any interference by the general government; except using its power by giving through its mint a specie currency, and by its legislation a standard value to keep the coin in the country." The following month when a delegation came from Philadelphia to ask him for relief from the credit stringency, the President admitted that there was distress among "brokers and stock speculators and all who were doing business on a borrowed capital," and that they would "suffer severely"; but he declared that "all such people ought to break." Moreover, he warned them: "Andrew Jackson never would restore the deposits to the Bank— Andrew Jackson would never recharter that monster of corruption. . . . Sooner than live in a country where such a power prevailed, he would seek an asylum in the wilds of Arabia."[31]

A committee from Baltimore came to urge that the government do something for relief from the current distress. "Relief, sir!" interrupted the President, "Come not to me, sir! Go to the monster. . . . It is folly, sir, to talk to Andrew Jackson. The government will not bow to the monster. . . . You would have us, like the people of Ireland, paying tribute to London. . . . The failures that are now taking place are amongst the stockjobbers, brokers, and gamblers, and would to God they were all swept from the land! It would be a happy thing for the country." But fortunately "Andrew Jackson yet lives," he vociferated, "to put his foot upon the head of the monster and crush him to the dust." The spokesman protested that the committee represented honest citizens, not gamblers and stockjobbers. The President, in a picturesque fury, either real or simulated, allowed him no comfort. "The mammoth, sir, has bled you." And he declared that he had "rather undergo the tortures of ten Spanish inquisitions" than that the deposits be restored or the monster rechartered.[32]

Of a delegation from New York, he demanded angrily, "Why am I teased with committees?" It was because of the Bank, he knew. "The abominable institution," he cried, "the monster! . . . I've got my foot upon it and I'll crush it. . . . Is Andrew Jackson to bow the

[31] Catterall, chap. XIII; *American Quarterly Review* xv (June 1834), 518; J. A. Hamilton, *Reminiscences*, 270; Congress, *Register of Debates* x, Part 3, 3073-74.
[32] Congress, *Register of Debates* x, Part 3, 3074-75.

knee to the golden calf as did the Israelites of old? I tell you, if you want relief, go to Nicholas Biddle." The spokesman for the committee replied: "Nicholas Biddle will tell us that he is following the recommendations of the Executive in winding up the affairs of the Bank by curtailing its discounts." This was striking home. "The rage of the President," the committee reported, "now increased, if possible, to a degree which we shall not attempt to describe. He continued: 'Did I advise him to interfere with elections and to corrupt the morals of the people? . . . I tell you I am opposed to all banks and banking operations from the South Sea Bubble to the present time. The Israelites during the absence of Moses to the mount made a golden calf and fell down and worshipped it; and they sorely suffered for their idolatry. The people of this country may yet be punished for their idolatry. Let the United States Bank relieve the community by issuing their notes, and I pledge myself that the state banks shall not oppress it!" Thus in successive breaths the President doomed the Bank to extinction and invited it to prolong its operations.[33]

As if it were not enough to endure the pressure of general business panic and political attack, Secretary Taney had his own bank and its president to worry him. After Ellicott's disgraceful performance the preceding autumn, their correspondence had been amicable still and the Secretary had asked Ellicott's advice from time to time. But by April things were as bad as ever, or worse. "I am disappointed and mortified at the condition of your bank," Taney wrote. "It is a most unpleasant position to find myself not only not able to draw on you the money you have but to be obliged to furnish you with even more to sustain your credit. . . . And it is not a little mortifying that your bank, in which I unfortunately have a small personal interest (which I wish was in the Dead Sea, or at the bottom of any other sea) is the only one of all the selected banks which has placed itself in the condition to require not merely forbearance but actual support."[34]

Ellicott's situation was so bad that Amos Kendall was much alarmed; Taney's interest in the Union Bank was known, and the bank's failure would be a disaster not to the Secretary of the Treasury alone but to the President and the party. In April 1834 Kendall warned Ellicott in sternly under-scored language: "The responsi-

[33] Congress, *Register of Debates* x, Part 3, 3073.
[34] Taney Papers, Taney to Ellicott, 18 April 1834, 29 May 1834.

bility of your situation is *immense*. We can stand the stopping of other banks, but if the 'Pets' begin to go, it is impossible to appreciate the consequences. . . . It is desirable to sustain other banks but not at any hazard to yourself. If there be the least danger to you, for Heaven's sake, fortify yourselves so that you *can stand amidst ruin*." There was more than an equal chance, Kendall said, that nearly all the Baltimore banks would fail. "*You must not, if all the rest do*." He particularizes about the bank's condition: "*You are not strong enough in specie*." Six weeks later Ellicott's bank had not failed but the situation was still serious, and Kendall wrote him, 28 May 1834, that Secretary Taney "is on all sides harassed almost out of his senses." Shortly thereafter Taney broke with Ellicott for good. For ten weeks he had been writing Ellicott about three times weekly, in his own hand.[35]

In the Senate, where Jackson's and Taney's enemies were in majority, the monetary distress intensified political anger at their having "seized" the public treasure and put it in the keeping of state banks. The Senate formally censured the President—a legislative act as extraordinary as the executive act which occasioned it but of no such moment. In the House of Representatives, however, a committee report was approved which found that the Bank ought not to be rechartered, that it ought not to receive the public deposits, that the federal government instead should use private banks as depositories, and that another congressional inquiry into the Bank's affairs should be made. The Senate could do nothing by itself beyond rejecting Taney's appointment to the Treasury. He was out. But Congress adjourned in June 1834 with any hope of recharter depending on nothing but some miracle—which, however, never occurred.

Meanwhile protests from the business world were being directed at the Bank, which by February in Professor Smith's opinion had surmounted the crisis presented by the shifting of the public deposits and by July was become again "so strong that it was ready to reverse its policy and begin to expand." Late in December even Thomas Wren Ward had written the Barings that, though the Bank had been abused, there was no reason for its keeping the money market in the state it was in. But Mr Biddle had been dealing with a serious threat and was unready to relax. In a letter to William Appleton of the Boston office, 27 January 1834, he said: "If the

[35] Taney Papers, Kendall to Ellicott, 15 April 1834, 28 May 1834.

Bank remains strong and quiet, the course of events will save the Bank and save all the institutions of the country, which are now in great peril. But if, from too great a sensitiveness—from the fear of offending or the desire of conciliating—the Bank permits itself to be frightened or coaxed into any relaxation of its present measures, the relief will itself be cited as evidence that the measures of the government are not injurious or oppressive, and the Bank will inevitably be prostrated. Our only safety is in pursuing a steady course of firm restriction—and I have no doubt that such a course will ultimately lead to restoration of the currency and the recharter of the Bank." A month later, 21 February 1834, he wrote: "The relief, to be useful or permanent, must come from Congress and from Congress alone. If that body will do its duty, relief will come—if not, the Bank feels no vocation to redress the wrongs inflicted by these miserable people. Rely upon that. This worthy President thinks that because he has scalped Indians and imprisoned judges, he is to have his way with the Bank. He is mistaken—and he may as well send at once and engage lodgings in Arabia."[36]

It is clear from these statements that Mr Biddle was concerned not merely to defend the Bank but to pursue its course in the hope of reversing the advantage gained by the President from vetoing the new charter and removing the deposits. In this he quite underestimated the strength of the popular conviction that the President had done something remarkable. He also over-estimated the patience of the business world. With respect to the latter he was admonished in March 1834 by the Union Committee of New York bankers and merchants, comprising Albert Gallatin and others of the eminently conservative and intelligent but not any of the pets.* The Bank had just been persuaded to alter its course when suddenly the Governor of Pennsylvania, who had been thought to be its friend, denounced it in a message to the legislature. The directors, alarmed at the very moment of tentative relaxation, hesitated to ease the Bank's policy,

---

* Other prominent members of the Committee were James Brown of Brown Brothers and Company; Philip Hone, a man of wealth and various public accomplishments; Gardiner C. Howland, merchant; James G. King, merchant and financier; D. W. C. Olyphant, China merchant; and John A. Stevens, merchant and later the first president of the Bank of Commerce. Union Committee, *Report*, p. 34.

[36] W. B. Smith, 164-65; Baring Papers, OC, T. W. Ward to Baring Brothers, 27 December 1833; Biddle, *Correspondence*, 219-20, 222.

and Mr Biddle informed "the New York committee that the conduct of the Governor of Pennsylvania obliged the Bank to look to its own safety." This reaction was reasonable, since the Governor's message, coming as it did, was seen by enemies and friends alike as a deadly blast. The committee persisted, however, and the Bank's directors agreed, 17 March 1834, "that no diminution up to the first of May next be made in the present amount of loans and discounts in the city and state of New York, and if practicable that an increase be made in the line of domestic bills of exchange discounted at the office in that city, and that the Bank will not call for the payment of such balances as may become due to it by the city banks up to the first of May next." In June and July, upon further advice from the New York committee and from a like group in Boston, the Bank abandoned its curtailments and prepared to enlarge its discounts moderately. In Professor Walter B. Smith's judgment, the Bank's reduction had been "moderate in view of the uncertainties of the situation."[37]

VI

Meanwhile the Union Committee had published a temperate and thoughtful report, 18 March 1834, reviewing the recent events. It showed that the public deposits in the Bank had been reduced from $7,600,000 to $3,100,000 between August 1833 and February 1834 and the private deposits from $10,100,000 to $6,700,000. This was a reduction in all deposits of nearly $8,000,000. In the same period the Bank's loans and discounts had been reduced from $64,200,000 to $54,800,000, a reduction of $9,400,000. The contraction of loans, the Committee thought, did not inordinately exceed the contraction of deposits. Curtailment of the Bank's loans was "a necessary consequence" of the change in depository, and the authority responsible for the change was "responsible for all the effects that may have flowed from the curtailments." Circumstances which, in the Committee's judgment, compelled the Bank to protect itself were the decidedly hostile attitude of President Jackson, the drafts secretly given the pet banks by Secretary Taney, and what appeared to be an attempt to break the Savannah branch by a sudden call for $300,000 in specie. The more general effects the Committee explained in a description of inter-related factors in the economy and especially of

[37] Biddle, *Correspondence*, 224-25, 242; Union Committee, *Report*, 5-6; W. B. Smith, 165, n56, 294-95.

the vital part played by credit; it emphasized the fact that business men were "at the same time debtors and creditors for sums generally far exceeding their respective capitals" and that the regular discharge of the enormous mass of intimately connected engagements spread over the whole country depended on "an uninterrupted continuance of the ordinary sales, payments, remittances, and credits." In fine, "the whole machinery by which business in its various branches is carried on is credit extended to its utmost limits. Whatever lessens the general confidence on which credit is founded must necessarily produce a fatal derangement and interruption in every branch of business."[38]

"It was with this state of things that, without any necessity or investigation, the Executive thought proper to interfere. . . . The threat of the removal of the deposits, and especially their actual removal, created apprehensions of danger, immediately to the Bank itself and more remotely to all the monied institutions and concerns of the country. . . . Men saw that the relations between the government and the Bank were thenceforth to be hostile; that between it and the selected banks they were to be those of mistrust; and that without a national Bank the stability and safety of the whole monetary system of the country would be endangered."

The removal of the public funds from the federal depository, according to the Committee, implied in the Executive—Jackson and Taney, that is—"gross ignorance of the system of credit which connects all the monied interests" of the country and "was at least wholly unnecessary." The current distress was due, moreover, not merely to the amount of credit curtailment but to destruction of confidence.[39]

The administration's course was scrutinized also in an essay in the *American Quarterly Review*, June 1834, entitled "The Public Distress." "The President," said the author, "informs us that by the Constitution gold and silver coins are the only legal currency of the country." And though economists for the past half century had been saying that bank notes were money as much as coins made of the precious metals were, "he adopts a construction which repudiates for the general government all superintendence over seven-eighths of the currency—the regulation of which constituted one of the most important objects of the federal union." The author thought

---

[38] Union Committee, *Report*, 11-18.
[39] Union Committee, *Report*, 9-10, 16; Niles xlvi (1834), 73-80.

it much easier to "prove" the state banks to be unconstitutional than to make out that the federal government lacked the power to incorporate an institution "either as the fiscal agent of the Treasury or for the regulation of the currency." He found it "not a little remarkable that no notice should have been taken, either in Mr Taney's report to Congress or in the cabinet paper of 18th September 1833, of the functions of the Bank as a regulator of the currency"; nor was any account taken of them in documents that followed. "The attention of the government seems to have been turned to the Bank only as a fiscal agency, which though an important, is far from being the most important, relation in which it stands to the nation." The current distress, therefore, "was occasioned by hostility to that very establishment which the foresight of the wisest statesmen had provided as a safeguard" against such distress.[40]

These events were mirrored a few years later in a satire, *Quodlibet*, by John Pendleton Kennedy, which Professor Parrington, in his *Main Currents in American Thought*, calls "the most vivacious criticism" of the Jacksonians "in our political library." In *Quodlibet* a set of speculators organize the Patriotic Copperplate Bank on democratic principles—"one dollar a share paid in, the rest in a note payable when convenient." They become a federal depository and receive a letter from Mr Taney, the Secretary of the Treasury, expressing to them, as to the other pet banks, the hope that "the deposits of the public money will enable you to afford increased facilities to commerce and to extend your accommodations to individuals." The Patriotic Copperplate Bank thinks highly of President Jackson and his administration, who are true friends to the people. "How careful they are of our great mercantile and trading classes! . . . No more low prices for grain . . . no more scarcity of money—accommodation is the word—better currency is the word—high prices, good wages, and plenty of work is the word nowadays . . . we are destined to become a great, glorious, and immortal people. . . . We must all make our fortunes." But, of course, "the Secretary expects, you know . . . that the accommodation principle, you know, is to be measurably extended, you know, in proportion to the democracy of the applicants." It is. Loans are made, notes are issued, shops are built, prices are bid up, and there are hopes of

[40] *American Quarterly Review* xv (June 1834), 518, 521.

being soon in Wall Street, when the cashier absconds to Europe with the bank's funds—and then it turns out that the bank was not a Democratic institution after all, but Whig, for "Democrats are poor, sir," and "banks are not made by poor men."[41]

Now, these acquisitive characters are no more agrarian than the *bourgeois gentilhomme* of Molière was a peasant—except that like most Americans of their day they had been reared on farms. Their interests are not agrarian but to get rich quick. Yet Professor Parrington says that *Quodlibet* was satirizing the agrarians! He calls it "a capitalistic counter to the agrarian attack on the rising money power." But so far from John Pendleton Kennedy's being a friend of "the rising money power," it is this rising money power that he satirized. He expresses the contempt of a cultivated, substantial conservative not for farmers but for up-start speculators and politicians, for "mushroom banks," and their "swarms of scrub aristocrats in the shape of presidents, cashiers, directors, and clerks." They were the aspiring Jacksonian *nouveaux riches* who were fast taking over America, seen by an aristocrat who also wanted to make money but would do it more respectably. Kennedy was satirizing the same thing as his friend Thackeray in the *Diary of C. Jeames de la Pluche* and as Thomas Love Peacock in his novels. Professor Parrington in calling *Quodlibet* a capitalistic satire on agrarians has been taken in by the Jacksonian clichés that the story ridiculed. For when Amos Kendall, David Henshaw, and their fellows expressed their rancor at the aristocrats whom John Pendleton Kennedy represented, they always made it appear that they were not capitalistic themselves but simple folk from the farm or poor mechanics trying to get on in the world. They did it so well that their assault against the federal Bank in the interest of easy money, *laisser faire*, and Wall Street became embedded in a fossiliferous tradition as the triumph of agrarians over the money power. If so, it was a triumph curiously short-lived considering its sublimity and odd in having as its most substantial consequence the position, which it helped establish, of Wall Street in the American economy.

Mr Kennedy's interests were shared by his great friend, Washington Irving, whose fastidious tastes also discriminated against the less dignified ways of making money. The kindly Irving, however, refrained from satire. Unlike his friend and the unworldly romanc-

---

[41] Parrington II, 55-56; Kennedy, *Quodlibet*, 33-36, 40, 182-86.

ers and Transcendentalists, he maintained a benign attitude toward the great American passion for making money.

He was a supporter of Andrew Jackson, a friend of Martin Van Buren, and a friend of John Jacob Astor. Writing from the latter's home, where he was a guest, to a friend in Congress, January 1838, he deplored disparagement "of the great trading and financial classes of our country," for he saw "how important these classes are to the prosperous conduct of the complicated affairs of this immense empire." He continued: "As to the excessive expansions of commerce and the extravagant land speculations, . . . I look upon these as incident to that spirit of enterprise natural to a young country in a state of rapid and prosperous developments; a spirit which, with all its occasional excesses, has given our nation an immense impulse in its onward career and promises to carry it ahead of all the nations of the globe. There are moral as well as physical phenomena incident to every state of things, which may at first appear evils but which are devised by an all-seeing Providence for some beneficent purpose. Such is the spirit of speculative enterprise which now and then rises to an extravagant height and sweeps throughout the land. It grows out of the very state of our country and its institutions and though sometimes productive of temporary mischief, yet leaves behind it lasting benefits."[42]

VII

Being without the government's deposits and the acquisition therefrom of claims against the state banks, the federal Bank had ceased to possess any effective regulatory powers over the currency of the country and the extension of bank credit. Mr Biddle knew it. "The Executive," he wrote 11 March 1834, "by removing the public revenues has relieved the Bank from all responsibility for the currency." It was the shift of the public deposits rather than the veto which, in a technical sense, "destroyed" the federal Bank; for the shift deprived the Bank at once of its essential powers, and changed it from a conservative force in the economy to an inflationary one. Its vast capital and resources, no longer employed in central banking, became employed simply in making money by the expansion of credit. The Bank, in Mr Gallatin's opinion stated in 1841, had "ceased to be a regulator of the currency as early as the years 1832-33, when its discounts and other investments were increased

---

[42] Irving II, 338-40.

from fifty-five to sixty-five millions, that is to say, at the rate of 85 per cent beyond its capital; whilst those of the sound banks of our great commercial cities did not exceed the rate of 60 per cent beyond their capital. . . . It is obvious that it is only by keeping its discounts at a lower rate than those of the state banks that these can be its debtors; and that it is only by enforcing the payment of the balances that it can keep them within bounds and thus regulate the currency."[43]

It is unfortunate that Mr Biddle did not stop when the Jacksonians tried to make him do so. But he too had a mission to perform. He must save the country from the "gang of banditti" in Washington. "I know these people perfectly," he said, "—keep the police on them constantly—and in my deliberate judgment, there is not on the face of the earth a more profligate crew than those who now govern the President. The question is how to expel them." So he continued for a while to watch for the possibility of recharter by the federal government, which would make him a central banker again. But it was no use. The year 1834 ended and 1835 passed with nothing to warrant hope; the Bank wavered between the prospect of liquidation and that of becoming a state bank. In February 1836 the charter expired and the federal Bank ceased to exist. A state charter, however, had been enacted a fortnight earlier by the Pennsylvania legislature, incorporating all the stockholders of the federal Bank, "excepting the United States and the Treasurer of the United States," as a state bank "to be called the United States Bank"—but not so called generally and in another section incorporated according to the practice still common as "the President, Directors, and Company of the Bank of the United States." The old Bank transferred its assets to the new, which assumed the corresponding liabilities.[44]

At their last meeting, 19 February 1836, the stockholders of the expiring Bank voted to give Mr Biddle "a splendid service of plate," betokening their gratitude to him. Apparently it was not completed and presented till two years later. At that time Philip Hone of New York, visiting in Philadelphia, 14 February 1838, made the following note in his diary: "I was shown this afternoon at the shop of Messrs Fletcher and Company in Chestnut Street the most superb service of plate I ever saw, to be presented by the directors of the

---

43 Biddle, *Correspondence*, 226; Gallatin III, 394-95.

44 Biddle, *Correspondence*, 255; 24th Congress, 2nd Session, HD 118, pp. 64-69; Biddle Papers, 1 PLB (1836), 354-55; W. B. Smith, 173, 179.

old Bank of the United States to Mr Nicholas Biddle. It is to cost $15,000.* The inscription recites all his valuable services to the institution and to the country at large and among other things his having 'created the best currency *in the world*.' He deserves all they can do for him, but the world is a big place."[45]

The history of the United States Bank of Pennsylvania is that of a different concern, operated in different circumstances by the same management as the deceased federal Bank. The distinction between the Bank of the United States, a corporation under federal charter with unique power and responsibility, and the United States Bank of Pennsylvania, a corporation under state charter with no peculiar power and responsibility, is far greater than the distinction between the first Bank of the United States and the second. Yet the accident that there was an interval of five years between the first federal Bank and the second, with a complete change of management, and that there was no interval and no change of management between the second federal Bank and the state-chartered United States Bank of Pennsylvania, has led to exaggeration of the difference between the two federal Banks and to something very like identification of the second with its private successor. This identification has been to the advantage of the Jacksonians, who very naturally believed and claimed that what happened in Chestnut Street in 1839 and 1841 justified what they had done from 1828 to 1833—though, in fact, the later events were largely a result of what they had done. It was a cardinal error of Nicholas Biddle to have been responsible himself for this identification; for though he recognized the difference, he did not stress it but instead let vanity and resentment build up the pretension that Andrew Jackson had been foiled after all in his attempt to destroy the federal Bank. Quite to the contrary, Andrew Jackson had irrefragably succeeded.

Indeed, it is the distinction between the state bank and the federal Bank, carrying with it great differences of practical moment, that goes far to explain why the brilliant career of Nicholas Biddle as central banker was followed by a career as private banker which was also brilliant in its first brief passages and then plunged into swift, spectacular disaster. For the Jacksonian account, full as it is of rhetoric and holiness, does not avail against the evidence of Nicholas

* It cost $30,000 according to Scharf and Westcott, *History of Philadelphia*, I, 647.

[45] W. B. Smith, 176; Hone, 301.

Biddle's earlier success. But with full allowance for Mr Biddle's brilliance, resourcefulness, and rationality, it was a fair weather success. So long as the Bank was operated as a central bank, his judgment was tempered by convention. But with that governance removed he became erratic. This was apparent in his effort to withstand the Jacksonians' demoralizing assault. Again, after destruction of the Bank's essential function, he wavered and drifted. Previously, in acquiring government securities and commercial paper for the Bank's portfolio, he could not so readily go wrong. But as the public debt was retired and as preparations were making for liquidation of the Bank upon expiry of the charter in 1836, "the policy was adopted of converting the active debt into loans upon the security of stocks, by which permanent investment might be provided for the capital of the bank during the long period of its anticipated liquidation." This was sensible in itself, an orderly and deliberate liquidation being anticipated, but when it was resolved to take a new lease on life under state charter, the policy was not changed; the bank consecrated itself to empire-building. Between March 1835 and March 1836 the loans upon bank stock (including the bank's own shares) and other personal security increased from $4,800,000 to $20,500,000. Like investments were made. "We have just purchased the Merchants Bank of New Orleans," Mr Biddle wrote a correspondent 28 September 1836. "Is there anything to be done in that way in Alabama?" By 1840 the bank had shares in more than twenty banks from New Orleans to New York, some of which it wholly controlled. Shares were acquired in railways, toll-bridges, turn-pikes, and canals; loans were made to these projects and on the security of their shares, and bonds issued by the individual states to finance them were purchased. Change in the bank's portfolio was hastened by the Pennsylvania charter, which was as much an act of extortion as a grant of powers. It was entitled "An act to repeal the state tax on real and personal property, and to continue and extend the improvements of the state by railroads and canals, and to charter a state bank, to be called the United States Bank." It burdened the bank with a bonus of about $5,000,000 to be paid the state and with participation in schemes for public works which the state itself was improvidently undertaking. The bank reported in 1841 that in five years it had diverted about $13,000,-000, over a third of its capital, "to purposes of the state." Banking of this sort afforded full play for Mr Biddle's weaknesses of judgment. Combat had made him in principle indistinguishable from his enemies.[46]

Yet recent historians and biographers, it seems to me, have been more interested in what he did after the Jacksonian assault than in what he did before, though it is in the light of the earlier performance that the wisdom and propriety of destroying the Bank must be judged. That he proved under pressure and provocation to be something less than a George Washington does nothing to alter his having been a devoted, conscientious, and exceptionally able manager of the federal Bank up to the time the President and his advisers decided to do away with her and him too. Consequently, whatever weaknesses he may have displayed after the attack do not relieve the Jacksonians of a heavy share in responsibility for what came to pass. They did not seek reform or correction. They sought to end the Bank's life, impelled by the entrepreneur's desire for abundant credit, the sectional politician's jealousy of federal powers, the self-made man's envy of those whom he had not yet supplanted, and New York's impatience with Philadelphia's remnant of financial primacy. Animated with those worthy emotions, the Jacksonians found the Bank defiant of the government and arrogantly independent of authority. This was their way of saying that the Bank's president answered charges that it was unconstitutional, useless to the government, and harmful to the economy; and resisted efforts to interfere with its management. What he did was lawful and in a democratic sense proper. Similarly, Andrew Jackson defied the Supreme Court and Congress. Both refused to be interrupted in the discharge of their responsibilities. But Andrew Jackson's "sagacious temerity" saw him through. Nicholas Biddle was not so lucky. Yet both, despite their forceful personalities, were pretty much tossed about by the economic upheaval of their time—an upheaval occasioned not by the dissatisfactions of a dying agrarian order but by a vigorous democracy's impatience to man the Industrial Revolution in America. We are still in the economy they created.

Though my own disposition is to deplore with Albert Gallatin, Ralph Waldo Emerson, and Henry David Thoreau the aggressive, intense, and rapacious growth of the American economy in the 19th century and its passion for money-making, yet I think there was never the ghost of a chance that the development could have been

---

[46] 29th Congress, 1st Session, HR 226, pp. 414, 532; Biddle Papers, 1 PLB (1836), 67; Knox, *History of Banking*, 75-76; W. B. Smith, 180-82.

other than what it was. The Bank of the United States was an important restraint and corrective, but to suppose that it could maintain itself in the teeth of the overwhelming inflationary tide established in the Jacksonian age and dominant over the American economy ever since, is illusory. The democracy, rapt in dreams of avarice, would brook no restraints. The course which history took was the ineluctable product of the opportunity afforded by American resources to European energy. Furthermore, the triumph of business enterprise has had advantages and need not be wept over. It may therefore be recognized for what it was and not as the agrarian reform it has been made out to be. The federal Bank was not destroyed by champions of the helpless contending against the money power, but by a rising and popular business interest that found the Bank doubly offensive for being both vested and regulatory—Wall Street, the state banks, and speculative borrowers dressing up for the occasion in the rags of the poor and parading with outcries against oppression by the aristocratic Mr Biddle's hydra of corruption, whose nest they aspired to occupy themselves.

I have narrated the federal Bank's misfortunes with so much detail that my readers may excuse a brief summary of the factors that brought the Bank to its end but that are far less important as such than as factors of the 19th century American economy's development in general. These factors, which of course inter-played, were the following:

1. The most important was the impatience of the state banks and of business enterprise with the federal Bank's restraint upon bank credit.

2. Paralleling this entrepreneurial resentment was the attitude of the agrarians, who hated all banks and distrusted the business world generally. A few of them understood that the federal Bank was a corrective for the evils of inflation and that for practical reasons it should have their support; but most of them got no further than the fallacy that the Bank of the United States was nothing but the biggest and worst "bank" of all. They blamed it for doing what its business enemies blamed it for not doing, i.e., making credit cheap and easy.

3. There was also the hostility of the states' rights politicians for a federal institution which penetrated the area of state jurisdiction and was conducted independently of state taxing and other authority.

4. The federal Bank was obnoxious to many not merely because it was a "bank" but because it was a corporation. This enmity, which ran back farther than the South Sea Bubble, was nursed by agrarians and also by business men who had not yet learned what a useful device the corporate form of business organization could be. The merchant world of the past had comprised individuals only, trading on their personal responsibility, and though the merchant world was now giving way to the complex world of multifarious business specialties, the idea persisted in many quarters that business should remain individualistic. This was the doctrine most militantly held by the Loco Focos.

5. A factor of more limited scope but of the greatest cogency was New York's determination to supersede Philadelphia. This was not a matter of mere vanity, by any means. New York's business community was the chief source of the Bank's funds, and yet the Bank was controlled by Philadelphians, who could say how much the New Yorkers might borrow "of their own money." Boston and Baltimore also, without desiring New York's preeminence, wanted Philadelphia's ended.

6. Another similar factor of limited scope but utmost cogency at the outset was the Jacksonian principle that to the victor belonged the spoils. The federal Bank was an organization to be manned by the faithful. This objective was soon supplanted by the view that the Bank, "as at present organized," in the words Andrew Jackson often repeated, should be brought to an end.

The Bank's enemies were animated in different degree by some or conceivably by all of the foregoing, as might have been a New York politician, for example, with local banking and business interests but still nominally loyal to his agrarian origins. Though agrarian enmity to the federal Bank was the oldest factor at work, it was no longer the most active or potent. The effective enmity at the outset of Andrew Jackson's administration was that mentioned first —the enmity of the state banks and the business world. Its purpose was to prevent recharter. The early purpose of the Jacksonian politicians, however—or some of them—was probably to get control of the Bank. Up to this point there is no evidence of any real Jacksonian plan and none at all of any purpose in General Jackson's own mind; though he was often moved by his conviction that banks were unconstitutional and his vague, congenital association of them with the South Sea Bubble. But in the fecund minds of the New Yorkers the various considerations coalesced into an intelligent and practicable program for ending the Bank's existence to the advantage of their state and city. On the destructive side, the attacks of the Jacksonian press should continue. Leadership should be given to the hostility which the states' rights politicians felt, and President Jackson himself should be animated to assume a position of definite hostility and to popularize it. The federal Bank's regulation of the state banks was presented to him as "oppression," as an aggrandizement of federal powers, and an offense to state sovereignty. His animosity was gradually aroused till the point was reached when it worked of itself.

Meanwhile, on the constructive side, the New Yorkers got their Safety Fund established, a general measure that was seriously marred by incidental blunders of draftsmanship but embodied an original scheme of bank regulation which a little more than a century later was revived and made national by the Franklin Roosevelt administration in the form of federal deposit insurance. Thus Mr Van Buren prepared not merely to end Philadelphia's financial primacy and the Bank of the United States but to have New York assume Philadelphia's place with the best banking system there was in the country.

VIII

"The Anglo-American world," Professor Joseph Dorfman observes of business relations about this time and a little later, "had an organic unity that made for the fluid movement of ideas, methods, and men across the Atlantic in both directions." This condition is illustrated in the coeval and parallel attacks upon the Bank of England and the Bank of the United States in their respective countries. The Bank of England's charter expired in 1833, the Bank of the United States' in 1836. Opposition to renewal rested in both cases, but in varying degree, upon similar considerations, viz., resentment against the government Bank's "monopoly," especially on the part of other banks and private business, and a *laisser faire* conviction that free or competitive banking would be not only more liberal of credit but self-regulatory. There were the significant differences between the two institutions that the Bank of England was wholly owned by private shareholders whereas a fifth interest in the Bank of the United States was held by the

American government, with participation in the Bank's management, and that the Bank of England had an actual though limited monopoly, whereas the Bank of the United States had none in any real sense.[47]

The monopoly of the Bank of England was a monopoly of note issue, originally in all England and Wales but since 1826 in London and within a radius of sixty-five miles thereof only. London, however, was just where competition was most eager to penetrate. Moreover, it was definitely both the trend and the purpose of the Bank of England under Horsley Palmer—as of the Bank of the United States less definitely under Nicholas Biddle—to take over the entire paper circulation, while holding the country's metallic reserves. Together, therefore, the country banks opposed the Bank of England because it threatened their part in the circulation and the would-be city bankers opposed it because it kept them out of London, except under restrictions.* The concern of both groups was roughly paralleled overseas by the state banks' resentment at the federal Bank's interference in their note issue and by the city banks' further resentment, in New York, Boston, and Baltimore, at the advantage its situation gave Philadelphia. In 1833 the English joint stock banks gained the right to establish themselves in London, provided that they did not issue notes, but the Bank of England was not destroyed. On the contrary, its control of currency and credit was improved.

Although complaints against the two Banks sounded much alike, they reflected different modes of central bank control, different competitive relations, and different public sensitivities. In America, the state banks issued circulating notes universally, and in consequence central bank pressure for their redemption was a regulatory measure universally felt. It was the United States Bank's chief regulatory device; the discount rate was not. In England, notes other than the Bank of England's had a much less general use, the Bank had a territorial monopoly such as the Bank of the United States never had, and its pressure for the redemption of country bank notes was less comprehensive and less palpable. Accordingly

* Banks established in London could not be joint stock banks with more than six partners. Note issue had been voluntarily abandoned by London banks, as it soon was in large part by the more important New York banks.

[47] Dorfman, *JEH*, xi (1951), 147; Dorfman, 604.

this mode of central bank control had not the importance in Britain that it had in the States.

On the other hand, though the basic metallic reserves of the American banking system were held by the Bank of the United States, this element of central bank responsibility was less developed in America than in Britain, and its importance was less generally recognized. The Bank of England, wrote a contemporary American observer, more than the Bank of the United States is "the national depository of specie." American business did not converge on Philadelphia or any other one American city as British business did on London, it was influenced by the Americans' passion for regional independence, and the conception of an organic, centralized credit system was psychologically distasteful to them, if recognized at all. Since the British country banker was inured to the focus on London, whose funds had a unique importance, he accepted the Bank of England's retention of the banking system's metallic reserves with a tolerance quite alien to what American bankers could feel.[48]

Transcending these differences and intensifying them, was the basic fact that the States, having great opportunities for investment but quite inadequate savings, had the greater development, the more avid demand for money, and more disposition to resent restraints upon credit than had Great Britain, which was a lending economy and much more mature. But by the same token, resentment toward the federal Bank's restraint was tempered by some recognition that the Bank increased the amount of local capital. Accordingly, the net difference in the situation of the two Banks, leaving aside their respective errors, was that hostility to the Bank of the United States was roused chiefly by its regulatory action and secondarily by its competitive advantages; whereas hostility to the Bank of England, it seems to me, was roused chiefly by its competitive advantages and secondarily by its regulatory action.

The assault on the Bank of England seems to have made a deeper impression on the Americans than was true the other way round. A writer in the *Southern Review*, November 1831, was encouraged in his opposition to the Bank of the United States by reports that the British were "heartily tired" of the Bank of England; and the Washington *Globe*, 12 July 1832, coupled announcement that the President had the day before vetoed the federal Bank's new charter with mention of the gratifying criticism of the Bank of England by

[48] *American Quarterly Review* xv (June 1834), 518.

The Times and the *Courier*, of London. "It will give great relief to the friends of our free institutions to perceive that these great and leading prints in the cause of reform in England take the same ground of opposition to the GRAND BANKING MONOPOLY there as is taken here to our Anglo-American Bank." Several years later the New York *Evening Post*, 11 March 1841, expressed its *laisser faire* interest in abandonment of banking regulation by noting that in England a choice was to be made "between a great artificial regulator on the one hand and the laws of trade on the other"; and it commended for the currency "the same wholesome freedom of action and competition which keeps all other pursuits of business in healthful order." Domestic friends of the Bank of the United States saw things the other way round: "What the Bank of England has done for the commercial credit of Great Britain," said a writer in the *American Quarterly Review* in 1834, "it would be in the power of the Bank of the United States to do for the great interests of this country, were it permitted to employ its resources not in protecting itself against the illegal acts of the government but in the performance of its appropriate functions."[49]

Though in the States, opposition to the central bank was voiced in a hypocritical jargon of agrarian and equalitarian idealism, in Britain it was more honest, intelligent, and realistic. In the Parliamentary hearings of 1832, John Easthope, Member of Parliament, a stockbroker, and former country banker, expressed opinions "decidedly against the exclusive privileges of the Bank of England." He preferred a system of "free banking" like the Scottish, or at any rate one which did not require that the Bank of England "should trouble themselves with anything but their own business." If the Bank's "exclusive privileges" were withheld, more banks would be established in London, and given competition and publicity they would check each other. The public would derive additional security and advantage from the establishment of a system of joint stock banking companies, "almost any system being preferable to the present system of the Bank of England."[50]

One may find defects in Mr Easthope's reasoning, but one recognizes that it was reasoning. British forensics were not without their

---

[49] *Southern Review*, November 1831, 36; Washington *Globe*, 26 September 1833; Hildreth, *Banks, Banking, and Paper Currencies*, 48, 113, 152-53, 171; *American Quarterly Review* xv (June 1834), 519.

[50] British Parliament, *Hearings, Bank of England Charter*, 3 August 1832, Queries 5785, 5845, 5854-55, 5858, 5894, 5928; Redlich, 168.

demagogy, however, thanks to the vivacious and irresponsible William Cobbett, Member of Parliament, who in this matter bestrode the Atlantic world like a Jacksonian Colossus. He had written an encomiastic, so-called *Life* of Andrew Jackson, and he had republished in London William Gouge's *History of Paper Money and Banking*. He had himself assailed the Bank of the United States when a Philadelphia journalist, he had since assailed the Bank of England back in his native country, and he now rejoiced in the heroism of the virtuous President whose heel was crushing the American monster's head. "The United States of America," he wrote, "and particularly the farmers and working men of those states, now headed by the bravest man of whom the history of the world affords us any knowledge; . . . those people have resolved to get rid of the blighting curse of paper money." (Actually, of course, getting rid of the Bank of the United States would be to get rid of only that paper money issued by the Bank, which was about one-quarter of the aggregate, and it would result, as it did, in a still greater volume of paper money than before.) "From the first," Cobbett went on, "from the issuing of the President's reasons for his veto, . . . I predicted that if the democracy of the country once clearly understood the matter, they would put an end to the paper money completely. And that would in a very short time put an end to our paper money. . . . The paper money crew are smitten with fear; their knees knock together; their teeth chatter in their heads. . . ." He had a right, he said, to glory in the events which were taking place. "Before the Bank was established, I warned the American Congress and the American people—fully warned them—of the dangerous consequences. . . . I said some time back that it must come to this, or that the people must go and take NICHOLAS BIDDLE and fling him out into the street and take all his books and burn them." Mr Cobbett could assure his readers that things were in train for a mighty change in America. "There is an organization of the working men," he said, "for the purpose of ridding the country of paper money, by the means of which they are fraudulently robbed of their earnings. They call the bank of NICHOLAS BIDDLE the 'BRITISH BANK'. Ah! they see through the whole of the conspiracy. They see who is at the bottom of the whole; they see that the base and cowardly imps of hell who are everlastingly seeking the destruction of freedom all over the world are the principals and that NICHOLAS BIDDLE and his crew are only the underlings; they see that the base and bloody-minded villains on this side of the water intended to destroy them or to make them slaves by means of this paper money."[51]

This sort of thing was fairly paralleled in the United States. President Van Buren in his annual message to Congress, December 1839, said that setting up a new bank in even "the most distant of our villages places the business of that village within the influence of the money power of England." His statement involved the perfectly innocent and objective fact that the English-speaking communities were economically a unit, the one in the Old World being creditor and that in the New, debtor. Putting a sinister and invidious light on the fact was demagogy.[52]

The like animosities which the Bank of England and the Bank of the United States had to face did not avail to fetch them together in mutual sympathy. They continually rubbed each other the wrong way, though the business men of the two economies—in London and in New York—got on for the most part as if they were one. The managers of the Bank of England, like most substantial business men, did not like Nicholas Biddle or trust his judgment. He was too facile and too unconventional for them. They had been drawn to the Bank from their counting houses, he from his study. That he was more advanced than they in formulating and assuming the responsibilities of the government Bank as regulator of the currency and of the money market, was not in itself a reason for their resenting the way he conducted affairs. But the originality and independence which characterized his conduct were bound to set him apart from the kind of men who make money by inspiring confidence in themselves and realize that in such matters confidence is seldom inspired by the talkative and unconventional. A final distinction is characteristic. Mr Biddle, an intellectual, sought painstakingly to explain and justify the play of the federal Bank in the economy. The managers of the Bank of England, drilled in the world of private business, said nothing they were not required to say. One is led by the respective outcomes to think that taciturnity is best.

* The American "working men" to whose organization Mr Cobbett refers were the Loco Focos, who will appear later.

51 Niles xlvii (1834), 4, 15.
52 Richardson iv, 1762.

CHAPTER 15

Panic, Suspension, Resumption

1837-1838

I. Debt, surplus, and specie circular — II. London and Phila-
delphia prior to suspension — III. The cotton transactions:
London versus Philadelphia — IV. New York's program —
V. Philadelphia's program — VI. The surplus — VII. The
Loco Focos

I

SUCH had been the growth of the American economy and so strong
the aversion to aggrandizement of federal powers, that by 1827 the
federal government's debt was being rapidly reduced and plans for
disposal of a surplus were being considered. The debt was fully paid
in 1835. Then in June 1836, Congress enacted a unique and curious
measure providing that the federal surplus be distributed to the
individual states.

The receipts and expenditures of the Treasury, 1828 to 1837,
were as follows (in thousands) :[1]

Year	Customs	Public Land Sales	Total Receipts*	Expenditures
1828	$23,200	$ 1,000	$24,800	$16,400
1829	22,700	1,500	24,800	15,200
1830	21,900	2,300	24,800	15,100
1831	24,200	3,200	28,500	15,200
1832	28,500	2,600	31,900	17,300
1833	29,000	4,000	33,900	23,000
1834	16,200	4,900	21,800	18,600
1835	19,400	14,800	35,400	17,600
1836	23,400	24,900	50,800	30,900
1837	11,200	6,800	25,000	37,200

* The total includes other, minor revenue.

In all of these ten years but the last, receipts exceeded expenditures by a large amount, and in 1836, the last year of Andrew Jackson's Presidency, total Treasury receipts were twice what they had

[1] Dewey, *Financial History*, 168-69, 217-22, 246.

been in 1829, his first year. Although the growth of receipts from the sales of public lands was impressive, the bulk of the surplus arose from customs; and although these fell sharply in 1834, when the lowered rates of the compromise tariff of 1833 became effective, they at once began mounting again from the lower level. Since the government's income was derived mainly from customs, since the customs were derived from the importation of goods, and since the importations put the economy in debt to Britain, the seeming prosperity of the American government was in fact incidental to prodigal purchases abroad; and liquidation of the federal debt was concomitant with an extravagant expansion of the debt owed to Europe by private business and by the individual states.

Importations, Mr Gallatin observed, had averaged $59,000,000 a year from 1822 to 1830; from 1831 to 1833 they averaged $83,-000,000, from 1834 to 1837 they averaged $130,000,000, and in 1836 alone they amounted to $168,000,000. Moreover the excess of imports over exports had risen rapidly from an average of $4,000,-000 a year in the first period to $61,000,000 in 1836. The official figures of exports and imports reported by the American customs service exhibited, said a British writer in 1837, "perhaps the most striking proof of overtrading ever given to the world." For the years 1830 to 1837 the excess of imports over exports, which meant an equivalent lent and invested in America by Europe, aggregated about $140,000,000. The eagerness of the New World to borrow was matched by the eagerness of the Old to lend. There was not only American speculation proper but also speculation in America by Europeans.[2]

The sale of public lands, though another important source of federal income, was more significant as a medium of speculation. The lands concerned lay mainly in the Mississippi and Ohio river valleys. They were fertile and included promising sites for urban and industrial development. They now comprise some of the wealthiest areas on earth. The government was selling them for $1.25 an acre. It kept the price low in order to avoid discrimination against settlers who were poor, but the low price was equally advantageous to professional speculators, who had already the advantage of being organized, alert, practiced, and catered to by their own banks. The latter were practically free of restraint. Each bank could count the notes of other banks as reserves and expand its loans accordingly; with

---

[2] Gallatin III, 386; [J. R. McCulloch], *Edinburgh Review* LXV (1837), 223.

the general result that the more the banks lent the more they mutually augmented their reserves and the more they were able to lend. No legal requirements governed bank reserves before 1837 either in amount or in composition, or long thereafter save sporadically, and there was now no federal Bank maintaining systematic pressure on the banks to redeem their notes. The more frequent and numerous transactions were, the easier to maintain the airy fabric of mutual debt and the less evident the risk to the individual participant who held the obligations of the others and supported his own by their aid.

Besides over-trading in government lands, "speculations in unimproved town lots, mines, and every description of rash undertakings increased at the same rate." The Jacksonian democracy was everywhere absorbed in schemes to make money hand over fist. The whole economy was in a fever of excitement and expansion, stimulated by streams of immigrants and capital goods pouring in from Europe.[3]

The total number of banks in the United States in 1836 was nearly 600, of which more than one-third had been set up in the previous three years.* There was an even greater expansion of bank liabilities. In the East, note issues increased 50 per cent during the three years mentioned, in the West about 100 per cent, in the South 130 per cent. This expansion of the liabilities of banks to the public meant, of course, a corresponding expansion of the public's liabilities to the banks. But in the prevailing enthusiasm, men's eyes were turned from the swelling volume of their liabilities to gleam with satisfaction on what the assets were doing.[4]

The current fiscal policy of the federal government was a product of the current over-trading, inflation, and speculation, but also a contributor thereto. For these evils, which Andrew Jackson aimlessly deplored, could not have been more effectively promoted by Jacksonian policies had that been their purpose. Thus retirement of the public debt, in which the General took great pride, as if it were a personal achievement—as indeed it was in a sense because the

---

* Records of the number of banks in this period are erratic, there being no systematic assembly of figures. Branches were often enumerated as banks. According to Secretary Woodbury, October 1835, "the whole number of banks chartered" was 568, with 122 branches. (Treasury Department, Secretary, *Reports on Finances, 1790-1849*, III, 665.) Gallatin reports 322 in 1839 and 659 in 1840. (Gallatin III, 369.)

[3] Gallatin III, 386.   [4] Knox, *History of Banking*, 82.

burden of it fell inequitably on the southern planters, of whom he was one—closed an important field of conservative investment and returned funds to investors who then had to find other uses for them.* In consequence the demand for other investments was intensified and their prices were driven up. A less direct but not less significant stimulus to over-trading arose from the illusion that payment of the public debt was the result of public thrift, honesty, and grit, whereas it was in fact the result of speculation, over-trading, and a protective tariff. A debt was being paid off in one quarter by the assumption of a larger one in another. But the performance was novel, and superficial views of it inevitably prevailed. Albert Gallatin himself had thought the retirement of the public debt would be a good thing; but he found instead that it was the "signal for an astonishing increase in the indebtedness of the community at large." A result he thought perhaps worse even than civil war "was the rapid decline in public economy and morality; the shameless scramble for public money; the wild mania for speculation; the outburst of every one of the least creditable passions of American character."[5]

In his first presidential message, 1829, General Jackson had expressed the expectation that once the federal debt was paid there would always be thenceforth a surplus in the Treasury "beyond what may be required for its current service." He repeated this expectation in his message the next year. Being opposed to enlarged federal powers and believing the Constitution did not permit use of the funds for public improvements by the federal government, he suggested their distribution to the states for that purpose according to their ratio of representation. The law enacted by Congress followed this original suggestion in substance, but since the General had changed his mind, the distribution was called a "deposit" in order to avoid his disapproval—i.e., the surplus was to be deposited with the states, not distributed, upon receipt from them of certificates expressing their obligation to repay the sums "deposited." The sum directed to be "deposited" was "the money . . . in the Treasury" on the 1st of the following January in excess of $5,000,000. What that sum would be was at the moment only to be conjectured. It was to

---

* Southerners of more perspicacity than the General in economic matters reasonably and loudly contended that the tariffs which retired the debt and supplied the surplus were an outrageous tax on the agricultural South for the benefit of northern manufacturers.

5 Henry Adams, *Gallatin*, 656.

be "deposited" with the several states "in proportion to their respective representation in the Senate and House of Representatives," and in four equal parts, on the first day of January, April, July, and October, 1837. The act was approved 23 June 1836. Senator Benton, who had preferred that the surplus be used for national defenses, said of the arrangement: "It is in name a deposit; in form, a loan; in essence and design, a distribution." Henry Clay, who wanted the funds distributed, said: "If in form it was a deposit with the states, in fact and in truth it was a distribution. So it was then regarded. So it will ever remain."[6]

At the President's direction, 11 July 1836, less than three weeks after approval of the distribution, Secretary Levi Woodbury issued the "specie circular," which directed land agents to accept only gold and silver in payment for public lands. This document was notable for being the only administrative act of President Jackson that was consistent with the hard-money doctrine absorbed from his agrarian background and always professed by him. It was a step toward blessing America, the most progressive and dynamic of economies, with an exclusively metallic circulation such as Europe had had in the Middle Ages; but its immediate purpose was to prevent "frauds, speculations, and monopolies in the purchase of the public lands and the aid which is said to be given to effect these objects by excessive bank credits." This purpose was laudable. But the measure itself was unconscionably clumsy and taken too late to do anything but harm. It was intended to protect poor settlers and to curb the land speculators, whom, however, it largely spared because they were better able to get control of specie than the poor settlers were; and, by permitting less public land to come on the market, it gave the speculators who had land in their possession already a further advantage. Though it checked the growth of the surplus, it was in conflict with the distribution, its tendency being to impound specie in the West, where the land sales were, while the distribution required the specie to be in the more populous East, where most of the surplus would go.[7]

The difficulties became lively the first of the year when the distribution began, the one favorable development being that the amount to be distributed was less than had been expected. Back in October it

6 Richardson III, 1014, 1077-78; Knox, *United States Notes*, 169-71; Benton I, 652; Bourne, 19-21.
7 Knox, *History of Banking*, 81-82; Niles L (1836), 337.

had looked as if the amount would be $50,000,000; in December it had looked more like $42,000,000; and by the first of January it was in fact $37,468,860. Each quarterly installment, in consequence, was to be $9,367,215. Some of this money was in banks situated in the states to which it was to be distributed. Much was not. Some banks had enough cash and collectible loans to enable them to make their payments. Many had not. Over the country as a whole, the banks that had received the surplus were not in general the banks that held the gold and silver in which the surplus was to be distributed, and the funds in the individual states did not match the amounts to be distributed to those states. The requirements of the specie circular, aggravated by the distribution, produced absurd disorder. It caused, in Mr Gallatin's words, "a drain of specie on the banks of New York at a time when it was important that that point should have been strengthened. It transferred specie from the place where it was most wanted, in order to sustain the general currency of the country, to places where it was not wanted at all. It thus accumulated so much in Michigan that, whilst it was travelling from New York to Detroit, the Secretary of the Treasury was obliged to draw heavily on Michigan in favor of New York and other seaports." Another contemporary wrote: "The monetary affairs of the whole country were convulsed—millions upon millions of coin were *in transitu* in every direction and consequently withdrawn from useful employment. Specie was going up and down the same river to and from the South and North and the East and West at the same time."[8]

The surplus had been accumulated in the form of balances due the government on the books of the pet banks, and the administration in Washington seems to have been under the impression that though the banks had lent the funds, as Mr Taney had encouraged them to do, they also retained them and could at any time meet heavy withdrawals in specie. Actually, as Jabez Hammond said of the situation in New York, the banks had "treated this immense amount of money as so much capital on which they could make loans," and consequently the order from the Treasury for the distribution was to them "extremely embarrassing." They "complained that the mode of distribution adopted by the secretary, Mr Woodbury, was unwise and unnecessarily oppressive." This was in New York, where the banks were hand in glove with the party and where moreover there

8 Gallatin III, 391-92; Bourne, 27-38.

would be a net gain of funds from the distribution. The western banks could complain far more. Government funds had accumulated in them to an amount double what they could keep under the distribution, and suddenly they were called on to surrender the excess in specie to be shipped east. The Jacksonians were not peculiarly responsible for the distribution, but they administered it in a crude fashion intolerably hard on the West. "The specie circular may have been harsh," writes Dr Carter H. Golembe in his account of western banking in this period, "but the withdrawal of deposits was fatal."[9]

II

Although the specie circular and the distribution were important domestic disturbances in the United States, they were minor beside other evils produced by years of speculation and hasty expansion in the transatlantic economy comprising Britain and America. These two jealous and touchy partners complemented each other to the immense concern of each. Britain had become the premier industrial and financial power of the world. She found in the States the premier market for her goods and for her capital and the premier source of cotton for her mills. Americans found in her their premier market for their cotton and their securities. With these they paid for what they obtained from her in goods. In June 1836, because her specie reserves were falling away rapidly, the Bank of England raised her discount rate from 4 to 4½ per cent. In August she raised it again from 4½ to 5 per cent. But not until after she undertook this action, apparently, did she become aware of the extent to which credit in the British money market was centered on American trade. About the same time she got word of the specie circular. Filled with alarm at the situation in the British market and at what the specie circular indicated was and would be the situation in America, the Bank took direct action in a letter to her Liverpool agent instructing him to reject the paper of certain specified houses with American interests. She allowed this discrimination to become known in an ill-considered and startling fashion that annihilated the credit of those houses and shook the whole trade. Thus within a few weeks the blow delivered the American market by President Jackson with the specie circular was paralleled by the Bank of England in the British market.[10]

9 Jabez Hammond ɪɪ, 469; Golembe, 208.
10 [J. R. McCulloch], *Edinburgh Review* ʟxv (1837), 232-33.

Each of these markets, which represented respectively the debtor and creditor halves of the transatlantic economy, was divided between the friends and the enemies of the other. At the same time that *The Times* in London was thundering about the perfidious Americans, British investors had been buying all they could of the Americans' securities; and while some Americans had been occupying themselves with the perfidies of Britain, others had been courting her for her money. One of these was Samuel Jaudon, second to Nicholas Biddle in the Bank of the United States. He, of course, deplored the Bank of England's proscription of American credit. "The Bank of England," he wrote to Baring Brothers from Philadelphia in October 1836, "having slept during the onset, wakes to the danger after a decided check has been given by other parties." He said that the effect of the stand taken against American stocks was severely felt in the States. But he blamed no less the Jackson administration's "absurd attempt to introduce a purely metallic currency." Confidence, he said, which had been maintained so long by the hope of better times, was beginning to give way "and failures have commenced among our mercantile and trading classes." At the moment the current ills may have been aggravated by the approaching national elections early in November, for during the early winter things did not rapidly grow worse. Mr Jaudon wrote to Baring Brothers again in December in a more cheerful mood; the United States Bank's stock, which had fallen to 115 in October, had got back up to 121. But in the spring things worsened again drastically. Thomas Wren Ward wrote the Barings 24 March that Nicholas Biddle's views regarding the Bank of England were kinder than his own; Biddle thought its course would have a good effect, because some failures in London would bring relief all around. That the Barings themselves, like Thomas Ward, took a more severe view of the Bank of England's action is suggested in a letter of Joshua Bates to Samuel Jaudon the 1st of March. Saying that bills amounting to three or four millions sterling might return to the United States under protest, he continued, "Whether this calamity is to be avoided now depends on a few individuals in the Bank parlour as little remarkable for their wisdom as for their liberality." A month later, 1 April 1837, Mr Bates declared himself "in a great fever" to liquidate the firm's commodity holdings, "tea and indigo and everything else"; and he reported that the Baron Rothschild, in Paris, had urged him to do all in his power to get an arrangement carried into effect between the Bank of England and the United States Bank, for "without that there can be no orders for goods, and business will be at a stand in three or four months."[11]*

The crisis came sooner than that. There was a contraction in the demand for cotton and a fall in its price. In consequence, early in March 1837, an important firm in New Orleans, Herman Briggs and Company, failed, being unable to realize enough from the sale of their cotton to pay the obligations they had incurred in purchasing it. A burst of similar failures followed in New Orleans and New York. The British had stopped buying, had stopped lending, and expected payment of what was due them. The Americans found themselves unable to sell, unable to buy, unable to borrow, unable to pay. Business was at the stand which the Baron Rothschild had apprehended.

The arrangement he had hoped would be made between the Bank of England and the United States Bank is evidently one which James Pattison, Governor of the Bank of England, had proposed to Nicholas Biddle in a letter of 22 March 1837. The proposal, doubtless, was initiated by Baring Brothers, one of whom, Sir Francis, was an influential member of the Bank's Court of Directors.

"It has been suggested to the Court of Directors," Governor Pattison wrote, "that facilities might be afforded to the Commercial interests in both Countries, and the disastrous consequences incident to the present state of credit be mitigated, by the conjoint interference of the important body over which you preside and the Bank of England. The Court of Directors, acting on this suggestion, has authorized me to communicate with you, and to express its readiness to concur in any measures feasible in themselves, and likely to produce the desired results.

"In the absence of intelligence as to the effects that may be produced in America by the state of things here and in the midst of many difficulties in which the subject is involved, we can only at present express a willingness to accept Bills to be drawn by the Bank of the United States on the Bank of England, to an amount not exceeding two Millions Sterling, one half of the amount drawn for

---

* This Baron Rothschild was James, who headed the Paris branch of the banking firm. All five of the Rothschild brothers were created barons by Emperor Francis I of Austria in 1822.

[11] Baring Papers, MC, 15 and 31 October, 7 December 1836; OC, 24 March 1837; AC, 1 March 1837; MC, 1 April 1837.

to be covered by a simultaneous transmission of bullion, the other half being covered by Securities consisting of Bills of Exchange and State Stock valued at the current price in America, such Stock to be redeemed within Six Months from the maturity of the Drafts, and the Advances to bear an Interest of Five per Cent per Annum.

"We hope that this arrangement by furnishing our Money Markets with Bills of an undoubted character, may facilitate the liquidation of the immense transactions now pending between the two Countries. Should any fresh notion strike us previously to the receipt of your reply, we shall not hesitate again to address you."*

Simultaneously with this proposal from Threadneedle Street, a different plan was being arranged in the States. Prime, Ward, and King, in New York, reported it in a letter to Baring Brothers dated 24, 25 March 1837, which would be a day or two after the Bank of England's letter to the United States Bank. Prime, Ward, and King reported "good prospects of an arrangement with the United States Bank at Philadelphia to issue their post notes against good paper—and so exchange a less for a more convertible security." The same would "also be done by the Morris Canal and Banking Company, and good will result to sustain those who have means and ought to be supported, whilst no false credit will be extended. . . ." What had happened is that a number of New York business men, not too jealous of Philadelphia to get help thence in a desperate situation, had taken counsel with Nicholas Biddle and concurred with him in measures to be taken at once—measures largely if not wholly devised by him.** Till cotton could be sold once more and at an accustomed price so as to provide funds with which to meet maturing American obligations abroad, it was imperative that something acceptable be offered in the foreign money markets to sustain American credit. What the Bank of England wanted was gold, as her letter of 22 March to Mr Biddle clearly showed, and to draw in gold she had raised the discount rate. But gold was about the last

* I am indebted to the Governor and Company of the Bank of England for extracting the text of this letter and permitting me to publish it.

** Thomas Wren Ward wrote to Baring Brothers from New York a few days later: "Land speculators are failing by dozens every day and weak jobbers and importers also." The United States Bank "is applied to by all the leading institutions and merchants of New York to aid by shipping specie, by drawing exchange, by issuing post notes here (to bring out the money of those who are afraid to trust the merchants), and to issue sterling bonds." Baring Papers, OC, 29 March 1837.

thing the American banks could let her have. The precious metals were going into hoards, public and private, and the American government, itself the largest transactor in the economy, was refusing to accept anything but those metals. In these circumstances the plan agreed upon in New York was that the United States Bank and several others, the Manhattan, the Bank of America, the Girard, and the Morris Canal and Banking Company, sell their own obligations, mostly in the form of bonds, in the London, Paris, Amsterdam, and domestic money markets. The amount to be sold ranged up toward $12,000,000, the press reports probably reflecting the uncertainty of expectations. The offering was to be supported by a shipment to London of $1,000,000 in specie from the United States Bank, sometime. These arrangements were made in the course of a few days and presumably communicated at once by Prime, Ward, and King and by Thomas Ward to Baring Brothers and through the latter to the Bank of England.[12]

Confirming them, 1 April, Mr Biddle wrote from New York to the Bank's correspondents in London, le Havre, and Amsterdam—respectively the Barings, Hottinguer and Company, and Hope and Company. His letter follows: "You will learn from other quarters what has occurred here during the last few days, and I need not therefore do more than add a few words in regard to our relations with your house.

"On my arrival here I found a state of things requiring very prompt and vigorous interposition. The disasters in New Orleans and in London had nearly destroyed all confidence in private bills and left no means of remittance except specie. Of this the supply in the banks was very small, for altho' much has undoubtedly come into the country, yet owing to the perverseness of the Government it had ceased to be available for the purposes of commerce. The crusade against banks and the discrimination at the Land Offices between specie and bank paper has not been without its effect on the less intelligent part of our population, whom it has inclined to hoard specie. This inclination is further encouraged by the fact that the entire absence of the gold coinage from our circulation has rendered gold coins an object of luxury and curiosity in the eyes of Americans in the interior, and now since they can be obtained they have been lost to the general circulation by their attractiveness as a species of medal. The Land Offices too have absorbed a large

[12] Baring Papers, OC, 24 and 25 March 1837; Niles LII (1837), 65, 81; Hidy, 219.

part of the specie, which has been thus carried beyond the mountains. The consequence was that the specie in the banks being low they had for some time been pursuing a very vigorous system of curtailment, which compelled the merchants to great sacrifices in order to comply with their engagements. They submitted to this cheerfully as long as their commercial paper could be cashed at any rate, but when the recent disasters made the importers unwilling to take private bills, and the demands were again turned upon the vaults of the banks so as to require further curtailments, the commercial community began to despair of escaping from their difficulties and were on the eve of a general suspension of specie payments. I say a general suspension because if it had been practicable to select those who ought to fail and let them fail, as victims of their own rashness, it would have been desirable. But in moments of financial panic such a discrimination was impossible, and all that remained was by some vigorous effort to rally back the spirits of those who were about to throw up every thing in a moment of despair. The cause of the trouble I believed to be temporary. The cotton bills, discredited for a moment, would soon become abundant and sound, now that the crop had fallen to its proper commercial value, and the dispersed coin would be restored to the commercial cities by the low prices of foreign goods wanted in the interior. The question was only to save the community from its own fears. For this purpose the Bank consented to issue its bonds payable in London, Paris, and Amsterdam at twelve months from the date so as to furnish means of remittance. Those for London are made payable with you. It was necessary to domiciliate them somewhere. Mr Ward I learn from Mr Jaudon saw—or made—no objection. We were unwilling to seek any new channel when the old was so familiar and so satisfactory, and as these bonds require no acceptance and imply not the slightest responsibility on your part, I trust that the arrangement will not be unsatisfactory to you.

"On the whole—and this is my chief purpose in writing—this movement of the Bank is one of emergency, wholly conservative in its character, and designed to dissipate an alarm calculated to do infinite mischief. To our friends abroad I deem it particularly important. The country is very able and very willing to pay its debts. The causes which delay the payment are accidental and temporary and I think it better for them to receive such remittances as the country affords at the moment, rather than hazard the injury to their interests inevitable from a commercial panic. The Bank in fact interposes as the common friend of the interests on both sides of the Atlantic and I have no doubt that as soon as the mercantile community recovers from this momentary despair, with the benefit of a severe lesson, everything will resume its accustomed course and the remittances be abundant and satisfactory. This will be the case the sooner, since the withdrawal of almost all the open credits and the scarcity of money here, which must be made to continue for some time, will oblige the country to buy only what it can pay for at once."*

This letter upon its arrival in England must have been taken as an unintended, indirect, and unwelcome reply to the Bank of England's offer, which, it would be clear, had not been received by the Americans when their plan was decided upon but had it been received would not have been accepted. The Bank of England had wanted to get the maximum of bullion and grant the minimum of credit—her terms had been a credit of $10,000,000 against $5,000,-000 of bullion. What the Americans had decided on was a credit of maybe $10,000,000 or more against $1,000,000 of bullion. The Americans were not at all in the appropriate attitude of prostrate debtors; instead Mr Biddle was addressing his country's creditors as if from a great height. That his plans might succeed, as in fact they did, would make them no more palatable. The London market, with a superfluity of securities already, was to get still more of them and the vague promise of some gold. The audacious Mr Biddle was offhandedly annexing the City of London to Philadelphia and producing emotions in the Bank parlours in Threadneedle Street that must have taxed all sense of decorum.

But Mr Biddle, who was often correct in the estimate of his own importance, realized that he had direct access to the British investor and did not too greatly need the Bank of England's help. The British investor liked American securities, the record of which so far had been good. Through his own banker, he could obtain them from numerous merchant-bankers in London who had accepted them as cover for credit to their American correspondents. Baring Brothers, though leading suppliers of American securities, had no monopoly by any means. And these houses that dealt in American

* The original of this letter is in the Baring Papers, Miscellaneous Correspondence, at Ottawa; the Bank's retained copy is in the Biddle Papers, the Library of Congress, Washington; 1 PLB (1836), 168-70.

investments could be looked to for no very eager support of the Bank of England's deflationary action; they preferred lenity and just such access to American securities as Mr Biddle wanted to the British funds to be had in exchange for them.[13]

Both Thomas Wren Ward and the firm of Prime, Ward, and King seem to have approved the Biddle arrangement. Mr Ward was never swept off his feet by anything and least of all by admiration for Nicholas Biddle, but he reported to the Barings, 9 April 1837, that "Mr Biddle is getting the Bank of the United States very strong by what he is doing. You will get very little specie from this side for months to come—of this be fully assured. . . . I have felt some uneasiness lately about our banks, but there is a right feeling here that the banks must at all hazards pay specie and that paper must be lessened and prices brought down. Mr Biddle is collecting specie, but it is a very slow process."[14]

Through April Thomas Ward was anxiously watchful of Nicholas Biddle's procedure and inspired by no growing confidence in it. "I have fears that Mr Biddle's general judgment is not equal to the exigency," he reported toward the end of the month. He repeated his misgivings and found the Bank over-extending itself every way. Meanwhile the letters of both Biddle and Jaudon overflowed with confidence, and their acts indicate their own belief in what they said.* Their one note of regret is with the failure to ease the pressure on their drawing account with the Barings. Yet the last day of April a letter was got off to Governor Pattison, which came before the Court of Directors 25 May, acknowledging the Bank of England's offer, 22 March, of a credit of two millions sterling and declining it on the obvious ground that the bullion it called for could not possibly be spared, and that "the measures which the Bank of the United States deemed it advisable to pursue in order to protect the common interests of this country and Great Britain"—viz., the sale of bonds in the London market—made the measure proposed by the Bank of England unnecessary. "This country," Mr Biddle repeated, in the sanguine, clairvoyant fashion customary with him,

---

* In fact on 29 April 1837, the day before writing the letter next to be cited, Biddle said that "on the adjournment of Congress, two of the members persuaded me to associate with them in one enterprize, north of the Ohio, which will absorb all my means for some time to come." Biddle Papers, 1 PLB (1837), 182.

13 Jenks, 78.   14 Baring Papers, OC, 9 April 1837.

"is abundantly able and perfectly willing to pay all its debts to Europe. It has ample means to discharge them in any proper proportion of produce and bullion." But, because of the government's proceedings at Washington, "the coin portion of our currency is in a great degree lost for commercial purposes." In these circumstances bullion could not be exported by the American banks without a "highly disastrous" curtailment of loans. Instead the sale had been arranged of long-term obligations, "which, while they inspired confidence here and will enable the Country gradually to collect its metallic resources, seemed to possess the advantage of not encroaching upon the means either of the Bank of England or of private bankers, as shorter drafts would have probably done."* By now the obligations which the Americans purposed to sell in London had arrived, and according to Professor Leland H. Jenks they created great excitement. "No one ventured to doubt their intrinsic security. Not even the Bank of England would decline to honor them. And it began to appear that that venerable institution was being outwitted by the clever Mr Biddle."[15]

A minor feature of Nicholas Biddle's letter is the irritating implication that the debtor had only to decide between long-term and short-term obligations without asking the creditor's possible preferences or whether any such measures at all were agreeable to him. A major feature is the absence of even the slightest foreboding of the complete suspension of specie payments by all American banks, including the United States Bank, the week following. No central banker should be endowed with such an unfailing eye for the bright side of things only.

But men with less of a squint were surprised too. For on 11 May 1837, Prime, Ward, and King reported to Baring Brothers that "contrary to the expectations expressed in our last, the banks here have been unable to sustain themselves and by a common movement yesterday were obliged to suspend specie payments." The letter continued: "The immediate cause of this movement was so great a want of confidence among the depositors that very large sums were withdrawn in coin during the last two days." Had the demands

* I am indebted to the Governor and Company of the Bank of England for the text of this letter and permission to publish it. No retained copy was found amongst the Biddle Papers in the Library of Congress.

[15] Baring Papers, OC, 24 and 29 April, 4 May 1837; MC, 8 April 1837; Jenks, 90, 95.

come from note-holders only, "no mischief would have resulted; but against a combined movement on the part of those using banks for depositing their unusually large balances in these times of difficulty, there was no recourse but the one adopted. . . . We entertain the greatest fears that the United States Bank will, like all the banking institutions of our devoted country, be forced to adopt the same course. Their amount of specie does not exceed $1,500,000, their deposits nearly $2,000,000 and their circulation (old and new) about $7,000,000." All this was the more to be regretted, they said, because measures "were just now in progress to bring about some connexion between the Bank of the United States and the United States Treasury. . . . This must in the end prove to be true, but great confusion must now be the consequence for some time to come. Specie has already been sold at 12-1/2 per cent premium. Stocks have suddenly risen and like every other article of sale must continue to rise . . . in our depreciating currency."[16]

The despondency of this conservative, objective, and wealthy house was not shared universally. From the United States Bank, four days later, Samuel Jaudon reported the same developments to Baring Brothers with something like elation. The suspension, he said, would have the effect of securing many of the debts due the bank "which could not have been promptly collected if the excessive pressure and prevailing panic had continued." Confidence was now returning, he said, "depositors are using their funds, and property is rising toward its real value. . . ." The bank's loss from failures would be small "and will not affect our dividend."[17]

This good news, which must have made the Baring Brothers shudder, was the rosy prelude to acknowledgment of the awkward fact that the United States Bank was still unable to put its account with the House in proper shape. It had nothing to offer but excuses, promises, and the assurance that everything was all right, except for the shortage of ready cash. By this assurance the Barings were unimpressed; they closed their credit to the bank, which in future would be permitted to draw only against remittances of specie, cotton, or bills of the payment of which it had been advised by Barings. "For the present," Mr Ward was informed, "until the accounts are fully covered, they must not issue drafts upon us against anything they remit. We think you will agree with us that

[16] Baring Papers, OC, 11 May 1837.
[17] Baring Papers, MC, 15 May 1837.

whenever a whole community ceases to pay in the medium in use between one country and another, all foreign credits for the transactions of that community should cease."[18]

III

From having been saucy and confident the year before because they had just discharged their public debt, the Americans had become angry, perplexed, and unable even to reduce their other external obligations currently. But they had in Nicholas Biddle a resourceful and energetic protagonist. Abroad their creditors were represented by the Bank of England. The conflict between them was not noisy, for Mr Biddle and the gentlemen in Threadneedle Street had little direct discourse with one another and that little was polite. But the facts behind their urbane language were that Mr Biddle was wrapping the London money market around his little finger and the Old Lady would not have it.

However, Mr Biddle by no means had all America behind him. Though on balance the country was a debtor, there was a growing class of creditors, especially in New England and New York. These more conservative business men found deflation in accord with their interest; and neither sentiment nor position inclined them to like the efforts of Nicholas Biddle to prevent it. He irritated them as much as he did their friends in the City of London. They were intelligent, but he was too intelligent. He was too persuasive and too audacious. He was not content with a normal opportunism. Instead of nibbling safely at the course of events, he had schemes for redirecting them. He talked too condescendingly, his manner was over-confident, and he was too ready to look after not only the New World but the Old.

The object of Mr Biddle's efforts, now that suspension had become a reality, was support of the market for cotton and other agricultural staples. As much as any one and more than most, he sought payment of foreign debts and restoration of American credit abroad, but that could not be accomplished by going down cellar and getting out some money laid away in the dark for such purposes. It could only be accomplished by the disposal of American products to foreign buyers at an adequate price. The sale abroad of bank bonds shortly before the suspension had anticipated an early restoration of the commodity markets and a prompt recovery of

18 Baring Papers, OC, 14 June 1837.

agricultural prices, but nothing of that sort had come to pass. When it became clear that cotton would not regain value if left to itself, Nicholas Biddle decided to corner it. He would hold it off the market and starve the foreign buyers into buying at higher prices. The procedure he designed was comprehensive. Agents in the South would buy cotton and ship it to other agents in Liverpool. There it was to be held back and sold gradually so as to force up the price. To finance the holdings, an agent in London would sell American securities, including obligations of the bank and of others, to British bankers and investors. A compact merchandising and financing organization would do by itself what in times of normal business activity was done by hundreds or thousands of buyers, sellers, shippers, and lenders pursuing individually their own interest but producing collectively an orderly progress from production to consumption and from savings to investment. The operations could be maintained if there were a demand for either American cotton or American securities; but the basic condition must be a demand for cotton. Until that was restored, the operations rested on borrowings to tide over and help terminate an emergency. The effort was brilliant, bold, napoleonic. To the annoyance and surprise of conservatives, British and American, it succeeded, for a matter of two years.

The first step was to buy cotton, and this the United States Bank would make possible. But since there were no borrowers daring and wealthy enough to initiate the undertaking and since the bank could not legally buy and sell commodities itself, the transactions were conducted in the name of Nicholas Biddle and other senior officers, who borrowed from the bank the necessary funds.* Legally the cotton was theirs and the profit and loss was theirs; and since the laws at that time neither forbade nor restricted loans to bank officers, the arrangement was permissible. Moreover, save on the score of its purpose and scope, it was not unusual. It was a matter of course in American banking, and always had been, that the directors and managers of a bank had first claim on its facilities; and the arrangement made in the cotton dealings was definitely

---

* All American and Canadian banks were forbidden by their charters, following the Bank of England's, to deal in commodities, as they still are by the banking statutes; except when title was to be taken to property acquired in satisfaction of debts.

animated by a less selfish object than loans made to further purely private undertakings.

The real fault with the arrangements was that they concentrated risk instead of dispersing it. They made everything depend on the bank in Philadelphia—upon its funds and upon the judgment of its managers. Normally the movement of cotton from grower to spinner was effected by a chain of participants, each of whom was not merely an agent in the physical movement of the cotton but guarantor of a contract for its transfer. The grower contracted to sell his cotton to a dealer, who, when he had acquired it and shipped it, drew a bill on the British house to which it was consigned and which contracted to take it and pay for it, and this bill was sold by the dealer with his endorsement to his bank, which sent it to a banker abroad for collection of the amount due from the British house, to which the cotton had been shipped, and this amount was credited to the American bank on the books of the British banker. Still more intermediaries than these would probably participate, the whole movement being broken up into specialties. The value of the bill or other negotiable instrument used in the chain of transactions depended not only on the value of the cotton itself but on the worth of the respective participants as guarantors behind either the sale of the cotton or its purchase. But in the existing state of business on both sides of the Atlantic, all these participants were beset with paralysis. Because the British spinner would not or could not buy, no dealer would or could buy, no bank would or could lend. No cotton was going into use, no money was being made, no debts were being discharged.

Nicholas Biddle broke this *impasse* by having the bank assume the lead. Its doing so was, of course, irregular. Banks, like women, are not supposed to take the initiative. They consider proposals and say yes or no. This spreads the risk inherent in enterprise; it subjects the judgment of enterprisers to independent scrutiny, and though the banks, if they acquiesce, take some risk, they retain recourse upon the enterprisers and their property if the projects fail. In its cotton transactions the United States Bank had no sharers in the risk, except its own officers and agents. Its only security lay in the commodity itself: if prices rose, all would be well; if they did not, the bank had recourse to no one outside its own organization.

Nicholas Biddle did not lead his bank into this situation recklessly or ignorantly. He knew well what he was doing and believed his course was warranted by the plight of American producers in general, of Southern cotton producers especially, and by the paramount necessity of rehabilitating American credit abroad. He respected the principle that a bank, being debtor as well as creditor, should amply secure itself against loss lest it sacrifice the interests of its creditors to those of its debtors. But he also thought that the economy should not be allowed to lie prone for want of courage and resourcefulness. The lesser evil, in his opinion, was to have the bank take the risk in the debtor interest, general welfare being more dependent on that course for the moment than on one in the creditor interest. Posterity, in similar circumstances, seems to have agreed with him.

The bank's advances on cotton were made, he explained, "not as in past years on the mere personal security of the merchants, which the confusion of all private credit would have rendered too hazardous, but on the actual shipment of the produce to an American house in England, willing and able to protect American property from the reckless waste with which it has been too often thrown into the market with an entire disregard of all American interests." Though the bank did not hold title to the cotton, the transactions were commonly spoken of as its own. The same was true of those undertaken rather commonly in the South, for the United States Bank was by no means the only bank dealing in cotton: it was but the principal one. The transactions were sometimes called advances on commodities and sometimes purchases of them. Between an advance and a purchase the distinction might be fine, and different banks had different procedures. The press, for example, reported that "purchases" of cotton by the Brandon Bank of Mississippi in the autumn of 1837 were about "eighty thousand bales, mostly in collection of debts due the bank, forty dollars a bale being advanced. . . ."[19]

Despite the United States Bank's great influence in the South, the transactions of southern banks were not undertaken at the bank's bidding or against any participant's better judgment. They must have seemed a reasonable and well-precedented measure justified by the need of restoring to producers a market for their products and to debtors a means of liquidating their debts with

---

[19] 29th Congress, 1st Session, HD 226, p. 407; Raguet, *Financial Register* I, 235.

something more suitable than the heart's blood. It had in fact been done before and was not unusual. Biddle was told in 1838 by Colonel Wilkins, president of the Planters Bank, Natchez, that recently his bank had sent 60,000 bales of cotton to England. For nearly two centuries the realization of funds in England from the shipment of staples for sale there had been customary. It had been long established when George Washington did it, building up his credit or deposit by the shipment of his tobacco to the London merchant who was his agent and virtually his banker. To many people, including those with something at stake, it was not obvious why a bank should refrain from doing what planters had done.[20]

Subsequent critics of Nicholas Biddle have talked as if the cotton operations were merely a speculation of his intended to make money. They were obviously more than that. They were intended to restore trade, pay what America owed abroad, and restore her credit in the Old World's capital markets. His contemporary critics did not call them personal speculations or anything less than what they were—an immense and skillful attempt to restore international markets for American farm products—and their criticism was not that he was making money, but that he was maintaining "artificial" prices. When *The Times*, London, called the United States Bank a "great trading and speculating corporation," it spoke for a community of creditors and consumers whose wishes were being over-ridden by an expert champion of borrowers and producers. The British were being forced not only to pay more than a "natural" price for cotton but also to finance the operations by which the price was raised. This might be to their ultimate advantage, as to the Americans', but if so it was not obvious, and the performance was distasteful to them.

The performance was also precarious for Mr Biddle. He was in the position of a man who is priming a pump and has only one pail of water to do it with: if the pump takes hold before his pail is emptied, well and good; if it does not, the operation comes to an end and he no longer has so much as the water he started with. For Mr Biddle's purposes, the British manufacturer would have to sell more cotton goods, the British investor would have to continue buying American bonds and stocks, and the resources of the United States Bank would have to be unfailing, like the widow's cruse of oil.

In these circumstances the position of the bank's agents abroad had its vicissitudes. These were Humphreys and Biddle in Liver-

20 Biddle Papers, 1 PLB (1836), 511.

pool—the junior being Nicholas Biddle's son—who were to sell the cotton, and Samuel Jaudon, in the London money market, who was to raise the funds needed to hold the cotton till the price was right. Mr Jaudon's was the difficult task. He had gone to London in October 1837 with letters from Mr Biddle that were perfect in form though perhaps not ingratiating in substance; and he also had been heralded by the carping announcement of Mr Thomas Wren Ward, who wrote Baring Brothers, 23 September, that Mr Jaudon was to embark for Liverpool soon to establish himself in London as agent of the United States Bank and that Mr Humphreys was going to Liverpool with the same object. "I presume," he said, "this move is in consequence in part of the withdrawal of your credit. The bank can do a great business in exchange, cotton, and stocks, and if all goes right may make much money. But the concerns of the bank are extended, and their proceeding as I now understand it, unwise. I think you were right in not placing yourselves in its power. They will be likely to make some great mistake. Mr Jaudon is clever but too speculative, and Mr Humphreys is clever on a small scale, but conceited, and not a man of straightforward purpose."[21]

As might be expected, Mr Jaudon's reception in London had been cool. He was allowed to open a deposit account at the Bank of England but was denied credit there, and in consequence his balance seems to have been such that he could hardly have faced the Bank's tellers without blushing. His function was to get money from British investors for the purpose of holding cotton and raising its price to British buyers. His capital was his trunkful of bank stocks, bonds, and other securities which he sold if possible or used as collateral. The London market was the world's market and as such must be hospitable to foreigners, but this American arrangement of Mr Biddle's put an egregious strain on its hospitality. Yet Mr Jaudon, suave, sanguine, irrepressible, and buoyant like his principal, carried things off astonishingly well. He was constantly asking his hosts for a loan large or small, constantly apologizing for not having repaid what they had already lent him, and constantly expecting something magnificent to turn up on the next boat. Toward the end he got to the point of fortifying his applications with the grievous assurance that failure to get the money he wanted, and at once, would make him unable to repay what he had already got.

[21] Baring Papers, OC, 23 September 1837.

Despite this, he was tolerated. For he represented an economy of astounding achievements and promise, on which the British money market could not turn its back. The Americans had a way of *demanding* that foreign capitalists invest in their country. This was exasperating, but, after all, investments had to be made somewhere and America was a very promising place to make them.

Mr Jaudon's agency in London was the occasion late in 1837 of an episode which reveals the sort of amity felt by the two principal banks in Christendom for one another. During the preceding summer the Bank of England had sent the United States Bank dishonored bills for collection. In line with the course of lenity it was following, the United States Bank paid little heed to these collections, and the Bank of England found itself the last of August "without any information from the United States Bank either as to what steps have been or are to be taken, or what progress has been made in the realization of any of the outstanding claims of the Bank of England on the citizens and merchants of the United States." In order to get both news and action, the Bank of England in September sent an agent to the States, Mr J. W. Cowell, who was received by Mr Biddle and furnished quarters in the bank in Philadelphia. It was shortly thereafter that Mr Jaudon arrived in London, presented his credentials in Threadneedle Street, and asked for some money; two and a half to three millions would do. He addressed Governor Curtis in the following friendly fashion, 13 November 1837:

"The letter of the 6th Octr from N: Biddle, Esquire, President of the Bank of the United States, which I had the honor of presenting to you a few days since, will have apprized you of my appointment as Agent of that Bank, and of its wish that I should establish relations of business with your Institution.

"I beg leave therefore to enquire whether it will be agreeable to the Bank of England to receive my account as Agent of the Bank of the U: States, on the usual terms with depositors and discounters generally.

"As it may sometimes suit the convenience of the Bank of the U: States to anticipate its remittances to me—and as I may occasionally want funds for the purchase of Bills on the U: States—I should be glad to know also whether your Bank will grant me a credit, either open or covered, of five or six hundred thousand Pounds—If covered, which can only be regarded as a mere matter of form, the securities which I could offer, would consist of Shares in the Bank of the U: States, and such State and Corporation Stocks as the Bank of the U: States may hold, knowing them to be safe and solid.—Considering however the ample security which the large Capital of the Bank of the U: States itself affords, and the confidence which you have already shewn by remitting to it for collection Bills to three times the amount of the sum which I have named, I should hope that any advances would be placed upon the more agreeable footing of an open credit."*

Three days later, 16 November 1837, the Court of Directors briefly resolved, at the recommendation of the Committee of Treasury, that Mr Jaudon's proposal be declined. When news of its action reached Mr Biddle in Philadelphia it evidently put him in a tart mood, for he wrote Governor Curtis, 12 January 1838, an excessively courteous letter in which he described the "somewhat anomalous" position in which the two institutions appeared to stand with respect to each other. He said, in part:

"The Bank of the United States is the Agent of the Bank of England, collects its debts, and remits the proceeds to the Bank of England by drafts on its Agent in London. But its drafts on that same Agent drawn in the course of its business in favor of all other persons are proscribed, and so far as that proscription has an influence, discredited, by the Bank of England.

"The Bank of the United States receives deposits for the Bank of England, the Bank of England declines receiving deposits for the Bank of the U: States.

"The Agent of the Bank of England is domiciled under the roof of the Bank of the United States, where he receives the constant and cordial assistance of its officers. The Agent of the Bank of the United States is not permitted even to keep an account in the Bank of England.

"The same packet which announces the refusal of the Bank of England to admit the Funds of the Bank of the United States brings fresh amounts of bills and securities which the Bank of the United States is expected to collect for the Bank of England."

In these circumstances Mr Biddle invoked "a rule . . . to permit no account with any institution which declines admitting a similar account. . . . Accordingly the account of the Bank of England in

---

* I am indebted to the Governor and Company of the Bank of England for the text of this letter and permission to quote it.

the Bank of the United States will be closed, the balance remitted, and the commission charged on all past collections refunded to the Bank of England. You will also have the goodness to abstain from all further transmission of bills and, with as little delay as may consist with your convenience, transfer to other hands the management of the concerns of the Bank of England hitherto under our charge."*

To this, Governor Curtis made an excessively temperate reply, 22 February 1838. He adverted first to the proposal of Mr Jaudon on a previous visit to London in 1836 that an arrangement be made whereby the United States Bank should draw upon the Bank of England "at sixty days' sight, remitting prior to maturity and enjoying the right of overdrawing the account to the extent of £500,000 on the deposit of state stock or shares of the Bank of the United States." The Bank of England had declined this proposal, he said, though offering an alternative. Since Mr Jaudon had been apprized, in "several discussions," of the reasons for the Bank's refusal, it was presumed that they were "perfectly known" to him and Mr Biddle. Mr Jaudon had been told also that the more recent proposals of the United States Bank must be refused "as falling within the clear principle already decided." At the same time, contrary to what appeared to be Mr Biddle's understanding, Mr Jaudon had been allowed to open a deposit account; "but, upon full consideration, the Court of Directors felt themselves bound not to grant him a discount account or to allow bills accepted by him as Agent of a foreign bank of issue to be made payable at the Bank of England, these being concessions which have in fact never been granted to any similar institution." Mr Jaudon had been told that "the Bank would decline to discount any bills drawn by the Bank of the United States upon him" and this information was given him, the Governor wrote with a grim look toward Philadelphia, "as a matter of courtesy and good feeling, fearing that the principle might be acted upon and he might hear of the fact from some third party without any explanation of the cause." The Governor made a distinction between the function of the agent his Bank had sent to America to collect funds due on account of advances made on American paper at a moment of crisis and the function of the United States Bank's agent sent to London to get more advances before the old ones were

---

* I am indebted to the Governor and Company of the Bank of England for the text of this letter and the reply and for permitting me to quote them.

paid. He said that he thought a break in relations was unnecessary, that he would sincerely regret it, but that the Bank of England's agent was being given power of attorney to adjust matters as he thought best. The prompt and maybe unexpected result of this communication was continuance of the old relations; Mr Biddle gave assurance of his "great anxiety to avert from the Bank of England any loss in consequence of her interposition to protect the commercial interests of the two countries," he kept silent about the refusal of the Bank of England to grant him credit, and his assistance to the Bank of England's agent went on.

It is evident that the Bank of England, notwithstanding its dissatisfaction with the United States Bank, had found as yet no agency it preferred and that its own representative, Mr Cowell, found himself on very friendly terms with the officers in Philadelphia. It is also evident that though Mr Biddle could talk very independently to the Bank of England, he had rather pull in his horns than break with it. The Bank of England was a useful institution to remain on speaking terms with even though it would lend him nothing.

The outcome suggests that he had been bluffing and that by his offer to the Bank of England of a break in relations—though as things stood a break was certainly more to its advantage than to his—he hoped not merely to signify his resentment but to force it into what he thought more constructive action. For, a week before he tossed his threat into the Bank's parlours, he wrote Samuel Jaudon, 6 January 1838, of his regret that the latter's overtures had been rejected, and continued: "It weakens the probability of an intimate and very confidential relation between the two institutions, which I had hoped to see for the mutual benefit of the two countries. I of course ascribe it to the force of routine in business and an unwillingness to do anything out of the usual line."[22] The gentlemen of the Court in Threadneedle Street would probably have concurred in substance with what he said, ascribing to him, however, too little respect for what he called "routine" and too great a willingness to do things that were out of the usual line. What seems most evident now is that the accord Nicholas Biddle desired would have been good for two countries with so much in common and that its having to be

[22] Biddle Papers, 1 PLB (1836), 306; Clapham II, 159-60; Bray Hammond, *QJE*, LXI (1947), 613.

sacrificed to a hopeless incompatibility of temperaments and convictions was most unfortunate for both.*

Although Nicholas Biddle's current efforts were being exerted on behalf of debtors—debtors who for the moment were in distress but whose borrowings had been productive and would be so again—his aim was payment of America's debts and restoration of her credit abroad. This was plain in what he said privately as well as publicly. Writing to Samuel Jaudon, 31 March 1838, that New York's plans for resumption were "rash and premature," he said he wished "the crop to go forward and pay our debts and settle all our domestic balances, and then we may talk about specie payments." He was an empire-builder, and no one was more aware than he of the importance of European money for American development. No one did more than he in the procurement of European money for the purpose, and nothing was more necessary for the future of his policy than resumption of European investments. His plan to defer the renewal of specie payments at home and to favor foreign creditors but at the same time enlist their aid was orderly, consistent, and intelligible. The more substantial and conservative part of the business world concurred in his aim but distrusted his method. They preferred a good, stiff, straight-forward, Old Testament deflation, with the weak going to the wall, where they belonged, and the strong gathering up what they left. There was still another school of opposition which concurred neither in Mr Biddle's methods nor in his aim. It was the xenophobic school which believed that "as between foreign and domestic creditors 'the preference, if any must be given, was due to our own countrymen, as well on the score of morality as patriotism.' " This was the sentiment of the Jacksonian warhorse, future millionaire, and captain of industry, Amos Kendall. The Bank of England and *The Times*, when annoyed with Nicholas Biddle, possibly did not know how much worse off their interests might have been at the hands of some other Americans.[23]

IV

While the cotton program with its invasion of the London money

---

* One may contrast this early failure of accord with that achieved eighty years later between Sir Montagu Norman and Mr Benjamin Strong, Governors respectively of the Bank of England and of the Federal Reserve Bank of New York.

23 Biddle Papers, I PLB (1836), 387-88; W. B. Smith, 227.

market was proceeding on the one hand, there proceeded on the other the domestic program against premature resumption of specie payments. Facing this wing of Mr Biddle's napoleonic plan was Wall Street. Mr Biddle had not foreseen the stoppage of payments, or sought it, or begun it. It had started in New York. Yet now it was Wall Street that pressed for resumption and Chestnut Street that held out for delay. London assisted Wall Street. Washington proclaimed its resolution to associate with none of the others—a resolution which London and New York accepted indifferently but which Nicholas Biddle resisted. With respect to New York his tactics were merely obstructive. He had only to stand out against New York as London stood out against him. Yet the initiative that Wall Street was taking against him impeded the initiative that he had taken against London. The hostility of London and New York gradually coalesced against him, and while this went on in one quarter, he was assailed in another by stones and imprecations from the caverns of Washington.

Bank suspension, it must be observed, differed greatly in 1837, as it had in 1814, from bank suspension in the 20th century. What it then interrupted, for most people outside commercial centers, was simply the conversion of deposits and bank notes into coin. In 1837 the banks did not close their doors, and stoppage of payments did not deprive people of their money. Instead it actually provided them more, correspondingly depreciated. It relaxed an obligation to convert certain forms of money, viz., bank deposits and bank notes, into coin; but it left the deposits and the notes still in use, and the obligation to convert them being relaxed, the way was free to create more deposits and more notes.

In the conflict of aims between the three centers, New York, Philadelphia, and Washington, New York followed what might be called a sound money program, lying between Philadelphia's easy money and Washington's hard money programs and sharing the saner parts of each. New York wanted to put the banking system back under the discipline of having to convert its obligations into silver and gold on demand. The objection to this was that it would be excessively painful. It would entail a severe liquidation of indebtedness in which debtors would lose their equities and often have to sacrifice their property in order to pay what they owed, fresh borrowing would become impossible, prices would fall, enterprise would languish. It was this fatal treatment of borrowers and producers that Nicholas Biddle sought to avoid. In paraphrase of later and more popular reformers, he would not crucify men on a cross of gold or of silver either. Instead, he would prolong the suspension and, by easing the bondage of debtors under the contracts they had made, enable them to work their way out of the slough they were in. He advocated what in effect his country accepted ninety-six years later in the administration of Franklin D. Roosevelt, when in a similar situation the dollar was depreciated by statute and gold was withdrawn from circulation.

New York's first step had been backward to safer footing. Nearly all of her banks were incorporated under the Safety Fund Act of 1829, which made their charters forfeit if they suspended. Since they had suspended, the Albany Regency got the action of the law postponed a year. Thus reprieved, the banks undertook in August 1837 to get agreement "on the time when specie payments should be resumed and on the measures necessary to effect that purpose." To their overtures, the Philadelphia banks replied that it would be better to await action by Congress, which was then about to meet in response to President Van Buren's call for a special session to deal with the monetary situation and with the problem of distributing a federal surplus which had ceased to exist. Accordingly, after adjournment of the session, a bank convention met in New York in November. Being unable to agree upon a date for resumption, the convention adjourned to April 1838. But in January the New York banks published a report of the convention's proceedings, in which they held away indignantly from the shocking idea that the merit of a protracted suspension should even be discussed. In February, in another report, they recommended that resumption be undertaken 10 May, the anniversary of suspension, and that in preparation for it the banks make themselves impregnable by restricting credit, diminishing loans, and retaining specie. At the reconvened meeting in April, which the Philadelphia banks abstained from attending, New York was without support from the others that did attend. The majority decided to recommend waiting till the end of the year and resuming January 1839. Only two groups voted nay to this: New York because January was too far away, Mississippi because it was not far enough.[24]

Left alone by the other banks but supported by the City of London, the banks of New York carried out successfully their inde-

[24] Gallatin III, 396-400, 462-88; Raguet, *Financial Register* I, 342-46, 352.

pendent resolution to resume 10 May 1838. The Bank of England fortified them by the shipment of £1,000,000 sterling, consigned to Prime, Ward, and King, and by the promise of as much again, if needed. The New York banks had reduced their liabilities to a minimum and filled their vaults with precious metal. They stood invulnerable, amidst a commercial community half-strangled by the ordeal but assured of a happy issue out of all their afflictions in time.

The consummation had been skillfully prepared. Nearly a month before, the restoration of confidence in Wall Street had been given encouraging publicity. The New York City correspondent of the Albany *Argus* made the following report 16 April 1838:

"Matters assume a cheering appearance here to-day. Information is in town that the Bank of England has remitted £1,000,000 in specie to New York to assist our banks in resuming, and it is said that Mr Gallatin read today in the bank convention a letter from one of the directors of that institution saying that they would transmit £2,000,000 instead of £1,000,000 if the latter amount should be deemed necessary.

"The Bank of England has a double object in this movement. First, to thwart the operations of Mr Jaudon's agency in London, which are exceedingly distasteful to the English as well as many of the American merchants; and second by restoring confidence here to enable us to resume our purchases, which have fallen off some 40 millions in the last year, and to pay the more readily the debts which we still owe. This step will increase general confidence in our ability to resume and continue specie payments, and New York will become the center of moneyed operations and a sound currency. The Bank of United States will be no longer feared."

Circumstances had become "eminently propitious," Mr Gallatin later wrote. "Not only had the foreign debt been settled or postponed, and all the exchanges, whether domestic or foreign, become decidedly favorable, but one million sterling in specie had been imported, under the auspices of the Bank of England, through the agency of a commercial house." The city banks "resumed with more than seven millions of dollars in specie, their gross circulation reduced to three millions, and their other liabilities payable on demand considerably diminished. . . . Above all, the sound and most powerful portion of the commerce of New York had now taken an active part in promoting an immediate resumption." Mr Gallatin went on: "The debtor-interest, which, combined with that of the United States Bank of Pennsylvania, and with the mistaken views of some and the unfounded apprehensions of others, had constantly attempted to impede the course pursued by the banks, was silenced. They resumed, sustained by that general support of the commercial community and by that general confidence which are indispensable for the maintenance of specie payments. They resumed in good faith and in full, redeeming the country paper which, during the suspension, had become the general currency of the city, freely substituting their own circulation, and paying without distinction, when required, all their liabilities. The resumption was effected without the slightest difficulty; and it is but just to add that no attempt was made to impede it, either by the United States Bank of Pennsylvania or from any other quarter."[25]

New York's lead was followed by Boston and other New England banks. The United States Bank and the other Philadelphia banks resumed in July and banks in the South and West soon thereafter.

The supposition has sometimes been expressed that the unwillingness of banks outside New York, and especially in the agricultural South and West, to hasten resumption of specie payments was the product of Mr Biddle's persuasive wiles, as if but for him they would all have toed the mark promptly. On the contrary, the banks dreaded deflation and needed no persuasions from Philadelphia to make them shun it. Few of them outside the business centers had been tempered to the independence and professional detachment a good banker should have. They were at heart debtors and enterprisers themselves and the creditor viewpoint, though well established in London, Boston, and New York, was alien to them. They could not endure to deny credit, depress prices, forgo earnings, accept losses, and curb in general the activity of the producers and merchants among whom they belonged. Resumption would force them into outright bankruptcy, which continuance of the suspension enabled them to avoid. They were impelled now by the same coercive self-interest that had protracted the general suspension of 1814-1816, which, with no leader advocating delay as Nicholas Biddle was doing in 1837-1838, had persisted far more stubbornly.

The supposition has also been expressed that Mr Biddle, in his effort to prolong the suspension, was moved by concern for his own bank. He should have been, but I doubt if he was. He felt too little

25 Gallatin III, 401.

anxiety about anything that he managed. It is true that the course
he chose accorded with the interest of his own bank, but more than
that inspired it. He was animated rather by a desire to make the
administration in Washington abandon the imposition of its monetary notions upon a modern dynamic economy, to restore values and
activity in trade, and to rehabilitate American credit abroad. Yet
of a statement by him that his plan was to avoid the low farm prices
that must attend the contraction of credit and the resumption of
specie payments, it was the comment of Nathan Appleton, one of
Boston's foremost economic royalists, that the plan involved "principles as false in political economy as its whole character was
objectionable on the score of mercantile morality." John Quincy
Adams, a personal friend of Nicholas Biddle but intensely conservative in his economics, identified suspension with counterfeiting. And
the New York banks, led by Albert Gallatin, Prime, Ward, and
King, and other conservatives, "insisted that it was monstrous to
suppose" that if banks could resume and sustain specie payments
they had any "discretionary right" to consider whether or not
resumption was in the national interest. These were the pious ex-
pressions of creditors, men of substance and of conservative outlook,
whom a depression of commodity prices did not so greatly hurt.
They had as much right to protest at the suspension as the debtor
interest had to defend it, but they had no monopoly of virtue, or of
economic principles. Whether correct or not in some absolute sense,
the argument of Nicholas Biddle in the debtor interest was no more
subterfuge than was that of his business opponents in the interest
of creditors. And it gains sympathy from the fact that the conservatives did not combat it on its practical economic merits but
called it, with pompous indignation, iniquitous.[26]

It was under pressure of these creditor interests that Thomas
Wren Ward expressed to his British principals congenial animadversions on the character and ability of Nicholas Biddle. "In Mr
Biddle's judgment and management of the bank," he said, "I have
never had confidence." He considered Mr Biddle "a man of talent
and resource" and "an intriguer and manager," who had "great
address in getting out of difficulties but not the wisdom to avoid
getting into them." Mr Ward would prefer "a plain and straight-
forward man of good judgment and prudence." Such judgments
were not the unmixed moral judgments they sound like; they were

[26] Appleton, *Remarks on Currency*, 16; Gallatin III, 398-99.

opinions expressed in moralistic terms about a course of action which was contrary to the economic interests and principles of business conservatives. That course may have been wrong, but in both purpose and method it was in accord with the dominant social trend of modern economic statesmanship. And it would fall today under the same condemnation by creditors and business conservatives that it did in 1837.[27]

I have alluded also to another element in Mr Biddle's program— his novel conviction that Congress had a duty in the matter. The fact that that duty, as he saw it, included restoration of a central bank does not make his contention merely one of self-interest. He was right, regardless of self-interest, and in time Congress did what he urged. Nothing is more firmly established in 20th century thought than that government has over-riding economic responsibilities, especially in respect to money. But in 1837 the influence of *laisser faire* doctrine was against all broadening of government responsibilities. Although Thomas Wren Ward and Prime, Ward, and King expressed privately the conviction that some governmental regulation of banking was necessary, most of their associates did not. The spirit of Wall Street's advocacy of resumption was one of contemptuous indifference to what the government might do or might not do. The business world could look after itself. The Jacksonian ideal of diminishing the responsibilities of Washington accorded with Wall Street's fully.[28]

How severe the strangling of business had been in preparation for the triumph of the New York banks is indicated by the rebellious action of the New York Board of Trade, dominated by debtors, which two days after the resumption invited Nicholas Biddle to establish a bank in New York that should be conducted with "the same enlarged views and the same enlightened and liberal policy" as the United States Bank's. The acceptance of this "invitation," which Prime, Ward, and King said was itself invited, was announced at a special session of the Board of Trade, where every one was rejoiced by the news and loudly cheered the statement that this was the brightest day to dawn upon New York in a twelvemonth. It was also reported that Mr Biddle would establish "branches" of the United States Bank in Rochester and Buffalo "under the new bank law"—news that was said to be "exceedingly acceptable to the en-

---

[27] Baring Papers, OC, 26 May, 27 September 1837.
[28] Baring Papers, AC, 15 September 1843.

terprising merchants of those cities," who "know the spirit of the Philadelphia financier" and would hail the day of his return. Three months later a charter was taken out under the Free Banking Act recently adopted by New York, 28 April 1838—and "the Bank of the United States in New York" was organized, being one of several banks, most of them in the South, controlled by the United States Bank in Philadelphia.[29]

Another thing worth incidental mention is that the City of London's generous assistance to Wall Street when resuming specie payments in May 1838 has had odd treatment by British historians. In Tooke and Newmarch's *History of Prices*, published in 1840, the rather remarkable error was committed of supposing that the Bank of England's loan was to the United States Bank. The Americans' intra-mural conflict over resumption was ignored and the Bank of England's action was condemned in the following mixture of fact and fancy: "However desirable it might be that the American banks should fulfil their engagements to their creditors by paying in specie, it was no part of the business of the Bank of England to hasten their doing so, nor was it for the real interests of the American public that the restoration of cash payments should be thus artificially accelerated. . . . The United States Bank, had it not received the countenance and aid of the Bank of England, would not have been in a condition so soon to renew its reckless course and would not in all probability have been enabled to aid and abet the southern and western banks in their preposterous attempts to obstruct artificially the legitimate operation of supply and demand in the article of cotton. . . ."[30]

The authors appear incensed at this "quixotic measure of the Bank of England"—an "eccentric operation" which is "most earnestly and strenuously to be deprecated and reprobated"—and consider it "an additional instance of the impatience which, as exhibited on former occasions, the Bank seems to have felt whenever there has been an accumulation of treasure in its coffers and of its resort to some unusual effort to get rid of it." I do not know if the Bank resented its being denounced for having done the opposite of what it actually did; but its historian, Sir John Clapham, does not offer to correct the charge. He merely says that the Bank of England made a profit of £18,930 on the shipment of the specie to New York—"a

[29] 29th Congress, 1st Session, HD 226, pp. 398, 541; Raguet, *Financial Register* II, 12-14, 44; Biddle, *Correspondence*, 321.
[30] Tooke and Newmarch III, 79, 80-81.

transaction about which little more is known." It seems unusual for the debtor to have a better record of transactions than the creditor. Sir John also seems to think that the resumption of specie payments in the States was premature, as Nicholas Biddle maintained; and he apparently concurs in the judgment of Thomas Tooke that "had the American banks resolutely contracted their liabilities and called in every dollar due to them, instead of suspending payment," the Bank of England's treasure "might not have seen it through the spring of 1837."[31]

V

The first account of New York's resumption was Mr Gallatin's in 1841. He was by temperament and conviction an "ultra-bullionist," to use his own term, and though a banker and thoroughly conversant with the business world, he deplored much as the poets, romancers, and Transcendentalists did the excessive and un-Jeffersonian commitment of America to money-making. For him personally scholarship was more important.* He was repelled by the fierceness of American enterprise and its clamor for exploitation. He had supported Nicholas Biddle while the latter was still a central banker restraining intelligently and efficiently the extension of bank credit, but much as he disliked Andrew Jackson, he also disapproved Biddle's tactics of counter-attack. Even more he disapproved the later expansionist policy that made the United States Bank of Pennsylvania the exponent of unrestrained enterprise, of easy money, and of an aggressive debtor interest. He approved the stern commercial statutes of his native Geneva which imposed the liabilities of deceased bankrupt fathers on their sons. It is not to be expected that his account of the conflict over resumption, in which he was a principal, would present very sympathetically the considerations and principles which Nicholas Biddle advocated in the debtor interest. Mr Gallatin knew the debtor interest, and nothing in his background, philosophy, or temperament disposed him to esteem it. He had dreamed, with Thomas Jefferson, of a very different America from the one which that interest, teeming and appetent, was aggressively creating.

* Mr Gallatin's writings on American diplomacy and banking grew out of his experience in those fields. What may be called his pure scholarship, less known but no less a professional achievement, was his pioneer work in the ethnography of American Indians.

[31] Clapham II, 161, 165.

Though Nicholas Biddle was not a humanitarian, the later program he turned to after destruction of the federal Bank belonged to the dominant, popular, and dynamic movement of his time—the democratization of business enterprise—and in its economic effects was related to the abolition of imprisonment for debt and the reform of bankruptcy procedure. These were in the interest of the debtor-entrepreneur and served to relieve him of the more crippling part of the risk he took in the development of the economy. Such relief was not the conscious purpose, but it was the end it served. The whole entrepreneurial movement found itself served indeed by many more factors, directly and indirectly, likely and unlikely, than can be catalogued. It drew into itself tendencies wholly unrelated to it in their origin. It disrupted Nicholas Biddle's earlier career, and then, having destroyed the conservative restraints on bank credit that he had been ably conducting, made a leading place for him, with no sense of irony, in its own expansive ranks, the most sanguine of empire-builders, the most aggressive, the most prominent.

Current American business enterprise was a force arising from the energy, ambition, and ingenuity of men selected by the rigors of migration from the most advanced and vigorous peoples of northwestern Europe, released from the social and political restraints of the Old World, and placed with free hands, with nothing more to lose, and with everything to gain, in a fresh and stimulating environment, spacious, inviting, and full of such natural wealth and natural facilities as with steam and credit at command had never before in the world offered so many men so many rewards for their effort.

The success of this entrepreneurial force is embarrassing to its critics; for it made America in the course of a century the most powerful nation on earth, populous, and endued with the highest standard of living for its people. Whatever dissatisfaction may be felt with its spiritual attainments, and sympathetic as one may be with the dreams of Thomas Jefferson, Albert Gallatin, Henry David Thoreau, and others who stood out against the dominant trend, one can not assert convincingly that the idealists were altogether right and the realists altogether wrong.

The outcome of the controversy raised by the bank suspension of 1837 and 1838 was a blending of the rival emphases which the borrowers and the creditors respectively sought to give the issue. It was learned that the economy could not be so wholly devoted to the debtor interest as Mr Biddle wished, lest the goose perish that laid the golden eggs. And the banks of New York swung back soon enough from the extreme creditor position to which they had been driven by the United States Bank's procedure. They fell again under the long-range dominance of the debtor-entrepreneur, who though thereafter he often enough got scotched still never got killed and never could reasonably contend that the American banking system failed to serve his interest with entire adequacy and sometimes superfluity.

VI

During the progress and retrogression of these events, the administration in Washington had been having a pitiful time, starting with the May morning, two months after Mr Van Buren became President, when his Secretary of the Treasury looked in the newspapers and found that all the banks—even the pets where the government's money was—were refusing to pay out coin.* He had had to give up distributing the federal surplus in specie and distribute the second installment in the notes of suspended banks. The Treasury's income dwindled—receipts from customs for the year were half what they had been in 1836, receipts from land sales were barely a quarter. But expenditures were higher than ever; for in the prosperity just passed, outlays had been authorized which made the Treasury spend twice as much in 1837 as it had spent in 1835. For the second time in less than twenty-five years it found itself stripped of cash in a crisis coincident with failure to continue the life of the federal Bank. By the end of summer, while still obliged to distribute a "surplus," the administration had in fact a deficit. So far from having anything to distribute, it lacked funds to meet current expenses. At the special session of Congress which met in September at President Van Buren's call, the legislators postponed payment of the third installment of the surplus then due, at the same time forbidding the Treasury to call for a return of the "deposits" already made. They also adopted the reluctant recommendation of the hard-money administration that current needs be met by issue of $10,000,000 of circulating Treasury notes, the large denominations bearing interest, the small bearing none. Even Senator

* It was said that the first bank to cease paying specie was a pet—the Dry Dock Bank in New York. Bourne, 39.

Benton—Old Bullion himself—was constrained to vote for these notes.[32]

Eight months later, May 1838, another issue of Treasury notes was authorized bearing interest at varying rates up to six per cent and re-issuable. Within one month nearly $5,000,000 went into circulation. In view of the fact that a generation later the Greenbackers—political offspring of the party of Jackson and Van Buren —began to advocate the regular issuance of government obligations for monetary purposes, it is interesting that the Van Buren administration scrupulously refrained from sanctioning these notes on any other ground than deplorable necessity. It based their issue on what was due the government from the depository banks, and Secretary Woodbury reported in 1839 that the amount outstanding had not exceeded half the amount authorized. The hard-money antediluvians had done the best they could.[33]

As for distribution of the surplus, this third installment in the fall of 1837 was the last ever paid, though the Treasury was frequently dunned by the states for the balance due. Nearly half a century later, in 1883, the state of Virginia sued in the Supreme Court for payment of the fourth installment and lost. The court's decision was that the federal government had not obligated itself by the act of 23 June 1836. The amounts distributed aggregated about $28,000,000, and on the books of the Treasury, in accordance with an act of Congress so late as 1910, they are still technically due the federal government from the states with which they were "deposited."[34]

The distribution was much derided throughout the country. In the southern states it was received with contempt as "a sop thrown them by the protectionists." In some places it was made *per capita*, and the amount being about two dollars a person, it was "as earnest a matter as the acquisition of two dollars is ordinarily regarded." Most of the money was squandered on "public improvements" unwisely undertaken. Some was used to establish permanent funds. The town of Groton, Massachusetts, received $4,115. "Just about the time this money was received," the town clerk subsequently reported, "a heavily loaded seven-horse team, driver and all, fell through a bridge over the Nashua River, causing a loss or damage of about

[32] Bourne, 40; Knox, *United States Notes*, 41-42.

[33] Knox, *United States Notes*, 43-46.

[34] Bourne, 43.

$3,000, and this $4,115 was regarded by many as a real Godsend to meet that occasion. . . ."[35]

While the resumption of specie payments followed the course I narrated from Wall Street's point of view, a separate series of events in Washington and Philadelphia enabled Nicholas Biddle to claim that the credit was really his; for in a way the federal government was forced at last to do what he all along had demanded. "On the 30th of May," to state the matter in his own words, and following resumption by the New York banks on the 10th, "the specie circular, requiring payments in coin in the land offices, was repealed by Congress. On the 25th of June the bill called the sub-treasury, requiring coin in all payments to the government, was negatived. In the month of July the government agreed to receive an anticipated payment of the bonds of the bank, to the amount of between four and five millions of dollars, in a credit to the treasurer on the books of the bank, and arrangements were made for the more distant public disbursements in the notes of the bank."* By this action the government avoided an imminent failure to meet its current obligations and again accepted the bank as its depository. These arrangements, he continued, "brought the government into efficient cooperation for the re-establishment of the currency and opened the way to a resumption of specie payments. That resumption accordingly took place throughout the middle states on the 13th of August and in many of the southern and western states soon after."[36]

Mr Biddle was elated. He had "beaten down the government and secured the ascendancy of reason for the future," he wrote to one correspondent, and to another: "The repeal of the specie circular and the defeat of the subtreasury are the results, exclusively, of the course pursued by the Bank of the United States. If we had done as the New York banks had, succumbed to the government and resumed when they did, it would have been a surrender at discretion. I was willing to risk the temporary overshadowing to have a permanent sunshine; and I think we shall soon have it." To still another friend he wrote: "I took a deliberate stand against the administra-

* The transaction constituted payment of $7,900,000 to the government for its stock in the Bank. The sum included a premium of about $1,000,000, besides which the government already had received dividends of over $7,000,000 during the twenty years of the Bank's existence.

[35] Bourne, 25, 34, 146-47.
[36] 29th Congress, 1st Session, HD 226, p. 407; Raguet, *Financial Register* II, 237.

tion, determined to do nothing until they were defeated, and I *know* that this opposition caused their defeat." Mr Biddle wished to avoid strutting in public, however, and urged his friends to enjoy the triumph with moderation. "I would specially avoid everything like exultation—everything like reproach to the administration as being forced at last to resort to the Bank. But on the contrary the administration should be treated as having done a good thing and should have credit for a pacification which can not fail to be useful to the country. It may be of some consequence to the administration to see that they do not expose themselves by this step to sneers and sarcasms from their political opponents."[37]

The bank's being again a government depository was a great feather in Mr Biddle's cap and impressed every one. "Mr Biddle has certainly obtained a triumph over the Treasury," Prime, Ward, and King told the Barings, "having in the purchase of his bond or bonds provided for his becoming a deposit bank. And the Treasury now draws upon 'the Pennsylvania Bank of the United States'. . . ." Yet in fact what had happened meant next to nothing. The bank was not made *the* federal depository by a merely unusual transaction which put a credit on its books in the Treasury's favor, nor had it gained any special regulatory power. Mr Biddle had been able to get some tired and impoverished Jacksonians to eat a few of their words, and that was all; he had regained nothing essential; and the Treasury's incontinent withdrawal of the balance in the next few months was merely somewhat less embarrassing to the bank than it might have been.[38]

VII

But Mr Van Buren had more than the government's fiscal affairs to worry about. He had also a schism in the Democratic party—a schism that was open and bitter in his own New York and that was potential everywhere. It was between the bank and the anti-bank Democrats. So long as the two wings had been working to destroy the federal Bank, the schism had been overlooked. Now that the Bank had been "destroyed," there was nothing to hold them together and much to drive them apart. To one wing of the party, destruction of the federal Bank had been in the interest of the state banks, but to the other wing it had been prelusive to destruction of the state banks too.

[37] Biddle, *Correspondence*, 315-17, 320-21.
[38] Baring Papers, OC, 16 August 1838.

Mr Van Buren's own interests were with banks, especially the New York banks. He was himself the patron and virtual founder of New York's Safety Fund system. The Albany Regency, his powerful party machine, was closely associated with leading banks of the system. But now the banks had all ceased to pay specie, though bound by gratitude and by the law adopted in the June preceding Mr Van Buren's election, which required that those which held government funds be specie-paying banks. This was a major embarrassment for the President, and the more so because it was for his revered old chief an opportunity. The pet banks were one blot on his agrarian consistency which Andrew Jackson could now expunge, and two months after the suspension, writing from the Hermitage, he had expressed himself, 9 July 1837, in the following forcible words:

"Now is the time to separate the government from all banks, receive and disburse the revenue in nothing but gold and silver coin, and the circulation of our coin through all public disbursements will regulate the currency forever hereafter, keep the government free from all embarrassment, whilst it leaves the commercial community to trade upon its own capital, and the banks to accommodate it with such exchange and credit as best suits their own interests, both being money making concerns, devoid of patriotism, looking alone to their own interests, regardless of all others. . . .

"The history of the world never has recorded such base treachery and perfidy, as has been committed by the deposit banks against the government, and purely with the view of gratifying Biddle and the Barings, and by suspension of specie payments, degrade, embarrass, and ruin if they could their own country. . . ."[39]

These were the General's personal views, in so far as his own ideas can be dissociated from the cant of Taney, Henshaw, and Kendall. He had avowed his distrust of all banks to Nicholas Biddle in 1829 and he had often restated it; though the exigencies of the assault on the federal Bank and the advice he got from the kitchen impelled him no less often to bed himself down with the state banks. Senator Thomas Hart Benton explained the matter frankly. He said that shortly after the first message, December 1829, questioning the Bank's constitutionality and usefulness, he had suggested to the President that the currency should be exclusively metallic and that the Treasury keep its funds wholly in its own vaults. "When these ideas were mentioned to him, he took them at once; but it was not

39 Jackson, *Correspondence* v, 495, 498, 500, 504ff; Raguet, *Financial Register* II, 58.

until the Bank of the United States should be disposed of that anything could be done on these two subjects; and on the latter a process had to be gone through in the use of local banks as depositories of the public monies which required several years to show its issue and inculcate its lesson. Though strong in the confidence of the people, the President was not deemed strong enough to encounter all the banks of all the states at once. Temporizing was indispensable—and even the conciliation of a part of them."[40]

The Senator's recollection of the source and form of the plan errs in detail, but the ideal itself—the venerable, vague, agrarian ideal of an exclusively metallic currency and an end of all banks of issue—this he reflects perfectly. So far Andrew Jackson had been actually faithful to that ideal only in issuance of the specie circular. A British observer who was discussing the circular in the *Edinburgh Review* in 1837, pointed this out in the following words: "The real error of General Jackson in his policy as to commercial affairs does not consist in his having issued this order, but in his having sacrificed the Bank of the United States. He always professed, and we believe truly, to be an enemy to the paper system, or at least to its abuse. But instead of attempting to improve it, by exerting the influence of government to prevent the multiplication of mushroom banks in all parts of the Union, he encouraged them, and exerted himself to suppress the only institution that deserved his patronage, that was a check on the wild and mischievous proceedings of the others, and on whose stability and good conduct the public might at all times depend."[41]

A 20th century critic, Dr Fritz Redlich, restates the matter in sharper terms. "A true statesman" with Andrew Jackson's anticapitalistic convictions, he says, but with understanding of the realities of his time, "would have preferred to check an unavoidable capitalistic development," which he could not expect to stop, "by strengthening the existing brakes instead of smashing them to pieces and thereby letting the mechanism run wild." But the General, though he could never forget his own adolescent ideas on the subject, could still less resist the sophisticated advice of his sycophant associates. The advice, when it favored the state banks, might be reconciled with expediency, but the General must often have yearned nevertheless for an opportunity to swing the axe against the state

[40] Benton I, 158.

[41] [J. R. McCulloch], *Edinburgh Review* LXV (1837), 227; Raguet, *Financial Register* I, 52.

banks the way he had swung it against the federal Bank. And in 1837, if he could no longer experience that spiritual joy himself, he might nevertheless relish it vicariously through Mr Van Buren.[42]

Whatever President Van Buren's own views, he knew that those expressed by Jackson were latent and powerful in the country at large. The schism in his own state, which for two years or more had been growing dangerously and now, in consequence of the suspension, had become exigent, was the work of the Equal Rights party, or Loco Focos, as they came to be called. These people carried on the pristine Jeffersonian principles. They were the original anti-bank Republicans, or "Democrats in principle," now become openly rebellious. But they were become distinctly urban and industrial also; their doctrine was a Jeffersonian and agrarian equalitarianism put in the urban and industrial form of their day. They were Labor, the nascent by-product of business enterprise and industrialization; they were those workers whom the Jacksonian revolution did not make capitalists but employees. So far, in America, cities had represented the mercantile and business interest with exceptional tradesmen and mechanics absorbed into it, but now that interest by its very success had generated a powerful and lasting labor opposition within its threshold. This opposition, inspired by William Leggett, a brilliant doctrinaire journalist, had revolted in 1835 from the political leadership of the Albany Regency over the party of Thomas Jefferson in New York and its alliance with the Safety Fund banks and other dominant business interests. According to their apologist, Fitzwilliam Byrdsall, the Loco Focos "regarded the banking system of the state of New York, with its Safety Fund league and restraining law as a hydra-headed monster whose overthrow was essential to human rights and human progress." And when President Jackson had destroyed the federal hydra they were impatient to get on with destruction of the hydras incorporated by the states. "We demand," they said, "that the state governments will no longer authorize the issuing of bills of credit, commonly called bank notes, in open violation of the Constitution of the United States." These were views irreconcilable with the authoritative statement of Roger Taney, when President Jackson's Secretary of the Treasury, that there was "perhaps no business which yields a profit so certain and liberal as the business of banking and exchange; and it is proper that it

42 Redlich, 171.

should be open so far as practicable, to the most free competition and its advantages shared by all classes of society."[43]

The Loco Focos held the contrary, orthodox belief that banks were privileged, aristocratic monopolies, as Thomas Jefferson and John Taylor of Caroline had said, though they held this belief in an invigorated, realistic form begot by Jacksonian banking expansion. In the period of prosperity leading up to the panic of 1837, they had begun to demand a lowering of commodity prices and rents, whose rise they ascribed to speculation, and speculation they ascribed to banks. With true Jeffersonian insight, they recognized that bank credit augmented the supply of money, diminished the value of the dollar, and raised the prices which they as consumers had to pay. "As the currency expands," they cried, "the loaf contracts." Here, again, an intelligent and sincere opposition to banks was being uttered—though less discerning than that of Erastus Root, who had recognized that the inflationary disposition of the banks had its most effective curb in the operations of the federal Bank. Still it was sagacious. And it was also antithetic to the interests of such Jacksonians as Henshaw and Taney, who had no Jeffersonian aversion whatsoever to banks but only to their regulation by the federal government.[44]

The overt mutiny of the Equal Rights people had occurred at a meeting they held in Tammany Hall, 29 October 1835, control of which the regulars attempted to seize. After a lively tussle on the platform to gain and hold possession of the chair, the regulars had been overcome, but they countered by going downstairs and turning off the gas which lit the hall. Thereupon the insurgents had produced candles and loco focos, as the recently invented friction matches were popularly called, and in what must have been a murky and fitful but impressive light, they had proceeded to adopt memorable resolutions. In these they not only had commended a strict interpretation of the Constitution with respect to enlarged federal powers and upheld the assault on the federal Bank but condemned paper money in general and "all bank charters granted by individual states," because they gave "impulse to principles of speculation and gambling," were "at war with good morals and just and equal government and calculated to build up and strengthen in our country the odious distribution of wealth and power against merit and equal

[43] Jabez Hammond II, 489ff; Byrdsall, 41, 140; Treasury Department, Secretary, *Reports on Finances, 1790-1849* III (1829-1836), 457.
[44] Byrdsall, 18-19, 99-100.

rights." Silver and gold, they said, "are the only legitimate, substantial, and proper circulating medium." From their resort to loco foco matches, which saved for them the course of their meeting, the Loco Focos had taken their name. Warfare with the regulars became sharp and continuous. The Democratic party in New York was split bitterly between its two wings. "The one," writes Professor William Trimble, "inclining to the philosophy of enterprise, defended the state banks, championed the extension of the canal system, and affiliated itself with the expansionists of the South; the other, holding fast to the principle of distributive justice, agitated the restriction of banks, tried to restrain canal promotion, and progressed toward 'free soil, free speech, free labor, and free men.' " Eventually, the one was the "Hunkers"; the other the "Barnburners."[45]

Early in 1837, the afternoon of a cold and windy February day —the Loco Focos had held an out-door meeting to investigate "the cause of the present unexampled distress," this being the period immediately preceding the panic. The prices of "bread, meat, rent, and fuel," they said, "must come down." They declared that "our monstrous banking system" was the cause of the current trouble; banks had "fostered extravagant speculations" in land and provisions. It was resolved that "the true remedy for the people, which will reduce the price of all the necessaries of life, is that every working man refuse paper money in payment for his services or demand specie of the banks for all notes paid to him." This course, however, had been too subtle and indirect for many; and when it was proposed to go at once and raid the provision dealers, the crowd had acquiesced, burst into warehouses, and dumped stocks of flour into the street. Considerable, it is likely, found its way into private homes. Three months later—3 May 1837—another mass meeting had been held, again to denounce the banks and "to adopt measures to retrieve our country from the desolating influence of paper money." Since runs on the New York banks followed a few days later and specie payments stopped, the Loco Focos seem to have supposed they had achieved something. But they were deluded if they supposed so, because it was large depositors, as Prime, Ward, and King observed, and not small note-holders who put the banks under the

<hr>

[45] Byrdsall, 26-27, 39, 57, 68; Jabez Hammond II, 491; Trimble, *AHR*, xxiv (1918-1919), 415.

pressure they could not withstand. The suspension owed less to the Loco Focos than they to it.[46]

This popular outburst in his own state against the banks and his own party organization had presented President Van Buren with a grave problem. To repudiate the banks and their organization was to sacrifice the machinery that had put him in the Presidency and was needed to keep him there. But to repudiate the Loco Focos and cleave to the banks would be worse, for it would mean repudiation of Andrew Jackson, whose name had a potency second to no known machine's. It was the public and not the banks that did the voting, and that put parties in and out of power. No one of Mr Van Buren's political sagacity, with experience of Andrew Jackson's popular strength, could feel disposed to toy with that elementary fact. But neither was Mr Van Buren the man to cast aside party organization and, starry-eyed, leave his fate in the laps of the people.[47]

The arrangement that he determined on, after what must have been the most anxious and careful thought, was a masterly fusion of the ingenious and obscure. It was recommended to Congress by him in the special session which met at his summons in September 1837. It breathed the sound and fury of Loco Foco distrust of banks but in substance proposed a course of action which subjected them to nothing worse than being called hard names. Otherwise it was a course to which they became reconciled fully in time and whose termination years later they did not welcome. Such was the ingenuity of Mr Van Buren's proposals, however, that they were quite misapprehended at the time by the state banks and party regulars, who took what he said at face value. They saw in his proposals only a surrender to their Loco Foco enemies, and they raised in consequence a din filled with sincerity, wrath, and heart-break. The Loco Focos, hearing the unhappy clamor, uncritically supposed that the banks were really being hurt. Mr Van Buren had confused both sides equally.

His proposal was that an independent Treasury, or sub-treasury system, be established, that the government accept and disburse only silver and gold coin, keep its funds in vaults of its own maintained in Washington and other leading cities, and make no use of bank credit whether in the form of bank notes or bank deposits. It is not astonishing that this program at first dismayed the bankers. According to Jabez Hammond, who was a contemporary, they had

[46] Byrdsall, 100-05, 109-113, 140-43.   [47] Trimble, *AHR*, xxiv (1918-1919), 410.

sustained General Jackson "with all their influence" in his veto of the federal Bank's renewed charter and in his removal of the federal deposits from its care; "but when Mr Van Buren recommended the removal of the deposits from the state banks, it was quite another matter." John Jay Knox, the 19th century banker-historian, wrote that "earnestly as the state banks had aided Jackson in pulling down the power of the Bank of the United States, they now with equal earnestness fought against the independent Treasury."[48]

But if the banks misunderstood President Van Buren's message, it was not because he omitted to say what he meant. For he reminded them that business did not require the federal government's intercession. In Europe, he said, the domestic and foreign exchanges were carried on by private houses. "There is no reason why our own may not be conducted in the same manner with equal cheapness and safety . . . and few can doubt that their own interest as well as the general welfare of the country would be promoted by leaving such a subject in the hands of those to whom it properly belongs. A system founded on private interest, enterprise, and competition, without the aid of legislative grants or regulation by law would rapidly prosper. . . ." It was an evil tendency to look to government for help. "It may indeed be questioned whether it is not for the interest of the banks themselves that the government should not receive their paper." Government was "not intended to confer special favors on individuals or on any classes of them, to create systems of agriculture, manufactures, or trade, or to engage in them. . . . The less government interferes with private pursuits the better." This was not grim advice for business men, nor should they have been alarmed by the President's pious repetition of the Jacksonian platitude that it was not the legitimate object of government to make men rich. It was enough to let them get rich.[49]

Mr Cambreleng in Congress the month following President Van Buren's message was still more reassuring. It is true, he declared, that the American banking system was "unquestionably the worst in the world" and that it was "impossible to imagine a system more discordant and more embarrassing to trade." But why was it so? Because there was too much governmental influence on it. British banks were having less current difficulty than American banks because they were freer and capital "flowed with astonishing rapidity"

48 Jabez Hammond II, 478; Knox, *History of Banking*, 86-87.
49 Richardson IV, 1547, 1558, 1561.

where it was most needed. Moreover, "that remnant of barbarism," the usury law, had been repealed. For, he said, the rate of interest, "the safety valve of business . . . should be permitted to rise and fall with the pressure upon the money market. In this country we have locked it down and doubly prohibited the free use of capital." Capital was not at liberty to flow into banking as in England and Scotland. Instead the quantity was regulated in each state. "Our state governments might with equal propriety and wisdom regulate the quantity of capital in every other branch of trade." And what was the consequence of this legislative interference with banking? Mr Cambreleng asked. It was that New York City, "the commercial emporium of the Union, the centre of circulation, . . . is permitted to employ in this branch of trade some twenty millions—about one-third of the banking capital of a neighboring city.* Such legislation is as absurd as it is unequal." Mr Cambreleng's solution, with allowance for his impressive vagueness, was a reservation of "currency" powers to the state and a dismissal of all "banking" powers from legislation. "Banking," he says, "legitimate banking, is a trade and should be as free as all other trades. . . . Currency, sir, is not a trade." The conclusion for banks to draw was that they should give up to sovereignty the issue of notes, which was unnecessary anyway to the well-managed banks and in fact unimportant to many of them, and by confining themselves to a deposit business be free of government control altogether. In short, Mr Cambreleng offered the banks freedom of all regulation if they would surrender the issue of notes; which would mean that banking to-day, since it no longer includes note-issue, would be as free of regulation as any other business. Whatever this might be considered now, it was in 1837 a reasonable and conservative proposal, familiar to economists and in principle approved by Albert Gallatin among others. It was wholly within the spirit of *laisser faire*. Yet to Loco Foco and banker alike it sounded drastic. Had it been understood, the Loco Foco should have cursed with frustration, and the banker should have grinned with complacence. In fact each did the opposite, taking his cue from his opponent's behavior: the banker was angry because he saw that the Loco Foco was pleased, and the Loco Foco was pleased because he saw that the banker was angry.[50]

So the bankers were not swept away by the subtle considerations

* He means Philadelphia, of course.

[50] Congress, *Register of Debates* xiv, Part 2 (1837), 1628-29.

which Mr Van Buren and Mr Cambreleng presented. *Laisser faire* they knew and liked; but *laisser faire* presented in the Jeffersonian language of the Loco Focos—desperate and destructive radicals— they failed to recognize. Only after a good, long breathing spell did they become reconciled to the independent Treasury and find in it more than ample compensation for the "loss" of the Treasury's business, which proved to be far more serious to the Treasury than to them. And the system was eventually extinguished, not at their instance but at that of the federal government, its real victim.* In 1837, however, their inertia and the partisan hostility of the Whigs to any Democratic measure deferred the hopes of the Loco Focos and the ingenious efforts of Mr Van Buren and Mr Cambreleng. The independent Treasury bill failed as yet to be enacted and Congress had adjourned, acquiescing in the stoppage of specie payments.

But the idea was by no means dead. The double objective of the Loco Focos—an "independent" federal Treasury and prohibition of banks by the states—was to achieve considerable success. It was the traditionary objective of the Jeffersonian agrarians in a fresh form, strengthened by the banks' own behavior. The identity of Loco Foco and agrarian doctrine is indicated by comparison of their sentiments already quoted with the following counsel of James K. Polk, later President of the United States, writing when he was governor of Tennessee in 1841 to an agrarian citizenry: "What the farmer or planter should most desire," he said, "is a regular course of policy, steadily pursued, by which prices may remain settled and not be subjected to great and sudden changes, often brought about by extended bank credits to a small class who have overtraded or engaged in visionary or disastrous speculation."[51]

Whether expressed by the urban mechanic or by the farmer, the complaint was the same. It was the venerable complaint that credit and speculation artificially disturb the normal values of things, in- flicting on the economy alternate fever and prostration and undoing the sober efforts of steady and honest men. How ancient the com- plaint is I do not guess, but since the South Sea Bubble at least it had been ever present in the Anglo-American economies.

* President Van Buren correctly called the measure "one of restriction, not of favor," with respect to the Treasury, which was refused by it "a discretion possessed by every citizen" and was required instead to accept payments of money only in specified form. Richardson, *Messages*, III, 341.

[51] W. B. Smith, 72, quoting Tennessee *Senate Journal*, 1841, Message of Governor James K. Polk, 7 October 1841.

CHAPTER 16

The Foundering of the United States Bank of Pennsylvania

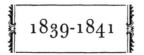

1839-1841

I. Nicholas Biddle's retirement — II. The United States Bank in trouble — III. The United States Bank's failure — IV. Criminal charges against Nicholas Biddle — V. His accomplishment — VI. Factors in his fall — VII. Persistence of his ideas and practice — VIII. The sub-treasury — IX. North and South; Britain and America

I

Toward the end of the same year, 1838, that the banks resumed paying their depositors and note-holders in specie, Nicholas Biddle announced that he would soon retire from the presidency of the United States Bank. "All that it was designed to do has been done," he wrote in a valedictory addressed to John Quincy Adams in December: "It was proposed to protect the character of the country from the first shock of the suspension, to effect the honorable discharge of our foreign debt with the least sacrifice of the property of the debtors, to vindicate the good faith of the state legislatures, to discourage all premature attempts to resume; but, by a cautious delay for those states which were less prepared, accomplish a universal resumption. All these are done, and the troubles of the country have happily ceased.

"Of the future it is difficult to speak; but in that future the Bank of the United States will no longer occupy its past position. The Bank of the United States had ceased to be a national institution in 1836, and was preparing to occupy its new place as a state bank when the troubles of 1837 forced it in some degree back into its old position, and it then devoted all its power to assist in carrying the country unhurt through its recent troubles. Having done this, . . . it . . . will take its rank hereafter as a simple state institution, devoted exclusively to its own special concerns."[1]

[1] 29th Congress, 1st Session, HD 226, p. 408.

When it came, Mr Biddle's retirement was anything but quiet and unobtrusive. On 26 February 1839 he was the guest of honor of President Van Buren in the White House. Another guest, James A. Hamilton, the son of Alexander Hamilton, observed: "This dinner went off very well, Biddle evidently feeling as the conqueror. He was facetious and in intimate converse with the President." A month later, 29 March 1839, he retired from the Bank, its affairs being, he said, "in a state of great prosperity and in the hands of able directors and officers." The same day the directors of the Bank were unanimous in describing him as one "who, having performed so much and so faithfully, leaves the institution with which he is identified prosperous in all its relations, strong in its abilities to promote the interests of the communities by which it is surrounded, cordial in its associations with sister establishments, and secure in the respect and esteem of all who are connected with it in foreign or domestic intercourse." Philip Hone, at this time, called Nicholas Biddle in his diary "the undaunted opponent of arbitrary power" and recorded the rumor that he was to be Secretary of the Treasury in Mr Van Buren's Cabinet.[2]

Six months later the bank had to stop specie payments. It resumed them, and then, after a year or more of struggle, dismayed inquiry, and recrimination, it suspended again. It closed its doors permanently in 1841 and went into the hands of trustees, bankrupt.

Though Mr Biddle spoke of his retirement in the lofty terms of a mission accomplished, the more substantial reason for it seems to have been the state of his health and the attraction of other interests. His health was so impaired by hard work and his sedentary life, he said in a letter to Samuel Jaudon, 19 April 1839, that if he kept on as he had, he must expect to be found some morning dead at his desk. He was suffering from a chronic disease that already had caused prolonged absences from his office and five years later caused his death.[3] A year or so before his retirement, he had given some thought to becoming a candidate for the Presidency of the United States, though not very much, apparently. After what happened in 1839 it was no longer to be dreamed of, but a little later he was inquiring about a diplomatic post, preferably Vienna.[4]

[2] J. A. Hamilton, *Reminiscences*, 312; Biddle, *Correspondence*, 337; Niles LVI (1839), 84; 29th Congress, 1st Session, HD 226, p. 486; Hone, 386.

[3] Biddle Papers, 2 PLB (1839), 127.

[4] Biddle, *Correspondence*, 272, 277-82, 296-97, 333.

II

But retirement proved to be something less than he might have supposed. It gave him leisure from the bank, though he came in frequently from Andalusia still and was consulted a great deal by his successors. One would expect no less. But things were not going too well with cotton, and he was drawn into a new series of transactions. "The foreign buyers keep back," he had been told in February from Liverpool, "and the Manchester people must, of course, abstain from purchasing the raw material until they can dispose of yarns. How long this contest will last, it is quite impossible to say. Meanwhile in the face of advices by every packet of diminished crop, arrivals come forward just about equal to the present scale of consumption. The market is daily teased . . . to the effectual defeat of any advance in price." And hence there is no reduction of inventory to report. Moreover, "All the Mississippi banks, whose interests the house protected by advancing upward of £700,000 and holding their cotton from four to eight months, by which they gained an immense benefit to their institutions and planters, are now sending the cotton under their control to other houses. . . , which is not only disgustingly ungrateful but somewhat mortifying, our counting house arrangements being on an expensive scale to compass another year's extensive business, which from present appearances will be reduced to less than one-fifth of the preceding." There had been a short cotton crop the autumn of 1838, but such advantages as it might bring were offset by plans in "all the cotton growing states" to resume specie payments, the banks there having lagged behind the resumption in the North months before. "This may make money scarce and counteract the effect of a diminished crop."[5]

It did tend to do so, but the real troubles now arising were abroad, not at home, and they began to operate with devastating effectiveness about the time of Nicholas Biddle's retirement. "Bullion in the Bank of England decreased from £9,336,000 to £2,525,000 between January and October" of 1839, and it was very commonly expected that the Bank would suspend specie payments. Commercial houses failed in Canton, Calcutta, Le Havre, and Brussels. Everywhere money was dear. In Britain, where America's cotton was to be sold, conditions were especially bad. There was a painful reaction from the over-building of railways and extravagant stock speculation, of which the past readiness to buy American securities was a part.

[5] W. B. Smith, 196-202; Biddle Papers 85, Folio 17726; 1 PLB (1836), 532.

Simultaneously, British exports to the Continent had fallen off severely, partly because of business recession and partly because the establishment of spinning mills in Belgium, Saxony, and Prussia had sensibly reduced the demand for British yarn. Harvests in the Isles had been poor in 1838, and in 1839 they looked worse; there was practically no summer at all. In the end the harvests did fail, in ruinous, torrential autumn rains, with the expected result that grain and other stuff to feed the population had to be imported. The imports cost £10,000,000, and with but £3,500,000 in gold in her vaults the Bank of England had to borrow from the Bank of France. The New York *Courier and Enquirer*'s correspondent, writing from London, 20 September 1839, catalogued the dismal realities of the worst British September "within the memory of man," the prospect that foreigners would take no more manufactured goods this winter than in the last, the likelihood of "another year of misery of every kind," and the impossibility of perceiving how the Bank of England was to avoid suspending.[6]

These things did not happen all at once but arose in a disheartening train, one mischance after another, from the summer of 1838 to the fall of 1839, when they reached their fatal peak. Their cumulative effect on the demand for Mr Biddle's cotton and on the United States Bank's credit was crushing. He had counted on recovery, with the optimistic but reasonable expectation that conditions, being bad, would improve; instead of which, being bad, they got worse. A high price for staples had been maintained, but it had been a nominal one. Much of 1838's cotton had lain untouched. And now the British spinners, made resolute by the domestic calamities, the loss of their Continental business, and the probability that the Americans could not hold out longer, stopped buying cotton and reduced production drastically. "A succession of events, political and economic," says Professor Leland Jenks, who has narrated these events illuminatingly from the viewpoint of the London market, "united to bring the Biddle system to disaster in 1839 and to wreck the credit which it had been the medium of restoring for a time to American enterprise. . . . Cotton recovered in price for a few weeks but then sank rapidly as the spinners held together and the rising discount rate of the Bank of England discouraged fresh enterprise. . . . England would buy neither cotton nor securities."[7]

6 W. B. Smith, 216; Jenks, 95-96; Hazard I, 269.
7 Jenks, 95-97; Niles LVI (1839), 351.

There had been doubt all the time whether Mr Biddle's plans would succeed and hopes that they would not. In January 1839, Mr Humphreys had been greeted with ironic courtesy in the Bank parlours on Threadneedle Street as an agent of the "master mind" in Philadelphia who was contriving "the monopoly of the cotton crop now coming forward"—a design "to secure the control of perhaps a million of bales and thus establish any future price that Mr Biddle chose to put upon it in Europe." The program was a commonplace in the press and in private correspondence. It was well understood that its success depended on favorable external conditions and an early recovery in trade. So as weeks and months passed through the fall of 1838, the winter, and the spring and summer of 1839, with no recovery and with a steady worsening of conditions throughout the world, it needed no grim fortune-teller to see that the bank's prospects were darkening. Apart from the staples program, it was known that since 1836 the bank's capital had been tied up more and more in ventures that must take years to mature and that a good many shrewd persons thought would never mature—nor were proper for a bank even if they did. In April 1839 the bank headed a public list of subscribers to a new steamship company with a subscription of $100,000 and then found the subscription to be illegal. It was known that London, New York, and Washington were all hostile to the bank and far readier to stick their knives into it if it got in trouble than to help it out. The bank had the watchful eyes of the market on it. High and resistant as was its prestige, distrust rose equally high, as men with neither Nicholas Biddle's talents nor his weaknesses appraised the bank's position and one by one drew clear of it. Month by month, the wise money slipped away.[8]

The result was a ceaseless suction on the bank's specie, which was drawn off faster than normal transactions would replace it. To meet the drain sometime in the early summer following Mr Biddle's retirement in the spring, the bank's managers turned to fresh sources of funds, which they found mainly among the unsophisticated and the avaricious. The procedure was to sell the bank's obligations in New York, Boston, and Baltimore, let the proceeds accumulate as deposits in the banks of those cities, especially in New York, and then when the deposits were sizable enough, suddenly demand their instant payment in cash, with the reasonable expectation that the

8 Biddle Papers 83, Folio 17389; 2 PLB (1839), 127-28.

demand could not be met. Instead the banks would have to suspend specie payments again, and in the general suspension that would follow, the United States Bank would have relief from its embarrassment. Meanwhile, if the pressure put on the other banks did not force them to suspend, it would at least squeeze out of them some cash for the empty coffers in Philadelphia.*

The obligations which the bank sold were post-notes and foreign drafts. The post-notes were its promissory notes due generally in six months' time, yielding interest, but sold usually at a discount as well. They were a bank liability equivalent in substance to time deposits, but since they could be sold aggressively as investments they were more readily expansible than deposits. They were a familiar form of obligation. They were now offered at such high yields and in such volume that they drove out other investment obligations. In order to reach small investors and sop up all the funds possible, they were issued in denominations as low as ten dollars and sold to yield as much as twenty per cent per annum. In these sales the Girard Bank of Philadelphia was associated with the United States Bank.

In Baltimore it was reported in August: "The whole floating capital of this city has been absorbed in the discounting of post-notes of the United States and Girard Banks. . . ." Philadelphia's action "has been of serious injury to us. Now no securities can be discounted at any price." The Boston money market was also invaded; "the Bank of the United States put its sucker into their pond in the shape of $800,000 of post-notes . . . and from a state of comparative ease, in three days the market was in an agony of pressure." The Boston *Courier* reported 28 August: "The rate of interest for the past week has been from one to one and a quarter per cent a month for the best paper. This high price for money has been, in a great degree, caused by the large amount of United States Bank post-notes which have been forced upon our market

* There seems to be no contemporary statement by the bank itself of its purpose, which may indeed have been no more than a hand-to-mouth grabbing of what it could get. My supposition is that its real objective was what I think it logically should have been, viz., to produce another general suspension, because only that offered it any real hope, the specie it got being certain otherwise to go as fast as it came in. But Professor Walter B. Smith, who is far more familiar with the bank's operations than I am, seems to emphasize its purpose to get specie, and the failure to get it. W. B. Smith, 215.

at one per cent a month discount. The proceeds have been, or are now about to be, taken from our city in specie. . . . These post-notes have been bought by those who have full confidence in all the transactions of this great institution. Are they acting for their own interest in making these investments? Is it not probable that before these notes are at maturity, the United States and Girard Banks, and all others south and west of Pennsylvania, may suspend specie payments?" How, it was asked, can the Philadelphia banks, now in straits for cash and selling post-notes to obtain it, be expected in six months to repay the notes? "By the sales of these post-notes and the consequent removal of the specie from this city, the power of our own banks is weakened, and hence our tradesmen, manufacturers, and merchants are distressed. And this may not be all the evil; for even those who have gathered up their coppers and bought these post-notes may have paid too dear for their whistle."[9]

Meanwhile sales of European exchange began also to be pressed, in the form of drafts on Hottinguer and Company, long the United States Bank's correspondent in Paris and Le Havre. The sales were profuse, and the source of the balances against which they were drawn was a mystery. "The United States Bank," reported the New York *Journal of Commerce*, 30 August 1839, "for sixty or ninety days past has supplied all demands for exchange on England. It has sold several millions of bills at least. What funds these bills have been drawn against for such very large amounts, seeing that American stocks have ceased to sell, we do not understand. . . . And why now the same bank or its most intimate companion is shipping great amounts of gold to England and still drawing bills at a heavy loss compared with the value of the gold it gets out, we are equally at a loss to understand."* In short, the bank was selling drafts on London and Paris, obtaining specie from their sale, shipping the specie to Europe to pay the drafts, and losing money on every draft it sold. "These bills," the New York *American* later reported, "were pressed on the market with great urgency, and the rates at which they were sold made it matter of easy calculation to ascertain that loss must result from the operation to the sellers, who were to remit the specie they produced in order to meet the bills. As, moreover,

* The "intimate companion" was presumably either the Girard Bank in Philadelphia or the United States Bank in New York. 29th Congress, 1st Session, HD 226, p. 541; Raguet, *Financial Register* II, 13-14.

[9] Boston *Corrier*, 26 and 28 August 1839; W. B. Smith, 214.

the bank was then a borrower in Europe, inquiry was naturally excited as to what these drafts could mean." According to the *Journal of Commerce*, the United States Bank was "constantly making great sacrifices at somebody's expense and for somebody's benefit, neither of which somebodies can exactly be found." A week later, 6 September 1839, the *Journal* observed skeptically that "the policy of the bank in drawing bills on England without funds there and shipping specie to meet those bills at maturity is put forth as a voluntary effort on the part of the bank for the public good . . . ," this "good" being the provision of exchange with which merchants could pay their debts in Europe and continue necessary importations. But however obscure the purpose, the sales were pressed still more hotly. The drafts were signed in blank in Philadelphia and rushed to New York "to be sold without limit."[10]

The sale of notes and drafts yielded the bank substantial balances; and during August it withdrew an estimated $1,250,000 in specie from the New York banks, the largest withdrawals being made in two successive days, the 26th and 27th. On the latter day, agents of the United States Bank, accompanied by notaries, entered various Wall Street banks half an hour before closing time, presented checks of which no previous notice had been given, and demanded instant payment.

"At the Bank of the State of New York, a draft for $80,000 was handed in. The teller said it should be paid as soon as possible. The presenter of the draft replied that it must be paid instantaneously, or the check be given back; that he had no discretion. The cashier being called, and informed of what was going on, said *he* had a discretion in the matter, and that he should *not* give back the check, and that it should be paid by three o'clock. Orders were given accordingly to count out the specie—which was not quite accomplished when the clock struck three. Upon the stroke appeared the notary, with a duplicate of the draft in the handwriting of Mr Young, the cashier of the United States Bank here, and prepared to protest it for non-payment. Seeing, however, the money was there, and forthcoming, the protest could not decently be made. . . ." Similar demands were also met by the other New York banks.[11]

In London, meanwhile, Samuel Jaudon was performing prodigies. He could still face brightly the officers of the Bank of England and

[10] New York *Journal of Commerce*, 30 August, 4 September 1839; New York *American*, 20 April 1841; 29th Congress, 1st Session, HD 226, p. 488.
[11] New York *American*, 20 April 1841; Niles LX (1841), 121.

ask for credit, undaunted by the cold body of his prospects which must have been present at every interview, swathed in crêpe. Here and there he went, between Paris and Liverpool, begging for money, and often getting it. On 22 August he wrote his allies in Liverpool, Humphreys and Biddle, in whose care the unwanted bales of cotton lay: "I must look to you for £50,000. . . . If I do not get this I get none; . . . everything, therefore, turns upon what you can do, for here I am exhausted. You must therefore work your hardest for me—life or death to the Bank of the United States is the issue." The following day he wrote for £50,000 more. Next the skies fell: Hottinguer and Company, associated for twenty years with the United States Bank and its predecessor but disliking the signs of the times and the goings-on in Philadelphia, refused to honor the drafts thence, drawn without advice or funds. Mr Jaudon energetically met the crisis by persuading the Paris Rothschilds to take them up—or a substantial part of them. This was a real feat, especially because the same house had declined two months before to join the Bank of France and others in the loan to the Bank of England. Their credit to the United States Bank was confirmed by the following letter to its president from Paris, 23 September 1839:

"We have the honour to inform you that we have arranged with Mr Jaudon to accept for your account the amount of 5,500,000 francs, your drafts on the Messrs Hottinguer, which remained in suspense. We take it for granted that Mr Jaudon will have informed you of the arrangements entered into by us with him for this purpose, and consequently consider it unnecessary to recapitulate them here, limiting ourselves to furnishing you, on the other side, a memorandum of such of your drafts as have been left in our hands to-day to be clothed with our acceptance.

"We are happy, Mr President, to have found an opportunity to give you a proof of our high consideration for the establishment over which you preside, and to have been able, at the same time, to arrest the disastrous effects which this refusal of acceptance on the part of Messrs Hottinguer was beginning to produce in our place, as well as in Lyons, by many holders of your bills, who, pressed by their necessities to an immediate realization of their funds, were offering to part with these securities at a loss over the discount.

"We shall correspond with Mr Jaudon in everything concerning our acceptance on your account, in conformity to his request made to us, so that we shall not be obliged to trouble you with details relative to this operation, except in case of new instructions on your part."[12]

I do not know why the Rothschilds did this and only conjecture that it served the purpose of some strategy aimed against London's dominance in American trade and undertaken at a moment of the City's weakness. The sum of 5,500,000 francs was not too much to stake on gaining America's business for Paris. Whatever its purpose, however, the Rothschilds' action must have proved to be a blunder in the end; but not so at the time. "This event has been the subject of extraordinary excitement, both in England and in France," it was reported from London to the *Courier and Enquirer* of New York. "But the numerous enemies of the Bank of the United States, who both in London and Lancashire and Yorkshire were exulting in the supposed downfall of the institution, have now found that, on the contrary, the result of the affair has eminently strengthened the credit of the institution; all parties now agreeing that if Mr Jaudon when suddenly called upon, . . . could substitute the greatest capitalists in the whole world for the comparatively unknown house of Hottinguer—that all this must redound most signally to the credit and solid power of the Bank of the United States." The report included no reason for the Hottinguers' action, which was merely presented as extraordinary; and its calling the house "comparatively unknown" was probably intended to minimize the significance of what it had done.[13]

But Mr Jaudon, on 26 September, three days after the Rothschilds' Paris letter, was turning again to the Bank of England. He needed more than to have the drafts from Philadelphia honored. He wanted £300,000 for three or four months, to be secured by American stocks. He said in part:

"This application of the bank has become necessary in consequence of the difficulties which the very unexpected refusal of Messrs Hottinguer and Company to accept the drafts of the Bank U. States has occasioned. That refusal was the more unfortunate as my letters of the 31st August from the cashier of the Bank state that about Fcs 1,800,000 were going to Messrs Hottinguer and Company by the packet of the 1st September and that others would follow in good time.

"The discredit however which that refusal has occasioned, not-

[12] 29th Congress, 1st Session, HD 226, p. 479; Hazard I, 335; Baring Papers, OC, 12 October 1839.

[13] Hazard I, 269; Burgess, *Circular to Bankers*, 20 September 1839, p. 93.

withstanding that I have made arrangements with Messrs de Roth-schild frères to protect the signature of the Bank U. States so paralyzes my operations that I am compelled to look to the Bank of England as the only power which can sustain me until the arrival of the Steamer Gt. Western on the 5th proximo. . . .

"But there is one point which I may be permitted to suggest, viz., that upon supporting the credit of the Bank U. States depends an operation which, if completed, will enable me to draw upon the Continent to the extent of six hundred thousand pounds and thus bring this large amount to co-operate with the exertions of the Bank of England to turn the exchanges in favor of this country. . . .

"P.S. In case any loan should be granted by the Bank of England, and it should appear after the Gt. Western arrives that the whole business of the Bank U. States cannot be carried out successfully in the opinion of an eminent House in London, I would make a stipula-tion that the first remittances from the Bank U. States shall be applied to the repayment of this loan, with the exception of £100,-000 already advanced to me by a friend who will be prepared, I believe even to postpone this claim in favor of the Bank of England."*

The Bank of England refused the application but offered "to advance an amount of Consols of the value of £300,000 for a period not exceeding one month . . . to be secured by the guarantee of Commercial Houses to be approved by the Committee of Treasury." This counter-proposal could give Mr Jaudon little comfort, and it was not accepted. A number of private individuals, however, united to support him and advanced "£800,000 in money, for the period . . . of a year and a half or two years, and upon the deposit of American securities only." These benefactors were presumably stockholders and creditors of the United States Bank who were willing to risk something more in order to prevent the monstrous loss which Mr Jaudon dangled before their frightened eyes.[14]

During September, things had been quieter on the western side of the Atlantic, with no repetition of the peremptory performance of August. According to the *Journal of Commerce*, 30 August, "a letter of conciliation was circulated yesterday . . . from the U.S.

---

* I am indebted to the Governor and Company of the Bank of England for the text of this letter and permission to publish it.

14 Jenks, 97; House of Commons, *Report from Select Committee on Banks of Issue* (1840), 149, 231; Niles LVII (1839), 162-63.

Bank full of assurances of good feeling and that no more specie will be drawn and all that." None would be or could be, the *Journal* was confident, because the post-notes were no longer selling, those sold were maturing, and the balance was the other way. It was indeed; about six weeks later, 9 October, the United States Bank suspended, being quite unable to meet her obligations to the money market she had been abusing. The other banks of Philadelphia also suspended with her, and the banks of the South and West rather generally followed their example. The day after the United States Bank suspended, the steamer from Liverpool arrived in New York with the news that Hottinguer and Company had refused the drafts the bank had drawn upon it. To make the coincidence more ironic, it also brought news of the Rothschilds' help. Thus news of Hottinguer's refusal of the drafts and Rothschilds' acceptance of them reached the States after the suspension in Philadelphia, and news of the suspension reached Europe after the affair of the drafts. Each world had its own share of the excitement and something to offer that must make the other stare.[15]

A fortnight later the United States Bank instigated a meeting in the City Hall, New York, at which merchants and other "honorable men" were urged to embarrass the New York banks with demands for the renewal of their discounts and with abrupt withdrawals of cash. But to this second attempt to break them, said Mr Gallatin, "the banks, as might well be expected, unanimously refused to yield." Of this whole sequence, Mr Gallatin, a witness and an intended victim, wrote shortly thereafter the following summary: "In September the bank drew largely on Europe without funds and partly without advice. In order, if possible, to provide funds for that object and also, as has been acknowledged, for the purpose of breaking the banks of New York, payment for the bills thus sold in that city was suddenly required in specie and the amount shipped to Europe. The attempt was a failure in both respects; the banks stood, and the bills were dishonored. On the 9th of October the United States Bank suspended its payments; and it is not improper to observe that, a fortnight later, another attempt was made under its auspices by the debtor interest of New York to compel the banks to expand their discounts, and thus prepare the way for another

---

[15] New York *Journal of Commerce*, 10 and 11 October 1839; Boston *Courier*, 11 and 12 October 1839; Boston *Atlas*, 12 October 1839.

general suspension. . . . From that time the fate of that institution was considered as sealed by every impartial observer."[16]

From October 1839 to January 1841, the bank continued in suspension, raising money as she could and arranging accommodations. Times were bad. Professor Walter B. Smith shows that export prices, especially of cotton, were falling and that business was worse than two years before. American stocks were still harder to sell abroad, partly because they had got a bad reputation and partly because London was still without funds. Yet the bank had to attempt the resumption of specie payments lest she lose her charter under the Pennsylvania law. The attempt was made 15 January 1841, after anxious preparation, and was continued about three weeks, till 4 February 1841, when her doors were closed finally and for good that afternoon at three o'clock, the regular closing time.* The directors found that "a feeling of hostility to the institution or, what was equally destructive, a pervading distrust of its credit and means, existed to an extent so great as to render the undertaking hopeless unless the bank was prepared to meet every dollar of her liabilities with a dollar of coin." Mr Gallatin considered this attempt to resume foredoomed; "it was impossible that it should not have failed," he said. "The element indispensable for sustaining any bank, *confidence*, was utterly lost. It seems incredible that it should not have been foreseen that, as soon as the United States Bank paid

---

* The other banks "foolishly attempted to stem the current and continue full payments of specie next morning," according to the report to Baring Brothers by Grant and Stone, correspondents of theirs in Philadelphia. "But the panic and rush was so overwhelming that a few hours finished the attempt, and all were reduced to the point they ought to have started from—paying their small notes only. If the banks had kept cool and refused all large sums, the effect would have probably produced another result; but paying deposits by *thousands* and *tens of thousands* alarmed other depositors that so reckless a course should be adopted, and knowing it could not be continued they did not mean to be left behind and drew also, receiving their money instantly, untold, in boxes of half dollars of $1000 each, in wheelbarrows, carts, etc.—not to be removed to another bank but to be hoarded up at home. This rapid movement was of short duration and highly amusing to the thousands of spectators and a few pickpockets, all in perfect good humor." (Baring Papers, MC, Grant and Stone to Baring Brothers, 26 February 1841.) This describes, one should note, not a run on the United States Bank but on the other Philadelphia banks the day following the United States Bank's closing.

16 New York *American*, 20 April 1841; Niles lx (1841), 121; Gallatin iii, 404; Baring Papers, OC, T. W. Ward to Baring Brothers, 12 and 18 October 1839.

in specie, every person who held its notes would instantaneously seize the opportunity of converting them into cash."[17]

III

In the universal wonder at the predicament of an institution, possessing, in the words of *The Times*, London, "a larger capital strictly applicable to the uses of industry and commerce than any other in the whole world," blame had soon begun to descend on the shoulders of Nicholas Biddle. When he had retired from the bank's presidency in the spring, then, with all his blushing honors thick upon him, he had told the world that he was leaving the bank in a state of great prosperity. Only six months later it was unable to pay its debts and floundering in difficulties from which it never extricated itself. In the summer of 1840 Mr Biddle was told that he owed the bank about $320,000 "over-advance" on the cotton accounts. He denied the debt on the advice of counsel. Yet, though he "did not recognize the claim" and though "neither law nor equity made it necessary to pay," he gave the bank the $320,000—mostly in bonds of the Republic of Texas. By this payment, he said, "I thought I was giving a strong proof how far ancient and kindly recollections of the bank prevailed over all selfish considerations." To help make up the amount, the sumptuous service of plate given him the year before was melted down for what it would fetch as bullion. Even this devoted offering did not avail. For one of Nicholas Biddle's quickness of mind, self-confidence, and vanity, it must have been bad enough to find his former admirers crossing the street to avoid him and to have to wrestle in his heart with the appalling fact that his career and accomplishments were in men's eyes a disgrace and his fortune his country's loss. A yelling mob could scarcely make things worse, nor the smug grins of the Jacksonians, who though they lost the election to the Whigs in 1840 and had to go home with Mr Van Buren, nevertheless could now demonstrate by Nicholas Biddle's own showing that their proscription of him had been deserved.[18]

In this miserable situation Mr Biddle produced and published in April 1841, following the bank's final collapse, a series of letters by way of apologia. They were prolix, specious, declamatory, bewildered —the painful protestations of a man who could not comprehend what

[17] W. B. Smith, 221; Gallatin III, 405; 29th Congress, 1st Session, HD 226, p. 472.
[18] Burgess, *Circular to Bankers*, 20 September 1839, p. 93; 29th Congress, 1st Session, HD 226, pp. 419-20, 475ff, 481, 523ff.

had happened but still must babble on. In them he declared that
the bank was prosperous when he relinquished management of it,
and that its subsequent ruin arose from "efforts to break down the
banks of New York." The bank's officers, he was told, believing a
storm was about to burst, had deemed it best, "instead of meeting
its full force at once . . . to make it fall first upon the banks of
New York." This news that the bank had "invited" its own suspension by trying to compel the New York banks to suspend, was
something, according to Niles' *Register*, "which Mr Biddle is the
first to announce." Philip Hone also indicates that the "precious
disclosure" just made by Mr Biddle was news to him. One would
expect Mr Hone to know the facts if many persons did. It is hard to
believe that the matter could have been a secret, but at any rate it
was now common understanding that in order to get other centers
heavily encumbered with demand obligations to Philadelphia, the
United States Bank had plunged into debt itself on obligations of
later maturities and had sought by both prolonged and sudden
withdrawals to force Wall Street into stopping specie payments. "If
the New York banks could have been made to refuse a specie draft,"
the New York *American* explained, "the alarm consequent upon
the notoriety of that fact, would, it was hoped, cause a run upon
them that would force a suspension, and then the Philadelphia
banks—and especially the Bank of the United States of Pennsylvania, which foresaw its inability to continue specie payments—
would have been preceded, and so far justified, in suspension, by
those of New York."[19]

Mr Biddle also reported that, to effect the bank's purpose, "large
means were necessary, and to procure these resort was had to the
sale of foreign exchange. . . . The proceeds of these immense sales
of exchange created very heavy balances against the New York
banks; which, after all, signally failed in producing the contemplated effect. The bills, not being provided for, nor even regularly
advised, as had uniformly been the custom of the bank, were dishonored;* and although the agent in London did everything which

* When banks sell drafts on their foreign correspondents, they are
supposed not only to have funds *already* on deposit with the correspondents
to pay the drafts but to inform, or advise, the correspondents of each draft

[19] 29th Congress, 1st Session, HD 226, pp. 480, 482, 486; Niles LX (1841), 121;
Hone, 540-41.

skill and judgment could accomplish, the credit of the bank was gone, and from that day to the present its effects upon the institution have been more and more disastrous." Here, said Mr Biddle, was the "real and secret cause of the disasters of the bank"; the whole trouble was the "neglect, or inadvertence, or omission" to apprise Messrs Hottinguer and Company of the drafts upon them.[20]

This is scarcely adequate. It ascribes the bank's difficulties merely to the kiting of drafts on Messrs Hottinguer; it omits entirely the sale of post-notes and the pressure on the bank itself for redemption of the matured notes. It omits the circumstance that the bank suspended the day *before* the ship arrived from Liverpool with the news of the Hottinguers' action and that the ship also brought the compensating news of the Rothschilds' assistance. If these omissions sound disingenuous, it is not because Biddle disapproved the raid on the other banks and sought to direct attention from it. For there is no reason to suppose that he did disapprove it. The raid was quite within the ethics of the time. His own acceptance of the practice is expressed in letters of his dated just before the general suspension, May 1837, when the bank had suffered some loss of specie. He had written Samuel Jaudon: "What we lose has gone to New York and as none goes abroad we may fairly make reprisals on the New York banks. My favorite scheme would be this. Sell sterling, or sterling bonds, or post-notes, or bank stock" and leave the funds in New York banks, "to remain in the hands of sundry depositors subject to our call in case of accident. I did this as you know once before, and it proved a great comfort." Whatever the occasion and the purpose, this involved compulsive pressure upon the debtor banks, though not apparently to the drastic extremes of 1839, through the sale of obligations and the accumulation of deposit credit. The following note is evidence, indeed, that he knew in 1839 what was going on. It is unsigned, but in the handwriting of his long-time friend R. L. Colt, and endorsed as Colt's by Biddle himself. It is dated in New York, 15 October 1839, within a week of the bank's stopping specie payments. "I am sorry you could do nothing further. We must wait for results. If our banks were not governed

---

drawn. And unless and until the foreign correspondents receive such advice they are not expected to pay the drafts. This was the established practice in 1839 as it always has been, and its disregard by the United States Bank was a flagrant part of its offense.

[20] 29th Congress, 1st Session, HD 226, pp. 488-89.

by false pride and a cabal that rules them, they would stop at once. They will make a desperate effort to hold on until after the Liverpool sails. If your banks could get hold of some New York funds almost at any cost, they ought to make a run. I am satisfied that our merchants will not hold out a week longer; the only wonder is that they have held on so long." It is probably not a mere coincidence that a week later, at the City Hall meeting already mentioned, the further attempt to embarrass the Wall Street banks occurred.[21]

But in 1839, banks were so indisputably under the same obligation as other creditors to meet their liabilities that the motives of those who called on them to do so were of no concern. A bank's promise was a promise. Hence Mr Gallatin said it was "monstrous" to suppose that they had any discretion in any circumstances about keeping their promises. This being true, it was next to monstrous to suppose that the motives of those who demanded performance of their promises should be questioned. Under the shelter of this unquestionable right of creditors to demand payment due from their debtors, banks, both Canadian and American, commonly sought to embarrass one another. The motive might seem bad, but the procedure was legal and defensible. In 1833 the Bank of the United States had itself been the object of a raid, instigated in New York, with the connivance—or more, as credibly rumored—of the Jackson administration. The fact that the demands of certain creditors, if pressed aggressively and maliciously, were opposed to the interests of other creditors was frequently recognized and belligerently acted on, especially if the demands were made by creditors from out of town; but yet the principle was not established that the general interest justified banks in refusing particular and importunate demands. Moreover, at a time when stoppage of specie payments impaired mainly the convertibility of notes but did not close the banks or prevent the use of bank credit, it was not the calamity it has become since the liabilities of banks came to be mainly or wholly in the form of deposits. The effort of the Philadelphia banks to embarrass the New York banks in 1839 may be condemned, as may the latters' reciprocation of the compliment in 1841 and their collusion in a similar attack on the federal Bank back in 1833, but it can not be under the same condemnation as if it were to occur now, after becoming through a century of evolution of worse consequence practically and, by statute and general regard, a crime.[22]

[21] Biddle Papers 88, Folio 20022; 1 PLB (1837), 181, 185-86.
[22] Niles xlv (1833), 297-99; Union Committee, *Report*, 15-16; Catterall, 299.

What Nicholas Biddle disapproved about the 1839 affair was, as he said, the sale of foreign exchange drawn without advice and without funds. And without approving the sales either of exchange or of post-notes, I agree with him that the difference between them was substantial. The sale of post-notes was domestic and involved no escape from responsibility within the American jurisdiction. It did not embarrass or affront foreign creditors and by so doing impair American credit. It did not involve the sale to innocent purchasers of obligations whose worth was known by the bank to hang by a thread. It kept the affair within the family, legally as well as economically, and the worth of the notes, though in the end no greater, hung at the time of their sale by something that was stronger than a thread even though not strong enough. So when Nicholas Biddle condemned the raids of 1839 simply because the bank sold foreign exchange drawn without funds and without advice, he condemned what he thought was wrong and nothing less.

In April 1841, at the time the letters of apologia appeared and two months after the final closing of the bank, the stockholders heard a clear and grim report that, as Professor W. B. Smith says in quoting from it, must have been bitter reading for Nicholas Biddle. They then authorized negotiations for settlement of the bank's affairs. Proposals were made and failed. Other banks refused to accept notes of the United States Bank on any terms. "In the meantime these notes continued to depreciate and became entirely unavailable to the holders except at a most ruinous sacrifice." Suits continued to be instituted almost daily; and as the bank had no legal defense to make, judgments were obtained readily. For the law now made the charter forfeit but provided no means of conserving the bank's assets equitably for the benefit of all creditors.[23]

The full result for the creditors appears indeterminable. John Jay Knox, who was a young contemporary of the liquidation, reported that payment of the bank's obligations was in full, principal and interest, though he errs in the date of the final settlement, which was 1866 or 1867. Professor W. B. Smith's account indicates that the surviving records fall somewhat short of either proving or disproving the statement made by Mr Knox. Altogether circumstances seem to indicate that the condition of the state bank in 1839 was no worse and possibly better than that of the federal Bank twenty years before,

[23] 29th Congress, 1st Session, HD 226, p. 536; W. B. Smith, 228-29.

from which Langdon Cheves had rescued it in no great time. Proper liquidation of the bank's assets required time and care and the forbearance of claimants, which they never got. The creditors snatched and litigated. The stockholders, in searching Mr Biddle's pockets as unintelligently as they had adulated him before, expended energy that should have been used in conserving the assets they had. The portfolio was immense, and it was liquidated largely in the '40's when buyers were not eager nor prices buoyant. These things magnified the disaster, how much it is impossible to say. In 1841 the stockholders insisted that the creditors could be paid in full and their own losses minimized if the state of Pennsylvania would stay its pressure on them, which it would not. The contention seems reasonable; but as things were, the stockholders never recovered anything. This, in the circumstances, is evidence that the bank though insolvent was not "rotten" as the Jacksonians asserted. There is no evidence that it was, unless rottenness, figuratively, is much less than the word signifies literally. What had happened, in brief, is that the Jacksonians, for selfish and materialistic reasons, had destroyed a useful institution ably managed. Nicholas Biddle, in rash but otherwise excusable reaction, had tried to frustrate their victory. In doing so he got the bank committed to the southern economy and to long-term credit generally. The market had grown suspicious of the bank's condition, and the wise money began to slip away. Then when cotton and securities ceased to draw from London the desperately needed current funds, the management's raids on the New York, Boston, and Baltimore money markets began. And when these failed, the bank, like one whose breath is stopped, fell over dead.[24]

Nicholas Biddle seems to have lost all his personal fortune, largely in meeting the bank's $320,000 claim. His wife's fortune remained, and he spent his last years "in elegant retirement," to the urbane editorial anger of William Cullen Bryant, who said he should have spent them in the penitentiary.

IV

Meanwhile Mr Biddle's payment of $320,000 had not satisfied the stockholders, and in June 1841 they directed that he be sued for $1,000,000 more. In September the amount was reduced to $240,000. The following January he and four others once officers

24 Knox, *History of Banking*, 79; W. B. Smith, 229-230; 29th Congress, 1st Session, HD 226, p. 533; Wainwright, 97-98, 102, 130.

of the bank were arrested on charges of criminal conspiracy and put on $10,000 bail each. The important charges were that they had "conspired to cheat and defraud the bank by obtaining therefrom large advances upon shipments of cotton to Europe, of the fortunate sales of which they retained the surplus proceeds or profits, while the losses were sustained by the bank"; and "by the unlawful receipt and expenditure of large sums of money, the application of which is not specified upon the books." The accused sued in the Court of General Sessions for writs of *habeas corpus*. The question for the court to decide was whether "probable cause" was established by the evidence for imputing to the accused "a concerted design to injure the Bank of the United States by false or corrupt means or to benefit themselves by measures of an illegal character." If it were found that the evidence supported the imputation of guilt and hence justified their being tried before a jury, the accused would be held for trial accordingly. If not, the court would discharge them. A fortnight was taken in hearing the evidence of the prosecution; twenty witnesses were examined and "all the books and papers of the bank brought into court, where they underwent a most searching investigation." The defense let its own case stand on the prosecution's evidence. "As soon as the testimony for the prosecution was finished, the counsel for Mr Biddle offered to leave the matter to the court without argument." This was presumably a play from strength, but the court in its opinion complained that its own task was rendered more difficult thereby. Though Mr Biddle's counsel made no formal argument, testimony must have been offered, at least in response to the court's questions. Otherwise the court's task would not have been difficult merely but impossible.[25]

With respect to the cotton operations, the evidence, according to the opinion, was that the advances had been made openly like any others; that the operations "were rendered indispensable by the liabilities of the bank in Europe and the failure or omission of the directors otherwise to meet their foreign engagements"; that they "were not only lawful in themselves but eminently useful to the bank and originally profitable to it"; and that "although, at their close, losses were occasioned by them growing out of the prevailing commercial distress, these were made good to the bank" by the defendants "upon terms which the directors considered, accepted,

25 Philadelphia *Public Ledger*, 11 and 30 April 1842; Philadelphia *Enquirer and National Gazette*, 10 May 1842; Biddle Papers 99, Folio 22371.

and thus closed their account." In the court's opinion, "it is rather the *amount* than the *character* of these advances on cotton to which objection seems to be taken." Excerpts from the opinion follow:

"In 1836, Samuel Jaudon, having been sent for that purpose by the directors to Europe, negotiated two loans for the Bank of the United States; the one of one million pounds sterling in London to be repaid by four equal instalments, two in 1837 and two in 1838; the other in Paris of twelve millions and five hundred thousand francs, payable in six equal instalments. . . . Again in March 1837, the bank contracted heavy additional liabilities upon the application of the merchants of New York to that institution for relief under circumstances of great commercial distress. These bonds thus payable in Europe arriving at maturity, the Board of Directors, though fully informed of this, had adopted no measures for their payment.

"The duty then of meeting these bonds devolved upon the officers. The directors as a body considered it the business of the Exchange Committee; the Exchange Committee in turn referred both the labor and responsibility to the officers of the bank; and these persons, in the decline of private credit, availed themselves of the obvious if not the *only* resource of shipping produce instead of purchasing bills of exchange. . . . There was then . . . but *one* method of making the desired remittances. . . . This was for the bank to make advances or purchase bills secured by pledges of specific shipments, to be forwarded to its creditors or agents in Europe, to be there sold and the proceeds applied in reimbursement of the advances. In such a case, the excess, if any, of the proceeds beyond the amounts advanced would belong to the borrowers; the deficiency, if any, would afterwards have to be made good by them to the bank. That this is a familiar arrangement in commercial business is well known. . . .

"The officers of the bank, therefore, bought merchandize of which they and not the bank were the owners. . . . The advances were all entered in full detail on the bill books. . . . From the bill books they passed regularly into the ledger. . . ."[26]

The opinion recited that in dividing the profits, Nicholas Biddle received one-half; Joseph Cowperthwaite, cashier, one-quarter; and John Andrews, assistant cashier, one-quarter. "But while these parties only were entitled to receive the surplus proceeds realized, it was their duty on the other hand to be prepared with the means

26 Biddle Papers 99, Folios 22371-74; Philadelphia *Public Ledger*, 30 April 1842.

of refunding the amount of any deficiency which might appear on the result of subsequent sales. . . .

"The surplus proceeds being thus divided, there occurred on subsequent shipments a deficiency equal to about two-thirds of what had been previously realized. Two of the parties at once admitted their liability for its repayment. One of them paid or secured satisfactorily the whole of his portion of the debt; the other was unable to do so in a manner equally satisfactory, but gave up to his creditors the whole of his property [a portion of which the bank accepted, the court said, in satisfaction of his liability]. The third party, Nicholas Biddle, had left the bank eighteen months before; and in answer to the application stated that he did not conceive himself bound to make up the deficiency, which had arisen, as he asserted, from sacrifices of his property made by the bank; but for the sake of peace, he agreed to pay his whole share without deduction. This was accordingly done. He paid the amount of the claim, obtained a receipt in full, and the account was finally closed."

The Texas bonds which were tendered in payment, the opinion recited, were not at par in the market; but "it is in evidence that the bank at the time of making the settlement with Mr Biddle possessed information that they would soon be of par value—probably more than par value." The Republic of Texas was then arranging a loan in London for their payment.

The charge that Biddle and his associates had conspired against the stockholders the court found to be untenable because nothing had been done to which the directors were not parties. The charge implied some concealment or deception of which the directors, the stockholders, and the bank were victims. There was no concealment or deception. There was too much careless bookkeeping, but in this also there had been general acquiescence, and in consequence it was a bit late to be putting all the blame on Nicholas Biddle even for that.

As to the charge of misapplied funds, the court found no evidence of misapplication by any one. "The only charge of fraud is that the application does not appear on the books; but this is shown to be in accordance with the routine of business and general usages of the bank—always prescribed or sanctioned by the directors; and it has been particularly shown to the court to be the case as to a vast number of items of which the actual, correct, and faithful application has been ascertained; and there is no evidence that it was incorrect or unfaithful in the items complained of."

Accordingly, having found that the evidence presented did not establish adequate grounds to warrant trial of the accused for having, as alleged, "criminally conspired to cheat and defraud the stockholders," the court discharged them. Of wrong doing they were exonerated.

The propriety and correctness of the court's opinion seem to me unquestionable—though I speak thus confidently without being a lawyer. I see nothing in this case or in anything pertaining to Nicholas Biddle and his career that shows corrupt motives or criminality in the conduct of the bank as alleged by the prosecution and by Nicholas Biddle's enemies in general. There were mistakes and in avoiding their acknowledgment there was a self-protective disingenuousness that would put fully half the population in jail if it were a statutory offense. But of purpose to get money by dishonest means, from the bank or any one, and put it in his pocket, there seems to me to be no evidence whatever.

As might be supposed, the events of 1839, 1840, and 1841 had the business world agog and plenty of things were said that conflict with the opinion I have just expressed. A week after the bank's stoppage of payments, 18 October 1839, John A. Stevens, president of the Bank of Commerce, New York, after the Bank of the United States the biggest in the country, had written to Baring Brothers: "The dishonour of the United States Bank in Paris, the precarious position of its agent in London, and its suspension if not bankruptcy at home before these events were known here, must stop, I think, its mischievous interference in trade, its attempt to regulate prices, its support of hazardous if not worthless undertakings and stocks of all sorts, and leave commercial affairs again to a regular and natural course."[27]

This was the voice of the conservative business world—of the Barings in London, of Thomas Wren Ward and Nathan Appleton in Boston, of Albert Gallatin, Jonathan Goodhue, and Prime, Ward, and King of New York—whose sturdy and sound views embraced the wholesome doctrine of *laisser faire* but no other rash novelties, and least of all the regulation of trade and prices and "absurd and gigantic schemes of internal improvements" for the general good. All during 1840, gossip about the situation in Philadelphia had

[27] Baring Papers, MC, 18 October 1839.

enlivened the correspondence and conversation of business men. Philip Hone had called the bank "an immense sack" into which every one put his hand and took out as much as he wanted, from Nicholas Biddle down. In 1841, after the final failure, the open recriminations, and the publication of the letters of apologia, gossip had bubbled with a fresh intensity. Joshua Bates, the American partner of Baring Brothers, had been back in the States on a visit that spring and had filled his letters to London with outbursts of contempt for the Philadelphians. He had had an average of sixty-five callers a day. "I have talked bank until I am now as tired of it as of the name of Biddle. What a precious set of rascals and swindlers the directors of the United States Bank have proved to be. The report of the committee and Biddle's letters astonish me very much. Jaudon will not be able to look any one in the face after this." Thomas Wren Ward, Mr Bates had said, "one of the soundest men in the country, . . . has been so right about the Bank and the quarrel amongst the Philadelphia rogues." Former President Van Buren, he had said, "called to-day; he seems to have got Biddle's letters by heart." The present directors "are Biddle's creatures," Mr Bates remarked; the United States Bank "has been under the management of fools and knaves, and it is mortifying that one did not discover their character sooner."[28]

Perhaps Mr Bates, like William Cullen Bryant, thought that Nicholas Biddle should go to jail, but I doubt it. If he did, I should set against his words those of Albert Gallatin, who though severe and well informed as any one in condemning the business judgment of the United States Bank, said that "the character" of its president and directors "was as irreproachable as that of the directors and officers of any of the banking institutions of New York." The vivacious language of Joshua Bates was that of a man who had always been annoyed by Mr Biddle and at last was disgusted by him. Mr Bates belonged to the business world by instinct and long training, and, like his friend John Stevens, he had no faith in interference with the "natural course" of things or in schemes for the regulation of trade and prices. He thought them mischievous. Yet he knew that there is considerable difference between a thief who steals money because he wants it himself and an innovator who tries to force his inventions on a reluctant, conservative world and in the effort runs disastrously beyond his powers. The loss may be the

[28] Hone, 521; Baring Papers, MC, 26 April, 31 May, 12 June 1841.

same, however, and in the rugged ethics of the business world a mistake need not be distinguished from a sin.[29]

That the cotton transactions would not be permitted nowadays seems to me irrelevant. To-day undertakings of the kind are conducted through distinct corporations, formed for the purpose. Such an arrangement, which had not been thought of in Nicholas Biddle's time, avoids what got him into trouble; it defines and limits responsibility. That, to be sure, could have been done anyway and should have been done. For Mr Biddle and his associates in the cotton corner to have anticipated their profit, to have committed it beyond easy recovery, and to have left the scene with a liability dangling to them, was inexcusably lax in any one who professed to be a business man. Still it was not a crime, subjectively or objectively. The question who was responsible for the loss in which the transactions ended is moot, but either way it was a responsibility of judgment, not of morality; and the blame it puts on Nicholas Biddle, as the ablest of many who participated in effecting the arrangement, is that the possibility of loss was overlooked. To Joshua Bates, of course, a shrewd and disciplined business man, that oversight would be itself a "crime."

Most persons seem to have found the court's opinion in the *habeas corpus* proceeding unconvincing. They were grimly positive that somebody was guilty of something and found no satisfaction in hearing that it had rained hard in England, that the spinning industry had been much extended in Saxony, and that Mr Biddle's efforts to spur economic recovery had been less successful than had been hoped. Dissatisfaction with the court's failure to see evidence of guilt was in part the defense's fault in taking a course that avoided a frontal encounter with the charges. The suit for writs of *habeas corpus* was heard by three judges, two of whom agreed in finding the evidence insufficient to warrant a trial by jury, the third dissenting. Two of the defendants, Samuel Jaudon and Thomas Dunlap, the latter Biddle's successor as president of the bank, had hearings apart from the others before a fourth judge and were also released. Thus four judges considered the charges, if one exclude the magistrate who on a preliminary presentment first bound over the accused, and three of the four found them insufficiently supported by the evidence. A good many persons would trust the judges more than they would trust a jury, but others, and especially those

29 Gallatin III, 442; W. B. Smith, 200-202.

prejudiced against bankers, would not; and even if they did, they would hold it against the defendants that instead of confidently taking their chances with the normal procedure, they elected a short cut, "avoided" a jury, and got the decision they wanted. This seemed to Nicholas Biddle's enemies just the sort of thing he always had been doing.[30]

But on the other hand the writs were sued for in circumstances for which *habeas corpus* procedure is designed. Such was the excited state of public feeling that the defendants might well shrink from letting the case take its normal course and prefer to seek a technical rather than a popular decision. Acquittal is fine if one can get it, but in some circumstances one may feel satisfied, even if innocent, with escaping prison. Once when Mr Biddle was robbed in the bank lobby by a pickpocket, it was amusing even though malicious to have the affair mentioned in the press as a transaction between financiers. But most of the malice was not amusing. The *Public Ledger*, which in January had criticized Biddle and his associates with asperity for their apparent efforts to evade a full and impartial trial, now protested in April at the savage feeling in the community, with thousands crying out to lynch him. The crowds, it said, which once jostled each other in the streets for the privilege of degrading themselves in Mr Biddle's presence were now jostling with equal violence for the privilege of tearing him in pieces. "Having never courted the money king, we can afford in behalf of justice to say a word for Nicholas Biddle, the respondent in a criminal and, as we believe, malicious prosecution." The business associations of Philip Hone, the New Yorker, did not incline him to take sides with Nicholas Biddle, "who lately was encumbered with the load of his greatness, to whom men's knees were bent and their beavers came off of their own accord," but he noted disdainfully that Biddle had been "indicted for high crimes and vulgar misdemeanors by a secret conclave of greasy householders," who a few months before had been reflecting back "the complacent smile of his good natured visage, . . . his animated step, and comfortable rotundity." *Old Nick's Song Book* published in Philadelphia in 1841 indicates the scurrility of common talk, which seems to have reflected not only the ill will of investors, creditors, speculators, and debtors who suffered losses through the bank's failure but also a popular sadism

---

[30] Washington *Globe*, 3 May 1842; Philadelphia *Public Ledger*, 17 and 18 January, 4 April 1842.

roused by the rare spectacle of the big banker, his own beaver knocked off, scuffling in the dirt for his reputation.[31]

These events and the comments of men upon them need of course to be considered in the light of the celebrity Nicholas Biddle had achieved. At home his political enemies had made his name known wherever Andrew Jackson's was. Abroad, and especially in Great Britain, few living Americans, if any, were more famous. Biddle personified to the Old World the astounding economic growth of the United States, the indispensable products she was supplying, and the tempting opportunities she afforded for investment. No one in the American business world rivaled him. The Rothschilds and the Barings were renowned for wealth and power, but they were European. Nicholas Biddle was the comparable banker of America itself and a brilliant, original, and striking one besides. Now he was fallen, with the largest bank in the world. The event was tremendous.

The tenacious effort to punish Nicholas Biddle was checked but not stopped by the *habeas corpus* decision. In July 1842, another suit for $400,000 was instituted. The stockholders filed a bill of equity in which they asked for an accounting and answers to certain questions. The bill was dismissed December 1844. The court held that those questions which might incriminate could not be asked. The others were of no consequence. Furthermore Nicholas Biddle was now no longer living. He had died ten months before, 27 February 1844, aged fifty-eight.[32]

In March 1842 Charles Dickens was in Philadelphia on his first visit from England and made the following note: "Looking out of my chamber-window, before going to bed, I saw, on the opposite side of the way, a handsome building of white marble, which had a mournful ghost-like aspect, dreary to behold. I attributed this to the sombre influence of the night, and on rising in the morning looked out again, expecting to see its steps and portico thronged with groups of people passing in and out. The door was still tight shut, however; the same cold cheerless air prevailed. . . . I hastened to inquire its name and purpose and then my surprise vanished. It was the Tomb of many fortunes; the Great Catacomb of investment; the memorable United States Bank."

[31] Philadelphia *Public Ledger*, 1 April 1842; Hone, 540, 576-77.
[32] Ingersoll II, 285-88; *Bank of the United States* v. *Biddle*, 2 Parsons 33.

V

Nicholas Biddle once remarked, when a very young man, that the desire to do a thing well too often prevents it being done at all. Too often, maybe, but not so very often. And if he feared lest perfectionism defeat his own ambition, it was most unfortunate. For it was from attempting too much and with too little care that he let the world's largest financial concern founder almost under his feet. Nevertheless I think he did more than anyone else after Alexander Hamilton to make banking and credit the major factor they have been in the prodigious growth of the American economy. Like Alexander Hamilton, he demonstrated the great difference there may be between an economic statesman and a successful moneymaker. He thought and worked in terms of the economic state, viewed its resources appraisingly, understood its organic functions and their inter-relations, provided mechanisms and media for those functions, and in particular developed the art of central banking both in restraint and in impulsion, to a degree of effectiveness that had not then been attained by the Bank of England and was not again attained by his own countrymen for a century.

Most of this has become apparent since his time and gives his work a significance that even his vanity did not perceive. What he sought was something less pretentious. It was, he said, "to make the currency as sound and the exchanges as equal over this immense territory as it was in the smallest and richest kingdom in Europe. My purpose was that in every section however remote of this nation every citizen should have his industry rewarded in what was equivalent to gold and silver, and if he exchanged the fruits of that industry with his most distant countryman, he should do it at less expense than the cost of transmitting that gold and silver." This was no inconsiderable purpose, and he achieved it—only to have the achievement recklessly denied and then undone.[33]

Though the crisis of 1837 led him into commitments that turned out disastrously and though his practical judgment was much at fault in making them, still it was in the course of what he did that he put principles into practice which have become the standard guides of financial statecraft. "We owe a debt to foreigners," he said in 1837, "by no means large for our resources but disproportioned to our present means of payment. . . . We have worn and eaten

[33] Biddle Papers 89, Folios 20193-94.

and drunk the produce of their industry—too much of all, perhaps —but that is our fault, not theirs. . . . The country is dishonored unless we discharge that debt to the uttermost farthing." But, he went on to say, it was evident "that if resort was had to rigid curtailments, the ability to pay would be proportionally diminished; while the only true system was to keep the country as much at ease as consisted with its safety, so as to enable the debtors to collect their resources for the discharge of their debts." This doctrine held for domestic obligations as well as foreign: prolongation of the suspension would give debtors a breathing spell and allow markets and prices to recover, whereas a forced resumption meant a sacrifice of everything else to the accumulation of gold and silver reserves by banks, with the probability moreover that in the absence of the necessary reforms by Congress the sacrifices would be in vain. Since the country was suffering from depression, credit should be eased. So long as the banks were relieved of the rigid obligation to pay their debts, there could be lenity for their debtors, foreclosures and bankruptcies would be avoided, and values protected from collapse. Suspension was "wholly conventional between the banks and the community" and arose from "their mutual conviction that it is for their mutual benefit."[34]

This was the doctrine that Nathan Appleton of Boston and the other economic royalists thought both unsound and immoral. To most persons, though not the most influential ones, it was sensible and welcome. It expressed something more constructive than the sterile eye-for-eye-and-tooth-for-tooth relationship traditionary between debtor and creditor. There was implicit in it a principle not merely humane but restorative and fecund. Credit was more than contractual, and the interests of society—certainly of an entrepreneurial society—were better represented by the debtor, who was typically creative and dynamic, than by the creditor, who, important as he was, must at times acknowledge considerations more weighty than his bond.

When the cotton transactions were undertaken in the summer of 1837, there was probably not a cotton dealer in the South solvent and operating. At the best there were too few, especially in New Orleans, the principal market, to move more than a few miserable bales. The only dealers and middlemen who saved themselves were

---

[34] Biddle Papers 89, Folio 20172; 29th Congress, 1st Session, HD 226, p. 404; Raguet, *Financial Register* I, 342; Niles LIV (1838), 98; Appleton, *Remarks on Currency and Banking*, 16.

those who shoved their hands in their pockets and did nothing. The producers were prostrated. In the northern commercial centers, importers were unable, such was the dearth of exchange, to purchase remittances for the protection of their credit in England. In this situation, the business conservatives in the financial centers and the political conservatives in Washington contented themselves with insisting on specie, denying credit when credit was needed most, and to no end but that prices must fall, producers' incomes shrink, and the dollar—if one had a dollar—appreciate in value. No one thought of anything to do that would check the destructive course of deflation or tried to do anything. It was the bears' turn. And their mournful conviction was that events must take their course, during which, however, some good bargains would doubtless turn up. The protection of agricultural markets and the disposal of farm surpluses is to-day a responsibility of government. A century ago it was not. One would be hard put to it to think of any administration in American history less disposed than Andrew Jackson's or Martin Van Buren's to undertake what Nicholas Biddle undertook—a major resort to monetary measures for the alleviation of economic disorder, inertia, and distress. The depression of the late 1830's, like that of the early 1930's, was dominated by low farm prices and an adverse balance of payments which in the 1830's was international and in the 1930's was inter-regional. Yet no contrast could be more striking than that between the paralytic helplessness of the Van Buren administration, clutching its inheritance of Jacksonian clichés, and the humming, untrammeled energy with which the administration of Franklin D. Roosevelt moved against a similar crisis ninety-six years later. The Roosevelt administration, as if animated by admiration for Nicholas Biddle's attempts and disgust with Jackson's and Van Buren's, let no grass grow under its feet, but depreciated the dollar, withdrew gold permanently from circulation, and expanded bank credit, accomplishing thereby what Nicholas Biddle had sought to accomplish by prolonging the suspension of specie payments; and it elaborated agencies to do for agricultural staples what Nicholas Biddle sought to do by advances on them. The social responsibility assumed by Mr Biddle is now assumed by the state, and the problem of profits, losses, and holding power no longer reflects the limitations under which a private corporation works. That his program failed is due in part to his own practical errors and in part to the extraordinary succession of adversities it ran into. And it was a malign continuance of these adversities that his own errors have been allowed to stand out as the sole matter of importance, his purpose and the impediments to it having been disregarded.

In 1839 the appeal of Nicholas Biddle's doctrine was again demonstrated. The day following the United States Bank's suspension, the *United States Gazette* of Philadelphia said, 10 October 1839: "The immediate effect of the suspension will be an ease in the money market, a cessation of those cares and disquietudes with which the business men of our community have been annoyed. . . . The great error . . . to which all subsequent errors are in a measure to be traced was in the premature resumption in August 1838. . . . The banks are just as good, and better and more solid under a season of suspension as under its opposite." The obligation to pay specie being ended, the pressure on debtors could be eased; the banks in Philadelphia had chosen to suspend rather than ruin the community, and the banks in New York had chosen otherwise. In New York the *Evening Star*, a paper friendly to the United States Bank, presented the following apologia: "The United States Bank . . . has been brought into its present position from attempting to do too much . . . from efforts to aid every section of the Union: the agriculture of the South, the trade of the West, the commerce of the North, the industry of the East. The United States Bank . . . in efforts to sustain commerce, trade, and manufactures, went beyond probably what was prudent and discreet and was herself compelled to stop."[35]

Contemporary British comment was similarly divided over Mr Biddle's program. The London *Morning Post*, in September 1839, said sympathetically that the United States Bank had come forward to the assistance of the mercantile interests of America in extraordinary circumstances "at a period of universal difficulty and derangement, and if it has not done all the good that was contemplated by it but probably partial mischief, the failure is not to be by any means interpreted in the light of a crime but simply in that of an error. The misfortune of the United States Bank is to have attempted more for the relief of commerce than in these times of financial pressure it has succeeded in effecting."[36]

The Times ridiculed this. It said that in the *Morning Post*'s

---

[35] Boston *Courier*, 12 October 1839; Boston *Atlas*, 12 October 1839, quoting Philadelphia *United States Gazette*; Niles LVII (1839), 140-41.

[36] Burgess, *Circular to Bankers*, 27 September 1839, p. 98.

article—"a dictation from the Bank parlour"—the Bank of England was defending the United States Bank because "the time is near at hand when indulgence is to be claimed for its own errors." *The Times* was Mr Biddle's unrelenting enemy:

"The United States Bank, . . . departing from the legitimate province of banking, . . . has constituted itself a great trading and speculating corporation, and . . . entering upon a field of operations too vast for its own capital, great as that is, has continued to trade and speculate upon credit until it finds itself encumbered with a large mass of stocks and securities of all kinds and a large quantity of cotton, the realization of all which is stopped by the state of the European money markets. . . .

"The United States Bank . . . has thought it an easy and a prosperous game to borrow as much money in Europe at low rates as it could congregate and to employ it in the United States in indirect purchases of stocks and of cotton or in advances upon such securities. . . . It is immaterial to consider whether the money was employed in purchases or in advances; when its recovery depends upon the sale of the commodities, the investment is almost equally dangerous and equally opposed to sound banking principles. Mr Biddle has shown himself a man of great ability and great resource in emergencies, but he has evidently exaggerated his power as well as mistaken his duty. He has supposed, perhaps from patriotic motives and national feelings, that he was placed in a position where he must by advances furnish funds to the planters, agriculturists, and producers of the great staple of the United States and at the same time furnish the means to states and companies for all their plans of internal improvement."[37]*

* Henry Burgess's *Circular to Bankers*, from which I have quoted the foregoing, was as consistently kind to Biddle, Jaudon, and the American interests in the London market as *The Times* was not. But it was severe toward the Barings and severer than *The Times* toward the Bank of England, though for opposite reasons. The Bank was blamed in the *Circular* for ruining the American houses in 1837 and making necessary the United States Bank's efforts to replace them. Britain's mercantile traffic with the Americans was at stake, it said; yet "twice within three years has the Bank been compelled to dash it to the ground in order to save herself." These and other authorities, it will be recalled from the preceding chapter, believed that the Bank of England had been saved by the credit *debâcle* in the States. Henry Burgess, *Circular to Bankers*, 20 September 1839, p. 93; 4 October 1839, p. 109; 11 October 1839, pp. 114-15.

[37] Burgess, *Circular to Bankers*, 20 September 1839, pp. 91-92; 27 September 1839, pp. 98-99.

This second and restorative exercise of central banking in 1837 and 1839 had been undertaken, as Nicholas Biddle himself remarked, after the central banking responsibility had been terminated. Loss of its former status had not impaired the bank's powers of expansion but only its powers of restraint; for, being no longer government depository, it was not receiving the public deposits of notes and checks that made it the creditor of the state banks and able to curb their lending. According to Mr Gallatin, the Bank of the United States had ceased to regulate the money supply as early as 1832, two years before it ceased to be government depository and four years before its federal charter expired. But to Mr Gallatin's way of thinking regulation meant only restriction; he did not conceive of the central banking function working both ways. Nicholas Biddle did; and unlike Mr Gallatin conceived expansion to be no less corrective, on occasion, than restraint.

With these significant and original exercises of central banking, the name of Nicholas Biddle has not been associated.* It is remarkable how quickly his fame died. Thomas Wren Ward in Boston, writing his customary letter to Baring Brothers the last day of February 1844, confined his report of Nicholas Biddle's death two days before to these few words: "Mr Biddle is dead. He has caused me a great deal of anxiety within ten years." Mr Ward's laconism was typical of the business world, which has a vigorous biological indifference to the past, and finds even its own, at best, no more than quaint; but besides that Mr Ward disliked the modern element in Nicholas Biddle's work. The politicians crowed a while and then turned to fresher things, finding it sufficient, to their lasting profit, to remember that a banker named Biddle had tried to resist Andrew Jackson. Sympathetic mention of him was fugitive. John Quincy Adams, his friend from their literary days on the *Port Folio* but many years his senior and on occasion his severe critic, dined with him *en famille*, 22 November 1840, and talked long with him. This was about the time the plate was melted down and added to the bonds

* Dr Fritz Redlich in his *Molding of American Banking,* published in 1947, has given discerning and pioneer attention to Nicholas Biddle as central banker. More recently, Professor Walter B. Smith, in his exacting and judicious work, *The Economic Aspects of the Second Bank of the United States,* has given fresh substance to Nicholas Biddle's career. There is support for the views of these two scholars and for my own in their having been arrived at independently; though the other two volumes preceded mine and have been very useful to me.

of the Republic of Texas in order to make up the sum whose return the bank demanded. "Biddle," Mr Adams wrote, "broods with smiling face and stifled groans over the wreck of splendid blasted expectations and ruined hopes. A fair mind, a brilliant genius, a generous temper, an honest heart, waylaid and led astray by prosperity, suffering the penalty of scarcely voluntary error—'tis piteous to behold." Duff Green, a more successful empire-builder and friend of the South, who left his country enriched with railways, factories, newspapers, and cities of his promotion, who had been the first outspoken enemy of the federal Bank among the Jacksonians and particularly critical of its restraint upon the liberal extension of credit by the state banks, consistently deplored in 1841 the attempt to impeach the integrity of Nicholas Biddle. In 1847 John Tyler, who two years before, as President, had accomplished the annexation of Texas, acknowledged in labored phrases the far-seeing support he had had from Nicholas Biddle to that end. "I was myself sustained and encouraged by the opinion of other distinguished citizens," he said, "among whom I take pleasure in mentioning the name of one who once would have commanded the respect if not the confidence of thousands, but who at the time rested under a cloud and spoke to me from the shades of Andalusia—I mean the late Nicholas Biddle, with whom I differed so widely on the subject of the Bank of the United States. His bright and accomplished mind did not fail to embrace in its full extent the value of the virtual monopoly of the cotton plant, secured to the United States by the acquisition of Texas—a monopoly more potential in the affairs of the world than millions of armed men."[38]

For an interval of some years after the Bank of the United States was destroyed, a genuine but constricted revulsion against banking lived on in the agrarian West, but in the country as a whole there was no abatement in the growing number of bankers and of banks, in the swelling volume of bank credit, or in the ardent conviction of its potency. The laborer and the agrarian gained no advantage from any Jacksonian monetary measure; capitalism and enterprise suffered no blow. It was rather the reverse. The destruction of the governmental agency of credit control was in time repaired by General Jackson's own party, which had established the Bank of the United States in 1816, which established the Federal Reserve

[38] Baring Papers, OC, 29 February 1844; J. Q. Adams, *Memoirs* x, 361; Biddle Papers 96, Folio 21703; Tyler, *Life and Times* II, 431.

Banks in 1913, in the administration of Woodrow Wilson, and which in 1935, in the administration of Franklin Roosevelt, enlarged and centralized Federal Reserve powers. The party's one and only positive achievement in banking and monetary policy under the General himself was the establishment of Wall Street's primacy in the country's financial affairs—and even that was an achievement qualified to the important extent that Wall Street's primacy was mainly ascribable to other factors than political ones.

VI

"The failures of statesmen," says Professor H. A. L. Fisher in his *History of Europe*, "are not ordinarily due to treason, felony, or misdemeanour, or to other faults which are the proper subject for judicial enquiry, but to errors of judgment, of temper, and of calculation." This seems to me true of Nicholas Biddle. I should ascribe his fall, perhaps the most dramatic and consequential in American history, to four things which are not matters of morals but are, very clearly, matters of judgment, of temper, and of calculation. The first was his temperamental inability to cope with the assault upon the government Bank which terminated the early and better part of his career; the second was his poor business judgment; the third was his having too much to do with the agricultural South and too little with the industrial North; the fourth was his predilection for easy money and the long-term capital market.

The assault upon the Bank involved Nicholas Biddle in a contest in which demagogy and cant had all the advantage. For neither had he any aptitude. He was an aristocrat with public spirit; an intellectual whose judgment was less moved by practical considerations than by reason and imagination. He lived untouched by adversity until it came into his life too late. He was a man of cultivation whom fortune had encumbered with an incorrigible *naïveté* toward men filled with prejudice, envy, and acquisitiveness. He was unused to opposition and could not take it philosophically or constructively. Such a man, if able and energetic, as Nicholas Biddle was, may be like a mechanism which performs wonders so long as it works in favorable conditions but becomes useless, or worse, when ruggedness, firmness, and impassivity are required.

Until he was first attacked by the Jacksonians and for a long time after their assaults and bedevilments continued, there was absolutely nothing in his conduct of the federal Bank to justify more than minor criticism, for it was not only one of the earliest examples of central banking in a modern economy but one of the best. The unreasonableness and absurdity of President Jackson's allegation that the Bank was unconstitutional and that the currency was unsatisfactory aroused in Biddle only an agitated incredulity. That there could be what his more sophisticated friends suspected at once, a deliberate conspiracy to end the Bank's existence, to the advantage of New York over Philadelphia in particular and in the interest generally of an inflationary expansion of bank credit, he was about the last person to recognize. He was confused and demoralized by the Jacksonians. Instead of seeing that he was unfitted for the encounter that was being forced upon him, he splashed excitedly ahead, never unintelligent but usually wrong. Being no longer in the rational, studious, and affable *milieu* in which he was at home, he progressed through error into fatuity and thence into tragedy. His downfall, which involved hosts beside himself, is something for which he can not be relieved of responsibility; but neither can the Jacksonians. Nor, it must be allowed, did they ever wish to be.

The second factor to which I ascribe Nicholas Biddle's fall—his want of practical business judgment—was something not so serious in his earlier career. The federal Bank, as contemplated by its original founder, Alexander Hamilton, was not managed for profit. The old Bank had not been so conducted and, save for a brief period under William Jones, neither had the second. Its peculiar nature and its responsibility to the economy were not understood as they are in the 20th century, but they were plainly recognized. As government director, Nicholas Biddle had been much influenced by President Monroe's Jeffersonian fear of inflation; and that conscious regard for maintenance of the federal Bank's proper and conservative force was never wanting in his earlier administration.

The case was different when the Bank had to be defended from the Jacksonian assault, and it was no better under state charter when Mr Biddle's responsibilities were to a bank conducted solely for profit. A want of business judgment was displayed in his attempting to operate at all under the barbarous conditions imposed by the Pennsylvania legislature. Yet when the possibility of obtaining the state charter arose, instead of refusing to touch it, he caught it up eagerly, without brooding over the augmented difficulties that must be encountered under outrageous obligations to the state, with too much capital, without a portfolio of readily marketable government securities, and in circumstances of an adverse trade balance with Europe that made the retention of specie reserves a chronic, major problem. What determined him to take the Pennsylvania charter, probably, was not that he meant to make money, or stabilize the economy, or avoid *ennui*; it was that he hoped to keep financial primacy from passing to Wall Street and wished to get even with Andrew Jackson—which required that the new bank be no whit less immense and imposing than the one that had been destroyed and so like it that no one should notice any difference. Temporarily and as revenge, this *riposte* with the state charter was pretty successful; and when the agile aristocrat escaped with his monster into the Pennsylvania sanctuary, whence they could gnash their teeth at him, the old hero was suitably exasperated. But the last laugh was not Mr Biddle's.

Having become a business man under these unbusinesslike conditions, Nicholas Biddle then conducted his business in an unbusinesslike fashion. The careless accounting methods at the bank were mentioned by the court in the *habeas corpus* proceedings. One imagines Biddle's bookkeepers having a desperate time trying to keep up with him; but he had never been through their discipline and probably never regretted it. He had no adequate respect for established routines, seeing too clearly their shortcomings and not clearly enough what safety, stability, and economy they bring to human employments. He valued too much the brilliant kind of thing he could do himself and too little the dull but essential kind of thing that others did.[39]

Nicholas Biddle seems to have had no proper sense of a working organization and no faculty for selecting co-workers who could complement and balance his abilities. He needed a capable executive assistant to attend to details of operation and staff discipline. He also needed a sagacious and seasoned committee on loans and investments. With the exception of Samuel Jaudon and perhaps one or two others his associates were men of conspicuous mediocrity. Presumably he could not work with his peers. Having come into the bank at the top, without experience or training, he neglected the training of others. He had the understanding of internal administration which an intelligent and industrious man can acquire but not the understanding which comes from having swept the floor, run

[39] Biddle Papers, 1 PLB (1836), 164-65, 354-55; W. B. Smith, 179, 210.

errands, and kept books. His management of the bank, consequently, had too much the air of a rich young person good-naturedly ordering the servants about.

He neglected reserves and in particular liquidity, as if he thought either that his analysis of the future and his specific provision for it were complete or if not that his resourcefulness would prove adequate when the need arose. He kept too close to the edge; he tried characteristically to do without sufficient margin; it was something that the Barings were always complaining of in his dealings with them. He neglected, in spite of the naval tradition of his family, to recognize the possibility of his being struck with all his sails set, no sea room, and all his powers extended. He assumed, for venture after venture, a lower incidence of mischance than probabilities warranted. He allowed too little time for investments to mature and too little free capital to carry them through. This was not, however, his conscious and professed practice. On the contrary, he expressed himself like a model of conservatism. But in practice what he deemed conservative generally turned out to be something that would make a real conservative's hair rise.

Often it has been alleged or supposed that Nicholas Biddle retired from the bank because he foresaw its foundering and tried to jump clear. I think, on the contrary, that no one foresaw its foundering and that if anyone had it could not have been Nicholas Biddle. If he possessed the *sang-froid* to retire in 1839 because he saw disaster ahead, it was the sole display of such qualities in his whole career. One less apt to conclude that his life's work was about to end in disaster can scarcely be imagined. To have appraised the future in such terms required a controlled, objective nature, alert to self-deception, which was not Mr Biddle's. Besides, he did not try to jump clear. He returned to the bank frequently, carried on correspondence from it, kept himself familiar with its operations, and advised its management. As is often the case with active men who "retire," he did not dissociate himself from his old interests but merely reduced his executive burden. Later, indeed, he tried to excuse himself for what happened, but this effort to evade responsibility was undertaken after trouble arose; he made no effort to evade it before. So far from apprehension, it is a fatuous self-confidence that he displays. His bullishness was never more evident than just before his fall, when he seems to have aspired to close his career in all the magnificence possible. His course was not heroic, but neither was it shrewd.

The third major source of Nicholas Biddle's misfortunes was his being associated too closely with the southern agricultural economy and too little with northern industry and commerce. His commitment to the South arose first from the federal Bank's having been a national institution conducting its operations throughout the country and being naturally drawn into most activity where it was most needed. In New England and New York there was more money, and the local banks left less occasion for the commercial operations of the federal Bank than there was in the South and West. In that quarter, particularly, lay the need of extensive facilities and immense credit for marketing cotton, which was the South's great staple, the country's principal export, and the North's chief source, other than borrowings and the sale of investments abroad, of the exchange needed to pay for the capital goods which it imported for the construction of its industrial plant and equipment. Wherever the cotton went, the facilities of the Bank accompanied and expedited its movement. The New Orleans office ranked next to Philadelphia in volume of business, and the offices in Charleston, Savannah, Mobile, and Nashville were employed in the same trade. No other agricultural product required such services or could be given them by any other organization; no other moved in such massive volume on so well established a course as cotton grown in the homogeneous South and destined for the mills of England. All other products in varying degree—tobacco, grain, and meat—were produced in more scattered and restricted areas, shipped in more different directions in less massive volume, and disposed of in more numerous markets, domestic and foreign.

But the South was economically vulnerable through the very dominance of cotton. She had virtually a colonial economy, producing one great staple, dependent upon the outside world for all she required in capital and consumer goods, and dependent upon that staple alone to pay for them. Slave labor made her economy rigid. With these vicissitudes and weaknesses the United States Bank of Pennsylvania was espoused. When the demand for cotton was vigorous, the South was affluent; but when it went slack, as it did in 1837, 1838, and 1839, the South's whole burden fell inertly on the bank. For a time a large part of the southern population was being fed by it. The burden was more than the bank could sustain.

The South, as it happened, was not grateful. Here and there she showed appreciation of Nicholas Biddle's interest but mostly not. I. C. Levy, a Charleston merchant, wrote him, 29 January 1839: "I can not but congratulate you that the great staples of the South have been sustained and its agricultural interest guarded and that these objects have been achieved by making foreign countries contribute to this end." The South should be grateful, he says, but instead a Democratic convention in Mississippi has just resolved that the influence of the United States Bank has been deeply injurious to the staple states by making them dependent on the money power of the North and transferring all their profits to it. Later, consistently with this view, Mississippi justified the repudiation of certain bonds by citing the "intentional and wilful fraud" of Nicholas Biddle in negotiating the sale of the bonds.[40]

Had Mr Biddle been able to associate the United States Bank of Pennsylvania to a greater extent with northern industry, his career might have ended more happily. In the North even farming was diversified and not dependent on one foreign market. But far more significant than that was the growth and prosperity of industry, which was steadily accumulating its secular advantages over agriculture. Given labor and capital now produced a far greater return when engaged in industry; and the financing of industry was both the safer and the more profitable. Moreover, the margin between them kept widening with time. Agriculture, which had been the country's only considerable source of wealth in 1800, was to fall behind industry, a wholly new interest, by 1900 and was to become relatively less efficient and profitable. Within the field of agriculture, cotton was especially risky and yet immensely important. It was when cotton—then a staple for less than the half century since invention of the gin—first glutted the world market that the United States Bank collapsed. On the other hand, it was Wall Street's entrenchment in northern industry and commerce that enabled her, with London's help and the Jacksonians', to emerge from the same crisis the financial leader of the American economy.

The fourth major source of Nicholas Biddle's misfortunes was the sanguine bias he shared with the majority of his fellow Americans toward easy money and long-term credit. This bias was restrained and tempered in the period of his success, when the federal Bank's operations required a conservatism that offended the state banks and

[40] Biddle Papers 84, Folios 17526-27; 29th Congress, 1st Session, HD 226, p. 875.

the Jacksonians. Later, the function of control having been disrupted, there was nothing to withhold him from expansiveness and everything to pitch him headlong into it. It was as if he were continuing under the spell of his first two employments, both Jeffersonian—his work in Paris on the Louisiana Purchase, and his narration of the Lewis and Clark expedition. He had too lively a sense of America's magnificent, continental future. Once committed to easy money—in the crisis of 1837—he could never relinquish it. Being more rational than practical, more imaginative than shrewd, and more sanguine than skeptical, he yielded without reserve to his country's seductive demand for long-term credit. Even his friendly critics ridiculed his "loans to corporations notoriously unworthy of credit," and his enthusiasm for "mulberry trees, town lots, coal and navigation companies, bank stocks, internal improvements," and anything congruous with the splendor of America's varied forms of potential wealth.* Imagination led him far into his country's future, where he was not engaged in business, and obscured the present, where he was.[41]

VII

John Jacob Astor told Joshua Bates that he once paid two and a half per cent a month for money—thirty per cent a year—"and gained more by the use of it than by any other operation in his life."[42] This was the enterprising use of credit that Americans typically understood, admired, and longed to emulate, though few had Mr Astor's skill. The agrarian who borrowed at all and did so because he had to, who saw in debt only a burden and its repayment a grim obligation which he must painfully discharge, as Andrew Jackson always did, was far less representative and influential than Mr Astor, before he became conservative, or Mr Biddle, after he ceased to be conservative, or the fabulous Colonel Mulberry Sellers, a generation later, who never was conservative but lived forever in

* Not long after his retirement he became president of the National Association for the Promotion of the Silk Culture in the United States. There was then an active interest in sericulture and much speculation in mulberry trees. But silk was not all. Later the same year Mr Biddle was requesting seed of a new clover from England, by which, he said, "a great sensation has been made among farmers." Biddle Papers 88, Folios 20046, 20061, 20084-85.

41 Philadelphia *Public Ledger*, 4 April 1842.
42 Baring Papers, MC, 26 April 1841.

to-morrow. These latter rather than either Albert Gallatin or
Andrew Jackson, at their respective poles of economic conservatism,
represented the millions who gave the stamp to 19th century America that the world has found distinctive and that provoked in protest
the poetry, the romances, and the idealistic philosophy that are
still the classics of American literature. Whether the country is
better represented by its economic behavior than by its idealism I do
not offer to say; but that she is more truly represented by it seems
to me indubitable. For the same reason, the monetary views of Albert
Gallatin and of Andrew Jackson are both obsolete, but Nicholas
Biddle's, thanks largely to the quite independent teachings of Lord
Keynes, are alive and orthodox. Nicholas Biddle sought to make
monetary policy flexible and compensatory rather than rigid. He
had a vision of national development to which abundant credit was
essential. The majority of his countrymen have agreed with him.
They have dismissed the man, but they have followed his ideas,
especially his worse ones. They have shared his bullishness and his
energy. They have no use for General Jackson's primitive ideals of
a simple, agrarian society, except in their nostalgic moods. They
have not understood Mr Gallatin's noble aversion for the fierce spirit
of enterprise. They have exploited the country's resources with
abandon, they have plunged into all the debt they could, they have
realized a fantastic growth, and they have slighted its cost. Albert
Gallatin personified the country's intelligence and Andrew Jackson
its folklore, but Nicholas Biddle personified its behavior. They closed
their careers in high honor—he closed his in opprobrium and bewil-
derment. A better apologist for him, I must say, would be one who
glories more than I do in the concept of Manifest Destiny and in
the 19th century expansion of the American economy; and yet,
though the spirit of enterprise has been to many persons not wholly
agreeable and has given the narrative of American growth more in
common with picaresque romances than with the lives of the saints,
still it has made the country what it is—powerful, extensive, and
rich. There can be no carping at history or nursing the agrarian
dreams of a past age, when steam and credit had not yet altered
the face of the earth and the character of civilization. This being so,
one can not help admiring in Nicholas Biddle, as in Alexander
Hamilton, the perspicacity and statesmanship to which the complex
potentialities of the American economy were so plain and the
imagination which formulated the means of realizing them. In the

20th century moreover, they may perhaps be admired the more because they were uncontaminated by the doctrine of *laisser faire*, which to the Jacksonians and their contemporaries seemed to be the last and sufficient word in economic and political wisdom. "The world is governed too much," the Jacksonians declared; "*laissez nous faire!*" Accordingly they did all they could—which was considerable—to undo what Alexander Hamilton and Nicholas Biddle had done to make the state effectively responsible in the economy, and much of subsequent governmental history in America is concerned with restoring and enlarging federal responsibilities over money which the Jacksonians uprooted.

VIII

Following the United States Bank's collapse in 1839 and the general suspension of specie payments precipitated by it in the South and West, the project for an independent Treasury, which had failed in 1837, was renewed. And in December 1839 President Van Buren again recommended it, the proposal being that the federal Treasury be independent of banks, that all its payments and receipts be in silver and gold coin only, and that its funds be held in its own vaults in Washington and in sub-treasuries situated in other cities.

The independent Treasury had the support of the Loco Focos, or anti-bank Democrats, whose radical, hard-money opposition to banks and paper money in general had been strengthened by the piling of 1839's experience on top of 1837's. They wanted an exclusive metallic currency and an end to bank credit in any form. The independent Treasury had also southern support. Senator Calhoun, fighting against the protective tariff and the relative decline of the southern economy, seems to have reasoned that withdrawal of the federal funds from the banks would hamper the North, where most of the banks were and most of the funds, and be consequently to the South's advantage. The northern Loco Foco and the southern landed aristocrat had each his grievance against the northern banks, and not only did the grievances, though become incongruous, have a common object but in their agrarian past they had a common source as well. Fitzwilliam Byrdsall, the Loco Foco leader of northern Labor, could join hands with John C. Calhoun, the conservative leader of southern slave-owners. Such support, however, was more curious than effective and did Mr Van Buren little good. The business world was still offended by his independent Treasury scheme.

After long debate the measure was enacted by only a narrow vote and became law 4 July 1840; but that autumn Mr Van Buren was defeated for re-election, the victim of his inability to unite the two disparate wings of his party. During President Jackson's administration these had had in common their determination, for quite distinct and conflicting reasons, to destroy the federal Bank, and they flew apart with mutual dislike when that aim had been achieved. The following summer the sub-treasury law was repealed.[43]

The Whigs were now in power, but in odd circumstances, for General Harrison had died a few weeks after becoming President, and John Tyler, who succeeded him, had no real bond with the party at all. He soon was at daggers' points with the Whig leaders in Congress, who, resenting the fortune that made him President, snubbed and infuriated him. When it repealed the Van Buren independent Treasury law, Congress had enacted in its stead a measure prepared by the Treasury establishing a "Fiscal Bank of the United States" much like the recent federal Bank but with branches to be established in such states as gave their assent. The President vetoed it. Thereupon, to meet his objections, a bill was prepared establishing a "Fiscal Corporation of the United States." It passed and he vetoed it also, three weeks after the first. The party was furious and the Cabinet resigned—all but Daniel Webster, Secretary of State, who was engaged in negotiations concerning the Canadian border which were consummated in the Webster-Ashburton treaty. Mr Tyler tried to work out plans for an "Exchequer Bank" that would satisfy Congress, his pride, and his conscience, but nothing came of it, and the Treasury, with practically all relevant statutes repealed by now from both sides, went back to where Secretary Hamilton had started in 1789. Over a half century's legislative attempts to adjust the fiscal affairs of the federal government to those of the economy were all but completely undone. The Treasury and its officials—many of whom had to keep its funds in their personal possession as best they could—got on this way till 1846, when the independent Treasury system was again established.[44]

The system was vitiated by two cardinal faults. First, it confined the federal government's monetary authority to control over coin, the minor part of the money supply, and left control of the major part, comprising bank credit, to be divided among an indefinite

[43] Hofstadter, 88; Calhoun, "Correspondence," AHA *Annual Report, 1899* II, 861, 940, 965, 1003.

[44] Dewey, *Financial History*, 240-43; Hepburn, 151-53; Kinley, 43-44; Richardson IV, 1916, 1921, 1937.

number of states, then twenty-nine and increasing. "The great error" in the measure, wrote a contemporary in *Hunt's Merchants' Magazine*, 1839, "is in the dereliction of duty: the voluntary abnegation" by Congress "of that control over the currency which it is the primary duty of every good government to secure in order that the people should not suffer." Viewed constitutionally, establishment of the independent Treasury system was one of the current victories for states' rights at the expense of the federal authority. "The whole constitutional argument against the use of banks by the government," said Professor Kinley in 1910, was "but a phase of the old doctrine of states rights and supremacy which prevented Congress from assuming such control over the banking system of the country as would have made it safe, would have prevented wild cat banking, would have saved the financial good name of the country, and would have made the sub-treasury system unnecessary by making the banks as safe for government use as they are to-day."[45]

This statement can bear some qualification. The independent Treasury did involve a "control" of banking and its more sophisticated advocates said so: cash held in the Treasury reduced the power of banks to enlarge their note circulation. But it was a power without purpose. The receipts and disbursements of the Treasury, whereever and whenever the one exceeded the other, either decreased the lending power of banks or increased it. For when specie went into the Treasury it decreased the reserves of banks and consequently their power to lend; and when it was disbursed by the Treasury it enlarged the banks' reserves and increased their power to lend. The result was not a control of banking but a haphazard contraction and expansion of bank reserves without reason, intent, or policy. In New York, for example, or in any other port, where and when there were large arrivals of goods from abroad, the importers would have to withdraw specie from the banks in order to pay the customs duties, and for every dollar withdrawn the lending power of the local banks would be diminished from five to ten dollars, that range covering roughly the effective ratio between bank reserves and liabilities. Contrariwise, wherever there was an Army post or a Navy yard or a concentration of payrolls, as in Washington, the Treasury's expenditures would normally exceed its receipts, the specie it paid out would enlarge local bank reserves, and the banks would have more funds to lend. The results were spotty and fortuitous fluctuations, now restrictive and now inflationary. This was in time cor-

45 *Hunt's Merchants' Magazine* I (1839), 497; Kinley, 48.

rected by three things of which the independent Treasury's advocates had not a flicker of foresight: the inflow of specie from Spanish America which had formerly gone to Europe, the specie brought into the country by immigrants, and after 1848 the production of precious metals in California and other parts of the West. The specie from these sources so greatly increased the gross amount in the country that the spasmodic influence of Treasury receipts and disbursements upon the reserves and the lending power of banks became apparent only in crises.

The independent Treasury's second fault, which embraced a number of technical objections, lay in its neglecting the fact that the federal government was the largest single transactor in the economy, receiving a far greater income and making far larger disbursements for materials and services than any millionaire or corporation. To have required that Mr John Jacob Astor make all his payments in silver and gold and accept none due him if not in those metals, would have seemed absurd to anyone; but it would have been economically less absurd than it was to do the same with respect to the government. It imposed upon the Treasury a clumsy and inefficient fiscal procedure which the country was rich enough to afford in normal times but not otherwise. The consequence was summed up by the system's opponents in the words: "Gold for the office holders; rags for the people"; but the federal government was the real victim. The banks, for their part, found in time that Mr Van Buren's arrangement was a very agreeable one. The Treasury had long been a difficult and pusillanimous customer, and the loss or diminution of its business was of little moment against the gain they derived from freedom of action and the immense growth of the economy.[46]

IX

It is relevant, I think, that the banking troubles of the late '30's co-incided with growing tension and ill will between North and South and between Britain and the United States as a whole. Between North and South there was the issue of slavery—an institution with which the southern economy was indissolubly intertwined. Being committed to cotton and to slavery, the South was a slave herself. Though she produced the bulk of the nation's exports and hence paid for the bulk of its imports, the profits on all she did inured to the vulgar, hustling, pullulating North, whose wealth and might more and more surpassed hers. And then, after strangling her

---

[46] Sherman, *Recollections,* 254.

with protective tariffs, and lording it over her commerce and finance, the North began to force upon her, with disgusting hypocrisy, the barbarities of the abolitionists. But the truth was that her "peculiar institution" put her intolerably on the defensive before the civilized world, and the consequences of her plight were no less deeply psychological than political and economic. She did not see how she could survive without slaves, for the cultivation of cotton demanded them. To make slave labor equally efficient with free labor and to make capital as remunerative when utilizing slave labor as free was impossible; yet the basic rivalry between agriculture and mechanical industry required that slavery be made efficient, and the effort to make it so produced self-defeating extremes of degradation and inhumanity. The realities of her impossible dilemma she could not face, and the result was desperate fear: fear of the slaves beneath her and of the North—industrial, commercial, financial, and abolitionist—above.

Though it was obvious that most of the North's economic employments, especially her manufacturing, could not be emulated by the South, it was not so obvious that the financing, shipping, and marketing of her cotton had to be alienated. Yet they were. Northern buyers and northern banks took a profit that business men of her own should have had. Most prominent of these invaders was the United States Bank, managed in Philadelphia, the home of the American Anti-Slavery Society. That the Bank had sought a high price for cotton amounted to little so long as northern business gained from it what southern business should. In the early days of the second federal Bank, the rift between North and South had not yet grown wide, and the Bank, though its head office was in the North, could still be thought a national concern, advantageous to agriculture, and a federal make-weight in the South's favor against the commercial and financial ascendancy of the North. This in fact it was, but not enough. As the South and West expanded territorially during the twenty years of the Bank's life and the five of its state bank successor, Philadelphia seemed to southern and western eyes more and more a northern and eastern center; and as the business power of the North and East grew in the same period, Philadelphia was absorbed more and more, to jealous southern eyes especially, in the predatory orbit of the North. This increasing identification of the Bank and its successor with interests alien to the South may help explain, I think, why the two Carolinians John C. Calhoun and Langdon Cheves turned against it. Both, in 1837, declared a federal

Bank unconstitutional and—what is more extraordinary—that they had never believed otherwise, even though one of them had sponsored the Bank's establishment and the other had been its able president and savior. Their assertions were the product of many influences, but pervasive among these was their morbid anxiety for the interests of the South, which northern business, northern tariffs, and northern sanctimony seemed sure to crush.[47]

As between the North and South, Great Britain's business interests were with the North, because they were with New York. From the British standpoint the South and the United States Bank were one in their demand for a higher price for cotton—not only a higher price but an artificial, extorted price. And Britain and New York were one in resisting it. It is true that the aristocracy and intelligentsia of Britain sympathized excessively with the South, where there were so many ladies and gentlemen with cultivated manners— Lord Acton, for example, took slavery for granted because of its virtues, or at least its necessity, and he confidently took for granted also the end of the federal union as soon as the South had said it was ended. But besides the aristocracy and intelligentsia in Britain, there were Manchester and the other commercial and industrial areas, where liberalism centered, and where the idea of slavery made men sick, as it did in the northern states, though they could stomach the exploitation of employed labor. These commercial centers, where conceptions of free trade and *laisser faire* prevailed along with Dissent and missionary efforts among the distant heathen, were those where in 1839 the spinners united against the artificial demands of the United States Bank and the southern economy. They were those where a quarter century later efforts to gain British aid in the southern states' secession were frustrated. For, when the South took up arms to make her economy and her institution politically her own, she found herself without the sympathy of the Midlands, whose people needed her staple for their spindles but not so much that they would let her have Great Britain's support against the industrial North.

In 1839, of course, the resentment was against the United States as a whole, for America's sectional schism was not yet impressed on Britain. The failure of the Americans to pay their debts and their simultaneous effort to make Britain pay higher commodity prices

[47] 25th Congress, 1st Session, *Congressional Globe* IV, Appendix, 32-36; Niles LIII (1837), 8-9; Biddle, *Correspondence*, 305, 306; Calhoun, "Correspondence," AHA *Annual Report, 1899* II, 377, 378-79; Baltimore *Merchant*, 14 September 1837.

than supply and demand would justify were two more exacerbations added to those produced by disagreement over the northeast boundary between Maine and the neighboring provinces, by the Mackenzie insurrection and the *Caroline* affair, and by rivalry and suspected rivalry in Oregon, California, and Texas. Texas and cotton were closely related and Nicholas Biddle's interest in the former, though less signal, must have been as well known at Whitehall as his interest in cotton was in the City. These things either settled themselves or were settled by the Webster-Ashburton Treaty in 1841; but meanwhile the spirit in which at least one of the participants in the cotton corner worked is expressed in remarks addressed to Nicholas Biddle by the senior partner of Humphreys and Biddle in Liverpool, 25 January 1839, about the time the transactions were being again renewed. "The grand move" of the United States Bank, it was stated, which in the period "of extreme low prices" in 1838, made it possible to sustain producers and also to keep the cotton out of the market, "affords a most striking illustration of its vital importance not only commercially but politically to England." Consequently, if the United States wishes to "inflict a deadly blow" on Britain, it "could not resort to a more summary and effectual process than by withholding, by purchase or otherwise, say one-third or more of any one year's cotton crop, from the European market. The immediate effect would be to force prices up in England to a point that would suspend consumption and thus throw out of employment an immense multitude of the most turbulent population in the world—when insurrection if not revolution might follow. And when we reflect on the serious consequences that would succeed such a step, we ought not to wonder at the extreme jealousy that has been manifested in high quarters towards the comparatively little that has been done tending to this point. . . . Cotton bags will be much more effectual in bringing John Bull to terms than all the disciplined troops America could bring into the field."[48]

Perhaps this bellicose spirit was not shared by other participants in the cotton transactions, but to the extent it was, they must have been arch-dissemblers indeed if they could suppress it wholly in their dealings with America's customers; and combined with the notion that only America was able to produce cotton—a notion with which the South grew more and more infatuated—it could scarcely have fostered that amity and trust in which commerce is supposed to flourish.[49]

[48] Biddle Papers 88, Folios 17492-93.   [49] E. D. Adams II, chap. x.

CHAPTER 17

The Suffolk Bank; the Safety Fund;
Briscoe v. Bank of Kentucky

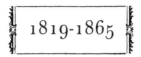

1819-1865

I. The Suffolk Bank — II. The Safety Fund — III. *Briscoe v. Bank of Kentucky*

I

THE Jacksonian process of forcing the federal government's banking responsibilities into desuetude was paralleled by a variety of procedures in the individual states. Some of the latter prohibited banks, some promoted them, some did one thing and then did another. Some achieved very satisfactory control of banking, except that it was necessarily incomplete, the jurisdictions being limited. But one of the oldest and most famous systems of control was wholly private, though it comprised banks under state charter. This was the Suffolk Bank system of New England.

Boston, like New York and Philadelphia, was already a substantial community when her first banks were established and could provide them real capital and able management. She was the metropolis of a region whose limited territorial expansion had nearly stopped, when that of the rest of the country was still beginning; and whose development was to be primarily industrial and financial. She was therefore spared to some degree the inflationary strain to which a then limitless westward expansion exposed New York and Philadelphia. But with the rise and multiplication of country banks she experienced as they did an inundation of country bank paper brought into the city by country merchants and other visitors. Everywhere, of course, out-of-town notes had to be accepted by the city merchants, though they were of varying and uncertain value, dirty, and hard to get redeemed. Being inferior to city bank notes, they drove the latter out of circulation. This was probably a major stimulus to the abandonment of note issue by the city banks and the growth of their deposits. Business men already familiar with the convenience of checks preferred them the more, for use among themselves, to the out-of-town notes. City bank notes could not compete with country bank notes, but city bank deposits could.

The city banks, however, exaggerating as every one else did the importance of circulating notes, failed to see compensation for their decline in the growth of deposits and sought to drive out the country bank notes in order to make way for their own. The obvious means to this end was to assemble the country bank notes, sort them, and take them to the issuing banks with a demand for their redemption. But this was expensive and required concerted action to be effectual, and concerted action was not easy to command; there were differences of opinion about the best procedure, and there were conflicts of interest. Of these the country banks took every advantage. They did not leave the circulation of their notes to hazard, but found means to force them into circulation. They purchased with their notes the short-term obligations of city merchants, offering a cheap kind of money which the cheap kind of merchant could borrow on cheap terms. The country bank notes were not universally unattractive, by any means, for the uncertainty of their value always afforded opportunities for the sharp trader to take them in sales for less than they were worth and to part with them in purchases for more than they were worth. Such traders were the kind of people who preferred to fish in troubled waters and who readily joined the country banks in outcries against the oppressions of the monopolistic city banks which were trying to deny them cheap credit and cheap money. Furthermore brokers found the buying and selling of country bank notes very profitable. They acquired an expert knowledge of them which the public did not possess; and though they provided a useful market for such notes and stabilized the dealings in them, they were not disposed to have all notes circulate at par lest their business disappear. So they fed their market by becoming agents of country banks, arranging loans to city borrowers in country bank paper, and at the same time providing themselves with more country bank paper to buy at a discount. They too resisted the efforts of the city banks to supplant a poor monetary medium with a better. In consequence of the impediments and the uproar raised by the various people who had a vested interest in depreciated money, metropolitan banks achieved only occasional and impermanent success in their efforts to expel country bank paper from their communities.

In 1804 the Boston Exchange Bank, organized for the purpose of dealing in out-of-town bank notes, had some promise of success but shortly was acquired by Andrew Dexter, jr., who used it, with several other banks, including the Farmers Exchange Bank of Glocester, Rhode Island, as I have already recounted, to demonstrate for the first time in the New World how to wreck a bank. In 1813 the New England Bank, representing some of Boston's best business men, essayed the elimination of country bank notes, buying them at a discount and systematically sending them home for redemption. In 1818 the Suffolk Bank entered the competition, and devised a new procedure less simple and obvious than the old but more efficient. Instead of getting the country bank notes first and then demanding redemption of them, it got the funds first and held them till the notes came in. For country banks as for others, circulation had to be large to be profitable, generally speaking, and there were two ways of enlarging it. One was to make redemption so easy and so certain that it was never demanded, in which case a bank's notes would continue to circulate because there was confidence in them. The alternative was to evade redemption by making it difficult for notes to find their way home. The first was preferable if a bank had enough funds to make it possible. Thus Isaac Bronson's bank in Bridgeport, Connecticut, as early as 1812, was maintaining with the Mechanics Bank in New York just such a balance as the Suffolk was now inviting. To this balance the notes of the Bridgeport Bank were charged as they reached the bank in New York, which was the known redemption agent, and the balance was replenished with specie weekly. Bankers who could not afford to put funds in New York or Boston for the payment of their notes, or who disliked to, could choose the alternative, which was to evade redemption by making it difficult; as was the case, obviously, if the notes were in Boston and the banks responsible for them were far away in Maine or Vermont.[1]

The Suffolk, on the basis of these alternatives, approached the country banks with an offer in one hand and a threat in the other. The offer was to let the country bank have the discount on its own notes if it would maintain a permanent balance of $5,000 with the Suffolk and enough besides to redeem such amount of its notes as the Suffolk received. The condition of a permanent balance of $5,000 was omitted for certain banks whose accounts the Suffolk already

[1] Redlich, 70, 71, 78.

had, if they would maintain all their balances with it. What this scheme meant to the Suffolk was that it got increased deposits. What it meant to the Suffolk's country correspondents was less certain: if the notes stayed at a discount, the country bank redeemed them correspondingly and profitably at less than face value; if the notes went to par the country bank could take pride in the fact. The threat, on the other hand, was that if the country bank refused the offer, the Suffolk would pursue it into the woods and demand redemption of its notes on the spot. This was annoying. Country bankers generally preferred the first alternative, though they liked neither. But even if they accepted the threat, they had to be prepared to meet it. In consequence, one way or the other, the prevailing discount on Massachusetts country bank notes was shortly brought down from one per cent to less than one-half per cent. The Suffolk found its scheme worked too well. By 1822 "the profits on the business had become so small that the directors felt obliged to reduce the expenses of the bank."[2]

At the same time that the Suffolk was dissatisfied, so were the other Boston banks. To have the discount on country notes lessened was fine for the public, but what the Suffolk wanted was increased deposits and what the others wanted was increased circulation. At the suggestion of the Suffolk, therefore, six of them agreed to employ the Suffolk as their agent for the collection of all the country bank notes they received and to maintain balances with it through which the country bank notes received by them should be cleared. This arrangement was begun in 1824.[3]

Since the Suffolk was now handling the country notes received by six other Boston banks as well as by itself, the country banks were under more pressure than before. They were still offered the alternative of maintaining a balance with the Suffolk for redemption of their notes or having their notes brought home to be redeemed at their own counters; but it was this alternative that they complained was "coercion." They called the Suffolk the Six-Tailed Bashaw and its agreement with its six accomplices the Holy Alliance. But the Suffolk went ahead and made them honor their obligations, one way or the other. It might have practiced an equivocal indulgence toward them and encouraged, as the brokers did, the inflationary practices on which it profited; instead of which it had a puritan conviction of the moral importance of its policy and pursued it with zeal. It scolded its country correspondents like bad boys and admonished them as if their souls and not merely its own earnings were at stake. As the enthusiasm of the economic democracy rose, as the number of banks increased, as bank credit grew more distended, and as the regulatory powers of the Bank of the United States waned and disappeared, the Suffolk had more notes to handle, its correspondents grew tardy in remitting for the replenishment of their balances, and they leaned more on it for credit. It grew more and more admonitory. It sent a circular "to such of its correspondents as it allowed to overdraw, informing them that on account of the scarcity of money and in order to have some control over its own funds, overdrafts must be limited to $10,000."* In September 1833 it wrote to correspondents in the following strain: "Your account is overdrawn about $16,000; and we shall send home your bills for specie on Monday next, if it is not made good on or before Saturday. We cannot permit any overdrafts on this bank in future and shall hereafter send your bills home for payment unless you have funds here to redeem them as fast as received. We can allow no overdrafts, because banks are so numerous and money so scarce, that it has become necessary for each bank to rely entirely on its own resources, and to limit its business accordingly."⁴

During the winter of 1835-1836, as Andrew Jackson's second term neared its end and the charter of the federal Bank was expiring, thirty-two new banks were chartered in Massachusetts alone, where, however, the speculation was less than elsewhere. In April 1836 the Suffolk wrote as follows to forty-four country correspondents whose accounts were overdrawn: "In consequence of the great increase of banks in the New England states during the past winter, and the scarcity of specie, it has become impracticable to allow any further overdrafts on this bank, or to hold your bills beyond the amount of funds to your credit. Your account is now overdrawn ———dollars, which we must rely upon your making good with as little delay as possible; and we shall be compelled to send your bills home for specie in future, unless you have funds here to redeem them. We regret the necessity of these measures, but the deranged state of money matters throughout our whole country renders them unavoidable."⁵ The Suffolk with all other Boston banks suspended,

* Interest was calculated for each day on debit or overdrawn balances. *Hunt's Merchants' Magazine,* September 1841, p. 261.

⁴ Whitney, 23-24.   ⁵ Whitney, 25-26.

12 May 1837, two days after the banks in New York. Though fairly secure itself, its correspondents were heavily engaged to it and unable to discharge their engagements; but by May 1838, when the New York banks resumed payments, the Suffolk and other Boston banks resumed also.

The Suffolk was in effect the central bank of New England. It was doing what the Bank of the United States should and might have done for the country as a whole. It was regulating the extension of bank credit, supporting the country banks, on occasion tightening the curb on them, and responsibly advising them what they should do and what not. In October 1842, its president, Henry B. Stone, warned a Vermont correspondent that it had lent too much "in accommodation paper, which can not be relied upon at maturity to meet your liabilities." The bank perhaps expected, he said, that means for it to reduce its debit balance at the Suffolk might "arise from the 'coming clip of wool in your state' and from the 'wisdom of our country assembled at Washington.'" The former "no doubt may afford you some relief, and we hope you may be aided by the latter." But "the experience of the last twelve years" indicated, in the Suffolk's opinion, that neither wool nor Washington was so safe a basis for bank circulation as cash and good mercantile paper. Meanwhile it was expected that flotation of a government loan and an advance in British exchange would be putting "severe pressure upon our money market" and obliging the Suffolk to call in its funds. "We hope, therefore," he concluded decisively, "you will take measures to reduce your balance immediately. Our discount sheet is entirely closed, and we do not even look at the applications." To another correspondent he said picturesquely: "I am glad you are so situated as to hear the thunder before the lightning reaches you."[6]

By 1850 the Suffolk, either directly or through the other Boston banks that kept balances with it for the purpose, was clearing notes for all the sound banks in New England, which then numbered about 500. The better banks both city and country were reconciled to it, its services were generally accepted, and though it was not loved, its prestige was high. In 1857, however, it was forced again to join the general suspension that attended the panic of that year. In 1858, when specie payments were resumed, it was confronted by a competitor, the Bank of Mutual Redemption, which was organized by groups that disliked the Suffolk and coveted its profits. The Suffolk,

[6] Whitney, 32, 35.

after years of vigilant success, had apparently become too deeply impressed by its own very substantial virtues to suit most people outside its sanctum. The new competitor, whose stockholders largely represented country banks, alleged that the Suffolk was engaged in a criminal conspiracy in accumulating country bank notes and demanding redemption in cash. It claimed, moreover, that its own charter made it the instrument of state policy and virtually outlawed the Suffolk, for the Massachusetts legislature had incorporated it for the specific purpose of redeeming New England bank notes, which the Suffolk was doing without such sanction. The Bank of Mutual Redemption was an unconventional and aggressive competitor and had the support of a growing number of country banks, who were at length accepting the principles of the Suffolk, but practicing them in a rival camp. The Suffolk did not at once give up the field but turned more and more to the customary commercial banking, to which it confined itself entirely after the National Bank Act, which owed some of its most useful features to the Suffolk's example, had set up a wholly new bank note system. Though its potentialities as a regulator were far less than those of the Bank of the United States, with which from 1818 to 1836 it was contemporary, its actual accomplishments were substantial and distinguished. In one important quarter of the country it imposed a salutary discipline on note issue for nearly half a century; the Bank of the United States did so in the whole country but only for the years that intervened between its earlier mismanagement and the Jacksonian attack.[7]

Aside from escaping the political enmity which ruined the federal Bank, the Suffolk had the advantage of a regulatory procedure that was technically superior to the others; that is, instead of being merely creditor of the banks it regulated, it became their debtor. They maintained balances with it to which their notes were charged. This kept them in a cash position, except when overdrawn, and prepared to redeem their notes. With the federal Bank, they were always behind or too easily became so, because it received their obligations *before* it received the funds for their payment. In being regularly a debtor to the banks it served and on occasion their creditor, the Suffolk was in the position of modern central banks such as the Federal Reserve Banks or the Bank of Canada. It apparently had not a flexible discount rate, and it was not government

[7] Whitney, 46, 54, 57; *Bankers Magazine*, November 1858, 389-90.

depository and fiscal agent. Yet without these customary stigmata of central banks it was nevertheless very effective. There was an insatiable demand for bank credit in the Suffolk's days that kept bank reserves under constant pressure and the banks themselves responsive, accordingly, to central bank control.

The operations of the Suffolk Bank showed *laisser faire* at its best. With no privileges or sanctions whatever from the government, private enterprise developed in the Suffolk an efficient regulation of bank credit that was quite as much in the public interest as government regulation could be. A New Yorker wrote in 1858 that his state, "even with aid of statutes and 'revised statutes,' " had a system "far inferior to that created by the voluntary Suffolk Bank system." At this very day, he said, "the bank bills of the interior of our own state are less valuable than those of New England in Wall Street—the discount on the former being ¼ per cent, while upon the latter the loss is only ⅛ per cent." The notes of New England banks, he said, "are at par throughout every town and village of those states, while, with all the aids of law, we have not yet been able to create a par currency in the Empire State."[8]

Though the Suffolk system profited by the earlier experience of New York, its greater success was owing to the greater earnestness with which note redemption was pursued in Boston, and this greater interest seems to have been but one reflection of the conservatism that prevailed there. The Suffolk's directors included Appletons, Lawrences, and Lowells. New York had its conservatives, too, but they never attained the ascendancy that their peers attained in Boston and Philadelphia. New York was always more hospitable to the new and experimental, and at the same time Rhadamanthine toward whatever turned out to be impracticable. But the Suffolk's procedure, like that of the Bank of the United States while it was still allowed to regulate the currency, was definitely deflationary; and it is natural that it should be found more tolerable in the capitalist and creditor community that Boston already was than in New York, Philadelphia, and other centers where the debtor and entrepreneurial interest was more representative.

II

It was in 1829, four years or so after the Suffolk's procedure had developed to its most efficient and characteristic form, that New

8 *Bankers Magazine*, November 1858, 384-85.

York established by law the state-wide Safety Fund system of banks, which relied on ultimate insurance of notes rather than their immediate redemption for its effectiveness. The Fund was first proposed by Joshua Forman, a lawyer, one of the most influential promoters of the Erie Canal, and the originator of improvements in the production of salt by evaporation. The occasion of his proposal was the imminent expiry of most New York charters within the next few years, no new ones having been granted after 1825 and the question whether the charters should be renewed and on what terms being already agitated. The Forman proposal embodied reasonable terms on which they might be renewed. It was based on the principle that since banks profited from the public's use of their notes as money, they ought to guarantee that the public suffer no loss from that use. This they were to do by contributing to a general fund in proportion to the amount of their capital, and their contributions were to be accumulated by the state government till needed to discharge the circulating note liabilities of any banks that failed. Mr Forman submitted his plan to Martin Van Buren, then newly elected Governor of New York, and Mr Van Buren recommended it to the legislature. "The propriety of making the banks liable for each other," Mr Forman said, "was suggested by the regulations of the Hong merchants in Canton, where a number of men, each acting separately, have by the grant of government the exclusive right of trading with foreigners and are all made liable for the debts of each in case of failure." The situation of the banks he found similar. "They enjoy in common the exclusive right of making a paper currency for the people of the state and by the same rule should in common be answerable for that paper." The charge upon the banks was to be compensated by limiting the grants of charters, by exemption from taxes, by relief from the imposition by the state of bonuses and similar burdens, and by permission to charge seven per cent on loans instead of six as theretofore. This permission, it may be recalled, created a new complaint against the Bank of the United States, whose offices charged only six per cent and consequently interfered with the New York banks' charging the higher rate allowed by law.[9]

The legislature adopted the Forman plan with several changes

---

[9] Jabez Hammond II, 298; New York Assembly Journal, 1829, pp. 178, 179; New York State, *Messages from the Governors* III, 230, 238.

for the worse. What was most important, it did not follow the suggestion that the Fund be used only for the payment of note liabilities. Instead, through what appears to have been sheer inadvertence or ignorance, it made the Fund available for payment of the "debts" of the banks. This, contrary to all intention, made it legally available for payment of deposit as well as note liabilities. Each bank, chartered or rechartered after 2 April 1829, was to pay into the Fund one-half per cent of its capital annually for six years. This distributed the burden in such way that the better banks, with large capital, had to pay relatively more than those with bad management and inadequate capital. The contributions should have been levied on the amount of liabilities being insured. The burden was still more inequitable from the consideration that the purpose of the legislators was to insure circulating notes; for the banks with large capital, mainly metropolitan, paid most though they had relatively less note circulation—some had none at all; and the small banks, the more numerous and mostly in the country, paid least, though they had relatively more circulation. The larger banks protested, but it did them no good. It had been proposed also that the notes of all the Safety Fund banks be issued in uniform amounts and counter-signed by a central agency, but this sensible provision had been omitted from the law in deference to individualism, and to the convenience of counterfeiters. The law also failed to limit the number of banks. At the same time, it retained various high-sounding but otiose provisions, some ancient and some recent, that were common in bank charters. One was the venerable limitation on liabilities with respect to capital, whose lineage ran back through Alexander Hamilton's work on the charters of the Bank of the United States and the Bank of New York to that of the Bank of England. Another was the more recent but no more effective limitation on loans and discounts with respect to capital. Yet another, still more recent in American bank legislation and still less effective, was the requirement that new banks hold their paid capital in silver and gold.[10]

These fifth wheels in the law left it sound in principle, though clumsy. Of prime importance was its embodiment of Joshua Forman's intelligent understanding that banks constitute a system, being peculiarly sensitive to one another's operations, and not a

[10] Chaddock, 268-69; Gallatin iii, 418-19.

mere aggregate of free agents.* The law introduced another important novelty in authorizing appointment of three bank commissioners, one to be chosen by the Governor of New York and two by the banks themselves. The commissioners were to inspect each bank at least once in every four months and any bank oftener if asked by three other banks to do so. They were to question bank officers under oath and satisfy themselves of each bank's solvency. On evidence of illegality or insolvency, they were to apply for an injunction against the delinquent bank and appointment of a receiver for it by the court. This commission seems to have been the first special supervisory authority established over banking in the States and the beginning, therefore, of a bureaucratic development which in somewhat more than a hundred years has achieved in American bank supervision an hypertrophy, complexity, duplication, confusion, and cost that even the ingenious Mr Van Buren might feel surprised to be the author of.[11]

The novel requirements of the Safety Fund Act inspired its opponents to denounce its interference with enterprise, its encouragement to careless banking, and its subjection of banks to "inquisitors" —criticisms that signalized some conflict between the growing popularity of *laisser faire* and the stubborn recognition that banking was a monetary function which *laisser faire* did not wholly seem to suit. The system, its defects notwithstanding, was creditable not only to Joshua Forman but to that group of promoters and politicians known as the Albany Regency which so ably advanced the interests of New York. The measure was a constructive one designed to strengthen New York's banking system at the same time that General Jackson's assault on the Bank of the United States was being encouraged as a means of breaking Philadelphia's financial primacy and erecting New York's. The New Yorkers were not mere wreckers by any means. It will be recalled that Mr Van Buren held the Governorship of New York only a few weeks, in the spring of 1829, resigning it to enter President Jackson's Cabinet. In those

---

* The act also relieved bank stockholders, other than directors, from personal liability for a bank's debts. But in 1846 the new state constitution made stockholders *personally* liable for the amount of their stock. This anomalous imposition, peculiar to stockholders of banks as compared with other corporations and known as "double liability," was generally in force throughout the country till after 1933, when the federal government and many states abandoned it as impracticable and unjust.

[11] Chaddock, 262.

few weeks the one important measure he recommended to the New York legislature was the Safety Fund. According to James Gordon Bennett in the New York *Herald* some years later, 3 May 1837, the Safety Fund proposal was taken up in the state Assembly by Abijah Mann, who urged it be adopted "on the ground of opposition to the United States Bank and in order to take the place of that institution." At the time this was written, just before the panic of 1837 broke, Bennett was flaying Van Buren, whom he blamed for the destruction of the Bank of the United States and the "wild, unregulated banking" it stimulated. "The Democrats," he said, "opposed all banking in Congress but carried it to all lengths in the states."

And in New York, as in some other states, they did not do badly, by any means. For about twelve years the Safety Fund went smoothly, and in 1841 Mr Gallatin wrote that the banking system of New York, since the Fund had gone into effect, had proved "superior to most and inferior to none of the plans adopted in other states." In 1834 the commissioners had urged that instead of letting new banks be established, those already in existence be strengthened, and in 1835 no charters had been granted. But in 1836 the pressure was more insistent; the Governor mentioned with alarm the publication of ninety-three applications for new charters—enough to double the number of banks. In 1837, before the general suspension which began 10 May, three banks in Buffalo failed, and the Safety Fund had to be called on for the first time. There was then belated realization that it could not be used till the assets of the banks had proved inadequate. Since this meant delay and a depreciation of the banks' obligations, the law was quickly changed to authorize use of the Fund first instead of last. Also in 1837 the charters of two other banks were repealed for violation of the law, and the Fund recovered all that it had to advance in payment of notes. It was not till after 1840 that the Fund suffered loss; and then just as Mr Gallatin was speaking of its good record, a series of bank failures began which prostrated it.[12]

Within two years eleven banks failed, and redemption of their notes depleted the Safety Fund far more rapidly than it could be replenished. Moreover in the court action incident to the first of these failures, it became established that under the law, now twelve years old, the Fund was liable for the claims of depositors as well as note-holders. The astonishing discovery that deposits were debts

[12] Gallatin III, 419; Chaddock, 276, 282, 302-04.

of banks as much as circulating notes were caused dismay. "This peculiar feature of the law," said the commissioners, "does not seem until recently to have been generally understood either by the public at large or even by those engaged in the business of banking." The language of the law may not have been known generally, but that the debts of banks included their deposit liabilities certainly had long been obvious to banks which had smaller circulation than deposits or no circulation at all. In order to correct the inadvertence, the legislature in 1842 hastily ended the liability of the Fund for deposits of banks that should fail thereafter. It was thenceforth liable for notes only, as originally intended. Existing claims of depositors still stood against it, however. In 1843 creditors of the first four banks to fail obtained an injunction restraining the use of the Fund to repay later creditors till their own claims—for notes and deposits both—had been satisfied. In 1845 the legislature authorized the issue of bonds by the state in an amount estimated to be sufficient to pay off all these claims. Between 1842 and 1854 the only Safety Fund bank to fail was the Canal Bank of Albany, and it was able to pay its debts without calling on the Fund. The next failure was that of the Lewis County Bank in 1854; its assets were wholly inadequate, but the Fund could do nothing for the creditors, being itself mortgaged to the state for the help advanced on account of the 1842 failures. In the panic year 1857 three more banks failed, throwing more claims on the Fund which it could do nothing about. In 1866, when the last Safety Fund bank charter expired, the Fund itself was terminated.* Its obligation to the state for the advances in 1845 had been paid, partly through contributions from the banks that had survived but mostly through disposition of assets of the banks that had failed, and there was a balance on hand. The sum was insufficient to meet all the unpaid claims for which the Fund was liable, but a large part of the claims had been lost, forgotten, or given up by the creditors, twenty-four years having elapsed since the oldest failures still unsettled had occurred and nine years since the latest. Thanks to this protracted liquidation, the sum on hand in the Fund was sufficient to pay all the claims actually presented, and about $10,000 remaining was transferred to the state treasury.[13]

* The old charters expired, but new ones were obtained by the banks that were continuing.

[13] New York Commissioners of the Safety Fund, *Report, 1841*; Knox, *History of Banking*, 409-10; Chaddock, 329, 330, 359, 360, 363, 365-67, 382.

This sorry consummation of the Fund was not the fault of the principle underlying it, which the Chinese had applied with so much more success than the hasty New Yorkers. The principle was put in effect in Vermont in 1831; in Michigan in 1837; in Ohio in 1845; in Iowa in 1858; in Canada, where it is still in force, in 1890; and in 1933—a hundred and four years after the original proposal by Joshua Forman—Congress put it in practice as federal deposit insurance for the whole United States.[14]

The trouble in New York was that the Fund was instituted in slip-shod fashion and then neglected; for soon after it was established and while its prospects still seemed bright, the legislature became fascinated by a new and inferior scheme, "free banking," which it adopted in 1838. The banks in the Safety Fund all had special legislative charters and for that reason were condemned by the Jacksonian democracy as wicked monopolies. The Fund became orphaned early and spent far the greater part of its dwindling existence in a painful, slow, and hopelessly complicated dissolution. In 1843 the office of the three commissioners who had supervised and examined the Safety Fund banks was abolished by the legislature for the over-simple reason that when bank officers were honest, commissioners were unnecessary, and when they were dishonest, commissioners were unavailing; though Mr Gallatin, two years before, had said that the work of the commissioners had been eminently useful. Year by year, while the number of banks of the new free system was increasing, the number of banks belonging to the Safety Fund and liable to its levies was growing less and less; no more could be chartered. Had the Safety Fund been properly restricted as to its liabilities in the first place and had it not been neglected for an inferior system, it would have been able to give the protection it was intended to give.[15]

The New York Safety Fund system was contemporary with all but the first ten years of New England's Suffolk Bank system and both came to an end in 1866. But their careers were very different. For the Suffolk, under intelligent and energetic managers, was too successful for its own advantage. It aimed at profits, but what it achieved was the public good. The Safety Fund sought the public good but under impossible conditions and achieved bankruptcy.

Although the Safety Fund principle was and is workable, I think

14 Federal Deposit Insurance Corporation, *Annual Reports*, 1950, 1952, 1953.
15 Chaddock, 326; Gallatin III, 420; Knox, *History of Banking*, 412-13.

it inferior to the principle of the Suffolk Bank. The reason lies in a condition remarked in 1832 by Isaac Bronson, when he wrote that there could be no sound currency without a central bank "so constituted that its own existence shall be made to depend on the exercise of such a controlling influence over the circulation of other banks as to preserve the whole in a sound condition." The Suffolk Bank was so situated, for its operations were inherently and automatically corrective. So were those of the Bank of the United States. Both, by pursuing their self-interest, exercised a governance *within* the banking process, where it was always active and nipping trouble in the bud. In the Safety Fund, on the other hand, reliance was placed on immobile resources drawn outside the banking process, held there, and re-injected after trouble had arisen. In principle this was much less efficient; in practice it may be best to have both. The Suffolk, to be sure, availed no more than the Safety Fund to prevent general suspension in 1837; nor—to anticipate—did the Federal Reserve System in 1933.* Yet though none of the three succeeded in preventing the misuse of bank credit, all three tended to do so. And it was this wholesome tendency that damned them. All three were displeasing to an enterprising democracy determined to exploit its matchless opportunities in the New World to the utmost and unwilling to let borrowing be made difficult by ideals of a sound currency and conservative growth.[16]

III

Though the general demand for easy money directly or indirectly impelled the legislatures to increase the number of banks, there was also in many states besides New York a successful desire to make the state banking systems responsible and efficient. These efforts had not been neglected even while the Bank of the United States was an effective regulator. On the contrary, state legislation shows from the very beginning a self-critical tendency to make bank charters more exacting and disciplinary—a tendency that was halting and erratic but significant. The earliest American charters were almost wholly plenary, but after Alexander Hamilton had made those of the

* Isaac Bronson rightly said that the Safety Fund could not have "any influence in preventing all the banks in the state from suspending payment at once." But the Suffolk, the Bank of the United States, and the Federal Reserve did have, or might have had, that influence.

[16] Raguet, *Financial Register* II, 12.

Bank of the United States and the Bank of New York lengthy with requirements and conditions, his example became the fashion. Charters also fell into established patterns. Thus New York after some modification of the charter of the Bank of New York enacted successive bank charters in the same pattern till 1825. There also arose the legislative practice of enacting general laws to which all banks subsequently chartered should be subject. The view customarily taken was that charters were inviolable contracts which could be altered only by mutual consent, but it was commonly possible to get banks to accept new restrictions in return for new powers. Such changes were toward uniformity and in time led directly to the enactment of banking laws to which banks generally, within a given state, were subject.

During all this development the question whether the Constitution allowed the states to incorporate banks remained unsettled but never pressing. The power of the states to form corporations other than banks was not disputed, for it inhered in sovereign powers that the states had never alienated, but since the states had surrendered the direct power to issue bills of credit themselves it was reasonable to contend that they could not lawfully grant it to their creatures. When the Constitution was fresh, the question probably occurred to no one, for people were familiar with bills of credit and with bank notes as quite distinct things that nothing in their experience or knowledge had ever associated. To identify the two as one under the terms of the Constitution would then have seemed metaphysical. But twenty or more years later, as banks increased in number and as their credit in the form of circulating notes came to provide a volume of currency which before could not have been imagined, the fact that the notes were money became obvious, and its unexpected implications began to emerge.[17]

They became clear under pressure of the opposition to the Bank of the United States. "With respect to state rights," said John Taylor of South Carolina in April 1810 in the course of the congressional debates on renewal of the Bank's charter, "I believe it is more easily to be demonstrated . . . that the states are constitutionally prohibited from erecting banks in their own states than this government from erecting the bank we are now discussing. I fancy these bank bills are but bills of credit after all, which the Constitution expressly prohibits the state governments from issuing; . . . ."

[17] ASP, Finance I, 49.

William Crawford of Georgia in February 1811 also "questioned the authority of the state governments to create banks"; before the states questioned the right of the federal government to establish banks, "they ought to have thoroughly examined the foundation on which their own right rested." John C. Calhoun of South Carolina argued in February 1816 that the federal convention of 1787 had intended to give Congress exclusive control of the monetary system; that subsequently there had sprung up great numbers of state banks; that as a result there had been "an extraordinary revolution in the currency of the country"; that "by a sort of undercurrent the power of Congress to regulate the money of the country had caved in"; that the state banks had usurped it, "for gold and silver are not the only money," since whatever is "the medium of purchase and sale" was the money of the country; and that the state banks should be caused "to give up their usurped power." They were not then caused to give it up; in fact Congress in April 1816 specifically authorized the Treasury's acceptance, determined by Alexander Hamilton twenty-seven years before, of the notes of specie-paying state banks.[18]

But the constitutional question remained alive, reiterated by the orthodox Jeffersonians, who hated all banks, and by their opponents who championed the federal Bank against the state banks. Daniel Webster said in the Senate in 1832: "It cannot well be questioned that it was intended by the Constitution to submit the whole subject of the currency of the country, all that regards the actual medium of payment and exchange, whatever that should be, to the control and legislation of Congress. . . . The exclusive power of regulating the metallic currency of the country would seem necessarily to imply, or more properly, to include as part of itself, a power to decide how far that currency should be exclusive, how far any substitute should interfere with it and what that substitute should be. . . . But notwithstanding this apparent purpose in the Constitution, the truth is that the currency of the country is now . . . practically and effectually under the control of the several state governments; . . . for the states seem first to have taken possession of the power and then to have delegated it" to the state banks. The year following, 1833, Justice Story, in his *Commentaries on the Constitution*, approved this derogation of "the doctrine that the

---

[18] Clarke and Hall, 459, 441-42, 631-32; Dewey, *Financial History*, 228.

states, not being at liberty to coin money, can authorize the circulation of bank paper as currency."[19]

That same year the question came before the Supreme Court. Not till 1837, in *Briscoe* v. *The Bank of the Commonwealth of Kentucky*, was it answered. During this period the contention that state banks were unconstitutional had not only the respectable support of the safest conservatives but the vociferous support of the Loco Focos, the wildest radicals of the day. The appearance of the question before the Court was evidently a reflection of the popular interest in it.

In 1820, in response to the demand for relief for debtors on land purchases, the legislature of Kentucky had established the Bank of the Commonwealth of Kentucky, which should be the property of the state exclusively, the president and directors to be chosen by the legislature. (This was the bank of which Francis Preston Blair was president before he was fetched to Washington in 1830 to replace Duff Green as editorial spokesman of the Jackson administration.) In the course of business the bank made a loan at its Harrodsburg branch to four co-borrowers, who subsequently defaulted. The borrowers had received notes of the bank in exchange for their own obligation, and when the bank sued for repayment, their defense was that the notes delivered to them were bills of credit issued by a creature of the state, that the notes contravened the constitutional prohibition on bills of credit, that the bank itself was unconstitutional, and that, the notes delivered by the bank being null and void, their own obligation to the bank was without consideration and therefore void. Whatever the defendants' politics, their defense rested on familiar Loco Foco doctrine. Historically it was clear, as I said in an early chapter, that when the federal convention in 1787 used the words "bills of credit," it had in mind the paper money that had been issued by the colonies, and later by the states and the Continental Congress. But nothing in the Constitution excluded bank notes from the prohibition, and the term "bills of credit" was not well defined. However, in *Craig* v. *Missouri*, 1830, the Court had decided that certain certificates issued by the state of Missouri were bills of credit and that as such they came within the prohibition. In 1833, on the basis of this decision, the Illinois Supreme Court held the notes of the State Bank of Illinois unconstitutional and void. These judgments foreshadowed some similar one

---

[19] Congress, *Register of Debates*, 22nd Congress, 1st Session, 957; Story, *Commentaries* III, chap. XVII, 19-20.

from the federal Supreme Court sooner or later. The opportunity was proffered in the case *Briscoe* v. *The Bank of Kentucky.*[20]

The case, first heard by the Supreme Court in 1834, was continued for rehearing the next term. "In cases where constitutional questions are involved," it was explained, "unless four judges of the Court concur in opinion, thus making the decision that of a majority of the whole Court, it is not the practice of the Court to deliver any judgment except in cases of absolute necessity." Two of the aged justices were physically unable to attend the hearings, and the other five were divided three to two. So decision was postponed. The next year it was postponed again for the same reason, there now being only six justices. Then again it had to be postponed, this third time because of an almost complete change in the membership of the Court. Chief Justice Marshall had died in 1835; other members had died or resigned; and in 1837 when the case finally recurred for hearing, all the members were new except Justice Story, all but he were appointees of President Jackson, and the Chief Justice was Roger B. Taney.[21]

The case was decided 11 February 1837, the last month of the Jackson administration, and the decision, according to Justice Story's vehement dissent, was very different from what the Court as it had been would have rendered. It was in effect that bank notes differed in name, in form, and in substance from bills of credit issued by a state and were "not bills of credit within the meaning of the federal Constitution." So state banks and their notes did not come under a ban after all.[22]

Historically, the best thing to be said for this decision is that the authors of the Constitution, when they said "bills of credit" in 1787, had certainly not meant bank notes. But by 1837, bank notes had certainly come within the scope of what had been meant, as the Jeffersonians and Loco Focos had long contended. And the Supreme Court under John Marshall had evidently been ready to agree with them in *Craig* v. *Missouri*, when it had defined bills of credit as "paper intended to circulate through the community for its ordinary purposes as money," and as "a paper medium intended to circulate between individuals and between government and individuals. . . ." Under this broad definition the Court had found the certificates of

---

[20] *Craig* v. *Missouri*, 4 Peters 424; *Linn* v. *State Bank of Illinois*, 1 Scammon 87; *Briscoe* v. *Bank of Kentucky*, 11 Peters 310.
[21] 8 Peters 115; 9 Peters 85. [22] *Briscoe* v. *Bank of Kentucky*, 11 Peters 326.

the state of Missouri to be bills of credit and accordingly forbidden. Missouri's calling them certificates had not helped; it had merely evoked Chief Justice Marshall's ironic enquiry whether the Constitution was to be openly evaded in one of its most important provisions "by giving a new name to an old thing."[23]

The Court's definition of bills of credit in *Craig* v. *Missouri* would have seemed odd in 1787 though the finding itself would not. But the definition now offered by the new Court in *Briscoe* v. *The Bank of Kentucky* would have seemed no better, when it was declared that a bill of credit to be forbidden "must be issued by a state, on the faith of the state, and be designed to circulate as money." The Convention of 1787 had had no such limited idea of a bill of credit, for to its members as to any one in the 18th century a bill of credit could be issued by any body, natural or artificial, for the purpose of borrowing, and the only reason for not intending to have the term include bank notes was that no occurrence or experience had yet suggested that it should. Experience since then, however, had clearly and emphatically suggested it, by exhibiting in bank notes substantially the same evils as in colonial and revolutionary bills of credit. The same evils, that is, if one saw them as evils, which the new Court evidently did not. The evil that seems to have impressed Chief Justice Taney and his Jacksonian associates was disruption of the state banking systems, to which as politicians they had long been tender. To avoid such catastrophe a suitable definition was found.

To John Marshall's Court, the Bank of Kentucky had been unconstitutional because it was but an aspect of the state of Kentucky; it was a "mere metaphysical thing," indistinguishable from the state itself. The Court had seen no distinction of constitutional significance between the state and an arm of the state called a bank. It was prepared to distinguish between such a bank and one privately owned, apparently, but what its opinion would have been with respect to the latter is moot. Roger Taney's Court, on the contrary, distinguished between a state and the arm of a state but made no such distinction between banks founded wholly on private capital and banks that were merely arms of the state. It showed no wish to confine the question to banks of the class to which the Bank of Kentucky belonged, state-owned and state-controlled, but boldly swept all state banks into salvation. According to its opinion, which

[23] *Craig* v. *Missouri*, 4 Peters 431, 433.

was read by Justice McLean, another former member of President Jackson's Cabinet, "if this bank be unconstitutional, all state banks founded on private capital are unconstitutional." To keep all state banks on a common footing was perhaps not very good jurisprudence, but it was expedient. For there was no difference between state banks in function no matter how different their ownership and organization, and a decision which made note issue by privately owned banks constitutional and note issue by state-owned banks unconstitutional would have been ridiculous to any one.

The Court was pragmatic therefore: it shied from concluding that state banks were unconstitutional—a conclusion which Justice McLean found "startling" and which would strike them "a fatal blow." The state banks had, he said, "a capital of near four hundred millions of dollars and, . . . supply almost the entire circulating medium of the country." This was a good reason for preserving them. A decision that the state banks were unconstitutional would have been incalculably deflationary. It would also have been a blow to the states. As it was, the decision validated the right of a state to do through a bank what it had not the right to do itself. This was what scandalized Justice Story. The state could not issue bills of credit, but who would care? For it could call one of its departments a "bank," this "bank" could issue notes, and the notes would serve exactly the same purpose as bills. So the decision in *Briscoe* v. *Bank of Kentucky* was not only conservative of vested rights but consistent with the prevailing political and economic preferences of the Jacksonian majority and their leadership—Martin Van Buren, Roger Taney, Amos Kendall, David Henshaw, and others. It was deferent to the states; it confirmed their monetary sovereignty save for the coinage and the definition of the standard of value, which was all that the Constitution, taken literally, gave the federal government. It was favorable to an increased number of banks and a greater abundance of bank credit. It enabled the Michigan legislature, a month later, to enact a free banking law, then pending, which authorized an unlimited number of banks to be set up, and the New York legislature to enact a similar law the year following; and these laws, which are the subject of the next chapter, began a greater expansion of banking than any America had yet known. The decision followed—probably more by instinct than design—the pattern of Jacksonian choices and acts, which, with a fidelity never acknowledged and quite contrary to the creed of agrarianism, served signally what it considered the interests of business enterprise. That creed, in the form contemporaneously held by the Loco Focos, it repudiated. Though the opinion was not Chief Justice Taney's, it reflected faithfully his concern for states' rights, property rights, and the rights of bankers in particular.

Yet the *Briscoe* decision gained no great repute, though it boldly turned its back on the opinion in *Craig* v. *Missouri,* one of the strongest Marshall ever wrote, according to Senator Albert J. Beveridge, and the only one "to be entirely repudiated" after his death. Later, when the legality of the State Bank of Arkansas came to be questioned, the Supreme Court of the state weighed the two relevant decisions of the federal Supreme Court—the *Craig* decision and the *Briscoe*—found them in conflict and decided that the state bank was constitutional, following the *Briscoe* precedent because it was the later though the worse law. The Arkansas "court evidently regretted that the case of *Craig* had been over-ruled, as it contained the sound and true constitutional doctrine," Chancellor Kent reported. President Van Buren, in his annual message, December 1839, seemed ready to share this regret. In a tone very different from the Supreme Court's, he deplored the conduct of the state banks, which that autumn had followed the United States Bank of Pennsylvania into a second general suspension in two years, and said: "By their means we have been flooded with a depreciated paper, which it was evidently the design of the framers of the Constitution to prevent when they required Congress to 'coin money and regulate the value of foreign coins', and when they forbade the states to 'coin money, emit bills of credit, make anything but gold and silver a tender in payment of debts', or 'pass any law impairing the obligation of contracts.' " With respect to the Supreme Court's concern in the *Briscoe* case for the state banks whose legality was in question, it may be mentioned that two state Supreme Courts, Michigan's and New York's, did not shrink a few years later from outlawing banks by the score on constitutional grounds—banks, as it happened, which a different decision in the *Briscoe* case would have kept from being formed. But, to be sure, their jurisdictions were smaller, the banks affected were fewer, and the record of banks had become much worse throughout the country than it had been when the *Briscoe* case was decided.[24]

The Supreme Court had announced its decision in February 1837,

24 Beveridge IV, 509; Kent, *Commentaries,* 1860 (10th edition), I, 456-57; Richardson IV, 1768; *Green* v. *Graves,* 1 Douglas 351; *De Bow* v. *The People,* 1 Denio 9.

just three months before the general suspension. Had the case been decided *after* that suspension, which aroused widespread resentment, made the Loco Focos most vociferous, and confounded the Jacksonian leaders, the Court might have decided it differently, as President Van Buren's words indicate that he might have done. For by refusing to pay their notes the state banks might well have seemed to be pleading with unclean hands. As things were, however, it took only some ingenuity to work out a decision favorable to the banks and consistent with the record of Justice Taney and the other Jacksonians who, though they did not themselves cause the suspension, had destroyed the federal restraints on bank credit, encouraged the state banks to over-expand, and fulfilled a program which in every important respect conduced to the suspension and to continuing monetary disorder.

Both the majority and minority thought no case come before the Court had surpassed the *Briscoe* in importance. In 1851 the decision was confirmed in *Darington et al.* v. *Bank of Alabama*. In 1865 Congress reversed it by ending the issue of notes by state banks; and in 1867 in *Veazie Bank* v. *Fenno* its action was upheld by the Supreme Court.[25]

[25] *Darington et al.* v. *Bank of Alabama,* 13 Howard 12; *Briscoe* v. *Bank of Kentucky,* 11 Peters 311, 349.

CHAPTER 18

Free Banking in New York and Michigan

1835-1865

I. Significance of free banking — II. Its background — III. Its legal obstacles — IV. Free banking in the courts — V. Its operation in New York — VI. Its operation in Michigan

I

UNTIL passage of the first free-banking law in Michigan in 1837, banks in the States could be incorporated only by specific legislative act, the power to issue charters not having been delegated to administrative authority. Thereafter, when delegated, the power to issue charters was practically without discretion. The law required that anyone who set up a bank comply with certain conditions; and, those conditions being met, the appropriate administrative authority had simply to record the fact and the issuance of a charter. Though the law made any one "free" to engage in banking, the freedom was qualified to the extent that one must have the necessary money to start and must meet certain other formalities. The result was that it might be found somewhat harder to become a banker than a brick-layer, but not much.

As an idea, free banking had its origin in England, but its native home as a practice was New York. It seems to have been proposed officially in that state first in 1825, when a legislative committee, disgusted by scandal after scandal in the enactment of special charters, recommended freedom to engage in banking on grounds of "the natural right which every citizen has to employ his time and money in banking operations either individually or in association." Besides ending the efforts to purchase privileges, the committee said, repeal of the existing restraints on banking would make it easier for credit to be obtained by "the merchant, the farmer, the manufacturer, and the mechanic." This proposal antedated New York's Safety Fund measure, which was enacted in 1828 and temporarily deferred free banking. In 1831 a free-banking measure was introduced, but not adopted, in the Maryland legislature. It was in New

York that the new idea had the most pertinacious support, though it was not translated into law till 1838. One of the measures previously pending in the New York legislature was enacted by Michigan in 1837.[1]

Free banking was an application of *laisser faire* to the monetary function. Banking, with its "certain and liberal" profits, should be open "to the most free competition and its advantages shared by all classes of society," as said by Secretary of the Treasury Roger B. Taney in 1834, in words already quoted. Fifteen years afterward, Millard Fillmore—later President of the United States—said in his 1849 report as Comptroller of New York: "The free-bank system . . . takes its name from the fact that all are *freely* permitted to embark in it who comply with the rules prescribed." Free banking meant, in effect, an indefinite and unlimited number of banks. It was a retrograde effort to restore to the individual the ancient common law right to be a banker.[2]

It broke with the Hamiltonian concept of banking and the principle that supervision of banking as a monetary function was a responsibility of the federal government. Its adoption was a victory for states' rights and, with destruction of the federal Bank and affirmation of the legality of state banks by the Supreme Court in the *Briscoe* case, an impairment of federal sovereignty. But this consequence was reversed when free banking, after adoption in nearly all the individual states, became in 1863 the principle on which the federal Congress based the National Bank Act. By 1863 the democracy had learned to seek its ends through federal rather than state action. Its ends themselves remained the same. And whether practiced under state authority or federal, free banking was the American democracy's choice of a permanent policy of monetary inflation—a policy that assures plenty of funds for all who wish to borrow, prices that rise in the long run persistently though haltingly, and a dollar that never ceases for long to shrink in value.

II

Free banking emerged as a political doctrine from an odd mixture of motives and convictions. The chief factor on one side was the Loco Foco demand that all banks be abolished; and on the other was the entrepreneurial demand for more and more of them. In

---

[1] New York Senate Journal, 1825, p. 100; Chaddock, 371.

[2] Treasury Department, Secretary, *Reports on Finances, 1789-1849*, III, 457; *Bankers Magazine* III (1849), 679.

between were the conservatives—the chartered banks already in business—who wanted neither the annihilation threatened by the Loco Focos nor the unlimited competition threatened by the Jacksonian entrepreneurs. These chartered banks were hand-in-glove with the Democratic party organization in New York, headed by the Albany Regency. It had long been difficult to get new bank charters in New York, because the Regency kept the number down conservatively. And whenever a new one was decided on, it had been the practice to appoint commissioners who were to assure that fair opportunities were afforded the public to purchase stock—provided of course that most of the stock went into the possession of Democrats. The banks themselves belonged to the Safety Fund system, Mr Van Buren's legacy to the state when he joined General Jackson's Cabinet, and the Albany Regency was itself largely a bankers' affair.[3]

This was an association which had become increasingly disliked, for both political and business reasons, from both sides. Erastus Root in 1832 had defied the Regency and defended the federal Bank, and Mr Cambreleng had in consequence to read him out of the party. The Loco Focos next attacked it along with the federal Bank, the destruction of which, in their view, as in Andrew Jackson's, was the proper prelude to destruction of the state banks. Their heresy had also to be condemned, and in 1835 their leader, William Leggett, was excommunicated by the Jacksonians for the additional error of offending Amos Kendall and advocating, "openly and systematically," the abolition of slavery.*

Loco Foco doctrine, as I have already said, was an urban and industrial phase of traditional agrarianism produced by the economic pressure which was exerted on the less fortunate part of the population by industry and enterprise, by steam and credit. It was the doctrine of men who had been till recently on farms but were now working in factories and had not as yet contrived a new language in which to express the ideas arising from their new experiences. Like their *laisser faire* employers, the entrepreneurs, who had also come but recently from farms, they railed at the traditional agrarian

---

* The excommunication of General Root, in 1832, it will be recalled, was also for rebelling against the Regency and Tammany, which the Loco Focos found, as the General seems to have done, "a nursery of brokers, where federalists, monopolists, and corruptionists are fostered." Byrdsall, 65.

[3] Jabez Hammond II, 447.

bugaboos—"privilege," "monopoly," "aristocracy," and "corruption." Unlike the official Jacksonians, however, they were not satisfied with stopping the federal Bank. They wanted all banking stopped. But it was more practicable for them to exert themselves against the granting of new charters than for the abrogating of charters already granted. This allied them, in effect, with existing banks. It also allied them on occasion with men who sought by an attack on banking to undermine the political advantage of existing banks and create a breach through which new banks might pour. It was a confusing and deceptive situation. It was described by Richard Hildreth in 1840 in the following words: "The local banks of the United States have doubled in number and capital since Jackson's veto upon the recharter of the United States Bank; and that too notwithstanding the gold currency party have acted in the meantime in strict alliance with the monopolists of bank charters and have most strenuously joined in the opposition to the creation of any new banks."[4] Consequently, an attack on the *evils* of banking might emanate from a banker or a would-be banker, or a doctrinaire enemy of bankers, and the language used would give no sure sign of its source. In Philadelphia back in 1829 a group of so-called "working men and others opposed to the chartering of any more new banks," had expressed in the following words the concern they felt that "in most parts of the Union the productive labourer, with the utmost diligence and frugality, is hardly able to lay by a sufficiency against the day of distress":

"The philanthropists who have recently investigated the condition of the labouring poor have perceived that suffering and want are as severe and as widely extended in proportion to the number of inhabitants as in Europe. There must be some blight in this country upon the industry of the people or this state of things could not exist.

"In searching for a cause for these evils, we have found it in a too great extension of paper credit. Vast numbers of men in every part of the country have legislative sanction for adding to the amount of circulating medium; this is the easiest and surest mode of obtaining wealth, at the expense of productive industry and the infallible means of making those men rich at the expense of the labouring poor.

"The amount of paper which can advantageously circulate is not greater than the amount of silver and gold which could be used for

---

[4] Hildreth, *Banks, Banking, and Paper Currencies*, 171.

the same purpose. . . . To increase the quantity of paper money beyond this amount is only to raise prices; but wages do not rise so easily in price as commodities; hence much loss to mechanics and every rise in price is a reduction of wages. . . .

"We are well aware that some persons suppose much of the prosperity the country at present enjoys is owing to the banks; but we can find sufficient causes for the increase of national wealth in the combined operations of capital accumulated by preceding generations with the exertions of an increased number of labourers in a country rich in natural resources, aided by improvements in the arts and discoveries in the sciences. . . . Those who maintain that banks enrich a country are bound to prove that speculation creates wealth. Till they establish this paradox, we shall continue to believe in the old-fashioned doctrine that wealth owes its existence to industry and economy."

Hence these "working men" wished to "put a stop to the increase of those contrivances called banks, which are insensibly though certainly enabling those who produce nothing to live on the wealth that is created by our industry."[5]

I suspect that bankers themselves had as much to do with the advocacy of these views as working men had, for they condemned the evils that might arise from either a monopoly or an excess of banks. Mr Gallatin could have said about the same things that working men did—stopping short of their sweeping conclusion, however—and Prime, Ward, and King also; for to conservative business men, speculators were as contemptible as to any one—perhaps more so.

The Loco Focos probably suffered less from direct external opposition than from penetration by enterprisers using Loco Foco language to mask their own efforts at defending or more probably supplanting the chartered banks. It was impossible to tell what a tirade against the latter might mean until one had looked up the speaker's sleeve. For example one candidate for Loco Foco leadership against the existing banks in New York declared that no other institution had "so strong a tendency to create and perpetuate the odious distinctions betwixt the rich and the poor as the paper money banks"; and that he "would sanction nothing but silver and gold as a circulating medium." But, he went on to say, "Bankers' notes of large denominations and bills of exchange, which must exist, can not come within my definition of circulating medium. My creed is to

[5] Raguet, *Free Trade Advocate* I (1829), 296-98, 315.

leave commercial men to manage their own affairs." Another who talked clockwise and counter-clockwise at the same time said it was the duty of the legislators "to protect the people against the evils of an expanded paper currency . . ." but, he went on to say in the spirit of those spotted Jeffersonians, David Henshaw, Roger Taney, and Amos Kendall, "the right of the people to compete with the incorporated banks in dealing in money and credit as currency ought to be restored to them by law." For the entrepreneurs the first step in this restoration, after destruction of the federal Bank, was repeal of the laws in restraint of banking.[6]

The earliest of these, in New York, had been enacted in 1804, when the Federalist legislature made it illegal for any person "unauthorized by law" to become a proprietor of a bank or member of a banking company. There had been at the time six chartered banks in the state besides an office of the Bank of the United States. In 1813 and 1818 the restraint had been restated and strengthened; and the law of 1818 not only forbade individuals to engage in banking but specifically included receipt of deposits in the forbidden function. In 1830 these prohibitions were renewed.[7]

The object of these acts according to the state Supreme Court in *New York Fireman Insurance Co.* v. *Ely* was to assure chartered banks "a monopoly of the rights and privileges granted to them, which had been encroached upon or infringed by private associations." In this case the state Supreme Court found that the insurance company had lent money illegally, and the finding was based in part on the reservation of banking to the incorporated banks. "Previous to the restraining acts," the Court said, "there was no power possessed by a bank not also allowed to individuals and private associations. They could in common issue notes, discount notes, and receive deposits; the only difference was that the former were not liable beyond their corporate property, while the latter were accountable in their persons and to the full extent of their private estate." But since 1804, because of the acts, banking had not been a common law right in New York; except when specifically authorized, it was illegal. There was a bounty of $500 for the conviction of every unauthorized banker, and promissory notes given to him for borrowed money were null and void.[8]

[6] Byrdsall, 75-76, 81-82.

[7] New York Statutes, *An Act to Restrain Unincorporated Banking Associations*, 6 April 1813; *An Act Relative to Banks, etc.*, 21 April 1818; Revised Statutes, 1830, I, 711-13; Jabez Hammond II, 448.

[8] *New York Fireman Insurance Company* v. *Ely*, 2 Cowen 678, 710, 712.

It is obvious that these restraining laws were a bulwark to the chartered banks and an offense to the democratic forces of enterprise which wished to get into the banking business themselves. To the Loco Focos, however, the restraining laws presented a dilemma. By supporting the restraints, they were loyal to their ideal of repressing and ultimately abolishing banks; but meanwhile, in effect, they were protecting the privileges of the chartered banks. If they flinched from doing this, they found themselves in the arms of the enterprisers who wanted the whole world thrown open to banks.

The ambiguity of the restraining laws—the uncertainty, that is, whether they restrained banking in the public interest or in the interest of the chartered banks—ran back through a century of legislation, Parliamentary, colonial, and state, to the Bubble Act itself. In that act the restraint evidently had been intended by its authors to make the privileges of the South Sea Company as secure as possible, since in effect it preserved the company from competition. But its terms were so sweeping and its tone so harsh that it was taken later —if not even at the time of its enactment—as a curse against all corporate business organization. This I described in the first chapter. The act was extended by Parliament to America in that spirit with the particular purpose of prohibiting the issue of paper money. That was likewise the purpose of the Virginia legislature, and it continued the restraint in 1776. But it was evidently not the purpose of the restraint by 1804 in New York. The purpose of the latter, like that of the Bubble Act in the first place, seems clearly to have been to protect existing privileges. It did protect them, and its beneficiaries fought for its retention accordingly; in Jabez Hammond's positive language years later, it gave "soulless institutions a power equal to the exclusive power of coining money."[9]

The ambiguity was increased when the revised state constitution of 1821 made "the assent of two-thirds of the members elected to each branch of the legislature . . . requisite to every bill . . . creating, continuing, altering, or renewing any body politic or corporate." To get a two-thirds majority of all possible votes was difficult. Though raised against any sort of incorporation, the measure according to contemporary evidence was antagonistic mainly to banks. It obstructed not only the chartering of new ones but also the amendment and renewal of charters already granted; thus it would be either difficult or impossible for a bank or any other corporation to increase

[9] Jabez Hammond II, 489.

its own capital even. But in the judgment of the traditional enemies of corporate privilege, the more discouraging the requirement, the better. Since corporations in general "were exceptions to the common law," the committee that proposed the requirement had said, and since "they could not be proceeded against in the ordinary way of prosecutions against individuals in courts of justice, they ought not to be increased but should be diminished as far as could be done consistently with the preservation of vested rights." And banks, of all corporations, were the worst. The disagreeable fact that all these restraints favored existing banks was the lesser of two evils.[10]

The principal and most immediate reason for this constitutional requirement, indeed, was the bribery which disgraced legislative action on bank charters. It had been especially scandalous when charters were enacted for the State Bank of Albany, 1803, the Merchants Bank of New York, 1805, and the Bank of America in 1812. It was the unconscionable behavior over the latter that had impelled the Governor to prorogue the Assembly. Yet in 1824, when the new constitutional safeguard against such things was but three years old and a charter to incorporate the Chemical Bank was being sought, it became apparent that the "only effect" of the new barrier was to increase the value of charters and hence "to increase the evil by rendering necessary a more extended system of corruption." The evidence found by a committee of the Assembly "afforded a most disgusting picture of the depravity of the members of the legislature. . . . The attempt to corrupt, and in fact, corruption itself, was not confined to any one party. It extended to individuals of all parties. . . . In short, it was evident that the foul and sickening scenes of 1812 had been re-enacted in 1824." Because of this experience, the proposal, already mentioned, was made the year following that banking monopoly be abolished by allowing any one to be a banker—a proposal that to the pure in heart sounded about as reasonable as a plan to abolish the crime of theft by allowing every one to steal.[11]

The proposal had been premature and in 1829 it was superseded by the Safety Fund, a more conservative measure wisely preferred by Mr Van Buren. But neither the Loco Focos, who sought the annihilation of banks, nor the enterprisers, who sought their mul-

---

10 *People* v. *Morris*, 13 Wendell 336.
11 Jabez Hammond I, 337; II, 178-79.

tiplication, would let the matter remain in the nice balance where the Albany Regency had it under the Safety Fund law. In 1835 another attempt was made to repeal the restraining laws, but the Loco Focos joined the chartered banks to defeat it, preferring monopoly to the flood.

III

Though the free-banking advocates were gaining ground, slowly but ineluctably, despite their failure to repeal the restraining laws in 1835, they had begun to face a more serious impediment in the state's constitution than in those laws. For the free-banking project contemplated enactment of a general law authorizing not one or two or any certain number of banking corporations but a wholly indefinite and unlimited number. And regardless of the democratic intent of such a measure, there was reason to suppose that it would come under the clause of the state constitution which stipulated that any laws creating bodies politic must be passed by a vote of two-thirds of all the legislators. The advocates of the measure could hope for no such support. Moreover Attorney General Bronson had rendered an opinion that, in effect, even a law which received a constitutional majority could not constitutionally authorize an indefinite number of bodies corporate to be validated, so to say, by some other agency at various times but was limited to the creation of one or a greater *definite* number at a time and by its own direct act. It looked, therefore, as if a requirement imperfectly intended to curb monopoly were about to prevent enactment of a measure intended to break it up completely. This, however, was on the assumption that the proposed free banks would be corporate—an assumption that was at once hopefully corrected by suggesting that they would not be corporations but "associations," with respect to which the constitution stipulated nothing. So far from being corporations, indeed, they were antithetic to them. Corporations, every one knew, were monopolies, and the new law was going to end monopolies. The free-bank people gained heart. In 1837 they succeeded in getting the restraining laws modified to the extent of permitting individuals to receive deposits and make discounts. This was less than they had attempted in 1835, when they sought repeal, but it was an achievement, not a failure. They also prepared and introduced free-banking measures styling the proposed free banks associations, not corporations. These failed to pass, but they gained more support than before.[12]

The main opposition to the free-banking people now seems to have come from the Democratic party regulars, who continued to defend the chartered banks and resist the proposed legislation. The Albany Regency was so thoroughly identified with the chartered banks and the Safety Fund system that it could hope for no survival apart from them. Accordingly, the state banking commissioners in a report, 27 January 1837, urged the Assembly not to enact the free-banking bill. The state of New York, they said, had "the best banking system in the world," and no more currency or banks were needed.

"Another plan which has been proposed," they said of the new bill, "is to surrender *all* legislative control over the subject, and permit every one, or any number who may choose to associate under certain general regulations, to enjoy all the privileges of banking now possessed by our banking institutions. This is also urged as a measure beneficial to trade, not injurious to the currency; and entitled to favor as the antagonist of the monopoly of banking. By some it is claimed as a natural right wrongfully withheld by the Government."[13]

This protest could scarcely have worried the free-banking champions; but a fresh and more serious impediment was put in their way a little later by the state's Attorney General, Samuel Beardsley, a new incumbent, whose opinion of the altered free-banking measure, authorizing "associations," had been requested. He delivered a blast of sound legal objections. First, the proposed "associations" would be corporations in fact no matter what name was given them. Second, the constitution did not permit the legislature to authorize an indefinite and unlimited number of corporations but only some specific number. Third, any law authorizing any number of corporations would be invalid unless given the affirmative vote of two-thirds of *all* the members of both houses of the Assembly—which of course might be substantially different from the ordinary two-thirds majority of all members present and voting. There was nothing in this to weaken the appeal of free banking or create affection for the Regency and the chartered banks, but there was much in it in the

---

[12] New York Senate Document 4 (1835), 13; Cleaveland, 49, n18; Jabez Hammond II, 464-65; Gallatin III, 428.

[13] 25th Congress, 2nd Session, HD 79, p. 235; New York State Bank Commissioners, *Report*, 27 January 1837.

form of practical, legislative difficulty for the free-bank advocates to overcome.[14]

However, this technical advantage for the New York party regulars and chartered banks was at once offset by the advantage which the free-banking cause gained from Michigan's enactment of a free-banking measure, March 1837, that was a copy of the one then before the New York Assembly. And whatever advantage the regulars and the chartered banks still had, vanished completely in the general stoppage of specie payments by the banks in May. It was a fine predicament for the chartered banks to be in—a fine predicament for the party regulars, the Regency, the Safety Fund, "the best banking system in the world." Nothing could have occurred more to the advantage of the free-bank people, who had a program of reform all ready based on the evils of privilege and the virtues of democracy. In New York the Democrats suffered a sharper embarrassment than in Washington, for the Regency was much more closely associated with the state system than the Van Buren administration was with the state banks, and even the pets, country-wide. But the state elections that fall foreshadowed the overturn in the national elections three years later, for despite President Van Buren's effort to rally Loco Foco support in his messages to Congress that fall on the shortcomings of banks, the Whigs won from the Democrats the lead held by the latter for years in the New York Assembly. This rejection of him by his own state within a year of his succession to the Presidency was sad business, but it was largely the result of the inflation of bank credit, stimulated by overthrow of the federal Bank, which he as much as any one—perhaps more—had instigated in the interest of New York's banks. Through what anfractuosities of his subtle mind and from what wrestlings of a Jeffersonian conscience there emerged the principle of "divorce of bank and state" and his adherence henceforth to Loco Foco doctrine—or what seemed to be Loco Foco doctrine—I do not know; but, leaving aside the tradition of Mr Van Buren's ingenuity, the pressure of forces and circumstances in this period was too complex for one to believe without careful confirmation that the change in Mr Van Buren's political views with respect to banking was as simple as it may seem. In any case, the "state" meant by him when he recommended a divorce of bank and state was not the state of New York but the federal government, and the effect to be reckoned on was a

---

[14] New York Assembly Document 303 (1837), 6; Document 304 (1837), 7.

diminution of the federal government's contact with the main currents of business activity to the advantage of the Union's individual members. The plan was a clever one but not clever enough to re-elect Mr Van Buren—or perhaps too clever, for it was probably never well understood till too late.

The incumbent Governor of New York, William L. Marcy, was a Democrat, but he interpreted the defeat of his party in the 1837 elections to mean disapproval not only of the chartered banks for having stopped specie payments but of his party's protection of their virtual monopoly of banking in the state. Accordingly he recommended to the new Whig legislature that it enact a free-banking measure such as the previous Democratic legislature had rejected. However, he thought the banks to be formed under such a law must be considered corporations and that though the state constitution did not explicitly forbid a law authorizing an indefinite number of corporations, it did plainly require that the law, to be valid, be passed by a two-thirds vote of all the legislators. But the advocates of free banking preferred the view that the proposed banking "associations" were not to be considered bodies corporate and that in consequence the law could be enacted by a simple two-thirds of the legislators voting. The measure was accordingly introduced. It was accompanied by a committee report, prolix and rhetorical, telling how bad inflation was, blaming it on the chartered banks, now in suspension, testifying to "the spontaneous recoil of every advocate of free institutions from the paralyzing grasp of monopolies," and implying that if banking were made a business open to all, inflation would never recur.[15]

The bill was taken up and put in shape by Abijah Mann, who nine years before had had charge of the Safety Fund measure and had since served in Congress as an active Jacksonian enemy of the federal Bank.* It passed the Assembly 18 March 1838, two days

---

* Abijah Mann is the hero of a story that when he was in Congress and member of a committee appointed to investigate the federal Bank, the committee was refused admittance to the latter's offices. Thereupon Abijah Mann hired some men with picks and shovels and started to tunnel his way in. This, it is said, so daunted Nicholas Biddle that he let the committee enter by the door. Why the Congressmen, instead of obtaining a proper writ, risked getting dirt on their clothes creeping through a tunnel, and why, if they were without a proper writ, Mr Biddle did not get a warrant against them

15 New York Senate Document 68 (1838), 1.

after the bank convention in New York City decided to resume specie payments 10 May. But, as had been apprehended, it failed to receive the votes of two-thirds of all the members of the Assembly. It had only a two-thirds majority of those voting, most of the Democrats being loyal to the existing banks and voting against it. So it seemed likely that if some future court decided the free banks authorized by it were corporations, there would be trouble, since it would follow that the law had not received the number of votes required to validate it. There also remained the question whether the constitution in any event permitted the authorization of an indefinite number of corporations. The majority who voted for the law, however, contended that it authorized not corporations but associations. And there, for a while, the matter lay.[16]

Legislatively, the Loco Focos seem to have been demoralized by the abhorrent alternative of siding with the chartered banks against free banks or with free banks against chartered ones, and their part in the law-making is obscure. Outdoors, however, they were still active; they were prominent in the public parks and in the runs on the New York banks that preceded the May 1837 suspension. In New York they seemed more formidable than they really were, and though they furnished most of the arguments used to establish free banking, the arguments were from their point of view misused. It was their misfortune to suppose that the Jacksonian assault on the federal Bank was really an assault on the "money power" and prelusive to the total abolition of banking instead of its immense expansion. In New York, confused and disillusioned, they mostly crept back into the Democratic fold, where they had arisen. In the West, as will be seen, they suppressed banking for a time with remarkable success. Yet in the country as a whole, thenceforth, the free-banking law under which the typical banks of Wall Street and eventually of the entire economy conducted their affairs was expounded and praised in characteristic Loco Foco language as a famous popular triumph over monopoly, privilege, and the money power. The continued existence of the money power was not explained.

---

on a charge of trespass and committing a nuisance—all this is left by Mr Mann's biographer to conjecture. *Appleton's Cyclopedia of American Biography* IV, 189.

[16] Jabez Hammond II, 484.

IV

But the law was barely a year old when in 1839 one of the free banks authorized by it sued a delinquent debtor, and the debtor's defense was that the bank had no legal existence. He pleaded that the law authorized the creation of an *indefinite* number of corporations at the pleasure of individuals, that it was therefore "unconstitutional and void," that the plaintiff bank as a creature of that law was itself "consequently illegal and void," and that a debt to a creditor whose existence was void must itself be void. The case was *Thomas* v. *Dakin*, the bank having sued in the name of its president, Anson Thomas—a procedure which was one of the things supposedly distinguishing the free-banking associations from incorporated banks. The case was heard by the state Supreme Court.[17]

In answer to this plea, the arguments of the bank's counsel leaned heavily on tradition. It was contended that the free banks were not corporations, because they were not creations of the sovereign power but of an administrative bureau and because the law gave them no name and no power to use a seal or pass by-laws. It was contended that an individual person authorized by the act to engage in banking certainly was not a corporation—and this point was later upheld.*
Counsel pointed to the specific exemption of shareholders from personal liability and to the specific grant of perpetual succession—characteristics possessed by corporations inherently without need of bestowal—and asked, "why such a provision if these associations are thought or intended to be corporations?" As for the constitution of 1821, free banks were "a new mode of union, unknown at the time of the adoption of the constitution, and falling within no description or definition of 'bodies corporate.'" The free-banking act was, in effect, counsel contended, merely a repeal of existing restraints on banking; it was wholly in accord with the spirit of the constitution

---

* In *Cuyler and Sexton* v. *Sanford*, 8 Barbour 225. The state Supreme Court said (p. 230): "It is sufficient to mention one indispensable characteristic of a corporation to show that an individual banker can not be one; and that is its principle of succession and perpetuity for the period of existence assigned to it by its creator." In 1857 the bank superintendent reported that though individuals had been permitted to operate banks, he considered the practice anomalous, objectionable, and of doubtful legality. There were then about forty individuals reported as "banks." 34th Congress, 3d Session, HD 87, pp. 111-112, 124-125.

17 *Thomas* v. *Dakin*, 22 Wendell 9.

in striking at monopoly, and "not within the mischief contemplated by it."

"Opening at once, to a whole community, the business of banking, allowing all to bank who choose, is a very different measure, rests on entirely different principles of policy, and must be followed by entirely different results, from increasing from time to time, under a strong external pressure upon the legislature, stimulated by individual interest, private and exclusive corporate privileges for banking...." In setting up the new system, counsel said, the legislature had carefully avoided authorizing corporations; and he insisted that "a judicial tribunal should hesitate in declaring that a legislative department had done that which they did not intend to do and expressly declared they had not done."

The Court decided otherwise. It held that the free banks were corporations. They had, it said, the essential powers and faculties of corporations, and therefore they were corporations no matter what name the legislators gave them.

This opinion, which was legalistic and reactionary in form, was pregnant and revolutionary in substance. It threw a stubborn interpretation of the constitution athwart the path of the popular will; but it also put the corporate form of enterprise in a very new light. It established an identity between two things that were generally regarded as antithetical—it asserted that the new instrumentalities of individualistic enterprise were legally one with the old instrumentalities of monopoly, however much they might differ in their advocates' opinion. By the same token it exhibited the corporation as a democratic device, with which *laisser faire* was to accomplish more than it ever could otherwise. This, it is obvious, was significant for enterprise in general and not for banking alone. And yet, though the Court found the free banks to be corporations, it did not find them to be unconstitutional; for it said, contrary to the earlier opinions of two Attorneys General, that the constitution allowed authorization of an indefinite number of corporations. There was another question, however, which the Court avoided: it being granted that the banks were corporations and that the law could have been constitutionally adopted, had it been so adopted in fact? It was notorious, of course, that it had not; but the Court contented itself with a statement that the law was constitutional if passed by a two-thirds vote and that one must presume that it had been so passed. "We must clearly do so until the fact is denied by plea. The requisite constitutional solemnities in passing an act which has been published in the statute book, must always be presumed to have taken place until the contrary shall be clearly shown."

In January 1840, a few weeks after *Thomas* v. *Dakin,* two new cases identical with it in issue came before the state Supreme Court. In each a free bank was suing a debtor for payment of a note, and in each the defense demurred that the banks were corporations and that they were formed under a law that was unconstitutional. In both, as in the previous case, the Court gave judgment to the plaintiffs, accepting the defendant's contention that the banks were corporations but rejecting their contention that they were unconstitutional. In both, that is, the banks won but on grounds that boded ill for their constitutionality. These two new cases, *Warner* v. *Beers* and *Bolander* v. *Stevens*, were immediately taken by writs to the Court for the Correction of Errors, which was then the highest court in the state. It comprised the state Senators, the President of the Senate, the Chancellor, and the justices of the Supreme Court. The Chancellor and Supreme Court justices could vote only on cases that had not previously come before them, and the president of the Senate voted only when there was a tie. All, however, could join in the discussion of cases. The members of the Senate, of course, were under no like restraint, and could vote as judges on matters on which they had previously voted as legislators.[18]

The pleas before the Court for the Correction of Errors in the two new cases were again that the banks were corporations and that the law was unconstitutional in authorizing an unlimited number of corporations, but there was also included the point omitted in the earlier case, viz., that the law had actually lacked a constitutional majority. Counsel for the debtors urged that "This court ought to, and will, as the Supreme Court should have done, take judicial notice without plea by what majority the act to authorize the business of banking was passed." The fact, he said, that the act was "published in the session laws by the printer to the state without the certificates of the manner of its passage, which appear on the act in the office of the Secretary of State, furnishes no reason for the court's indulging presumptions against the truth, or omitting to look into the original act in the office, or shutting their eyes against its publication in the state paper, or for professing ignorance of what they are presumed to know and do in fact know."

18 *Warner* v. *Beers, Bolander* v. *Stevens,* 23 Wendell 103; Scott, 322-24.

This language challenged the members of the Court directly and personally, reminding them of what had happened among them as members of the Senate. Yet the challenge was eluded. In formulating their judgment, they followed the argument of Chancellor Walworth that the constitution was "not in all cases to be construed literally," but "according to its spirit and intent, so as to carry into effect the will of the convention and of the people." The Court must contemplate "the evil intended to be remedied" by the constitution. This evil was monopoly. The constitutional restriction was intended to guard against the increase of corporations with "exclusive privileges not enjoyed by the citizens at large" and "placed beyond the reach of general legislation either for a modification of their powers or the repeal of their charters." The law of 1838, according to the Chancellor, did not conflict with this intent. The constitutional restriction had "clearly failed to secure . . . the benefits proposed," and it was therefore all the more improper to make it interfere with a law wholly congenial to it in spirit or intent—a law "which neither creates monopolies, nor secures to any individuals privileges which may not be enjoyed in the same manner by all others."

This was soundly and factually reasoned, save for the conclusion, which ought to have been not that the law was constitutional but that the constitution was at fault and should be amended so that the law might be constitutional. Instead, following the Chancellor both right and wrong, the Court of Errors affirmed the judgment of the Supreme Court that the two banks were entitled to recover the money they had lent but repudiated its opinion that they were corporations. It "resolved" that the act of 18 April 1838, authorizing the business of banking, was valid and constitutionally enacted, although it may not have received the assent of two-thirds of the legislators. It next resolved that the banks formed under the law were "*not* bodies politic or corporate, within the spirit and meaning of the constitution."

This was intended to put the Supreme Court in its place and settle the point that free banks were not corporations; but it failed. For the same year, 1840, the Supreme Court repeated, in *Delafield* v. *Kinny*, that the free banks *were* corporations. Then one of the banks in Watertown, hearing that it was not a corporation, declined to pay a corporate tax. When this case came up, *The People* v. *Assessors of Watertown*, 1841, the Supreme Court, uncowed, declared that the bank was a corporation, regardless of what the Court for the Correction of Errors might resolve. The Chief Justice, Greene

C. Bronson, used these astounding words: "An association under our general laws for a village library, or to tan hides, possesses all the essential attributes of a corporation in as great perfection as the Bank of England or the East India Company." He said further: "It may be true, as has been argued, that the legislature intended to make a legal being and give it all the essential attributes of a corporate body, and yet that it should not be a corporation. That the legislature could not do. . . . The constitution of things—the order of nature—forbids it. Human powers are not equal to the task of changing a thing by merely changing its name." In the three years following, the Supreme Court reaffirmed its position three times: in *Willoughby* v. *Comstock*, in *The People* v. *Supervisors of Niagara*, and in *The Matter of the Bank of Dansville*. In the second of these cases, again, a bank resisted payment of a corporate tax. The decision was against it, and it appealed. The Court of Errors, in 1844, notwithstanding its declaration that the free banks were not corporations within the meaning of the constitution, now found that they were corporations within the meaning of the tax law.[19]

This was a dangerous distinction, it played directly into the Supreme Court's hands, and the Supreme Court made the most of it in 1845, when, in *De Bow* v. *The People*, the familiar questions were again presented. De Bow was a person who had been convicted in a lower court of having in his possession counterfeited notes of the Bank of Warsaw, New York, and of passing them with fraudulent intent. His defense was that the act under which the bank was formed was unconstitutional and void because it had not received a two-thirds majority, and that there was no body existing in law by the name of the Bank of Warsaw capable of being defrauded.[20]

The Supreme Court agreed with him. Chief Justice Bronson paid his respects in advance to the Court of Errors by declaring that "no judge could ever respect himself after holding that these banks are corporations within the meaning of the tax law and yet that they are not corporations within the meaning of the constitution." Moreover he said irreverently that the higher court's resolution to the effect that the free banks were not corporations within the meaning

[19] *Delafield* v. *Kinny*, 24 Wendell 345; *The People* v. *Assessors of Watertown*, 1 Hill 616; *Willoughby* v. *Comstock*, 3 Hill 389; *The People* v. *Supervisors of Niagara*, 4 Hill 20; *The Matter of the Bank of Dansville*, 6 Hill 370; *Supervisors of Niagara* v. *The People*, 7 Hill 504; Cleaveland, 297-325.

[20] *De Bow* v. *The People*, 1 Denio 9.

and spirit of the constitution, was merely "entitled to some weight as expressing the views of several gentlemen of great respectability on a question of public importance," but was not to be considered a judicial decision. He also pointed out that the question whether the law were constitutional could at last be determined. "It is now settled that it is the business of the court to determine what is statute as well as common law; and for that purpose the judges may and should, if necessary, look beyond the printed statute book and examine the original engrossed bills on file in the office of the secretary of state; and it seems that journals kept by the two houses may also be consulted." The conclusion of the Court was emphatic. "Having examined and ascertained that the general banking law did not have the assent of two-thirds of the members of either house, it follows that so far as it authorized the forming of corporations or associations it is utterly void; and the banking companies which have been organized under it have no legal existence."

These were major words. They deprived half the banks in the state of legal being. And they were confirmed in the next case that came up, *Gifford* v. *Livingston,* where a bank sued for payment of a note, the defendant demurred that the bank had no legal existence, and the Supreme Court held accordingly. So far as that court was concerned the banks could neither defend themselves from counterfeiters nor collect what was due them from debtors; there was only the slender comfort that being without legal existence they might not have to pay taxes.[21]

This case also went to the Court for the Correction of Errors, 1845, and that court again bestrode the issue, under the Chancellor's ingenious leadership. The Chancellor said that in *Warner* v. *Beers* it had been decided that the banks were not corporations within the meaning and spirit of the constitution, and that if ever there was a case in which the principle of *stare decisis* was to be applied, it should be in this. Echoing the United States Supreme Court's opinion in the *Briscoe* case eight years before when it recoiled, startled, from the idea that the state banks, which had a capital of $400,000,000 and supplied nearly all the country's circulating medium, could be unconstitutional, the Chancellor spoke of the millions of dollars that had been invested in free-bank stock, of the notes of the banks in circulation "to an immense amount," of the loss to the creditors of the banks if the banks were to be found without legal existence, and of

---

21 *Gifford* v. *Livingston,* 2 Denio 380.

the other existing legislation that must be invalid if the free-banking act were found to be unconstitutional. The Chancellor had the Senators with him. They continued to hold that the banks were not corporations within the meaning and spirit of the constitution. They declared that in *Warner* v. *Beers* it had been decided that the free-banking act was "valid and was constitutionally enacted, although it may not have received the assent of two-thirds of the members elected to each branch of the legislature; and that the decision in that case is conclusive."*

This decision, 30 December 1845, was one of the last pronounced by the Court for the Correction of Errors, for by the new constitution of the year following that court was abolished, and a Court of Appeals, purely judicial, replaced it. The new constitution also omitted the requirement of a two-thirds majority for all laws creating corporations. It stipulated in Article VIII that the term "corporation" should include associations and joint stock companies; and that "the legislature shall have no power to pass any act granting any special charter for banking purposes; but corporations or associations may be formed for such purposes under general laws."[22]

This settled a question that had been in doubt for a matter of eight years, during which time what the law was depended on which court the question was before. The free banks had survived a deliberate and well-considered judgment that they were without legal existence; and the corporate form of business organization, as a result of insistence on its legal essentials, had completely changed its political skin—it had become dissociated from monopoly and identified with *laisser faire* and individualism. In 1850 Chief Justice Bronson, now sitting on the new Court of Appeals, said of the free banking associations that they had been adjudged corporations directly and expressly, by the highest courts in the state. "They are

---

* The New York *Tribune* referred to the decision of the Court of Errors in *Gifford* v. *Livingston* in an editorial in its issue of 3 January 1846, under the caption, "All Right with the General Banking Law." It said: "This decision is final, there being no higher tribunal to appeal to. So the General Banking Law stands firm. We regard this as a most just and salutary decision and congratulate the People of our State that this long vexed question is at last put at rest."

In its issue of 3 May 1845, the *Tribune* had noticed and condemned in its commercial and financial news an attempt, allegedly of the chartered banks, to get the general banking law repealed.

[22] Scott, 324.

not corporations in a qualified sense, as within the intent and meaning of some particular statute; but are corporations to all intents and purposes. If anything can be settled by judicial decisions this is settled." The learned Justice, one observes, did not cite the constitution's statement to the same effect. It was presumably in his mind that the law is not what the constitution says but what the judges say the constitution says.[23]

Since the free banks were corporations, the term "association" was now otiose. Yet it remained in the law, defined as the synonym of the word whose antonym it had originally been. And the state and national banking laws in America still, over a century later, denominate banks "associations" as the original free-banking statute did, though the only present effect of doing so is to raise a question and necessitate an answer.*

It is not often that a conflict between statute and constitution is resolved by altering the constitution; and that it was done in this instance indicates the strength of the spirit of free enterprise. Even the judges who repeatedly condemned the statute were in sympathy with its purposes. In *De Bow* v. *The People* Justice Bronson had acknowledged, as had many other jurists, that the constitutional restriction frustrated its own social aims. He had said, "I hope the day is not very distant when this and other kindred laws which needlessly shackle men in their lawful pursuits will either be greatly modified or wholly erased from the statute books." But "where the constitution speaks in unequivocal terms and tends to no great evil or absurdity it should be followed at all events—leaving the work of making amendments to the people, to whom alone it rightfully belongs." Thus the path was cleared for the free banks by the Justice's conservative denial of their plea that they were not corporations. For being corporations they were and are better off than if they had continued as an anomalous legal entity, neither fish, flesh, nor fowl.

---

* A good many national banks, being required by law to include the word "national" in their titles, use also the word "association" in order to retain an older, original name intact. Thus, for example, the New Haven Bank National Association can comply with the law without losing the value of the name it has borne for a century and a half and still popularly bears— "the New Haven Bank." Likewise the "Bank of America," San Francisco, is formally the Bank of America National Trust and Savings Association.

[23] *Gillet* v. *Moody*, 3 Comstock 485.

V

Looked back upon more than a century later, New York's free-banking act of 1838 was a remarkable measure, in which there converged a number of trends of wide significance.

For one thing, it marked a stage in the evolution of laws from individual and special enactments into general statutes of uniform and comprehensive nature. It was not the first of general laws, but it was one of the most important of the first ones. The trend toward uniformity had begun with the earliest charter enactments, which had soon fallen into a set pattern, followed by charter after charter year after year. Often a single act had incorporated several banks at once. This trend had gone further in a revision of the statutes in 1827, which embodied provisions uniform in their applicability to banks. It went still further in the Safety Fund act of 1829. A much shorter development had brought about a general definition of banking powers in the new act. The earliest bank charters had not defined banking powers; an act creating a corporation and calling it a bank gave it in blank whatever powers a bank was supposed to have, as if those powers were somewhere defined. But they were not defined —certainly not in New York and probably not elsewhere—till 1825 when the charter of the Commercial Bank of Albany authorized it "to carry on the business of banking by discounting bills, notes, and other evidences of debt; by receiving deposits; by buying gold and silver bullion and foreign coins; by buying and selling bills of exchange, and by issuing bills, notes, and other evidences of debt"; and granted "no other powers whatever." The definition passed into other acts, was included in the free-banking law, and is still basic in American banking legislation, state and federal.[24]

For another thing, the free-banking law departed from the executive type of enactment, complete in itself, so to speak, and became purely legislative in that it defined certain powers to be exercised in designated circumstances and by an administrative agency to which it delegated the execution of what it authorized. "A general law," it was stated a little later by a Michigan court, "by which individuals . . . could multiply indefinitely monied corporations was unknown in the history of legislation, either in this state or any other state or country. It is an invention of modern times." In the absence of such a law, as in the contemporary absence of general divorce

---

[24] *The People* v. *The President, etc. of the Manhattan Company*, 9 Wendell 351; Cleaveland, xvi, xxvii.

laws, for example, a special act of the legislature was necessary in order to incorporate a bank as to divorce a husband and wife. The appearance of such laws on the statute books was attended by the addition of one administrative agency after another to the governmental structure, with results evident in the size and complexity of 20th century government.[25]

Again, the free-banking law surrendered to democracy and to *laisser faire* a business hitherto set apart in general estimation and by special laws privileged and restricted. Banking had got into this peculiar position by accident. It was because Alexander Hamilton, being in need of a government Bank to fit into the structure of fiscal powers he was designing for the federal government, drew up a plan, based on the charter of the Bank of England, which was so well done that it became at once the nearly universal pattern of American bank charters and of Canadian charters too. This occurred in spite of the fact that the Bank of England and the Bank of the United States were properly unique in their economies, each being *the* government bank; whereas the ordinary banks required for the private business of the country should have been modeled on the private banking houses of the Old World. But being private and without the documentation which described the Bank of England, these were too little known to be imitated. They represented individuals, partnerships, and families of wealth in established and mature economies where the uses to which money could be put were tried and known. In America capital had to be scraped together collectively and every adventitious aid to that end had to be availed of, including particularly the aid of government, in the form of a corporate charter, at the least. This was the more expedient, because banks were needed because they created money, the money they created was generally recognized only in the form of bank notes, and to give the notes acceptability a corporate charter was important. And because money was so important, laws governing the banks that provided it were necessary. All these things had worked together to give banking in America a peculiarly public nature that it lacked in Europe. And hence Albert Gallatin, familiar with banking as it was conducted privately in the Old World, and inclined philosophically to *laisser faire* besides, could think it anomalous that banking should not be at all a private business in America. He had denounced

---

[25] *Green* v. *Graves*, 1 Douglas 355.

the restraining laws accordingly for denying to Americans the right to engage in banking without charters of incorporation.[26]

Mr Gallatin's sentiments were better informed and qualified than most men's but otherwise substantially the same. The traditional dislike of special privileges, with or without special responsibilities, was sharpened among men at large by a tardy realization that America had cultivated an abuse which even the Old World—that hive of injustices—did not know. The result was a revolution that in common with other revolutions wasted more than it accomplished and instead of building intelligently on what had been attained fell back as far as possible into the primitive and crude. "The people," according to a court opinion, had "demanded that the right to deal in money should be as free in its exercise as that of dealing in wheat or in cotton bales, having always a due regard to the soundness and safety of the currency." It might well be argued that this approach to the problem was entirely wrong, any disposition to overlook the unique character of money and put it in the same class with wheat and cotton being bound to lead to trouble; but with that consideration aside and with the criticism confined to what was purposed, there is still the objection that "due regard to the soundness and safety of the currency" was not had in the free-banking act.[27]

Such regard was sought, of course, in the requirement that notes issued by free banks be secured by the pledge of bonds lodged with the supervisory authorities. The bank notes were to be prepared under the control of state officials and to be obtained from them by the banks upon surrender of bonds equal in dollar amount to the bank notes. Rigidly limiting the issue of notes to the amount of bonds pledged to secure them seemed at the time to be a safeguard against inflation as well as a guaranty of individual note issues. But as such it amounted to nothing. It merely put a movable limit on the amount of notes each bank could issue—for the more bonds it bought, the more notes it could put out and the more bonds it could buy—and it put no limit on the number of banks. On the contrary, it multiplied them. And most important of all, it did absolutely nothing about deposit liabilities, which were a far more dangerous medium of inflation.

Moreover, even as a guaranty and when they were "good," as the bonds accepted in New York usually were, their market value in a

26 Gallatin III, 428.
27 *Warner* v. *Beers,* 23 Wendell 178.

period when banks were in trouble was apt to be low and to be driven still lower by their sale in large amounts at the hands of bank supervisors seeking funds for the redemption of defaulted issues. Knowledge that the fund existed might make the public suppose itself secure, and to that degree make it secure, but the pledged bonds otherwise could do nothing to prevent suspension and little to mitigate it. Altogether, the free-banking law was a step backward from the Safety Fund, not forward. But it was a great thing politically. It was all things to all men. It promised more business opportunities, more banks, more money, and protection for the public. It also established a new market for bonds at a time when enthusiasm for public improvements was producing a flood tide of bond issues.*

It was an oddity of the New York law that though governed and animated by the principle that control of bank credit could be achieved by requiring bank notes to be secured by the pledge and deposit of bonds, dollar for dollar, it also recognized a rival principle, then barely emerging into notice, that control should be sought through the medium of required reserves. This, of course, is the medium that in the 20th century prevails, after a long and complex evolution. Following a Virginia statute of the year before, the New York law required each free bank to keep specie on hand in ratio to its note circulation. But the ratio was only twelve and one-half per cent, the requirement was tacked on at the end of the statute, as if by chance, and two years later it was repealed.[28]

The new law was taken to enthusiastically. The number of free-banking associations set up in the first three years nearly doubled the number of banks in the state. A hundred and thirty-four were chartered in about twenty months—and this in a period when times were hard. Over fifty applicants for free-bank charters were ready in the first six months, and how sanguine they were about the future is indicated by requests in all but four cases for charters to run at least 100 years; fourteen sought a corporate life of 400 years or more, and of these, two specified 1,000 years and one 4,050 years. But of the eighty or so first organized, more than twenty failed to survive even three years. Mr Gallatin saw in the statute "internal evidence that it was prepared by speculators." Thomas Wren Ward said that there were "openings to fraud" in it and that the associa-

---

* At first the law authorized the pledge of mortgages also, but it was soon amended to authorize the pledge of bonds only.

[28] Cleaveland, 106, 116.

tions it authorized were not intended "for investing capital so much as for speculative purposes and borrowing money." He also thought it likely that similar laws would be enacted in other states and so far as he could see at the moment "there is no danger from the establishment of *good* banks under them." He expected frauds and losses.[29]

Furthermore, both the terms of the law and its administration gave unreasonable advantages to the new banks as compared with the old. Being under a political condemnation as aristocratic monopolies, the chartered banks got much the same vindictive hounding that the Bank of the United States and the United States Bank of Pennsylvania had got, though their alleged monopoly was a transparent fiction. It was "extraordinary," Albert Gallatin said, that intelligent men should still think the chartered banks had exclusive privileges. It had merely been far harder for them to get charters than it now was, they could do less than the free banks could, and they were under more restrictions and burdens. They had to redeem their own notes at par, for example, whereas the free banks could buy both the chartered banks' notes and their own at a discount, which was very profitable. Yet whenever a chartered bank sought to renew its charter, reduce its capital, or even move from one address to another, it was carped at as a "privileged body" and told to convert itself into a "free association"; which, however, it could not do without dissolution and loss of corporate identity.[30]

In these circumstances the capitalists who already had charters were properly punished for their possession of them and made to realize that the new ones authorized by the free-banking act were better. The result was that the banking community shifted as fast as it could from aristocracy to democracy. Even those who wished their banking to be conducted properly found nothing in the new act that would force their banks to be bad. The most important of these new organizations was the Bank of Commerce, New York City. The law was only about three weeks old when Prime, Ward, and King reported to the Barings, 16 May 1838, a disposition on the part of business men with whom they were congenial to avail themselves of the privileges granted by the law, which, they said, "are of the largest character and extent." The firm was inclined to join in forming a bank such as the statute authorized, to be "under

[29] Redlich, 202; Gallatin III, 434, 438, 443; Baring Papers, OC, 12 January, 21 February 1839.
[30] Gallatin III, 442, 444.

the management of able and experienced and prudent men . . . , one to be hemmed in and kept under control, yet with full utility, upon old fashioned principles." In January 1839 Thomas Wren Ward of Boston, despite his first misgivings, advised the Barings to take $100,000 of stock in the new bank; he was taking $30,000 to $40,000 himself. "I really think," he wrote from New York, "that this institution will be important in keeping the banks in order. The Bank of America and the Manhattan and the Bank of Commerce by uniting can keep the other banks in this city right and I think act strongly on Philadelphia and Boston for the same object." The Barings' interest in the Bank of Commerce, he wrote a week later, would tend to identify them "more and more with the safe and solid part of the city of New York and of the country at large. . . . It will be a conservative money bank in which your friends, correspondents, and others, the best men in the city of New York, have a large stake. . . . The bank will have its London account with you but will not require a credit and will not issue bonds." These prognoses were correct. The Bank of Commerce, New York, was for nearly a century to follow one of the most prominent and honored in the country; in 1929 it was amalgamated with the Guaranty Trust Company.[31]

Free banking in time became general throughout the country. It was the culmination of Jacksonian banking policy, which was instigated by Martin Van Buren on behalf of New York and began with destruction of the federal Bank, then housed invidiously in Philadelphia. It proceeded with transfer of the federal funds to the books of state banks at the hands of Amos Kendall and the Secretary of the Treasury, R. B. Taney. At the same time, Jacksonian policy encouraged the formation of still more state banks, the business being singularly profitable in Secretary Taney's words, and suitable for all classes to participate in. Free banking was furthered in the *Briscoe* case, which judicially quieted the doubt of state bank constitutionality. It was a program with two underlying aims: first, to advance states' rights in the economic field at the cost of federal powers, and, second, to diffuse and expand the opportunities for business enterprise. This policy was formulated in the spirit of *laisser faire* and expressed in the vocabulary of agrarianism. It was a belated triumph of Thomas Jefferson over Alexander Hamilton, in a way. Hamilton,

[31] Baring Papers, OC, 16 May 1838, 31 January 1839, 6 February 1839; Knox, *History of Banking*, 256.

however, would have recognized the defeat far more readily than Jefferson could have recognized the victory, for it involved a misuse of Jeffersonian ideas and less a Jeffersonian correction of the Hamiltonian structure than a replacement of it with something anarchic. The results of this Jacksonian revolution were obvious in monetary inflation, in speculation, in wasted labor, in business failures, in abandonment of an efficient means of credit control, and in corruption of a sound monetary system. They also included the final shift of financial primacy to Wall Street and the incubating of a new and bigger generation of millionaires.

It is perhaps ironic that gentlemen in Wall Street thought banking needed to be regulated and deliberately sought to have the Bank of Commerce do what the Bank of the United States had done. But it was only the more conservative who thought so. And more than size was needed. The Bank of Commerce was not a government bank and was under no such impulsion to regulate the banking system as the Bank of the United States had been, with an immense stream of federal revenue coming to it in the form of bank checks and bank notes that had to be converted into funds expendable anywhere from the St Croix to the Mississippi. To be sure, like the Suffolk Bank in Boston, the Bank of Commerce in New York could have built up a central banking responsibility even without the impulsion the federal Bank had been under and without the peculiar status in the London money market derived by the Bank of England from its charter and its century and a half of life. But the task would have been difficult at best, and the interests of the bank's managers were governed by greater opportunities in other directions.[32]

Mr John Jacob Astor and Mr Gallatin were considered for the presidency of the Bank of Commerce but a younger man, John A. Stevens, was chosen after a temporary tenure by Samuel Ward of Prime, Ward, and King. The bank issued no notes, though organized under a law of which note issue was a cardinal concern. Its influence on American banking was largely exercised through close relations with banks throughout the country which maintained their New York accounts with it. The bank's capital was $5,000,000, which, as Wall Street's best judgment of what its most important bank should have, throws a painful light on the fantasies prevailing in Philadelphia, where the United States Bank of Pennsylvania was still wallowing under a capital of $35,000,000.

[32] Raguet, *Financial Register* ii, 7, 9, 10, 12.

But New York's free-banking law had also given Mr Biddle an opportunity. It was in May 1838, as soon after enactment of the law as Prime, Ward, and King had expressed to the Barings an interest in the proposed Bank of Commerce, that certain New Yorkers not in Prime, Ward, and King's circle had got an invitation off to Mr Biddle, to help provide New York with a banking association under the terms of the new law, to be "managed with the same enlarged views and the same enlightened and liberal policy" as the United States Bank. Prime, Ward, and King were contemptuous of this rival project, which they considered speculative and bound for trouble. Mr Biddle, they told the Barings, had solicited the invitation, which is very probable. Biddle wrote Daniel Webster that the United States Bank was going to have an "agency" in New York City which he thought would "do as well as the new monster projected under the presidency of Mr Gallatin." But it could not legally be a branch, and instead an association called the "Bank of the United States in New York" was organized. It was owned by George Griswold and Richard Alsop and was under contract as an agency of the bank in Philadelphia, which paid all its expenses and a compensation of $12,000 a year.[33]

VI

Michigan, organized as a territory in 1835, with numerous and influential settlers from western New York who brought their political and economic ideas with them, had included in her territorial constitution the clause of the New York constitution of 1821 which stipulated that any act incorporating any body politic must, to become valid, have the votes of two-thirds of all the members of the legislature. In 1836, still as a territory, she authorized a system of Safety Fund banks like New York's. These seem to have been the first to acquire the epithet "wild cat."* Next, upon her admit-

---

* The promoter of one of these banks, according to Dr Carter H. Golembe, arranged as follows with a correspondent bank for the funds required by law to be on hand when the new bank opened. "I do not conceive," wrote the new bank's promoter, "that 'tis necessary to have the specie actually here but only a certificate of deposit in your bank; which will not interfere with your report of specie and will go for as much in our stock." Accordingly both banks would report the same specie in their possession. The following instructions were given for the design of the new bank's notes:

[33] Baring Papers, OC, 16 May 1838; Biddle Papers, 1 PLB (1838), 407, 436, 439; Raguet, *Financial Register* II, 13, 14, 44.

tance to statehood the year following, Michigan enacted as law, 15 March 1837, the free-banking measure then pending before the New York Assembly. Free banking, therefore, went into effect first in Michigan and thirteen months later in New York.

Of her free-banking measure, Michigan's Governor said, "The principles under which this law is based are certainly correct, destroying as they do the odious features of a bank monopoly and giving equal rights to all classes of the community." Within a year of the law's passage, more than forty banks had been set up under its terms. Within two years more than forty were in receivership. Thus America grew great.[34]

This performance gave free banking its first notoriety. Contemporary accounts make it sound typical of the Michigan free banks that they monetized the state debts by purchasing bonds with their own circulating notes and then disappeared in order to avoid having to redeem the notes. They had to be hunted for in the woods, among the retreats of wild cats. Their cash reserves were sometimes kegs of nails and broken glass with a layer of coin on top. Specie exhibited to the examiners at one bank was whisked through the trees to be exhibited at another the next day. According to the state banking commissioner's report, 18 January 1839: "The singular spectacle was presented of the officers of the state seeking for banks in situations the most inaccessible and remote from trade, and finding, at every step, an increase of labor by the discovery of new and unknown organizations. . . . Gold and silver flew about the country with the celerity of magic; its sound was heard in the depths of the forest; yet, like the wind, one knew not whence it came or whither it was going. . . ."[35]*

In Michigan, as in New York, the constitutionality of the free-banking law had been in doubt and for precisely the same reason.

"Get a real furioso plate, one that will take with all creation—flaming with cupids, locomotives, rural scenery, and Hercules kicking the world over." Golembe, 20, 31.

* The device of moving treasure ahead of the investigators and thereby making a dollar of bank reserves do the work of a dozen belongs among the most venerable of monetary manipulations. Thucydides (VI, xlvi) records a like performance in Sicily in 415 b.c., when the Athenian ambassadors were taken in by it at Segeste.

[34] Albany (New York) *Argus*, 9 February 1838; Knox, *History of Banking*, 733, 735.

[35] 25th Congress, 3rd Session, HD 227, pp. 641-42.

According to legal opinion, the free banks it authorized in indefinite number were corporations, the state constitution did not permit the authorization of an indefinite number of corporations by any one act, and it did require that any act of incorporation be passed by the vote of two-thirds of all the legislators, which the free-banking law could not command and did not command. In order to avoid these constitutional impediments, the law had designated the free banks "associations," as in New York, and not corporations. In this form and without a constitutional majority of votes, it passed, as in New York. Then, when trouble began, one of the banks being in receivership and one of its debtors being delinquent, the receiver sued him. The debtor demurred that the bank was a corporation, that the act authorizing it was unconstitutional and void, that the bank was in consequence without legal existence, and that he therefore could not owe it anything and did not. The case, *Green* v. *Graves*, came before the Michigan Supreme Court in 1844, was identical with *De Bow* v. *The People*, which came before the New York Supreme Court a year later, and was accorded the same decision. For what was left of the free-banking system in Michigan, however, the decision was a *coup de grâce* and was not survived as it was in New York, where the free banks remained in operation and in political favor. In the Michigan Court's opinion the free-banking act was "that law whose history was blackened with frauds and perjuries; under the operation of which individual and state credit staggered and at last fell; a law which brought odium and reproach upon the state within a year after its enactment." The Court held that the law was "unconstitutional and void" and that the banks organized under its authority "never had any legal existence." Even the receiverships were without legal status, for having had no legal existence the banks could have no creditors to account to, and such receivers as were in possession of assets could pocket them. "It is to be lamented," the Court said, "that the grave question we are now called upon to decide was not presented to this court at an earlier period and immediately after the passage of the obnoxious act. Our decision would have stayed the torrent which has swept over the state with effects so desolating, and preserved individual and state credit from the stigma and reproach which befell both."[36]

The Court's indignation was directed ill. The law was unconstitu-

[36] *Green* v. *Graves*, 1 Douglas 351, 366, 372; Knox, *History of Banking*, 736.

tional, to be sure, but its worse fault was its bringing unneeded banks
into being at a most unpropitious time. It was adopted in March
1837 when the tightness was already oppressive that was to become
panic two months later and force specie payments to be suspended.
Philadelphia and New York were concerting on measures to ease the
tension. The United States Bank was about to initiate the sale of
post-notes in London in order to relieve the demand on the States
for specie and Nicholas Biddle was about to undertake his operations in support of cotton. There was specie in the western banks—
or had been—but passage of the free-banking act was coincident
with distribution of the first installment of the federal "surplus."
The distribution was hardest on the West, for under Jacksonian
policy an unduly large proportion of the federal surplus had
accumulated in western pet banks, which had now suddenly to surrender it in specie. It was especially hard on Michigan, where the
government deposits had been unusually high and where, because
of the sparse population, the amount due was low. To organize over
forty new banks in such conditions and equip them each with a stock
of specie was a chimerical undertaking, even if normal conditions
in the new state warranted so many banks. The frauds and perjuries
which incensed the Supreme Court were not merely permitted by the
law but instigated by it.

However, the Michigan Supreme Court found the free-banking
law unconstitutional not because it was bad, but, as New York's
Supreme Court was to find a year later, because it had not received
the legislative assent prescribed by the constitution. The Court took
cognizance of the argument that the free-banking law was anti-
monopolistic, complied with "the doctrine of equal rights and equal
privileges," and harmonized in spirit and purpose with the constitutional restriction; but was unimpressed by it. Justice Whipple in
delivering the Court's opinion found the reasoning plausible but
doubted its soundness. "All corporations," he said, "are to a certain
extent monopolies," and he quoted with approval the opinion of
another court that "exercise of the corporate franchise is restrictive
of individual rights." He failed to see that corporate "monopolies"
authorized wholesale were any the less monopolies.[37]

The Court, one observes, found the free-banking law not only
wanting in compliance with the constitutional restraint but in conflict with its spirit. The New York Court found it wanting in com-

[37] *Green* v. *Graves,* 1 Douglas 366-67.

pliance but recognized its concord in spirit. Perhaps the Michigan justices in *Green* v. *Graves* were moved too little by the purpose of the law and too much by the results of it. In Michigan, to be sure, the results were bad, whereas in New York nothing so untoward happened; the difficulties that arose were legal only, not economic. Plainly the law itself was not at fault, for in New York it succeeded. The fault lay in supposing that a new and inchoate community had the wealth and the credit to support such an unreasonable number of banks. Where wealth existed and credit was established, banks gave them greater utility; where they might some day exist but as yet did not, banks could not create them.

CHAPTER 19

The West:

Monopoly, Prohibition, Laisser Faire,

and Regulation

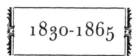

I. Absence of banking in the West — II. The agrarian
purpose — III. Banks restricted — IV. Banks prohibited —
V. Free banking — VI. End of traditional agrarian policy
— VII. Frontier and western conservatism

I

IN 1852 the Secretary of the Treasury reported that there were "no
incorporated banks in regular and active operation" in Arkansas,
California, Florida, Illinois, Iowa, Texas, and Wisconsin—seven of
the thirty-one states then in existence—or in the two organized
territories, Minnesota and Oregon, or in the District of Columbia.
In most of these jurisdictions banking was under constitutional prohibition; in others it was kept out by alert opposition. At the same
time, in Indiana and Missouri, it was restricted to a state-controlled
monopoly, as it was a little later in Iowa.[1]

The political sentiment responsible for this remarkable showing
corresponded to what had been called Loco Foco in New York, and
it was often called Loco Foco in the West. But whereas in New York
it had been the urban and industrial variant of an agrarian doctrine,
in these jurisdictions where it now prevailed it was wholly agrarian.
It continued that original tradition, dominant in colonial times,
cultivated by Thomas Jefferson and John Taylor of Caroline, professed by Andrew Jackson personally, though not by his entrepreneurial associates, and dominant again in the West, where frontier
conditions favored it as they had in the colonies. Even in the District
of Columbia the absence of incorporated banks was due to agrarian
sentiment operating through Congress; for anti-bank members were

[1] 32nd Congress, 1st Session, HD 122, p. 1.

able to prevent renewal of the charters of the four incorporated banks situate there, though these upon the expiry of their charters in 1844 continued as private banks organized either as partnerships or as trusteeships.[2]

II

The area from which banking was barred was probably as great in 1852 as at any time; and by 1863, when it was entirely opened up to banking under federal law, all the states concerned but Texas and Oregon had abandoned prohibition, mostly for free banking. Oregon's prohibitory clause still stands in her constitution as it did a century ago, but it was interpreted in 1880 to prohibit only the issuance of bank notes to circulate as money and so is without real force, their circulation being impossible anyway under federal law. Oregon's prohibition, which was substantially the same as that in effect elsewhere, derives in spirit from that acquired long before, adventitiously, by the Bubble Act; it derives in form from the law of 1741 extending that act to the colonies and from the Virginia statute of 1777 based thereon. It is as follows:

"Article XI. Section 1. The legislative assembly shall not have the power to establish or incorporate any bank, or banking company, or monied institution whatever; nor shall any bank, company, or institution exist in the state with the privilege of making, issuing, or putting in circulation any bill, check, certificate, promissory note, or other paper, or the paper of any bank, company, or person, to circulate as money."[3]

In a sense the jurisprudence which confined this prohibition, despite its comprehensive terms, to incorporated banks issuing notes to circulate as money, adhered to its probable intent. For the prohibition belongs to a setting wherein banks were commonly thought of as concerns whose essential function was the issuance of notes; although it was common knowledge that banks existed which did not issue notes and that with many note issue was of minor importance. It is impossible to say exactly what was meant, because nothing exact was meant. People did what they usually do when they feel that they must deal with a problem even though they have no clear understanding of it. They believed that note issue was bad and they believed that it was the function of banks to issue notes, and so they

[2] Proctor I, chap. xxviii.

[3] Thorpe v, 3013; *Oregon v. Hibernian Savings and Loan Association*, 8 Bellinger 399-402.

forbade banks. What they would have done had they believed something else, there is no way of knowing; but it is possible that they might have forbidden note issue only and sanctioned deposits. In fact they never discriminated thus, so far as I know, except in California, where the constitution of 1849 reads as if deposit banks were permitted though there were no such banks in the state in 1852.*

The agrarians, with characteristic love of stability, forbade banking because it was a source of instability. William Gouge described it in language that seems to me substantially correct, the only question being whether he was describing something good or something bad. "Anything," he said, "that excites the spirit of enterprise, has a tendency to increase the amount of bank issues. Whatever damps the spirit of enterprise or of speculation has a tendency to reduce the amount of bank issues. As the wild spirit of speculation has in most cases its origin, and in all its aliment, in banking transactions, these various causes operate in a circle. The banks, by expanding their issues, give aliment to the wild spirit of speculation when it begins; and by their contractions they aggravate the evils of the natural reactions." He denounced Nicholas Biddle's idea that "the value of bank medium consists in its elasticity—in its power of alternate expansion and contraction to suit the wants of the community." The flexibility or elasticity of bank credit, he averred as Thomas Jefferson had, "is not an excellence but a defect." For, "if banks at any time make money more plentiful than it would be if only gold and silver circulated, they diminish its value in increasing its quantity."[4]

Although Gouge speaks only of "issues," what he says is just as true of deposits; and the evil attributed to note issue was attributable to deposit credit no less. This was unapparent to him because it was not realized that deposit credit arose from lending exactly as note circulation did and that, banks being taken as a whole, there was more bank credit extended in the form of deposits than of notes. Consequently if notes were bad, deposits were worse; and if notes deserved to be prohibited, deposits deserved it still more. The Oregon

---

* Places where miners might take their dust and their nuggets were certainly needed in California, but these places were not banks. The value of the gold depended on its being transported, not kept in California, and so it was delivered by the miners to express companies. From one of these is descended the Wells Fargo, one of San Francisco's best-known banks.

4 Gouge, Part i, 45, 62-63, 186.

court, therefore, in limiting the force of the Oregon prohibition to note issue probably did violence to what the preceding generation had intended and certainly did violence to what it should have intended.

In the States, of course, prohibition was as old as banking itself. The agrarians who repealed the charter of the Bank of North America in Pennsylvania in 1785 were seeking prohibition, and the aim had recurred in the case of every bank charter refused or enacted since then. When banking became common the aim was enlarged correspondingly. The Governor of Kentucky in 1819 recommended that the legislature propose an amendment to the federal Constitution providing that "no incorporated bank should exist in the United States. . . ."; and a resolution was introduced declaring it to be "the duty of the general government and of every individual state composing it (gradually if necessary but ultimately and certainly) to abolish all banks and monied monopolies. . . ." Banks were objectionable to the agrarians not only as banks but as corporate bodies— that is, not only because of what they did but because of their very nature. All corporations set up for business purposes were bad. Individual merchants and business men were the agrarians' traditional enemies, but still they were individual human beings. Corporations, however, were impersonal, privileged, artificial, and soulless. They were aggregates of the worst in man. They were devices by which covetous persons avoided payment of their just debts and enriched themselves at the expense of the honest and diligent. They had neither "bodies to be kicked nor souls to be damned." They should have no place in a democracy of free-born farmers and mechanics who lived manfully by their own labor and ruggedly shouldered without evasion their own responsibilities.[5]

Banks were all this and more. They were the worst of corporations, the most aggressive and the most vicious. They were the "*principal* cause of social evil in the United States," wrote Mr Gouge. They corrupted legislation; they ruined private morals. They were money-lenders and usurers, whose grasp was to be avoided like the fiend's. They did not await only those who came voluntarily to submit to them as borrowers—no. They reached with their filthy paper money the souls and bodies of those who never came near them. They drove real money out of use, replacing it with trash of their own issue, whose value no one knew and whose holders were at the mercy of

[5] Gouge, Part II, 100-01, 234; Benton I, 158.

wily schemers and scoundrels. In a democracy of plain, honest folk, the only proper money—the only money permitted by the Constitution—was silver and gold, whose worth was known and whose volume, like that of the rain from heaven, was determined for the inscrutable good of man by an all-wise, benevolent Providence.

Though traditional agrarianism was mainly responsible for the resistance to banking, it was greatly helped by motley interests aroused against banks from no permanent convictions but from ephemeral self-interest, chagrin, and excitability. In the United States Senate, 2 October 1837, during the special session called by President Van Buren to deal with the general suspension of specie payments begun by the banks the previous May, Senator John C. Calhoun said angrily that the effect of banking was "to discourage industry and to convert the whole community into stock jobbers and speculators," but that "its most fatal effects" bore "on moral and intellectual development." If the community, he said, allotted its "honors and rewards" to "intelligence, knowledge, wisdom, justice, firmness, courage, patriotism, and the like," then those virtues "are sure to be produced." But if they were allotted where inferior qualities are required, the higher virtues would decay. "I object," he said, "to the banking system because it allots the honors and rewards of the community, in a very undue proportion, to a pursuit the least of all others favorable to the development of the higher mental qualities, intellectual or moral"; it worked to the disadvantage of "the learned professions, and the more noble pursuits of science, literature, philosophy, and statesmanship, and the great and more useful pursuits of business and industry." And he commiserated "the youths who crowd our colleges and behold the road to honor and distinction terminating in a banking house."[6]

At a lower intellectual level than Senator Calhoun's, the aversion to banks found less dignified expression. In Cincinnati, for example, in 1842, rioting was set off by the judicial outlawry of the notes of some unauthorized banks and by the suspension of specie payments by certain other local banks. The following account was communicated to the Philadelphia *Public Ledger* and printed in its issue of 18 January 1842:

"Before eight o'clock on yesterday morning, a number of citizens, principally mechanics, and residing in what is called 'Flat-iron Square,' were noticed at the corner of Main and Third streets. The

[6] Congress, *Register of Debates* XIV, Part 1, 476-77.

crowd gradually increased to several hundred by 9 o'clock. Their object was to exchange the notes of the Bank of Cincinnati, a galvanized concern, and others, for the paper of some other and less suspicious institutions, and apparently determined to revenge themselves, in case the Bank should refuse or be unable to make the desired exchange. At the hour of opening, a notice was stuck on the door of the Banking house, notifying the public, that in consequence of the failure of the Miami Exporting Company's Bank, (which had made an assignment the day before) the Bank of Cincinnati had suspended payment for twenty days. This was enough—the crowd immediately entered the Bank *vi et armis*, and commenced the demolition of every thing they could lay their hands on. Books, papers, desks and counters were thrown into the street, together with reams of unsigned sheets of bank notes. The mob then attacked with crowbars, sledge hammers, etc. During this operation the Sheriff made his appearance, and called on the citizens for aid, but none was afforded—they seemed delighted with this summary process. He then endeavored to make a speech, but he might as well have 'preached to the winds, and reasoned with despair.' The work on the vault was now resumed, while a detachment of the rioters drove the Sheriff off the ground. There was by this time (11 o'clock) probably three or four thousand men present. All the stores in the vicinity were closed, and the upper windows in the neighborhood were filled with spectators. About this time the mob broke into the Miami Bank, commonly called the 'Old Cow,' and situated two doors above the Bank of Cincinnati. Here every thing they could lay their hands on was destroyed by the mob—the furniture and fixtures were smashed—the books and papers were torn up and cast into the street—and finally the vault was forced open and rifled of a considerable amount of money in notes and specie, which was, however recovered, and the robbers arrested and sent to prison.

"The bills receivable of this Bank were removed the day before by the assignees, and are consequently safe. As soon as the mob learned that the Bank had gone into liquidation and was to be wound up, it was again shut. During the day the Exchange Bank, owned by the notorious John Bates, (who has swindled the people out of tens of thousands of dollars through the West Union Bank) was thronged by an anxious and angry crowd, demanding the redemption of Otis Arnold & Co's Nashville checks, put into circulation by Bates, and which he had advertised to redeem. These demands were complied with while his notes lasted, and he then paid out specie for them until they were all taken in.

"The crowd now required him to redeem the West Union notes, of which there is a large amount in the hands of the citizens, but this he positively refused to do. The mob then commenced and completely gutted the Exchange Bank, drove off Bates, and broke into the vault; but he had a few minutes before secretly taken out about $6000, in gold, and conveyed it to the Mayor's office near by. An attack was now made on Lougee & Co's broker's office, on the opposite corner. This Lougee had put into circulation a large amount of irresponsible paper which came under the decision of the Court in Bank alluded to above. This building was also destroyed, and the safe opened by violence, but every thing valuable had been removed hours before, as the attack had been anticipated. During these proceedings, Charles Fox, Esq., a lawyer of this city, attempted to read the riot act, when the mob dismounted him from his hobby, and made him take to his heels; he was chased by about three hundred men to the Pearl Street House, where he obtained shelter. . . . Soon after this the Sheriff again appeared, with about a dozen of the 'Citizens' Guard,' the rest of the volunteers having refused to turn out, in consequence of the censure heaped upon them for their alleged remissness of duty during a late riot. The Sheriff and 'Guards' were so severely pelted by the mob with sticks and stones, that they soon beat a retreat, and left the ground. As the rear files left the scene of action, being hard pressed, they turned and fired a volley on the crowd, wounding two or three men. . . . The Mechanics' and Traders' Bank, in the vicinity, an 'Individual Responsibility' concern, was run on all day, until 6 o'clock, P.M., when it shut up with the promise to open this morning at eight o'clock."

This again was an urban affair, like the Loco Foco riots in New York, and reflected feelings on the reverse side of enterprise, which though not themselves agrarian, worked toward the same end, brewing a vague but pervasive hostility against banking among persons who had little opportunity to get any direct and recognizable benefits from banks. The dislike manifested in California and Oregon for banks and bank paper seems to have arisen not only from agrarian sentiment, which it is likely most fortune-seekers derived from their backgrounds, but more immediately from the disdain felt for paper money by producers of gold.

III

Though the agrarians hoped they could abolish banks entirely, their first measures in the West were restrictive, not prohibitory. Indiana, which obtained statehood in 1816, Illinois, which obtained it in 1819, and Missouri, which obtained it in 1821, each authorized in its constitution the establishment by the legislature of a single state bank with branches but forbade the incorporation of banks otherwise. The idea of one state bank with branches was obviously derived from the Bank of the United States, to which many people had only the objection that it was unconstitutional, the practical advantages of a single responsible bank, directly amenable to the government and acting as its depository, being plain to them.

But it was eighteen years before Indiana exercised her power and sixteen years before Illinois or Missouri did, the people preferring to be without banks. There was a branch of the federal Bank of the United States in St Louis most of that time, however. In 1834 Indiana at length set up the bank permitted by her constitution, basing its charter on that of the Bank of the United States. The state subscribed half its capital and chose its president and a minority of its directors, leaving the management of the bank outside of politics. The bank had ten branches at first, but this number was later increased to thirteen, each branch serving a specified district. The branches were examined at least twice a year from the central office, the function of which was to administer the whole organization, all actual customer transactions being performed at the branch or banking offices. It was the only bank permitted in the state till near the end of its existence; it was the Bank of Indiana.

Illinois, after an unsuccessful effort in the twenties, followed the example of Indiana in 1835. But the State Bank of Illinois, unlike its Indiana prototype, became entangled in public improvement schemes and an effort to help the city of Alton outstrip St Louis as a commercial center and river port. It went bankrupt in 1842. There was also a Bank of Illinois at Shawneetown, which failed shortly after the State Bank did. Illinois was then without any incorporated bank for ten years or so, except for an unimportant one, the Bank of Cairo, at Kaskaskia, which seems to have closed some time before the ten years were up.

In Missouri a bank like Indiana's was formed in 1837, the year of the panic. The state owned two-thirds of the capital and chose the bank's president and six of its twelve directors. Besides the head office in St Louis, there were offices in five other towns. These branch offices had not the autonomy of the Bank of Indiana's branches, and the head office was itself engaged in banking as well as in supervision. In its early years it was much preoccupied in protecting itself from its sister institution, the State Bank of Illinois, whose notes it refused to accept. This incensed the St Louis merchants, who declared the Bank of Missouri's restrictions were ruinous to them, resolved that it should be held no discredit to a merchant if his obligations to it went unpaid through its refusal to accept notes of the State Bank of Illinois, and set about withdrawing their deposits. The Bank of Missouri had to yield, but in 1843 it had the satisfaction of surviving the derelict State Bank of Illinois, which it sued to have put in receivership.[7]

In the territory of Wisconsin, which was organized in 1836, the legislative majority was for years determined to tolerate no banks of issue, and in every corporate charter it enacted—even one for a church—it included a stipulation that nothing in the charter should be construed to authorize the business of banking. Despite this chronic suspicion, three bank charters or so were enacted, how and why being unclear, but to no very important consequence anyway. A charter of great consequence, however, was obtained in 1839 by George Smith for the Wisconsin Marine and Fire Insurance Company, which became one of the most important banks in the United States. The company was specifically denied "banking privileges," but in the same sentence it was specifically authorized to "receive deposits" and to lend money. It received deposits in amounts of one dollar or more and gave the depositors certificates similar in form to bank notes and equally suitable for circulation, being payable "on demand to the bearer." Its charter and practice were based on the example of a similar institution in Chicago, where moreover a large part of the Wisconsin company's business was done.[8]

The Wisconsin Marine and Fire Insurance Company was performing a valuable service and doing it in the best spirit of free enterprise, but it was also evading the law. After considerable fuming, the legislators repealed its charter in 1846, but the act proved ineffective, for the company, which by now had a record of about eight years' punctilious dealings, declared publicly that the repeal was illegal and that it would continue to do business and to meet its

[7] Cable, 180-84; Hazard i, 379-81; Primm, chap. ii; F. Cyril James i, 142, 160.
[8] Knox, *History of Banking*, 726-27, 740-41; F. Cyril James i, 201-04, 226-31.

obligations as usual. Farmers who wished to sell grain, dealers who wished to ship it, and merchants who wished to trade went on using the company's obligations and the legislature could do nothing.[9]

IV

In 1845, Texas became a state with a constitution in which banking was prohibited absolutely. Elsewhere, so far, prohibition had been qualified by the authorization of banking in special circumstances. In 1846, Iowa and Arkansas were admitted to statehood with similar absolute prohibitions. Iowa's prohibition was typical. All the authors of her constitution had immigrated thither from some older jurisdiction; over half of them were farmers and the views of most of the others were agrarian. Their orthodox convictions were hardened by many more years of experience with banks than their forerunners in Indiana, Illinois, and Missouri had had. In the intervening period, there had been general suspensions of specie payments, bank credit had abounded, pockets and tills had been crammed with depreciated and worthless bank notes. Memories were fresh of the bankruptcy of the United States Bank of Pennsylvania, of the failure of the near-by State Bank of Illinois, of the free-banking fiasco in Michigan, and of other recent events of like import. Against these experiences the excellent performance of the Bank of Indiana, the Bank of Missouri, and the Wisconsin Marine and Fire Insurance Company counted for nothing. Iowa's agrarians were convinced that banking was a "mad, untamable beast," the "common enemy of mankind," a "withering and blighting curse," and that nothing else "ever devised by mortal man was so successful to swindle the people."[10]

The constitution composed by these Iowa hard-money agrarians had the following to say on banking: "No corporate body shall hereafter be created, renewed, or extended with the privilege of making, issuing, or putting in circulation any bill, check, ticket, certificate, promissory note, or other paper, or the paper of any bank, to circulate as money. The General Assembly of this state shall prohibit by law any person or persons, association, company, or corporation from exercising the privileges of banking or creating paper to circulate as money. . . . The General Assembly shall provide by general laws for the organization of all other corporations

9 Hadden, 171.
10 Shambaugh, 68-70, 74-75, 102, 197, 405-15; Gallatin III, 384.

except corporations with banking privileges, the creation of which is prohibited. . . ."[11]

Before the constitution was ratified, a critic had pointed out that with no banks of its own the state would find itself buying and selling with the paper issues of banks in other states. Iowa would become "the plunder ground of all the banks in the union," he declared. "Instead of the hard money promised the people, we shall have not only a hard currency but one well mixed, for it will consist of the issues of those institutions which have no credit at home and whose paper is thus driven abroad for circulation. Instead of a currency free from expansion or contraction, as hard money is alleged to be, we shall have a circulation constantly liable to explosion and irredeemable in its character." The majority had no answer for this warning, which was supported by common experiences, but the temptation to take a stern and defiant position was irresistible, and the prohibition was adopted as "a decisive indication of public sentiment against all banking institutions of whatever name, nature, or description."[12]

As may result from too drastic efforts, the interdict stimulated the evil it was intended to prevent, and investigators, who were struck ten years later by the volume of bank notes circulating in a state where banking was forbidden, counted in Iowa City alone— then the state's capital—the notes of more than 300 banks. Many of these notes were issued by companies incorporated in the neighboring territory of Nebraska, which itself had a law forbidding the issue of notes for circulation but chartered eight institutions for the purpose of circulating them in Iowa, where "agencies" were maintained—the agents being the banks' owners, presumably. The principal one was the Western Exchange Fire and Marine Insurance Company whose president was Thomas Hart Benton, jr. This company echoed the name of George Smith's Wisconsin Marine and Fire Insurance Company and also the provision in its charter for the issuance of certificates of deposit, which circulated like notes; but, unlike its namesake, Benton's bank failed. Besides the papers of these Nebraska corporations, money was issued within Iowa by townships, cities, and counties, and by merchants and business corporations. Two produce buyers purchased pork and wheat with their own notes, which were engraved like money and became "an important part of the local circulation." A stagecoach company

[11] Thorpe II, 1132. [12] Shambaugh, 351; Preston, 47.

issued its own money to pay its operating expenses. These concerns were exercising the common law right to borrow and furnish their creditors with evidence of the obligation, and the constitutional prohibition did not stop them.[13]

Though specie was not abundant in the region to which Iowa belonged and could not be accumulated because it had to be spent for the goods that had to be purchased outside, still the region seems to have been better supplied with it than the colonies had been and was consequently in less need of paper money. This was obviously true of California and Oregon, where the precious metals were produced and the prohibition of banking worked no great hardship so far as currency was concerned. Specie found its way into the upper Mississippi valley from three sources. From Spanish America it arrived at New Orleans and was carried thence up the river in payment for the produce shipped down to New Orleans' markets. From California, after 1848, it came overland. It came from Europe in the possession of immigrants. Hugh McCulloch of the Bank of Indiana wrote that he had been a banker fourteen years, from 1835 to 1849, before he "handled or saw a dollar in gold except the ten-thaler pieces which were brought into this country by German immigrants." J. S. Gibbons, a New York banker, wrote in 1858: "A very large amount of foreign gold is brought into the United States by immigrants and travellers from Europe. It is mostly taken to the west. . . . It is quite usual for our city banks to receive from some thriving town beyond the Mississippi river a well-ironed box of 50 lbs. weight, filled with an indiscriminate mixture of half the coinages of Europe, to the value of nearly ten thousand dollars."[14]

In 1857, a year of severe monetary panic throughout the country, Iowa adopted a new constitution which permitted the establishment of banks provided the pertinent legislation be ratified by popular vote. Two measures were so ratified, one being a general banking law and the other incorporating a Bank of Iowa. The requirements of the general banking law were so severe that no banks were ever formed under its provisions. The Bank of Iowa, however, was organized at once. It was authorized to have not more than thirty branches (it established fifteen), not more than one in a single town, and

---

[13] Preston, 61-62, 67-68; Knox, *History of Banking*, 765, 807; *Bankers Magazine*, November 1855, pp. 372-73.

[14] McCulloch, 119; Gibbons, 256.

none in towns of less than 500 persons. The branches were mutually responsible for each other's note liabilities. Circulating notes were provided each branch in the ratio of $150 for each $100 of stock, one-half of which was to be paid up in gold or silver, the metal to be in the branch's actual possession and its *bona fide* property. Each branch was also under the requirement that it have vault reserves equal to twenty-five per cent of its outstanding notes and deposits. Payment of interest on deposits was forbidden. Loans were to be for no more than four months.[15]

The Bank of Iowa, like its sister institution in Indiana, was more than *a* bank; it was a system of autonomous branches or banking offices under a head office whose duties were supervisory. It could— and it did—take over any branch that was in difficulties and call on other branches for aid in rehabilitating or liquidating it. It continued in operation only about seven years, from 1858 to 1865, when under pressure of federal law it went into liquidation, most of its branches becoming national banks.[16]

Banking was prohibited in Texas from 1845 to 1904, except for the period 1869 to 1876, during which a carpet-bag constitution permitted it. In Iowa it was prohibited from 1846 to 1857 and in Arkansas from 1846 to 1864. In California it was prohibited from 1849 to 1879, and in Oregon from 1857 till about 1880, when, as already observed, the prohibition was interpreted not to mean what it said.

V

It was not till 1851 that the easy-money craze of the enterprisers and speculators began finally to supersede the conservatism of the western agrarians. By that time, supposedly, recollection of Michigan's experience had receded far enough into the past for free banking to be tried again. It had worked well in New York for thirteen years and had been adopted by New Jersey and by the province of Canada in 1850. In 1851 it was adopted by Ohio and Illinois and in 1852 by Wisconsin, Tennessee, and Indiana. In Ohio and Tennessee, banking had been neither conspicuously bad nor conspicuously good, and free banking did not change the record materially. In Illinois, where prohibition of banking failed by one vote in the constitutional convention of 1847, a provision was adopted

---

[15] Thorpe II, 1150; Knox, *History of Banking*, 766-68; *Bankers Magazine*, June 1858, pp. 953-54; Preston, 83-84, 90-91.
[16] Preston, 85.

which forbade the state to participate in banking and required that all banking legislation be submitted to the people. In 1851 a free-banking law fashioned after New York's was submitted to popular vote and approved. Illinois then had an experience with wild cat banks that was similar to Michigan's. In 1859 William Gouge found the ratio of specie to liabilities lower in Illinois than in any other state: it was less than 4.25 per cent. "The perfection of paper money banking consists in dispensing with specie altogether," said Mr Gouge; "to this pitch of excellence the banks of Illinois have not yet arrived, though they seem to be in a fair way to attain it." In 1860 there were 110 free banks in the state; in 1864 there were only 23. Chicago, in 1861, had "no incorporated commercial banks" but private banking houses were numerous.[17]

In 1848, Wisconsin had become a state; her new constitution continued to prohibit any authorization of banking by the legislature, unless such authorization were ratified by popular vote. Under this condition a free-banking law was put into effect in 1852. Wisconsin now recapitulated the experience of Michigan and Illinois. Speculators purchased bonds with a small down-payment—preferably southern states' bonds that were selling at discounts of ten to twenty per cent—had them delivered to the state Comptroller, obtained from him the notes authorized by the law, and with these notes paid the remainder due on the bonds. "Thus a bank with $100,000 capital could be created with not to exceed an outlay of $5,000, often less, according to the commission charged for advancing the money for bonds, plates, and printing." The remaining care of the proprietors was to find a shady nook in the deep forest, perhaps in an Indian reservation, where a cabin could house their inaccessible "bank," and a guard could frighten away or misdirect such hardy note-holders as came too close in their quest for the gold and silver to which they were entitled. In 1858 the bankers of Chicago refused to accept the notes of twenty-seven Wisconsin banks, some or all of which were "located at inaccessible points, having no capital, doing no banking business, providing no means whatever for the redemption of their issues, and in many instances having not even an office."[18]

Indiana had had notable success with her bank for eighteen years

---

[17] Thorpe II, 1006, 1041; *Bankers Magazine*, July 1859, p. 7; Knox, *History of Banking*, 725-28; F. Cyril James I, 215-19, 338.

[18] Thorpe VII, 4093; Knox, *History of Banking*, 747; Sumner, *History of Banking*, 451.

when in 1852 she turned and headed for equally notable trouble. In 1850 when her constitution was revised, the bank had found itself assailed from both sides; on the one, agrarian hard-money extremists got the state's retention of stock in the bank forbidden; on the other, speculators and promoters got authorization for the legislature to permit free banking and also the establishment of a privately owned bank with branches, which should supplant the old bank. Under the first of these provisions, the legislature in 1852 enacted a free-banking law. Within two years, about 100 banks were established. The Bank of Indiana, while affording the only banking service in the state, had provided a circulation of $3,500,000; the new banks ran theirs up to $9,500,000.[19]

"Anybody," wrote Hugh McCulloch, "who could command two or three thousand dollars of money could buy on a margin the bonds necessary to establish a bank, to be paid for in its notes after its organization had been completed." Otherwise the principal outlay was for the notes, which of course had to be fancily printed lest no one accept them as money. Then a room might have to be rented for banking quarters and a counter put up to keep strangers at a proper distance from the bank's reserves. To the extent that such expenses had to be paid, banking was not, strictly speaking, free. Hugh McCulloch tells of a gentleman with $10,000 and two associates with nothing who bought, "mostly on credit, $50,000 of the bonds of one of the southern states." These were deposited with the Treasurer of Indiana and paid for with circulating notes as soon as the notes were printed and delivered. "This transaction having been completed, more bonds were bought and paid for in the same manner; and the operation was continued until the financial crisis of 1857 occurred; at which time, this bank, which had been started with a capital of $10,000, had a circulation of $600,000, secured by state bonds, on which the bank had for two or three years been receiving the interest." The interest at 5 per cent or more was at least $30,000 a year, or 300 per cent of the bank's capital.[20]

This was common enough to be a scandal or a joke, whichever way one looked at it. The notes, having been paid to the broker who sold the bonds, were by him either delivered to the Treasurer of the debtor state or turned into other funds for him. Every transaction was at a discount, and the notes themselves were as much a means of

19 Knox, *History of Banking*, 697, 703.
20 McCulloch, 125.

haggling as a means of payment. From these original transactions they percolated into circulation, at almost any stage of depreciation, according not only to the takers' reluctance to accept them but to the payers' eagerness to trade them for something else. And it is to be supposed that the bank received the interest on its bonds in a sum worth far less in gold than the $30,000 nominally due it.

Such magnitudes mean little, for one may be sure that few persons in Indiana or anywhere else failed to discriminate, though perhaps imperfectly, between bank notes that were as good as gold —as the Bank of Indiana's were—and those that were as good as paper. It is in such uncertain terms that the reputed gains and losses in such matters must be appraised. Mr McCulloch said that Indiana and Illinois lost "millions of dollars" by their free banking experiments; "and yet," he says, "the growth of the states was not greatly retarded by them." No—because much of the loss was like that which is sustained when one writes a check for $1,000,000, signs it, and puts it in the fire. But not all by any means. Too many of the more innocent, confused and taken in by the pretentiousness that surrounded the so-called business dealings of the quacks and slickers that were helping America to become great, gave constantly more than they received. And it is no proper extenuation of the injustice that what they lost was still part of the wealth of the country, though in some one else's pocket.[21]

Indiana's plague of free banks was picturesque but brief. For a while the country was "shingled" with them, according to another observer. "One bank was made the basis of another, and that of a third, and that of a fourth. . . . By these cunning operations, three or four banks could be organized in four widely separated corners of the state, inaccessible during the winter season; and by the use of each other's bills, at the remotest point, they easily managed to keep in circulation a large amount of currency." Of the ninety-four organized by the time the free-banking law was three years old, the same observer lists fifty-one that failed in that time. These, he said, had had no funds to lend, having them all invested in state bonds; they had had no deposits; and many of them had had no directors. A legislative committee reported of one such bank that it opened its doors but twice a week; and it recommended respectfully that "every bank be compelled to have a regular banking office" and to keep this office "open a certain number of hours each day." It is

21 McCulloch, 127.

said, perhaps facetiously but to some point nevertheless, that a firm of Wall Street promoters who made it their "particular study to organize free banks," wrote to a prospective client in Wisconsin in 1857 that out of forty-three banks organized in Indiana by a rival firm "forty-one have failed, while of those we have got up— twenty-seven—only fourteen have failed."[22]

In 1855 the Indiana law was corrected to require "banks to have regular hours for business daily from 10 to 3 o'clock," to be situated in towns of at least 1,000 inhabitants, to have at least eleven stockholders, with a majority of the stock owned by resident citizens, and to have redemption agencies in Indianapolis. These and other changes in the law made things better, but the state's real relief came the hard way from the panic of 1857, in which most of its wild cat banks were choked off.[23]

Meanwhile, the promoters of the new "Bank of the State of Indiana," who were politicians of both parties united to make a little money for themselves, had got their charter, despite a veto that had to be over-ridden. But they found their course more difficult outside the legislature than in, for though their charter was one of the best ever enacted in the country it could not make bankers of them. Besides, their "corruption and wire-working" had become known and set public opinion against them. The result was that they ran into more trouble than they had expected; but they contrived a way out. They opened negotiations with the managers of the old bank, already in liquidation, the latter purchased the charter, and the business of the old bank was transferred to the new one. This was early in 1857, before the panic. The net result of the episode was that the politicians and promoters made some money with misuse of their power in the legislature, the old bank—with a new charter and slightly different name—continued after all, and the state's proprietary interest in banking ended. Yet, though the new bank was privately owned, its organization and policy remained practically the same as before. Hugh McCulloch was its president. It had twenty branches. It continued as one of the most distinguished and honored financial institutions of the country until the national bank law came into effect and most of its branches became national banks. Its existence ended in 1865.

[22] *Bankers Magazine*, September 1857, pp. 166-67, 170-71; August 1859, p. 153; *Hunt's Merchants' Magazine*, February 1858, pp. 261, 264.
[23] *Bankers Magazine*, September 1857, pp. 173-74.

Missouri avoided wild cat banks, but she did modify the state bank's monopoly. By 1857 St Louis had become the eighth largest city in the United States, and its business men felt themselves balked by the conservative credit policy of the Bank of Missouri, whose cash reserves were 37.5 per cent and whose portfolio held mostly bills of exchange. In order to permit the establishment of more than one bank, the constitution was amended, and in 1857 a statute was adopted which authorized the chartering of nine institutions, including a rechartered and reorganized state bank, in which the state retained an interest for nearly ten years. Each bank was required to have at least two branches; to maintain reserves of gold and silver not less than 33⅓ per cent of circulation; and to accept for deposit or in payment of debts due it only gold, silver, and notes of other specie banks in Missouri.[24]

The panic of 1857, which occurred the last of September, interrupted the organization of some of the banks the new law authorized and threw into suspension most of those that were already open. The terms of the law made a bank lose its charter if it remained in suspension more than ten days, but this requirement, as universally happened, was not enforced. By 1859 all the nine banks authorized by the law were in operation, seven having their head offices in St Louis, one in St Joseph, and one in Lexington. These nine banks had in all forty-one branches in thirty-five towns. The state bank was still the largest and had ten branches, the most of any. It continued in business till 1866, when the state's interest was sold and the several offices became national banks.[25]

VI

Agrarian monetary and banking policy had begun with the negative conviction that credit was bad for farmers and for honest men generally. Banks, therefore, since they throve on the provision of credit, should not be tolerated. When funds are plentiful, a Virginia Congressman had argued in 1811, there arises competition among banks to lend; and this "fictitious credit . . . will expose the farmers and planters to the most serious injury." He said that in Baltimore available bank funds had always exceeded the demand by solvent customers, and hence had gone to the accommodation of "mere speculators." A Pennsylvania legislative committee in 1821 had observed that before the establishment of banks "in the interior,"

24 Cable, 254-55.   25 Cable, 265-66, 290-91.

farmers "who possessed credit and character" had no difficulty in borrowing on their simple bond. "Embarrassments and failures, in those days, were scarcely known among our husbandmen, and society moved on by a regular, sure, and happy march." In the cities, on the contrary, "where loans have been made chiefly by incorporated banks," bankruptcies occurred regularly. Were credit confined to legitimate demand, "banking long since would have been abandoned as an unprofitable trade." I have already quoted Governor Polk of Tennessee, who in 1841 complained of the "great and sudden changes" in prices of which farmers and planters were the victims and of which the over-trading and speculation of "a small class" were the cause. What the farmer and planter should desire, he said, was settled prices. The men who secured the ban on banking in Iowa in 1846 were of the same opinion; only "when there was a gold and silver circulation," they said, "there were no fluctuations; everything moved on smoothly and harmoniously." Such views accorded with an old-fashioned belief that farm incomes were scarcely adequate to meet the interest charges on indebtedness and to retire principal. "The profits of agriculture are so moderate," Mr Gallatin wrote in 1831, "at least in the Middle States, and the returns so slow, that even loans on mortgage are rarely useful"; and he indicated that in the West the ability to discharge farm indebtedness would be still less. Since about 1830 or earlier, when the Loco Focos emerged, these typically agrarian opinions had been shared by labor too, but with an industrial rather than agrarian cast, of course, and to the extent that there was as yet in the West any conscious labor sentiment distinguishable from agrarianism.[26]

Traditional agrarian policy with respect to money and banking, after it attained striking success in the West, disintegrated when the agrarian interest at last gave way before enterprise and speculation. And this occurred with the triumph of northern business enterprise and nationalism coincident with the Civil War. For more than two hundred years, the "frontier," whether colonial or national, was manned by agrarians on the defensive against business enterprise and especially against banks, once they were introduced. Now, somewhat past the middle of the 19th century, agrarian conservatism succumbed, and there was repeated in the upper Mississippi valley what had happened already in the colonies and in the East, where

[26] Gouge, Part II, 45, 53, 138; Clarke and Hall, 147; Shambaugh, 70; Gallatin III, 317.

business interests were long in the minority but in time got the ascendant and turned an economy originally agrarian into one that was industrial and monied, dominated by steam and credit. Till then agrarian conservatism had been strong enough to prohibit or restrict bank credit for varying periods in different regions, depending largely on the origins and convictions of the population. It evidently had been weak in Michigan, the more influential part of whose people brought with them from New York the spirit of enterprise that was triumphing there. In Iowa a decade later the agrarian spirit was stronger partly because of the banking troubles in Michigan and the freedom from them, comparatively, in Illinois and Missouri, where there had long been no banks and never very many.

Consistently with these views, the Governor of Iowa said in 1850 that the growth and prosperity of the new state were largely due to her having no banks; and in 1858, Arkansas ascribed her avoidance of the panic the year before to the same happy condition. Contrariwise, the Governor of Florida, in 1841, lamented the condition that banking had got the people of Florida into and said that if their young and blooming territory had never chartered a bank, the evils under which they were laboring would probably have been avoided. This was before the blessed state of banklessness had been attained that Florida was to enjoy ten years later.[27]

Bank issues were the specific object of agrarian attack because paper money was issued in no other form; in principle the agrarian repugnance to government issues was quite as great. According to William Gouge, "The business of lending money is no part of the duty of any government, either state or federal," and the issue of government obligations as money would encourage "extravagance in public expenditures in even the best of times, would prevent the placing of the fiscal concerns of the country on a proper basis, and would cause various evils." In 1837 when the Treasury had found itself absolutely strapped as the result of a unique combination of circumstances—the federal debt having been paid off in full, the federal surplus being in process of distribution to the states, payment for public lands being required in specie, and specie payments being universally suspended—the agrarians were galled by the necessity of issuing Treasury notes. These notes bore interest, they were not legal tender, and they were redeemable in a year; yet it hurt the

---

[27] 29th Congress, 1st Session, HD 226, p. 685; Preston, 70; *Bankers Magazine*, January 1859, p. 586; Sumner, *History of Banking*, 453.

agrarian conscience to use them. Half a century later, when the Supreme Court announced that the Constitution empowered Congress to issue paper money and make it legal tender, the venerable George Bancroft, who had been one of the Jeffersonian intellectuals among the Jacksonians, was shocked. "Our federal Constitution," he declared, "was designed to end forever the emission of bills of credit as legal tender in payment of debts, alike by the individual states and the United States."[28]

But the maintenance of such noble convictions became increasingly difficult. The pressures and temptations of enterprise grew and overcame resistance. The West remained agricultural and its population still comprised farmers mostly. But farming itself was becoming a business, it could not be conducted without capital equipment, and capital equipment could not be maintained without abandonment of the ancient agrarian ideals—one sheep, as Thomas Jefferson had said, to clothe a family of five—and conformance to a world remade by the Industrial Revolution. Reapers and other farm machinery, as they were invented, had to be bought, and to buy them cash and credit were required. Clothing and tools could no longer be made economically on the farm, they too had to be bought, buying them called for money, and money made it necessary to have banks. Yet it was not banks alone; they were but one prominent factor in a new sort of economy that made it impossible for men to survive competitively without recourse to things that agrarians had traditionally done mostly without: machinery, equipment, science, imports, credit, and cash. Banking did not come apart from these things but with them, indissolubly.

It is likely, however, that the areas where banking was prohibited were all the time served more than they realized by incorporated banks elsewhere and by unincorporated banks in their own midst. The latter, being private business firms, conducted their affairs with becoming adherence to the same unprivileged conduct as merchants, mechanics, and farmers engaged in; and not being involved in politics or law-making, they left fewer records for posterity to know them by. But how important they were is indicated by the following comment in the June 1843 issue of *Hunt's Merchants' Magazine*. After observing that areas comprising six states and two territories, with a population exceeding 2,200,000, were "comparatively without banks," the commentator said that the business was

[28] Gouge, Part ii, 230; Knox, *United States Notes*, 41-46; Bancroft, 1.

"falling into private hands." This was a good thing, he thought. "Private houses have a great advantage over corporations in the economy, precision, and skill with which the business is conducted. They contain within themselves, also, a conservative principle which constantly counteracts a tendency to overtrading." They require obligations to be paid when due, they restrain credit extensions, and they make the merchant "careful not to buy more than he thinks he can sell." In some areas, however, they were outlawed, as they had been in New York by the restraining acts. Yet there were "unauthorized banks" everywhere. Besides partnerships and individuals operating as banks without corporate charter, there were also corporations without the name of banks that were engaged in discounting, sale of exchange, and extension of deposit credit. In St Louis, for example, the insurance companies and the St Louis Gas Light Company had very substantial deposit liabilities. To the extent that bank credit was supplied from such sources, it was conservatively supplied in all likelihood and genuinely useful.[29]

Considering the agrarians' boycott on credit, their prohibition of banking, and the restricted scope of the private houses and other lenders, I should say that the early West flourished on a paucity of credit. And even when the agrarians swung round to an acceptance of banking, it was to banking of a highly restricted sort. On this basis they were well off. Credit wisely extended was profoundly useful to them; it facilitated the exchange of their products for the products they needed from other regions and countries. When its volume was insufficient, they were at a disadvantage in producing and marketing their crops. When it was over-extended, when indebtedness was created on the basis of inflated prices, and when the means of payment were of false or uncertain value, the farmer was worse off than with no credit at all. So I should say that although the people of Iowa were better off with a state monopoly than with banking prohibited, because they then had a supply of sounder money, yet even with it prohibited they were better off than the people of Michigan, Wisconsin, Indiana, and Illinois were with banking free. And I also think that Iowa was better off in 1850 with no banks than she was seventy-five years later when she had about 1,600 of them, and more than 1,200 were to fail in less than ten years.[30]

29 *Hunt's Merchants' Magazine*, January, April, June 1848, pp. 79, 368, 563; Larson, chap. IV; Cable, 185.
30 Federal Reserve Board, 1943, *Banking and Monetary Statistics*, 26, 284.

VII

Notwithstanding the conservatism of agrarian credit practice in the early West, it seems to have been wholly supplanted in the conventional view of historians by wild cat banking. This is extraordinary. The anti-bank, hard-money policy of the western agrarians produced, particularly in Indiana, Missouri, and Iowa, some of the best banking in American history. Its banks were under a double limitation because the states which established them were neither absolute sovereignties nor independent economies. Yet they won distinction not as governmental institutions but simply as banks; they met the standards of private business at its best. And while they flourished—from about 1835 to 1865—they represented the West more truly than did the wild cats hiding in the woods.

The latter, presumably, have been taken as the more typical, because they seemed in accord with picturesque notions of frontier life and also with the conventional view that any one developing a new region will put the sources of credit under a strain. Thus, fancy and theory have gone hand in hand to exaggerate the wild cat banks' importance. Moreover, because most of the wild cats were western and the West was agrarian, it seems to have been concluded that wild cat banking was agrarian. There is no evidence I know that it was, beyond the geographical. The wild cats lent no money to farmers and served no farmer interest. They arose to meet the credit demands not of farmers but of states engaged in public improvements. And they certainly were not managed by farmers. No mentality could be much farther from that of a tiller of the soil than that of a fly-by-night skilled in the get-rich-quick artistry of wild cat banking. The latter sought seclusion not because he loved nature but because the hardships of his business required him to establish as remote an address as possible. His real activities were conducted among the haunts of men, where he negotiated his questionable obligations and the doubtful securities traded for them. The business centered in cities and was an affair of money-shavers, brokers, speculators, and engravers of bonds and bank notes, whose printing, issue, and subsequent manipulation were sources of profit. Wild cat banking had too much importance but not so much as its appeal to the imagination makes it seem to have had. It belonged to the realm of quackery, and its activities had much the same significance in the workings of the economy that noise has in the running of a railway train.

Yet the most sober of historians have been so susceptible to the antics of the wild cats that they speak as if there had been nothing else. Professor Frederick J. Turner said that the monetary record of the frontier, from the 17th century settlements onward, had been wholly bad—a craze for easy money and a lax commercial morality having followed the frontier's westering from colonial days to his own. Yet he lived in the region where banking had still been under severe restriction barely thirty years before he spoke. The agrarian record in colonial days, the agrarian resistance to banking wherever it arose, and the agrarian advocacy of hard money and hard money only show plainly that easy money was not early American. And what the agrarians so long contended for was realized best in the frontier states in the three decades before the Civil War. There they achieved a conservative monetary régime with a minimum of credit, though the enemy made awful inroads on their régime and eventually triumphed. Hugh McCulloch said with proper pride that "In nothing was the wisdom, the practical good sense, of the representatives of the people of Indiana . . . more strikingly exhibited" than in the charter of the State Bank; which, "although established in a new state and committed to the charge of inexperienced men, . . . was so managed as largely to increase the wealth of the state and secure for itself a reputation for honorable dealings and fidelity to its engagements which placed it in the front rank of wisely and honorably conducted banking institutions."[31]

To be sure, punctuality in paying debts was never the virtue in agrarian communities that it was amidst the tense and critically inter-dependent relationships peculiar to a commercial or financial community—nor need it be; but on no other ground, in my opinion, can it be said that business honor and financial integrity were lax on the frontier. Andrew Jackson was neither business man nor financier, but no one would presume to call his honor and integrity lax in money matters or to deny that he was typical of the frontier. And so far from advocating easy money, the agrarians or frontiersmen, whichever they may be called, consistently and conservatively opposed anything of the sort. For generation after generation they loudly and ably fought paper money, banks, and bank credit; and when in the West they sensibly yielded enough to sponsor the Bank of Indiana, the Bank of Missouri, and the Bank of Iowa, they spon-

[31] Turner, 32; McCulloch, 114, 121.

sored as conservative, constructive, and admirable a banking practice as was ever seen in this country or anywhere else.

It is significant of the completeness of the revolution after the Civil War which converted a farm population thoroughly to an enthusiastic sense of the blessings of easy money and abundant credit, that their ever having thought otherwise was at once forgotten. It seemed as if the American farmer as Populist and advocate of greenbacks and free silver must always have been what he now was. In large part this assumption was due to the eloquence and fervor of William Jennings Bryan, who made his followers and his opponents think that he was still within a tradition—as he undoubtedly thought himself. In reality he was leading the agrarians finally away from their traditional but no longer tenable hard-money position and converting them from opponents of business enterprise on the score of easy money to rivals of business enterprise for the benefits of easy money. The result was unanimity in the conviction that nothing was more essential to prosperity than abundance of cheap credit and nothing more contrary to economic welfare than deflation.* The unanimity, though established with some violence to historical fact, ended a conflict that during two centuries or more had been responsible for a major part of domestic political controversy. It distorted rather than vindicated Alexander Hamilton's economic views but Thomas Jefferson's it quite repudiated, though without affecting in the least the popular opinion of either statesman.

The West of the middle and late 19th century was the last frontier, and as such it was a place where many odd things happened. It still had a spaciousness and freedom which older communities had lost. I do not wish to deny its exciting attractions either to small boys or to historians. But it is perhaps not a waste of time to insist that the early West abounded in men of substance, sobriety, integrity, and conservatism. It had vigilantes as well as desperadoes. It had conspicuously strong and capably managed banks as well as

---

* Statements by the United States Treasury and by the Federal Reserve are always phrased in harmony with easy-money gospel no matter which way their action tends. This accords with the fact that current Treasury and Federal Reserve action in the field of money and credit is never condemned popularly except when it is restrictive. Now and then, however, when enough time has elapsed, it may be criticized for not having been restrictive in the past. It is easy to commend restraint after it has become too late to exercise it.

weak and fantastic ones. It had the most restrictive and responsible monetary statutes the country has ever known. George Smith and Hugh McCulloch belonged to the West as much as Sam Houston and Davy Crockett, though the first retired immensely wealthy to live in London and the other became for a while an investment banker there, achievements for which plenty of other westerners envied them. To a few people who went west the frontier was a paradise where one did as he pleased, or where, as Fanny Wright and Robert Owen would have done, Utopia was to be set up. But to most it was an undeceptive wilderness where known comforts, familiar institutions, and an inherited culture were to be established as soon as possible. Samuel Merrill, the Bank of Indiana's first president, read the Bible through every year of his life from the age of twelve; and every branch of his bank, with its portico and Corinthian columns, was a bit of classic yearning in the wilderness. Between Corinthian taste and the Holy Scriptures are palpable incongruities, but to the pioneers both were old and betokened civilization. They were precious to men who were not primitives or fugitives or iconoclasts but builders and missionaries. They hoped for something better for themselves in the West to which they had come, but it was to be something better in a world like that they had known. They sought opportunity, but with the piety of Aeneas carrying with him his memories, his affections, and his household gods. With a fond nostalgia amidst new and deficient surroundings, they used friendly and honored place names, set up conventional structures, read Plutarch, Milton, and the Bible; and while they laughed at the effete manners of the East and of the Old World, they never ceased to worry lest they appear ridiculous without them. And when Walt Whitman, himself an easterner, saluted the New World's unconventional merits with his barbaric yawp, no one shuddered more than westerners among the people he idealized.

The conspicuous and ingrained conservatism displayed in western banking practice is not anomalous, therefore, or negligible, or atypical. Neither, to be sure, is it everything. It was dominant, however, and though it broke down under the pressure of an infatuate over-expansion in the early years of the 20th century, it recovered itself and became at one again with the rock-ribbed, continental conservatism—both agrarian and capitalistic in its origins—that was to become a major characteristic of the Middle West.

CHAPTER 20

Banking in Canada before Confederation

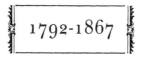

I. The situation in the Provinces — II. Impediments to bank-
ing — III. The first efforts at banking, 1792-1808 — IV. The
War of 1812 — V. The first banks in Lower Canada — VI.
The first banks in Upper Canada — VII. The first banks in
the Maritimes — VIII. Reserve and other requirements —
IX. Canadian and American policy

I

THESE doings in the States that I have been recounting drew the
utmost attention above the border, as American affairs always did.
In 1829 the cashier of the Bank of Montreal told the legislative
committee of Lower Canada that he did not know anything about
the banking practices of the Bank of England, or any other British
banks, but he was able to give very accurate information about
banking in the United States. Such knowledge of American affairs
was not exceptional or peculiar to bankers. Every Britisher in the
provinces shared it in some degree. "The influence of the United
States surrounds him on every side," Lord Durham wrote ten years
later, "and is for ever present. It extends itself as population aug-
ments and intercourse increases; it penetrates every portion of the
continent into which the restless spirit of American speculation
impels the settler or the trader; it is felt in all the transactions of
commerce, from the important operations of the monetary system
down to the minor details of ordinary traffic; it stamps, on all the
habits and opinions of the surrounding countries, the common
characteristics of the thoughts, feelings, and customs of the American people."[1]

Approached from Europe, the continent of North America above
Mexico comprised three zones or regions suitable for quite different
economic development. The southern, extending westward beyond
the Mississippi and southward to the Gulf of Mexico from the

---

[1] Shortt, *JCBA*, VIII, 145-46; Durham II, 311.

latitude of Delaware Bay—or what became established as Mason and Dixon's line, the border between Maryland and Pennsylvania—has been from the beginning adapted primarily to the production of agricultural staples. The intermediate, likewise extending westward to the Mississippi and beyond, was also in its pristine state adapted mainly to agriculture, but to shipbuilding and commerce too, and this with its possession of great mineral resources, both ores and fuels, led in course of time to its becoming primarily industrial and financial. The northern zone, now Canada, lying about and above the Bay of Fundy and the Great Lakes, has had the disadvantage of its high latitude and the lesser accessibility of its resources, which for technical and geographic reasons could not be reached and developed so readily as the resources of the southerly regions. Though the three zones became peopled by a homogeneous European stock, they sharply diverged in their later courses, economically and politically.

Of the three the southern zone, comprising the British colonies and later the states of the American Union south and west from Maryland, was the first to accumulate wealth from exports, these being in the main tobacco, indigo, and cotton. From the northern zone, now Canada, the exports of furs, fish, and timber were for a long time the outstanding sources of wealth, relatively little of which, however, inured to the region whence it came; shipbuilding and commerce were important in Nova Scotia, but what Nova Scotia had was repeated many times over in the States, save only that the port of Halifax was the one nearest Europe. The middle zone, now the northern part of the American Union, was notable for the diversity of its economic interests and its accumulation of capital. Its wealth was acquired less simply than by the export of staples to waiting markets where they were already in demand. Its wealth grew to a greater extent by ingenuity, enterprise, invention, technology, finance, and the rise of markets for manufactured products. It grew by the same conditions that gradually impaired the monopoly the South had long had for its products. Canada was dependent still more than the northern part of the Union on what the future would do for her. She had to await railways, peopling, and the exploitation of more accessible areas before her western prairies, reaching toward the Arctic Circle, began to yield their wealth. She had to await the exploitation of resources elsewhere and the greater advance of techniques, before her minerals could be drawn forth profitably. And for a long time—even into the 20th century—a relatively large volume of her savings was invested abroad, rather than at home in a domestic development that would have been premature.

In these circumstances economic dynamism centered during the 19th century in the northern zone of the United States. There the prosperity was greatest. There the most money was made. There change was swiftest. There the economy was most complex and contrived. There the distribution of wealth was most general. This rich and powerful community rose in ominous fashion above its neighbors on either side—the states to the south, the provinces to the north—who envied, feared, and resisted her. The South made a suicidal effort to free herself; Canada lived for generations in a fascinated dread. Both, by comparison, were backward, simple, conservative, and agrarian. Both were shackled to their own institutions and their dislike of enterprise. The South, indeed, retrogressed, being worse off in the latter part of the century than in the first. Canada progressed, but slowly, biding her time so to speak. The nature of her population reflected her economic situation and conditioned her politics. When the American states became independent, what is now Canada was far less populous than they were, most of her people were French, and her complete subjection to British rule was very recent. Canada proper, now the province of Quebec, was wholly French. Nova Scotia, which then included what is now the province of New Brunswick, was still a racked and half-formed colony no longer occupied by the Acadians and not yet more than sparsely settled by the British. Prince Edward Island also was barely a handful. The provinces received their first substantial English-speaking accretions from loyalists who departed from the revolted colonies, where they were known and vilified as tories. Most of these—some 28,000—populated New Brunswick, which was separated from Nova Scotia in 1784. Some 10,000 others crossed into what was subsequently Upper Canada and is now Ontario.*

The loyalists were welcomed, formally, by the British authorities, but they and their claims, though in sentiment a source of pride,

---

* The distinction I try to observe between provinces considered severally and the Provinces considered as a whole—that is, as a nation—is marked by the use of the capital letter P. The same is true of states and the States, the latter in my idiom being a short name for the United States. The Provinces and the States are both federal unions, of provinces and of states respectively.

were in fact a burden. To the original Canadians, who were French, Catholic, and fixed, the loyalists were still Americans and therefore abominable. And not unreasonably so; for they were Protestant and enterprising. They were also politically restless despite their loyalty to the British Crown. The two races were sorely antipathetic and jealous. At the time of the conquest in 1763, the British authorities had committed themselves to lenity and indulgence toward the French, who at first were far more tractable subjects than either the Americans or the British immigrants, both of whom had economic ambitions and political notions of which the simple *habitants* were innocent. Too soon, however, reacting to the peculiarity of their position, the French also became refractory. There then was something like anarchy, which reached its height about 1837, the French and English bristling at one another and both being froward with the British authorities, who were themselves something less than perfect. In these circumstances political impediments to economic growth combined with geographic. But it was also in these circumstances that the Earl of Durham wrote his brilliant and superb report, which led in particular to the present union of the British North American provinces as Canada and enlightened everywhere the colonial and the imperial policy of Great Britain. The change was marked by recognition of the value of the provinces, which it had been the fashion in some British quarters to deny.* Indeed, the improved political relations, though followed in turn by improved economic conditions, had been impelled by what the provinces were already doing economically. This, though less spectacular than what was happening in the States, was diverse and substantial. It had given pressure to demands for reform, it then justified the reforms once they were made, and it put the value of the provinces to the Empire beyond question. The benefits of the turn were confirmed by Britain's repeal of the corn laws and enactment of preferential tariffs which improved the market for Canadian grains and other products.

Till 1867 the name Canada belonged only to what are now, roughly speaking, the provinces of Quebec and Ontario; in that year

---

* Lord Brougham, animadverting in 1840 on the current "Canadian policy of liberal governments," ascribed to them the "senseless folly of clinging by colonies wholly useless and merely expensive, which all admit must sooner or later assert their independence and be severed from the mother-country." Henry Lord Brougham, *Statesmen Who Flourished in the Time of George III*, London, 1840, i, 65.

the Dominion of Canada was created by the confederating of three provinces—Nova Scotia, New Brunswick, and old Canada, the latter becoming divided thenceforth into Quebec and Ontario. Four other provinces which later joined the Confederation at first remained outside it—Newfoundland, Prince Edward Island, Manitoba, and British Columbia. By "Canada," therefore, one must mean different things at different times: to Lord Durham, "Canadian" meant French Canadian; it did not include Nova Scotian; and "the Canadas" did not include Newfoundland, New Brunswick, or Prince Edward Island, their sister colonies.

Between the Provinces and the States as two neighbor groups, there were from the outset ties as well as antipathies. Trade was practically free and moved more naturally over the uncertain international boundary than it did over some of the forest and mountain barriers that divided the Provinces and States within themselves. Montreal had long been the port and trading head not only for much of nearby Vermont and New York lying up the Richelieu River, but for the Ohio and Great Lakes regions, and the fur-producing areas of the Mississippi valley. The St Lawrence and the Ottawa had been the principal means of access to the interior of the continent, and made Montreal's economic hinterland extend naturally to the west and southwest; her influence in the interior was only gradually shrinking under the exigency that the lands which drained toward her lay within the spreading political boundaries of the United States and were being occupied by American settlers.* Later, with the Erie Canal in 1825 and then with the building of railways, access to Ontario from the sea became readier by way of New York, and the communities separated by the Niagara River were in fact separated by little. The Maritimes—Nova Scotia, Prince Edward Island, and New Brunswick—were remote, in a practical sense, from the Canadas proper, but close to New England and the northern American ports. Though the dominant movement of population was

---

* "The physical condition of the interior of the country made it necessary that certain portions of the United States should find an outlet through Canada and some parts of Canada an outlet through the United States. Thus Montreal became the natural port of entry and outlet for Vermont and northeastern New York; and before the opening of the Erie Canal much of the trade of the western portion of New York state and of all trading posts in the territory bordering on the lakes and as far west as the Mississippi River found its natural outlet through the Detroit, Niagara, and Kingston route, finally centering at Montreal." Shortt, *JCBA*, iv (1896), 8.

westward and within the territory of the United States, nevertheless migration and occasional travel of all classes—farmers, merchants, and professional people, rich and poor—to and fro between the States and the Provinces was always important. But the States exercised more influence both positive and negative than was exercised upon them.

II

Within the scope of these general conditions I have described there had continued from the 17th and 18th centuries certain more specific deterrents to enterprise and banking in the Provinces than had had to be faced in the States. One was that government in nearly every province tended to be strongly oligarchic. Political power was not so fluid as in the United States, where a swelling and turbulent population produced greater political instability. The strength and conservatism of the oligarchies were intensified first by the rebellion of the States from British rule and then by the French Revolution, the reaction to these two events being strong in both the French and British parts of the population, though for somewhat different reasons. The provincial governments became more royal than the King, and Westminster repeatedly had to restrain its despotic subordinates.

In Lower Canada (Quebec) power belonged to the Chateau Clique, representing the great feudal seigneuries which continued from the mighty days of 17th century France. This aristocratic set was supported by the humble *habitants*, and the two together constituted an agrarian interest which was by nature centripetal, Catholic, and averse to speculation and enterprise. Agrarianism in French Canada, like its counterpart in the States, had no great hankering for debt and easy money schemes. It was governed by as potent a tradition, and besides that the land resources then accessible were not so rich as were those of the States, being pocketed sparsely in river valleys between the Laurentian shield and the sea. The men who settled them had a passion to hold fast to what they had rather than grasp with borrowed money for more and newer holdings. When a demand for bank credit did arise, in the first decade of the 19th century, the agrarian interest opposed it in a less dramatic way than in the States but with a steady, consistent effectiveness that curbed the number of banks and restricted credit expansion by those that were allowed. As in the western States, when the agrarians permitted banks they maintained a wholesome and conservative discipline over them.

In Upper Canada (Ontario), power belonged to a group known as the Family Compact, in derisive analogy to dynastic arrangements in Europe. The group was not at all an affair of family relationships, but was extremely compact in devotion to its own privileges. Like the Chateau Clique, it was a landed and ecclesiastical interest, but Anglican, not Roman. Its outstanding personality was John Strachan, a clergyman of remarkable character and abilities, like the "combination of Churchman and statesman common in the Middle Ages." He was the most energetic member of the Governor's Council, champion of the Clergy Reserves, founder of the University of Toronto, and eventually Bishop of Toronto.* The Compact, with somewhat the same dislike of free enterprise as the Chateau Clique's in Quebec, wanted to keep banking in its own hands and out of the hands of others.[2]

In the Maritimes, power belonged to less conspicuous oligarchies, whose interests were markedly commercial but who inclined to foster banking only so long as it was done by themselves. The most important of these was the Council of Twelve in Halifax, whose power in business and in local government enabled it to withstand not only the common run of Nova Scotians but even the Crown.

Another factor, closely related to the foregoing, was the structure of the provincial governments. The legislatures had limited powers, and the Governors could obstruct law-making either by veto or by the time-killing reference of measures to Whitehall for signification of the royal pleasure. Nearly all the first bank charters were pawns in some such game. The typical Governors sent out by the Crown were military officers with no war to occupy them, or others for whom places had to be found. They usually fell under the congenial influence of the established oligarchic group, took its advice, and became its instrument; or else they were frustrated by it. The Governors being typically military and the oligarchies typically landed, except in Nova Scotia, the merchant class had no such weight as in

* The Clergy Reserves were large areas of virgin land set aside in 1791 for support of the "Protestant clergy." The uncertainty as to whom a Protestant clergy included, doubt if it deserved such benefits, and the interference of the Reserves with settlement and cultivation made them long a major political issue.

[2] Egerton, *History of Canada*, 128.

the States and in the colonies that preceded them. Henry Boulton, a lawyer, considered it a merit in the Family Compact's bank, then the only one chartered in Upper Canada, that merchants had little to say in its management. Though Whitehall was friendly to the merchant interest, because it wished to encourage trade, it was too far away for more than occasional appeals to reach it effectively, and its benevolence was complicated by paternalistic notions. The following comment by Professor Adam Shortt shows the nature of Whitehall's interest and its tendency to repeat in its early 19th century dealings with the provinces the same mistakes it had made with the rebellious colonies to the south in the century before, particularly with respect to monetary matters. "Sometimes the tendency of the British authorities to direct or to restrict Canadian legislation on these subjects was very active and persistent, while at other times there was a disposition to allow the colonies to work out their own salvation, or destruction, as the case might be. These variations, however, in the paternal mood depended upon the attitude of the British public toward their own monetary affairs, rather than on the danger or safety of the particular colonial measure or practice. Neither the banks nor the colonial governments took very kindly to these evidences of paternal solicitude for their welfare."[3]

Still another factor in provincial banking history was the monetary experience antecedent to banks. This may be said to have begun in 1685 when the French Intendant, having no funds with which to maintain his troops during the winter, when ice in the St Lawrence prevented the arrival of vessels from France, cut playing cards into four pieces each, gave the pieces various denominations, and on his own responsibility issued them as money. In the spring when ships came with specie, he redeemed the cards. This expedient was reasonably successful, the purpose being merely to finance the government and reflecting no such impulse to augment the money supply for economic reasons as developed in British colonies to the south. Later, a more sophisticated currency was introduced, but it deteriorated with governmental difficulties, and when French rule came to an end, in 1763, it was much depreciated. During the American Revolution, the Canadians got the worst impression from the continental bills of the insurgent colonies. These experiences confirmed a distrust of paper money, especially among the French, who had a peasant aversion to it congenitally, and supported an

---

[3] Shortt, *JCBA*, VIII, 4; Ross II, 390-91.

opposition to banks and bank notes like that in the United States. Meanwhile, however, the Provinces, like the States, were dependent upon the use of foreign coins too numerous in their variety and scanty in their volume. The English pound, shilling, and pence constituted the money of account, though they were a negligible part of the actual circulation. Moreover, conversion rates between the pound and the confusing variety of foreign coins varied in different provinces. In the St Lawrence valley, New York monetary values were used; in the Maritimes, Massachusetts values, known, however, as "Halifax currency" and not a currency but a money of account or system of conversion values between foreign money and pounds. Counterfeits of provincial money were produced in the United States and of United States money in the provinces.[4]

The weightiest factor in the early development of banking in the provinces was the direct example of banking in the States. Its influence worked in opposite ways, encouraging some people to want banks and others not to. But even the advocates, who tended of course to be the persons who wished to go into banking themselves, shrank from the excesses visible to them from below the border; and while they saw good in the banking function, they discriminated between the good and the equally evident evil. Those merchants who sought to be bankers were the most positive factor of all. They were in the trading centers—Montreal, Quebec, Kingston, York (now Toronto), Halifax, and St John—where interest in credit institutions in the early 1800's was like that in Philadelphia, New York, Boston, Baltimore, and Charleston in the late 1700's. But outside the Maritimes, they had not the influential position merchants had had in the States, where commerce had been less monopolistic and yet more powerful in government.

Except for the example of banking in the States, the influences I have recounted were either anterior to the start of banking in the Provinces or contemporary with its early years only, and the governmental reforms instituted in 1841 ended the capricious political impediments to which provincial banking had been subject till then. Thenceforth the influences differentiating the development in the Provinces were more recondite. They are summed up in two general conditions, viz., the less profuse and accessible native resources, which imposed a more modest rate of exploitation, and the greater

---

[4] Lester, chap. 2; Ross I, 4, 28-29, 31-32, 37; 25th Congress, 2nd Session, HD 79, pp. 108, 245; Felt, 160.

conservatism of the Canadian character—a conservatism which the environment required and which the people themselves were disposed to cultivate. Otherwise they would have become Americans.

For such reasons, it was harder to get banking started in the Provinces than in the States, and the start came some thirty-five years later: the Bank of North America, Philadelphia, was opened in 1782, the Bank of Montreal in 1817. In time the peculiar obstacles in the way of the first provincial banks disappeared; yet the Canadians did not attempt such numerous experiments as the Americans, or manifest such impatience, or fall into such excesses. They took the best of American experience for a pattern, and they stuck to it.

III

Although banking in the Provinces made its permanent start with establishment of the Bank of Montreal in 1817, an abortive start had been made long before. In 1792, a year in which eight banks, including the Bank of the United States, were set up in the States, merchants in Montreal and London had formed the Canada Banking Company. An announcement of it, dated in London, 17 March 1792, was published in the Quebec *Gazette*, 9 August 1792, and from time to time thereafter for several months. It was signed by three firms, the first, Phyn, Ellice, and Inglis, domiciled in London, and the other two—Todd, McGill, and Company and Forsyth, Richardson, and Company—in Montreal. Having experienced great inconvenience in Canada from the deficiency and variety of the money then current, they said in language such as American merchants had often used, "and knowing the frequent loss and general difficulty attending receipts and payments," they had resolved to establish a bank in Montreal, to be called the Canada Banking Company. The business of the bank would be that "usually done by similar establishments"; it would be "to receive deposits of cash, to issue notes in exchange for such deposits, to discount bills and notes of hand, and to facilitate business by keeping cash accounts with those who choose to employ the medium of the bank in their receipts and payments."[5]

Save for this brave beginning, there is a strange silence in the records about the Canada Banking Company of 1792. It is said, apparently on no positive evidence, either to have been no more than

[5] Shortt, *JCBA*, iv, 238-40.

an "attempt," as implied by Professor Adam Shortt in 1896, or to have been "a private bank only, chiefly of deposit, not of issue," as stated in an account in 1876 by James Stevenson, of the Literary and Historical Society of Quebec.* No effort seems to have been made to get a corporate charter. The sponsors, according to their announcement, purposed extending operations to every part of the two Canadas and presumed that the bank would be "particularly beneficial" to Upper Canada; but they had their office in Montreal only. It seems reasonable to think, as Professor Shortt explained, that the ephemeral institution of 1792 was premature. Lower Canada, thanks to its French population, had a fairly adequate accumulation of specie and an agrarian dislike of paper money that as yet was unrelaxed; Upper Canada was still a wilderness with few settlements. The Canadians in these circumstances were not yet ready to sustain an institution specialized in banking but fell back upon the granting of credit by merchants and upon the use, for remittances, of the drafts drawn by them upon the merchants to whom they sent exports for sale.[6]

Locally, according to an account by Professor Shortt in 1897 that pictures a state of trade probably true of many North American frontier towns in the early 19th century, "all kinds of goods were supplied by one merchant," and "all kinds of surplus products were purchased and exported by the same merchant." In what is now Ontario, "a typical trading centre consisted of a flour mill, still, sawmill, general store, tavern, and blacksmith shop. In more important places a woollen mill or at least a carding machine was added." Since the settlers needed supplies all the year round but had products to sell mostly in the autumn, "it was customary for the merchants, on the one hand, to give credit for supplies to be paid for in products later on, or on the other hand, in the case of those who brought products in advance, to issue due-bills or *bons*, to be ultimately redeemed in goods or partly in goods and partly in cash." These due-bills "together with ordinary promissory-notes, which enjoyed a considerable local circulation, . . . supplemented the

* However a note for five shillings (or "pour 5 chelins"), No. 6803, captioned "Canada Bank," dated 10 August 1792, "for the Canada Banking Company," and signed by John Lilly, Junior, is in the possession of the Canadian Bank of Commerce. Ross I, 7-8.

6 Literary and Historical Society of Quebec, *Transactions, 1876-77*, 121-22; Ross I, 7-8.

metallic money in the settlements and . . . furnished a fairly effective medium of exchange."[7]

"The merchants, for their part, in obtaining their goods and disposing of their accumulated products usually dealt with a few large importers at such places as Queenstown and Kingston. The merchants in these places also acted as bankers and bill brokers for the local merchants, receiving deposits, obtaining from their customers orders drawn upon various persons, and permitting their customers to draw orders upon them. These wholesale merchants sold as much as possible of the produce sent to them to the Government agents for the supply of the military and Indian posts, exporting the remainder to Montreal and importing from Montreal the supplies with which they furnished the local merchants. As the imports were greater than the exports, the balance was met by bills of exchange on London from the commissariat officers, vouchers for pensions, and other miscellaneous bills coming from all parts of the province.

"The large importers in Montreal acted also as bankers for the wholesale men in the upper province, receiving deposits, making payments to order, and not infrequently advancing loans or credits to be met later on by produce, exchanges, or cash, though we find very little of the latter passing."

This inclusion of the monetary function with that of exchanging goods was proper in a fairly undeveloped economy but inadequate in one more mature. And in March 1807 another attempt at formal banking was made both in Montreal, the commercial capital, and in Quebec, the political one. A petition for establishment of a bank in the two cities was laid before the legislature, but too late to be given attention. A year later, February 1808, a second petition was submitted, the petitioners praying that they might be incorporated as the Bank of Canada in Quebec and Montreal. After consideration of the matter by a committee, a bill of incorporation was introduced and ordered to be printed, but failed to pass. It was contended, as in the States, that the bank "would encourage a spirit of gambling and speculation founded on false capital"; it was also contended, with more originality, that most people were illiterate and could too readily be imposed on by a bank. Whatever was decisive in the matter, no further action seems to have been taken. In 1812, war with

[7] Shortt, *JCBA*, IV, 241-42.

the United States began, and it was several years before banking again came before the provincial parliament.[8]

But this rejected bill of 1808 to incorporate the Bank of Canada is of permanent interest because it followed, in the main word for word, the charters of the Bank of the United States and the Bank of New York, prepared by Alexander Hamilton, 1791; and because it was the matrix of all subsequent banking laws in Canada, being enacted, with appropriate changes, as the charter of one Canadian bank after another. The "Canadian banking system," said Professor Adam Shortt, "is a much more direct and legitimate descendant from the plan drawn up by Hamilton than is the present banking system of the United States."[9]

Though the merchants in Montreal seem to have been discouraged for the time being by the collapse of their efforts in 1808, the merchants up the St Lawrence at Kingston, in Upper Canada, initiated a like attempt two years later. They were influenced perhaps by their immediate proximity to the state of New York, where there were banks in operation across the river from them, and by the circulation of American bank notes in the province. Before their activities reached the legislative stage, however, the Bank of the United States was let die; this probably dampened their interest, and mounting animosity between the Empire and the United States made progress with their plans impracticable. In Nova Scotia also, efforts to establish banking had aborted. In Halifax in 1801 a bank had been proposed, but the Nova Scotia legislators would not grant a monopoly and the projectors would not go forward without one. Ten years later the effort was repeated, with the same result.[10]

IV

The War of 1812 caused a reversal of the economic situation in the Provinces and in the States. The Provinces had shared with Britain the burdens incident to withstanding the long and taxing aggressions of Bonaparte; and yet at the same time, their trade with Britain being impeded by the conflicts in Europe, they had been driven into a one-sided dependence upon the United States, with a balance of payments usually adverse. The Americans, on the other

[8] Shortt, *JCBA*, IV, 248-50; Literary and Historical Society of Quebec, *Transactions, 1876-77*, 132.
[9] Shortt, *JCBA*, IV, 19; Ross II, 389.
[10] Shortt, *JCBA*, IV, 250; Ross I, 37-39.

hand, though harassed by both the British and the French, had thriven as neutrals on the wartime needs of both.

But the American embargo of 1807 and the War of 1812, by suffocating the foreign trade of the United States, roughly disturbed American prosperity, threw the economy into confusion, and nearly tore the Union apart. Toward the end of the war, the British invasion precipitated the suspension of specie payments, and the country found itself with an inconvertible and depreciated currency. Meanwhile the Provinces had their turn to thrive. They became bases for the British military, whose needs maintained an immediate market for Canadian products and a uniform and dependable currency in the form of "army bills." The bills were signed by the Commander of the Forces and were payable at the Army Bill Office in Quebec in cash or in drafts on London. They were accepted with surprising readiness, considering the agrarian preference for real money; but there was a need for them, and they were known to be regularly redeemed. The bills themselves were a useful currency, but more important was the prevailing prosperity which the war brought the Canadians. It was the American War Hawks— John C. Calhoun, Henry Clay, Felix Grundy, and others, western and southern—who had courted war, with their eyes largely on provincial territory; but the war brought the States reverses with no overbalancing gain, and to the Canadians it was a "veritable godsend."* Its stimulus to trade and production was very great. In the States, it diverted energies toward internal trade and production, to the eventual advancement of the country's wealth, but these gains lagged behind current troubles. They were obscured and minimized by the loss of foreign trade, which had long been the country's most prominent and princely business interest. The Canadian gains, on the other hand, were immediate and unqualified—except along the New York border where the housewives suffered some loss of teaspoons and other domestic possessions to the ungentlemanly invader. And besides their economic gains, the Canadians could be thankful for salvation "a second time from the fangs of the neighboring Republic."[11]

* Of the Americans it is fair to say that their aim was not land and conquest merely—such projects seldom are. It was "liberation" of the poor Canadians from the yoke of George III.

[11] Literary and Historical Society of Quebec, *Transactions, 1876-77*, 122; Shortt, *JCBA*, ɪv, 344.

In these circumstances, when the war ended in the winter of 1814-1815, prospects were more favorable for the establishment of banks in the Provinces than they had ever been; for the close of the war meant an end to the army bills, the need of a substitute for them, and an opportunity for banks to provide it. Experience with the bills had diminished agrarian prejudice against paper money and fostered the belief of others in its benefits. Many persons, indeed, had got an exaggerated and illusory notion of those benefits and attributed Canadian prosperity to the generous supply of army bills rather than to war demands, which had produced both. Yet there were also misgivings based on American experience. The notorious failure of the Farmers Exchange Bank in Rhode Island had occurred in 1809, and the legislative scandals over the Bank of America charter in New York in 1812. The general suspension in the States continued from the late summer of 1814 to the late winter, 1816. The Quebec *Gazette*, 9 November 1815, gave its readers a monitory account of current experiences in the States. "How long the derangement of the American currency will continue is uncertain," it said. "The banking system has long been excessive in that country. It has indeed become a system of swindling and political intrigue. Nothing is more common than to see the directors and stockholders of bankrupt banks rolling in luxury, while thousands have been ruined by their mismanagement or villainy. Still the system has gone on." Such a mixture of plain and embroidered truth could make it appear that the British Provinces were happier without banks, and the longer they could be without them the better.

V

Nevertheless a banking project seems to have been on foot in Lower Canada even before the war ended, for in February 1815 a bill to incorporate a bank was considered by the legislature. It was dropped, but at the next session, February 1816, a bill was again introduced and was being favorably considered when the legislature was abruptly prorogued by the Governor, Sir Gordon Drummond, over another question. When the legislature sat again, the same thing happened again: a bill to incorporate a Bank of Lower Canada was introduced a third time and was being discussed, February 1817, when the legislature was suddenly prorogued once more, this time by the new Governor, Sir John Sherbrooke. The merchants of Montreal, hopeless about the legislative *impasse*, decided to proceed anyway. They signed articles of association, 19 May 1817, and in November opened their bank without a corporate charter. This was the Bank of Montreal. The procedure accorded with familiar American precedent, the earliest being that of the Bank of New York, which had opened in 1784 with articles of association prepared by Alexander Hamilton. The Montreal articles of association were derived from him also; they were substantially the same as the rejected bill of 1808 and followed the 1791 charters of the Bank of the United States and the Bank of New York. The bank's notes were issued in dollars. One of its officers was sent from Montreal to get experience in the new Bank of the United States. Another had had banking experience already in the States. The year following, 1818, organization of two other banks was undertaken, the Quebec Bank, in the city of Quebec, and the Bank of Canada, in Montreal. Their articles of association were the same as the Bank of Montreal's. The Bank of Canada was formed with American capital.[12]

Agrarian opposition to these banks, which was mainly French, of course, this being Lower Canada, was passive rather than aggressive—unlike what it was in the United States—and worked to the bank's advantage. For the "country people," according to Professor Shortt, when bank notes came into their hands, obeyed their preference for metallic money and steadily converted the notes "into specie on the first opportunity and thus tended to prevent the banks from overissuing until they had gained experience and corrected their first large ideas about the capacities of paper money. This was an advantage which the first banks in Upper Canada did not enjoy and for lack of which they suffered." The *habitants*, that is, performed the regulatory function the way the Bank of the United States did. Another advantage of being in the midst of these hard-money folk was that their holdings of specie were substantial and, some of the wealthier being coaxed to become stockholders, their hoards were a principal source of the banks' cash reserves. Thus the French Canadians furnished the Lower Canada banks both discipline and substance.[13]

All three of the banks formed in Lower Canada during 1817 and 1818 asked to be incorporated. An act to that effect for the Bank of Montreal was passed early in 1818 but was reserved for the King's assent and never heard of again. Like measures for the Bank of

12 Shortt, *JCBA*, IV, 347-51, 354-55; Ross II, 389-90, 393.
13 Shortt, *JCBA*, IV, 351.

Quebec failed to pass. While these matters were still pending, the Quebec *Gazette* offered the following wary observations, 30 March 1820, taking into account British and American experience: "In England during the late war, the banking system was much overdone and such an immense quantity of notes thrown into circulation by discounting all kinds of accommodation bills, thereby assisting and encouraging wild speculation, immediately ruinous to those embarked and ultimately so much so to the banks that in the years 1815 and 1816 above 240 country banks stopped payment. . . . For the last twelve months there has been very great and very general distress in many parts of the United States arising from the maladministration of their banks. The charters of these banks are in their general provisions good but the direction fraudulently bad. Before any of our banks obtain charters, it is certainly proper to have the subject well canvassed and viewed by the public in every bearing, so as the legislature may have information both as it may operate for and against the country and the banks."[14]

Finally, in 1821, charters were enacted by the legislature at Quebec for each of the three banks in Lower Canada and were given the royal assent the year following. Incorporation of the Bank of Montreal was proclaimed 22 July 1822 and of the Quebec Bank and the Bank of Canada, 30 November 1822. Like the first banks in the States, these Lower Canadian banks were definitely commercial. The Bank of Montreal established offices in Quebec, Kingston, York, and New York—where it dealt largely in foreign exchange. The Bank of Canada, a "direct rival to the Bank of Montreal," had been established by some "speculative Americans, attracted to the country by the prosperity of the war period. . . ." It "was not very firmly rooted in the stable financial interests of the province, depending apparently on the exchange business with the United States." It closed in the "severe depression of the early twenties," and the Bank of Montreal took over its business, with loss to the stockholders but none to the customers.[15]

The Bank of Montreal's charter was to expire in 1831 and its renewal was desired. But awkwardly for the bank, the unfriendliness of merchants and others displeased with her either on principle or because she was an ungenerous lender raised up charges that she was a source of "inconvenience and loss" to the public, maintained an

[14] Shortt, *JCBA*, iv, 356.
[15] Ross i, 14; Shortt, *JCBA*, iv, 354-56, 360.

office in Quebec without sanction, monopolized exchange dealings, etc. An investigation of her operations by the Assembly was demanded. The bank wavered before a temptation to resist this outrage to her dignity, and then in a happy access of common sense turned and welcomed investigation with the expressed hope that she would be exonerated of the charges and her corporate life continued. Her hope was realized, though the charter was extended to 1837 only. About the same time the Bank of Quebec's charter was extended to 1836. The province was in the world-wide state of prosperity that ended in 1837 and new bank charters were sought, but only one—that of the City Bank, Montreal, 1833—was granted. The jealousy of the banks already corporate and the opposed attitude of the popular Assembly and the executive, with Whitehall an unpredictable third factor, made the path to new corporate charters one of anything but primroses. There were unincorporated or private banking houses, however, and there were offices in Montreal and Quebec of the Bank of British North America, a joint stock bank organized in Great Britain in 1838 and admitted by the individual provinces to operate within their jurisdictions. It brought them fresh capital and a staff trained in banking.[16]

In 1837 the panic embarrassed the banks in the Provinces, but none failed to survive and the suspension of specie payments was shorter and less general than in the States. The panic coincided with the violent outbursts of political disorder which occasioned Lord Durham's mission; and in the midst of this the charters of the banks expired. The Bank of Montreal, for an interval, reverted legally to the status of an unincorporated association, and the other two got their charters extended temporarily by emergency action at Whitehall and Quebec. This was the posture of affairs till the union of the two Canadas in 1841.[17]

VI

Meanwhile in Upper Canada a tangled situation had arisen. The principal commercial town in the province was Kingston, but the political capital was York (subsequently renamed Toronto). Early in 1817 some Kingston merchants asked the Upper Canada legislature for a bank charter, mentioning the great number of banks in

---

[16] Shortt, *JCBA*, VIII, 148, 153, 158-59, 161, 163; Ross I, 22; II, 430-31; Breckenridge, *History*, 37-38.
[17] Ross I, 17.

the United States and the benefit that the Americans derived "from the ready aid afforded by their banks to carry on their establishments and improvements in their western territory, which although of a much more recent date, is in a more flourishing state than any part of this province." In March 1817, complying with the request, the legislature enacted a charter incorporating the Bank of Upper Canada, to be in Kingston. The Family Compact had decided meanwhile that the bank should be theirs and situated at York instead of Kingston; and through the Reverend John Strachan, of the Governor's Council, they had requested a charter of incorporation for a proposed Upper Canada Banking Company. They had not yet got the dominance they later achieved, and their request had been ignored, the Kingston charter being enacted instead, with the provision that the stockholders have till January 1819 to organize their bank. The Lieutenant-Governor, however, Sir Peregrine Maitland, reserved the charter for the King's approval and sent it to Whitehall, where it lay so long that it expired. The Kingston merchants, having waited a decent interval, followed precedent and organized their bank without a charter, adopting articles of association in July 1818 like those of the Bank of Montreal a year before. They were doubtless impelled to this action by the establishment, meanwhile, of a branch in Kingston by the Bank of Montreal and of another by the Bank of Canada. Their own bank opened in Kingston in April 1819 as the Bank of Upper Canada. Less than a month later, word came that the charter had been given the royal assent after all, regardless of the fact that it had expired. Whatever the opinion in Whitehall, the opinion in York was that the assent was of no avail, except as evidence of what the King's pleasure would be if a fresh charter to the same purpose were submitted. Yet not quite to the same purpose, as it happened. For the new charter for the Bank of Upper Canada at Kingston had barely been introduced, 12 June 1819, when on the 16th the Family Compact's representatives again requested a charter for their own projected Upper Canada Banking Company. Again the legislature ignored them and enacted the Kingston charter. The Council, where the Compact was stronger, then requested a conference, from which the Kingston charter emerged with amendments that changed the domicile of the bank from Kingston to the "seat of government," which would be York, and substituted the subscribers at York for those of Kingston. In other words, the charter was taken from the hands of the Kingston merchants and put into those of the Family Compact. This maneuver was, of course, to the glory of God and the sanctity of the Clergy Reserves. The Compact, being fair-minded as well as pious, at the same time transferred to their more worldly rivals down the lake the charter intended originally for themselves at York, altering it appropriately to incorporate the "Bank of Kingston." Both charters were enacted 8 July 1819. An important difference between them was that the original charter—intended for Kingston—was deemed to be already assured of the royal assent and included an authorization for the provincial government, whose funds the Family Compact largely controlled, to take stock in the bank.[18]

But Lieutenant-Governor Maitland disobligingly decided that the bill which the Family Compact had captured for its proposed bank in York was no longer the same as the one which the King had approved for the merchants in Kingston, notwithstanding its subject was still nominally the Bank of Upper Canada; and that the other bill, which incorporated the Bank of Kingston, was really the one for which the royal assent was intended. Accordingly he himself gave assent to the Kingston charter, 12 July 1819, and reserved the one for York. But besides giving their bank a new name, the Kingston charter imposed conditions which the merchants had not the financial resources to meet. So, leaving their new and approved charter in desuetude, they continued the business of their still unincorporated bank under its original name.

Meanwhile, as months passed, while the royal assent to the Compact's Bank of Upper Canada at York was awaited in vain and the unincorporated Bank of Upper Canada at Kingston was unable to meet the conditions of the charter proffered it as the Bank of Kingston, the province remained without an incorporated bank. Upper Canada was "over-run with American paper" according to Lieutenant-Governor Maitland in 1819, but it was a nuisance and nowise took the place of a proper domestic currency, such as every one remembered the army bills to have been. To meet the need of a medium of exchange, as had happened earlier in the States, it was proposed that provincial loan offices be set up where bills of credit might be lent on real estate mortgage security; but this project was adjudged illegal in 1821 by a legislative committee on the ground that Parliament's act of 1764—4 George III, c. 34—forbade it. (In fact, it only forbade making them legal tender.) Yet this measure,

[18] Shortt, *JCBA*, v, 2-3, 8-12.

aimed particularly at practices in the colonies which had since then become independent, had been repealed in substance in 1773—13 George III, c. 57—as I said in Chapter 1; and apparently under the sanction of that repeal, or amendment, as mentioned later, Nova Scotia had been issuing similar bills ingenuously and to its advantage since 1812 and was to continue doing so till Confederation in 1867, calling them Treasury notes.* The proposed Upper Canada loan office issues were also condemned by the 1821 committee for not being based on specie; and this was probably the real objection, for a "provincial bank" was proposed in place of the loan offices, and the legislature promptly adopted the proposal by authorizing such an institution to be called the Bank of Upper Canada—a title used a confusing number of times in unconsummated measures and already borne by the unincorporated bank in Kingston. In the minds of its contemporaries this new charter was based in some way, no longer clear, on the charter of the Bank of Kingston, already approved by Lieutenant-Governor Maitland. It received the royal assent, apparently at the hands of the Lieutenant-Governor himself, 14 April 1821. But a day or so later there arrived from Whitehall the royal assent to the earlier charter of the Bank of Upper Canada which the Family Compact had captured from the Kingston merchants for its own use in York. It took precedence over the proposed "provincial bank," because there could not be two Banks of Upper Canada at York even if two banks by any name. So the provincial bank was dropped. The Compact promptly organized the bank that had been approved at Whitehall and opened it for business July 1822. Its legal name was the Bank of Upper Canada, but it was generally known as the "York Bank," a designation which distinguished it from the unincorporated Bank of Upper Canada at Kingston. The latter now began to be called the Pretended Bank of Upper Canada. It had bad management as well as bad luck and, about the time the bank in York opened, it closed for good. This was Canada's first bank failure. But for years statutes concerned with its prolonged liquidation continued to stigmatize it "The Pretended Bank of Upper Canada," while agents of the government engaged in settling its affairs, Dr Adam Shortt said, "covered acres

---

* In 1839 the "Imperial authorities" are said also to have refused to let Upper Canada issue bills—on what ground I do not know, but I imagine it was on particular grounds of policy rather than general grounds of legality. *JCBA*, ii, 315-18.

of paper with all manner of bewildering calculations, lists of names, claims, and counter claims; carefully rolling up interest against the bankrupt, the vanished, and the dead; fulminating with lawyers' letters; and otherwise living beyond their income."[19]

Meanwhile the "legitimate" Bank of Upper Canada at York had a monopoly in the province, qualified only by the presence of the Bank of Montreal's offices in York and Kingston. It tried to force the latter bank out of Upper Canada by accumulating its notes in large amounts and suddenly presenting them with a demand for immediate payment. The Bank of Montreal retaliated, and neither being able to break the other by these legal and honorable raids, so frequent in the States, they mutually forbore in time. Otherwise the Family Compact was more successful, for, having control of the legislative council, it was able to achieve nearly everything it wanted and to prevent nearly everything it did not. Of the fifteen directors of its bank, nine had important stations in the government, including the Honorable and Reverend Dr John Strachan. The bank was strong, carefully managed, and prospered in the Lord. Its business was principally the discount of ninety-day promissory notes and the purchase and sale of exchange.[20]

The greater its success, however, the fiercer the opposition to it became. In 1829 it had to frustrate an effort of its enemies to have the Bank of England invited to establish an office in Canada. In 1830 William Lyon Mackenzie, whose comments upon the Jacksonian Democrats during his later sojourn in the States I have mentioned, prepared a bill for the regulation of banking, which would mean regulation of the Compact's bank. Mr Mackenzie was an intelligent man of passionate and reckless sincerity and a skillful writer much given to gross and disgraceful vituperation. He was a member of the Assembly and chairman of the currency committee. The Compact, failing to get his bill thrown out, tried to get him thrown out himself. It failed in its first attempt, but the year following it secured his expulsion by a charge of libel. His constituents elected him again, he was again expelled and again elected. His charges against the bank were not that it exercised a monopolistic restraint upon credit but that it was inflationary and irresponsible, conducting business on the "visionary basis of two shillings in the

[19] Shortt, *JCBA*, v, 9, 12, 18-20; viii, 3; Breckenridge, *Canadian Banking System*, 215-18; Ross ii, 397.
[20] Shortt, *JCBA*, viii, 5, 229.

pound." Had Whitehall approved what the Compact sought, he said, "we should have had nearly four millions of paper money afloat next year in Upper Canada and the farmers, labourers, and mechanics exchanging their wheat, labour, and industry for paper rags. . . ." Mr Mackenzie spoke for "agriculture, the most innocent, happy, and important of all human pursuits"; and he voiced the traditionary agrarian view, held since the South Sea Bubble, which associated monopoly with speculation and depreciation—not with restraints upon enterprise.[21]

"The American banking system," said the report of a committee in 1830 of which he was chairman, "may be defined to be a paper currency unsupported by an adequate metallic basis—a continuation of the delusive systems adopted in the Thirteen Colonies and France during their revolutionary wars." The report said it was "a mistaken notion that to increase the number of banks upon the American system and to encourage the unlimited circulation of their notes will enrich the tradesman and the farmer. . . . The prosperity of the farmer does not depend upon the amount of money or bank bills in his possession but upon the quantity of the necessaries and comforts of life which the profits of his farm and labor will procure for himself and family. It is favorable to an industrious people that wages and produce should be at a moderate money price and that money should command abundance of the necessaries and comforts of life." This dear-money orthodoxy, so far from exemplifying an agrarian radicalism, exemplified traditionary agrarian conservatism.* It was exactly what the Loco Focos were crying aloud in New York.[22]

The same conservatism had an unexpected display a little later in Mr Mackenzie's stand against a proposed competitor of the Compact's bank in York, current prosperity having spurred the

---

* In his interesting volume, *The Government of Canada*, page 499, Professor R. M. Dawson says that the Clear Grits of Canada were influenced "by the successors to the Jeffersonians, the Jacksonian Democrats," and like them "favoured soft money." But the Loco Focos and other Jeffersonian and Jacksonian "Democrats in principle"—including Jefferson and Jackson—did *not* favor soft money. They were hard-money fanatics. But for Professor Dawson I should have supposed that the Clear Grits also were. William Lyon Mackenzie was certainly not an advocate of soft money.

[21] Lindsey I, 181-82; Shortt, *JCBA*, VIII, 14, 229-41, 306; Mackenzie, *Sketches*, 456-58.
[22] Upper Canada, Journal of House of Assembly, Appendix, *Report on the State of the Currency*, 5 March 1830, pp. 21, 24.

ambition of rival interests in Kingston to be incorporated as the Commercial Bank of the Midland District. To this the Compact made a stubborn resistance. Mr Mackenzie, instead of aiding the newcomers against the Compact, fought them with even more energy and determination than did the Compact itself. Indeed, the latter soon found it expedient to acquiesce in the new institution. But Mr Mackenzie did not. In 1832, when the charter passed the Assembly and was approved by the Lieutenant-Governor, Mr Mackenzie went to England, as he had threatened to do, and besieged the ministries so effectively that to the astonishment of the provincial authorities it began to look as though the charter might be disallowed—which however it was not. Mr Mackenzie's intransigent and paradoxical conduct seemed to most people merely crazy. On the contrary, though fanatic, it was entirely consistent with his beliefs and his character. He held the venerable opinion that corporate privileges were evil, particularly the exemption of the owners of a corporation from personal liability for the debts of the corporation. For one group to be so favored was bad enough; for two groups to be so favored was worse. Like innumerable men of intelligence he could not believe, corporations being privileged, that a multiplication of corporations would destroy privilege. Mr Mackenzie's views were again those of the contemporary Loco Focos in New York, who made the bitter choice of continuing the monopoly of existing banks rather than have more banks.[23]

Society has benefited from the exemption of stockholders from liability for the debts of the corporations they own, as it has benefited from bankrupt laws that excuse men, in certain circumstances, from the obligation to pay their debts; but it seems to me remarkable that these victories over a simple and primitive moral logic have been achieved. Both were resisted, but the bankrupt had the spirit of humanity to help him against a rigid morality; whereas the exemption of stockholders from personal liability became established in subterranean fashion with almost no formal advocacy and with very little formal recognition—quite as if it were something men liked but were ashamed of. Consequently, that Mr Mackenzie should have resisted a convention that made it so easy to escape responsibility seems to me natural; an immense number of persons resisted what they considered the immoral innovations of business enterprise for the same reason. And he would not extend that innovation merely

[23] Ross II, 398-400.

to spite a group of men who wished to monopolize it. His idealism was ingenuous and impractical perhaps, but there was no smell of sanctimony about it.[24]

Yet there were plenty of things about which Mr Mackenzie was confused. The rebellion led by him owed much to the coveting in Upper Canada of the material prosperity that attended business enterprise among the Americans. Though repelled by certain features of business enterprise, he was attracted by its fruits; and he failed certainly, so long as he remained in Canada, to distinguish his own opposition to the Bank of Upper Canada from the Jacksonian opposition to the Bank of the United States—though the Bank of Upper Canada was privileged in fact, its owners being "a junto of government officers, enjoying a monopoly of the paper currency," and the second being a federal institution regulating a private banking system. But when the failure of his violent efforts to overthrow British and Family Compact authority drove him to take refuge in the United States, the spectacle of Jacksonian democracy as it really was chastened his ambitions and impelled him to alter his opinion that the Provinces should emulate the States.[25]

In 1835 the desirability of setting up a provincial bank in Upper Canada was again considered. A select committee held hearings and reported favorably on the project. It found that the far larger banking resources of New York State enabled its agriculturists, tradesmen, and mechanics—"although subject to higher taxes, higher prices for land, with a soil and climate by no means superior, with the additional expense of transportation"—to compete successfully with the inhabitants of the province in their own markets. After considering free banking, which the committee called "unrestricted private banking," then being advocated in New York and soon to be adopted there, the committee recommended instead a provincial bank, as had been done in 1819, finding reason to believe that it would "operate as a most salutary check on all chartered as well as private banks, by regulating or restraining any undue issue of paper money; and it will also by lessening the profits of banking prevent so many from entering into the business." This measure also was opposed by William Lyon Mackenzie, presumably again because the stockholders would not be responsible for the corporate debts.[26]

[24] DuBois, 93-94.   [25] Mackenzie, *Sketches,* 459-60.
[26] Upper Canada, Journal of House of Assembly, Appendix, *Committee Report on a Provincial Bank,* 13 February 1835.

The same year, 1835, the Family Compact was again subdued when it had to acquiesce in chartering the Gore Bank, of Hamilton. The proposed bank's chief sponsor had been associated with the Compact, and when the latter tried to obstruct his charter he began to divulge information about its inner workings, to the delight of its enemies and the public and to its own embarrassment. Besides the Compact's obstruction of new charters, there was a strengthened tendency in general to eschew the experience of the United States, whose banking practice, once thought worthy of emulation, no longer seemed so. As a consequence of this, of the panic conditions that supervened in 1837, and of the inoperable state to which provincial government was falling—with William Lyon Mackenzie leading armed rebellion in 1838—no new charters were granted till the union of the two Canadas in 1841; and in the upper province till then the incorporated banks, including the offices of the Bank of British North America, were barely a half dozen. In 1837 all the banks suspended but none failed for good, and in the few years succeeding "no permanent changes materially affecting the development of the Canadian banking system took place."[27]

VII

In the Maritimes a charter had been granted, 25 March 1820, to the Bank of New Brunswick, St John; it was the first fully effective charter in British North America—that is, the first enacted, approved, and used. This expedition may explain why there seems to be nothing more to tell of it. The American origin of this charter was obvious, as Professor Shortt observed years ago, but it followed the New England variant of the Hamiltonian pattern. New Brunswick incorporated her second bank, the Charlotte County Bank, at St Andrews, across the St Croix River from Maine, 17 March 1825, with a charter like that of the Bank of New Brunswick. In 1834 and 1836 three other banks were chartered, but one was absorbed in 1839 by the Bank of New Brunswick. No other bank seems to have been chartered for nearly twenty years.[28]

In Nova Scotia, as already said, attempts of merchants in 1801 and 1811 to obtain a bank charter had failed. In 1818 the provincial legislature forbade corporate issues altogether and in 1820 forbade

[27] Ross I, 23, 175; II, 404-05; Shortt, *JCBA*, VIII, 311-12, 317-18, 325.
[28] Breckenridge, *JCBA*, II, 320-21.

issue by individuals of notes of less than twenty-six shilling denomination. These prohibitions, which preceded those in the States, were evidently intended to protect the province's issue of Treasury notes, which were receivable for dues to the provincial government, bore six per cent interest, and were not re-issuable. There were further issues in 1813, 1817, 1820, and thereafter occasionally till Confederation in 1867, at which time the outstanding notes were assumed by the Dominion. The issues seem to have been redeemable in practice though not by legal requirement, and in general they served the province well. They were the last of those colonial issues of paper money which began in Massachusetts in the early 17th century, reflected a prevailing need in the New World, and displayed the self-reliance, intelligence, and resourcefulness of the colonists. They were imperfect and at times abused in the pressure of the New World's growth, but their merits far exceeded their imperfections. Their use continued for two and a half centuries, and for much of that time they were the occasion of ill-natured disagreement between the new economies that had need of them and the mature, well-capitalized economy overseas that could not understand such need. And though they were a device of the business world, they have been not only denigrated but ascribed to farmers.[29]

Before the issue of paper money was undertaken in Nova Scotia, a Halifax merchant of substantial wealth, Enos Collins, had built up considerable business in private lending and foreign exchange. This became more important than his merchandising. In 1825 he and his associates, including Samuel Cunard, subsequently the founder of the Cunard line of steamships, asked the legislature for a charter in some respects similar to what had been refused in 1801 and 1811 and in other respects similar to the charters of the Bank of New Brunswick and the Bank of Montreal and contemporary American charters. They asked for a monopoly, however, and the measure, like its two predecessors, failed to pass the Nova Scotian legislature. But the organizers this time went ahead and that same year, 1825, set up a bank, the Halifax Banking Company, under a partnership. Its president and cashier, before it opened, visited Boston and the principal banks there for the purpose of learning how the business should be conducted. The company continued as a partnership for nearly fifty years, with apparently no inconvenience from the lack

29 Ross, I, 38-39, 411-22; Breckenridge, *Canadian Banking System*, 205, 215-18.

of a charter. Its business was largely in exchange, Halifax being an important international shipping center.[30]

The Halifax Banking Company was the financial heart of the merchant and Anglican oligarchy which corresponded in Nova Scotia to the oligarchy of the landed Catholic French in Lower Canada and of the landed Anglicans in Upper Canada, but was the strongest of the three. Five of the banking company's partners were members of the Council of Twelve, which virtually controlled executive and legislative powers in the province. But as elsewhere, the Halifax group did not represent by any means the entire business community, and the dissidents were active. From the business quarter arose a group which wanted to establish a bank of its own, under corporate charter; and from the political quarter arose Joseph Howe, a statesman whose discontent was much like William Lyon Mackenzie's in Upper Canada but whose temper was more moderate and whose conduct was more sensible and effective. Against the established but unchartered Halifax Banking Company lay the charge of monopoly; in its favor was the defense that its liabilities were supported by the entire personal fortune of each of its wealthy owners, whereas the owners of the proposed bank would be without any personal liability. And the frequent, notorious failures of chartered banks in the States were cited in evidence of the practical importance of the distinction. The argument was one that might have appealed to William Lyon Mackenzie in his agrarian surroundings, but it was not so persuasive in a business and financial community. The Council of Twelve obstructed the charter but could not prevent its being granted, in 1832, and the new concern, the Bank of Nova Scotia, was organized. Its charter, like those in New Brunswick, was a Boston variant of the American pattern. For some time the two banks followed the usual temptation to mistreat one another all they could by accumulating one another's notes and making peremptory demands for specie.[31]

The controversy over enactment of the Bank of Nova Scotia's charter had "much to do with stirring up the political struggle for responsible government, which did not end until the partners of the Halifax Banking Company had been deprived of their seats on the Council"—as they were in 1840, when the new Lieutenant-Governor, Lord Falkland, pursuant to the new spirit raised up by Lord Dur-

[30] Ross I, 46-49, 59; II, 426-30.
[31] Egerton, *History of Canada*, 157-58; Ross I, 65, 84; II, 428-30.

ham, obtained their resignations. This action was an achievement which Joseph Howe and his associates had been seeking for years— an achievement which led to responsible government, their further objective, and eventually, with corresponding movements elsewhere, to Confederation.[32]

Yet the tenacity of the Halifax oligarchy and of like groups in other provinces had the conservative and beneficial effect of restraining the infectious ardor for banking, which, had provincial government been more popular and unstable, might have spread from the States. By the time government became popular and responsible, the people of the Provinces had observed to their profit the extravagant course followed in the States and had become satisfied with a modest and patient development adapted to their relatively illiberal environment. The Americans could afford their wastefulness; the Canadians could not.

In 1837 the two banks in Halifax suspended, but for two or three months only—which is better than any other community in the Provinces or States could do. For years they were the only banks in Nova Scotia, except for the office of the Bank of British North America.

VIII

It will be recalled from an earlier chapter that the restriction on the liabilities of the Bank of the United States, 1791, read as follows:

> "The total amount of the debts which the said Corporation shall at any time owe, whether by bond, bill, note, or other contract, shall not exceed the sum of ten millions of dollars over and above the monies then actually deposited in the bank for safekeeping."

In the charter of the Bank of New York, 1791, the restriction had read:

> "The total amount of the debts which the said corporation shall at any time owe, whether by bond, bill, note, or other contract, over and above the monies then actually deposited in the bank, shall not exceed three times the sum of the capital stock subscribed and actually paid into the bank."

[32] Ross I, 70-71, 85-90.

In the unsuccessful bill of 1808 to incorporate the Bank of Lower Canada the restriction had read:

> "The total amount of the debts which the said Corporation shall at any time owe, whether by obligation, bond, bill, or note, or other contract whatsoever, shall not exceed treble the amount of gold and silver actually in the bank arising from the capital stock (but exclusive of a sum equal in amount to that of the gold and silver actually in the bank arising from other sources than the said stock. . .)."

The charters enacted for the Banks of Upper Canada and for the Bank of Kingston departed from the Lower Canada version and followed the Bank of New York restriction *verbatim*. However, the only one of these charters which came into use, it will be recalled, was that of the Bank of Upper Canada at York, opened in 1822. Meanwhile in Lower Canada the articles of association of the Bank of Montreal, 1817, contained a restriction which was repeated *verbatim* in the consummated charters of that bank, of the Bank of Quebec, and of the Bank of Canada—all three proclaimed in 1822—except that in the articles the bank was called "the company" and in the charters, where the restriction read as follows, it was called "the said corporation":

> "The total amount of the debts which the said corporation shall at any time owe, whether by bond, bill or note, or other contract whatsoever, shall not exceed treble the amount of the capital stock actually paid in (over and above a sum equal in amount to such money as may be deposited in the bank for safe-keeping)."

In the Maritimes, where bank charters followed the Massachusetts pattern rather than New York's, the liabilities of the Bank of New Brunswick, 1820, were restricted as follows:

> "The total amount of the debts which the said corporation shall at any time owe, whether by bond, bill or note, or other contract whatsoever, shall not exceed twice the amount of the capital stock actually paid in. . . .

This version, used also in the charter of the Charlotte County Bank, St Andrews, 1825, differs from the versions followed in the Canadas in that the restriction is to twice the paid capital, not treble, and in omitting to exempt or even mention deposits. It is nearly identical with the restriction in the charter of the Philadelphia Bank, 1804:

> "The total amount of the debts which the said corporation shall at any time owe, whether by bond, loan, bill or note or other contract, shall not exceed double their capital."

Although a restriction to twice the paid capital was typical of Massachusetts, it was not unusual elsewhere, but the omission to say anything about deposits is extremely unusual, either in Pennsylvania or elsewhere. The authors of the earliest Maritime charters must have got a copy of the Philadelphia Bank charter to have reproduced it so closely. In this restriction, they vary from it only to omit the word "loan," which appears in the Philadelphia charter but in no other so far as I know, and to add at another point the word "whatsoever," which was typical of Canadian charters.

All these early provincial charters imposed the same range of conditions as charters in the States and in much the same words. Whether enacted above or below the border, all belonged to one legal family. Reports of condition were customarily required to be submitted, and official inspection was also authorized, but less commonly. The issue of notes below a minimum denomination was usually forbidden, and the failure to redeem notes was usually penalized in one way or another. The one conspicuous difference between state and provincial charters was that the former commonly authorized stock ownership by government and the latter rarely did. Only the charter of the Bank of Upper Canada—the "York Bank" of the Family Compact—had such an authorization; other charters omitted it. And they were doing so before any of the numerous banks in which states had interests had got into trouble from the connection.

Branches, which became ultimately a cardinal characteristic of Canadian banking, were in this early period no more peculiar to provincial charters than to American ones. They were authorized for the two banks at Kingston and York, but apparently no other provincial charters gave specific authorization; the two New Brunswick charters of 1820 and 1825 rather pointedly did not, permitting the directors to "remove" the respective banks to new locations and thereby implying that the bank was to be confined to some one spot. The Bank of Montreal and at least one other bank in Lower Canada were not authorized to have branches but did have them. The proposed Bank of Lower Canada charter of 1808, like its model the Bank of the United States charter, had contained an authorization for branches, but it had been omitted from the 1817 articles of association, and when the latter were taken as a basis of the charter enacted in 1822, the original authorization for branches was not restored, though the bank had branches then in Quebec, Kingston, and New York. Not till 1841 apparently were banks in Canada proper given generally a specific authority to maintain more than one office.[33]

Until the late '30's, bank legislation in both the Provinces and the States, though proliferating in details, remained unaltered and homogeneous in the main. Two patterns were discernible, the New York and the New England, but otherwise from the substance of any given charter, one could not tell where it belonged. All alike were the work of Alexander Hamilton, gradually modified. But in the tense period marked by the destruction of the Bank of the United States, the panic of 1837, the establishment of free banking in Michigan and New York, the political disturbances in the Provinces, Lord Durham's report, and union of the two Canadas in 1841, divergence between bank legislation in the States and that in the Provinces became distinct. The difference arose in the States, where the Jacksonians sought to establish *laisser faire*. In the Provinces the established pattern was not abandoned; nor from that time has any important banking innovation of the Americans been taken over by the Canadians. The result is that though the handiwork of Alexander Hamilton practically disappeared from American banking, it survives still in the Dominion, where it has undergone the changes incident to a long evolution but has retained a continuity otherwise unbroken. To this fact, however, there is the important qualification that the original pattern in the States was itself derived by Hamilton from the British act of 1694 authorizing incorporation of the Bank of England. Banking in British North America, therefore, came from a British source by way of the United States and its first Treasury head.

IX

The divergence established between American and Canadian banking by 1841 was a matter of both policy and structure. In policy American banking had become committed to free competition and

[33] Ross II, 395-405.

easy money. Federal regulation had been tried, abandoned in 1811, tried again, and in 1836 again abandoned. *Laisser faire* had won. The structure of American banking changed accordingly. The restriction inherent in chartering banks only by legislative act was given up, and free banking laws encouraged the establishment of new banks in unlimited number. In the Provinces and especially in Upper Canada, which was most susceptible to the spirit of American enterprise, the new trends in the States made some appeal but not very much. The Canadians were aware of the contention that "fictitious capital" in the form of bank credit had "advanced the prosperity" of the Americans and "that though much capital has been lost and many individuals ruined, yet the general state of the people has improved"; but they preferred to stick to the pattern that in the States was going out of fashion.[34]

This decision was not merely voluntary. In the States, the ready accessibility, volume, and diversity of natural resources supported a reckless monetary expansion. In the Provinces, geography prevented anything so spectacular and even impeded more modest progress. Moreover, as if geographic impediments were not enough, just at the time that American enterprise was turning itself gloriously loose under the expansive leadership of the Jacksonians, the Provinces were half-strangled in strife with their respective oligarchies and the British ministry.

It was to correct this situation, which in both Lower and Upper Canada had sunk to a stage of animosity and bloodshed such as had hardened the Thirteen Colonies in rebellion sixty years before, that the Earl of Durham, in one of the happiest decisions ever made in British statecraft, was sent out to investigate the condition of the two Canadas, taking account also of Her Majesty's other North American provinces. He acted so promptly that Whitehall and Westminster turned on him in anger and closed his career in five months. But in those five months he set things in train that not merely saved Canada for the Empire but assured the protracted prosperity of both and their ability to meet unconceived difficulties generations thence. The essentials of his recommendation were responsible self-government and union of the provinces.

These were not achieved fully for about thirty years, the difficulty of deferring regional interests and sovereignties to the general

[34] Upper Canada, Journal of House of Assembly, Appendix, *Report on the State of the Currency,* 5 March 1830, p. 24.

interest being almost as stubborn and menacing as in the States; but the tensions were relieved and improvement began at once. Lower and Upper Canada were united as the Province of Canada in 1841, but further union did not take place till Confederation in 1867.* Responsible government, however, long exercised by British subjects in Britain itself and vainly claimed in Virginia by George Wythe and Thomas Jefferson before the Revolution, was soon established in the separate provinces generally and successfully. In the Provinces as in the States the virtues of independence were not alone that it was naturally craved but also that the people of North America had a tradition of self-discipline which enabled them to give more fruitful attention to their own affairs than people could who, however excellent, were far across the sea and interested in something else. Lord Durham reported that though dissension had been worst in the two Canadas, it had been almost as bad in the other provinces. "The most serious discontents have only recently been calmed in Prince Edward Island and New Brunswick; the Government is still, I believe, in a minority in the Lower House in Nova Scotia; and the dissensions of Newfoundland are hardly less violent than those of the Canadas. It may fairly be said that the natural state of government in all these colonies is that of collision between the executive and the representative body." Though occasional collisions between the Crown and the Commons had occurred in Britain since the Revolution of 1688, they had been "rare and transient"; in British North America they were "frequent and lasting." Since, in the New World, the services of government had to be enlisted in providing society with institutions and facilities which the Old already possessed, Lord Durham was inclined to attribute much credit to the American government for that "amazing progress and that great material prosperity which every day's experience" showed the British North Americans was "the lot of the people of the United States." This sounds plausible. Yet the greater governmental efficiency which British North America acquired in consequence of Lord Durham's efforts bore its fruits not in a material prosperity equal to that of the United States but in a greater tranquillity.[35]

* The provinces of Lower Canada and Upper Canada, united in 1841 as the province of Canada, were again separated under their present names, as the provinces of Quebec and Ontario, when the Dominion of Canada was formed in 1867.

[35] Durham II, 62, 73, 90.

Yet there was prosperity too and a gradual laying up of capital. Economic employments became more diverse, exports increased, and capital came in more plentifully. Establishment of the Bank of British North America, in the light of what happened later, was of considerable significance. It was an early and major movement of British capital into the Provinces. It presaged greater future investments, and in a sense it anticipated federation, taking economic unity for granted and setting up in fact as well as in name a bank of British North America, inter-provincial or national, as other banks so far were not. It was an impressive step by Great Britain as Imperial participant in the internal development of Canada and dominant external influence upon her institutions. It indicated, like Lord Durham's mission and the reforms that followed it, an awakened spirit in the mother country. It occurred at a time, roughly coincident with the Jacksonian revolution, when American example ceased to inspire Canadians as much as it had.

Yet the path to be followed in Canadian development was by no means foregone. There was great doubt in Britain, even in responsible circles, whether it were practicable to hold the Empire together. There was doubt whether the immense area of British North America could ever prove valuable save in spots or ever be drawn into feasible unity. And when as late as 1867, the Americans bought Alaska and actually paid Russia $7,200,000 for it, there were gentlemen in the British Isles who wanted advantage taken of such extravagance in order to get rid of Canada.* To have parted with Canada politically would not have stopped British investment there, any more than independence prevented British investment in the States. But it would have meant a different interest. British capital in the Provinces was accompanied by much more managerial responsibility. This fostered the conservatism of Canadian business, which found itself backed by British conservatism—particularly in banking. British capital had gone into American banking in great volume at first, but after the United States Bank of Pennsylvania foundered and altogether too many other American banks besides, much investment was diverted to Canada, and British distrust of the American banking apparatus was added to Canadian distrust of it.[36]

* Whether they could have succeeded is doubtful, for many Americans thought Alaska no bargain, and in the United States Senate its purchase was very nearly prevented.

[36] Breckenridge, *History*, 23ff, 47ff.

Just before the difficulties of 1837, the Jacksonian prosperity in the States had been highly useful to those British North Americans most determined on political reform. "A people," exclaimed Joseph Howe of Halifax in March 1837, "who numbered but three millions and a half at the time of the Revolution—who owed then seventy-five million dollars—and who, though they purchased Florida with five millions and Louisiana with fifteen and owed one hundred and twenty-three million dollars at the close of the last war, are now not only free of debt but have an overflowing Treasury." America presented "an aspect of political prosperity and grandeur, of moral sublimity and high intellectual and social cultivation," which greatly impressed him. But two months after Mr Howe wrote this, the banks in the States stopped specie payments and six months after it the Jacksonians' Treasury was empty, the "surplus" had disappeared before they could finish "distributing" it, and the country was unable to meet its current debts abroad. Mr Howe's heart could not have been broken, for his words had been moved less by admiration for the Americans than by a polemist's need of things to cast at his adversaries. His position was presumably the same as William Lyon Mackenzie's, out in Upper Canada, who had also been citing the splendid example of how things were done in the States but after a sojourn there and a close view of his heroes was ready to take back much of what he had said and quietly become a Canadian once more.[37]

Yet even though political and economic ties with the mother country improved, there still were enticements to cultivate American interests and imitate American ways. These arose only to prove secondary, however, and for the most part abortive, as it was with free banking.

Free banking had been advocated in Upper Canada before the debacle of 1837 and almost as soon as in New York. A measure "to regulate banking" was introduced in the legislature of Upper Canada in 1831, a measure "to make general the privilege of banking" in 1833-1834, and a measure "to establish an uniform system of banking" in 1835. But as in the States, Michigan's experience dulled the interest in free banking till 1850, when it came again to life, the experience in New York having meanwhile been encouraging. In that year a bill "to establish freedom of banking in this province"

[37] Howe I, 135.

was enacted by the legislature of Canada.* In a memorandum referring the act to the British Governor, Lord Elgin, 7 December 1850, the Inspector General explained: "In the state of New York a system of free banking was established some years ago which has been eminently successful and is likely to be adopted in several other states. It presents the double advantage of effecting . . . security to the bill holder and of creating a home market for the public securities." This Canadian free-banking law preceded all the like measures in the States that, beginning in 1851, also followed New York's example. But at this point all similarity to the progress of free banking in the States ceased. Three banks were established under the Canadian law, but in 1855, having obtained special charters, they abandoned their free-banking status. Only two others chose it. The law was practically dead. Its repeal was first proposed in 1857 and in 1866 was effected. Obviously the Canadians did not like free banking.[38]

That they did not care for the farce of free banking in Michigan, Wisconsin, Indiana, and Illinois need arouse no wonder, for contemporary Americans did not like it either. But that they made no good use of free banking at all may seem strange, since American banks did and most were good banks though not required by the law to be. The explanation apparently is that, in the States, free banking usually tolerated no alternative, whereas in Canada, though free banking was authorized, special legislative charters continued to be granted. So long as there was a choice, a good banker was apt to prefer a special charter, for besides the feeling that one conferred according to ancient practice by special legislative act had greater prestige than a new-fangled one handed out at a window by an administrative officer, the free-banking emphasis on note issue was either useless or burdensome. Special charters, in the States and Provinces, invariably authorized note issue, but with no specific requirements. Under free banking, however, notes could not be issued until a quantity of bonds had been purchased and lodged with the state or provincial government, notes obtained from the latter, and agencies arranged for their redemption. To Americans who could get a bank charter on no other terms these requirements were accept-

---

* Province of Canada, 10 August 1850, 13 and 14 Victoria, c. 21.

[38] Breckenridge, *History*, 34, 58, 61-62; Ross II, 412-16; 13 and 14 Victoria c. 21; 29 and 30 Victoria c. 10; Journals of Legislative Assembly, Province of Canada, 1851 (15 Victoria), Appendix ZZ.

able; but to Canadians with a choice they were a nuisance. For if incorporated by special charter, a bank need buy no bonds—and banks in Canada seem to have found it either difficult or unprofitable to maintain a bond portfolio—it need maintain no redemption agencies, and it need have little to do with the provincial regulatory authorities. Intelligent bankers knew that note issue was of minor importance and were less and less interested in charters loaded with obsolescent terms. The Bank of Commerce, New York, the largest and most important bank in the States after 1838, was organized under the free-banking act but never issued any notes and according to Mr Gallatin would have preferred a special charter had it been possible to obtain one. Most bankers in the States and Provinces still felt it worth while to have at least a small circulation; but in the province of Canada they chose to have it without free banking and there is a strong presumption that in the States the preference of the best bankers would have been the same.[39]

There is still the question why the Canadian legislature did not discontinue the issuance of special charters when it authorized free banking, as was done in the States. I suppose it was because of doubt whether the old arrangement should be wholly abandoned. The Canadian Assembly was under no great pressure to issue many charters though under pressure to issue some. In the States, however, the demand was excessive, and every charter caused a fight. Recourse to bribery was notorious. In New York, indeed, the association of special charters with bribery had been a major reason for making banking free and removing temptations. In Canada there had been no experience to give this consideration force.

The divergence between American and Canadian banks has involved, among other things, the restriction on liabilities to which I have given prominence. The restriction, being one of liabilities to a multiple of capital, assumed that the capital would be held in specie. In the States, when it became recognized that the assumption was vain, then legislative efforts to enforce the retention of specie became common. They took their most important form in 1837 when Virginia enacted the requirement that a bank's specie holdings be not less than twenty-five per cent of its liabilities, which was the reciprocal of a limitation of liabilities to four times capital. Reserve requirements became in time the chief means of credit control in the States, but not in Canada. The difference is one of many that arose,

---

[39] Breckenridge, *History*, 61-62; Gallatin III, 484.

as American banks multiplied in number and the machinery of control was enlarged correspondingly, while the Canadians held to what they had.*

The Lords of the Treasury in Whitehall were not struck with admiration for Canada's free banking act of 1850, and the less because it followed American precedent, which Their Lordships thought by no means a safe example for imitation in matters of currency and banking. Instead they criticized directly the two elements of the law that had been called its merits, viz., the security given note-holders and the demand created for bonds. In place of securing note issues by the deposit of bonds they thought it preferable to require cash reserves of one-third, and they doubted the wisdom of creating a market for bonds in the manner intended; "the price thus raised by a fictitious demand would be dependent on the maintenance of circulation based on the deposit of the securities. . . ." Their preference for a reserve requirement to a bond security was, however, academic, for what they really approved, and wisely, was a single bank of issue; and while the Americans made assurance doubly sure by requiring both bond security and cash reserves—but always with care to insure the requirement's not being too effective—both the Provinces and Great Britain herself continued to profit from a sound banking practice under no statutory requirements of the sort at all.[40]

In 1841 there were less than a dozen chartered banks in the Provinces, and over a century later there are still less than a dozen. In the States, with perhaps ten or twelve times the population of the Provinces, there were then more than 700 banks, and now, somewhat more than a century later, there are about 14,000.** The average size of Canadian banks was already much greater than that of American banks. By about 1857 or a little later the Bank of Montreal was larger than any American bank and probably the largest and most powerful transactor in the New York money market, where

---

* In very recent years, however, reserve requirements have been a more important factor in Canadian central banking procedure than previously. There has also been a greater tendency among Canadian banks to lend on documents, as in the States, rather than on overdraft, as in Britain and elsewhere in the world.

** In both Canada and the United States the number has in the interval been much greater than it is now midway in the twentieth century.

[40] Journals of Legislative Assembly, Province of Canada, 1851 (15 Victoria), Appendix ZZ.

it maintained and employed immense sums. This raised the criticism that the bank, by taking Canada's precious funds abroad to deal with foreigners in Wall Street, was neglecting the domestic borrowers and the Provinces' interest. It was sacrificing Canada to the States. Canadian business and farming struggled as best it could with insufficient credit, America prospered, and Canadian bankers so far from redressing the balance worsened it.[41]

The earth, Thomas Jefferson said, belongs to the living. But it belongs to them a very short time, its condition always determined by the past and its possession indentured to the future. Canadians of the mid-19th century could reasonably complain that the Americans seemed to be having all the fun and making all the money, while their own resources were left in desuetude and their lives were narrowed. But perhaps their mistake was to have lived when they did and not later. In the mid-20th century, Canada's resources have a value and her children have a future that are certainly no less for her backwardness a hundred years earlier. They are perhaps greater. I fancy the Canadians of 1850 did better by lending their money in the United States than they would have done in a rash and premature effort to surpass her advantages. It might even be contended that a presiding wisdom restrained Canada in the 19th century while America burnt her candles at both ends, and that in the 20th century Canada is having her turn. This implies that wisdom depends on what century one lives in.

[41] G. Hague, "The Late Mr E. H. King," *JCBA*, iv (1896-97), 20, 24.

CHAPTER 21

Practice and Panic

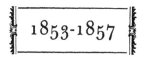

1853-1857

I

THE development of the American economy in the 19th century was the business of a vigorous, acquisitive, and ingenious people, drawn mostly from the British Isles and northern Europe and stimulated by natural resources in the New World of extraordinary abundance, variety, value, and accessibility. The spread of these people was the last of the great migrations, so far, that have filled three millennia of Western history with conflict, accomplishment, destruction, and change; but of all great migrations it displaced the least and was the most wholly constructive. It displaced the least because there was practically nothing to be displaced but some unfortunate savages, their game, and the wilderness they both lived in. It was not an affair of nearly matched, rival races such as have collided so often and so stormily in Europe, but a collision between very primitive aborigines and newcomers from the most advanced civilization in the world. The accomplishments of the newcomers, for two hundred years, were small beside the startling things they were to do in the third hundred. In the two earlier centuries the New World's attractions had been far less considerable. Its resources had been imperfectly known, and not yet of sufficient usefulness to be in pressing demand. But by the end of that period, they had become the object of intense development. For this steam and credit became available. Wonders began to be worked.

Yet these were not all. It was as if a force had been established to which one thing after another arose by some blind prearrangement

671

and contributed. In the decade between 1846 and 1857 especially there occurred a remarkable series of events. First was the Mexican War, which expanded American territory with a great, fresh sweep and intoxicating ease. Though the affair was carried through with a palpable hardening of the heart and an idealism not of the traditional sort, the economy was exhilarated by it and, like a strong man, rejoiced in its strength. In the last previous war, that with Great Britain in 1812, the federal Treasury had been nearly paralyzed by the difficulty of obtaining money that the economy either did not have or would not trust it with. But now, such was the solid accumulation of means within one generation, the government's loans were taken at a premium and in specie. And this was before the acquisition of California and the discovery two years later of its gold. The latter event gave the country another great resource of immediate and most exciting value. Accretions of a very different order arose from famine in Ireland and political revolution on the Continent, which through intensified migration increased the labor, the energy, the brains, and both the productive and the consumptive power of the American economy. At the same time, in the building of railways, there occurred an effect of these and other factors that was in turn a prodigious factor in still further achievements. Between 1850 and 1857 the railway mileage of the country tripled; a continuous line was completed running from New York to Chicago; and the process of drawing together territory that had just been vastly extended was well under way, absorbing labor and materials as of the prosperous moment, creating permanent wealth, and making the economy more compact and efficient for the future.[1]

That the economy in 1846 had been able to subscribe a war loan in specie did not mean that it was itself beyond the need of borrowing. Far from it. The demand of business enterprise for credit grew, because the successful use of borrowed money impelled the debtor to ask for more and the creditor to let him have it.

Roughly speaking, the credit was of two kinds—long-term and short-term—the long-term credit being employed in permanent works and undertakings, the short-term in the current monetary payments incident to the exchange of goods and to the expenditures incident to projects soon to be refinanced with long-term credit. From their beginning in 1782, the banks had been more or less able to provide the short-term credit because their liabilities in the form

---

[1] Dewey, *Financial History*, 255-57.

of deposits and notes, supported by the goods pledged to them, were acceptable as money required for the purchase and sale of the goods. The country having wealth in the form of commodities such as cotton, wheat, meat, and timber that were readily disposable, the banks could provide their credit as the medium of exchange needed for trade. But the case was very different with long-term credit. More steel was needed for her railways than the economy could produce, and it must therefore be obtained abroad. More was needed than could be paid for with American exports, great as were the sales abroad of cotton and other staples. But the means of payment provided by American banks for use within the American economy was of no use to British producers of steel and unacceptable to them. Credit usable and acceptable in Britain had to be provided in Britain, and since the railways would not pay for themselves within many years, it had to be provided in long-term credit. In other words, the American economy itself could do pretty well in providing short-term credit, for it was more or less a matter of people's trusting one another, through the medium of banks, from day to day. And as wealth was accumulated and means of production were enlarged, the economy could itself provide more and more long-term credit; but never in the 19th century anywhere near enough. For the country as a whole, which was a debtor, the attempt to do so was an effort to get the use of savings that had not yet been saved. It could not succeed. The only place for America to get capital was in the Old World, where it had been accumulated. Her chief source was the London money market and British industry.

Because a people developing a new economy of any but a primitive sort are necessarily dependent upon others for goods, materials, and equipment which they can not produce as yet for themselves, foreign long-term credit is indispensable. What they need, moreover, is much in excess of what they are able at present to pay for, because, being undeveloped, they must import more than they can export currently. Had Thomas Jefferson's wishes been realized and the economy remained agrarian, foreign credit would have been fairly unimportant, for there would have been no industrialization, no imports of materials for industrialization, and no imports in excess of exports. The habits of Americans would have been simple, their tastes cultivated, and in exchange for the farm products they sent abroad they would have contentedly received farm implements, books, musical instruments, and the few things they could not advisedly cultivate, such as rubber for their lead pencil erasers and sage with which to season their pork sausage. But since it was the ideas of Alexander Hamilton that prevailed, industrialization and immense public improvements were undertaken, materials required therefor were imported eagerly, American tastes became fanciful and expensive, imports exceeded exports, and the difference had to be borrowed abroad.

Some of this credit was obtained by American importers from their British suppliers, some by borrowing from Old World lenders, such as the Barings. Such credit was or should have been short-term credit. Long-term credit was obtained by the sale abroad of bonds, mostly federal and state, and of shares in American corporations. In this field and in the facilitation of American exports to the same general end, the federal Bank of the United States and still more its successor, the United States Bank of Pennsylvania, had been active and of cardinal importance. Some other corporate banks had emulated these two, but not many; and for the most part foreign credits had become by 1857 the specialty of unincorporated bankers in the States and in London. This left the great body of American banks engaged, as I said, in providing domestic credit exclusively. Some wisely confined themselves further to providing the funds with which to buy the goods and produce traded and shipped about within the country. These funds were normally borrowed for the limited time the borrowers must have the produce and goods on hand between their purchase and their sale. That this specialization was proper for banks in the 19th century American economy is confirmed by the success of the many prominent banks that not only professed it but practiced it; and by the failures of those which undertook to provide long-term credit, of which the most conspicuous was the United States Bank of Pennsylvania. These latter yielded to the demand for permanent capital and while their deposit and note liabilities remained quick they accepted assets that were slow. The pressure upon them was often political, the financing of certain projects in which politicians were interested being required by law. They provided capital by making accommodation loans, by lending on mortgage, and by the purchase of bonds and even of shares. It was something that at that time banks could not prudently do, because the economy as a whole had not accumulated the capital for such investments, and what the whole could not do the parts could not do. Some of the parts could, exceptionally, because even in an economy which was on balance a debtor, individual persons and institutions were able to acquire a preponderance of long-term claims on others and so become permanent creditors. Few banks could do this, however, and only in relatively small amounts.

In a mature economy where savings are adequate for the maintenance and enlargement of the physical plant—the factories, carriers, power-generating works, laboratories, schools, hospitals, and all the other equipment of a modern society—it is reasonable to think that the provision of permanent capital need not be separated from the provision of the money supply; but in the immature American economy of the 19th century where savings were adequate for only the latter, it was quite beyond the power of banks to do both. In the 20th century economy there is a complexity, a balance, and a self-sufficiency that greatly reduces the seasonal and regional differences of income and specialization typical of the 19th century. Regions that were formerly agricultural only are now industrial as well; transportation, processing, and refrigeration enable products to be moved in continuous and less varying volume. More of the economy's business is independent of particular seasons and regions, with the result that banking is less a matter of transactions moving forward in a stream than of transactions moving about in a lake. The abundance of the monetary supply leaves less occasion than formerly for capital demand to conflict with seasonal and regional monetary demand. Another circumstance is that the use of credit money has become universal, and the public is no longer legally able to deprive the banking system of its reserves and stop its operation by demanding conversion of the credit currency into gold. Bankers are able to conduct their business in greater security.

But at the middle of the 19th century banks had still to stand on their own. There was no longer a federal Bank restraining the expansion of their liabilities, and the insurance of those liabilities after an imperfect attempt had been abandoned. To the United States government, banks had become untouchable, and though they were under conservative restraint in some states, they were mostly at large in a jungle of *laisser faire*. Too many let themselves be tempted into taking risks that were incongruous with the nature of the economy in its current stage. When business was good too many thought it was bound to be still better, and when they judged it might be poor it proved to be worse. This was the fault of undisciplined and unsophisticated temperaments; but transcending it was the failure to recognize what was basically to their interest and what was not, especially when the choice was between individual and common action. So in the extraordinarily dynamic period of business enterprise extending from the election of Andrew Jackson in 1828 to the election of Abraham Lincoln in 1860, blunders in banking were profuse. So was dishonesty, though neither blundering nor dishonesty predominated. Banking was both good and bad. From the point of view of governmental responsibility and what the monetary system should have been, the imperfections were awful, mainly because of the anarchic destructiveness of the Jacksonians, who had ended control of a function inherently requiring control. Yet from the point of view of the economy, things were not bad enough to check the country's growth. There were more banks that helped than hindered.

II

On the question whether banks should confine themselves to short-term credit and the monetary function or provide long-term credit and permanent capital, opinion reflected two categories of practice. There were bankers who rushed to serve the demand for long-term credit and could easily justify themselves by asserting their confidence in the future of America. There were also bankers who cautiously selected the sort of earning assets that came due very soon, that were pretty certain to be paid when due, and that gave them a collateral security they could readily turn into cash if the obligor proved to be unable to pay; they could say that the present should be put before the future. They eschewed mortgages and loans on personal security for speculation or for relief from existing indebtedness. They eschewed also the bonds of states, municipalities, railways, factories, and so forth—such investments being as yet without the standard, familiar values that staple commodities had and there being no markets where they could be so readily sold.

This had been the empirical practice at the very outset of American banking, when, as Thomas Willing wrote, the managers of the Bank of North America found themselves without experience in banking, without knowledge, and without literature, but went ahead on the basis of their experience as merchants and confined the bank's extensions to short discounts that they knew were certain of repayment. They were not conscious of adopting an orthodox banking procedure or something with a well-formulated theoretical justification; they were merely deciding to lend in a manner to which common sense allowed no alternative, circumstances being what they were. Fifty years later the managers of the first Bank of Indiana were in the same situation. "None of the directors or officers of the bank or of its branches had made banking a study or had any practical knowledge of the business," according to Hugh McCulloch, "and yet no serious mistakes were made by them. Cautious, prudent, upright, they obtained, step by step, the practical knowledge which enabled them to bring the transactions of the branches into close accord with the public interests and to secure for the bank a credit ... which was never shaken." When the bank began business in 1835, said Mr McCulloch, and "the agricultural productions of the state did not much exceed the demand for home consumption, a large part of the loans were necessarily to men who were buying and improving lands. No considerable losses were sustained on these loans, but they were sluggish and unreliable. . . . The managers of the branches were not slow in discovering this fact, and the lesson which it taught was so sharply impressed upon them by the financial crisis of 1837 and the terrible depression which followed, that from the time when business began to revive, the loans which they made were mainly confined to bills of exchange, based upon produce shipped to Eastern or Southern markets. . . . What the state needed was the means for sending its agricultural productions to market. What the bank needed in order to be able at all times to meet its liabilities, was what was called prompt paper." It abstained from engagements involving it beyond the next crop and from putting its funds into highways, docks, and canals whence they could not be readily extricated. Its management reported to the legislature in 1836 the belief that the products of the state should in general "be disposed of within their season" and that it was "unbecoming an intelligent people" that they should incur obligations that could be paid only when high prices were obtainable. The Bank of Indiana's choice of policy was a pragmatic one, such as may arise from experience impinging on brains. And so it must have been for hundreds of bankers who avoided the entanglements of long-term credit in which so many of their intelligent and patriotic contemporaries made spectacles of themselves.[2]

It did not follow that the Bank of Indiana's only debtors were exporters of the state's products and importers of the goods its

[2] McCulloch, 116-17, 118-19; 25th Congress, 2nd Session, HD 79, p. 788.

people bought. In 1840 its discounts to merchants did not quite equal its discounts to manufacturers, mechanics, farmers, and all others combined, but these seem also to have been for short term and to have rested on the marketing of products. It is evident that by now farmers were among the important borrowers. By loans which enabled them to buy cattle and hogs to fatten on their surplus corn, and which were taken up 'by bills of exchange drawn against shipments," the bank "greatly stimulated and increased production." It seems to have lent on crop loans, which though longer in general than mercantile loans would be seasonal nevertheless. A legislative committee commenting in 1839 on the bank's credit policy, however, had complained that though "the farmers constitute about three-fourths of the people of the state and possess a corresponding amount of its property," they got "but one-fourth of the State Bank credit; whilst the merchants, not much more than one-fiftieth in number, enjoy about twice as much as the farmers." The committee was aware, it said, of the opinion maintained by some "that bank discounts ought to be confined chiefly to merchants and men of business"; but it thought otherwise. The more credit merchants got, the more "articles of show and luxury" they offered, "beyond the wants and the ability of the community," and the more they sold on credit. "The effect has been to stimulate a love of indulgence and display and to increase the consumption of the country beyond its production. The state, therefore, is impoverished and the habits of the people vitiated by the policy of stimulating the import trade of the state by bank credit." Ignoring the moralistic and sumptuary bias of this criticism, the bank could reply that not all merchants were importers of luxuries and that it sought, in its own interest as much as the state's, to extend its credit to exporters and hold obligations of theirs that facilitated sale of the state's products in New Orleans and procurement of funds therefrom. Two years before, a Missouri legislative committee had recommended a "policy of compelling the banks . . . to lend money in small sums to small dealers" (the term "dealer" was the old equivalent of "customer") and peevishly declared that "the importance of lending small sums to every merchant, every mechanic, and every farmer who may desire money and offers a well secured note appears not to have arrested the attention of banks."[3]

[3] McCulloch, 117; 26th Congress, 2nd Session, HD 111, p. 1381ff; 26th Congress, 1st Session, SD 172, p. 895; 25th Congress, 3d Session, HD 227, p. 607.

Not only in the West were there critics of the preference for short-term lending. In Connecticut in 1841, the banking commissioners said that the practice followed by some banks of confining their discounts "exclusively to business paper or paper that is subject to no renewal is a great innovation and denies to a worthy class of borrowers those facilities and advantages to which they are entitled in common with those of more various and extended business." The Connecticut commissioners were pretty poorly informed if they thought the practice new, but their argument clearly reflected the interests of an entrepreneurial democracy in resistance to commercial tradition.[4]

Yet again in the agrarian West, in Kentucky, short-term credit found defense in 1837 with a legislative committee which vigorously advocated the preponderance of the "bill line" over the "note line" in the business of banks. "While the bank deals in real bills principally, . . . it is not so likely to run into excessive issues as when it deals in notes and discounts. The bill business is limited by the actual operations of commerce, the accommodation business is as limitless as the want of money, the rage of speculation, or the spirit of gambling. . . . The past experience of this country when bank paper obtained upon accommodation loans had been attempted to be invested in real estate and permanent improvements has given bitter proof of the fact that banks, properly understood, are strictly commercial instruments, a part of that machinery by which the annual productions of the labor of men are circulated to the points destined for their consumption."[5]

In a later report it was said: "Bank paper is not capital, but credit. . . . Bank paper, being credit, the purity of which depends upon its always being met upon demand, is from its nature designed to circulate and exchange the annual and marketable products of industry; and is therefore an unfit subject for long loans and permanent investments."[6]

The same doctrine was being preached in 1843 by W. M. Gouge, the popular Jacksonian writer on banking, enemy of federal monetary regulation, and apostle of strict short-term bank lending as a means of self-regulation. The object of banking, he contended, should be "to confine so many of the operations of the bank as are

4 Sumner, *History of Banking*, 39.
5 25th Congress, 2nd Session, HD 79, p. 762.
6 26th Congress, 2nd Session, HD 111, pp. 1122-23.

based on its deposits and circulation, to business paper having but a short time to run, making it an inflexible rule never to renew the same." A bank's paper "is a mere medium for transferring commodities from producers to consumers." A bank does not lend capital but credit. Its proper function is monetary. He gave point to his argument by narrating the experience of a bank, which I surmise was Isaac Bronson's in Bridgeport, and which from 1807 to 1832, he said, followed with success the "solitary but inflexible rule" that its paper must never have more than sixty days to run, that every obligation must be paid at maturity, and that there should be no renewals or substitution of fresh discounts. After twenty-five years, the president of the bank, who declared that he had "rather find a counterfeit than an accommodation note among the bills receivable," chose to sell his stock, the bank's policy was changed, and within four years, Mr Gouge said, it failed.[7]

III

Specialization in short-term credit became most explicit and binding in New Orleans, where it was stipulated in the Louisiana banking act of 5 February 1842. This act and New York's free-banking act of 18 April 1838 were the products of the demands being made upon American banks for short-term and long-term credit respectively. Free banking sought a means whereby the supply of bank credit might be indefinitely enlarged for either long-term or short-term purposes and yet be protected by the pledge of fixed capital values in the form of government bonds. The Louisiana act confined banks to the provision of bank credit for short-term monetary purposes, save that a bank might acquire long-term assets equivalent to the amount of its liabilities to its shareholders—that is, to the amount of its capital. The New York act took the bold step of resting the value of money on political authority; and opened the way to the relegation of gold to a mystical arcanum where the State is absolute and the individual never enters to touch the precious stuff. The Louisiana act rested the value of money on gold and its volume on the volume of consumable products moving through the markets; it sought to make the value of money independent of the State or of political action. It became, in consequence, archaic, whether good or bad.

The author of the Louisiana act of 1842 was Edmond J. Forstall, a banker in New Orleans and agent of Baring Brothers. New Orleans

---

[7] Gouge, *Hunt's Merchants' Magazine* VIII (April 1843), 313-21.

was then fourth in rank among the world's shipping centers. It was there that the bulk of America's cotton exports were shipped, with other products of the Mississippi valley, and it was there that the bulk of her bullion imports were received; for after Mexico overthrew the Spanish viceroyalty in 1821, the silver and gold she produced became diverted to New Orleans. The immediate occasion of the 1842 banking act was a crisis in which all the banks of New Orleans had suspended. No new banks were authorized, but the old ones were continued on condition they comply thenceforth with certain rules "declared to be fundamental." These rules, which were obviously the work of a business man and not of politicians or lawmakers, reflect the counting house and especially the usage of English banks. They divided bank assets and liabilities each into quick and slow, which were denominated respectively "movement" and "dead weight," and bank funds were distinguished according as they were provided by shareholders or by depositors and note-holders. The books of each bank would be kept, therefore, in a form which showed the assets and liabilities appropriate to the shareholders apart from the assets and liabilities appropriate to the general creditors—the depositors and note-holders, that is. The rules declared to be fundamental were in part as follows:

"1. Each bank shall separate its loans on capital paid in from its loans on deposites; the loans on capital to be composed of accommodations on personal security or on mortgage, loans on stock, . . . and of all other investments of whatever nature not realizable in ninety days.

"The loans on deposites and specie, representing the paper money issued by the bank, shall be restricted to paper payable in full at maturity, and such paper shall form a component part of the specie basis intended to meet the circulation and deposites, and shall be restricted to ninety days, so as to effectually insure a rapid movement in the daily receipts.

"The loans and investments on the capital shall be denominated the 'dead weight.'

"The loans on deposites shall be denominated the 'movement of the banks.'

"2. No bank shall increase the investment in its dead weight so long as the whole of its cash liabilities shall not be represented by one-third of the amount of such responsibilities in specie, and at least two-thirds in satisfactory paper, payable in full at maturity and within ninety days. . . .

"3. That the account of the maker or endorser of any note or acceptor of any bill of exchange offered and discounted as paper strictly payable at maturity, who shall apply for a renewal of said paper, or for an extension of time, shall be closed in the bank where such transaction shall have originated, and notice thereof shall be immediately given by such bank to the other banks."

In other words, the capital of a bank might be invested in long-term assets, *viz.*, loans on personal and on collateral security, mortgages, bonds, and other such obligations.

The funds owing to depositors and note-holders should be invested to the extent of two-thirds in short-term assets maturing in ninety days or less, the other one-third being in specie. This was a requirement of a 33⅓ per cent specie reserve against deposit and note liabilities.

If any borrower or other obligor failed to pay a short-term obligation at its maturity, his account would be closed and the other banks in the city would be informed of what had happened.

Another rule was that every Saturday each bank in New Orleans report to the state's Board of Currency its dead weight in detail, and its movement in detail, to wit: "Loans on paper payable at maturity and intended to meet the two-thirds of cash liabilities unrepresented by specie; Circulation; Deposites and other cash liabilities; Specie and cash assets." The last statement each month must be published. It disclosed not only the relative positions of the individual banks but also the general condition of the New Orleans money market.*

The following is a consolidated statement of the commercial banks in New Orleans, then five in number, 30 October 1852, ten years after the enactment of the law:[8]

* Professor William G. Sumner in his *History of Banking* seems to have found the Louisiana act the only piece of American banking legislation he liked. He said it was "the most remarkable law to regulate banks which was produced in this period in any state. . . . It is drawn in remarkably clear and direct language, entirely free from legal verbiage. . . . It obviously proceeded from very mature study of the principles and practice of banking and may justly be regarded as one of the most ingenious and intelligent acts in the history of legislation about banking." Sumner, *History*, 387-89.

I agree with Professor Sumner. The Louisiana banking act of 5 February 1842, which Edmond Forstall drafted, seems to me in substance the wisest adaptation of practice to environment in any banking law I know.

[8] 32nd Congress, 2nd Session, HD 66, pp. 276-78.

MOVEMENT OF THE BANKS
Cash Liabilities

Circulation	$ 4,397,000
Deposites	10,545,000
Due to banks	810,000
Other cash liabilities	329,000
Total	$16,081,000

Cash Assets

Specie	$ 5,827,000
Loans on deposites payable in full at maturity	11,116,000
Due from banks	2,437,000
Other cash assets	1,649,000
Total	$21,029,000

DEAD WEIGHT
Liabilities

Capital paid in	$10,934,000
Total	$10,934,000

Assets

Capital of branches	$ 1,405,000
Real estate	893,000
Public improvements	1,149,000
Loans on capital:	
On stock	935,000
Long loans, mortgages	1,907,000
Other discounts	2,987,000
Other assets not available in 90 days	946,000
Protested paper	633,000
Total	$10,855,000

The circumstance that the law properly gave the general creditors a protection the shareholders did not have is reflected in a small excess of dead weight liabilities over dead weight assets that indicates capital impairment somewhere. In the movement there is a large surplus of assets over liabilities.

The New Orleans system continued in operation from 1842 till the Civil War. Thereafter it was superseded by free banking, partly through organization of national banks and partly through organization of state banks under a new law. The available evidence is that the system operated with distinguished success. An anonymous writer in the *Bankers Magazine* in November 1877 reports that he inquired of old bank officers in New Orleans as to the practical working of the law: "whether in fact its stringent provisions were maintained and whether any set of bank officers had the nerve to enforce those provisions against their customers." He was assured, he says, "that the provisions of the law were strictly carried out; that any renewal of three months' paper was regarded as equivalent to protest and the maker of it publicly dishonored; that the reserve of specie and the proportion of short paper were rigidly adhered to; and that when the specie fell below 33⅓ per cent discounting was stopped until the deficiency was made good." The prohibition on renewals, however, seems to have been relaxed in the later years of the system, but not the specie and short-term credit requirements. In the winter of 1861-1862, the first under the Confederacy, there was some political and military interference with payments, but it does not seem to have arisen from any weakness of the banks, and they resumed specie payments in April 1862 at the very time Captain Farragut was shelling Forts Jackson and St Philip and the city's fall was imminent.[9]

Something still more creditable is recorded by Hugh McCulloch; New Orleans being the market in which the bulk of the products of the northern part of the Mississippi valley were sold, the New Orleans banks currently held immense amounts due northern banks in payment for what had been shipped there. When war began, according to Mr McCulloch, then president of the Bank of Indiana, the New Orleans banks, "against the remonstrances of the secession leaders and in disregard of threatened violence," continued remitting to the northern banks what was due them as it matured. "Not a dollar was withheld. No more ably and honorably conducted banks existed in the Union than were those in New Orleans before the war." No more ably and honorably conducted banks existed anywhere, one supposes. But their honesty and defiance of the ethics of warfare would be tolerated by no enlightened government in an advanced age like the 20th century.[10]

Although the banks of New Orleans were well known throughout the country for their strength and integrity, the law governing them was not generally emulated. Too many American banks were situated where both the specie and short-term paper requirements of the New

[9] *Bankers Magazine* xxxii (November 1877), 352.
[10] McCulloch, 139.

Orleans banks were out of their reach. As a Louisiana legislative committee report said in 1837, "the position of New Orleans is unique," her banks being sustained "by the annual receipt of the produce of the valley of the Mississippi, amounting now to at least $75,000,000, and increasing annually with the population. . . . There is no place on the globe possessing so many elements and sounder materials for banking."*

IV

When recognizing as Virginia had already done that a bank's capital was not usually held in specie and that specie rather than capital was the more sensible basis for control of credit expansion, the Louisiana act of 1842 also recognized capital as an organ of long-term credit supply. It did this by permitting the capital funds of the New Orleans banks to be invested in "accommodations on personal security," in mortgages, and in loans and investments "of whatever nature not realizable in ninety days." This let the bank's specie holdings derive entirely from its depositors and recognized a long-established leaning of southern banks to use the landed estates of their shareholders as the source of their capital funds. But the arrangement, though it positively authorized the New Orleans banks to lend on mortgage and otherwise provide long-term credit, limited quite as positively the volume of such lending, which was permitted to absorb what was due the shareholders but not what was due the general creditors. In the statement presented earlier, the dead weight assets were half as much as the quick assets, and though the nature of the dead weight assets is not evident, it looks as if a substantial part of them, while not maturing within ninety days, were still not what would ordinarily be called long-term. In a general way, Mr Forstall seems to have modified the arrangement which invested the capital of the Bank of England in long-term credit, the

---

* What happened in time to the 19th century Anglo-American banking orthodoxy which informed the Louisiana banking act of 1842 is disclosed in the contemptuous words uttered in 1903 by Mr Andrew J. Frame of Waukesha, Wisconsin, then a major oracle of American banking. "It would take a powerful glass," said Mr Frame, "to spy out a gallery of bankers that would stand such ridiculous rulings as those." Hull, 333. Though Mr Frame exaggerated, I can support from memory his opinion of the chance of finding many American bankers willing or able to follow the New Orleans rules, for I began to learn banking myself in the neighboring state of Iowa the year after he spoke.

difference being that the capital assets of the Bank of England were more readily marketable than those of the New Orleans banks appear to have been. It was an arrangement, adapted to the needs of the States, which enabled the banks to provide some long-term credit but deferred their extension of such credit to their extension of definitely short-term credit, the increase of the dead weight assets being permissible only so long as the movement of the banks included specie equal to one-third the quick liabilities and paper maturing in ninety days or less equal to two-thirds.

The capital accounts of both American and Canadian banks had begun early to be the means of obtaining long-term capital abroad, for the shares of the Bank of the United States, both the first and the second, and of some New York banks, especially the Manhattan, had been largely held overseas, and the capital of the Bank of British North America was mainly if not wholly British. In the period of Nicholas Biddle's leadership, some banks obtained funds abroad by the sale of bonds, so-called, though not often of long-term. Some southern states which took stock in their banks paid for it by the surrender of bonds, which the banks sold abroad; some guaranteed the bonds of the banks themselves. The Union Bank and the Citizens Bank, both of New Orleans and established in 1832 and 1833 respectively, received bonds of the state secured by land mortgages supplied it in exchange by the banks, which in turn obtained them from the stockholders. These bonds were sold abroad, the proceeds supplying the banks with foreign balances. The Barings were interested, and their agent, Edmond J. Forstall, was president of the Citizens Bank. But these banks were generally unsuccessful and it was their stopping specie payments that gave Mr Forstall occasion to draft the banking act of 1842.

Of the southern bond-financed banks, or plantation banks, as Dr Redlich calls them, perhaps the most unfortunate was the Real Estate Bank of Arkansas, incorporated in 1836. Its bonds, as in Louisiana, were guaranteed by the state, which was in consequence painfully involved in its protracted bankruptcy. Arkansas had no major seaport like New Orleans with a great commerce of outgoing staples and of incoming silver and gold, in the stream of which it could establish its banks. So, its fingers badly burnt and with no encouraging alternative, the state chose the conservative, agrarian course and in 1846 forbade banking.

The State Bank of Indiana did better. "As there were no capitalists and few men of more than very moderate means in Indiana," said Hugh McCulloch, the bank's charter arranged that a subscriber for a certain number of shares in the bank at $50 each should pay $18.75 on each share but might borrow the remaining $31.25 from the state (not from the bank). The state was to be secured for the amount lent by a mortgage on land and buildings at one-half the appraised value. The borrower paid six per cent on his loan, and all dividends on his stock were credited on the principal. The state sold bonds in the London money market bearing five per cent interest and secured by the mortgages given it by the borrowing shareholders. "Long before their maturity" the state was ready to retire them, but their owners would not give them up, "although a handsome premium was offered for them." Meanwhile the shareholders had repaid their loans from dividends and had their investment clear. The only thing to regret about the arrangement was the smallness of its scope, but that, of course, was a factor in its success.[11]

The capital of banks in the first half of the 19th century usually bulked much larger in their balance sheets than it does a century or more later. Albert Gallatin, having the statements of more than 300 banks about 1830, could not find one whose loans amounted to *three* times its capital or whose note liabilities amounted to *twice* its capital. Since note and deposit liabilities were then about equal, he might have found the two combined were about *four* times the capital. A century and a quarter later, the loans and investments of American banks are about *ten* times their capital (including surplus and other capital accounts), and deposit liabilities are about *twelve* times their capital. There was then more fictitious capital but not enough to alter the fact that bankers counted much less upon their liabilities to the public than they have come to do since then. They counted upon them so little, indeed, that the dust raised over the circulation privilege seems rather absurd when one considers how much more expansible deposits have proved to be than circulation was. But that bankers could do relatively much less business on what they owed the public and that they had to provide relatively more of their funds themselves seems to be entailed in the fact that business was then much more an individualistic matter and much less a social one. Certainly the incorporated bank seems to have had much less advantage over the private lender than was commonly thought. Isaac Bronson, an authority on banking, was a large stockholder in

---

[11] McCulloch, 114-15.

a bank in Bridgeport, Connecticut, but he was mainly a private lender, which he presumably would not have been had he found bank stockownership more profitable than lending.[12]

V

When American banking was new, deposit credit had seemed to most men, save for occasional realization of the facts behind appearances, simply book credit testifying to the actual, physical *deposit* at the teller's window of silver, gold, circulating notes, or bank checks. Alexander Hamilton's observation that it arose also from bank loans recorded what every one familiar with banking must have known, but it failed to establish a recognized principle; though by 1858 at least one New York banker could ask what right depositors had to demand coin, since they were usually borrowers and had not given the banks coin but "a form of credit." Its full significance was missed even by Hamilton. Men continued to think of deposits as simply something deposited, regardless of the fact that in actual practice bookkeepers in banks were making deposits include what had been borrowed at the bank and left there to be checked out. Deposits continued to be identified with specie, though it was obvious that they exceeded specie several times. So confused and fallacious was the understanding of this perplexing subject, which, of course, still eludes the efforts of most people to comprehend it and then keep it comprehended, that in 1831 the minority report of the Clayton committee, which supposedly was prepared with the help of Nicholas Biddle, could make the statement that a bank's circulation was the only portion of its responsibility that need worry a banker; because "The deposits, except in periods when all commercial confidence is lost, so far from being properly regarded as a debt for which the bank should make provision as for its circulation, are universally considered by all banks as a fund upon the faith of which they may safely issue their paper to an equal amount."[13]

This was terrible. It virtually said that deposits were assets and professed that a bank could base its note liabilities on its deposit liabilities. When the first American banks were established, their depositors had been almost identical with their shareholders, always substantial, and well known to the banks' managers; consequently, being more or less in the family, so to speak, they could perhaps be

[12] Gallatin III, 312; Venit, *JEH*, v (November 1945), 201.
[13] Gibbons, 390; 22nd Congress, 1st Session, HD 460, pp. 311-12.

counted on as the holders of bank notes could not be. Whether this was ever true, it was by 1840 an illusion, supported only by two quite irrelevant circumstances. First, the word "deposits" sounded as if it must denominate something material, like gold, that was deposited or laid down with the help of gravitation on the bank's counter; and second, aggregate deposit liabilities and aggregate note liabilities happening at the time to be about equal in amount, it was easier to maintain a false notion of their relationship. Yet the idea that a bank's circulation was the only portion of its responsibility that need worry a banker and that deposits were a tranquil liability was clearly belied by contemporary experience. Deposits were far more volatile than circulation. Depositors were the larger creditors, the more sophisticated, the nearer at hand, and the fewer in number. They could clean out a bank in no time. Note-holders were small creditors, scattered, and ineffective. In reporting to the Barings, 11 May 1837, the suspension of the New York banks the day before, Prime, Ward, and King said the "immediate cause" was "a want of confidence among the depositors." Had the withdrawals been confined to note-holders, "no mischief would have resulted"; but against the demands of depositors with "unusually large balances . . . there was no recourse." Prime, Ward, and King said the same in 1841: "it is the depositors who demand coin"; and of certain "sound" banks, "they have no circulation." It was also reported by Grant and Stone, correspondents of the Barings in Philadelphia, that it was the withdrawals by depositors that closed the United States Bank of Pennsylvania and other Philadelphia banks in February 1841. Instead of being dependable, as Mr Biddle reasoned, deposits were flighty, and as demonstrated a century later in the bank failures of 1932 and 1933, the larger the deposit the greater its menace; the "wise money" was the first to slip away.[14]

Yet in the minds of many bankers and writers, the fallacy that circulating notes were the more volatile liabilities seems to have lived on with the conflicting notion that they were nevertheless more profitable, because it was harder for them to find their way home for redemption. Both notions could not be true, but what the elephant was supposed to look like depended on the part of him the blind man had his hands on when giving his testimony. No one in banking had more intelligence than Nicholas Biddle and Albert Gallatin, but both understood this part of their profession very imperfectly. Albert

[14] Baring Papers, OC, 11 May 1837, 8 February 1841; MC, 26 February 1841.

Gallatin could make the correct observation that note and deposit liabilities were interchangeable, with no difference of substance between them, but he could also say that though note liabilities should be under government control, there was no reason why deposits should be. And it long remained generally true that men could overlook not only the importance but the existence of deposits. The New York legislators had done this in 1829 when they set up a Safety Fund to insure bank notes but made it insure the "debts" of the banks, as if there were no such debts but the notes. The weak hold of the facts on men's minds is illustrated by two statements of Daniel Webster: The first, made to the Senate in 1832, was that "The power of issuing notes for circulation is not an indispensable ingredient in the constitution of a bank merely as a bank. The earlier banks did not possess it, and many good ones have existed without it." The second statement, made to the Supreme Court in 1839 when he was arguing the case *Bank of the United States* v. *Primrose*, was that the power "without which any institution is not a bank and with which it is a bank . . ." is the "power to issue promissory notes with a view to their circulation as money." Had the second statement been made first, it might have been said that Mr Webster was learning, but as things were, the longer it followed the first, the more mistaken he was.[15]

The Louisiana law of 1842, without lapsing into exposition, metaphysics, or argument, formally disposed of the matter in a fashion that was practicable and effective. It clarified no theories of banking and it left the nature of deposits as little understood as ever. It merely joined notes and deposits on the same footing, factually and indissolubly, as they should be. Mr Forstall proposed as law what might have been a resolution of his bank's board of directors: the bank's cash reserves were to be kept at not less than one-third of its cash responsibilities, comprising deposits as well as circulation.

For the first two decades or so of their use in America, bank notes had been simply promissory notes or evidences of debt. They were not money but promises to pay money. This was true in common parlance and in terms of law; for on each note, over the signature of its officers, the issuing bank promised to pay the holder of the note a stated amount of money either on demand or, as came to be the case less often, at some specified date. If the owner of such a

[15] Gallatin III, 268, 428; 22nd Congress, 1st Session, *Debates*, 984; *Bank of the United States* v. *Primrose*, 13 Peters 564.

note presented it at the bank which issued it, requested to be paid in coin the amount stated, and was refused, he could and sometimes did sue in the courts for the payment to which he was entitled. In principle and in law nothing could seem simpler than his right to judgment. In practice it was very unlikely that he would get his money. The courts, caught between what was clearly the law and what was clearly inequity, looked for technicalities to take refuge in and usually found them.

More than one thing impeded the individual claimant's suit. For one, public opinion was against him. He was usually a stranger and a broker who had bought bank notes at a discount and came into town to carry off the specie of the local banks to the hurt of the whole community. The banker found it easy to persuade his fellow townsmen that these strangers were their enemies, for it was obvious that the silver and gold they carried away to New York or to some other big, wicked city weakened the local bank and impaired its power to lend. The broker's occupation was therefore a hazardous one, and in Maryland, in 1841, banks were explicitly released by law from the obligation to redeem notes presented by brokers with a demand for payment. The effect of such feeling was to make demands by local note-holders something like treason; for payment to one creditor benefited him to the detriment of his neighbors. And few courts would fail to share this prejudice or to look on the plaintiff as any better than a sort of Shylock whose claim might be legal but whose motives were low.[16]

There were at least three contradictory views of the importance of note redemption and of its opposite, the stoppage of specie payments. One was the original, moral, legal, and respectable view that what banks promised they should be made to perform, that their failure or refusal to redeem their notes was dishonorable, and that the laws should authorize severe penalties therefor. Conservative bankers, and notably Albert Gallatin, shared this austere view. The second was the concessive, reasonable, expedient, and amoral view that the banks, whatever their faults, provided the people their money and could not be punished without punishing the people more. The third view, entrepreneurial, enlightened, and constructive, was that stoppage of specie payments was really a good thing, because it liberated the money supply from an arbitrary limitation, made it ample and expansible, and fostered enterprise. This view

16 Dillistin, *Bank Note Reporters*, 9; Bryan, 108-09.

was expressed as early as 1814 by the Pennsylvania manufacturer and Jacksonian politician, Samuel Ingham, who later, as Secretary of the Treasury, opened the attack on the federal Bank. These three views exercised conflicting influences on laws and public policy. In a stern mood legislators would declare that if banks failed or refused to redeem their notes, their charters would be forfeit. Then the banks would fail or refuse to redeem their notes, whereupon the minatory law would be suspended by the legislature and the bank's unlawful action legalized. The futility or the impolicy of procedure against banks for not paying their notes was generally recognized. Of events in 1815, a writer in the *North American Review* in 1831 asked rhetorically "what was the popular feeling toward those few individuals who resorted to their rights and asked the banks to fulfil their promises?" In 1832 a Parliamentary committee at Westminster heard that in the States "it is a generally understood thing that the banks are to be protected from demands in cash, except for the convenience of making fractional payments," that demands for specie were "rare," and that instances were known "where banks have privately interceded with merchants to suspend such demands." In 1837 the Vermont bank commissioners acknowledged themselves "aware that under the existing laws the banks can not be proceeded against in so full and ample a manner by those holding their notes as may be done by one individual against another," but they were "not fully agreed" what should be done about it. In 1838 a court dismissed a suit against the United States Bank of Pennsylvania, which then with all other banks was refusing to redeem its notes and hence was plainly violating the law; the grounds for dismissal being that the plaintiff had not "substantiated the facts" of his case.[17]

In such circumstances most suits seem to have been brought in times of a general stoppage of specie payments when the most people were discommoded and public opinion was most exasperated against the banks. The courts might be moved by the current opinion, as already said, but even so they were deterred by realization that they were dealing with a peculiar kind of obligation, which affected hundreds or thousands of absent creditors for each one importunate enough to go to law with his claim. They were not considering iso-

[17] *North American Review* xxxii (1831), 554; British Parliament, Minutes of Evidence, *Bank of England Charter*, 1832, Queries 5512, 5513; 25th Congress, 2nd Session, HD 79, p. 103; Raguet, *Financial Register* ii, 121-27; Gouge, Part ii, 84.

lated, ordinary contracts, such as involve designated parties and performance of a designated task for a designated consideration, but contracts affecting an untold number of creditors besides the one in court. The latter could not be awarded payment or the bank be declared insolvent without possible and very probable impairment of the claims of others. Nor could the court fail to see that bank notes, whatever they had been originally in law, were now in fact the circulating medium of the country and as such entailed considerations with which contracts were not concerned.*

In 1849 the New York legislature enacted a statute whose purpose was evidently to authorize corrective action against delinquent banks but which in the panic of 1857 the courts would not so use. The banks having agreed in that crisis not to convert their notes into specie on demand, a note-holder brought suit against the Bank of New York for its refusal to redeem notes issued by it which he owned and had presented for payment. This case was *Livingston* v. *The Bank of New York*. The plaintiff, alleging that the bank was insolvent, as indicated by its refusal, asked the court to institute proceedings for it to be put in receivership. The court refused. Traditionally and in principle, a debtor who openly and flatly refused to pay an obligation was culpable, and the legislature had evidently adopted the law under some such conviction. The court, however, took a different view. It would not admit the refusal to be evidence that the bank was insolvent, especially when all the banks were united in action. This was tantamount to judicial recognition of the fact long established in practice and accepted by all but the most conservative business men, agrarians, and die-hard theorists, that bank notes were money and no longer simply promissory notes to be dealt with as individual obligations between debtor and creditor.[18]

That the American prejudice against persons who demanded

* Another circumstance of uncertain weight is that corporate bankruptcy was not a condition for which the laws provided from the first. There were jails for individual debtors and laws for individual bankrupts but nothing of the like for delinquent corporations till well along in the 19th century. Chancellor Kent observed in his *Commentaries* (4th edition, II, 314) that the New York act of 1825 "to prevent fraudulent bankruptcies by incorporated companies" was an unusual measure, "for the English bankrupt laws and the general insolvent laws of the several states never extended to corporations," except, as he later noted, for a New Jersey statute of 1810 dealing with banks.

[18] *Livingston* v. *Bank of New York*, 26 Barbour 304.

specie of banks was not peculiar to the New World is indicated by the remark of Great Britain's Lord Chief Justice in 1801 in a case involving interpretation of the Restriction Act of 1797, which relieved banks of the obligation to redeem their notes in most circumstances but not all. A note-holder who demanded payment of a bank note in specie and was refused sued in the courts and was upheld, the circumstances being of the sort where payment in specie was still obligatory. But the court begrudged the plaintiff his judgment; a note-holder was not prevented by the act, said His Lordship with regret, from "captiously demanding a payment in money," and he added, "Thank God few such creditors as the present plaintiff have been found since the passing of the Act."* This judicial sentiment accords with the opinion of Lord Mansfield in *Miller* v. *Race*, 1758, which I mentioned in an earlier chapter. It was expressed when Britain was under pressure of war, but that seems to me of no peculiar significance; it illustrates that in war as in peace an economy in process of becoming modern would circumscribe the right of individuals to hoard specie and thereby diminish the general money supply by as many times the amount hoarded as the current credit expansion exceeded the specie stock.

In the 19th century, banks were so often spoken of as "putting their notes in circulation" that it sounds as if their doing so were an end in itself and presupposed nothing more than perhaps their thrusting the notes out the window to be caught by the wind. Quite to the contrary, the circulation was necessarily incidental to the accomplishment of loans, purchases, or other transactions that gave the bank earning assets in exchange. For most reputable banks it was sufficient that they got to use their notes in cashing the checks drawn on them, thus continuing to be in debt to their customers one way instead of another. For some banks that were reputable and for those that were not this was insufficient, and they took pains to press their notes into use. A common procedure to this end was for two banks remote from one another to exchange large blocks of notes. Each would then pay out the other's as called on, instead of its own, and the notes being far from home when they went into use would be a long time getting back. Some would never get back. A more speculative procedure was to advance a block of notes to an officer

* This is quoted from Mr J. Keith Horsefield's essay "The Duties of a Banker," in *Papers in English Monetary History*, edited by T. S. Ashton and R. S. Sayers, pp. 20-21.

or director with instructions to make a trip somewhere, buy commodities, sell them, and return home with the money before the notes did. In the case of free banks, the notes could be used to pay for the bonds that secured them, and the "bankers" either could draw interest—six per cent or better—on say $100,000 of bonds acquired with an outlay of $10,000 in cash, or could sell the bonds at a profit if they advanced, deposit enough to retire the notes, and pocket the gains. Since bank notes circulated not simply at par but sometimes at a premium and sometimes at discounts ranging off to ninety-nine per cent, there was always the adventitious possibility of dickering over their value and getting more for them than they were worth. The advantages, for example, of putting Chicago notes in circulation in Savannah or *vice versa* might be worth ten per cent and warrant their being shaved proportionally in attractive circumstances. That many fortunes were actually made in undertakings like this, I very much doubt, but that many men were tempted into them by the possibility of easy gain is evident. This corruption of the currency had been encouraged, of course, by destruction of the Bank of the United States and termination of federal control over note issue.

VI

The requirement in the 1842 Louisiana banking act of a one-third specie reserve was the highest set by any statute and the first against deposits as well as notes. It was not the first against notes alone. Virginia in 1837 had required a 25 per cent reserve against notes and New York in 1838 a timid 12½ per cent, which it shortly after abolished. The insertion of any ratio in the statutes was something of an achievement, because bankers themselves declared that no one general ratio existed. Nicholas Biddle said very truly in 1810 that what proportion of specie should be held by banks "to answer the calls" upon them for payment of their obligations was one of the "questions of commercial economy yet undetermined." Recent studies by Mr Keith Horsefield show how true this had been in Britain, and it was still truer in the States. "All practical men agree," it was said, that there could be "no settled proportion" of cash prescribed for all banks at all times. There was doubt in particular whether America with a chronic adverse balance of payments could possibly keep the ratio of specie reserves that Great Britain could with a chronic trade balance in her favor. New Orleans could, but not the whole country.[19]

The first ratios of reserves required by law, as I said in an earlier chapter, were the reciprocals of the limitation set in the first American and Canadian charters upon the expansion of liabilities relative to capital, i.e., to specie. Or it would be better to say that those limitations were the reciprocals, first devised by Alexander Hamilton, of the ratios between specie and liabilities which Adam Smith and other writers thought typical of good banking practice and to which in 1837 the statutes began to return. The Louisiana requirement of 33⅓ per cent reserves was the reciprocal of the Hamiltonian restriction of liabilities to thrice capital. Following Louisiana's example, Missouri in 1857 required 33⅓ per cent reserves against notes only, and Iowa in 1858 required 25 per cent against notes and deposits both. There was as yet no such requirement in the East. But Massachusetts adopted one in 1858 and Governor King of New York suggested in a message of 6 January, the same year, that New York require 25 per cent specie reserves. Under a law with a similar requirement, he said, "the chief banks of New Orleans, alone of all the banks of the country, were enabled to resist the pressure of universal suspension elsewhere and maintain their integrity" in the panic of 1857. Besides the states that emulated the Louisiana requirement, though with varying ratios, the federal government did so in the National Bank Act, 1863.[20]

This shift from a limitation on liabilities in terms of capital to a requirement of cash reserves in terms of liabilities established a device of credit control on which, in the century since, more and more emphasis has been placed. It was a shift from a static base to a moving one; for capital could not readily change, especially when fixed by law, whereas liabilities and cash were always changing. The shift was probably induced by realization that specie and capital were not the same thing, as Alexander Hamilton seems to have assumed they were, and that it would be more practicable to require specie reserves in proportion to liabilities than it had been to require capital to be paid in specie and then kept in specie. Efforts had long been made to insure the latter by having some state official count and certify the specie paid in as capital before a new bank could

[19] Ashton and Sayers (J. K. Horsefield), 50ff; William Hamilton, *Debates*, 31; South Carolina Legislature, *Compilation*, 688.
[20] 35th Congress, 1st Session, HD 107, p. 159.

open for business and by obtaining sworn statements from the bank's directors that the specie paid in was to be kept, so that the bank's capital would always be in the bank. Several states had such requirements and banking was little the better for them. An order or certificate calling for gold could be counted as gold, with the result that one bank might have a certain sum actually in gold and another might have an order for that gold and each might count the gold as in its possession. A less subtle procedure is described by Senator Thomas Hart Benton, who wrote in 1858 that some promoters in Kansas, who were organizing a bank with $50,000 capital, met the requirements of the law by borrowing $2,000 in coin, which they put in two valises and brought to the state capital for certification. They kept one valise outside, took the other into the Governor's office, and asked him to count what was in it. When he had done so, they brought in the second valise, asked him to count its contents, and took out the first. Then when he was through with the second, they brought in the first again, and took out the other. When this had been done twenty-five times, the Governor had counted $50,000 and was ready to give the promoters the certificate they needed. Thus America grew great.[21]

It had been Albert Gallatin's observation that the common statutory limits on liabilities in ratio to capital were nugatory because they were never reached; but Mr Gallatin was thinking of note liabilities only, which were relatively shrinking while the real expansion was in deposit liabilities. In terms of deposits, the limit based on capital would have been reached and in an expanding economy it would have become confining and incongruous. On the other hand, the requirement that specie reserves be kept above a fixed ratio with liabilities, both being freely expansible, was congruous with the demands of an expanding economy. It had also the administrative merit that compliance with it could be ascertained at any time by official examiners. Though the new requirements were more sensible and useful than the old, they alone did not produce the improvement in practice. What improved practice was the increased wealth of the country, its accumulated savings, its greater stock of specie—things for which the diligence of the Americans was responsible. Most men prefer substance to pretense, and when they were able to keep specie on hand they were very glad to do so. Though the Americans had rather have banks without specie than

21 *Bankers Magazine*, January 1858, p. 562.

have no banks at all, they preferred still more to have banks with specie. And as soon as they could, they did. The legal requirement was a practical affirmation of the preference.[22]

VII

In the year 1857 there were some 1,500 to 1,600 banks in the United States. They were being conducted with every degree of merit and demerit from the best to the worst. Banking was highly regarded in most quarters, but disliked and forbidden in others. There were also partnerships and individuals engaged in banking on their personal responsibility, unincorporated; and there were brokers, merchants, and corporations not primarily engaged in banking whose business nevertheless shaded off into it. The typical sign of banking, as loosely conceived by the public and by legislators, was the bank note, but many banks, and especially the important ones, issued few or no notes, and many concerns not banks issued certifications, drafts, etc., that were indistinguishable from notes. Banking practice covered a confusing range of varied activities. I have sought to confine myself to the essential function, viz., the lending of bank credit as a form of money, but what one found along the streets were banks and others engaged in far more than that.

In the main the practice of banks about the year 1857 comprised the following: the provision of deposit credit and of bank notes by lending; the purchase and sale of exchange in the form of bills drawn for the sale of goods; the purchase and sale of exchange in the form of bank notes, checks, and drafts; the underwriting, purchase, and sale of investment securities providing capital funds for industry and government.

In commercial centers lending was typically confined to short-term on the security of actual sales of merchandise in the commodities markets. According to the New Orleans figures shown earlier for 1852, bank credit was mostly in the form of deposits. The same was generally true of New York. In these centers circulation did not pay. "The high premium" on bonds, it was said, "and the labor and expense of maintaining the circulation are poorly compensated by its profits." Though lending on short term was not prescribed by law elsewhere than in New Orleans, it was the rule in commercial cities. In New York there was also lending on call and otherwise on

[22] Gallatin III, 312.

the security of stocks and shares, but it was frowned on. Banking practice at this time was entertainingly described by a New York banker, James S. Gibbons, whom I have just quoted on the profits of note issue. According to him the New York City banks did not discount paper until it was within two or three months of maturity.* "Merchandise," he wrote, "is sold from first hands to the jobber on a credit of eight months, more or less, for which the latter gives his promissory notes. The jobber sells in smaller quantities (by the piece or single package) to the retailer, on a credit of six months." Most traders of all classes were heavy borrowers, few having capital enough to pay till paid; and this condition supplied the banks with promissory notes, "the discount of which is their principal source of profit. Commerce, in its broadest sense," Mr Gibbons said, "is carried on by promissory notes. The multiplication of this form of credit is beyond all control. . . . The retailer purchases goods of the jobber and gives his note in settlement. The jobber gives notes to the wholesale merchant and he in turn to the manufacturer or producer. The manufacturer gives notes for the raw material. The factor is already under acceptance to the grower, and the grower's notes are given to the banks long before his fields 'are white unto harvest.' . . . The market carries millions of notes for what is already consumed and millions more for what is not yet sprouted in the furrow." These promissory notes were commercial currency, Mr Gibbons said, and had commonly been transferred already by endorsement from one merchant to another in settlement of debts by the time they came into the bank's possession.[23]

This New York account of lending practice agrees and disagrees with an account from Philadelphia nearly twenty years before left by Condy Raguet. Writing in 1838, Mr Raguet had said that "thirty years ago it was not the general practice of the banks of Philadelphia to discount notes that had more than sixty days to run." But there had been an increase of bank capital, "employment for which on short paper could not be found," he said, and this had "introduced the custom, here and elsewhere, of discounting paper at four and six months." He thought the general suspension of 1837

* Discounting was not yet formally and regularly delegated to the officers of banks but still, as in the 18th century, was done mostly by the directors, who met twice a week or so to consider the offerings left by applicants with the cashier. Gibbons, 20, 26, 27.

[23] Gibbons, 18-19, 59-60, 214-15.

attributable to these longer maturities but also to "the pernicious extent of credits on merchandise sold, to which our importers and manufacturers are reluctantly obliged to submit." This describes somewhat longer maturities in Philadelphia in 1838 than in New York in 1857, which may or may not be so, the differences not being excessive or obviously improbable and the reports themselves being in terms too general for precision. For both periods, however, it appears that bank credit was mainly being used in the movement of products.[24]

The second common function of banks about 1857—the purchase and sale of exchange in the form of bills drawn for the sale of goods—combined the transfer of funds with lending. It involved an efficient and useful employment of bank credit in the basic and massive movement of the country's products. Dealing in exchange fetched the banks a fee or discount for the service as well as interest on the credit advanced. That is, a bank that purchased a bill which was drawn by a manufacturer of furniture in Philadelphia on a dealer in furniture in St Louis and which was payable in nine months, would charge interest for the time it owned the bill and had to wait for repayment and would charge also for getting the money transferred from St Louis to Philadelphia. This practice, already long established in foreign trade, was extended to domestic trade by the Bank of the United States and adopted by banks generally, though it annoyed their customers to pay what seemed to them a double charge for a single service. But transferring money—which for the beneficiary is the same as having it transported, say from St Louis to Philadelphia—and lending money are two different things, each entailing a cost and justifying a profit. The transfer entailed a cost far greater then than now, for in the early 19th century before there were telegraphs, the distance between St Louis and Philadelphia in terms of communication was astronomical compared with what it is now. Any communication between the two cities might take three weeks. A telegraph message, in three weeks, could travel farther than I see any sense in reckoning. So in terms of transportation could an airplane moving at the speed of sound. Because scientific techniques have made the cost of a single transfer microscopic, though the preliminary conversation about it may cost something, banks do not charge for the bulk of monetary transfers. But in 1857 they still did. Thirty years before that, when the service

[24] Raguet, *Financial Register* II, 9, 15.

was new to them, Nicholas Biddle, 4 December 1824, had explained the views of the Philadelphia directors to the federal Bank's New Orleans branch as follows: "More particularly it appears to us that the discounting domestic bills at the mere interest of the money without any charge for the exchange is not an adequate profit for the risk and must have so injurious a tendency on the purchases of foreign exchange that it would be preferable for the Bank to decline such discounts unless at least one per cent were added to the interest."[25]

Although the financing of international trade had at first been an important part of the business of chartered banks, most notably the Bank of the United States and the United States Bank of Pennsylvania, it had become by the middle of the century the special medium of unincorporated banking houses, such as the Browns of Baltimore and their affiliated houses. One of this firm's later partners, John Crosby Brown, has written:

"Up to the time of the Civil War, and indeed until the establishment of regular telegraphic communication by cable, the business of the firm had been confined within very strict limits. Purchase and sale of sterling exchange, advances against cotton and other produce from Southern and other ports of the United States consigned to the Liverpool firm for sale, granting of credits to merchants for the importation of goods from all parts of the world, and the issuance of circular letters of credit to travellers, formed the major part of the business.

"It was one of the maxims of the older members of the firm, . . . that the distinction between domestic and foreign banking should be strictly maintained. It was for this reason that in the older days deposit accounts from domestic concerns were discouraged, in fact rarely received, and as far as possible all purely domestic banking business was declined. . . . My father used to say that deposits from domestic concerns were a poor reliance for a foreign banker, for in an active money market money needed for foreign purposes was always drawn out for home use.

"The course of exchange for years before the Civil War was mainly affected by the condition of the crops (chiefly the cotton crop) and by the magnitude and volume of the exports and imports. . . . During the spring and summer, when there was little cotton for export, exchange would usually be high, and low during

[25] Biddle Papers 11, Folio 2215; Golembe, 72-73.

the fall and winter, when cotton was freely shipped. It was custom-ary, therefore, when exchange was high, to draw very largely upon the Liverpool house and to use the money in New York to discount good mercantile paper falling due in autumn and winter. The paper discounted was largely that of Southern merchants, which usually commanded very high rates. In the autumn and winter, when ex-change was low, the process was reversed; large amounts were bought, not only with the proceeds of the paper discounted, but also by borrowing largely from banks."[26]

The purchase and sale of domestic exchange in the form of bank notes, checks, or drafts was also a function—the third of those common in 1857—in which unincorporated houses typically though not exclusively were engaged.* It involved an enormous and con-tinuous volume of small domestic transactions, whereas exchange in the form of bills involved fewer but larger ones, to a considerable extent seasonal and either foreign or inter-regional. One of the best-known houses engaged in the domestic field, and in physical terms engaged particularly in the discounting and collection of bank notes, was the firm of E. W. Clark and Company of Philadelphia. "The exchange business of the Clarks from 1842 to 1857 consisted of the usual purchase and sale of all kinds of funds on all sections of the United States and Canada." The bulk of these dealings were in bank notes, which were bought, sold, or sent back to the issuing banks to be redeemed. The firm had affiliates and correspondents in various parts of the country, through which notes acquired in one quarter could be transferred readily for collection or for use in another. At the outset of his career, Jay Cooke, later one of Amer-ica's most famous financiers, was an employee of the Clarks and an expert on bank notes. This meant that he could recognize at sight notes from all over the country, could distinguish the spurious and the counterfeit, and knew the varying value of those that had value. The varieties of money—not counting counterfeits and the worth-less notes of bankrupt issuers—were innumerable. The value of bank notes varied from bank to bank and place to place; and it was common for banks to have it understood with their customers in what sort of money deposits were to be withdrawn and with what sort

---

* The earlier brokers who dealt in bank notes commonly dealt in lottery tickets also. Dillistin, *Bank Note Reporters and Counterfeit Detectors.*

[26] John Crosby Brown, 279-80.

promissory notes were to be repaid. Nowadays banks deal with but one kind of currency.[27]

Jay Cooke wrote of his firm as follows in 1839 and 1840: "Our office is continually crowded with customers, and we do a tremendous business. We buy and sell at from ⅛ to ¼ for commission and thus in doing $50,000 per day you will see it pays well. We often make one per cent on a large amount in one day.... We keep money all over the United States."[28]

The circulation of bank notes occasioned the publication of reporters which attempted to list and evaluate all issues of bank notes and to describe all spurious issues and counterfeits. These publications, which were got out weekly and of which Thompson's in New York seems to have been the best, were indispensable to the merchant and banker, for notes of unknown and uncertain value were constantly being offered in payment everywhere. The Clarks published such a reporter themselves for a time.* They discounted and they had deposit liabilities, but they issued no notes, lest being unincorporated they violate the laws of some of the states in which their obligations might be used. They did issue "drafts," however, engraved as bank notes were, set up in denominations, and drawn by a Clark firm in one part of the country on another Clark firm in another part, and put in circulation by a third Clark firm somewhere else. The drafts were known, trusted, accepted, and a better currency than those emitted by many banks under specific authority of some law. They resembled the "certificates of deposit" issued by George Smith's Wisconsin Marine and Fire Insurance Company, even to the device of paying them out far from home; for Mr Smith seems to have had an arrangement for putting notes in circulation in Atlanta, Georgia, that had to get to Chicago, Illinois, to be redeemed, these two cities being about as remote from one another in those days as any two in the country.[29]

The Clarks were also dealers in stocks and bonds. They sold bonds of the federal government, for example, to finance the Mexican War, and this experience was useful to Jay Cooke twenty years later when he was similarly engaged during the Civil War. The sale of invest-

* For an account of these publications and much information of the conditions that made them necessary, see Dillistin, *Bank Note Reporters and Counterfeit Detectors*.

[27] Larson, 57-58.   [28] Oberholtzer I, 57-58.
[29] Larson, 61-63.

ment securities, like the financing of foreign trade, became more and more the eminent and characteristic function of firms that had begun as specialists in foreign trade, had established access to the foreign investment markets, and in time became specialists in the procurement of capital and long-term credit, both at home and abroad, for American industry. The Bank of the United States of Pennsylvania seems to have been the last incorporated bank which in the 19th century was prominently engaged in this function. While the farmer was gradually outgrowing the agrarian taboo on debt, and beginning to emulate the business man's recourse to the banks for it, industry was already learning that the banks were unsatisfactory sources of the long-term credit which it required. Small industry—which would mean the miller, the distiller, the cooper, the wheelwright, the blacksmith—would still seek credit at the bank or anywhere likely, but the railways, which were the first exemplars of large scale industry, were depending on Europe and their financing was largely done by banking houses originally engaged in foreign trade.[30]

Of the four practices I have described, all but the provision of deposit credit by lending either have disappeared entirely from the practice of banking or have become very minor; thus, for example, the transfer of funds has become almost wholly incidental to the deposit function. Moreover interest rates have fallen and investment securities vie with loans as earning assets. To replace the obsolete functions and maintain income, banks have been impelled to charge for the service of carrying deposit accounts subject to check and to undertake new functions that may be conveniently associated with banking proper but have nothing to do with it in principle and that in the middle of the 19th century and long after were seldom associated with it in practice. These new functions have included most commonly the rental of safety deposit boxes and most importantly the management of trust funds. The central and essential function of banks nevertheless remains what it was in 1782, the lending of money in the form of deposit credit.*

* It is perhaps advisable to repeat that though bank deposits originate mostly in lending, most depositors are not borrowers but receive the money they deposit from others who are; they receive it in payment of wages, salaries, and purchases.

30 Larson, 69; F. Cyril James i, 340-41.

VIII

In the situation just described as of the middle of the century, there developed two events of very different nature. One was establishment of the New York Clearing House in 1853; the other was the country-wide panic of 1857.

Within the few years preceding 1853, the number of banks in New York City had increased from twenty-four to sixty. Every day each bank might receive checks and notes from its customers on every one of the other fifty-nine, and sixty clerks might be calling at each of the sixty banks and collecting money at each for checks they were carrying about. Each bank might be paying the other fifty-nine in turn and being paid by them. Before drifting into this absurdity, they arranged instead to debit and credit each other daily and then settle their net balances with gold once a week.* But even this weekly settlement was bad enough. Sixty porters from sixty banks were all out at once, calling on one another's banks, receiving specie at some and leaving specie at others. (The porter was not what the word now signifies but the employee at each bank who had custody of its specie, the handling of which required heft as well as trustworthiness and mentality.) At the end of their rounds they met at the "Porters' Exchange" on the steps of one of the Wall Street banks for a final settlement with one another, whence each could return to his own bank pulling on a hand-truck whatever specie he had received and carrying receipts for whatever he had paid. The arrangement had the directness and simplicity of that which is said to have been worked out by the American Indians when each had a path leading from his tepee to every other Indian's tepee.[31]

Though clumsy, the procedure could not be readily abandoned for a better. Some bankers wanted nothing better, confusion and uncertainty having advantages. Others could not agree on what was better. But arrangements for a clearing house were at last accepted and put into effect in October 1853. Each bank sent a settling clerk and a specie clerk to the Clearing House daily at set hours, the first to be paid by the specie clerks of the other banks, the second to pay the

---

* Gold, by now being produced abundantly in California, "was the only legal tender (except for sums under $5) and was also the currency of the government, since the Treasury of the United States, under the Independent Treasury Law of 1846, was not permitted either to receive or to pay except in coin." Dunbar, 270.

[31] Gibbons, 292-94.

settling clerks of the others. These clerks, according to Mr Gibbons, by an orderly and simultaneous procedure accomplished in six minutes what had taken hours. The improvement was mainly a matter of meeting in one place and having each specie clerk settle successively for his bank with settling clerks of the others. Business in New York City was "transacted mostly by checks," Mr Gibbons wrote, and the average daily clearances were soon twenty-five millions. The circulating note issue of the local banks "is but seven millions," he said, "which is principally absorbed in the retail trade."[32]

Much more important than the saving of time in clearances were the tonic effects upon the participating banks of a daily settlement. The expulsion of any bank from the Clearing House or its failure to settle at once what it owed its associates was something for it to dread as fatal. This alone impelled it to conduct its affairs prudently. Moreover concealment from its associates of any weakness in its condition was extremely difficult. A law enacted in New York shortly before the establishment of the Clearing House required each bank in the city to publish every Tuesday a sworn statement of its "average amount of loans and discounts, specie, deposits, and circulation" for the preceding week. The conditions of membership in the Clearing House made this statement factual and potent. As had been the case in New Orleans for ten years or more, the arrangement revealed the reserve position of each bank and effected a "restriction of loans by the necessity of maintaining a certain average of coin from resources within the bank." By *producing* that average— not merely requiring it as the law might do—the Clearing House of New York exercised "a restrictive power over the general currency of trade" throughout the country. The original idea of the Clearing House had been simply to facilitate exchanges. But by 1857 Mr Gibbons said: "It has already added to this many other advantages and uses which were not contemplated; and more are suggested. It has put an end to speculative banking in New York. It has exerted a powerful influence to arrest speculative commerce. It has set the example of *positive liquidation,* which henceforth must spread and increase. Especially in the organization of accounts, it has gained results which were before thought to be out of reach. There is probability, at least, that the New York Clearing House leads the way in a practical use of statistics and commercial facts far beyond our

[32] Gibbons, 114, 296, 308-09.

present attainments and for which there has long been great need."[33]

The establishment of a clearing house in New York had been proposed by Albert Gallatin in 1841. He had said: "Few regulations would be more useful in preventing dangerous expansions of discounts and issues on the part of the city banks than a regular exchange of notes and checks and an actual daily or semi-weekly payment of the balances. It must be recollected that it is by this process alone that a Bank of the United States has ever acted or been supposed to act as a regulator of the currency. Its action would not in that respect be wanted in any city, the banks of which would by adopting the process regulate themselves. It is one of the principal ingredients of the system of the banks of Scotland. The bankers of London, by the daily exchange of drafts at the Clearing House, reduce the ultimate balance to a very small sum and that balance is immediately paid in notes of the Bank of England. The want of a similar arrangement amongst the banks of this city produces relaxation, favors improper expansions, and is attended with serious inconveniences. The principal difficulty in the way of an arrangement for that purpose is the want of a common medium other than specie for effecting the payment of balances."[34]

This want, Mr Gallatin had thought, might be met by setting up a "cash office" which should hold specie deposited in it by each bank and which could issue certificates representing the specie deposited. Mr Gallatin's proposals contained, said Mr Gibbons, "the whole germ of the clearing house system." They comprehended, "essentially," the manner of its action—the proposed cash office becoming the coin depository, and the "common medium other than specie" for effecting the payment of balances becoming the coin certificates which the individual banks received in evidence of their contributions to the coin depository and which they transferred to one another by way of settlements instead of transferring specie.[35]

The banks in Boston established a clearing house in 1856, and the banks in Philadelphia in 1858.

IX

Great as the benefits of the New York Clearing House were and much as it accomplished in correcting "relaxation" and "improper expansion," as Mr Gallatin had thought it might, and in exercising

[33] Gibbons, 321-22, 328.
[34] Gibbons, 339-40; Gallatin iii, 424.
[35] Gibbons, 299-300, 316-17, 340-41.

"a restrictive power over the general currency of trade" throughout the country, as Mr Gibbons observed, it did not prevent or obviously mitigate, four years later, the panic of 1857.

In the East there was no such dislike of banks and no such restraint upon the establishment of them as in the West; and after a slow recovery during the '40's from the Jacksonian credit debauch, their number more rapidly increased in the '50's. The capital of the newcomers, in the judgment of their established competitors, who were prejudiced but not necessarily mistaken, was "mostly fictitious—merely paper—nothing in fact but the creation of a book debt, with hypothecated stock certificates as collateral security." This designation of the capital as nothing but book debt hardly gets to the bottom of the trouble, however, for most debt is "book debt" and yet serves very satisfactorily as the blood stream of a modern economy. But in this new capital there unquestionably was fiction and excess. In New York City, according to Mr Gibbons, "More than half of it was of this character, and at least another fourth was in excess of the commercial want; but it was legally organized, and it attracted or hired deposits and so created a larger basis for more credit in the shape of loans, which in August 1857 were extended to over forty millions of dollars. It is safe to say that two-thirds of this prodigious debt was a grievous burden super-imposed on the legitimate debt of the community and that instead of benefit it brought embarrassment and injury to the trade and labor of the city."[36]

Throughout the country the trend was similar, save that in the West, where there were few banks, the expansion of credit was greater than in the East. It was supplied by the East. "The credits given to Southern and Western buyers were necessarily long at any time, and there is ample evidence that in the few years before 1857 they had seriously increased," wrote Professor Charles F. Dunbar, reviewing the occurrences less than twenty years later. "The lengthening of the credit given to the consumer had brought in its train a longer credit given to the merchant who supplied him, a longer credit by the jobber to the merchant, and by the manufacturer or commission merchant to the jobber, and so on through the whole chain of intermediate dealers from the consumer to producer or importer." If this were not the sort of thing that induced agrarian

[36] Gibbons, 369-71.

Iowa to abandon the prohibition of banks for restricted or monopoly banking, it might well have been.[37]

Since 1849, gold had been coming out of California at a prodigious rate, and the export of it had reduced but not prevented its depreciation. Gold production was already increasing elsewhere too and enhancing confidence in the beneficent control of its supply by the Almighty. As its output increased, its value fell, and prices rose. The economy was stimulated from within and without. The rise in prices, Professor Dunbar reported, "was a new spur to enterprise and a new incentive to the anticipation of gains likely to accrue in the future. In spite of the partial revulsion of 1854 and 1855, nearly every branch of domestic business was driven to the extreme point to which the competition of a singularly active and pushing class of men could force it, and this process was accompanied by an extension of mercantile credits in length as well as in amount." In all, the situation at the outset of 1857 was one wherein "the foreign trade of the country . . . was stimulated to a high degree of activity. Internal trade had been pushed forward with a great expansion and lengthening of credits; the railroad system in its rapid growth had absorbed much circulating capital and had also contributed a large share toward the increase of the vast system of credit on which our domestic affairs rested. And finally this mass of credit was managed by the aid of a great number of banks established upon unlike and often insecure systems, acting upon no common principle, and with no important guaranty for the faithful and prudent discharge of their functions." Yet now, by the summer of 1857, when it became known that the "madness of railroad building was arrested," Mr Gibbons said, the decrease was interpreted as optimistically as the increase had been. "Stock companies could no longer send an agent to Europe with five millions of credit tokens and receive the money for them within sixty days from the engraver's press." And this was tranquillizing. In New York, "the common sentiment was that we had passed the dangerous point in railway credits and with the immense productions of the year at our doors, there was little probability of serious financial disturbance. The most sagacious of our city bank officers saw no indications of an unusual storm in the commercial skies. When the loans reached the unprecedented height of one hundred and twenty two millions of dollars on the eighth of August,

[37] Dunbar, 269-71.

they pointed to the annual reduction of ten or twelve millions in the autumn months as one of the regular ebbs to which the market is subject, but they had no foresight of extraordinary pressure and no dreams of panic. Credit was extended, but 'the country never was so rich.' " This was the way gentlemen had talked in 1837. Though banks began to contract their loans—this was still early in August—and the stock market fell, Wall Street was not upset. "The failure of a heavy produce house was explained by the depression of that particular interest in the market. A report of dishonest jobbing and of the misuse of funds in a leading railway company caused partial excitement without seriously disturbing confidence in mercantile credit."[38]

But the straws were at last piled on that broke the camel's back. On 24 August the New York office of the Ohio Life Insurance and Trust Company suspended and closed its doors. It was the branch of a Cincinnati corporation but seems to have been conducted with little supervision. It was really a bank in function but the more highly reputed "because it was not a bank of issue." Drafts on it were sold in the West, which it borrowed currently in the New York money market to meet. Consequently, nearly all the other New York banks were its creditors, either for the drafts on it sent in by western merchants to the New York suppliers or for funds lent it directly. It was therefore the bankers who were frightened first and started the liquidation. The failure was like an explosion in their midst, and bank officers, in the judgment of James S. Gibbons, participated in the intense excitement "with unusual sensitiveness and want of self-possession." Desperate panic seized the city, prices dropped, and values disappeared. There were daily bulletins of business failures. One of the Clearing House banks fell into default. The banks practically stopped discounting and street rates for money, even on unquestionable securities, rose to three, four, and five percent *a month*. On ordinary commercial paper, such as promissory notes and bills of exchange, money was not to be had at any rate. House after house failed and among them several banking firms, but still no Clearing House banks closed. The Clearing House settlements were watched anxiously, but there were no new defaults among the members.[39]

For some weeks of unrelaxed liquidation the banks held the initia-

38 Dunbar, 269, 273-74; Gibbons, 343-44.
39 Gibbons, 345, 349-51; McCulloch, 133.

tive, reducing their loans right and left. But it was an initiative of desperation. Being without any leadership and without any lender of last resort such as the Bank of England was to British banks and such as the Bank of the United States might have become to American ones, they had no choice but to strip their borrowers in order to save themselves. Efforts to allay the panic were attempted, but as soon as any one bank showed signs of forbearance, others seized the chance to increase its burden to their own advantage. "It was alleged and was believed by many that the attempt to enlarge discounts had been defeated by a few of the stronger banks which were not unwilling to drive their weaker neighbors into liquidation and to confine the business of banking to fewer establishments." This is the comment of Professor Dunbar, but Mr Gibbons, himself a banker and closer to the events, said that it was the newer and less seasoned banks that led the panic. Though he did "not pretend to find a complete apology for the older banks," nevertheless, he wrote, underscoring his words, these older ones, "almost without an exception, *maintained their discount lines nearly unchanged*." So, he adds, did some—"judiciously managed"—of the new ones. Among sixty banks a variety of behaviors is scarcely incredible. Meanwhile the panic had spread. Western merchants who were using drafts on the Ohio Life Insurance and Trust Company to pay their bills in the East had been struck by the same blow as the New York banks. Then it came out that most if not all the company's capital had been "virtually embezzled." Alarm generally throughout the country grew deeper with news of subsequent happenings in New York, where the despair had been blackened still more by the unseasonable delay of steamers fetching gold from California and by the loss of one, the *Central America*, which sank at sea with $2,000,000 of gold aboard— nearly a fifth as much as Wall Street had when the panic began. Toward the end of September the banks in Philadelphia and Baltimore suspended, then in Pennsylvania, Maryland, and Virginia generally, then in New England.[40]

The initiative had now passed from the city banks to their customers and first to the country banks—the "country correspondents"—which were heavy depositors of their reserve funds in the New York banks. The telegraph system which Mr Amos Kendall was energetically building began to fill the latter with imperative orders from the country banks for return of their deposits in gold.

[40] Dunbar, 280-82; Gibbons, 335, 350, 370-71.

The New York City depositors could not stand this and formed in line themselves. Heavy runs on all the city banks began 13 October; the day following all of them stopped specie payments except the Chemical, which held out two days longer. The Boston and New England banks generally stopped the 15th. The stoppage soon prevailed everywhere in the country, *except* in the Mississippi valley, a primitive region which, according to historical convention, was given over to agrarian radicalism, paper money crazes, and lax business morality. There the state-wide Bank of Indiana, the banks of Kentucky, and four of the five banks in New Orleans remained on the specie basis that Wall Street and the sound, conservative, capitalistic East abandoned. These hard-money banks, alike in their strength and in the ability of their managers, were oddly unlike in other respects. New Orleans was one of the chief commercial cities of the world; Indiana and Kentucky were wholly agricultural. The farmers in both these states had had a good year and the banks, as was their wont, were well provided with liquid assets. The directors of the Bank of Indiana, secure themselves and seeing "not a cloud in the sky," had been astounded to receive a telegram informing them of the stoppage of specie payments in New York by the Ohio Life Insurance and Trust Company, which they had thought carefully and judiciously conducted. They decided to risk continuing specie payments and were able to do so throughout the panic. The bank's notes were at a premium. Kentucky's banks had the same success. In both Indiana and Kentucky there were two favoring conditions. One was that the banks' creditors were mainly noteholders widely dispersed on farms and less able as well as less apt than the alert depositors in New York to stab their bankers with sudden, concentrated demands. The other was that the banks in Indiana and Kentucky besides being strong were few in number and able therefore to unite on a program in a fashion impossible for the more numerous banks in New York City. This advantage held for the banks in New Orleans too. Though their heavy deposit liabilities made them more vulnerable than the banks of Kentucky and Indiana, their small number—ten or so—enabled them to act in concert and refrain from the demoralizing, panicky liquidation into which the eastern banks had plunged; and by sparing their debtors they themselves were spared.[41]

The banks of Canada also passed through the 1857 crisis with

41 Gibbons, 357; McCulloch, 132-35; Dunbar, 283.

little scathe, though under severe pressure from it. Canadian banks were generally good. The American banking system, though excellent in numerous spots, had too many weak concerns that were a constant menace to their betters. American banks were also too numerous for reasonable agreement on important questions. The Canadian banks, like those of New Orleans, could act readily and sensibly in concert. "Considerable credits in London strengthened their resources and by avoiding any unnecessary curtailment of loans they prevented any panic among their customers and depositors. . . ."[42]

As usual, the immediate effect of stopping specie payments in the States was ease. The banks, relieved of having to pay their own debts, ceased their harsh pressure on their borrowers. The general understanding that specie payments must sooner or later be resumed impelled a continuance of liquidation but of milder sort. Individual banks, by refusing to lend, could not strengthen themselves at the expense of their liberal neighbors. Specie payments were resumed sooner than in the suspension of 1837 and 1838 and with less bickering, for then the banking system had had the unsettled rivalry of New York and Philadelphia to impede its decisions. Payments were resumed in New York and New England in December, in Philadelphia and Baltimore in February, and by the summer of 1858 everywhere.[43]

In March 1858, three months after their resumption, forty-two of the New York City banks agreed to keep on hand severally "coin equal to not less than twenty per cent of our net deposits of every kind, which shall be made to include certified checks and all other liabilities except circulating notes."* This voluntary requirement became binding on all members of the New York Clearing House. It manifested a change of mind on the part of bankers, who had formerly objected that no single ratio was practicable for general observance. But for sixteen years now a requirement of $33\frac{1}{3}$ per cent reserves had been successfully imposed by law on the banks of New Orleans, and these banks had done better in the panic of 1857 than the banks of New York. James S. Gibbons' discussion of the New York bank reserves shows an unquestioning acceptance of their cardinal import-

---

* The practice of certifying checks was extremely common and much abused. Banks had let themselves get committed to the practice without adequate protection for the risk they took.

[42] Dunbar, 284.　　　[43] Dunbar, 288.

ance. During the year ended July 1855, he said, the specie reserves of the New York Clearing House banks had been "kept at 25 per cent of the deposits." But for the twelve months ending July 1856, the ratios of 1855 being taken for normal, loans showed an excess of $15,000,000, a year later an excess of $35,000,000, and in August 1857, when the panic started, an excess of $45,000,000. "These results," he wrote, "are astounding. If such a departure from equilibrium does not foreshadow the suspension of specie payments as inevitable, it lessens our surprise that it should have occurred (to borrow the words of the Bank-Superintendent) 'with overflowing granaries, exemption from pestilence, neither internal insurrection nor foreign invasion, and our country at peace with every nation on earth.'" The state superintendent of banking, of whose naive surprise Mr Gibbons makes mock, was expressing a notion long cultivated in the States. If people were rich enough, in good health, and at peace, why should anything go wrong? The same astonishment had been expressed in 1837 and in other crises. For a nation of Bible-readers, the Americans failed grievously to pick up anything from the Book of Job.[44]

As Mr Gibbons described it, the force of an approved reserve ratio is corrective and admonitory. "A fair proportion of the resources of a bank," he said, "should be reserved in coin to meet immediate liabilities." What the immediate demand might be varied with circumstances, but a "fair proportion" to meet the probabilities was a matter of judgment. Traditionally it hovered between a fifth and a third. Whatever was decided on became in practice a point of warning, lest "immediate" demands exceed what the banks had ready. Moreover, to those concerned, both in the banks and outside them, anything short of the ratio signified that credit expansion had gone too far. "The market," Mr Gibbons remarked, "is uneasy with high loans and low specie." The money market comprises not only the bankers themselves but other business men, users of money, who are as canny as the bankers who lend it and as deft in reading the oracles. What makes them all uneasy is not that the banks have cash enough to pay only a fifth of their liabilities, say, instead of a third; it is rather that a five-fold expansion of credit means something substantially more than a three-fold expansion. It means that confidence is becoming over-confidence, that borrowers have contracted an amount of debt that it will tax them to repay, and that

44 Gibbons, 365-68.

the earning assets of banks, on which and not on cash their solvency mainly depends, are going to be harder to liquidate. Of all this, low cash reserves relative to liabilities or to earning assets were indicative. Their position had much the same significance as that of the mercury in a thermometer, the degree of which does not induce or prevent extremes, but reflects them. The market, recognizing the reflection, becomes uneasy. Inside the banks and out, the more sagacious and sophisticated dislike the look of things. They quietly prepare to jump. No one wishes to jump, but if he must he wishes to be among the first. Some incident—in August 1857, the failure of the Ohio Life Insurance and Trust Company—breaks the equilibrium, and the trouble begins. The rest of the country, rapt in contemplation of its overflowing granaries and other blessings, happy in its freedom from pestilence, at peace with all the world, and too much impressed by other fortunate circumstances irrelevant to the fact that monetary weakness has developed, is filled with astonishment and consternation. To most people the maintenance of a proper ratio of bank reserves—if considered at all—seemed a formality whose practical importance was obscure, since at best the reserves were adequate to repay only the first few depositors who got inside the door. But to the market and the expert transactors comprising it, the quiet fall of reserves below the line of safety was as effective as a whistle blast. "The market is uneasy with high loans and low specie"; and that is adequate reason for banks to avoid such a condition. For the market is not made up of that part of the people who can be fooled all of the time.[45]

X

Besides the voluntary action of the Clearing House banks of New York in assuming the requirement that each member keep gold on hand equal to twenty per cent of its deposits, the Massachusetts banks were put under a requirement by law to keep 15 per cent on hand. These eastern requirements fell palpably short of New Orleans' 33⅓ per cent and of those in force in Missouri and Iowa.

This evidence of the West's conservatism is supported by the record of what reserves were actually held. The following table shows the liabilities of banks in various states, January 1859, their specie, and the ratio thereof to their liabilities.[46]

45 Gibbons, 366.
46 *Bankers Magazine*, July 1859, p. 30.

Ratio of Specie to Deposits and Circulation of the Banks in Twenty-seven
States on 1 January 1859

State	Deposits and Circulation	Specie	Ratio to 100
Louisiana	$ 30,916,547	$16,218,027	52.46
Missouri	9,192,742	3,921,879	42.66
Alabama	10,481,784	3,371,956	32.17
Minnesota	61,774	15,272	31.12*
Pennsylvania	38,035,048	11,345,536	29.83
Indiana	7,103,776	1,869,000	26.31
Tennessee	11,132,631	2,863,018	25.72
Kentucky	19,490,575	4,984,141	25.57
Maryland	13,006,635	3,120,011	23.99
Georgia	17,005,505	3,751,988	22.06
Massachusetts	51,377,591	11,112,715	21.63
New York	138,973,788	28,335,984	20.39
South Carolina	13,068,173	2,601,414	19.91
Virginia	17,742,043	3,077,687	17.35
North Carolina	7,704,938	1,248,525	16.20
Ohio	12,430,155	1,845,441	14.85
Nebraska	47,094	6,629	14.08
Delaware	1,793,503	217,342	12.12
New Jersey	8,294,005	952,231	11.48
Maine	6,269,449	663,754	10.59
Connecticut	9,520,335	915,814	9.62
Rhode Island	6,449,156	608,833	9.44
Wisconsin	7,717,554	706,009	9.15
New Hampshire	4,185,563	294,423	7.03
Vermont	3,640,015	178,556	4.91
Michigan	887,671	42,018	4.73
Illinois	6,347,106	269,585	4.25

Illinois and Michigan, which are western, are at the bottom, but
five New England states, with Wisconsin, are next to them. Louisiana, Missouri, Minnesota,* Indiana, Tennessee, and Kentucky—all
in the Mississippi valley—stand above New York. Arkansas, California, Florida, and Texas are not included, banks being prohibited
there. Iowa had authorized them too recently for any to have been
established, and Oregon did not become a state till later in the year.
Had the table shown figures for earlier years, there is no reason to

* The figures for Minnesota are plainly incorrect. One must not expect
too much of 19th century bank statistics.

think that the distribution of ratios would have been very different, though specie reserves for the country as a whole were probably higher than usual that year. The West, I should say, shows up very well, manifesting a conservative monetary restraint that scarcely suggests it was to be in the latter part of the century the home of Populism, greenbacks, and free silver.

CHAPTER 22

Federal Monetary Control Restored

1863-1865

I. Disunion — II. War and money — III. The National
Bank Act — IV. Resistance of the banks — V. Coercion —
VI. Like action in Canada and unlike

I

ABRAHAM LINCOLN was elected President of the United States
November 1860. When he went into office four months later seven
states had seceded from the Union and had formed a new, Confederate government. Numerous members of President Buchanan's
Cabinet and officers of his administration were secessionist, and during the interval, while the process of secession was going on, they
either abandoned their loyalties to the Union or were generally
supposed to be doing so. In consequence, the North was in a panic
of incertitude and alarm, only tempered by a failure to believe that
the situation was really as bad as it appeared.

When the new administration came in, it faced the need of an
immense amount of money to quell disunion, the fact that there was
nothing in the Treasury, and the difficulty of obtaining funds from
a frightened money market. The source of the fright was not merely
political, nor was there the slightest idea of what it was going to
cost to regain the seceded states. Its most substantial cause was the
enormous indebtedness of southern banks and business men to
northern banks and business men. Every one of the latter must face
the lively possibility that what was due him from the South for
merchandise and collections might never be received. Even delay
with the receipts might mean ruin, for there were debts to be paid
with those receipts. The commercial world was critically dependent
upon punctual payments and the uninterrupted passage of funds
from hand to hand in an endless net-work of debtor-creditor inter-
relations. Here the country's greatest inter-regional balance of
payments was suddenly at stake in absolutely unprecedented fashion.

Every business man saw his solvency threatened by a possible though not conceivable stoppage of payments in all directions.

The difficulties that faced President Lincoln and the North, however, turned out to be more recondite than this matter of what was owing from the South. As already said, the remittances thence, especially from New Orleans, the greatest commercial and banking center, continued for some time in spite of the efforts of the Confederate government to stop them, the southern bankers having a different sense of obligation from the southern politicians. The North's real difficulties were caused by the rudimentary state into which federal powers had been allowed to lapse for two decades while the economy waxed greater and greater. In that interval, railways and factories had been built. Science, invention, ingenuity, labor, skill, and capital had been concentrated on the enlargement and improvement of the country's productive means. There was now an impressive diversity of resources and employments that put the nation near to self-sufficiency. There was power, prosperity, and wealth. This wealth was well distributed. The people had a high standard of living. The federal government, by comparison, was a cave-dwelling affair. If it had made any movements at all since Amos Kendall had thrilled the democracy with the statement that the world was governed too much, it had made them backward. Mr Kendall himself, after helping reform the government in the direction of passive simplicity, had since then been pushing the economy in the opposite direction, building telegraph lines, and making money. The government had extended its authority and its prestige by virtue of the territorial acquisitiveness of its people and their economic energy; Congress had been loud during a generation of debates on slavery and states' rights; but otherwise the federal government had withdrawn into the modest performance of minor routines. It had turned virtuously away from the policies of Alexander Hamilton and neglected even the humane projects of Thomas Jefferson and Albert Gallatin. It had hesitated to assume responsibility for the Smithsonian Institution. Steamships had been crossing the ocean for thirty years and navigating rivers and lakes, but the little American Navy was still largely under sail and very beautiful to look at. It had less than 10,000 officers and men. The Army had less than 20,000, which was about enough to watch the Indians.

If this were all it might not have been bad, because it might reflect the pacific instincts of a noble people. What it reflected rather was pusillanimity. Departmental organization was antediluvian; the civil service belonged to the politicians; and the business administration of the government's affairs might as well have been directed from Kamchatka so little was it influenced by the energy, adaptability, and efficiency of the economic world around it. This was nowhere more conspicuous than in the fiscal and monetary responsibilities of the government, which were trailing so far behind the progressive world outdoors that they had barely braved the turn from the 18th century into the 19th made by the rest of creation sixty years before. One result of this, and perhaps the one most appalling, was that when Mr Lincoln entered office in March 1861, confronted by the worst exigency, material as well as spiritual, in the country's experience—an exigency requiring ships, guns, men, food, and all the needs of an immense physical effort—his Treasury was empty.

II

It was this rudimentary state of federal powers that prolonged the war. The South's advantages were the North's unreadiness and inability to pull itself together, the decisiveness and energy of the southern leadership at the outset, and the military genius of General Robert E. Lee and his associates. Only one of these advantages was lasting. The advantages of the North were all lasting. She had the population, the wealth, the resources, the commerce, the equipment, the diversified productivity, and the diversified skills. If the war were prolonged, she was bound to win. But the condition of the government was such when Mr Lincoln became President that she could win only if it were prolonged.

Mr Lincoln's Secretary of the Treasury was Salmon P. Chase of Ohio, an able, intelligent, and distinguished lawyer with no experience of fiscal affairs. He found on hand less than $2,000,000, all of which was appropriated ten times over. He calculated that he needed $320,000,000, as he reported to the Congress that met in July in response to the President's call. He had sold some bonds meanwhile which the money market would take only at a discount forbidding to the Treasury, and he had issued some Treasury notes. With the authority obtained from Congress, he first arranged to borrow $150,000,000 from the banks of New York, Philadelphia, and Boston. The bonds received by the banks might be resold by them to the public. The banks expected the Secretary to take the proceeds of the loan in deposit credit on their books as any other borrower would do and as Congress had specially authorized him to do when it authorized him to borrow. But Mr Chase, presumably because he lacked familiarity with banking practice and because the authority conflicted with the requirements of the sub-treasury act without repealing or suspending it, declined to accept deposit credit. He wanted the whole $150,000,000 in gold. This was like killing the goose that laid the golden eggs. By refusing bank credit and demanding cash, the Secretary was forcing the banks to abandon banking. But like a good lawyer he was sticking to what he considered to be the law's demand. The banks indeed did not have $150,000,000 in gold, and those in some states were forbidden by law as well as common sense to strip themselves of cash. The saving condition was that the gold was not taken all at once, though the Secretary would have preferred it so. Instead it was taken from time to time, which avoided strangling the banks completely but allowed them to continue half-strangled. Passing to the Treasury, the gold was thence disbursed, and a substantial part of it was returned to the banks by depositors. But much was not, and the total active supply passing through the Treasury and banks gradually shrank as more and more was put in hiding by the public. The federal laws required the Treasury to use gold, the state laws required the banks to use gold, and for present needs there was not enough for either. To meet the worsening shortage, the Secretary issued more Treasury notes. These being a partial legal tender could be used by the public instead of gold. So the public used the notes and hoarded more gold. This made things still harder for the banks; they could not use the notes as legal reserves but gold only, and gold grew grimly scarcer.[1]

In November 1860, just after the election, the New York Clearing House banks had pooled their specie reserves. This was a remarkable improvement over their cut-throat conduct three years before, in the panic of 1857, when it was each for himself with hopes that the devil would take the hindmost. The banks "agreed that for the purpose of enabling them to expand their loans, the specie held by them should be treated as a common fund," each bank holding Clearing House certificates for the amount of its share. "The effect of this arrangement was that any bank which experienced an unusual demand for specie was supported in meeting it by the whole of the

---

[1] Dewey, *Financial History*, 276ff; Dunbar, 294ff.

common stock and that the debt which it thus incurred it could meet by a pledge of its securities. Whatever course might be taken, each bank was as strong as the rest in specie, nor could any bank, by holding back its loans, strengthen itself at the expense of the others, since the specie which it might thus collect must by the agreement be held for the general benefit." This was wise, it became useful in time, but for the moment it was inadequate.[2]

In only a matter of months, the war already had outlasted all expectation, the number of seceded states had increased from seven to eleven and disunion was menacing in three or four others; arsenals, Navy yards, custom houses, mints, ships, arms, and men had gone with secession. Fort Sumter had been given up, and the first battle of Bull Run had been lost. By December, when Congress met again, it was plain that far more money than had been supposed was going to be needed, and that more effectual means of getting it must be found. Harsh necessity required that the government and the economy be reunited; the happy divorce they had long enjoyed must end. The first step sadly taken toward this reunion was the stoppage of specie payments by the banks and the Treasury at the close of the year. Secretary Chase, instead of learning with surprise of the banks' suspension and then complaining ignorantly about it as his predecessor in President Van Buren's Cabinet had done in 1837, resignedly concurred in its inevitability.

The reform that was needed was both constitutional and practical. It must entail the undoing of two Jacksonian triumphs. Not only was the federal government obstructed, under the Jacksonian legacy, from exercising an essential function—it was forbidden to act normally and to its own advantage as a transactor in the economy. No meeting ground between a government and its people is of more vital importance than that of monetary payments; yet the federal government was denied the use of the money the people used. Any business corporation or individual could borrow at banks, but the government could not. Even in a time of terrible need, the Treasury was forbidden to touch the common means of payment, either as borrower, as payor, or as payee. It might have been confined, with less serious results, to ox carts for conveyance, to quill pens, and to candle light.

This practical fencing-in was rendered suddenly intolerable by the war, which was also intensifying the anomaly of the federal

2 Dunbar, 307-08.

government's impaired control over the monetary system. In terms of the Constitution and of common sense, control of the monetary system irrefragably belonged to sovereignty and if there were any reason at all for federal union, no single one was more basic than that it was needed in order that it might supply the economy a uniform circulating medium. In theory this was recognized, of course: the federal government defined the gold content of the dollar and supplied coins for circulation; and some persons still tried to contend that the coins were the only money. This was ridiculous. The coins were far surpassed in volume and aggregate value by the circulating notes of the state banks and again by the deposit liabilities of those banks transferable by check. Coins were indispensable, but effected only a fraction of all monetary payments. Though the Congress defined the value of the dollar, its definition involved no slightest attempt to control the value of the bank notes which the public had no choice but use. Each note, though conventionally the equivalent of a certain number of dollars, might be in fact the equivalent of anything more or anything less, depending on the reputation of the bank that issued it. And, what was of less substance but seems to have made the worse impression, the notes were neither uniform in size and style nor readily replaced with new ones, with the result that counterfeits abounded and the aged paper, circulating till worn away in powder, was so repulsively soft and filthy that a fastidious person might rather be without money than have to handle bank notes and put them in his clothing. Some of these evils were minimized by states with good banking laws properly administered, but no state could prevent the impairment of its standards by other states. The situation of a good banker was about as secure as that of a person trying to be good enough not to get small pox. The federal government itself could not make all banks sound, but it could achieve improvements that no other authority could come near.

In his first annual report Secretary Chase made proposals aimed at restoring the federal government's monetary responsibilities and the monetary bond between it and the economy. Secretary Chase was one of many men who for some time had felt dissatisfied on both political and practical grounds with an arrangement which, in disregard of the Constitution's plain intent, had pared the federal government's monetary responsibilities down to almost nothing and left the monetary system in fact under no authority at all but free to be toyed with by as many states as might be formed. In a field quite apart from the monetary, federal and state authority were met in bloody combat; it was in accord with a transcendent logic that men taking the federal side in that combat should be disposed to restore to the federal authority that control over the monetary function of which, a quarter century ago, it had been deprived in the centrifugal passion of the Jacksonians for *laisser faire* and states' rights. Mr Chase, who was later to be Chief Justice of the Supreme Court in succession to Roger B. Taney, disregarded the Court's decision in the *Briscoe* case defending the legality of the notes of state banks: "Such emissions," he said to Congress in his report, "certainly fall within the spirit if not within the letter of the constitutional prohibition of the emission of 'bills of credit' by the states and of the making by them of anything except gold and silver coin a legal tender in payment of debts." But whatever the question of the states' power, he found it "too clear to be reasonably disputed that Congress, under its constitutional powers to lay taxes, to regulate commerce, and to regulate the value of coin, possesses ample authority to control the credit circulation which enters so largely into the transactions of commerce and affects in so many ways the value of coin." Mr Chase did not propose that a new federal Bank be established but, in effect, that a system of banks with national charters be authorized on terms like those authorized by the free-banking laws of the states. Under such an arrangement Congress would take up again its monetary responsibilities and provide the uniform, controlled circulating medium which the country had been without since the federal Bank had been destroyed.[3]

Later it was also urged that the proposed national banks would be important buyers of federal bonds, which they would need as security for their note issues, but in his first proposals Mr Chase did not make much of this prospective advantage. Thinking still that the war would soon be ended and that enactment of a law and establishment of a system of national banks must take altogether too long a time for the new demand for government bonds to be of help in the current financing, the Secretary seems to have been moved less by immediate objectives than by the anomaly of a sovereign authority waging war in defense of its sovereignty without possessing that most ancient and elementary attribute of sovereignty—control of the monetary system.

[3] Sherman, 270-71.

In his next annual report, December 1862, the war still going on, Secretary Chase repeated and amplified his proposals for a system of national banks. The project had gained ground. Various considerations favored it and most of all the growing sense of nationalism which the war itself fostered. But Mr Chase now stressed, besides the need of a national currency, the need of a market for federal bonds which the proposed national banks would create and the convenience to the federal Treasury of the banks as depositories. He wanted the government to make use of banks again, like any other transactor in the economy. It must conduct its business the way the rest of the world did. The gap between the Treasury and the economy should be closed.

III

The congressional leaders in charge of the administration's new banking measure were Senator John Sherman of Ohio and Representative Samuel Hooper of Massachusetts. Mr Hooper first brought up the proposal in the House 19 January 1863. The reception was discouraging. Then Senator Sherman took it up, introduced on the 26th a bill "to provide a national currency," and gave it a forceful presentation in the Senate. With the energetic backing of President Lincoln's administration, it was passed 20 February. The performance was astonishing for a measure that in Senator Sherman's words was "so radical in its character and so destructive to the existing system of state banks"; it is explicable only as an incident of war. The banks had found the measure most unwelcome and their views were well represented in Congress, principally by Senator Collamer of Vermont. But the public liked the proposals, and the objections of the banks had little force.[4]

"The issue of circulating notes by state banks," wrote Senator Sherman in his *Recollections*, "had been the fruitful cause of loss, contention, and bankruptcy, not only of the banks issuing them but of all business men depending upon them for financial aid. . . . Long before I became a member of Congress, I had carefully studied the banking laws of the several states. . . . My study and experience as a lawyer in Ohio convinced me that the whole system of state banks, however carefully guarded, was both unconstitutional and inexpedient and that it ought to be overthrown. When I entered Congress I was entirely prepared not only to tax the circulation of state banks but to tax such banks out of existence."[5]

4 Sherman, 294.   5 Sherman, 282, 284.

In his arguments supporting the new measure in Congress, Senator Sherman described the banking and monetary system as it was and reviewed the constitutional question of monetary control. "There were 1642 banks in the United States, established by the laws of twenty-eight different states. . . . With this multiplicity of banks, . . . it was impossible to have a uniform national currency, for its value was constantly affected by their issues. There was no common regulator. . . . There was no check or control. . . ." At the moment the government's legal tender notes were "the basis of an inflated bank circulation, . . . and there was no way to check this except by uniting the interest of the government, the banks, and the people together by one uniform common system."[6]

Senator Sherman quoted from the 1815 report of Secretary Dallas recommending re-establishment of the Bank of the United States and affirming that under the Constitution the power of the federal government over money, whether coin or bills of credit, must be deemed an exclusive power. "Congress," the Senator contended, "has the power to regulate commerce; Congress has the power to borrow money, which involves the power to emit bills of credit; Congress has the power to regulate the value of coin. These powers are exclusive. When, by the force of circumstances beyond our control, the national coin disappears, . . . Congress alone must furnish the substitute. No state has the power to interfere with this exclusive authority in Congress to regulate the national currency. . . ." Furthermore—like Secretary Chase and in fine disregard of the Supreme Court's opinion in *Briscoe* v. *The Bank of Kentucky* and of the opinion presumably still held by Roger B. Taney, still presiding over the Court—the Senator said: "As the states were forbidden by the Constitution to authorize the issue of bills of credit, they were equally forbidden to authorize corporations to issue circulating notes, which were bills of credit. Upon this point," it seemed to Senator Sherman, "the authorities were absolutely conclusive. That position was taken by the most eminent members of the constitutional convention, by Joseph Story in his Commentaries, by Daniel Webster, and other great leaders of both parties since that time"— including John C. Calhoun, Thomas Jefferson, and Andrew Jackson, he might have said, but not Chief Justice Taney.[7]

Congress, the Senator acknowledged, might legally exercise its power by making the federal government's bills of credit the national currency. But this he thought unwise. History showed "that the

---

6 Sherman, 289, 290, 296.   7 Sherman, 289, 291.

public faith of a nation alone is not sufficient to maintain a paper currency." Following the reasoning of Alexander Hamilton, he said "there must be a combination between the interests of private individuals and the government." That combination the Senator would effect in the proposed system of national banks, whose liabilities would provide a national currency based on concrete values and supervised by the government. The notes issued by these banks "would be convertible into United States notes while the war lasted and afterwards into coin; . . . the currency would be uniform, of universal credit in every part of the United States. . . ." The system would furnish a market for government bonds. The banks would give up their state charters and become national, "with severe restrictions as to the amount of notes issued." The Senator "insisted that the passage of the bill would promote a sentiment of nationality. . . . The want of such nationality," he declared, "was one of the great evils of the times; and it was that principle of state rights, that bad sentiment that had elevated state authority above the great national authority, that had been the main instrument by which our government was sought to be overthrown."[8]

Mr Hooper spoke in the same strain; "It is justly said," he told the House, "by an eminent financial writer who was once distinguished as the head of the Treasury Department that this abdication by the government of its power to control the currency of the country has furnished one of the main supports of this rebellion. . . ." The New York *Tribune* said in support of the new measure: "There can be no stronger argument in its favor than that it tends to strengthen the Union by closely interwoven ties of common interest in the permanence and credit of the National Government."[9]

Senator Sherman spoke 26 January on a closely related measure, and on the bill itself 9 February. It was adopted 20 February, and President Lincoln approved it 25 February. This was 1863, in the twenty-second month of the war.

IV

The new act was a free-banking measure, derived from the original free-banking law enacted in New York in 1838 but modified by the variations thereof in other states. Its virtues were encompassed in its main purpose—to make banking a federal responsi-

[8] Sherman, 297-98.
[9] A. M. Davis, *Origin of National Banking System*, 111-12.

bility—and did not extend far into its specific provisions, which, as in the states, permitted good banking in favorable circumstances but did not require or insure it. The expectation was that existing banks would surrender their state charters and re-incorporate under the terms of the new law with national charters.

According to Hugh McCulloch, the president of the Bank of Indiana, the existing banks objected to the new federal law on four grounds: they believed it would foster banks of circulation only; they feared the federal government might lose the war; they feared Congress; and they were unwilling to give up the names they had and take a number as a national bank.[10]

All four of these objections were reasonable, and the better the bank, the more reasonable the objection. The trend of banking was away from circulation and banks of circulation only were the wild cats that had been notorious under the free-banking statutes of several western states. Except as it was subordinate to a commercial banking business with deposit liabilities, note issue was disreputable; it implied evasion, counterfeiting, dirt, raggedness, and note-shaving. The idea of accepting the terms of a wild cat law was disagreeable to good bankers who had circulating liabilities and more so to those who had none.

In the second place, fear lest the federal government lose the war was not incompatible with the hope that it would win and the effort to help it to do so. Bankers felt no assurance that they could serve the country better under a federal charter, and they might serve themselves worse if it lost.

Thirdly, fear of Congress was a deterrent whether the government won or lost. Fear of the Treasury accompanied it. Some bankers could remember how they had been solicited by Amos Kendall and Roger Taney thirty years before when the federal Bank was being put to death and how a little later they were being reviled by politicians of the same group and deprived of the government's business. They had become fully reconciled to the loss, for it had ample compensations. The politicians had made the Treasury a difficult customer; and now, after seventeen years of the new arrangement, which Mr Van Buren had told them at the very beginning was in their own interest, the bankers did not wish to go back to the old. Mr McCulloch indicates that many bankers may have felt so, finding themselves embarrassed by government de-

10 McCulloch, 168.

728

posits, which were always impelling expansions and then imposing contractions. One, he says, the president of the Bank of Michigan, Detroit—for years "managed with great prudence, meriting the confidence which it enjoyed"—had sought to surrender the Treasury account and dissolve connection with the government. This had been in 1836 and his bank was one of the Jackson administration's pets. The directors overruled him, loans were expanded, and the bank went down in 1837, "hopelessly insolvent." Bankers had had their lesson, and now, after having been free for years of the Treasury's caprices, they found it proposed not merely that they have the federal government as a customer again but that they have it as a boss. They did not like it.[11]

The fourth of the objections the bankers had to the new measure was that it required them to give up their names and take numbers. The requirement was indeed absurd. One wonders that Secretary Chase, a man of intelligence, should have made it at all, and much more that he should have given it up reluctantly. For the government it obviously accomplished nothing, and for the bankers it was an affront to what was most human in them. Any respectable banker prized his bank's name. Nevertheless, the proprietors of the Bank of North America, for example, and the Bank of New York were expected to surrender the distinguished names they had borne ever since they were the first banks in the country eighty years past and become the First, or Tenth, or Thirty-third National Bank of Philadelphia, say, or of New York, respectively, according to the order of their conversion to the national system. The foolish requirement was soon abandoned.[12]

The metropolitan banks, which as a group were the most influential, could have found little in their dealings with Secretary Chase to reassure them in their fear of what his proposed national system held out for them. Short of giving him their assets and rendering themselves insolvent, they were doing all they could to help him finance the war. Not even the worst exigency could close at once a gap opened by the law and widened by custom. The bankers found the Secretary ill informed about practice and inclined to be an over-conscientious interpreter of the law. They thought he could accept bank credit, and he thought he could not. Yet it is clear that Mr Chase's dissatisfaction was not with them but with the law and with the situation as a whole. With allowance for his not being a

11 McCulloch, 60.   12 McCulloch, 169-70.

financier nor understanding probably half of what they said about their business, he took on the whole a generous and appreciative view of their position. He could not blame them for wanting to hold their specie or for stopping specie payments when they had given it up. Later he wrote to Mr Hooper, sponsor in the House of the new banking measure, that "sufficient stress" had not been laid, "in arguments for the national banking system, upon the absolute necessity of a currency in which the transactions of the government as well as those of the people can be conducted." With such a currency, he said, the loans required to carry on the war might have been obtained without suspending specie payments. To be sure. Had the Treasury been able to accept bank credit, as any citizen could do, it could have got its $150,000,000, or more, in the summer of the first Bull Run with no difficulty. It, not the banks, was the victim, except that the banks had to yield to the Treasury's need, give up their reserves, and then suspend.[13]

The situation was such that the Secretary wanted to change it fundamentally and permanently, whereas the banks preferred to weather the crisis the best they could and then revert to the independence they had so long enjoyed. Hence they resisted the new banking measure, both before and after enactment. They resisted it in part for excellent reasons, free banking being a most imperfect vehicle for a major reform, and the law having been hastily and faultily prepared. They resisted it also for selfish but pardonable reasons. Their alternative proposal was that the specie clause of the sub-treasury act be repealed so that the government could accept bank credit, that the war be financed with it, the suspension of specie payments being legalized, and that the government "issue no paper except upon an interest of six per cent, or higher if the money markets of the world demanded more." It was, Senator Sherman said, "the plan substantially adopted in the war of 1812, . . . a plan of carrying on the operations of our government by an association of banks over which Congress had no control and which would issue money without limit so far as our national laws affected it." The Senator thought this alternative which the bankers proposed "pretentious and even ludicrous."[14]

After enactment of the law a committee of the New York Clearing House was given three questions to consider, one of which was the following: "What is this scheme to provide a national currency?"

[13] A. M. Davis, *Origin of National Banking System*, 97-98.
[14] Sherman, 286-87.

Its answer was that the new law encouraged banks of circulation only, known as wild cats, that the currency it authorized would depreciate, and that this currency would "supplant a like amount of legal tender notes which the government could issue free of all interest and which amount the government would have to borrow and pay interest on at six per cent. This loss on $300,000,000 would amount annually to $18,000,000." The report was accepted by the Clearing House. It looks as if the Populists might have got from Wall Street the greenback doctrine they were soon advocating. Among the bankers who opposed the new measure was Hugh McCulloch, whose statement of their objections I have outlined. "In 1862," he says, "I went to Washington to oppose the passage of the bill to establish a national banking system, which if it passed might be greatly prejudicial to the state banks, of one of the largest of which I was president." Mr McCulloch considered the law a wild cat measure. Secretary Chase heard his complaints, accepted what suggestions he could, convinced Mr McCulloch that the new system was needed, and asked him to take charge of its organization as first Comptroller of the Currency; which after considerable astonishment and reluctance he did.[15]

In 1864 Congress corrected the law extensively, largely with changes recommended by Mr McCulloch as Comptroller, and enacted a new statute in its stead, entitled the National Bank Act, approved 3 June. The new law deprived state banks of the authority incongruously given them at first to issue a national currency while retaining their state charters. It continued the important authorization for the Secretary of the Treasury to use national banks as depositories, though it did not discontinue the system of sub-treasuries set up in 1846. It modified the reserve requirements which the older act had established, sensibly though not very logically; for the principle being followed was that the circulating notes to be issued by the banks were fully secured by the pledge of bonds. This, though a wooden sort of arrangement, was considered the soul of the currency reform. The requirement that banks also maintain reserves proportional to their liabilities was considered less important. In fact it was all-important. It embodied in the law what good bankers had always observed, voluntarily. It made the pledge of securities a pretentious and cumbersome formality. A step of great evolution-

---

[15] Knox, *History of Banking*, 100; McCulloch, 163-64.

ary significance was taken, also in half-conscious, incidental fashion, by providing that required reserves might be partly in the form of bank credit. Thus banks outside New York and other reserve centers might count the deposit balances they maintained with banks in those centers as part of their reserves, the remaining part to be in gold in their own vaults. The banks in the centers, however, must maintain their reserves wholly in gold. The adoption of this arrangement, itself a product of an evolution begun when Alexander Hamilton in 1790 ruled that the liabilities of specie-paying banks could be accepted by the Treasury as the equivalent of specie, has led to the stage reached in the 20th century where the reserves of banks, as required by federal law, comprise no specie or other cash whatever, but exclusively amounts due from the Federal Reserve Banks.

V

Initial progress under the law was disappointing. Though it had been purposed that the system comprise old state banks converted to national, in fact nearly 700 new national banks were chartered before the first conversion. It became evident that the state banks, if they could not be enticed, must be driven. Their notes, to this end, were subjected to a prohibitive tax.

A tax had been proposed by Secretary Chase even before the national system, though apparently for revenue rather than reform. In July 1861, he had included bank notes with ale, beer, and tobacco, as suitable objects of taxation, but with the thought that the tax besides producing revenue would relieve the nation of excessive note issue. When he proposed a system of national banks in his first annual report, December 1861, he again recommended a tax on state bank notes. The recommendation was repeated in December 1862, and Senator Sherman, to the same end, introduced an appropriate amendment to the pending revenue bill. There was so much opposition that he withdrew the amendment to save the bill but brought it up again next month, January 1863. He "stated distinctly that the purpose of the bill was not merely to levy a reasonable tax on banks but also to induce them to withdraw their paper in order to substitute for it a national currency." He reviewed "the history of our currency legislation from the act chartering the first Bank of the United States." He cited President Madison's statement that a "uniform national currency" was essential and that establishment of the second Bank of the United States was for that purpose.[16]

But it was evidently concluded at this point that action against the state bank currency should be deferred till after a national bank currency was created; the positive step should be taken before the negative; for it was shortly thereafter that the Senator took up the national bank measure already introduced in the House by Representative Samuel Hooper. Thereafter, the national currency measure having been adopted but the state banks ignoring it, popular impatience with them arose, especially in the West. "Tax the banks out of existence," the Chicago *Tribune* exhorted Congress. The project was resumed, but now, instead of the two per cent that had been proposed in 1863, it was a tax of ten per cent. Speaking for his measure 27 February 1865, Senator Sherman said: "The national banks were intended to supersede the state banks. Both cannot exist together; yet while the national system is extending, the issues of state banks have not materially decreased. Indeed, many local banks have been converted into national banks, and yet carefully keep out their state circulation. . . . If the state banks have power enough in Congress to prolong their existence beyond the present year, we had better suspend the organization of national banks."[17]

There was a brief, bitter, and unsuccessful opposition. The measure meant, as its opponents said, the destruction of the state banks, and no bones were made about it. The bill passed, and President Lincoln approved it 3 March 1865, the day before his second inaugural, a month before the fall of Richmond, six weeks before his murder.

The immediate effect was the desired conversion of large numbers of state banks to national charter. The tax was a powerful agency in that direction but not a compulsive one. About half the state banks, being already without note liabilities or now terminating them, continued under state charter. And save for the first few years the number of state banks has always been far greater than the number of national. The tax was compulsive only upon banks that wished to maintain their note circulation, but even then it was not the only influence. Nationalistic sentiment had grown greatly. The Bank of

16 A. M. Davis, *Origin of National Banking System*, 97; Sherman, 271, 287.

17 Sherman, 293; A. M. Davis, *Origin of National Banking System*, 96; 38th Congress, 2nd Session, *Congressional Globe*, 1139; F. Cyril James I, 328-29.

Commerce, New York, had already taken a federal charter voluntarily for that reason. But since note circulation was still of importance in men's minds, the imposition of a prohibitory tax by Congress was momentous. It was an extreme assertion of federal sovereignty. It deprived the states of a monetary power they had exercised for eighty years and in effect undid the Supreme Court's *Briscoe* decision in 1837 that the power was exercised constitutionally. It deprived them, however, only of what was in fact minor and obsolescent. It failed, as had happened before, to take account of deposit credit as the principal form of money. In principle and intent it was a resounding victory for the federal control of the monetary supply. In practice, since it omitted the major part of the monetary supply, it proved to be highly imperfect. It assured the economy of a paper currency that was uniform in appearance and value, difficult to counterfeit, and clean. It enabled the government and the public to use the same money. It permitted the government to use bank credit, to have bank accounts, to draw bank checks, and to accept them. All this was considerable. But it failed to give the federal government control of the amount of money supplied or more than partial regulatory powers.

In 1869 the tax on state bank notes came before the Supreme Court in *Veazie Bank* v. *Fenno*. Mr Chase, now Chief Justice, himself read the opinion. It had been his fortune as Secretary of the Treasury to lead in restoring the federal monetary powers that Roger Taney, in the same position, had repudiated; it was now his fortune, at the head of the Supreme Court, to nullify in effect the monetary powers of the states that Roger Taney in the same position had upheld. The opinion settled the Court back in the Hamiltonian channel from which the Jacksonians had deflected it. The opinion took cognizance of the argument that the tax was intended to destroy the state banks and would destroy them but held that it was fully within the constitutional powers of Congress nevertheless. It affirmed in substance the ability of Congress to do what it sought —extend its exclusive authority over all the recognized components of the monetary system. Had circulating notes been the only liabilities of banks, the aim would have been achieved. But just as the intent of the Constitution had been frustrated by state banks of issue, it was still to be frustrated by state banks of deposit.[18]

18 *Veazie Bank* v. *Fenno*, 8 Wallace 533.

VI

Meanwhile, above the northern border, action had been taken in British North America that reflected and paralleled what was happening currently in the States both in advancement of the federal principle and in the placing of monetary powers. Till the moment, there had never been much disposition in the Provinces to federate; and Lord Durham had preferred a simple legislative union, which Upper and Lower Canada effected in 1841. But this form of union, which left the two former provinces no autonomy, proved disappointing and made a federate union seem preferable. So, odd as it seems, federation was generated in the Provinces just at the time they had the spectacle before them of the American Union torn bloodily in two by war. But the American troubles seem to have inspired a fresh Imperial loyalty and a feeling that it was again possible to do better than the States had done. By 1865, however, it was not American troubles only that counted: there was then the growing likelihood of northern victory, which to observant persons in the divided provinces suggested the disagreeable possibility of a new and triumphant nationalism in the American North as dangerous to its neighbors eventually as it was already to a defeated South. As these considerations imply, Canadian confederation was autochthonous. It was devised at home, not in Great Britain. The battle had been won in Britain a quarter-century before when the principle of responsible government in British North America was recognized. The task since then had been a provincial one, and Britain had only to approve and welcome its results.[19]

The first direct step had been toward an improvement of the terms on which Lower and Upper Canada were united, but it was taken with a sense that opportunity might be found at the same time to create a more extensive federation. A coalition government was formed in Canada committed to such a program. Meanwhile in the Maritimes a similar interest was alive, and in the late summer of 1864 representatives of Nova Scotia, New Brunswick, and Prince Edward Island met in the latter's capital, Charlottetown, to discuss a federal union of the three. There they were joined by official visitors from the province of Canada, with whom they agreed upon a more ambitious conference to consider the federating of all the Provinces.

[19] Egerton, *History of Canada*, 227ff; Durham, 270, 304-07; Pope, *Macdonald* i, 22-25.

This was convened in Quebec in October, where resolutions were adopted which included the following statements:

"1. The best interests and present and future prosperity of British North America will be promoted by a Federal Union under the Crown of Great Britain, provided such Union can be effected on principles just to the several provinces.

"2. In the federation of the British North American Provinces the system of government best adapted under existing circumstances to protect the diversified interests of the several provinces and secure efficiency, harmony, and permanency in the working of the Union, would be a general government charged with matters of common interest to the whole Country, and local governments for each of the Canadas and for the provinces of Nova Scotia, New Brunswick, and Prince Edward Island, charged with the control of local matters in their respective sections; provision being made for the admission into the Union on equitable terms of Newfoundland, the North West Territory, British Columbia, and Vancouver."[20]

Conformably to this proposed assignment, the new general Parliament was to "have power to make laws for the peace, welfare, and good government of the Federated Provinces (saving the sovereignty of England)." This federal power was to extend especially over specific, listed subjects which included "Currency and Coinage" as item nineteen and "Banking, Incorporation of Banks, and the issue of paper money" as item twenty. In the corresponding list of provincial powers nothing of the sort was included.[21]

The objectives of the Quebec conference of 1864 were debated and discussed both in the Provinces and at Westminster during 1865 and 1866; and not without reverses, especially in the Maritimes, where there was a strong leaning toward a separate union apart from the Canadas. They were finally ratified in the British North America Act, 1867, federating the Canadas, Nova Scotia, and New Brunswick as the Dominion of Canada. Other provinces joined later. The act specifically included currency and coinage, banking, the incorporation of banks, and the issue of money among the classes of matters declared to be under "the exclusive legislative authority" of the federal Parliament; and it is of interest that this assignment had remained absolutely unchanged through all the several successive drafts of the measure from the Quebec resolution

20 Pope, *Confederation Documents*, 38-39.
21 Pope, *Confederation Documents*, 43-44, 46-48.

of October 1864 to enactment, July 1867.* Nor was the assignment casual. Although there seems to have been no discussion of authority over money and banking, as there had been in the convention at Philadelphia in 1787, there was every emphasis upon the importance of dividing powers so that the federal government and the provincial governments should have respectively those appropriate to them. This emphasis occurred at every stage—in Charlottetown, in Quebec, in Ottawa, and in Westminster—and the cogent reason often repeated for it was the mistake the United States had made in assigning limited powers to the general government and leaving all the residue to the states.

Sir John Macdonald, who was the Dominion's first premier, took in the federative negotiations a position like that of Alexander Hamilton in the convention at Philadelphia eighty years before. Like Hamilton, he preferred a unitary legislative union to a federation of components. And like Hamilton, when he found his preference utterly unacceptable he worked with all his might for such union as could be attained and became its chief artificer. But in respect to the allocation of residual powers he got established at once what Hamilton failed to get. For, in the words of Lord Bryce, "whereas in the United States, Congress has only the powers actually granted to it, the state legislatures retaining all such powers as have not been taken from them, the Dominion Parliament has a general power of legislation, restricted only by the grant of certain specific and exclusive powers to the provincial legislatures."[22]

"In framing the constitution," Mr Macdonald had said in the course of the task, "care should be taken to avoid the mistakes and weaknesses of the United States' system, the primary error of which was the reservation to the different states of all powers not delegated to the general government." Otherwise, the Dominion would be adopting the worst features of the United States. "We have strengthened the general government. We have given the general legislature all the great subjects of legislation. We have conferred on them, not only specifically and in detail, all the powers which are incident to sovereignty, but we have expressly declared that all subjects of general interest not distinctly and exclusively conferred upon the local

---

* The new act established Dominion authority over eighteen banks in Ontario and Quebec, five in Nova Scotia, four in New Brunswick; and over the Bank of British North America, which was inter-provincial.

[22] Egerton, *British Colonial Policy*, 371.

governments and local legislatures, shall be conferred upon the general government and legislature."[23]

With respect to monetary and banking matters, in particular it was observed that British North American Confederation as planned established "a central authority which it will not be within the power of any of the local governments to interfere with or rise up against." It has "avoided the errors into which the framers of the American Constitution not unnaturally fell." The Provinces, he said, "have profited by the experience afforded in the case of our American neighbor."[24]

Yet the sagacity of the founders of the Dominion might conceivably have been frustrated had money and banking not been specifically assigned to the general government, for the tendency of jurisprudence since then has been away from the original major intent, and toward increased provincial powers. Whether, therefore, the British North America Act would be interpreted to sanction the Dominion government's exercise of exclusive power over banking, if the power had not been specifically granted already, is doubtful. The tendency that has prevailed is like that in the United States but moves in the opposite direction. In the United States a Constitution that sought, as James Madison and Thomas Jefferson contended, only very limited powers for the federal government and an otherwise unlimited residue for the states has in fact been employed to sanction a Hamiltonian aggrandizement of the former and limitation of the latter. In Canada a constitution that sought to allow but limited powers for the provinces and an otherwise unlimited residue for the federal government has not in fact achieved the continuing centralization that was to have been expected. But Canada's allocation of responsibility for money and banking has remained a settled matter, whatever the vicissitudes of other responsibilities, whereas in the States that responsibility has fluctuated in fogs of uncertainty that sometimes have lightened but never have been wholly dispelled, intent and understanding never having balanced one another. The intent in the National Bank Act, 1863, and in the act of 1865 which put a prohibitory tax on the notes of state banks was commendable and clear; but the understanding needed to make it effectual was dim. The moral on both sides of the border appears to be that

23 Pope, *Macdonald* I, 269; *Confederation Debates*, 33 (quoted by Dawson, 35).
24 *Confederation Debates*, 404.

peoples disposed to union should unite, because the advantages of doing so outweigh the disadvantages. But they should not expect an end of the troubles to which flesh is heir or that evolution will follow the path they think they have given it.[25]

[25] Egerton, *History of Canada,* 241-43; Dawson, 37.

WHEN the first American bank was established, at the end of the Revolutionary War, the American business world was engaged almost wholly in the export and import trade and in domestic merchandising. It was a well-to-do, intelligent, compact, energetic, and influential minority, comprising maybe a tenth of the population. The great majority was agrarian. Alexander Hamilton was spokesman of the one, Thomas Jefferson of the other.

Eighty years later, at the beginning of the Civil War, the business world had steam and credit at its command. It had expanded and become diversified. The urban population, though still the less, had increased five times faster than the rural. Business was no longer a matter of dealing in merchandise almost wholly, but a matter of manufacturing innumerable kinds of things by new processes incomparably more productive than the old; it was a matter of railway and steamship transport, of mining, of the telegraph, of power printing, of banking, insurance, brokerage, and investments. And the new business world was not a mere expansion of the old. It was not dominated by descendants of the merchants who had dominated the old or by their traditions. It was dominated by self-made men born on farms and reared in the spirit of agrarian democracy. These men exulted in their humble origins and acquisitive achievements. The spirit of enterprise was fierce in them. Their ideal was *laisser faire*. Their employment of power and resources to serve material human needs altered the people's ways of living. Their business success alienated them insensibly from their origins, however, and from uncontaminated Jeffersonians. It was the despair of the poets and Transcendentalists.

The Jacksonian revolution was largely the conquest of the economy by these self-made men; and a prominent political crisis—the Jacksonian attack on the Bank of the United States—was produced by their intolerance of restraint upon their use of bank credit. The ambitious, farm-born entrepreneur, envious of the rich and set to become rich, wanted credit for his enterprises; his banks wanted to provide it. But the "aristocratic" federal bank situated in conservative Philadelphia restricted bank lending. The restraint was resented especially in New York, otherwise Philadelphia's superior rival, and in Boston and Baltimore. Taking advantage of the traditional agrarian aversion to banks and of President Jackson's particularly, the entrepreneurial rebels attacked what they called the monopoly and the tyranny of the federal Bank, ended its existence, neutralized the federal government's constitutional responsibility for the currency, made banking a business free to all, and thereby insured to enterprise an abundance of banks and of bank credit.

Their rebellion was a popular and democratic one but not agrarian. It accomplished the antithesis of agrarian aims. It was led by men whose skill in propaganda, in cant, and in demagogy was supported by envy and an uncritical belief that the divine blessing was on their efforts. "There is perhaps no business," said Roger B. Taney, Andrew Jackson's devoted aide, "which yields a profit so certain and liberal as the business of banking and exchange; and it is proper that it should be open, as far as practicable, to the most free competition and its advantages shared by all classes of society" —sentiments strangely incompatible with those of Thomas Jefferson, of John Taylor of Caroline, and of Andrew Jackson himself when expressing his own convictions.

It is superfluous evidence of the ineluctable, pervading strength of the spirit of enterprise that, after sweeping from Nicholas Biddle the conservative responsibilities that had been his as head of the federal Bank, it absorbed him as the head of that Bank's state-chartered successor, letting him become one of its most sanguine practitioners and one of the most impractical. Except for his intelligence and industry, he lacked the tougher, hard-headed qualities needed in business enterprise and so conspicuously possessed by the men who were his undoing and the federal Bank's—Amos Kendall, David Henshaw, Isaac Hill, Churchill C. Cambreleng, Samuel Ingham, Martin Van Buren, and others self-made but humbly born on farms, prototypes of American success, and patterns of what, to the rest of the world, the true American seemed to be.

Having ended federal restraint on bank lending and federal responsibility for the monetary system, the Jacksonians gloried in what was a triumph for *laisser faire* in a field where *laisser faire* had no place. Sovereign and unified control of the monetary system is needed in any economy, whatever freedoms may be proper otherwise. Consequently, from possession of what was generally considered the best monetary system in the world, the country fell back into one of the most disordered. But the period was one of such prodigious growth in population, territory, natural wealth, and accumulated wealth that the cost could be borne. The Americans, Professor

Charles Dunbar said shortly after the last events with which this book has dealt, are the only people who with a light heart have trusted to the energy of growth to insure them against the effects of their mistakes.

The economy could endure such mistakes, but the federal government could not—at least when war had to be waged. For after the Jacksonian enterprisers deprived the federal government of its constitutional control over the monetary system, they even forbade it access to ordinary bank facilities and the principal means of payment employed by the people at large. So what had been done away with in the administrations of Andrew Jackson and Martin Van Buren had to be restored in an altered form by the administration of Abraham Lincoln. What had been taken from the federal government and left to the individual states had now to be recovered by the federal government incidentally to a war over the larger but logically corresponding issue of federal sovereignty and the indissolubility of the Union.

The restoration was not accomplished soon enough to help much in the war; but it was helpful for the future, and though it owed little to common sense and much more to the passionate spirit of nationalism for nationalism's sake, it brought about something necessary. Not perfectly, of course, by any means, or finally. The intent was determined and by good fortune well directed. The understanding, as observed before, was dim.

ACKNOWLEDGMENTS

HAVING worked on this book a long, long time, I have come under countless obligations to so many persons that to name them all would seem like listing the better part of my acquaintance. Moreover, I know that I must have failed to come up to the level of many who have helped and advised me, and that these persons may blush at my mention of them, preferring my silence to my thanks. So I make my acknowledgments with anxiety lest I seem to some not grateful enough and to others more grateful than they like.

My first obligation, however, is to one no longer living, Professor F. W. Taussig of Harvard. I knew him only by correspondence and through mutual friends, but he made himself so real and wrote so confidently of an undertaking which I then looked at askance that I fear I shall find no reader to fill his place. Years later Professor Edwin B. Wilson of Harvard and the late Professor Robert Warren of the Institute for Advanced Study in Princeton interposed to keep me going on the task Professor Taussig had set. No wish can be more sincere than that this finished work be worthy of these friends.

To Dr Louis B. Wright of the Folger Shakespeare Library and to Professor Lester V. Chandler of Princeton I am obliged for their generous interest and quite indispensable encouragement. It is painful to think what I should have done without them. To Professor James O. Wettereau of New York University, I am obliged for invaluable criticism and for information derived from his own studies in much the same field as mine and given me generously. Professor Joseph Dorfman and Professor Richard Hofstadter, both of Columbia, have helped me with advice, judgments, and moral aid for which I am most grateful. It has been my good fortune also to find Mr J. Keith Horsefield of Richmond, Surrey, interested in my work and unfailingly helpful. Being an historian of British banking, he could give me advice and information and raise profitable questions. I have also had the use of his excellent library. Professor John Munroe of the University of Delaware has put me under endless obligation by reading my text in proof, setting me right where I have slipped, and admonishing me about my errors of a more general and subtler sort.

At the Federal Reserve Board, where I was employed for many years until my retirement, my obligations are of course abundant.

I can acknowledge only the most specific of them—to the Board itself; to Mr Chester Morrill, the Board's former secretary and my generous superior; to Mr Winfield W. Riefler, an unfailingly perceptive and helpful mentor; to Mr Howard H. Hackley, by whom I have been patiently enlightened on questions of law; and to Miss Alvern Sutherland, the Board's librarian, who has been of invaluable assistance in various ways and particularly in procuring for me research material not otherwise accessible. I am obliged also to Mr Samuel I. Katz and Mr Frank M. Tamagna, both of the Board's staff, whom I have always consulted to my profit.

In following certain paths into Canada and back, I have had the kind and indispensable advice of Mr A. F. W. Plumptre of Ottawa. I am also under obligation to Mr Joseph F. Parkinson of Ottawa and to the Research Department of the Bank of Canada. Besides making valuable use of the collections in the Parliamentary Library, I consulted the Baring Papers in the Public Archives at Ottawa, where Mr Norman Fee and others of his staff were kindness itself; and I gratefully acknowledge the courtesy of the Public Archives in permitting me to quote from the Baring Papers.

Others whose kindnesses it is a pleasure to acknowledge are Mr John Garland of the Commonwealth Bank of Australia, Professor R. S. Sayers of the London School of Economics, Dr Edward M. Riley of Colonial Williamsburg, Professor Howard S. Ellis of the University of California, Professor Ralph W. Hidy of New York University, Professor Edward C. Kirkland of Bowdoin, Professor Arthur H. Cole and Professor Alvin H. Hansen of Harvard, Professor Frank W. Fetter of Northwestern, Professor C. H. Danhof of Tulane, Dr Clark Warburton and Dr Carter H. Golembe of the Federal Deposit Insurance Corporation, Dr Charles M. Wiltse of Washington, D.C., Mr T. G. Tiebout and Mr Albert C. Agnew (retired) of the legal staffs of the Federal Reserve Banks of New York and San Francisco respectively, and Mr Karl Bopp of the Federal Reserve Bank of Philadelphia.

The collections of the Library of Congress have been most fruitful sources—especially the papers of Alexander Hamilton, of Nicholas Biddle, and of Roger B. Taney. And amidst the courtesies I have had at the Library, I wish to mention especially the kindness of Mrs Dorothy Eaton and Dr Percy Powell in the Manuscripts Division, of Mr J. G. McEwan and Mr James Elder in the Legal Division, and of Mr Gordon W. Patterson and Mr David J. H. Cole in the Reading Room.

The library of the Historical Society of Pennsylvania has materials invaluable for my work, and I am most grateful to Mr N. B. Wainwright for access to its collections, for permission to use material from them, and for his own repeated kindnesses. I am indebted also to Miss Grace M. Sherwood and to the Rhode Island State Library, under her charge, for access to important material and permission to use it; to the Historical Society of Maryland for the use of its library; and to Dartmouth College for access to the comprehensive collection in the Baker Memorial Library.

During residence abroad it was my fortune to do considerable work at the British Museum, where besides kind and intelligent attention I found every book I wanted, mostly American of the early 19th century. I am happy to thank Mr F. C. Francis and members of his staff and to recall gratefully the pleasure of working in their magnificent institution. It was also my privilege to have access to the library of the Royal Empire Society and the library of the London School of Economics; to both I am obliged.

For certain manuscript material quoted or used otherwise I make acknowledgment in appropriate places; but I wish to record especially my deep obligation to the Governor and Company of the Bank of England for the text of correspondence had with the Bank of the United States and for permission to use it.

Some chapters of this book include material I have adapted from essays of mine previously published. For leave to do this I am indebted to the Harvard University Press and the *Quarterly Journal of Economics*, in the November 1934 and August 1947 issues of which, respectively, appeared my "Long and Short Term Credit in Early American Banking" and "The Chestnut Street Raid on Wall Street, 1839"; to the New York University Press and the *Journal of Economic History*, in the May 1947 and May 1948 issues of which, respectively, appeared my "Jackson, Biddle, and the Bank of the United States" and "Banking in the Early West: Monopoly, Prohibition, and Laissez Faire"; to the University of Chicago Press and the *Journal of Political Economy*, in the April 1936 issue of which appeared my "Free Banks and Corporations"; and to the American Economic Association and the *American Economic Review*, in the December 1933 issue of which appeared "The Banks, the States, and the Federal Government."

The Canadian Bank of Commerce and Brown Brothers, Harriman, and Company, respectively, have kindly assured me that I may quote from the *History of the Canadian Bank of Commerce* by Mr Victor Ross, and from *A Hundred Years of Merchant Banking* by Mr John Crosby Brown. I am obliged to them for their courtesy. I am also obliged to the *Canadian Banker* for leave to quote from Professor Adam Shortt's accounts of Canadian banking published in its early volumes; and to Longmans, Green and Company for leave to rearrange items from tables in Professor Davis R. Dewey's *Financial History of the United States*.

Finally and most gratefully, I acknowledge the substantial encouragement given me by the John Simon Guggenheim Memorial Foundation and the warm, heartening interest of its secretary general, Mr Henry Allen Moe, in what I have been doing.

BRAY HAMMOND

ABBREVIATIONS

AHA	American Historical Association
AHR	*American Historical Review*
ASP	American State Papers
JPE	*Journal of Political Economy*
JEH	*Journal of Economic History*
JEBH	*Journal of Economic and Business History*
JCBA	*Journal of the Canadian Bankers Association*
PMHB	*Pennsylvania Magazine of History and Biography*
QJE	*Quarterly Journal of Economics*
PLB	President's Letter Book (Biddle Papers)
OC	Office Correspondence (Baring Papers)
MC	Miscellaneous Correspondence (Baring Papers)
AC	Additional Correspondence (Baring Papers)
HR	House Report (Congress, USA)
SR	Senate Report (Congress, USA)
HD	House Document (Congress, USA)
SD	Senate Document (Congress, USA)

WORKS CITED

Abernethy, Thomas P. "Early Development of Commerce and Banking in Tennessee." *Mississippi Valley Historical Review* xiv (1927-1928), page 325.

Abernethy, Thomas P. *From Frontier to Plantation in Tennessee.* Chapel Hill, 1932.

Adams, Henry. *History of the United States of America.* New York, 1921.

Adams, Henry. *Life of Albert Gallatin.* Philadelphia, 1879.

Adams, Ephraim D. *Great Britain and the American Civil War.* London, 1925.

Adams, John. *Works of John Adams.* (Charles Francis Adams, editor). Boston, 1856.

Adams, John Quincy. *Memoirs.* Philadelphia, 1874-1877.

American Antiquarian Society. *Proceedings.* Worcester, Massachusetts.

American State Papers, Finance. Washington, 1832.

Andrews, Charles M. *The Colonial Period of American History.* New Haven, 1934-1938.

(Anonymous). "Churchill Caldom Cambreleng." *Democratic Review* vi (1839), pages 144-158.

Appleton, Nathan. *Banking System of Massachusetts.* Boston, 1831.

Appleton, Nathan. *Remarks on Currency and Banking.* Boston, 1841.

Arnold, Samuel G. *History of the State of Rhode Island and Providence Plantations.* New York, 1859-1860.

Ashton, T. S., and Sayers, R. S. *Papers in English Monetary History.* Oxford, 1953.

Baldwin, Loammi. *Thoughts on the Study of Political Economy, etc.* Cambridge, Massachusetts, 1809.

Bancroft, George. *A Plea for the Constitution of the United States of America, Wounded in the House of Its Guardians.* New York, 1886.

Baring Papers. (Baring Brothers), Office Correspondence (OC), Miscellaneous Correspondence (MC), Additional Correspondence (AC). National Archives, Ottawa.

Barker, Jacob. *Incidents in the Life of Jacob Barker.* Washington, 1855.

Barnard, Daniel D. *Speeches and Reports in the Assembly of New York at the Annual Session of 1838.* Albany, 1838.

Bartlett, John R. *History of the Wanton Family of Newport, Rhode Island.* Providence, Rhode Island Historical Tract 3, 1878.

Bartlett, John R. *Records of the Colony of Rhode Island and Providence Plantations.* Providence, 1856-1865.

Bassett, John Spencer. *Life of Andrew Jackson.* New York, 1931.

Bates, Frank G. *Rhode Island and the Formation of the Union.* New York, 1898.

Bates, William N. *Nicholas Biddle's Journey to Greece in 1806.* Philadelphia, 1919.

Beard, Charles A. *Economic Origins of Jeffersonian Democracy.* New York, 1949.

Behrens, Kathryn L. *Paper Money in Maryland, 1727-1789.* Baltimore, 1923.

Benton, Thomas Hart. *Thirty Years' View.* New York, 1864.

Beveridge, Albert J. *Life of John Marshall.* New York, 1916-1919.

Biddle, Charles. *Autobiography.* Philadelphia, 1883.

Biddle, Nicholas. *Correspondence of Nicholas Biddle.* (R. C. McGrane, editor). Boston and New York, 1919.

Biddle Papers. (Nicholas Biddle), Folios, President's Letter Books (PLB). Manuscripts Division, Library of Congress, Washington.

Biddle, Nicholas. *History of the Expedition under Lewis and Clark.* (Paul Allen, editor). Philadelphia, 1814.

Biddle, Nicholas. *History of the Lewis and Clark Expedition.* (Elliott Coues, editor). New York, 1893.

Biddle, Nicholas. *Ode to Bogle.* Philadelphia, 1889.

Bishop, Hillman M. "Why Rhode Island Opposed the Federal Constitution." *Rhode Island History* VIII (1949), page 1.

Blodget, Samuel. *Economica: A Statistical Manual for the United States of America.* Washington, 1806.

Bogart, E. L. "Taxation of the Second Bank of the United States by Ohio." *American Historical Review* XVII (1912), page 312.

Bourne, Edward G. *History of Surplus Revenue of 1837.* New York, 1885.

Boyd, Julian P. "John Sergeant's Mission." *Pennsylvania Magazine of History and Biography* LVIII (1934), page 213.

Bradley, Cyrus P. *Biography of Isaac Hill.* Concord, New Hampshire, 1835.

Brant, Irving. *James Madison.* Indianapolis, 1941-1948.

Breckenridge, Roeliff M. "Canadian Banking History." *Journal of the Canadian Bankers Association* II (1894), page 320.

Breckenridge, Roeliff M. *Canadian Banking System, 1817-1890.* New York, 1895.

Breckenridge, Roeliff M. *History of Banking in Canada.* Washington, National Monetary Commission, 1910.

British Parliament. *Hearings, Bank of England Charter.* London, 1832.

British Parliament. *Hearings, Expediency of Resuming Cash Payments.* London, 1819.

Brooks, Van Wyck. *World of Washington Irving.* New York, 1944.

Brown, John Crosby. *A Hundred Years of Merchant Banking.* New York, 1909.

Brown, Kenneth L. "Stephen Girard, Promoter of the Second Bank of the United States." *Journal of Economic History* II (1942), page 125.

Brunhouse, Robert L. *Counter-Revolution in Pennsylvania, 1776-1790.* Philadelphia, 1942.

Bryan, Alfred Cookman. *History of State Banking in Maryland.* Baltimore, 1899.

Bullock, Charles J. *Essays on the Monetary History of the United States.* New York, 1900.

Burgess, Henry. *Circular to Bankers.* London, 1826-1846.

Burnaby, Andrew. *Travels through North America.* New York, 1904.

Byrdsall, F. *History of the Loco Foco or Equal Rights Party.* New York, 1842.

Cable, John R. *Bank of the State of Missouri.* New York, 1923.

Calhoun, John C. *Works.* New York, 1854-1860.

Carey, Mathew. (editor) *Debates and Proceedings of the General Assembly of Pennsylvania on the Memorials Praying a Repeal or Suspension of the Law Annulling the Charter of the Bank.* Philadelphia, 1786.

Carr, Cecil T. *Select Charters of Trading Companies, 1530-1707.* London, Selden Society, 1913.

Catterall, Ralph C. H. *The Second Bank of the United States.* Chicago, 1903.

Chaddock, Robert E. *The Safety Fund System of New York.* Washington, National Monetary Commission, 1910.

Cheetham, James. *Remarks on the Merchants Bank.* New York, 1804.

Chevalier, Michel. *Lettres sur l'Amérique du Nord.* Paris, 1838. Translation (T. G. Bradford): Chevalier, Michael. *Society, Manners, and Politics in the United States.* Boston, 1839.

Chitty, Joseph. *A Practical Treatise on Bills of Exchange, Checks, etc.* (from the 5th London edition). Philadelphia, 1821.

Clapham, Sir John. *The Bank of England, a History.* Cambridge, England, 1944.

Clarke, M. St. Clair, and Hall, D. A. *Legislative and Documentary History of the Bank of the United States.* Washington, 1832.

Cleaveland, John. *The Banking System of the State of New York.* New York, 1857.

Confederation Debates. Quebec, 1865.

Congress, USA. *Annals,* 1789-1824.

Congress, USA. *Register of Debates,* 1824-1837.

Conrad, R. T. "Nicholas Biddle" (in Longacre, James B., and Herring, James, *National Portrait Gallery of Distinguished Americans,* volume 4). Philadelphia and New York, 1839; revised, Philadelphia, 1854.

Conway, Moncure D. *The Life of Thomas Paine.* New York, 1908.

Crèvecoeur, J. Hector St. John. *Letters from an American Farmer.* New York, 1925.

Crowl, Philip. *Maryland during and after the Revolution.* Baltimore, 1943.

Dallas, George M. *Life and Writings of Alexander James Dallas.* Philadelphia, 1871.

Danhoff, Clarence H. "Farm Making Costs and the Safety Valve, 1850-1860." *Journal of Political Economy* LXIX (1941), page 317.

Darling, Arthur B. *Political Changes in Massachusetts, 1824-1848.* New Haven, 1925.

Davis, Andrew McF. "Boston 'Banks'—1681-1740—Those Who Were Interested in Them." *New England Historical and Genealogical Register* LVII (1903), page 274.

Davis, Andrew McF. *Calendar of Papers and Records, Land Bank of 1740.* Boston, Colonial Society of Massachusetts, 1910.

Davis, Andrew McF. *Colonial Currency Reprints.* Boston, Prince Society, 1910-1911.

Davis, Andrew McF. *Currency and Banking in Massachusetts.* New York, American Economic Association, 1901.

Davis, Andrew McF. *Origin of National Banking System.* Washington, National Monetary Commission, 1910.

Davis, Joseph Stancliffe. *Essays in the Earlier History of American Corporations.* Cambridge, Massachusetts, 1916-1917.

Davis, Matthew L. *Memoirs of Aaron Burr.* New York, 1855.

Dawson, Robert M. *The Government of Canada.* Toronto, 1948.

Dewey, Davis R. *Financial History of the United States.* New York, 1936.

Dewey, Davis R. *State Banking before the Civil War.* Washington, National Monetary Commission, 1910.

Dewey, Davis R. *The Second United States Bank.* Washington, National Monetary Commission, 1910.

Dillistin, William H. *Bank Note Reporters and Counterfeit Detectors, 1826-1866.* New York, 1949.

Dillistin, William H. *Historical Directory of the Banks of the State of New York.* New York, 1946.

Domett, Henry W. *A History of the Bank of New York, 1784-1884.* New York, 1884.

Dorfman, Joseph. "Anglo-American Finance." *Journal of Economic History* XI (1951), page 147.

Dorfman, Joseph. *The Economic Mind in American Civilization.* New York, 1946.

Douglass, (Dr) William. *A Discourse concerning the Currencies of the British Plantations in America.* Boston, 1740.

Douglass, (Dr) William. *A Summary, Historical and Political, etc., of the British Settlements in North America.* Boston, 1747.

DuBois, Armand B. *The English Business Company after the Bubble Act, 1720-1800.* New York, 1938.

Duke, Basil W. *History of the Bank of Kentucky, 1792-1895.* Louisville, 1895.

Dunbar, Charles Franklin. *Economic Essays.* New York, 1904.

Durham, The Earl of. *Lord Durham's Report on the Affairs of British North America.* (Sir Charles P. Lucas, editor). Oxford, 1912.

Egerton, Hugh E. *A Historical Geography of the British Colonies.* Volume v. Canada, Part II, Historical, Oxford, 1908.

Egerton, Hugh E. *Short History of British Colonial Policy.* London, 1910.

Elliott, Jonathan. *Debates on Adoption of the Federal Constitution.* Washington, 1836.

Emerson, Ralph Waldo. *Journals.* Boston and New York, 1909-1914.

Esarey, Logan. *State Banking in Indiana, 1814-1873.* Indianapolis, 1912.

Farrand, Max. (editor) *Records of the Federal Convention of 1787.* New Haven, 1937.

Felt, J. B. *Historical Account of Massachusetts Currency.* Boston, 1839.

Findley, William. *Review of the Revenue System Adopted by the First Congress.* Philadelphia, 1794.

Fisher, H. A. L. *A History of Europe.* London, 1949.

Ford, Paul Leicester. (editor) *Pamphlets on the Constitution of the United States, Published during 1787-1788.* Brooklyn, 1888.

Ford, Thomas. *History of Illinois, 1818-1847.* Chicago and New York, 1854.

Formation of the Union. (Tansill, Charles C., and Meyer, H. H. B., editors). 69th Congress, 1st Session, House Document 398, Washington, 1927.

Franklin, Benjamin. *Writings.* (Albert Henry Smyth, editor). New York, 1907.

Gabriel, Ralph H. *The Course of American Democratic Thought.* New York, 1940.

Gallatin, Albert. *Writings.* (Henry Adams, editor). Philadelphia, 1879.

Gallatin, James. *Diary of James Gallatin.* New York, 1916.

Gibbons, James S. *The Banks of New York, Their Dealers, etc.* New York, 1858.

Gilchrist, Agnes A. *William Strickland, Architect and Engineer.* Philadelphia, 1950.

Golembe, Carter H. *State Banks and the Economic Development of the West, 1830-1844.* Doctoral Dissertation, Faculty of Political Science, Columbia University, New York, 1952.

Gouge, William M. *A Short History of Paper Money and Banking in the United States.* Parts I and II. Philadelphia, 1833.

Gouge, William M. "Commercial Banking." *Hunt's Merchants' Magazine* VIII (1843), page 313.

Gouge, William M. *Journal of Banking.* Philadelphia, 1841-1842.

Gould, Clarence P. *Money and Transportation in Maryland, 1720-1765.* Baltimore, 1915.

Gras, N. S. B. *Massachusetts First National Bank of Boston.* Cambridge, Massachusetts, 1937.

Green, Duff. *Facts and Suggestions.* New York, 1866.

Hadden, Clarence Bernard. *History of Early Banking in Wisconsin.* Madison, 1895.

Hamilton, Alexander. *Works.* (James C. Hamilton, editor). New York, 1850-1851.

Hamilton, Alexander. *Works.* (H. C. Lodge, editor). New York and London, 1904.

Hamilton Papers. (Alexander Hamilton), Manuscripts Division, Library of Congress, Washington.

Hamilton, James A. *Reminiscences.* New York, 1869.

Hamilton, William. (reporter) Debates in the Pennsylvania Legislature, 1810-1811. Lancaster, Pennsylvania, 1811.

Hamlin, Talbot. *Greek Revival Architecture in America.* New York, 1944.

Hammond, Bray. "Free Banks and Corporations." *Journal of Political Economy* XLIV (1936), page 184.

Hammond, Bray. "Long and Short Term Credit in Early American Banking." *Quarterly Journal of Economics* XLIX (1934), page 79.

Hammond, Jabez D. *History of Political Parties in the State of New York.* Syracuse, 1852.

Harding, William F. "The State Bank of Indiana." *Journal of Political Economy* IV (1895-1896), page 1.

Harlow, Alvin F. *Old Bowery Days.* New York and London, 1931.

Harper, Robert Goodloe. *Exhibit of Losses, etc., and Report of the Conspiracy Cases Lately Decided at Bel Air, etc.* Baltimore, 1823.

Hart, Freeman H. *Valley of Virginia in the American Revolution.* Chapel Hill, 1942.

Haskell, Louise P. *Langdon Cheves and the United States Bank.* American Historical Association, Annual Report, 1896, volume I.

Hazard, Samuel. *Commercial and Statistical Register.* Philadelphia, 1839-1840.

Hening, William Waller. *Statutes at Large of Virginia*. Richmond, 1809-1823.

Henshaw, David. *Remarks upon the Bank of the United States*. Boston, 1831.

Hepburn, A. Barton. *History of Currency in the United States*. New York, 1924.

Hidy, Ralph W. *The House of Baring in American Trade and Finance*. Cambridge, Massachusetts, 1949.

Hildreth, Richard. *Banks, Banking, and Paper Currencies*. Boston, 1840.

Hildreth, Richard. *History of the United States of America*. New York, 1880.

Hofstadter, Richard. *The American Political Tradition*. New York, 1948.

Holdsworth, John Thom. *The First Bank of the United States*. Washington, National Monetary Commission, 1910.

Hone, Philip. *Diary of Philip Hone, 1828-1851*. (Allan Nevins, editor). New York, 1936.

Horsefield, J. Keith. "The Cash Ratio in English Banks before 1800." *Journal of Political Economy* LVII (1949), page 70.

Howe, Joseph. *Speeches and Public Letters*. (Joseph Andrew Chisholm, editor). Halifax, 1909.

Hubert, Philip G., jr. *Merchants National Bank of New York City*. New York, 1903.

Hull, Walter Henry. *Practical Problems in Banking and Currency*. New York, 1907.

Hunt, Thomas P. *Book of Wealth, in which it is proved from the Bible that it is the Duty of every man to BECOME RICH*. New York, 1836.

Huntington, Charles C. *A History of Banking and Currency in Ohio before the Civil War*. Columbus, Ohio Archaeological and Historical Society, 1915.

Ingersoll, Charles J. *Historical Sketch of the Second War between Great Britain and United States*. Philadelphia, 1849.

Irving, Pierre M. *Life and Letters of Washington Irving*. Philadelphia, 1872.

Jackson, Andrew. *Correspondence*. (J. S. Bassett, editor). Washington, 1926-1933.

Jackson Papers. (Andrew Jackson), Manuscripts Division, Library of Congress, Washington.

James, F. Cyril. *Growth of Chicago Banks*. New York, 1938.

James, Marquis. *Life of Andrew Jackson*. Indianapolis and New York, 1938.

Jefferson, Thomas. *The Papers of Thomas Jefferson.* (Julian P. Boyd, editor). Princeton, 1950-.

Jefferson, Thomas. *Writings.* (Paul Leicester Ford, editor). New York, 1892-1899.

Jefferson, Thomas. *Writings.* (Memorial edition, Lipscomb and Bergh, editors). Washington, 1903.

Jenks, Leland Hamilton. *The Migration of British Capital to 1875.* New York and London, 1927.

Journals of the Continental Congress, 1774-1789. (Gaillard Hunt, editor). Washington, 1904-1937.

Kemmerer, D. L. "Colonial Loan Office System in New Jersey." *Journal of Political Economy* xlvii (1939), page 867.

Kendall, Amos. *Autobiography.* Boston, 1872.

Kendall, Amos. *Circular to Stockholders of the American Telegraph Company.* New York, 1860.

Kennedy, John P. *Quodlibet.* Philadelphia, 1840.

Kent, Frank R. *The Story of Alexander Brown and Sons.* Baltimore, 1950.

Kent, James. *Commentaries on American Law.* Boston, 1860, 10th edition.

Kimball, Fiske. "Bank of the United States, 1818-1824." *Architectural Record* lviii (1925), page 581.

King, Charles. *Memoir of the Construction, Cost, and Capacity of the Croton Aqueduct.* New York, 1843.

King, Charles R. *Life and Correspondence of Rufus King.* New York, 1894-1900.

Kinley, David. *The Independent Treasury of the United States and Its Relations to the Banks of the Country.* Washington, National Monetary Commission, 1910.

Knox, John Jay. *A History of Banking in the United States.* New York, 1903.

Knox, John Jay. *United States Notes.* New York, 1899.

Larson, Henrietta M. *Jay Cooke, Private Banker.* Cambridge, Massachusetts, 1936.

Lester, Richard A. *Monetary Experiments—Early American and Recent Scandinavian.* Princeton, 1939.

Lewis, Lawrence, jr. *A History of the Bank of North America.* Philadelphia, 1882.

Libby, Orin Grant. *The Geographical Distribution of the Vote of the Thirteen States on the Federal Constitution, 1787-1788.* Madison, 1894.

Lindsey, Charles. *William Lyon Mackenzie.* Toronto, 1862.

Literary and Historical Society of Quebec. *Transactions.* 1876-1877, Quebec.

Lobato Lopez, Ernesto. *El Crédito en México*. Mexico, 1945.

McCaleb, Walter F. *Present and Past Banking in Mexico*. New York, 1920.

McCulloch, Hugh. *Men and Measures of Half a Century*. New York, 1889.

McCulloch, J. R. "Crisis in the American Trade." *Edinburgh Review* LXV (1837), Article IX, page 227.

McGrane, Reginald C. *The Panic of 1837*. Chicago, 1924.

Mackenzie, William L. *Life and Times of Martin Van Buren*. Boston, 1846.

Mackenzie, William L. *Lives and Opinions of B. F. Butler and Jesse Hoyt*. Boston, 1845.

Mackenzie, William L. *Sketches of Canada and the United States*. London, 1833.

McLaughlin, Andrew Cunningham. *A Constitutional History of the United States*. New York, 1935.

McMaster, John Bach. *Life and Times of Stephen Girard*. Philadelphia, 1918.

Madeleine, Sister M. Grace. *Monetary and Banking Theories of Jacksonian Democracy*. Philadelphia, 1943.

Madison, James. *Writings*. (Gaillard Hunt, editor). New York, 1901-1910.

Marshall, John. *The Life of George Washington*. Philadelphia, 1840.

Martineau, Harriet. *Retrospect of Western Travel*. London, 1838.

Massachusetts Historical Society. *Proceedings*. Boston.

Mayo, Bernard. *Henry Clay*. Boston, 1937.

Minot, George R. *History of the Insurrection in Massachusetts, 1786*. Boston, 1810.

Monroe Papers. (James Monroe), Manuscripts Division, Library of Congress, Washington.

Morse, Samuel F. B. *Letters and Journals*. (Edward L. Morse, editor). Boston and New York, 1914.

Moulton, R. K. *Legislative and Documentary History of the Banks of the United States, 1781-1834*. New York, 1834.

Munroe, John A. *Federalist Delaware, 1775-1815*. New Brunswick, 1954.

New York City. *Minutes of the Common Council of the City of New York, 1784-1831*. New York, 1917.

New York State. *Messages from the Governors*. Albany, 1909.

Niles, Hezekiah. *Weekly Register*. Baltimore, 1813-1841.

Nolte, Vincent. *Fifty Years in Both Hemispheres*. London, 1854.

Oberholtzer, Ellis P. *Jay Cooke, Financier of the Civil War*. Philadelphia, 1907.

Osgood, Herbert L. *The American Colonies in the Eighteenth Century.* New York, 1924.

Paine, Thomas. *Writings.* (Moncure D. Conway, editor). New York and London, 1894-1896.

Paine, Thomas. *Complete Writings.* (Philip S. Foner, editor). New York, 1945.

Parks, Joseph H. *Felix Grundy.* Baton Rouge, 1940.

Parrington, Vernon L. *Main Currents in American Thought.* New York, 1927.

Parton, James. *Life of Andrew Jackson.* Boston, 1883.

Pomerantz, Sidney I. *New York, an American City, 1783-1803.* New York, 1938.

Pope, Joseph. *Confederation Documents.* Toronto, 1895.

Pope, Joseph. *Memories of the Life of Sir John A. Macdonald.* London, 1894.

Porter, Kenneth W. *John Jacob Astor.* Cambridge, Massachusetts, 1931.

Potter, Elisha R., and Rider, Sidney S. *Bills of Credit or Paper Money of Rhode Island.* Providence, Rhode Island Historical Tract 8, 1880.

Pownall, Thomas. *The Administration of the British Colonies.* London, 1768.

Preston, Howard H. *History of Banking in Iowa.* Iowa City, State Historical Society of Iowa, 1922.

Price, Richard. *Observations on the Nature of Civil Liberty, etc.* London, 1776.

Primm, James N. *Economic Policy in the Development of a Western State, Missouri.* Cambridge, Massachusetts, 1954.

Proctor, John Clagett. (editor) *Washington, Past and Present—A History.* New York, 1930.

Radoff, Morris. *Calendar of Maryland State Papers.* Number 2. Annapolis, 1947.

Raguet, Condy. *The Financial Register of the United States.* Philadelphia, 1838.

Raguet, Condy. *The Free Trade Advocate.* Philadelphia, 1829.

Ramsay, David. *The History of the American Revolution.* London, 1791.

Redlich, Fritz. *The Molding of American Banking.* New York, 1947.

Reid, James D. *The Telegraph in America.* New York, 1879.

Rhode Island Assembly. *Report of the Committee Appointed . . . to Inquire into the Situation of the Farmers' Exchange Bank in Glocester Published by Order of the General Assembly.* March 1809.

Richardson, James D. *Messages and Papers of the Presidents*. New York, 1897-1927.

Riddel, William R. "Benjamin Franklin and Colonial Money." *Pennsylvania Magazine of History and Biography* LIV (1930), page 52.

de Roover, Raymond A. *The Medici Bank*. New York, 1948.

Rodney, Richard S. *Colonial Finances in Delaware*. Wilmington, 1928.

Ross, Victor. *History of the Canadian Bank of Commerce*. Toronto, 1920-1934.

Rush, Benjamin. *Letters*. (L. H. Butterfield, editor). Princeton, 1951.

Schachner, Nathan. *Alexander Hamilton*. New York, 1946.

Scharf, J. T., and Westcott, Thompson. *History of Philadelphia*. Philadelphia, 1884.

Schlesinger, Arthur M., Jr. *The Age of Jackson*. Boston, 1945.

Schultz, F. W. "The Declining Economic Importance of Agricultural Land." *Economic Journal* LXI (1951), page 125.

Schwartz, Anna J. "Beginning of Competitive Banking in Philadelphia." *Journal of Political Economy* LV (1947), page 417.

Scott, Henry W. *The Courts of the State of New York*. New York, 1909.

Shambaugh, Benjamin F. (editor) *Fragments of the Debates of the Iowa Constitutional Conventions of 1844 and 1846*. Iowa City, State Historical Society of Iowa, 1900.

Shepard, Edward M. *Martin Van Buren*. Boston, 1899.

Sherman, John. *Recollections of Forty Years*. Chicago, 1895.

Shortt, Adam. "Canadian Currency, Banking, and Exchange." *Journal of the Canadian Bankers Association* VII (1899-1900), pages 209, 311; VIII (1900-1901), pages 1, 145, 227, 305.

Shortt, Adam. "Early History of Canadian Banking." *Journal of the Canadian Bankers Association* IV (1896-1897), pages 129, 235, 341; V (1897-1898), page 1.

Smith, Adam. *Wealth of Nations*. (Edwin Cannan, editor). London, 1930.

Smith, Walter B. *Economic Aspects of the Second Bank of the United States*. Cambridge, Massachusetts, 1953.

South Carolina Legislature. *Compilation of Acts, Resolutions and Reports, etc., in relation to the Bank of the State of South Carolina*. Columbia, South Carolina, 1848.

Sparks, Jared. *Life of Gouverneur Morris*. Boston, 1832.

Spiller, Robert E., Thorp, Johnson, and Canby. *Literary History of the United States*. New York, 1949.

Stetson, Amos W. *Eighty Years; an Historical Sketch of the State Bank, 1811-1865; the State National Bank, 1865-1891*. Boston, 1893.

Stock, Leo F. (editor) *Proceedings and Debates of the British Parliaments respecting North America.* Washington, 1924-1941.

Story, Joseph. *Commentaries on the Constitution.* Boston and Philadelphia, 1833.

Sumner, William G. *Andrew Jackson.* Boston, 1882.

Sumner, William G. *The Financier and the Finances of the American Revolution.* New York, 1892.

Sumner, William G. *History of Banking in the United States.* New York, 1896.

Swisher, Carl Brent. *Roger B. Taney.* New York, 1935.

Taney Papers. (Roger B. Taney), Manuscripts Division, Library of Congress, Washington.

Taus, Esther Rogoff. *Central Banking Functions of the United States Treasury, 1789-1941.* New York, 1943.

Taylor, John, of Caroline. *An Inquiry into the Principles and Policy of the Government of the United States.* New Haven, 1950.

Taylor, John, of Caroline. *Principles and Tendency of Certain Public Measures.* Philadelphia, 1794.

Taylor, Robert J. *Western Massachusetts in the Revolution.* Providence, 1954.

Thorpe, Francis Newton. *The Federal and State Constitutions, Colonial Charters, etc.* Washington (59th Congress, 2nd Session, House Document 357), 1909.

Thwaites, Reuben G. *Story of Lewis and Clark's Journal.* American Historical Association, 1903, Annual Report, volume 1.

de Tocqueville, Alexis. *Democracy in America.* (Phillips Bradley, editor). New York, 1945.

Tooke, Thomas, and Newmarch, William. *A History of Prices.* London, 1840.

Trimble, William. "Diverging Tendencies in New York Democracy in the Period of the Locofocos." *American Historical Review* xxiv (1919), page 396.

Trimble, William. "The Social Philosophy of the Loco-Foco Democracy." *American Journal of Sociology* xxvi (1921), page 705.

Trotter, Alexander. *Financial Position and Credit of the States of the North American Union.* London, 1839.

Tucker, George. *The Theory of Money and Banks Investigated.* Boston, 1839.

Turner, F. J. *The Frontier in American History.* New York, 1950.

Tyler, Lyon G. *Letters and Times of the Tylers.* Richmond, 1884-1896.

Union Committee. *Report.* New York, 1834. (Also in Niles' Register lxvi [1834], pages 73-80).

Upper Canada, House of Assembly. "Committee Report on the State of the Currency (W. L. Mackenzie, Chairman)." *Journal of the Assembly*, 5 March 1830, Appendix.

Upper Canada, House of Assembly. "Committee Report on Establishing a Provincial Bank." *Journal of the Assembly*, 13 February 1835, Appendix.

Usher, Abbott Payson. *Deposit Banking in Mediterranean Europe.* Cambridge, Massachusetts, 1943.

Van Buren, Martin. *Autobiography.* Washington, 1920.

Venit, Abraham H. "Isaac Bronson." *Journal of Economic History* v (1945), page 201.

Viner, Jacob. *Studies in the Theory of International Trade.* New York, 1937.

Wainwright, Nicholas B. *The Philadelphia National Bank, 1803-1953.* Philadelphia, 1953.

Walsh, John Joseph. *Early Banks in the District of Columbia, 1792-1818.* Washington, 1940.

Walters, Raymond, Jr. "The Making of a Financier." *Pennsylvania Magazine of History and Biography* lxx (1946), page 258.

Walters, Raymond, Jr. "Origins of the Second Bank of the United States." *Journal of Political Economy* liii (1945), page 115.

Walters, Raymond, Jr. "Spokesman of Frontier Democracy." *Pennsylvania History* xiii (1946), number 3.

Wandell, S. H., and Minnigerode, M. *Aaron Burr.* New York, 1925.

Warren, Charles. *The Supreme Court in United States History.* Boston, 1935.

Washington, George. *Writings.* (John C. Fitzpatrick, editor). Washington, 1931-1940.

Washington, George. *Writings.* (Worthington C. Ford, editor). New York, 1889.

Watkin, Sir Edward W. *Canada and the States; Recollections 1851-1886.* London and New York, 1887.

Webster, Pelatiah. *Political Essays.* Philadelphia, 1791.

Wettereau, James O. "Branches of the First Bank of the United States." *Journal of Economic History* ii (Supplement 1942), page 66.

Wettereau, James O. "Letters from Two Business Men to Alexander Hamilton on Federal Fiscal Policy, November 1789." *Journal of Economic and Business History* iii (1930-1931), page 667.

Wettereau, James O. "New Light on the First Bank of the United States." *Pennsylvania Magazine of History and Biography* lxi (1937), page 263.

White, Horace. *Money and Banking.* Boston and New York, 1911.

White, Leonard D. *The Jacksonians.* New York, 1954.

Williamson, Harold F. *Growth of the American Economy.* New York, 1944.

Wilson, Janet. "The Bank of North America and Pennsylvania Politics, 1781-1787." *Pennsylvania Magazine of History and Biography* LXVI (1942), page 3.

Wiltse, Charles M. *John C. Calhoun, Nullifier, 1829-1839.* Indianapolis and New York, 1949.

Wiltse, Charles M. "From Compact to National State." In *Essays in Political Theory,* presented to George H. Sabine. Ithaca, 1948.

Woolny, William W. ("Spectator.") *Concise View of the late Proceedings of the Clintonian Party for Suppression of the Merchants Bank.* New York, 1804.

INDEX

INDEX

Bank of North America, 48, 49, 50, 51, 52,
53, 54, 56-63, 65, 66, 78-79, 87, 103, 104,
119, 129, 197, 676, 729
Bank of Nova Scotia, 658
Bank of Pennsylvania, 164-65
Bank of Prince Edward Island, 136
Bank of Quebec, 646-47
Bank of Scotland, 129
Bank of South Carolina, 168
Bank of Spain, 4
Bank of St Louis, 340
Bank of the State of Georgia, 272-73
Bank of the State of Indiana, 621
Bank of the State of South Carolina, 168,
171
Bank of Stephen Girard (*not* Girard
Bank, q.v.), 226
Bank of the United States (both I and
II), 112, 128, 196, 198, 206-07, 393, 553-
54, 594, 599, 701; constitutionality, 104-
06, 205, 207, 214, 233-37, 265-68, 374,
377, 395, 428; fiscal agent and depository, 208; foreign interest, 223-25, 314;
government interest, 207, 427, 440; regulatory, *see* central bank action
B.U.S. I (1791-1811), 41, 83, 114, 115, 118,
122-23, 125, 126, 128-29, 132, 139, 142,
145, 161, 162, 165, 178, 197, 204-05, 209-
10, 227, 238; architecture, 126; balance
sheet, 208; branches, 126-27; restriction on liabilities, 131ff, 659-60
B.U.S. II (1816-1836), 111, 231-32, 233,
240, 241ff, 249, 251ff, 279, 286ff, 330,
343, 353, 442-43, 559-60, 655; architecture, 298-300; Baltimore office, 260ff;
bills of exchange, 316-20; branch
drafts, 397-404; branches, 256, 312-14,
392; Canada, 320-22; charter powers,
243-46; Clayton report, 388, 390, 393ff;
contrast with Bank of England, 445-
50; discounts, 315-17, 434; expediency,
378; fiscal agency, 310-12, 436; government's stock, 412; loans to editors and
Congressmen, 424-25; loss of central
banking powers, 438; party alignment,
239-241; proxies, 245, 257, 261-62; recharter, 383, 385-86, 389-91; removal of
federal deposits, 341, 412ff, 417, 419-23,
429, 435, 598; publications, 425-26; sale
of exchange, 318; Savannah office, 434,
516; specie capital, 255; stock premium,
406-07; stockholders, domestic, 408;
stockholders, foreign, 407; veto, 352,
379, 385, 388-89, 391, 405-10
Bank of the United States v. *Deveaux*,
127, 222, 264

Bank of the United States v. *Planters
Bank*, 272-74
Bank of the United States v. *Primrose*,
690
Bank of the United States of Pennsyl-
vania (1836-1841), *see* U.S. Bank of
Pennsylvania
Bank of Upper Canada, 649-51, 655, 661
Bank of Venice, 68
Bank of Vermont, 171
Bank of Warsaw, New York, 589
Bank of Washington and Warren, Sandy
Hill, New York, 342
Bankers Magazine, 684
banking in America, origins, 4
banking function, 10
banking practice, 698ff, 704
banking system, 197
"banks," colonial, 9, 10, 17-18, 19, 24. *See
also* bills of credit, colonial and state
Barbour, James, 237
Baring Bros., 39, 125, 189, 207, 226, 252,
255, 263, 318-19, 321, 411, 458-59, 461,
464, 466-67, 522, 674
Barker, Jacob, 214, 232, 330, 342
Barlow, Joel, 293, 294
Bates, Joshua, 458, 523-24, 540
Bayard, James A., 225
Beardsley, Samuel, 581
Behrens, Kathryn L., 30
Belcher, Jonathan, 24
Bennett, James Gordon, 346, 560
Benton, Thomas Hart, 37, 259, 297, 330,
340-41, 364-65, 386, 388, 400-01, 455, 487-
88, 491-92, 697
Benton, Thomas Hart, jr., 615
Bevan, Matthew L., 372
Beveridge, Albert J., 570
Bibb, William W., 237
Biddle, Charles, 287, 290
Biddle, Nicholas, 261, 276-79, 287ff, 334,
343, 345, 350, 354, 357-60, 366, 369ff,
411ff, 427, 432-33, 438-42, 446, 458-65,
467ff, 478ff, 486, 489, 503ff, 513ff, 527ff,
540-41, 600, 603, 607, 686, 688-89, 695,
701, 741; causes of failure, 534ff; cotton and the South, 538; criminal
charges, 519; in Greece, 288; literary
work, 288, 289, 292-93, 294; meeting
with Andrew Jackson, 372-73; renominated by Andrew Jackson, 378; retirement, 500-01
Biddle, Thomas, 385
bills of credit, 91ff, 103, 105ff, 726; Canada, 650-51, 657; colonial, 10ff, 18-22,
25, 61, 650-51, 657; revolutionary, 14,
29, 41, 60, 95; state, 58, 138, 349-50, 568,

762